World Wide Web Directory

Kris Jamsa, Ph.D.

Ken Cope

JAMSA
P·R·E·S·S ™
...a computer user's best friend ™

a division of Kris Jamsa Software, Inc.

World Wide Web Directory

Published by
Jamsa Press
2975 S. Rainbow Blvd. Suite I
Las Vegas, NV 89102
U.S.A.

For information about the translation or distribution of any Jamsa Press book, please write to Jamsa Press at the address listed above.

World Wide Web Directory

Printed in the United States of America.
987654

ISBN 1-884133-20-7

Publisher Debbie Jamsa	**Technical Editor** Ken Cope	**Technical Advisor** Phil Schmauder
Copy Editor Larry Letourneau	**Indexer** Kris Cope	**Cover Design** Caroline Kinsey
Composition Ken Cope	**Cover Photograph** O'Gara/Bissell	**Proofer** Rosemary Pasco Linda Linssen

Traversing the World Wide Web

If you have heard about "surfing the Internet" or if you have joined the millions of users who travel the information highway, you will find the World Wide Web the coolest (and most informative) experience your computer has given you yet. If you've traversed the Web before, this book gives you an essential road map, with directions to thousands of sites that contain millions of documents!

If you are new to the Web, this book gives you everything you need to get started! To begin, we'll first introduce you to the Web and discuss how you use it (the pros refer to finding information on the Web as "surfing the Web"). Next, you will learn how to use the software we've included on the CD-ROM to access the Web for free! In fact, within minutes, you'll be connected to the Web, possibly for your first time!

In short, within this book and CD-ROM, you will find:

> Web browsing software that lets you access the Web
>
> Offers from online services and providers for free connect time
>
> A list of over 8,000 Web sites
>
> Everything you need to "surf the Web"

WHERE THE WORLD WIDE WEB GETS ITS NAME

The World Wide Web consists of millions of related (and interconnected) documents that form a web of information that spans the globe. Regardless of the information you need, you'll find corresponding topics on the Web. As shown in Figure 1, Web documents reside at computer systems dispersed throughout over 130 countries.

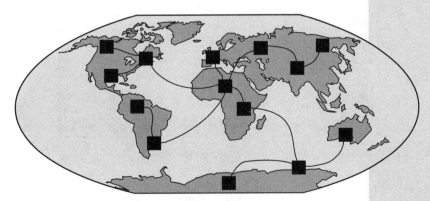

Figure 1 Web documents reside in over 130 countries, worldwide.

HOW YOU ACCESS THE WORLD WIDE WEB

To access documents on the World Wide Web, you use special software called a Web *browser* (the CD-ROM that accompanies this book includes browser programs you can use). Using your browser, you specify the Web address of the document you desire. Your browser, in turn, will display the document's content on your screen. Users refer to a site's document as a *home page*. For example, Figure 2 illustrates the White House home page.

Figure 2 *The White House home page (Web address:* ***http://www.whitehouse.gov***).

From within the White House home page, you can find information about the President and first family, as well as information about the Executive Branch of government, the Vice President and the Congress. In short, the White House home page gives you a starting point from which you can access a wealth of information about our government. Across the Web, thousands of companies, universities, and even individuals have home pages. For example, Figure 3 illustrates the Jamsa Press home page which contains information about our books, CD-ROMs, and company.

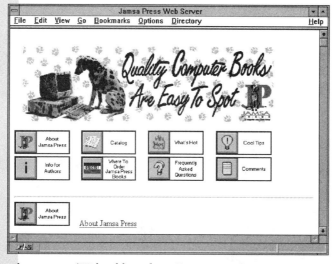

Figure 3 *The Jamsa Press home page (Web address:* ***http://jamsa.com***).

In this case, the Jamsa Press home page provides you with a starting point from which you can obtain our catalog, order products, or even read sample chapters of our books! Every home page on the Web has a unique address. To access a site, you simply tell your browser the location you want. This book lists the addresses for over 8,000 Web sites! As you traverse home pages on the Web, you will encounter *hyperlinks* that connect you to millions of documents!

WHAT'S ALL THIS ABOUT HYPERLINKED DOCUMENTS

Across the Web, home pages give you a starting location from which you can begin your search for information. As you view a home page, you may find links to other documents. Web documents display such links as icons or underlined text. If you click your mouse on a link, your browser will immediately display the linked document's contents. By clicking your mouse on document links, you move from one document to another, across the Web. For example, if you click your mouse on the Executive Branch link that appears on the White House home page, your browser will display the Executive Branch home page as shown in Figure 4.

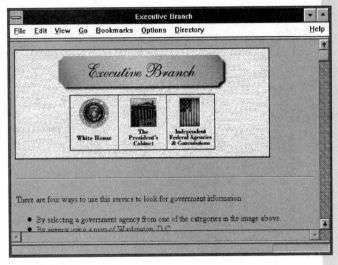

Figure 4 The Executive Branch home.

As you examine the home pages this book presents, you will find home pages for a wide variety of topics. You might for example, find a home page from which you can order books, flowers, or even pizza. Likewise, other home pages will contain information on large and small companies. If you are looking for a college, you can tour many universities right from your PC!

Most home pages will contain links that take you to other documents. For example, if you are looking at the home page for a university, the home page might have links to each of the school's departments, as well as a link that takes you on a picture-based tour of the campus! If you are looking at a company'S home page, you will encounter links that display the company's products and services. For example, if you click on the Catalog link at the Jamsa Press home page, your browser will display information on Jamsa Press books and CD-ROMs. From the catalog document, you can click on links that take you to documents that describe a specific book or CD-ROM as shown in Figure 5.

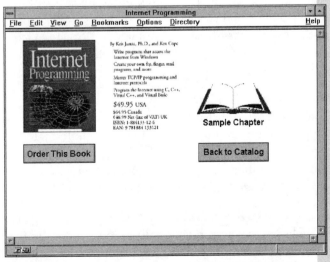

Figure 5 Using a link to access information on Jamsa Press books and CD-ROMs.

World Wide Web Directory

Links within a Web document are so named because they join (or interconnect) related documents. Across the Web, links interconnect millions of documents! Because the links let you move quickly from one document to another, users call the links, *hyperlinks*. Web documents, therefore, are *hyperlinked documents*.

TO TRAVERSE THE WEB, YOU NEED INTERNET ACCESS

As you have learned, you use your Web browser (a software program) to traverse the Web. Before your browser can access documents on the World Wide Web, you must connect your PC to the Internet. As shown in Figure 6, you connect your PC to the Internet using your modem and standard phone lines to dial into an *Internet provider* or *online service* (such as CompuServe or Prodigy).

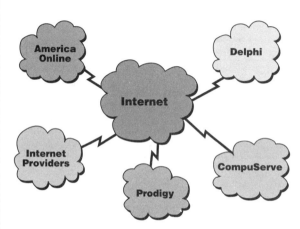

Figure 6 You connect to the Internet using an online service or Internet provider.

Internet providers are companies, who, for a monthly fee, let you access the Internet (and hence the World Wide Web) through their physical connection to the Internet. In short, the provider's computer is physically connected (by cable or by satellite) to the Internet. Using your modem and standard telephone lines, you dial into the provider's computer to gain Internet access. After you connect to the Internet, you use your browser to access Web documents.

USING AN ONLINE SERVICE

In addition to using an Internet provider, you can also access the Web (and various Internet components) using an online service such as CompuServe and Prodigy. One advantage to using an online service to access the Web is cost. The online services are normally less expensive than a provider. Second, depending on where you live, you may not have provider access. Because the online services are so large, you can normally connect to the service (from most cities) using a local phone call. Lastly, the online services may offer more for you (and your family) to do "online" than a provider.

The disadvantage of using an online service for Internet or Web access is speed. Your connection to the Web using an online services is normally slower than a provider-based connection. Because many Web documents contain graphics (which require the transmission of large amounts of information), speed is very important. If your Internet connection is slow, you may get frustrated waiting for your browser to load and display graphics. As such, if you find yourself becoming a "net surfer" who spends hours on the Web each day, you should connect to the Internet via a provider and enjoy the faster performance.

If you already connect to an online service such as Prodigy, CompuServe, or America Online, you can use your service to access the Web. Note, however, your online service may require that you have their latest software before you can access the World Wide Web. To obtain the latest software from your service, contact your service's technical support.

USING AN INTERNET PROVIDER

If you have already selected an Internet provider or online service, you can use the service to access the World Wide Web. Depending on your provider, the steps you must perform to access the Web may differ. To use your Internet provider to connect the Web, you need to insure that you have a SLIP- or PPP-based provider account (contact your Internet provider for more information). The SLIP and PPP software let you access the Internet using your modem from within Windows. Next, you will need special software you run from within Windows that dials your provider and establishes your SLIP or PPP connection. In some cases, your provider may require (or strongly recommend) that you use specific software. Contact your Internet provider and ask them to tell you the specific steps you must perform to connect to the Web and also if they provide specific software. After you establish your SLIP or PPP connection, you can use your browser to traverse the Web.

TRY OUT THE WORLD WIDE WEB FOR FREE!

To make it very easy for you to connect to the Internet and to access the World Wide Web, Jamsa Press has teamed with several major Internet providers and key online services to get you *free* access time on the Internet or significantly reduced startup costs! In other words, using software provided on the CD-ROM that accompanies this book, you are only minutes from connecting to the World Wide Web for free! We invite you to try out Web access on each of the providers and services we've included. Each offers advantages to users with different desires and levels of expertise. By test driving each provider, you can access the World Wide Web for over a month, for free!

If you live outside of the United States, pay close attention to the providers who have teamed with Jamsa Press. As discussed, the Web's presence is worldwide. Jamsa Press worked hard to support our international readers by obtaining free connect time or reduced startup fee offers from providers around the world!

COOL THINGS YOU CAN DO ON THE WEB

If you've never been out on the Web, or if you've been there, but only to a few sites, you are in for a real treat! There are thousands of sites across the Web and this book shows you where those sites are. For starters, you might want to visit the White House home page previously shown in Figure 2. After that, you can visit a Mars space exhibit and view pictures of the planets as shown in Figure 7.

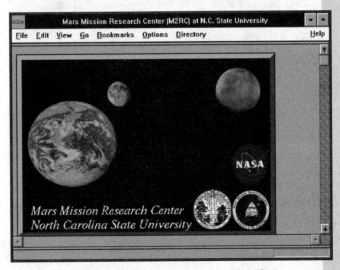

Figure 7 A Mars space exhibit (Web address: http://www.mmrc.ncsu.edu/)

After that, you might visit an on-line zoo where you can view live images of the animals (not photos). For example, Figure 8 shows a live image of a tropical fish tank that is taken by a video camera and later sent out across the Web!

Figure 8 Viewing live images of a tropical fish tank (Web address: http://www2.netscape.com/fishcam/fishcam.html)

In this case, the video camera constantly films the fish tank. Once or twice a minute, the site displays a new image of the fish. As you traverse the Web, you will encounter live video cameras that let you view Seattle, San Diego, and even Norway!

Lastly, if you are interested in shopping, you will find hundreds of online catalogs from which you can order clothes, flowers, books, or even Chinese food or pizzas! Figure 9 illustrates an online catalog.

Figure 9 Online catalogs let you shop via the Web (http://www.omix.com/).

HOW TO USE THIS BOOK

As discussed, this book contains the Web addresses for over 8,000 sites. This book organizes Web sites by category, presenting each category in alphabetical order, much like a phone book. To use this directory, start with your topic of interest. For example, if you are interested in music, you would turn to the "M" categories to locate the Music sites. Within each category, you will find a range of sites. As shown in Figure 10, each site includes a set of keywords that further describe the site. Using the site keywords, you can quickly differentiate between sites that discuss classical music and those sites that feature punk rock.

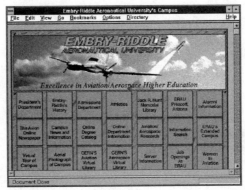

Site Keywords

http://macwww.db.erau.edu/
Embry-Riddle Aeronautical University

Figure 10 *Keywords further describe each site.*

After you find the site you desire, you simply specify the site's Web address to your browser. Web site addresses start with the characters **http://** as shown in Figure 11. As you type in a site address, be careful to type the address exactly as it appears within the book or on the CD-ROM.

Site Address

http://and.com/realbeer/rbp.html
Beer; Brewers; Homebrewing; Microbreweries

Figure 11 *Web site addresses immediately follow the home page graphic.*

Because books don't have an unlimited number of pages, we've presented home page graphics for 4,000 Web sites at the front of the book and a categorized listing of over 4,000 more sites at the back of the book! Take time now to examine the site listings presented at the back of this book. Note the wide variety of site categories.

USING THE CD-ROM THAT ACCOMPANIES THIS BOOK

The CD-ROM that accompanies this book contains software you can use to access the Web as well as a full-color directory of over 8,000 Web sites! Using the CD-ROM directory, you can search for sites by topic, keyword, or by any text you type. Regardless of your topic of interest, if you search the Web Directory CD-ROM, you should find a related Web site.

World Wide Web Directory

INSTALLING THE WEB DIRECTORY CD-ROM

Before you can use the Web Directory CD-ROM, you must first install software that lets you view the CD-ROM files from within Windows. To install this viewer-support software, select the Program Manager File menu shown in Figure 12.

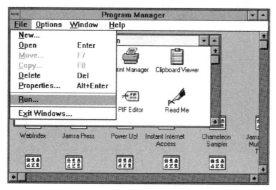

Figure 12 The Program Manager File menu.

Select the File menu Run option. Windows will display the Run dialog box. Type **D:\SETUP**, replacing the drive letter D with the drive letter of your CD-ROM drive. For example, if your CD-ROM drive is drive E, you would type **E:\SETUP** as shown in Figure 13.

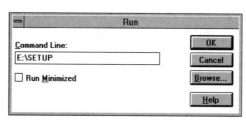

Figure 13 Installing the Web Directory viewer files.

The Setup program will copy the files to your hard disk, eventually displaying a dialog box that tells you the installation is complete. Choose OK. Your screen will now contain the World Wide Web Directory group window as shown in Figure 14.

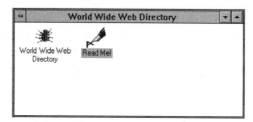

Figure 14 The World Wide Web Directory group window.

To use the Web Directory CD-ROM, double click your mouse on the World Wide Web Directory icon. Windows will display the directory's opening screen as shown in Figure 15.

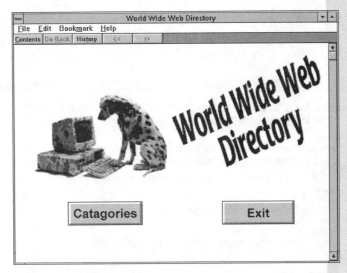

Figure 15 *The World Wide Web Directory's opening screen.*

BROWSING WEB SITES USING THE CD-ROM

When you view Web sites using the CD-ROM, you are not connected to the Web. Instead, you use the Web Directory CD-ROM to look up sites that contain the information you desire. Think of the Web Directory CD-ROM as a phone book. Before you place a phone call, you use the phone book to look up phone numbers. Likewise, before you connect to the Web, you can use the CD-ROM to locate the sites you need.

Just as you can use a phone book to look up numbers while you place other calls, you can use the Web Directory CD-ROM to lookup sites while you are connected to the Web. For example, assume that you are surfing the Web looking for job opportunities. Using the Web Directory CD-ROM, you can search for sites that discuss jobs or careers. Once you find a site in the directory, you can type in the site's Web address into your browser to view the site's document.

VIEWING SITES BY CATEGORY

The CD-ROM directory contains over 8,000 Web sites that we've grouped into almost 100 categories. To view sites by category, click your mouse on the Categories button. The Web Directory, in turn, will display its list of site categories as shown in Figure 16.

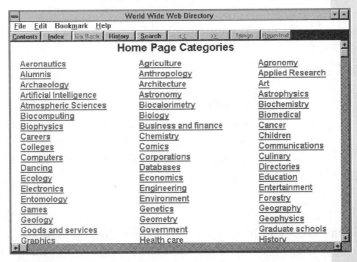

Figure 16 *The Web Directory site categories.*

World Wide Web Directory

To view a category's sites, click your mouse on the corresponding category. For example, if you are looking for information on plants and animals, you might click on the Biology category. The Web Directory, in turn, will display the first site in the category as shown in Figure 17.

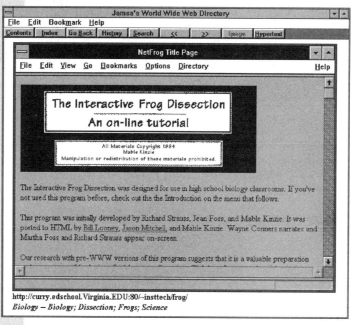

Figure 17 The first site in the Biology category.

Beneath the site screen image, you will find keywords that describe the site. In addition, you will find the site's Web address (the address starts with the letters **http://**).

The toolbar near the top of the Web Directory window contains two buttons you can use to move forward and backward through a category's sites:

If you click your mouse on the button containing the right-facing arrows (>>), the directory will display the next site in the category list. If you click your mouse on the left-facing arrows (<<), the directory will display the previous site. If either of these buttons becomes dim, you have reached either the first or last site in the category list and you cannot move further in that direction.

RETURNING TO THE CATEGORY LIST

You can return to the category list from a site at any time by clicking your mouse on the toolbar Contents button. Because the category list is too long to fit in a window, you can use the vertical scroll bar (that appears along the window's right edge) to view additional categories. To return to the Web Directory's main window, click your mouse on the Contents button from within the category list window.

PRINTING A SITE

When you find a site within the Web Directory that you later want to visit using your browser, you can write down the site's address, or you can print a copy of the site and its address. To print the current site, select the Web Directory File menu and choose Print Topic.

VIEWING A SITE'S HTML DOCUMENT

To build a home page, users create a document that uses a special programming language called HTML (hypertext markup language). Using HTML, users specify the home page graphics, text contents, title bar, and so on.

In addition to providing you with the screens from over 8,000 sites, the Web Directory CD-ROM also provides you with each site's HTML document. By including the HTML on the CD-ROM, we let you search for topics within over 8,000 HTML documents! In this way, if one of our keywords does not match your search topic, you are very likely to find your topic within an HTML document!

If you examine the toolbar, you will find a button titled Hypertext. To display the HTML for a site, click you mouse on the Hypertext button. Likewise, to display a site's screen image, click your mouse on the toolbar Image button. Figure 18, for example, illustrates the HTML document for the White House home page.

Figure 18 *The HTML document for the White House home page.*

SEARCHING FOR A WEB SITE

The fastest way to list Web sites that discuss your topic of interest is to click your mouse on the Search button. The Web Directory, in turn, will display the Search dialog box shown in Figure 19.

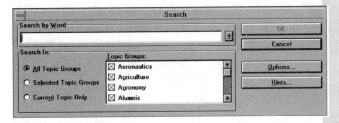

Figure 19 *The Web Directory Search dialog box.*

Within the Search by Word field, type in your topic of interest. If you are interested in Windows 95, for example, you would type in Windows 95 and press Enter. The Web Directory, in turn, will display a Search

World Wide Web Directory

Results dialog box similar to that shown in Figure 20 that lists the titles of sites that discuss Windows 95. By sizing the Search Results dialog box, you can view each site's complete title. To size the window, simply drag the window frame using your mouse.

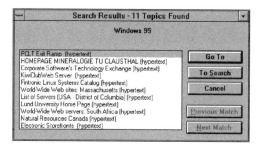

Figure 20 *The Search Results dialog box listing sites that discuss Windows 95.*

Within the Search Results sites list, double click your mouse on the title of the site you desire. The Web Directory will display either the site's screen image or the site's HTML document, depending on whether it found your topic within the keyword list or within the HTML text. If the Web Directory displays the site's HTML, click your mouse on the Image button to display the site's screen.

If the site contains the information you desire, click your mouse on the Cancel button to close the Search Results dialog box. Otherwise, double click your mouse on a second site.

CONTROLLING SEARCH OPERATIONS

By default, the Web Directory will search all 8,000+ sites for your topic text. Using the Search dialog box previously shown in Figure 19, you can restrict your search operations to specific site categories. For example, if you are a Doctor, you might want to restrict your search operations to Medicine, Healthcare, and Science. To constrain your search, click your mouse on the check boxes that correspond to the specific categories you want to search.

Depending on your topic, there may be times when a search operation yields hundreds or even thousands of matching sites. For example, assume you are interested in sites that discuss universities, but only those universities in the state of Washington. To perform such a search, you can direct the Web Directory to look for two words, universities and Washington as shown in Figure 21.

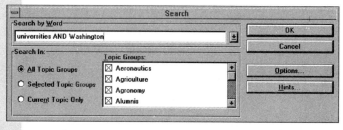

Figure 21 *Searching for two words.*

To learn more about advanced searching techniques, click your mouse on the Search dialog box Hints button. The Web Directory will display the Search Hints dialog box as shown in Figure 22.

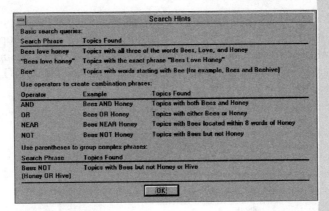

Figure 22 *The Search Hints dialog box.*

As you can see, you can use the words AND, OR, NEAR, and NOT to perform sophisticated search operations.

USING AN INDEX TO SEARCH

To find information within a book, you can turn to the book's index to determine which pages discuss the topics you desire. In a similar way, the Web Directory CD-ROM contains an index of terms. To use the Directory's index to locate sites that discuss your topic of interest, click your mouse on the Index button. The Web Directory, in turn, will display the Index dialog box as shown in Figure 23.

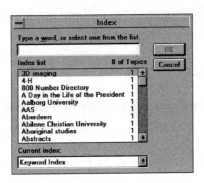

Figure 23 *The Index dialog box.*

To locate sites that discuss a specific topic, type in the topic you desire. As you type, the index will display words that match the letters you have typed. For example, if you type the letters **Boo**, the Index will display index entries shown in Figure 24.

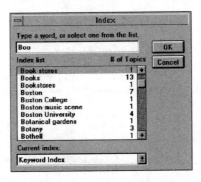

Figure 24 *Index entries matching the letters Boo.*

World Wide Web Directory

To the right of each index entry, you will find the number of sites that discuss the topic. Next, double click your mouse on topic you desire. The Web Directory, in turn, will display the Topics Indexed dialog box, shown in Figure 25, that contains the titles of the sites that discuss the topic. Again, by sizing the window, you can read the complete site title. Double click on the site you desire. The Web Directory will display either the site's image or HTML.

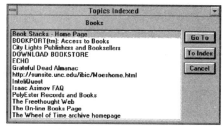

Figure 25 The Topics Indexed dialog box.

Selecting an Index

The Web Directory CD-ROM lets you search for information by category, keywords, and by text contained in a site's HTML document. To control your search operations, the Web Directory uses three different indexes as described in Table 1.

Index	Contents
Keyword	Contains the keywords that appear beneath the site graphic.
Category	Contains a listing of the site categories.
Web Site Index	Contains words found in the site HTML documents.

Table 1 The Web Directory search indexes.

To search a specific index, open the Index dialog box Current index pull-down list and click your mouse on the index you desire.

ANNOTATING A SITE ADDRESS

Over time, Web sites may change or cease to exist. If you are using the book version of the World Wide Web Directory, you can make an appropriate note on the page of the book that contains the site. Likewise, if you are using the Web Directory CD-ROM, you can make annotations to a site.

To annotate the current site, select the Edit menu Annotate option. The Web Directory, in turn, will display the Annotate dialog box as shown in Figure 26.

Figure 26 Annotating a site address.

xvi

Type in your annotation, such as a new site address, and select Save. The Web Directory, in turn, will display a small paper clip above the left-hand corner of the site's screen image. To display the annotation, click your mouse on the paper clip.

VIEWING A PREVIOUSLY VIEWED SIGHT

As you click through the sites in the Web Directory CD-ROM, there may be times when you want to view a site that you saw earlier, but whose category you no longer remember. In such cases, click your mouse on the toolbar History button. The Web Directory, in turn, will display the History dialog box similar to that shown in Figure 27 that contains a list of sites you have previously viewed. Double click your mouse on the site you desire.

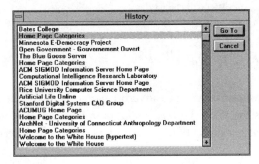

Figure 27 *The History dialog box.*

MARKING YOUR FAVORITE SITES

If you use the book version of the World Wide Web Directory, you may find yourself marking the pages of the sites you use on a regular basis. In a similar way, you can place bookmarks on your favorite sites within the Web Directory CD-ROM. After you assign a bookmark to a site, you can select the site quickly from the Bookmark menu. To assign a bookmark to the current site, select the Bookmark menu and choose Define. The Web Directory will display the Define dialog box. Choose OK.

EXITING THE WEB DIRECTORY CD

To exit the Web Directory CD-ROM, select the File menu Exit option or click your mouse on the Exit menu button that appears on the Directory's opening window.

OUR WEB SITE DISCLAIMER

The World Wide Web is a dynamic entity that constantly changes. In fact, the number of new Web sites created each day now numbers several hundred! As we studied the behavior of sites on the Web, we found that sites change and sometimes cease to exist. When we made our site selections for this book, we worked hard to choose stable sites. Unfortunately, despite our best efforts, you may periodically encounter a site address that is no longer valid. Luckily, based on the shear number of sites (over 8,000) that we've given you, we are very confident that you will find ample sites that discuss your topic of interest.

ADDING YOUR HOME PAGE TO A FUTURE EDITION

Jamsa Press is very interested in obtaining "cool" or "content rich" home pages for future editions of this book. To include your home page in a future edition, simply send us an e-mail message that contains your

World Wide Web Directory

Web site address (send to homepage@jamsa.com). For example, to include the White House home page in a future edition of this book, the President would send the following e-mail message:

```
Send: homepage@jamsa.com

Subject: Add our home page

Message

    Please add the following home page:

    http://www.whitehouse.gov

    Thanks, The President
```

CREATING YOUR OWN HOME PAGE

If you have a business with products you want to advertise, you can create your own home page that is accessible to millions of users across the Web. To create your own home page, you need to format a home page document using a special language called HTML. Second, you need Web server software that lets other users access your home page.

To make it easy for you to perform these operations, Jamsa Press has created a multimedia CD-ROM titled *Instant World Wide Web Access*. The CD-ROM contains 45 minutes of video that teaches you how to use HTML and how to use Web server software. In addition, the CD-ROM includes all the software you need! You will find *Instant World Wide Web Access* (ISBN: 1-884133-20-7) at fine bookstores and computer stores. For more information on *Instant World Wide Web Access*, connect to the Jamsa Press home page (Web address: http://jamsa.com).

ACCESSING THE WEB FOR YOUR FIRST TIME

If you don't currently use an online service or Internet provider, your first step is to choose one of the services this book makes available to you. As discussed, Jamsa Press has teamed with services who will give you free connection time to the Web or who will significantly reduce your startup costs. Use the descriptions that follow to connect to and try out each service. In this way, you not only get a chance to access the Web for free, you get to choose the service that best suits your needs.

Note: Over time, the services and discounts that the providers and online services offer may change. In some cases, a company's promotion may become even better than those offered here (more free hours or further reduced costs). The companies that follow are free to change their promotional offers at any time. Jamsa Press is not responsible for, nor can Jamsa Press control such changes. Jamsa Press makes these companies available to you in an attempt to simplify your first Web connection. We will continue to seek out such partners in the future who are committed to providing services to our valued customers.

ACCESSING THE WEB USING PRODIGY

Prodigy Information Services is one of the largest online services in the world. Using Prodigy, you can shop, get the latest sports, travel, and financial news, chat with or send electronic mail (e-mail) to users from around the world. In fact, with Prodigy you may converse with politicians, athletes, musicians, and even TV and movie stars! Your major motivation for using Prodigy is that it provides something for everyone in your family!

Prodigy also lets you access various parts of the Internet such as e-mail, newsgroups, but most importantly, the World Wide Web! Because Prodigy supports a wide range of users, each with different levels of expertise, you will find Prodigy one of the easiest ways to access the Web.

To give you a chance to test drive the Web, as well as, Prodigy's standard services, Prodigy will let you try them out for 10 hours, for free! For instructions on installing and using the Prodigy software, double click your mouse on the Read Me! icon that appears within the World Wide Web Directory group window. Windows, in turn, will open the Write word processor displaying the document's contents. Scroll through the document (which contains much of this text) until you locate the section on Installing the Prodigy Software. The document will walk you through the steps you must perform to try out the Web and the Prodigy services for free!

ACCESSING THE WEB USING PSINET

PSINet is one of the largest and fastest growing Internet providers in the world. Using PSINet, you not only gain access to the World Wide Web, but also to all Internet resources such as e-mail, ftp, gopher, online chatting, and newsgroups! To make it easy for you to access the Internet (and the Web), PSINet lets you connect to and test drive the Internet for seven days, for free!

For instructions on installing and using the PSINet software, double click your mouse on the Read Me! icon that appears within the World Wide Web Directory group window. Windows, in turn, will open the Write word processor displaying the document's contents. Scroll through the document (which contains much of this text) until you locate the section on Installing the PSINet Software. The document will walk you through the steps you must perform to connect to the Internet and to try out the Web using PSINet for free!

ACCESSING THE WEB USING NETCOM

NETCOM is one of the largest and fastest growing Internet providers. When you connect to NETCOM, you not only gain access to the World Wide Web, but you can access all Internet resources as well, such as e-mail, ftp, gopher, WAIS, and so on! To make it easy for you to connect to the Internet, NETCOM has waived their standard start-up fees for readers of the World Wide Web Directory! As discussed next, it's very easy to connect to NETCOM. Within minutes, you will be connected to the World Wide Web.

For instructions on installing and using the NETCOM software, double click your mouse on the Read Me! icon that appears within the World Wide Web Directory group window. Windows, in turn, will open the Write word processor displaying the document's contents. Scroll through the document (which contains much of this text) until you locate the section on Installing the NETCOM Software. The document will walk you through the steps you must perform to try connect to NETCOM.

ACCESSING THE WEB USING COMPUSERVE

CompuServe is one of the leading online services worldwide. Using CompuServe, you can shop, chat with or send e-mail to other users worldwide, get the latest sports, news, and travel information, and much more! In addition, CompuServe provides you with access to the World Wide Web. To make it easy for you to access their standard services as well as the Web, CompuServe will provide you with one free month of access and a $15.00 credit against expenses you incur while traversing the Web!

For instructions on installing and using the CompuServe software, double click your mouse on the Read Me! icon that appears within the World Wide Web Directory group window. Windows, in turn, will open the Write word processor displaying the document's contents. Scroll through the document (which contains much of this text) until you locate the section on Installing the CompuServe Software. The document will walk you through the steps you must perform to try out the Web and the CompuServe services for free!

ACCESSING THE WEB USING I-LINK

I-Link is a US-based Internet provider with plans to expand worldwide over the next year! When you connect to the Internet using I-Link, you gain access to the World Wide Web, and all other Internet resources such as e-mail, ftp, gopher, WAIS, and so on! To make it easy for you to connect to the Internet, I-Link will give three days free access for readers of the *World Wide Web Directory!* As discussed next, it's very easy to connect to I-Link. Within minutes, you will be connected to the World Wide Web.

For instructions on installing and using the I-Link software, double click your mouse on the Read Me! icon that appears within the World Wide Web Directory group window. Windows, in turn, will open the Write word processor displaying the document's contents. Scroll through the document (which contains much of this text) until you locate the section on Installing the I-Link Software. The document will walk you through the steps you must perform to try connect to I-Link.

ACCESSING THE WEB FROM AUSTRALIA

To access the Web from Australia, use AUSNet Services, one of Australia's largest Internet providers. To make it easy for you to try out the World Wide Web, AUSNet offers readers of the *World Wide Web Directory* 10 free hours of access!

```
AUSNet Services Pty. Ltd.
Suite 4, Level 9, Gold Fields House
1 Alfred Street
Circular Quay, NSW 2000, Australia
Tel: 61-2-241-5888
Fax: 61-2-241-5898
Web: http://www.world.net/
```

For instructions on installing and using the AUSNet software, double click your mouse on the Read Me! icon that appears within the World Wide Web Directory group window. Windows, in turn, will open the Write word processor displaying the document's contents. Scroll through the document (which contains much of this text) until you locate the section on Installing the AUSNet Software. The document will walk you through the steps you must perform to try connect to AUSNet.

ACCESSING THE WEB FROM CANADA

To access the Web from Canada, you can use the Prodigy Information Service or the CompuServe Information Service previously discussed. To obtain an account with an Internet provider, contact:

```
Alberta Supernet Inc.
10909 Jasper Avenue
Suite 325
Edmonton, Canada T5J3L9
Tel: 405-441-3663
Fax: 405-429-0743
```

ACCESSING THE WEB FROM THE UNITED KINGDOM

To access the Web from the United Kingdom, contact the following Internet providers:

```
Demon Internet Ltd
Gateway House
322 Regents Park Road
Finchlay, London N3 2QQ UK
Tel: 44-(0)-181-371-1000
Fax:44-(0)-181-371-1150
```

Demon Internet Ltd has different subscription promotions. Let them know you learned about their service through the World Wide Web Directory.

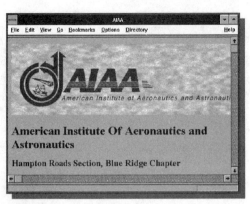

http://asmsun.larc.nasa.gov/
American Institute of Aeronautics and Astronautics

http://aviation.jsc.nasa.gov/
Aviation; Education; Flight Planning; Simulators; Weather

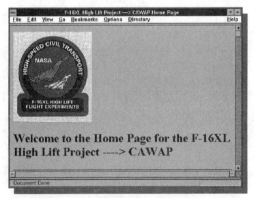

http://dval-www.larc.nasa.gov/F16XL/index.html
F-16XL; High speed transport; Test flights

http://ecf.hq.eso.org/ST-ECF-overview.html
European Southern Observatory; European Space Agency

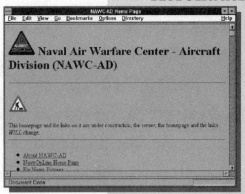

http://foghorn.nadc.navy.mil:8000/
Aircraft; Aviation; Navy; Weapons

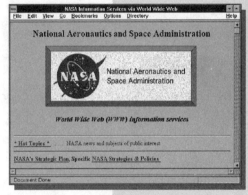

http://hypatia.gsfc.nasa.gov/NASA_homepage.html
Aeronautics; NASA; Planets; Space

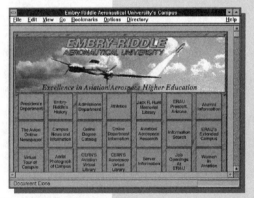

http://macwww.db.erau.edu/
Embry-Riddle Aeronautical University

http://mosaic.larc.nasa.gov/larc.html
Langley Research Center; NACA; NASA; Space

1

Aeronautics

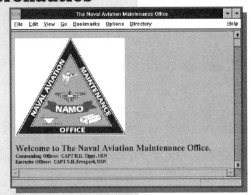

http://namopdc.nawcad.navy.mil/
Naval Aviation Maintenance

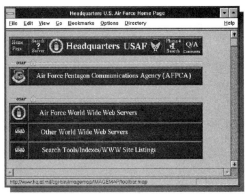

http://www.hq.af.mil/
Directories; Government; Headquarters; Military; U.S. Air Force

http://newproducts.jpl.nasa.gov/magellan/
Magellan; NASA; Planets; Space; Venus

http://www.ksc.nasa.gov/shuttle/missions/missions.html
Astronauts; Images; Shuttle; Space

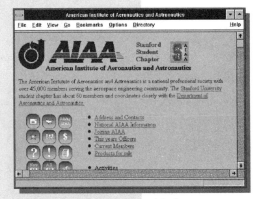

http://www-leland.stanford.edu/group/aiaa/
American Institute of Aeronautics and Astronautics

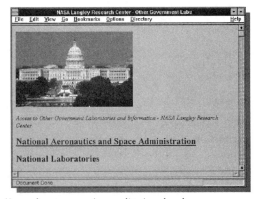

http://www.larc.nasa.gov/nasaonline/gov.html
Government; NASA; Policy; Space

http://www.dfrf.nasa.gov/dryden.html
NASA Dryden Flight Research Center

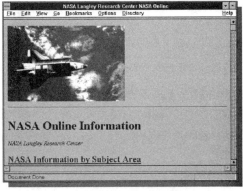

http://www.larc.nasa.gov/nasaonline/nasaonline.html
NASA; Research; Shuttle; Space

http://ccf.arc.nasa.gov/dx
Ames Research Center; NASA; Public Affairs

http://clementine.s1.gov/
Clementine Mission Overview; Images; Space

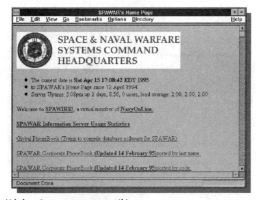

http://dolomite.spawar.navy.mil/
Aviation; Space; Technology; Warfare

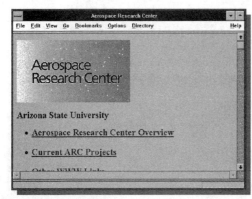

http://enws229.eas.asu.edu:80/
Aerospace Research Center

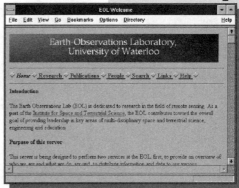

http://glenn.uwaterloo.ca/eol.html
Earth science; Education; Engineering; Physics; Remote sensing

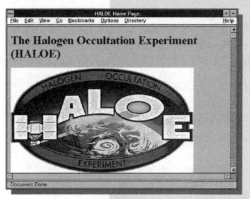

http://haloedata.larc.nasa.gov/home.html
Halogen Occultation; NASA; Technology

http://hypatia.gsfc.nasa.gov/GSFC_homepage.html
Goddard Space Flight Center; NASA

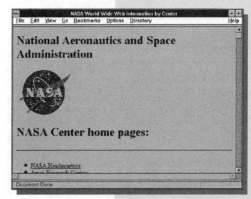

http://hypatia.gsfc.nasa.gov/nasa_centers.html
NASA headquarters; Space; Technology

Aerospace

http://images.jsc.nasa.gov/html/home.htm
Digital Image Collection; JSC; NASA

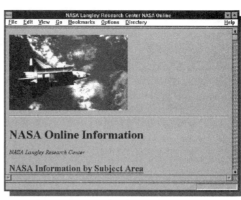

http://mosaic.larc.nasa.gov/nasaonline/nasaonline.html
Langley research; NASA information

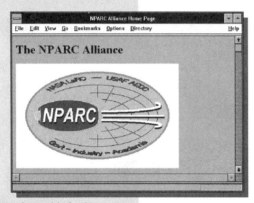

http://info.arnold.af.mil/nparc/
Alliance; Computational fluid dynamics; Government

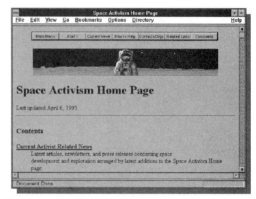

http://muon.qrc.com/space/start.html
News; Newsletters; Space activism

http://mesis.esrin.esa.it/html/esa.html
European Space Agency

http://newproducts.jpl.nasa.gov/calendar/calendar.html
JPL; Space calendar

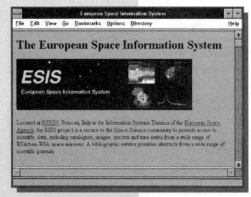

http://mesis.esrin.esa.it/html/esis.html
ESIS; European Space Information System; Physical science

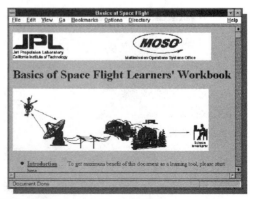

http://oel-www.jpl.nasa.gov/basics/bsf.htm
Basics of space; JPL; Learning tool; MOSO

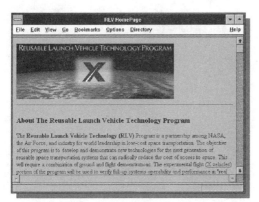

http://rlv.msfc.nasa.gov/rlv_htmls/rlv1.html
Reusable Launch Vehicle Technology Program

http://sti.larc.nasa.gov/RandT/Contents.html
Aeronautics; Aerospace technology; TM-4575

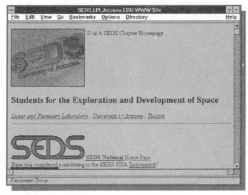

http://seds.lpl.arizona.edu/
Students for the Exploration and Development of Space

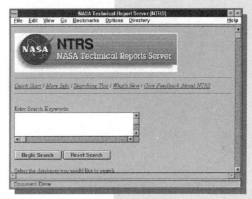

http://techreports.larc.nasa.gov/cgi-bin/NTRS
Document server; NASA; Technical reports

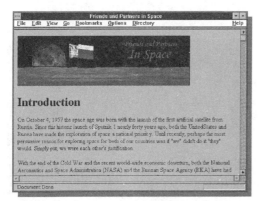

http://solar.rtd.utk.edu/~jgreen/fpspace.html
NASA; RKA; Space; Sputnik

http://techreports.larc.nasa.gov/ltrs/ltrs.html
Langley research; Search and retrieve; Technology reports

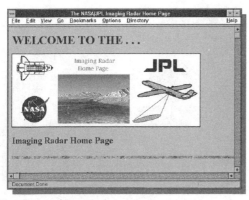

http://southport.jpl.nasa.gov/
Aeronautics; Imaging radar; JPL; Space

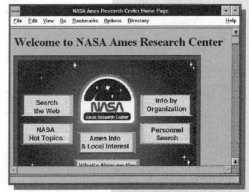

http://www.arc.nasa.gov/
Ames Research Center; NASA

Aerospace

http://www.dlr.de/
DLR; Germany; Large-scale aerospace researching

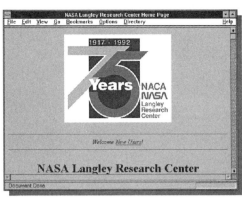

http://www.larc.nasa.gov/larc.html
Langley Research Center; NACA; NASA; Space

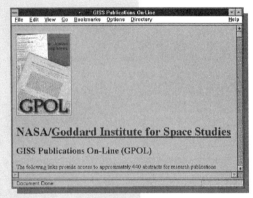

http://www.giss.nasa.gov/GPOL/
Goddard Institute; NASA; Space studies

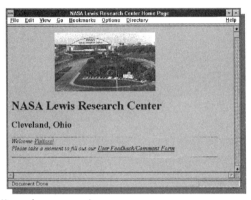

http://www.lerc.nasa.gov/
NASA; Propulsion; Research; Space

http://www.gsfc.nasa.gov/GSFC_homepage.html
Goddard Space Flight Center; Mission; NASA

http://www.mmrc.ncsu.edu/
Mars; Research; Space; Voyager

http://www.jpl.nasa.gov/
Jet Propulsion Laboratory; JPL

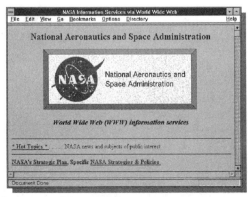

http://www.nasa.gov/
Aeronautics; NASA; Space Administration

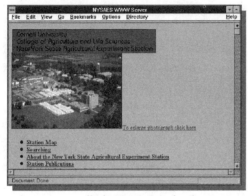

http://ag.arizona.edu:80/
College of Agriculture; Education; University of Arizona

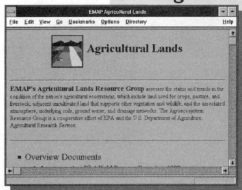

http://earth1.epa.gov/emap/html/resrcgrp/agroland/
Agricultural Lands Resource Group; EPA; Status; Trends

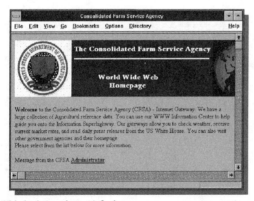

http://aruba.nysaes.cornell.edu:8000/geneva.html
Agriculture; Cornell University; Life Sciences

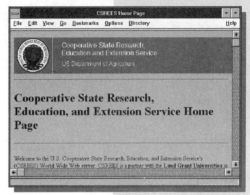

http://eos.esusda.gov/
Agriculture sciences; Education; Food; Research

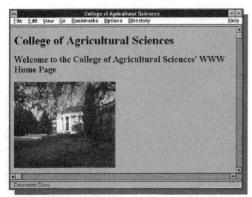

http://bbskc.kcc.usda.gov/cfsa.htm
Agriculture; Farm; Government; Market rates

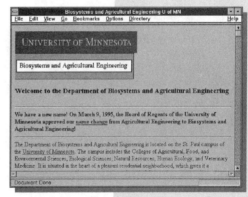

http://gaia.ageng.umn.edu/
Agricultural Engineering; University of Minnesota

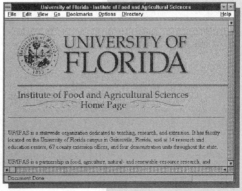

http://bluehen.ags.udel.edu/
Agricultural Sciences; University of Delware

http://gnv.ifas.ufl.edu/
Agriculture; Food; Research; University of Florida

Agriculture

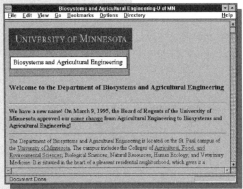

http://gold.uni-miskolc.hu/
Agriculture; Biology; Biosystems; University of Minnesota

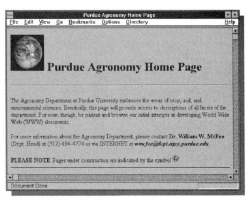

http://info.aes.purdue.edu/agronomy/agny.html
Agronomy; Purdue University

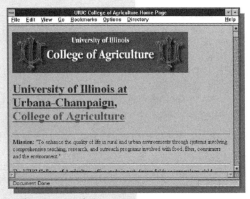

http://gopher.ag.uiuc.edu/
Agriculture; University of Illinois; Urbana-Champaign

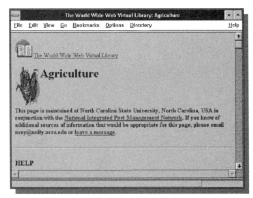

http://ipm_www.ncsu.edu/cernag/cern.html
Agriculture; North Carolina State University

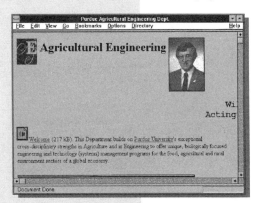

http://hermes.ecn.purdue.edu:8001/http_dir/agen/start.html
Agricultural Engineering; Purdue University

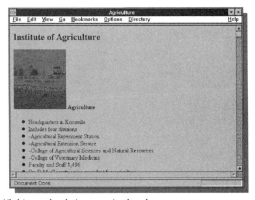

http://loki.ur.utk.edu/campus/ag.html
Agriculture; University of Tennessee

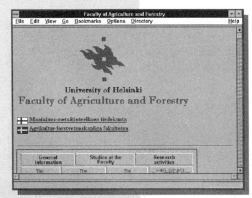

http://honeybee.helsinki.fi/index.html
Agriculture; Forestry; University of Helsinki; Finland

http://organic.com/Non.profits/F2F/
Agriculture; Farming; News; Publications

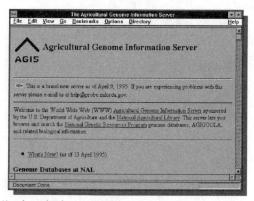

http://probe.nalusda.gov:8000/
Agriculture; Biology; Genome; Genome databases

http://www.abe.msstate.edu/cahe/cahe.html
Agriculture; Home Economics; Mississippi State University

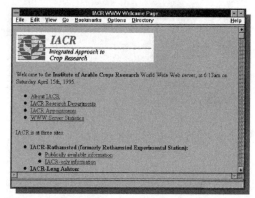

http://resc9.res.bbsrc.ac.uk/
Arable crops; Research

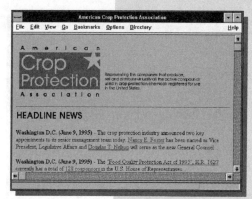

http://www.acpa.org/
Agriculture; Chemicals; Crop protection industry

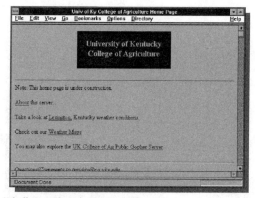

http://shelley.ca.uky.edu/
Agriculture; University of Kentucky; Weather

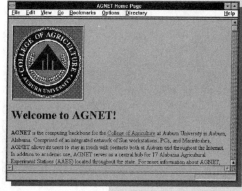

http://www.ag.auburn.edu:80/
Auburn University; College of Agriculture; Education

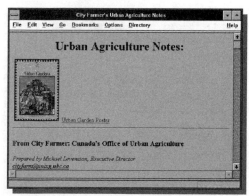

http://unixg.ubc.ca:780/~cityfarm/urbagnotes1.html
Farming; Office of Urban Agriculture; Urban food production

http://www.atlantic.com/ctguide/durham
Agricultural Fair; Connecticut; Durham

Architecture

http://alberti.mit.edu/ap/ap.html
Architecture; Education; MIT; Research

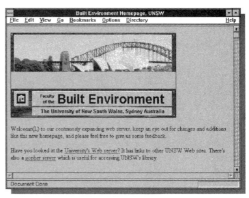

http://www.arch.unsw.edu.au/
Architecture; Library; Sydney Australia

http://arcrs4.saed.kent.edu/Architronic/homepage.html
Architecture; Kent State University

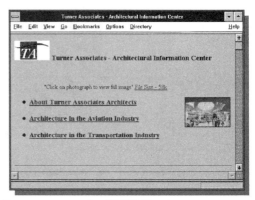

http://www.asa-net.com/nss/005/005.html
Architectural information; Turner Associates

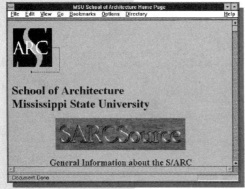

http://sarc.msstate.edu/
Architecture; Mississippi State University

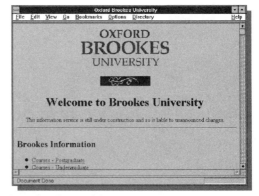

http://www.brookes.ac.uk/
Architecture; Oxford; Oxford Brooks University; UK; University

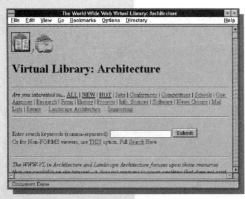

http://www.clr.toronto.edu:1080/VIRTUALLIB/arch.html
Architecture; Landscape engineering; Virtual library

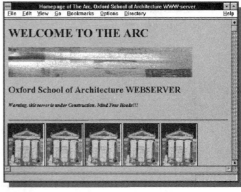

http://www.brookes.ac.uk/arch/archome.html
Education; Oxford School of Architecture

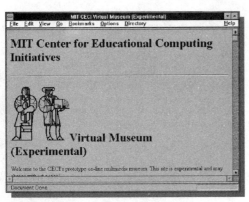

http://abelard.mit.edu/cgi-bin/museum-entrance/
Edgerton; Photography; Virtual museums

http://amanda.physics.wisc.edu/outside.html
Galleries; Links; Video

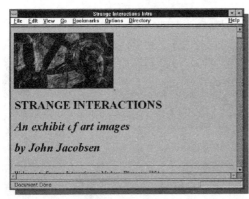

http://amanda.physics.wisc.edu/show.html
American art; Artists; Exhibits; John Jacobsen

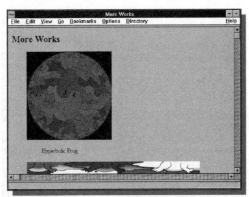

http://andro.sfc.keio.ac.jp/~aly/escher/more.html
Art; Graphics; Design

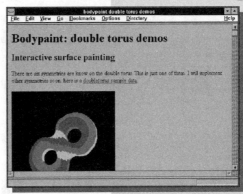

http://andro.sfc.keio.ac.jp/~aly/software/bodypaint/double.html
Double-torus; Graphics; Painting

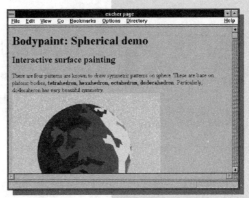

http://andro.sfc.keio.ac.jp/~aly/software/bodypaint/sphere.html
Interactive instruction; Painting

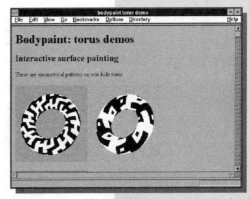

http://andro.sfc.keio.ac.jp/~aly/software/bodypaint/torus.html
Graphics; Instruction; Painting; Torus

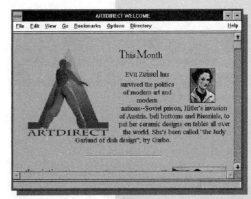

http://artdirect.com/
Art; Directories; Links; People

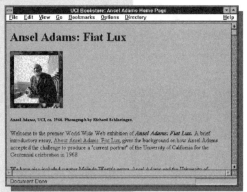

http://bookweb.cwis.uci.edu:8042/AdamsHome.html
Ansel Adams; Fiat Lux; Photography

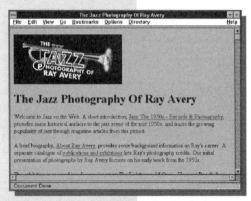

http://bookweb.cwis.uci.edu:8042/Jazz/jazz.html
History; Jazz; Photography; Ray Avery

http://brains.race.u-tokyo.ac.jp/RACE.html
Environment; Japan; Sculpture; Technology

http://ccat.sas.upenn.edu/arth/arth.html
Art; History; University of Pennsylvania

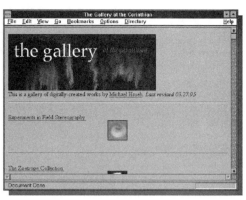

http://corinthian.mac.cc.cmu.edu/
The Corinthian; Digital art; Michael Hsueh

http://cruzio.com/arts/scva/scva.html
Index; Santa Cruz; Visual Arts

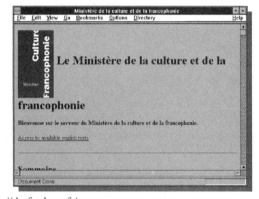

http://dmf.culture.fr/
Culture; France; French; French museums

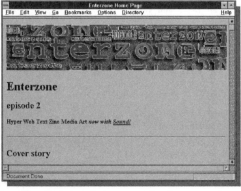

http://enterzone.berkeley.edu/enterzone.html
Computer graphics; Fiction; Hyperzine; Magazines; Philosophy

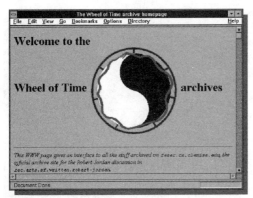

http://faser.cs.olemiss.edu/jordan/jordan.html
Authors; Books; Wheel of Time

http://kspace.com/
Artists; Contemporary music; Magazines; Pop music; Web services

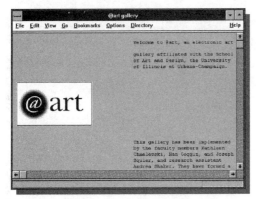

http://gertrude.art.uiuc.edu/@art/gallery.html
Art; Education; Gallery

http://mailer.fsu.edu/~bfiallo/fiae.html
Art; Education; Florida State University

http://isaac.exploratorium.edu/
Exploranet; Fine arts; WWW Server

http://metaverse.com/index.html
Entertainment; Metaverse; Music

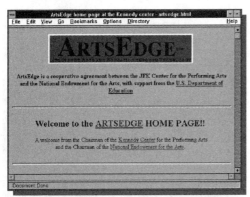

http://k12.cnidr.org/janice_k12/artsedge/artsedge.html
Education; Performing arts; Technology

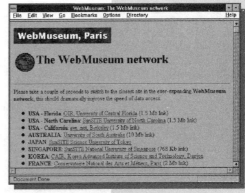

http://mistral.enst.fr/~pioch/louvre/
France; Japan; Korea; WebMuseum

13

Art

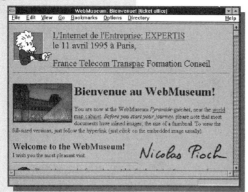

http://mistral.enst.fr/louvre/
Louvre; Museums; Exhibits

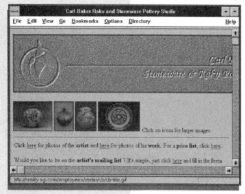

http://reality.sgi.com/employees/raster/cb/index.html
Stoneware Pottery Studio

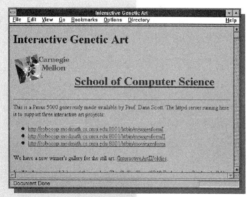

http://robocop.modmath.cs.cmu.edu:8001/
Carnegie Mellon; Gallery; Genetic art

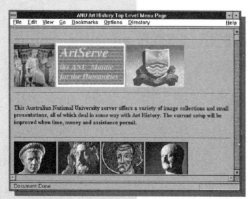

http://rubens.anu.edu.au/
Art; Exhibitions; History; Presentations

http://sunsite.unc.edu/expo/expo/bookstore.html
Goods and services; Vatican library

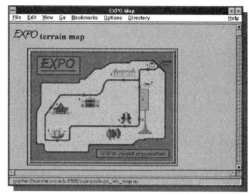

http://sunsite.unc.edu/expo/expo/expo_map.html
Electronic exposition; Maps

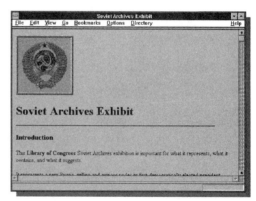

http://sunsite.unc.edu/expo/soviet.exhibit/soviet.archive.html
Soviet archives; Exhibitions

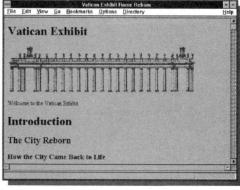

http://sunsite.unc.edu/expo/vatican.exhibit/Vatican.exhibit.html
Catholicism; History; Vatican

Art

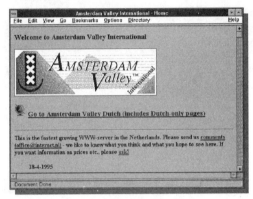

http://usa.net/home/art.html
Directories; Links; Visual Art

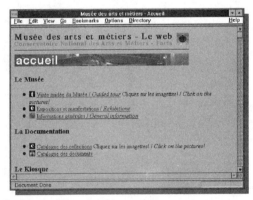

http://valley.interact.nl/av/int/home.html
Art galleries; Holland; The Netherlands

http://web.cnam.fr/museum/
Arts; Expositions; France; French museums

http://wimsey.com/anima/ANIMAhome.html
ANIMA; Arts Network for Integrated Media Applications

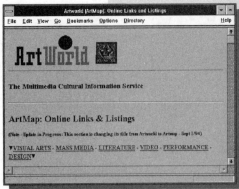

http://wimsey.com/anima/ARTWORLDonline.html
ArtWorld; Literature; Online magazine; Video; Visual arts

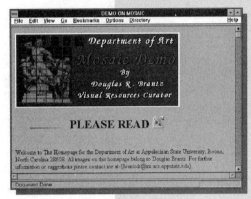

http://www.acs.appstate.edu/art
Appalachian State University; Douglas Brantz

http://www.advantage.com/EAG/EAG.html
Canada; Galleries; Paintings; Roy Henry Vickers

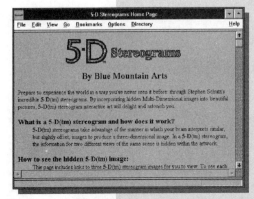

http://www.ais.net:80/netmall/bma/
5-D Stereograms; Multi-Dimensional images

15

http://www.ananda.com/plg/cindys/
Artists; Cards; Photographers; San Francisco

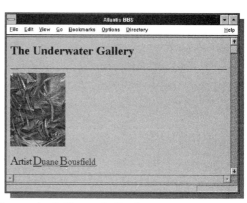

http://www.atlantis-bbs.com/gallery.htm
Atlantis BBS; Underwater Gallery

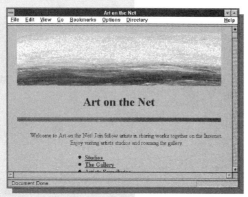

http://www.art.net/
Art; Artists; Gallery; Sculptors; Studios

http://www.cgrg.ohio-state.edu:80/mkruse/osu.html
Artists; Modern art; Pop Art

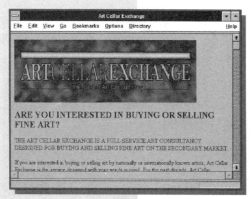

http://www.artcellarex.com/ace/
Collectors; Consultancy; Exchange; Fine art; Secondary market

http://www.chin.doc.ca/
Canada; Heritage; History

http://www.artnet.org/iamfree/IAMFREE/html/elecart.html
Electronic art; Image; Picture

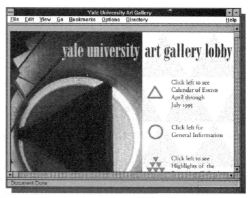

http://www.cis.yale.edu/~yups/yuag/lobby.html
Art gallery; Events; Images; Yale University

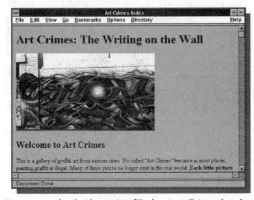

http://www.cs.brown.edu:80/fun/bawp/
Performances; Poetry; Spoken word

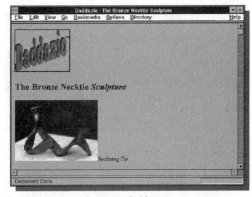

http://www.gatech.edu/desoto/graf/Index.Art_Crimes.html
Art crimes; Graffiti

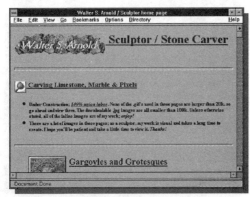

http://www.gems.com/showcase/daddazio/
Modern art; Sculpture

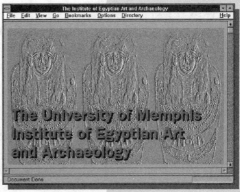

http://www.memst.edu/egypt/main.html
Archaeology; Egyptian art; University of Memphis

http://www.msstate.edu/Fineart_Online/home.html
Discussion; E-Mail; Fine art; News

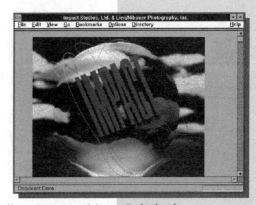

http://www.netaxs.com/~impact/index.html
Images; Photographs; Photography

http://www.mcs.com/~sculptor/home.html
Carving; Sculpting; Walter S. Arnold

http://www.primenet.com/art-rom/museumweb/
Art-ROM; Gallery; Museum

Art

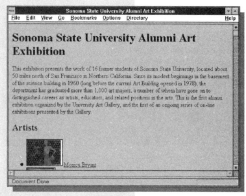

http://www.sccsi.com/Stewart/craig_stewart.html
Craig Stewart; Illustration; Photography

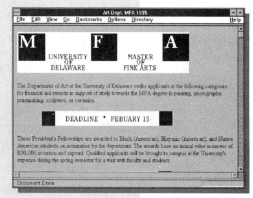

http://www.sonoma.edu/exhibits/alumni/
Artists; Exhibits; Graphic art; Paintings

18

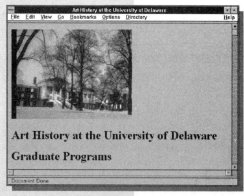

http://www.udel.edu/jeffers/ArtDept/MFA/MFA.HTML
Art; University of Delware

http://www.udel.edu/jeffers/ArtHistory/Brochure94.HTML
Art History; University of Delaware

http://www.ugcs.caltech.edu/~werdna/grotesque/grotesque.html
Death; Fantasy; Gothic; Grotesque; Horror

http://www.uiah.fi/
Finland; UIAH; University of Art and Design

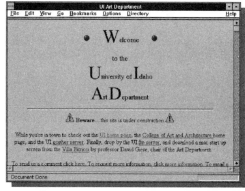

http://www.uidaho.edu/~art/
Art; University of Idaho

http://www.uky.edu/Artsource/artsourcehome.html
Architecture; Art; ArtSource

http://ai.iit.nrc.ca/ai_point.html
AI; Artificial Intelligence Resources

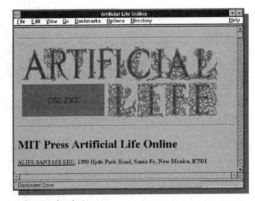

http://ai.iit.nrc.ca/misc.html
Artificial Intelligence; Index

http://alife.santafe.edu/
Artificial Life; MIT; AI

http://hitchhiker.space.lockheed.com/aic/
Lockheed Artificial Intelligence Center

http://maas-neotek.arc.nasa.gov/
NASA Ames Intelligent Mechanisms Group

http://reading-room-www.lcs.mit.edu/rr/
AI; Artificial Intelligence; Cognition; Computing; Learning

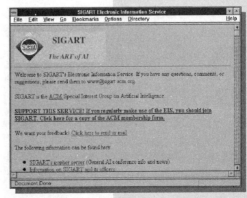

http://defiant.gsfc.nasa.gov/aiconf/AI-conf-General.html
Artificial intelligence; Goddard Space Flight Center; NASA

http://sigart.acm.org/
ACM; AI; Artificial intelligence

Astronomy

http://adswww.harvard.edu/
Astronaut; Astronomy; Astrophysics; NASA; Space

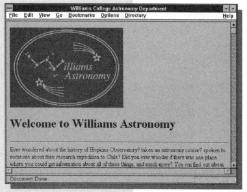

http://albert.astro.williams.edu/
Astronomy; Williams College

http://aquila.uni-muenster.de/
Astronomisches Institut; Education; Universitat Munster

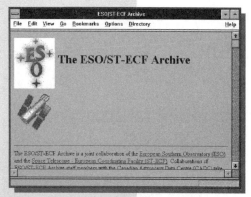

http://arch-http.hq.eso.org/ESO-ECF-Archive.html
Database; European Southern Observatory; Telescopes

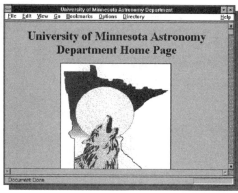

http://ast1.spa.umn.edu/
Astronomy; University of Minnesota

http://astrowww.astro.indiana.edu/
Astronomy; Indiana University

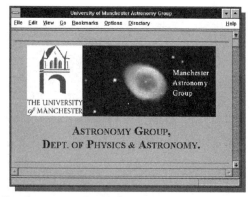

http://axp2.ast.man.ac.uk:8000/
Astronomy; Physics; Space; University of Manchester

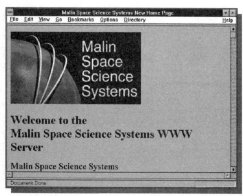

http://barsoom.msss.com/
Astronomy; Planets; Science; Space

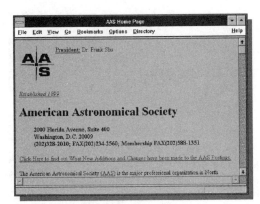

http://blackhole.aas.org/AAS-homepage.html
AAS; Astronomy; Astrophysics; Science

http://boas3.bo.astro.it/dip/DepHome.html
Astronomy; Italy; University of Bologna

http://cadc.dao.nrc.ca/ADASS-homepage.html
Astronomical Data Analysis Software and Systems; Canada

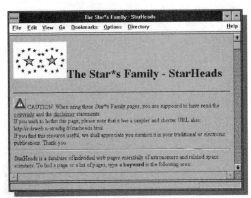

http://cdsweb.u-strasbg.fr/~heck/url2.htm
Astronomers; Astronomy; Science; Space; Stars

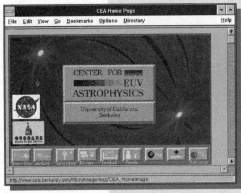

http://cea-ftp.cea.berkeley.edu/
Astronomy; Astrophysics; Goddard; NASA; Satellite

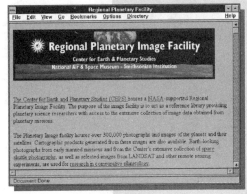

http://ceps.nasm.edu:2020/rpif.html
300000 photographs; Regional Planetary Image Facility

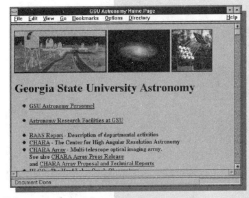

http://chara.gsu.edu/
Astronomy; Georgia State University

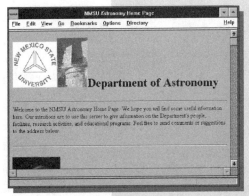

http://charon.nmsu.edu/
Astronomy; New Mexico; Space

21

http://ctio.noao.edu/ctio.html
Astronomy; Chile; CTIO; Observatories; South America

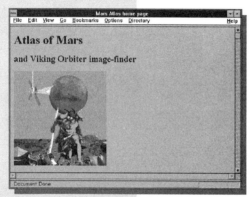

http://fi-www.arc.nasa.gov/fia/projects/bayes-group/Atlas/Mars/
Image; Mars; Orbiter; Viking

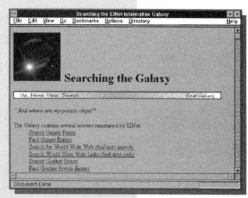

http://galaxy.einet.net/search.html
Galaxy; Planets; Search; Space

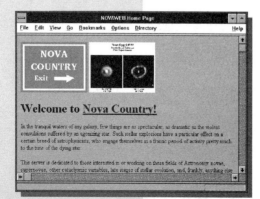

http://goodricke.astro.upenn.edu:8001/
Astronomy; Stars; Supernovas

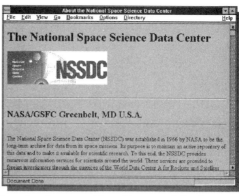

http://hypatia.gsfc.nasa.gov/about/about_nssdc.html
Archive; NASA; National Space Science Data Center

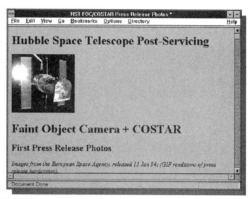

http://hypatia.gsfc.nasa.gov/hst/foc_costar_pr.html
COSTAR; Faint Object Camera; Photos

http://hypatia.gsfc.nasa.gov/hst/wfpcII_pr.html
Hubble Space Telescope; Photos; Planetary Camera

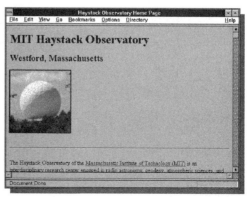

http://hyperion.haystack.edu/haystack/haystack.html
Massachusetts Institute of Technology; Observatory; Westford

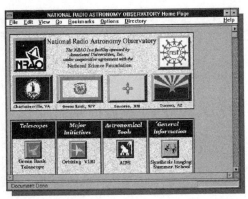

http://info.aoc.nrao.edu/
Astronomical tools; National Radio Astronomy Observatory

http://iuesn1.gsfc.nasa.gov/iue/iuedac_homepage.html
NASA; Physics; Robot; Satellite; Space

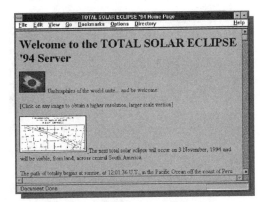

http://macjy.stsci.edu/
Space; Sun; Total solar eclipse

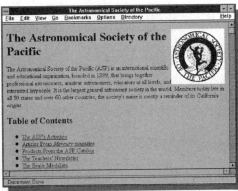

http://maxwell.sfsu.edu/asp/asp.html
Astronomical Society of the Pacific; Astronomy

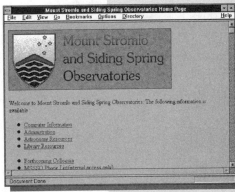

http://meteor.anu.edu.au/
Astronomy resources; Observatories; Space

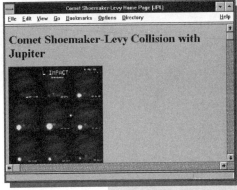

http://newproducts.jpl.nasa.gov/s19/s19.html
Astronomy; Comet; Nasa; Shoemaker-Levy; Space

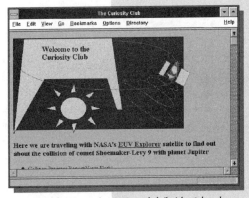

http://nisus.sfusd.k12.ca.us/curiosity_club/bridge1.html
Astronomy; Children; Curiosity

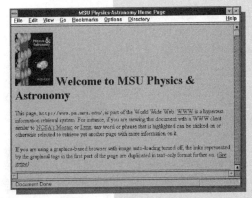

http://pads1.pa.msu.edu/
Michigan State University; Physics-Astronomy

http://planxty.stsci.edu:1024:/dogs/dogs.html
Galaxy; Milky Way; Space

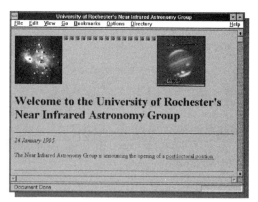

http://sherman.pas.rochester.edu/URNIRHome.html
Near infrared astronomy; Space

http://ringside.arc.nasa.gov/
NASA; Planets; Science; Space science

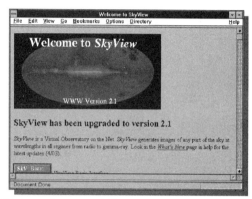

http://skyview.gsfc.nasa.gov:80/
Gamma-rays; Radio; SkyView; Virtual observatory

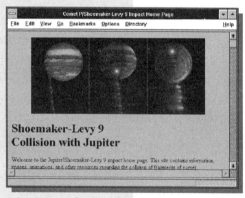

http://seds.lpl.arizona.edu/sl9/sl9.html
Astronomy; Comet; NASA; Shoemaker-Levy; Space

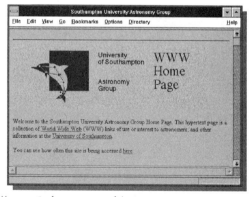

http://sousun1.phys.soton.ac.uk/
Astronomy; United Kingdom; University of Southampton

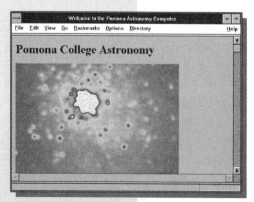

http://shanti.pomona.claremont.edu/
Pomona College Astronomy

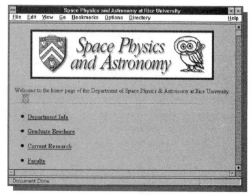

http://spacsun.rice.edu/
Astronomy; Rice University; Space Physics

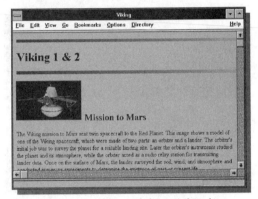

http://stardust.jpl.nasa.gov/
Measurements; Planetary missions; Planetary Data System

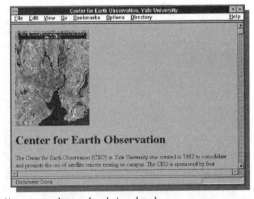

http://stardust.jpl.nasa.gov/planets/welcome/viking.htm
Images; Mars; Planetary exploration; Viking 1; Viking 2

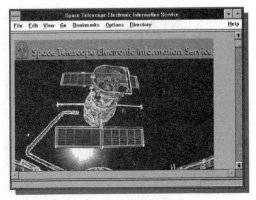

http://stormy.geology.yale.edu/ceo.html
Earth observation; Yale University

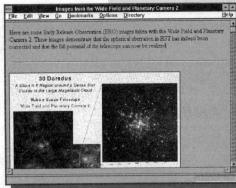

http://stsci.edu/wfpc2-images.html
Hubble Space Telescope; Space

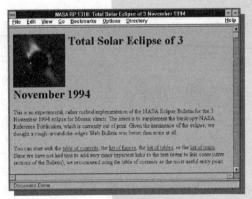

http://umbra.gsfc.nasa.gov/eclipse/941103/rp.html
NASA Eclipse Bulletin; Total solar eclipse

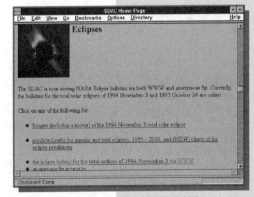

http://umbra.gsfc.nasa.gov/sdac.html#ECLIPSES
Eclipses; Images; Total solar eclipse

http://usa.net/cge/nancyhad.htm
Amateur Astronomers; Newsletter

Space Telescope Electronic Information Service
http://stsci.edu/top.html
Observatory; Space; Telescope

Astronomy

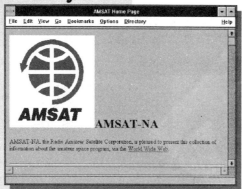

http://www.amsat.org/amsat
Amateur radio; AMSAT; Ham radio; Satellites

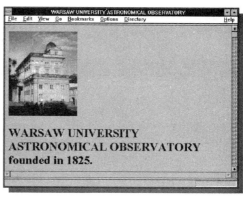

http://www.astrouw.edu.pl/
Astronomy; Observatory; Space; Warsaw

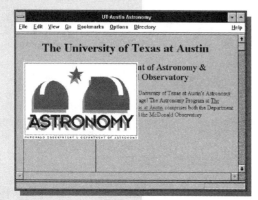

http://www.as.utexas.edu/
Astronomy; Austin; Science; Space; University of Texas

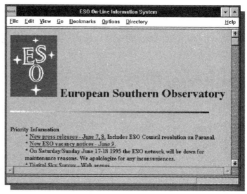

http://www.hq.eso.org/eso-homepage.html
European Southern Observatory; Information; News

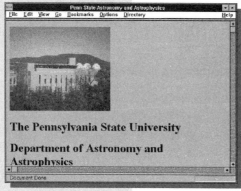

http://www.astro.psu.edu/
Astronomy; Astrophysics; Penn State University

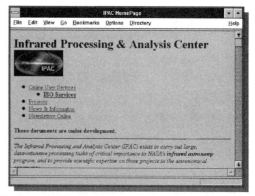

http://www.ipac.caltech.edu:80/
Astronomy; Infrared processing and analysis; NASA

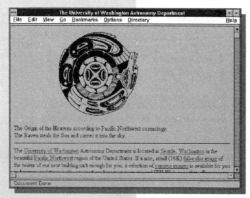

http://www.astro.washington.edu/
Astronomy; University of Washington

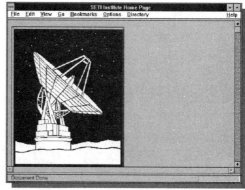

http://www.metrolink.com/seti/SETI.html
Satellites; SETI; Space

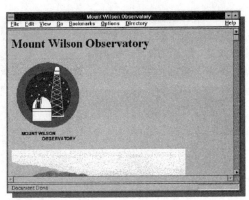

http://www.mtwilson.edu/
Mount Wilson Observatory; Planets; Space; Telescopes

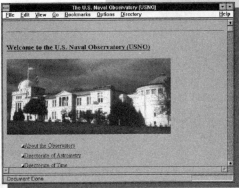

http://www.usno.navy.mil/
Astrometry; Space; US Naval Observatory

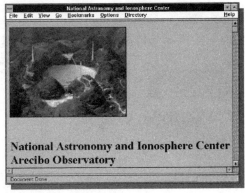

http://www.naic.edu/
Arecibo Observatory; Ionosphere Center; National Astronomy

http://www.usp.br/iag/iag.html
Astronomy; Brazil; Portuguese; University of Sao Paulo

http://www.noao.edu/kpno/kpno.html
Astronomy; Kitt Peak; Observatories; Space

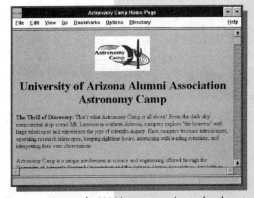

http://zeno.as.arizona.edu:8000/astro_camp/camp.html
Arizona; Astronomy; Education; Science

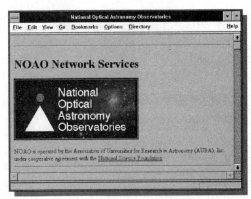

http://www.noao.edu/noao.html
Astronomy; Observatories; Space; Telescope

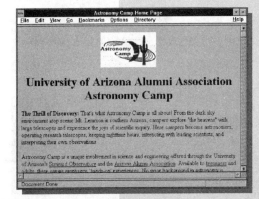

http://zia.geog.buffalo.edu/GIAL/netgeog.html
Astronomy; Space; Telescopes

Biology

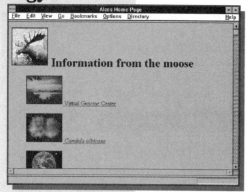

http://alces.med.umn.edu/start.html
Candida albicans; Virtual genomes

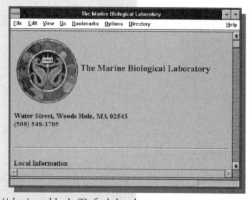

http://alopias.mbl.edu/Default.html
Marine Biological Laboratory; Marine science; Ocean studies

http://arnica.csustan.edu/
Biological sciences; California State University

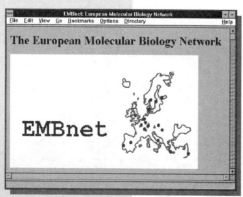

http://beta.embnet.unibas.ch/embnet/info.html
Europe; Molecular biology

http://bimcore.emory.edu/
BIMCORE; Biomolecular computing; Genetics; Software

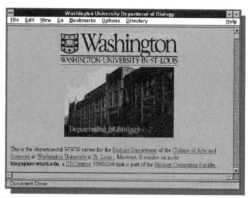

http://biodec.wustl.edu/
Biology; Missouri; St. Louis; Washington University

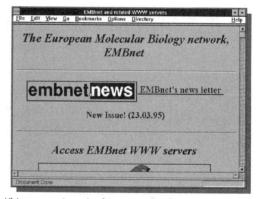

http://biomaster.uio.no/embnet-www.html
Biology; Biotechnology; Molecular biology

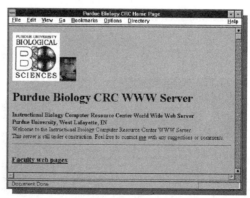

http://bogie2.bio.purdue.edu/
Biology; Indiana; Purdue University

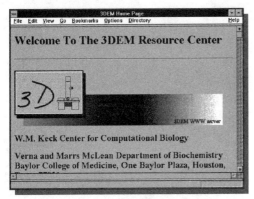

http://cns.bio.com/brni.html
Careers; Research; Vendors

http://condor.bcm.tmc.edu/3DEM/3dem-home.html
Baylor; Computational biology

http://condor.bcm.tmc.edu/home.html
Biology; Molecular Biology; Research

http://condor.bcm.tmc.edu/SCBMB/scbmb.html
Computational biology; Molecular biophysics

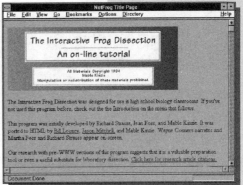

http://curry.edschool.virginia.edu/~insttech/frog/
Biology; Frog dissection; High School

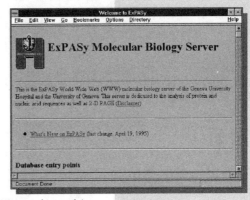

http://expasy.hcuge.ch/
Medicine; Molecular biology; Protein

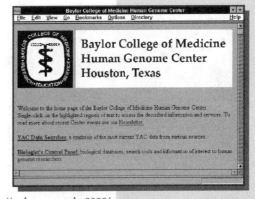

http://gc.bcm.tmc.edu:8088/
Baylor; Biological databases; Human genome

http://giles.ualr.edu/
BioFluids Dynamics; Little Rock; University of Arkansas

Biology

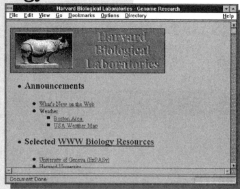

http://golgi.harvard.edu/
Botany; Harvard Biological Laboratories; Harvard University

http://hagar.biosci.ohio-state.edu/
Biological Sciences; Ohio State University

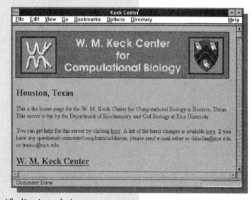

http://helix.rice.edu/
Cell Biology; Computing; Department of Biochemistry

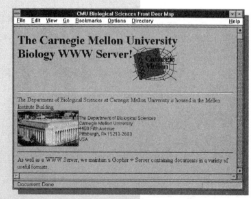

http://info.bio.cmu.edu/
Biology; Carnegie Mellon University

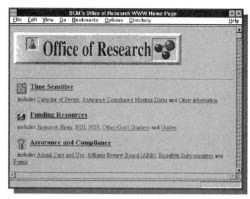

http://johnson.bcm.tmc.edu/
Assurance; Compliance; Funding resources

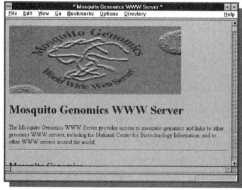

http://klab.agsci.colostate.edu/
Biotechnical information; Mosquito genomics

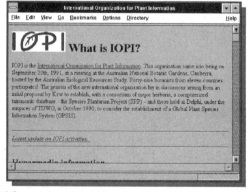

http://life.anu.edu.au/biodiversity/iopi/iopi.html
Botany; IOPI; Science; Taxonomy

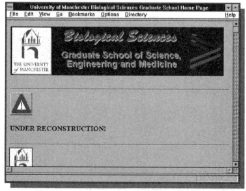

http://mbisg2.sbc.man.ac.uk/homepage.html
Biological sciences; University of Manchester

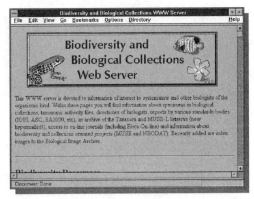

http://molbio.umn.edu/cbs.html
Biological Sciences; University of Minnesota

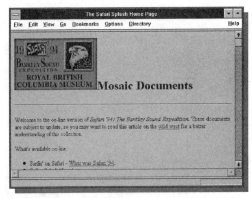

http://muse.bio.cornell.edu/
Biocollections; Biodiversity; Cornell University

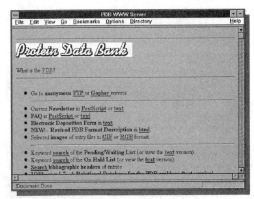

http://oberon.educ.sfu.ca/splash.htm
Animals; Biology; Safari

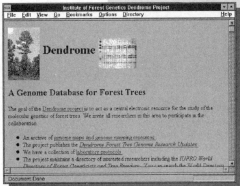

http://s27w007.pswfs.gov:80/
Forest; Forestry; Genome database; Trees

http://salk.edu/
Biological studies; Medicine; Neuroscience; Salk Institute

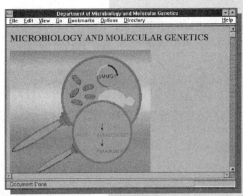

http://salus.med.uvm.edu/mmg/mmg.html
Microbiology and Molecular Genetics; University of Vermont

http://pdb.pdb.bnl.gov:80/
Biology; Data bank; Protein

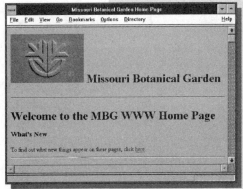

http://straylight.tamu.edu/MoBot/welcome.html
Botanical gardens; Botany; Gardens; Missouri; Plants

Biology

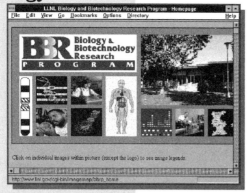

http://www-bio.llnl.gov/bbrp/bbrp.homepage.html
Biology; Biotechnology; Research

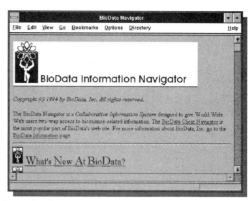

http://www.biodata.com/
Biodata; Bioscience; Biotechnology; Science

http://www.bio.bris.ac.uk/
Biological; Biology; Schools; Science; University of Bristol

http://www.bioweb.com/bioweb/__0ddf70c4/index.html
Biologists; BioWeb; Information Resource

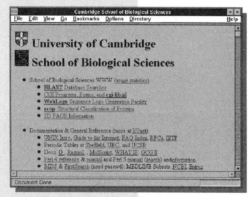

http://www.bio.cam.ac.uk/
Biological Sciences; Cambridge University; United Kingdom

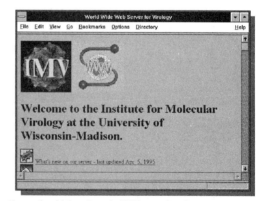

http://www.bocklabs.wisc.edu/Welcome.html
Biology; Diseases; Medicine; Viruses

http://www.bio.cornell.edu/
Biological Sciences; Cornell University

http://www.calpoly.edu/delta.html
Biological sciences; Databases

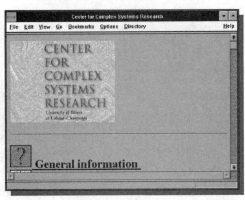

http://www.ccsr.uiuc.edu/
Biology; Mathematics; Physics; University of Champaign

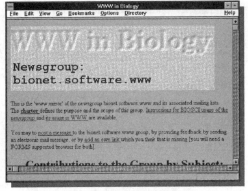

http://www.ch.embnet.org/bio-www/info.html
Bionet; Newsgroups

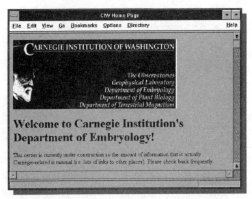

http://www.ciwemb.edu/
Bioscience; Carnegie; Embryology; Research; Science

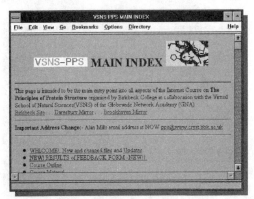

http://www.cryst.bbk.ac.uk/PPS/index.html
Biology; Protein structure; Science

http://www.gdb.org/Dan/catal/milli-intro.html
Biology; Images; Supplies

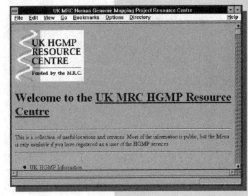

http://www.hgmp.mrc.ac.uk/
Biology; Gene; Genome; HGMP

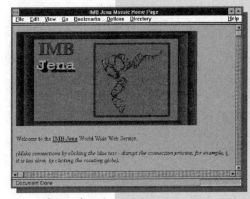

http://www.imb-jena.de:80/
Biotechnology; IMB Jena; Molecules

http://www.ncbi.nlm.nih.gov/
Biotechnology; DNA; Genes

Biomedical

http://biomed.nus.sg/
Biomedicine; National University of Singapore

http://opal.vcu.edu/html/biomede/bio-science.html
Biotechnology; Life sciences; Virginia Commonwealth University

http://bmes.mc.vanderbilt.edu/homepage.htm
Biomedical Engineering; Vanderbilt University

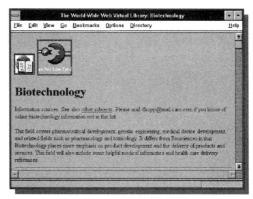

http://www.cato.com/interweb/cato/biotech/
Biotechnology; Virtual Library; World-Wide Web

http://ibc.wustl.edu/
Washington University Institute for Biomedical Computing

http://www.nlm.nih.gov/lhc.dir/lhncbc.html
Biomedical Communications; Biomedicine; Lister Hill

http://isdl.ee.washington.edu/ABME/annals.html
Biomedical engineering; Journal; Medicine

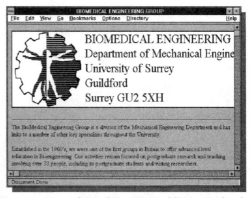

http://www.surrey.ac.uk/MechEng/BioMed/homepage.html
Education; University of Surrey Guildford Surrey

Business and Finance

http://140.174.161.1/sprintbiz/
Business; Cyberspace; Sprint

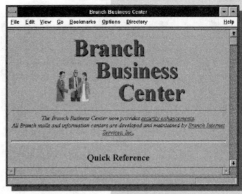

http://branch.com/business.htm
Communications; Computer Products; Electronics; Legal; Services

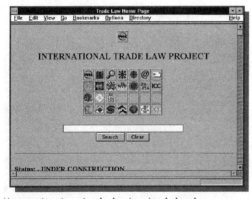

http://192.160.127.230/cgi-bin/vmarket
Business; Internet; Virtual Market

http://ccnet.com/~tloker/
Business solutions; Problem solving

35

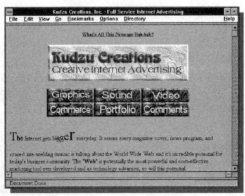

http://ananse.irv.uit.no/trade_law/nav/trade.html
Commerce; Law; Trade

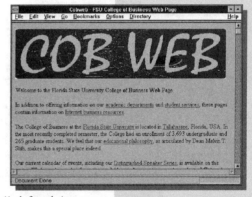

http://cob.fsu.edu/
Business; Florida State University; Tallahassee

http://atl1.america.net/com/kudzu/kudzu.html
Advertising; Business; Internet

http://colette.ogsm.vanderbilt.edu/
Computer; Marketing; Vanderbilt University

Business and Finance

http://crash.cts.com/cts/market/
CTSNET; Goods and services; Links; Products

http://cybermart.com/boisecc/
Boise; Chamber of Commerce; Idaho

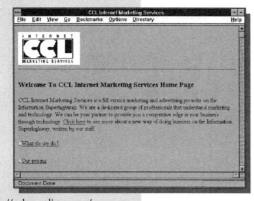

http://cyber.cclims.com/
Advertising; CCL Internet Marketing Services; Marketing

http://digicash.support.nl/
DigiCash; E-cash; Money; News; Products; Publications

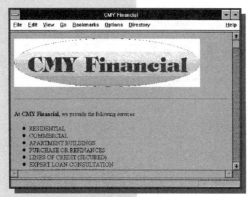

http://cyber.cclims.com/comp/cmy/cmy.html
Apartment buildings; Commercial; Credit; Loans; Residential

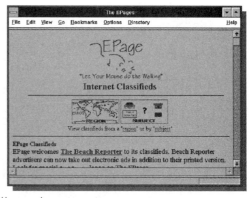

http://ep.com/
Announcements; Classified ads; EPages

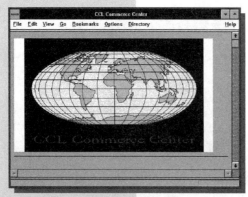

http://cyber.cclims.com/mall/commerce/commerce.html
Business directory; Commerce; Links

http://fccm.com/
Banking; Finance; First Chicago Capital Markets Inc.; Investment

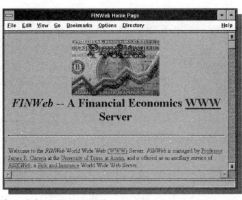

http://finweb.bus.utexas.edu/finecon.html
Economics; Finance; FINWeb

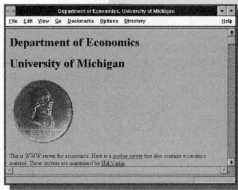

http://gopher.econ.lsa.umich.edu/
Economics; Education; Finance

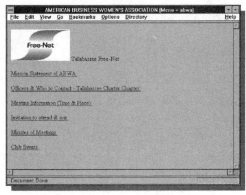

http://freenet3.scri.fsu.edu:81/ht-free/abwa.html
American Business Woman's Association; Mission statement

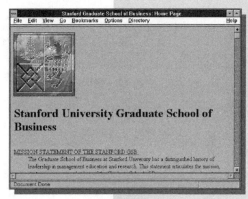

http://gsb-www.stanford.edu/home.html
Business; Graduate School; Stanford University

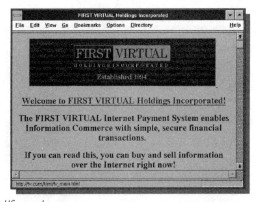

http://fv.com/
FIRST VIRTUAL; Internet Payment System; Secure transactions

http://hampton.roads.net/nhr/
Business; Commerce; Hampton roads

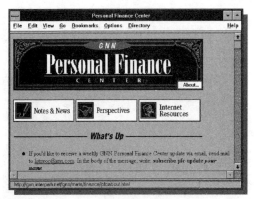

http://gnn.interpath.net/gnn/meta/finance/
GNN; Internet resources; Personal finance

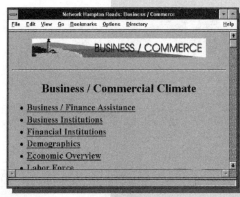

http://hampton.roads.net/nhr/business.html
Business; Commerce; Hampton Roads; Virginia

Business and Finance

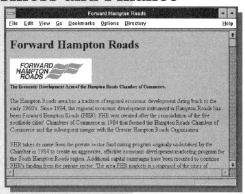

http://hampton.roads.net/nhr/fhr/home.html
Economic development; Hampton Roads; Virginia

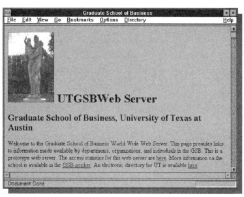

http://kiwiclub.bus.utexas.edu/
Austin; Business; Graduate School; University of Texas

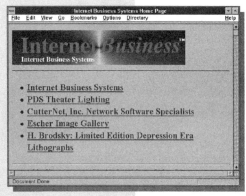

http://inetbsystems.us.com/Home-Page.html
Business; Business Information Systems; Images; Lithographs

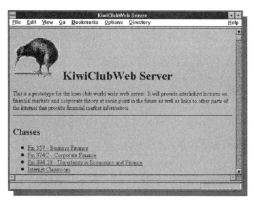

http://kiwiclub.bus.utexas.edu/finance/kiwiserver/kiwiserver.html
Economics; Finance

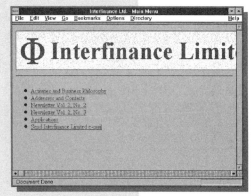

http://intergroup.com/interfinance
Banking; Finance; Investments; Real estate; Venture capital

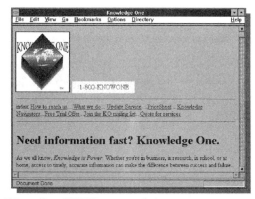

http://KnowOne_WWW.sonoma.edu/
Business; Information; Knowledge One; Research; School

http://kbt.com/cardservice
Cashless Society; Software processing

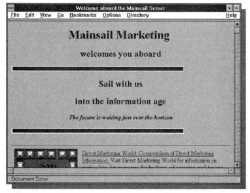

http://mainsail.com/
Information systems; Internet; Marketing; Web

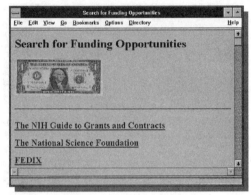

http://market.net/market/index.html
Directories; Information; Links; Market.NET

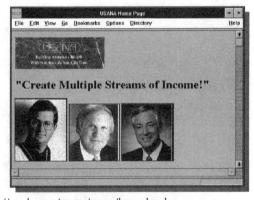

http://medoc.gdb.org/best/fund.html
Federally funded research; Grants; Search

http://merkury.saic.com/usana/home.html
Home-based business; USANA

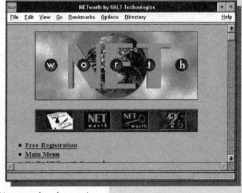

http://mmink.com/mmink/dossiers/tmg/tmg.html
Equipment; IBM; Mainframes; Midrange; OEM; Service

http://moneyforte.com/
Finance; Investing; Money Forte

http://nctn.oact.hq.nasa.gov/SBIR/SBIR.html
Events; Opportunities; Small business innovation

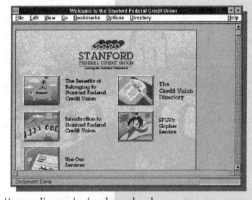

http://netmedia.com/cu/cu_home.html
Banking; Credit unions; Stanford

http://networth.galt.com/
Internet resource; Investors; Mutual funds

Business and Finance

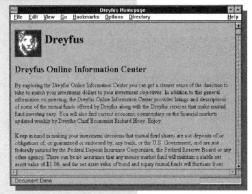

http://networth.galt.com/dreyfus/4134
Dreyfus; Financial markets; Investment

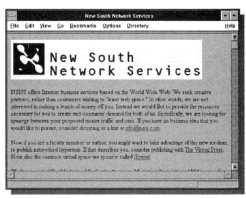

http://nsns.com/
Internet business services; New South

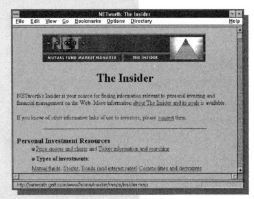

http://networth.galt.com/www/home/insider/insider.htm
Investment resources; Mutual funds

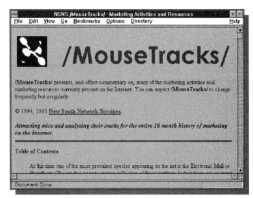

http://nsns.com/MouseTracks/
Commentary; Marketing activities; Marketing resources

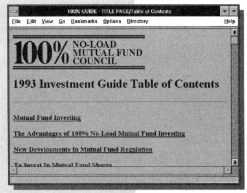

http://networth.galt.com/www/home/mutual/100/100guide.htm
Investment; Mutual funds; Guide

http://nw.com/bahnware/classifieds/classifieds.html
Classified Advertisements; Search

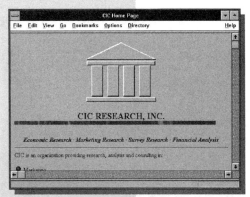

http://noc.thegroup.net/cic/
Analysis; Consulting; Economics; Marketing; Research

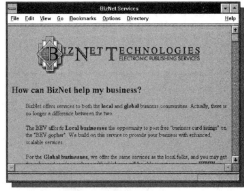

http://oscar.bnt.com/services.html
Business services; Electronic publishing; Global; Local

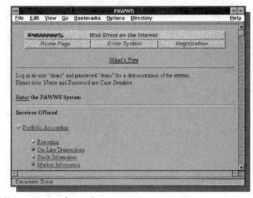

http://owens.ridgecrest.ca.us/
California; Community and Economic Development; Ridgecrest

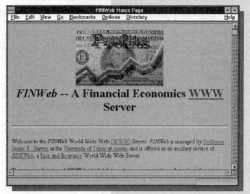

http://riskweb.bus.utexas.edu/finecon.htm
Economics; Finance; Insurance

http://pawws.secapl.com/
Online transactions; Stock market; Wall Street

http://riskweb.bus.utexas.edu/riskweb.htm
Insurance; RISKNet; RISKWeb

http://programs.interop.com/
Conference; NetWorld+Interop; SOFTBANK Exposition

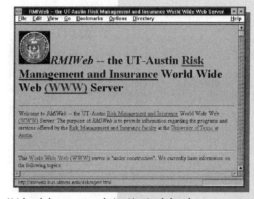

http://riskweb.bus.utexas.edu/rmi/rmiweb.html
University of Texas at Austin; RMIWeb

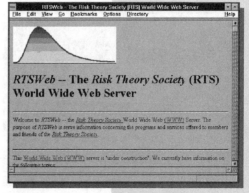

http://risc.cpbx.net/IOL/about.html
Finances; Investing; Newsletter

http://riskweb.bus.utexas.edu/rts/rtsweb.html
Insurance; Risk Theory Society

Business and Finance

http://riskweb.bus.utexas.edu/whataria.htm
Insurance; Risk; Services

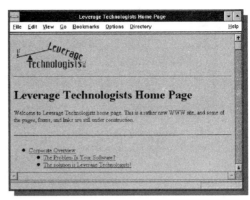

http://stout.levtech.com/
Consulting; Internet; Services; Tools; Training

http://silcom.com/
California; News; Santa Barbara; Silicon Beach Communications

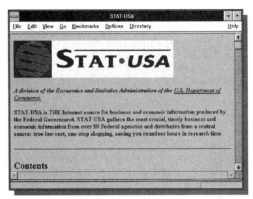

http://sunny.stat-usa.gov/
Business and economic information; Department of Commerce

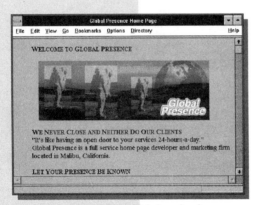

http://smartworld.com/globalpres/globalpres.html
Consulting; Home page developer; Internet presence; Web services

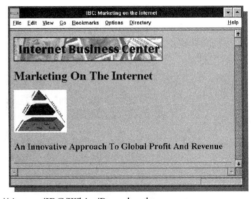

http://tig.com/IBC/White/Paper.html
Global; Internet Business Center; Marketing

http://smartworld.com/intmedia/imedia.html
Artists; Composers; Consultant; Multimedia; Production

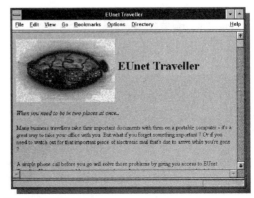

http://Traveller.EU.net/
EUnet; Europe; Internet

http://usa.net/home/business.html
Business; Directories; Links

http://webnet.pic.net/
Marketing; WebNet Technologies

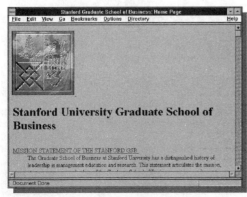

http://wsodeman.usi.edu/
Business; University of Southern Indiana

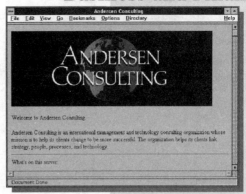

http://www.ac.com/
Consulting; Management; Strategy; Technology

http://www.accel.com/
Entrepreneurs; Investments; Venture capital

http://www.accessnv.com/postnet
Postal and Business Services; PostNet

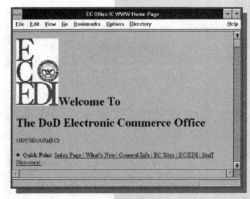

http://www.acq.osd.mil/ec/ecic_hpg.html
Electronic commerce; Government; Information Center

http://www-gsb.stanford.edu/home.html
Business; Stanford University Graduate School of Business

43

Business and Finance

http://www.adage.com/
Advertising; Business; Marketing

http://www.admarket.com/
Advertising; Directories; Marketing; Media; Public relations

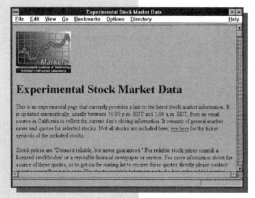

http://www.ai.mit.edu/stocks.html
Investment; Stock market; Ticker tape

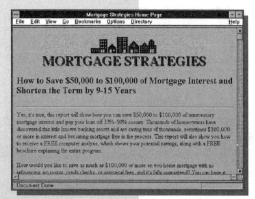

http://www.ais.net:80/netmall/mortgage/mortgage.html
Banking; Finance; Mortgages

http://www.amark.com/amark/
Auctions; Coins; Collectibles; Investments; Manuscripts; Stamps

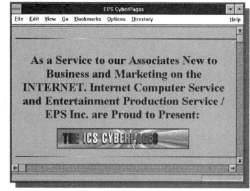

http://www.amug.org/~eps/cyber.html
Business; Internet; Marketing

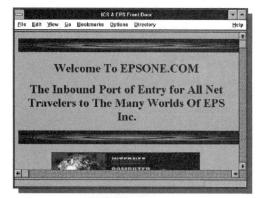

http://www.amug.org/~eps/index.html
Concerts; Consulting; Entertainment; Training; Multimedia

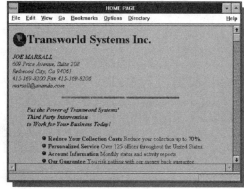

http://www.ananda.com/plg/marsall/
Collection agency; Credit; Services

http://www.and.com/and.html
And Communications; Information; Services

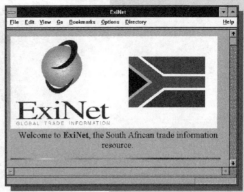

http://www.aztec.co.za/exinet
Resource; South Africa; Trade information

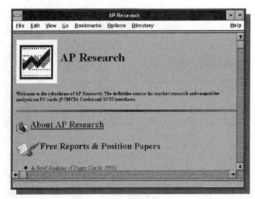

http://www.apk.net/look/
Economics; Private; Science; Technology; Trends

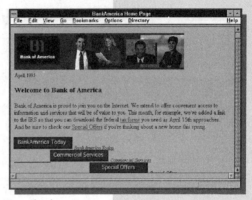

http://www.bankamerica.com/
Banking; Bank of America; Finances

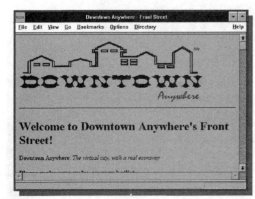

http://www.apresearch.com/
Competitive analysis; Market research

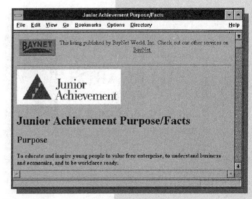

http://www.baynet.com/junior/intro.html
Business; Economics; Free Enterprise; Young People

http://www.awa.com/
Gifts; Online malls; Virtual downtown

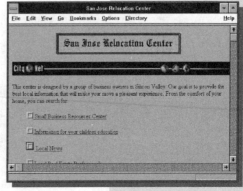

http://www.best.com/~hungtran/index.htm
Community information; News; Relocation; San Jose

Business and Finance

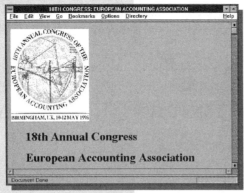

http://www.bham.ac.uk/business/eaacong.html
Accounting; European Accounting Association; Finance

http://www.blarg.com/webweavers
Marketing; Web presence; WebVertising

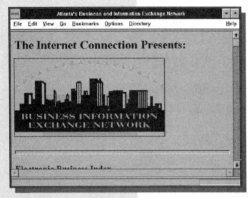

http://www.bie.net/
Atlanta; Businesses; Internet connection

http://www.bnt.com/~crc/
Economic development; Virginia Tech Corporate Research

http://www.billboard.com/
Advertising; Billboards; Companies; Directories; Services

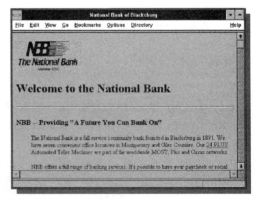

http://www.bnt.com/~nbb/
Full services community bank; National Bank; Virginia

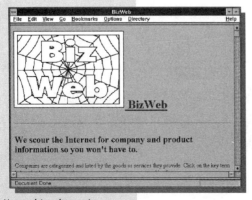

http://www.bizweb.com/
Company information; Product information; Service

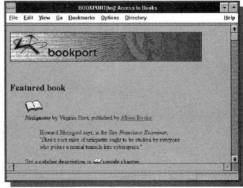

http://www.bookport.com/
Books; Publishers; Editors; Business

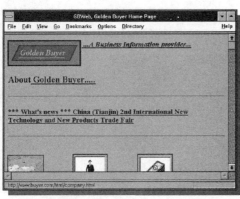

http://www.buyer.com/
Business Information provider; Golden Buyer; News

http://www.catalog.com/rmg/bbc.htm
Business owners; Pacific Beach.; Professionals; Sales reps

http://www.camcord.com/
Information; Statistical stock reports; Stock charts; Technology

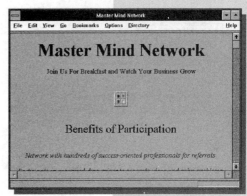

http://www.catalog.com/rmg/mm_net.htm
Business contacts; Networking; Parties; Presentations; Referrals

http://www.capmkt.com/
Consulting; Financial; Risk management; Services

http://www.catalog.com/rmg/scnba.htm
Business promotion; Business strategies; Non-profit organization

http://www.catalog.com/napmsv
Information resource; News; Purchasing; Supply Management

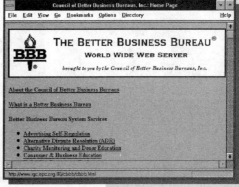

http://www.cbbb.org/cbbb
Better Business Bureaus; Consumer and Business Education

Business and Finance

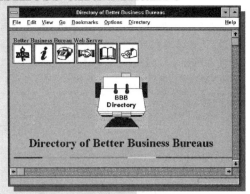

http://www.cbbb.org/cbbb/bbb-dir.html
Better Business Bureaus; Directories

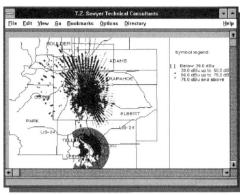

http://www.clark.net/pub/tzsawyer/tzsawyer.html
Technical Consultants; T.Z. Sawyer

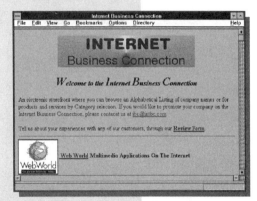

http://www.charm.net/~ibc/index.html
Internet Business Connection; Multimedia applications

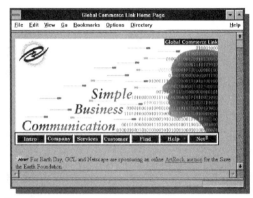

http://www.commerce.com/
Business; Commerce; Communication

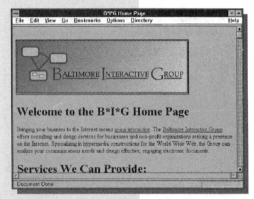

http://www.charm.net/~sam/BIG_Home.html
Baltimore Interactive Group; Business; Consulting; Design

http://www.commerce.net/
CommerceNet; Products and services

http://www.cityscape.co.uk/
Commerce; European business; Directory; News

http://www.commerce.net/directories/directories.html
Business; Commerce; Communication; Directories

http://www.connectinc.com/
Business presence; Virtual billboards

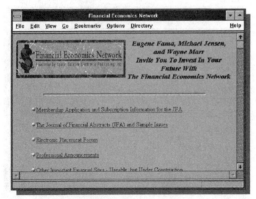

http://www.creacon.com/Q4Q/index.html
Deming; Engineering; Management; Quality; TQM

http://www.crimson.com/fen/
Economics; Finance; Investment

http://www.ctron.com/
Electronic magazines; Online magazines; Periodicals

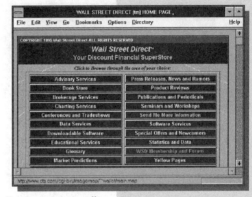

http://www.cts.com/~wallst
Financial; Investment; Wall Street

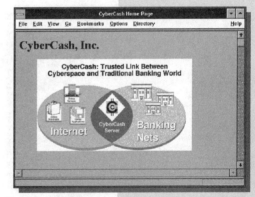

http://www.cybercash.com/
CyberCash; Online banking; Secure transactions

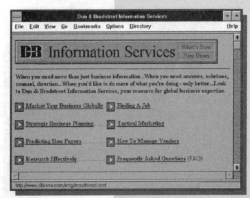

http://www.dbisna.com/
Business planning; Collections; Dun and Bradstreet

49

[image of New Brunswick site]
http://www.csi.nb.ca/econ-dev/
Investments; Canada; Economic development;

Business and Finance

http://www.directory.net/lexis-nexis/sba
Advertising; Business presence; Starting a business

http://www.fe.msk.ru/infomarket/rinacoplus/overview.html
Financial investments; Russian securities

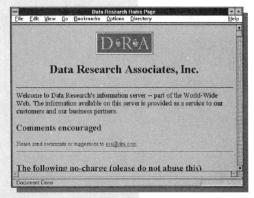

http://www.dra.com/
Data Research Associates Inc.; Research; Statisticians

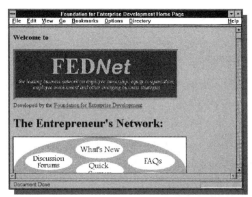

http://www.fed.org/fed/
Resources; Entrepreneur; Foundation for Enterprise Development

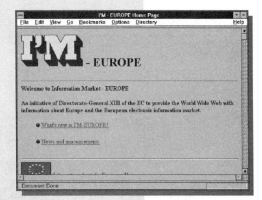

http://www.echo.lu/
Europe; European electronic information market

http://www.fid-inv.com/
Brokerage services; Fidelity; Investments; Tools; Mutual funds

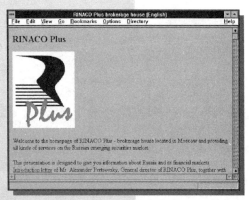

http://www.fe.msk.ru/infomarket/rinacoplus/
Financial; Russian; Securities market

http://www.financenet.gov/
Finance; Government

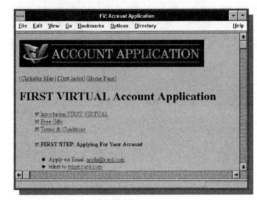

http://www.fullfeed.com/mosaicm/
Consulting; Internet advertising; Netopia; Publishing

http://www.global.net/
Company information; GeoNet; Products; Services

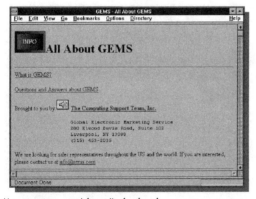

http://www.fv.com/setup.html
Account; First Virtual

http://www.hexadecimal.com/fi/
Banking; Business services; Consumer services; Economics

51

http://www.gems.com/about/index.html
Audio; GEMS; Marketing service

http://www.homefair.com/homefair/vawhatis.html
Guaranteed loan; Lenders; Loans; Mortgages; Real estate; VA

http://www.gems.com/showcase/lsma
Copyrights; Patents; Protection; Trademarks

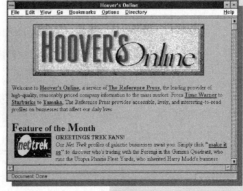

http://www.hoovers.com/
Business; Company information; Company profiles

Business and Finance

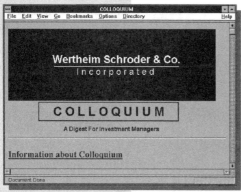

http://www.hydra.com/wertheim/colloquium.html
Investment; Management; Newsletters

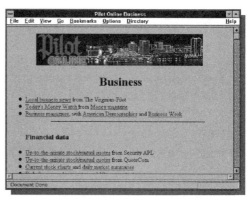

http://www.infi.net/pilot/biz.html
Business Week; Money magazine; Pilot Online

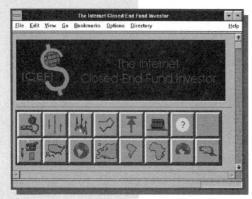

http://www.icefi.com/
CEF; Closed-End Funds; Investments

http://www.infi.net/pilot/how2ad.html
Pilot Online; Put your business online

http://www.iisys.com/www/iishome.htm
Contacts; International Business Guide

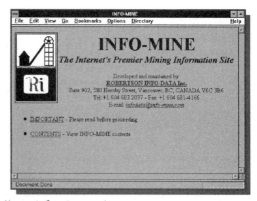

http://www.info-mine.com/
Canada; Mining information

http://www.infi.net/collegemoney
Education; Signet Bank Student Loan

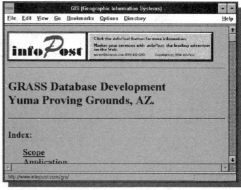

http://www.infopost.com/gis/index.html
Advertiser; Arizona; InfoPost

http://www.internet-is.com/myers/in-iis.html
Home Mortgage Loans; Myers Equity Express; Rates

http://www.internetmci.com/
Internet; MCI mail; Services

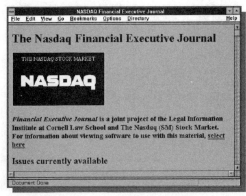

http://www.kiae.su/
Communications; Russian

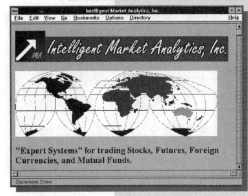

http://www.marketmind.com/
Futures; Investing; Market analysis; Mutual funds; Stocks

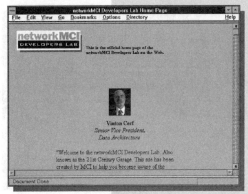

http://www.mci.com/developerslab
Data Architecture; MCI Developers Lab; Research

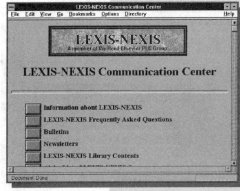

http://www.meaddata.com/
Accounting; Auditing; Communications; Filings; Publications

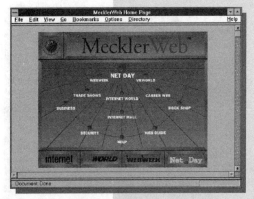

http://www.law.cornell.edu/nasdaq/nasdtoc.html
Investing; Nasdaq Financial Executive Journal; Stocks

http://www.mecklerweb.com/
Books; Business; Internet

53

Business and Finance

http://www.melanet.com/melanet/
Business; Commerce; Information

http://www.netpart.com/
Consulting; Internet; NetPartners; Systems integration; Tools

http://www.microserve.net/
Company Information; MicroServe Information System; MIS

http://www.nortel.com/
French; German; Networks; NORTEL; Resources; Spanish

http://www.nationsbank.com/
Banking; Finance; NationsBank; Olympics

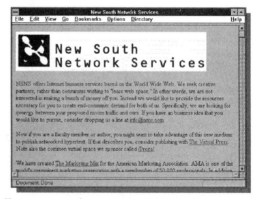

http://www.nsns.com/
Business service; Marketing; New South Network Services

http://www.netmarket.com/
Business solutions; Gifts; Online shopping; Services

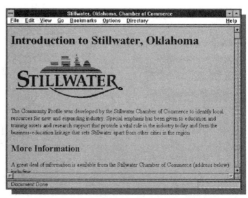

http://www.okstate.edu/stillwater/introduction.html
Business; Chamber of Commerce; Education; Stillwater Oklahoma

http://www.onramp.net/~atw_dhw/home.htm
Email; Forums; Planning; Services; Strategy

http://www.quote.com/
Investment; Stock Market

http://www.openmarket.com/
Commerce; Online shopping; Open market

http://www.sbaonline.sba.gov/
Resources; SBA; Small Business Administration

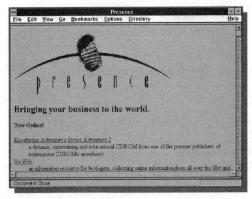

http://www.pcxpress.com/
Express Net; Products; Support

55

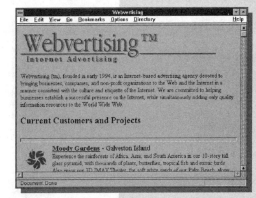

http://www.sccsi.com/welcome.html
Advertising agency; Business presence; Webvertising

http://www.presence.com/
Biologists; Business presence; Internet; Web sites

http://www.scubed.com:8001/tax/tax.html
Accounting; IRS; Tax forms; Tax law

Business and Finance

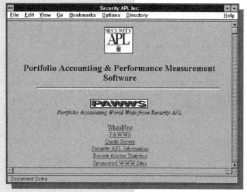

http://www.secapl.com/
PAWWS; Portfolio Accounting; Security APL; Quote server

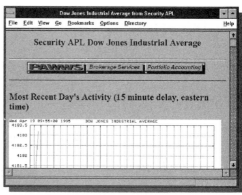

http://www.secapl.com/secapl/quoteserver/djia.html
Dow Jones; Economics; Finance; Stock Market

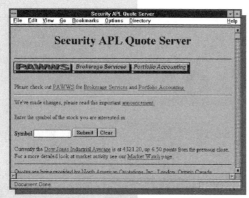

http://www.secapl.com/cgi-bin/qs
Brokerage service; Dow Jones; Stock market

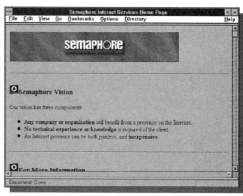

http://www.semaphore.com/
Business presence; Semaphore Vision; Web publishing

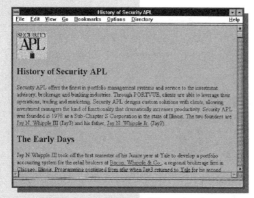

http://www.secapl.com/secapl/history/history.html
Investment; Portfolio management

http://www.service.digital.com/
Business; Consumer services; Digital; Products

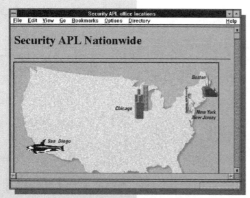

http://www.secapl.com/secapl/location/top.html
Investment; Security APL

http://www.sii.com/sales.and.marketing/salesover.html
Sales and marketing; System Integrators

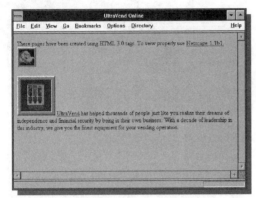

http://www.sri.com/
SRI; Stanford Research Institute

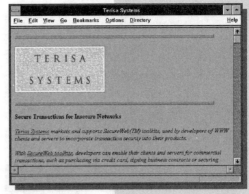

http://www.terisa.com/
Networks; Secure transactions; SecureWeb

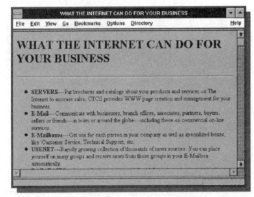

http://www.srv.net:8001/UltraVend.html
Business startup; UltraVend Online; Vending

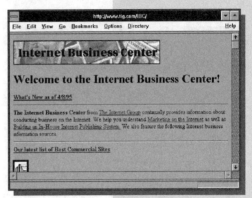

http://www.tig.com/IBC/
Business; Commerce; Marketing

http://www.sunbelt.net/hypervision/internet.htm
Advertising; Communications; E-mail; News

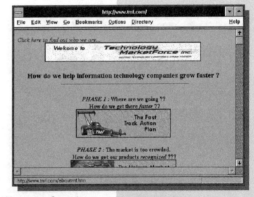

http://www.tmf.com/
Company support; Technology MarketForce Inc.

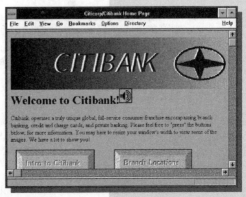

http://www.tdbank.ca/tdbank
Investment; Small business; TD Bank

http://www.tti.com/
Audio; Banking; Credit

Business and Finance

http://www.uswest.com/
Internet; Products and services; Telecommunications; US West

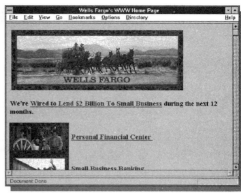

http://www.wellsfargo.com/
Banking; Finance; Small business

http://www.visions.com/netpages
Canada Net Pages; Canadian business and finance

http://www.wimsey.com/Magnet/mc/index.html
Brokering; Finance; Inventions

http://www.webcom.com/~lewrose/home.html
Advertising; Law; Marketing

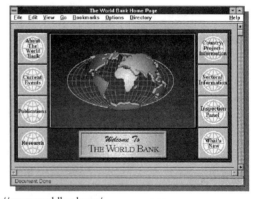

http://www.worldbank.org/
Current events; Publications; World Bank

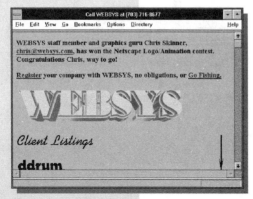

http://www.websys.com/
Client listings; Netscape Logo/Animation contest; WEBSYS

http://www.worldtrade.com/
GATT; NAFTA; WorldTrade Consortium

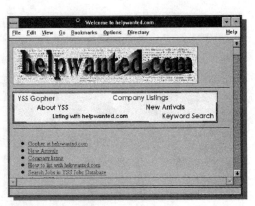

http://helpwanted.com/
Company listings; Employment; Help wanted; Jobs

http://supermall.com/cwcd/cwcdhome.html
Mail order business startup information

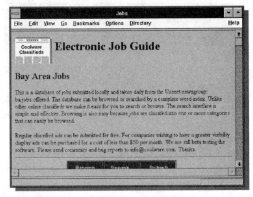

http://none.coolware.com/jobs.html
Database; Electronic Job Guide; Search

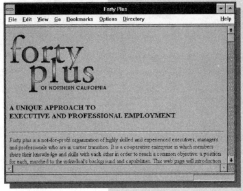

http://web.sirius.com/~40plus/
Executive; Non-profit organization; Professional employment

59

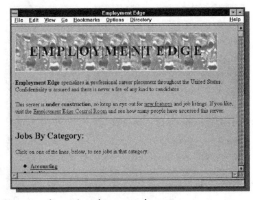

http://sensemedia.net/employment.edge
Career placement; Employment; Job listings

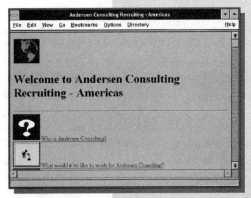

http://www.ac.com/recruit/welcome.htm
Andersen Consulting; Employment; Recruiting

http://stimpy.cen.uiuc.edu/comm/expo/
Employment; Engineering; Jobs

http://www.adnetsol.com//jsearch/jshome1.html
Database; Jobs; Search; Southern California

Careers

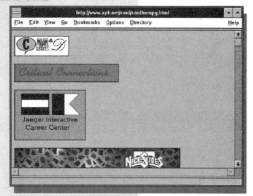

http://www.apk.net/cmd/cmdhompg.html
Jaeger Interactive Career Center

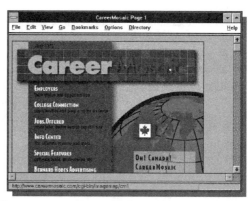

http://www.careermosaic.com/cm/
Directories; Employers; Jobs; Links; Resumes; Search; Services

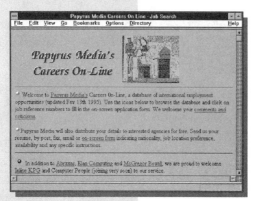

http://www.Britain.EU.net/vendor/jobs/main.html
International job opportunities; Resumes

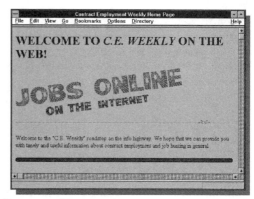

http://www.ceweekly.wa.com/
Contract employment; Job hunting

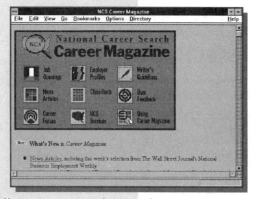

http://www.careermag.com/careermag/
Career information; Job searches; Employers

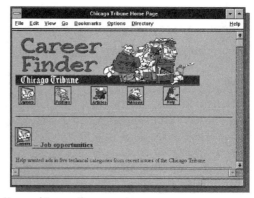

http://www.chicago.tribune.com/
Career Finder; Employment; Job opportunities

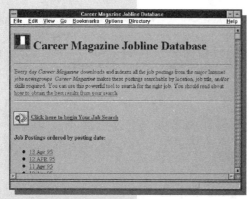

http://www.careermag.com/careermag/news/index.html
Job listings; Locations; Titles; Skills

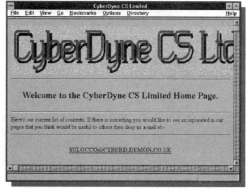

http://www.demon.co.uk/cyberdyne/cyber.html
Africa; Asia; Australia; Contracts; Europe; Job listings;

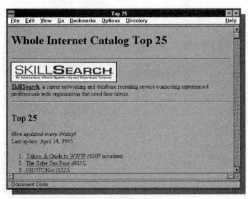

http://www.digital.com/gnn/wic/top.toc.html
Images; Internet catalog; Recruiting service

http://www.ipctech.com:80/
Computer companies; Employment; Training

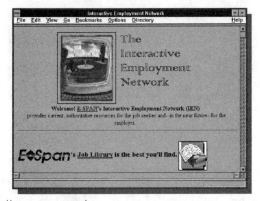

http://www.espan.com/
Employment; Job seeking; Career network

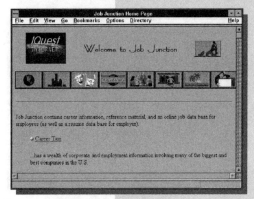

http://www.iquest.net/iq/jobjunction.html
Career information; Job database; Resumes

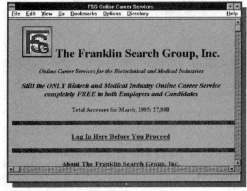

http://www.gate.net/biotech-jobs/
Boitechnical; Career services; Medical

http://www.monster.com/
Career fairs; Job services

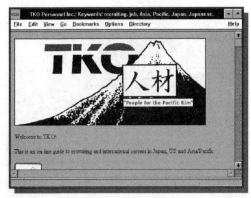

http://www.internet-is.com/tko/csites.html
Japan; TKO; TKO Personnel

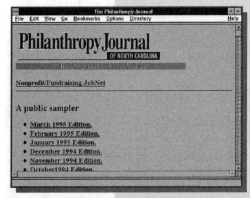

http://www.nando.net/philant/philant.html
Job listings; North Carolina

Chemistry

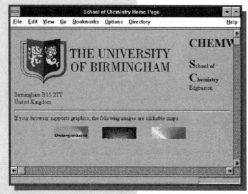

http://chem-www.mps.ohio-state.edu/
Chemistry; Ohio State University

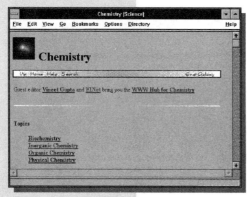

http://chemwww.bham.ac.uk/chemistry_home.html
Chemistry; University of Birmingham

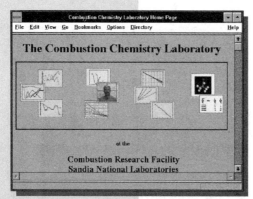

http://galaxy.einet.net/galaxy/Science/Chemistry.html
Biochemistry; Chemistry; Inorganic chemistry

http://mephisto.ca.sandia.gov/
Combustion; Laboratory; Sandia National Laboratories

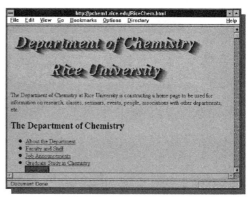

http://pchem1.rice.edu/RiceChem.html
Chemistry; Rice University

http://sbchm1.sunysb.edu/
Chemistry; Research; Science

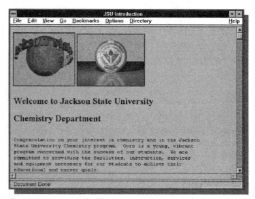

http://tiger.jsums.edu/html/homepage.html
Education; Jackson State University

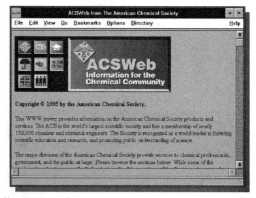

http://www.acs.org/
Chemical; Chemists; Engineers; Information; Science; Services

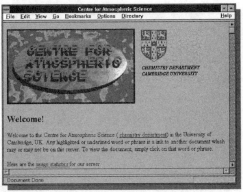

http://www.atm.ch.cam.ac.uk/
Chemistry Department Cambridge University; Education

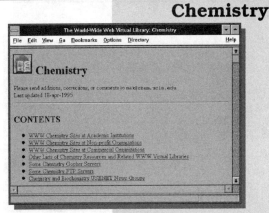

http://www.chem.ucla.edu/chempointers.html
Biochemistry; Chemistry; Science

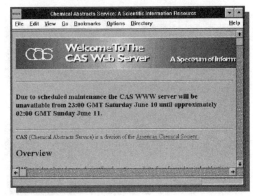

http://www.cas.org/
Chemical Abstracts Service; Scientific information resource

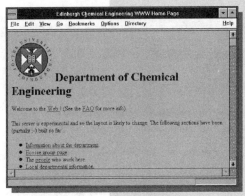

http://www.chemeng.ed.ac.uk/
Department of Chemical Engineering; University of Edinburgh

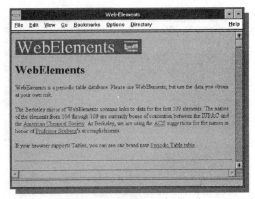

http://www.cchem.berkeley.edu/Table/index.html
Atomic numbers; Elements; Physics

http://www.cray.com/apps/UNICHEM/Mainpage.html
Computers; Cray Research; Simulations; Supercomputing

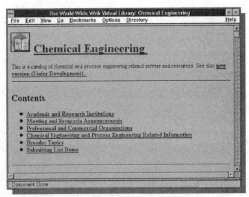

http://www.che.ufl.edu/WWW-CHE/index.html
Chemical Engineering; Process engineering; Research

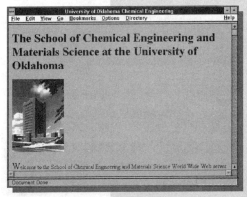

http://www.uoknor.edu/cems
Chemical Engineering; Materials Science; Univ. of Oklahoma

Children

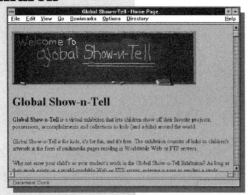

http://emma.manymedia.com/show-n-tell
Exhibition; Kids; Show-n-tell

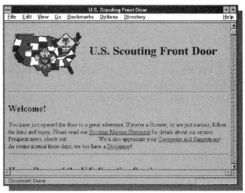

http://iquest.com/~hyper/usscouts.html
Activities; Boy Scouts of America; Boys; Cub Scouts; Kids

http://flsig.org/SIGkids/index.html
ACM SIGGRAPH; Children; Computing; SIGkids

http://k12mac.larc.nasa.gov/hpcck12home.html
Education; K-12; NASA

http://freenet3.scri.fsu.edu:81/ht-free/phfriend.html
Child safety; Kids; Phone friend; Tallahassee Free-Net

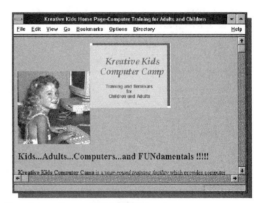

http://merkury.saic.com/kkids/kkids.html
Adults; Children; Computer training

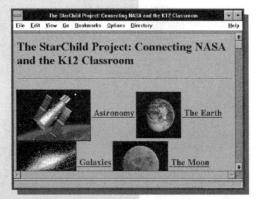

http://guinan.gsfc.nasa.gov/K12/StarChild.html
Astronomy; Education; K12; NASA

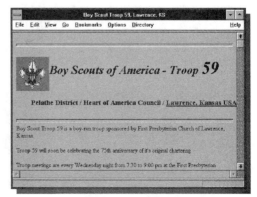

http://po-main.allenpress.com/troop59
Boy Scouts; Kansas; Lawrence

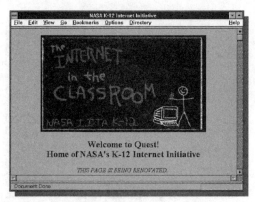

http://quest.arc.nasa.gov/
Education; K-12; Teachers

http://SchoolNet.Carleton.ca/
Canada; Children; Education; Internet; Schools

http://seawifs.gsfc.nasa.gov/JASON.html
Education; Electronic field trip; Jason Project; Kids

http://supermall.com/kids/page1.html
Children; Educational; Kids Universe; Parents; Software; Toys

http://www.childsoft.com/childsoft
Children; Educational software; Software

http://www.clark.net/pub/journalism/kid.html
Education; Kids

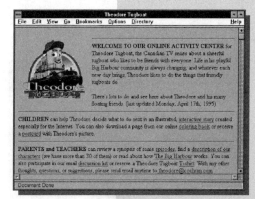

http://www.cochran.com/TT.html
Kids; Parents; Teachers; Tugboat

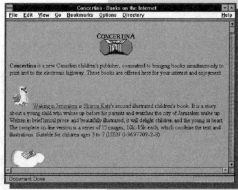

http://www.digimark.net/iatech/books
Canada; Children's books; Kids; Online books

Colleges

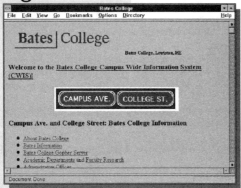

http://abacus.bates.edu/
Bates College; Lewiston; Maine

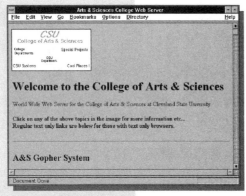

http://bones.asic.csuohio.edu/
Arts and Sciences; Cleveland State University

http://business.kent.edu/
Business Administration; Kent State University

http://dragon.union.edu/
Union College

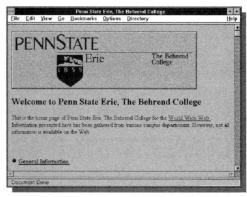

http://euler.bd.psu.edu/
Behrend College; Math; Penn State University

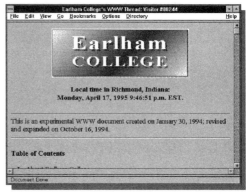

http://http.earlham.edu/
Earlham College

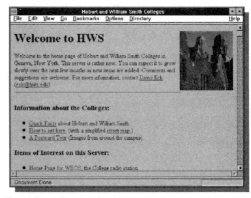

http://hws3.hws.edu:9000/
Geneva; Hobart and William Smith Colleges; New York

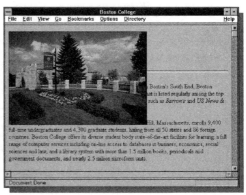

http://infoeagle.bc.edu/
Boston College; Massachusetts

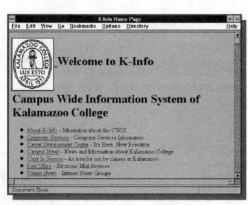

http://kzoo.edu/
Kalamazoo College

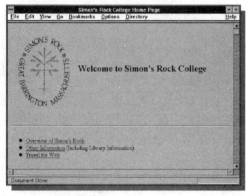

http://plato.simons-rock.edu/
Simon's Rock College

http://sci.dixie.edu/
Dixie College

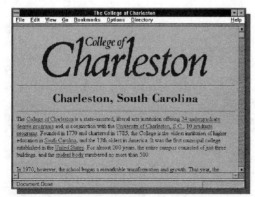

http://stono.cs.cofc.edu/
College of Charleston; South Carolina

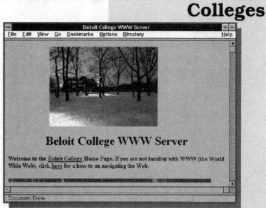

http://stu.beloit.edu/
Beloit College

http://STU.beloit.edu/ad.html
Beloit; Colleges

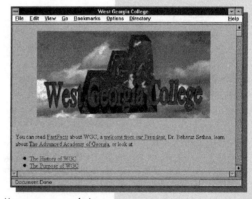

http://sun.cc.westga.edu/
West Georgia College

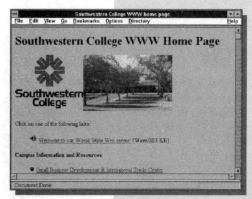

http://swc.cc.ca.us/
Southwestern College

Colleges

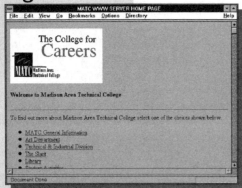

http://ted.ele.madison.tec.wi.us/
Madison Area Technical College

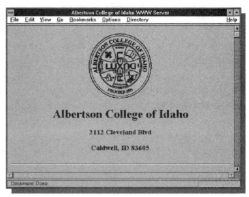

http://www.acofi.edu/
Albertson College of Idaho; Caldwell

http://utopia.mercy.edu/
Mercyhurst College

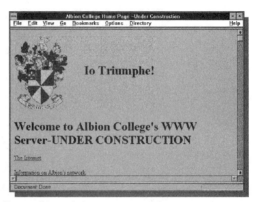

http://www.albion.edu/
Albion College

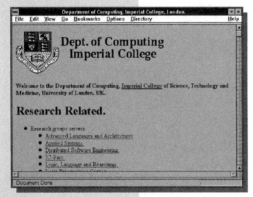

http://web.doc.ic.ac.uk/
Imperial College

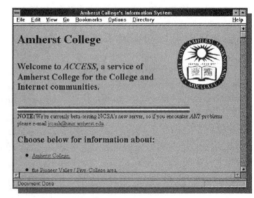

http://www.amherst.edu/start.html
Amherst College

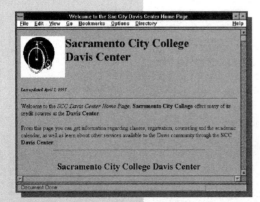

http://wheel.ucdavis.edu/~btcarrol/sac_city/Sac_City.html
California; Sacramento City College

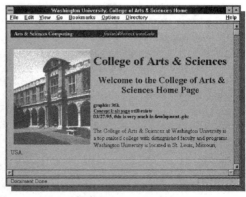

http://www.artsci.wustl.edu/
Arts & Sciences; Washington University

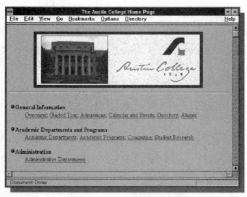

http://www.austinc.edu/
Austin College

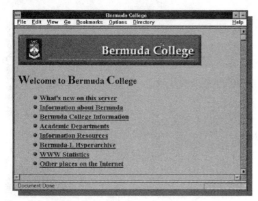

http://www.bercol.bm/
Bermuda College

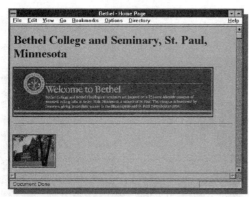

http://www.bethel.edu/BethelIntro.html
Bethel College; Minnesota; Seminary; St. Paul

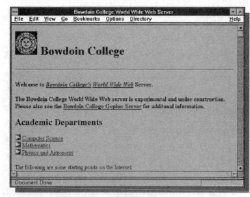

http://www.bowdoin.edu/
Bowdoin College

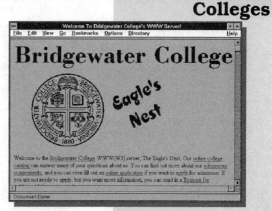

http://www.bridgewater.edu/
Bridgewater College

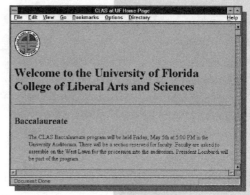

http://www.clas.ufl.edu/
Liberal Arts; University of Florida

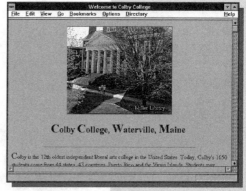

http://www.colby.edu/
Colby College Waterville Maine

http://www.dana.edu/
Dana College

69

Colleges

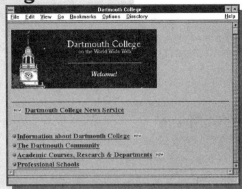

http://www.dartmouth.edu/
Dartmouth College

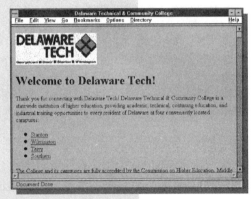

http://www.dtcc.edu/
Delaware Technical & Community College

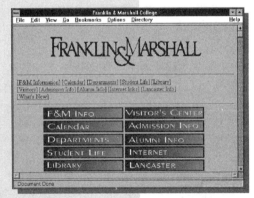

http://www.fandm.edu/
Franklin and Marshall College

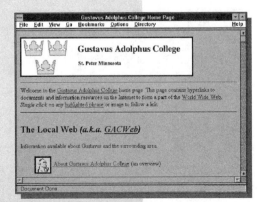

http://www.gac.edu/
Gustavus Adolphus College

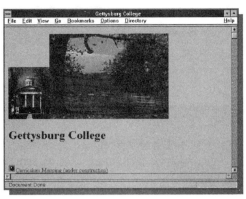

http://www.gettysburg.edu/
Gettysburg College

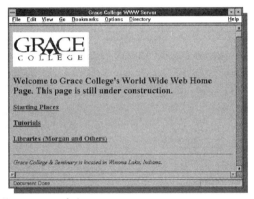

http://www.grace.edu/
Grace College

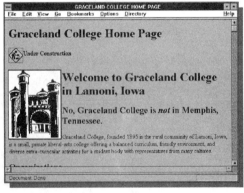

http://www.graceland.edu/
Graceland College; Iowa; Lamoni

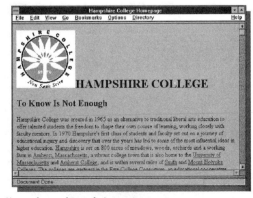

http://www.hampshire.edu/
Amherst; Hampshire College; Massachusetts

http://www.hanover.edu/
Hanover College

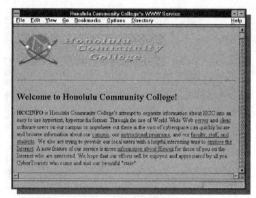

http://www.hcc.hawaii.edu/
Education; Honolulu Community College; Schools

http://www.hiram.edu/
Hiram College; Ohio

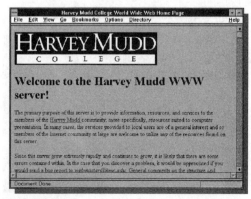

http://www.hmc.edu/
Harvey Mudd College

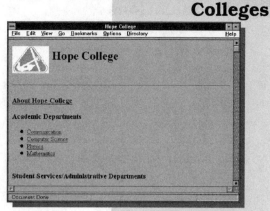

http://www.hope.edu/
Hope College

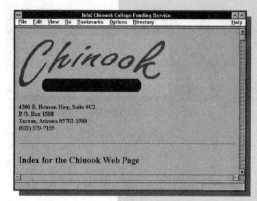

http://www.indirect.com/user/chinook2/
College scholarship; Student funding

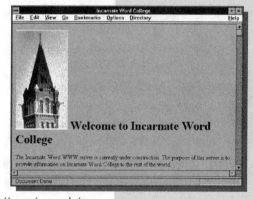

http://www.iwctx.edu/
Incarnate Word College

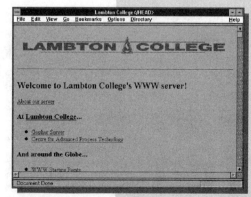

http://www.lambton.on.ca/
Lambton College

71

Communications

http://actlab.rtf.utexas.edu/
Austin; Communication Technologies; University of Texas

http://dworkin.wustl.edu/
Communications Research; Computer; Washington University

http://airpcs.com/airpcsHome.html
AirTouch Communications PCS Group

http://fcc.gov:70/0h/AAA_HOMEPAGE.html
Communication; FCC; Government

http://arctique.int-evry.fr/
Paris France; Telecommunications

http://futures.wharton.upenn.edu/~ahrens26/ivc.html
Internet VoiceChat; Telecommunications

http://carmen.artsci.washington.edu/default.html
Communications; University of Washington

http://gatekeeper.dec.com/pub/doc/sigcomm/ccr/overview.html
ACM; Communications; Special Interest

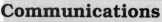

http://isdntek.com/
Digital phone system products; ISDN

http://kronos.lerc.nasa.gov/acts/acts.html
Advanced Communication Technology Satellite; Space

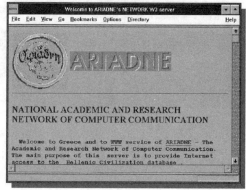

http://ithaki.servicenet.ariadne-t.gr/default.html
Academic; Research; Network; Communication; Greece

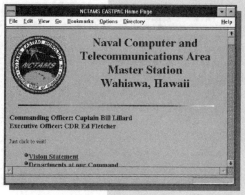

http://nctamsep.navy.mil/
Naval Computer and Telecommunications

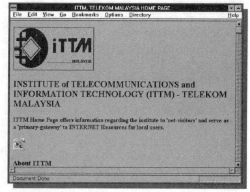

http://ittm.com.my/
Malaysia; Resources; Telecommunications

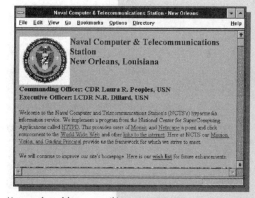

http://nctsnola.nalda.navy.mil/
Naval Computer & Telecommunications Station; New Orleans

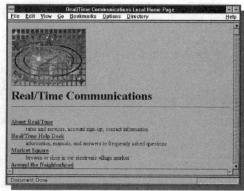

http://kaleidoscope.bga.com/
Information services; Real Time Communications

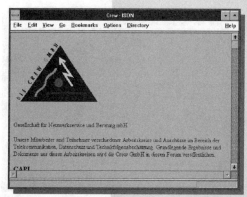

http://nda.net/nda/crew/isdn.html
Crew - ISDN; Germany

Communications

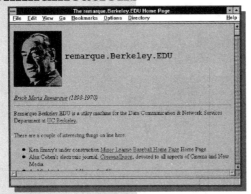

http://remarque.berkeley.edu:8001/
Data communications; Network services; UC Berkeley

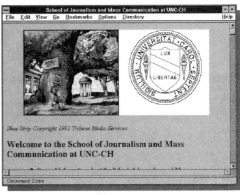

http://sunsite.unc.edu/ranjeev/jomchome.html
Journalism; Mass Communication; University of North Carolina

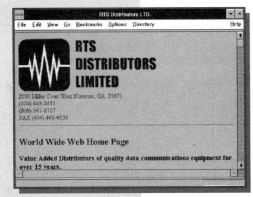

http://rtsdist.com/rtsdist/
Data communications equipment

http://tcomeng.com/
Telecommunications Engineering Associates

http://spiderman.bu.edu/
Hypermedia; Multimedia Communications Laboratory; Projects

http://town.hall.org/sponsors/persoft.html
Internet Multicasting Service; Persoft; SmarTerm 420

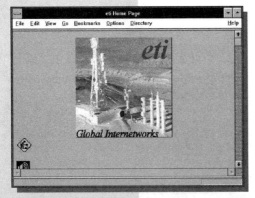

http://starbase.neosoft.com/~eti/
Internet presence; ISDN; Wireless

http://traveller.EU.net/TeleAdapt/
Adaptors; European; Product catalog; Telecommunications

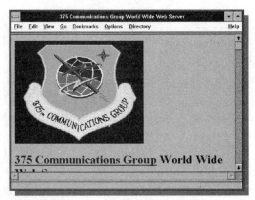

http://warlord.safb.af.mil/scott/375cg/375home.html
375 Communications Group; Newsletter; Scott AFB

http://www.3com.com/WhatNew/3Comimp.html
3Com; ISDN; External Digital Modem

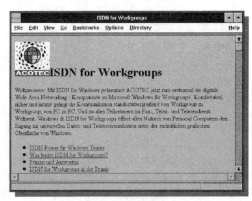

http://www.acotec.de/deutsch/ifw311/
Berlin; Germany; ISDN; Software; Windows; Workgroups

http://www.acotec.de/deutsch/ifwnt/
Berlin; Germany; ISDN; Software; Windows NT; Workgroups

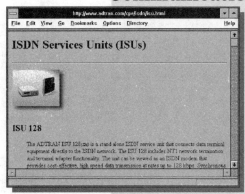

http://www.adtran.com/cpe/isdn/isu.html
Hardware; ISDN; Networks

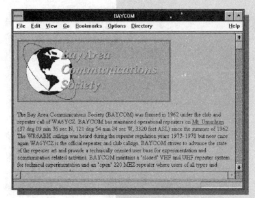

http://www.arasmith.com/baycom/index.html
Bay Area Communications Society; Experimentation; Repeaters

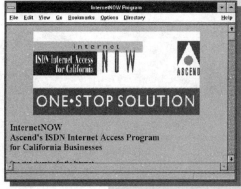

http://www.ascend.com/conews/i_now10.html
Ascend; Hardware; Internet services; ISDN; Software; Turnkey

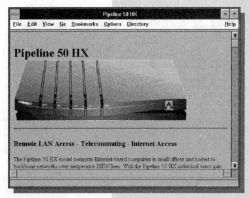

http://www.ascend.com/prodinfo/pipeline/P50HX.html
Internet Access; Remote LAN Access; Telecommuting

Communications

http://www.att.com/home64/
High speed; ISDN; Residential

http://www.ba.com/isdn.html
Bell Atlantic; FAQ; Integrated Services Digital Network; ISDN

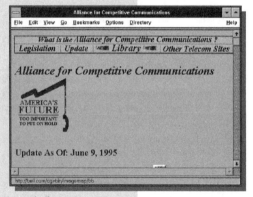

http://www.bell.com/
Competition; Legislation; Long-Distance market; News

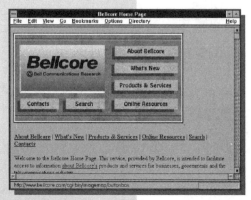

http://www.bellcore.com/
Products and services; Telecommunications

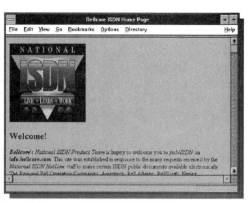

http://www.bellcore.com/ISDN/ISDN.html
Information; National ISDN HotLine; Pricing

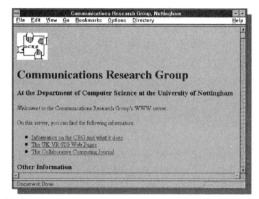

http://www.crg.cs.nott.ac.uk/
England; UK Web sites; WWW

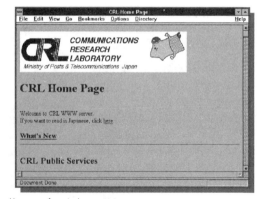

http://www.crl.go.jp/
Japan; Laboratory; Research; Telecommunications

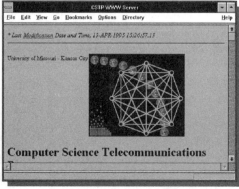

http://www.cstp.umkc.edu/
Computer science; ISDN; Optics; Telecommunications

http://www.ctr.columbia.edu/
Columbia University; Internet; Research; Telecommunications

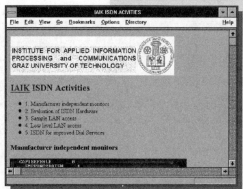

http://www.iaik.tu-graz.ac.at/ISDN/isdn_ia.html
Austria; Graz University of Technology; ISDN

http://www.deltanet.com/accessplus/access.html
Broadband communications; PCS licenses

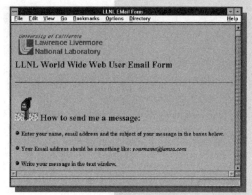

http://www.llnl.gov/llnl-bin/feedback/jed@llnl.gov
Email; Lawrence Livermore National Laboratories

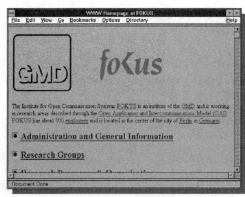

http://www.enst-bretagne.fr/
France; Telecommunications

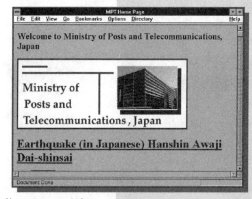

http://www.mpt.go.jp/
Earthquake; Japan; Telecommunications

http://www.fokus.gmd.de/
Fokus; OAI; Open Communication system; Research

http://www.netcom.com/
Internet service provider; NETCOM

Computers

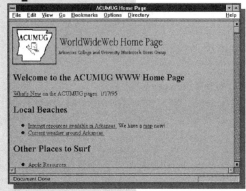

http://acumug.ualr.edu/
Little Rock; Macintosh Users group; University of Arkansas

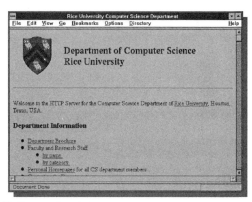

http://bellona.cs.rice.edu/
Computer Science; Rice University

http://akebono.stanford.edu/users/cad/group.html
CAD; Computer Aided Design; Stanford University

http://carol.fwi.uva.nl/~andy/mermaid.html
Computers; Modeling; Research; Simulation models

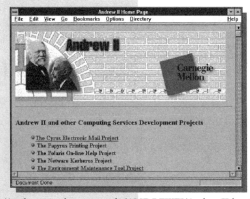

http://andrew2.andrew.cmu.edu/ANDREWII/AndrewII.html
Carnegie-Mellon University; Papyrus; Polaris

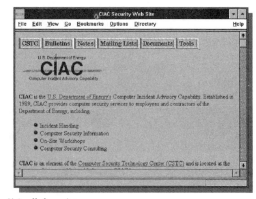

http://ciac.llnl.gov/
Security; US Department of Energy

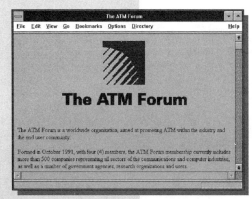

http://atmforum.com/
Asynchronous Transfer Mode Forum; ATM

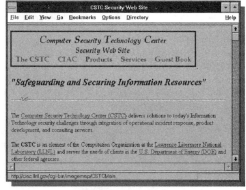

http://ciac.llnl.gov/cstc/CSTCHome.html
Consulting services; Incident response; Product development

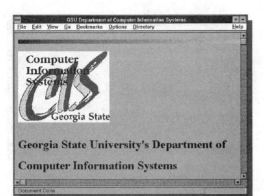

http://cis.gsu.edu/
Computer Information Systems; Georgia State University

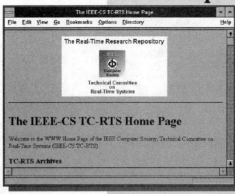

http://cs-www.bu.edu/pub/ieee-rts/Home.html
IEEE; Real-Time Research

http://coral.cs.jcu.edu.au/
Department of Computer Science; James Cook University

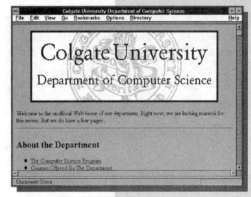

http://cs.colgate.edu/
Colgate University; Computer Science

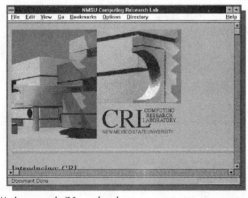

http://crl.nmsu.edu/Home.html
Computing Research; New Mexico State University

http://cs.nyu.edu/
Computer Science; New York University

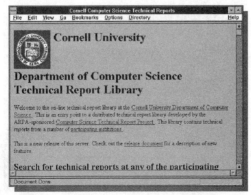

http://cs-tr.cs.cornell.edu/
Computer Science; Cornell University; Technical Reports

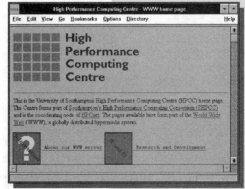

http://cs1.soton.ac.uk/
High performance computing; Parallel computing

Computers

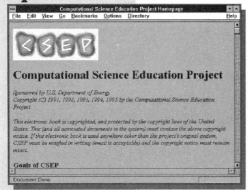

http://csep1.phy.ornl.gov/csep.html
Computer science; Education; Engineering; Teaching materials

http://fas.sfu.ca/1/cs
Canada; Computing Science; Simon Fraser University

http://cuisg13.unige.ch:8100/
Computer animation; MIRALab; Research

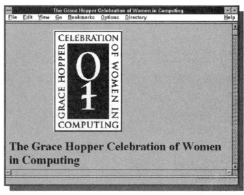

http://gatekeeper.dec.com/pub/doc/hopper/grace.html
Computing; Grace Hopper; Women

http://cybermart.com/scuzzy/index.html
DAT drives; Optical drives; SCSI hard drives; Wholesale

http://gozer.idbsu.edu/business/nethome.html
Archive; Delta; Distributed Electronic Telecommunications

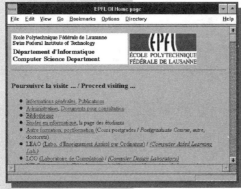

http://diwww.epfl.ch/
Compilers; Swiss Federal Institute of Technology

http://groucho.gsfc.nasa.gov:80/
Data systems technology; Goddard; NASA

http://hardy.fciencias.unam.mx/
Spanish; Web server

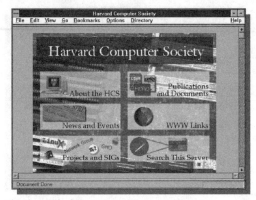

http://hcs.harvard.edu/
Computer Society; Harvard University

http://ice-www.larc.nasa.gov/ICE/ice.html
Integrated Computing Environment; Portability

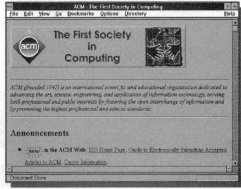

http://info.acm.org/
Association of Computing Machinery; Hardware; Software

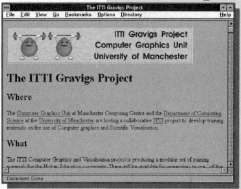

http://info.mcc.ac.uk/CGU/ITTI/gravigs.html
Engineering; Graphics; Medicine; Research; Science

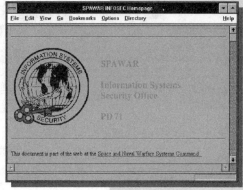

http://infosec.nosc.mil/infosec.html
US Navy Space and Naval Warfare Systems Command

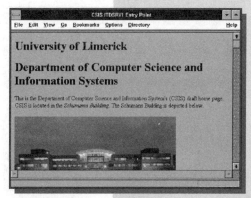

http://itdsrv1.ul.ie/CSIS/csis-home-page.html
Ireland; University of Limerick

http://kestrel.edu/
Computer Science; Kestrel Institute; Research; Software

Computers

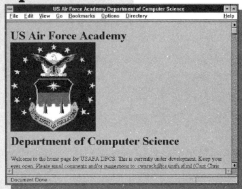

http://kirk.usafa.af.mil/
Computer Science; United States Air Force Academy

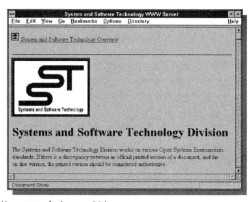

http://nemo.ncsl.nist.gov:80/
Open systems; Software technology; Systems

http://mls.saic.com/
Products and services; SAIC; Security

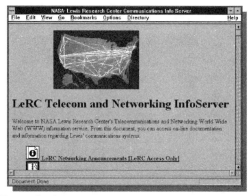

http://netgopher.lerc.nasa.gov:80/
Lewis Research Center; NASA; Networking; Telecommunications

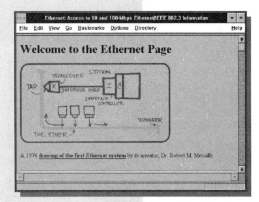

http://mojo.ots.utexas.edu/ethernet/ethernet-home.html
Ethernet; IEEE 802.3; Network Technology

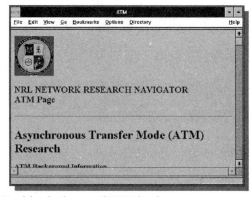

http://netlab.itd.nrl.navy.mil/ATM.html
Asynchronous Transfer Mode; ATM; Research

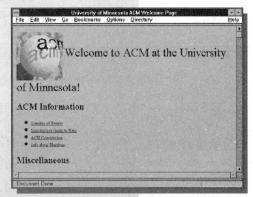

http://monopoly.cs.umn.edu/
Association for Computing Machinery; University of Minnesota

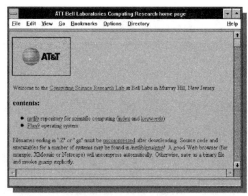

http://netlib.att.com/
ATT Bell Laboratories; Computing; Research

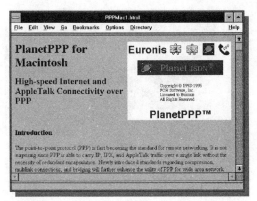

http://nw.com/satusa/PPPMac1.html
Appletalk; Hardware; Internet connectivity; Macintosh; PPP

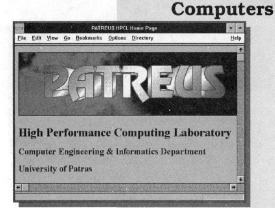

http://phaethon.cti.gr/Welcome.html
Greece; Parallel processing; University of Patras

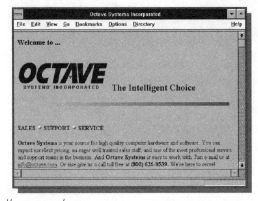

http://octave.com/
Computer; Hardware; Software

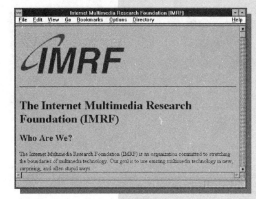

http://physics.purdue.edu/~sho/imrf.html
Multimedia; Research

http://olympic.jpl.nasa.gov:80/
Communications; High performance computing; JPL

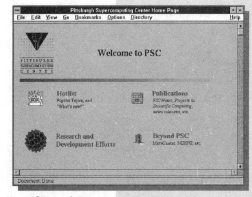

http://pscinfo.psc.edu/
Carnegie Mellon University; Pittsburgh Supercomputing

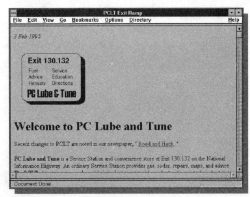

http://pclt.cis.yale.edu/pclt/default.htm
Computers; Education; Software

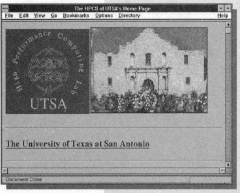

http://rabbit.cs.utsa.edu/Welcome.html
High performance computing; San Antonio; University of Texas

Computers

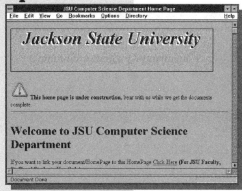

http://riscman.jsums.edu/jsucs.html
Jackson State University Computer Science

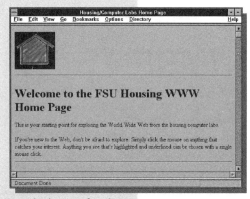

http://romulus.housing.fsu.edu/
Florida State University; Housing Computer Labs

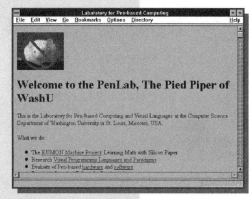

http://schiller.wustl.edu/
Hardware; Paradigms; Pen-based Computing; Visual Languages

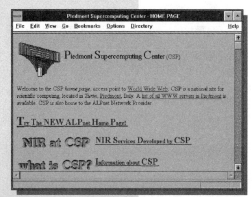

http://services.csp.it/welcome.html
Internet resources; Italy; Piedmont Supercomputing Center

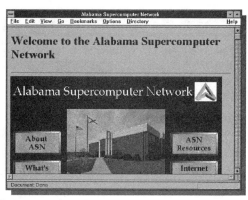

http://sgisrvr.asc.edu:80/
Alabama Supercomputer Network; Supercomputing

http://smartworld.com/macbyte/macbyte.html
Buy; Macintosh; Sell; Trade

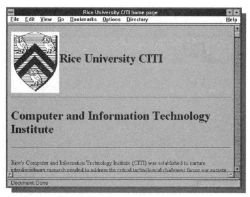

http://softlib.cs.rice.edu/CITI/
Computer and Information Technology; Rice University

http://src.doc.ic.ac.uk/
Northern Europe; Sun Microsystems

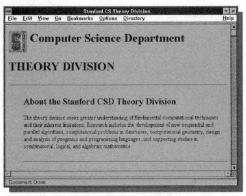

http://theory.stanford.edu/
Computer Science; Stanford University; Theory

http://tron.is.s.u-tokyo.ac.jp/RTCSA95/
Real-Time Computing Systems and Applications

http://unicode.org/
ASCII; Code Page 437; EBCDIC; ISO Latin 1; JIS; Unicode

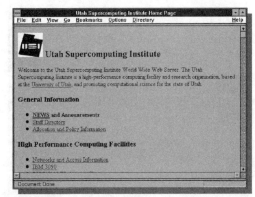

http://ute.usi.utah.edu/
Supercomputing; University of Utah

http://web.msi.umn.edu/WWW/wwwstart.html
Supercomputer Institute; University of Minnesota

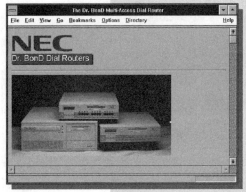

http://web.nec.com/products/datacomm/drbond/index.html
Multi-Access Dial Router

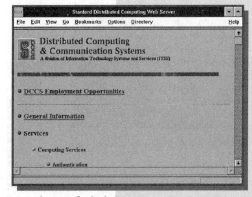

http://www-dccs.stanford.edu/
Communication; Information Technology

http://www-flash.stanford.edu/
Computing; Multiprocessor; Stanford

Computers

http://www.ac.duke.edu/
Duke University

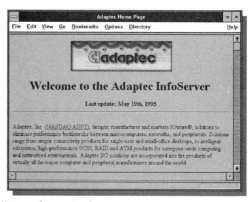

http://www.adaptec.com/
ATM; Design; Networks; Peripherals; RAID; SCSI

http://www.acc.com/
Advanced Computer Communications; Routing services

http://www.adnetsol.com/
Links; Networking products; Services

http://www.acl.lanl.gov/
Advanced Computing Lab; Los Alamos National Laboratory

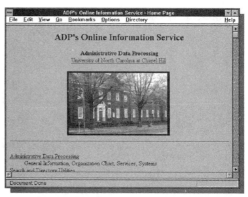

http://www.adp.unc.edu/
Chapel Hill; Data Processing; University of North Carolina

http://www.acs.ohio-state.edu/macforum/index.html
Apple; Hardware; Mac; Software

http://www.ai.mit.edu/people/ellens/gender.html
Computing; Women and Computer Science

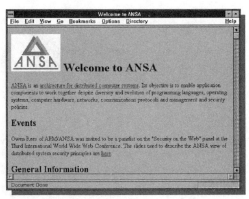

http://www.ansa.co.uk/
Management; Programming languages; Protocols; Security

http://www.apple.com/
Apple; Computers; Macintosh

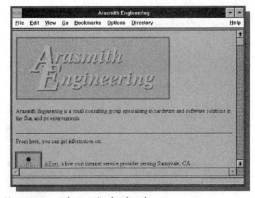

http://www.arasmith.com/index.html
Consulting; Hardware; Software; Sun :PC

http://www.arc.umn.edu/html/ahpcrc.html
Army; High performance computing; Parallel processing

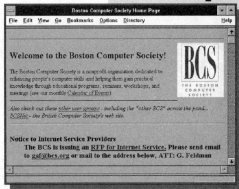

http://www.bcs.org/bcs/general_info.html
Education; Nonprofit; Seminars; Workshops

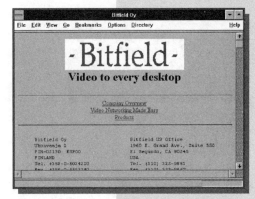

http://www.bitfield.fi/
Finland; Products; Video Networking

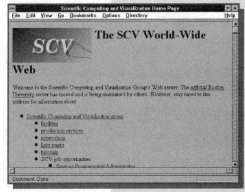

http://www.bu.edu/
Production services; Scientific Computing; Visualization; Tutorials

http://www.buslogic.com/
Advanced SCSI; Products; RAID

87

Computers

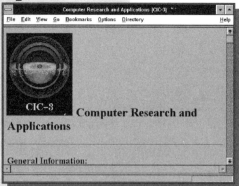

http://www.c3.lanl.gov/
C3; Computer research; Future computing; Graphics

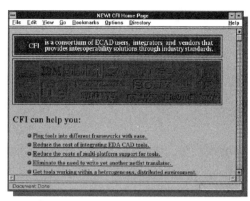

http://www.cfi.org/
CAD; Communications; Multi-platform; Software

http://www.calpoly.edu:80/
California Polytechnic State University; Education

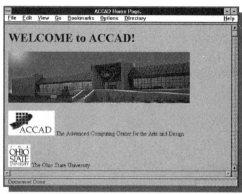

http://www.cgrg.ohio-state.edu/
Advanced Computing for the Arts and Design; Education

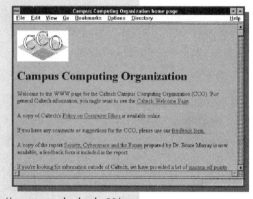

http://www.cco.caltech.edu:80/
Caltech; Campus computing; Cyberspace

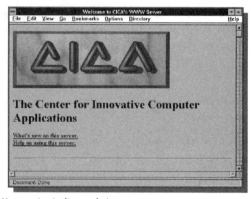

http://www.cica.indiana.edu/
Application; CICA; Computer

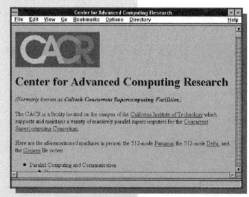

http://www.ccsf.caltech.edu/ccsf.html
Concurrent Supercomputing Consortium; Parallel computing

http://www.cica.indiana.edu/projects/Police/index.html
Criminal Justice; Police video image enhancement

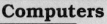

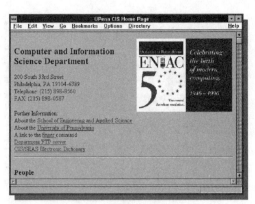

http://www.cis.upenn.edu/
Computer and Information science; Universities

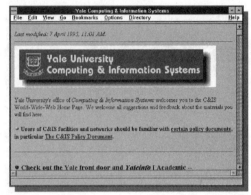

http://www.cis.yale.edu/
Computing and Information Systems; Yale University

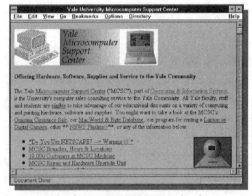

http://www.cis.yale.edu/~mcsc/MCSCHome.html
Microcomputer support; Yale University

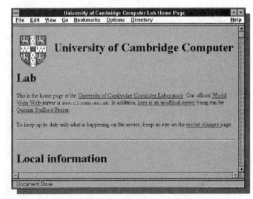

http://www.cl.cam.ac.uk/
Education; University of Cambridge

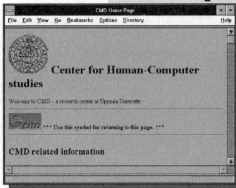

http://www.cmd.uu.se/
Human-Computer studies; Uppsala University

http://www.combinet.com/index1.html
Internet; On-demand networking; Remote access

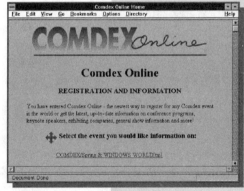

http://www.comdex.com:8000/
COMDEX; Expositions; Trade shows

http://www.comptons.com/
Encyclopedias; Interactive; Multimedia; Software

89

Computers

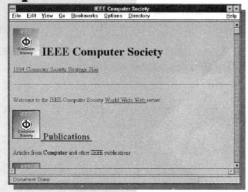

http://www.computer.org/
EE; Electronics; Hardware; IEEE Computer Society; Software

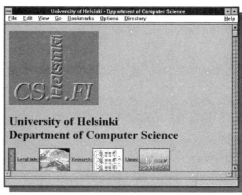

http://www.cs.helsinki.fi/
Computer Science; University of Helsinki

http://www.cpsr.org/home
Computer Professionals for Social Responsibility; CPSR

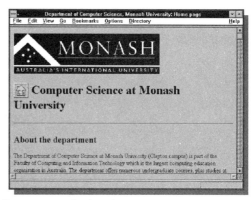

http://www.cs.monash.edu.au/
Computer Science at Monash University; Education

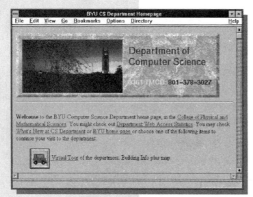

http://www.cs.byu.edu/homepage.html
Brigham Young University; Department of Computer Science

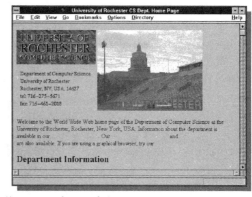

http://www.cs.rochester.edu/
Computer Science; Education; University of Rochester

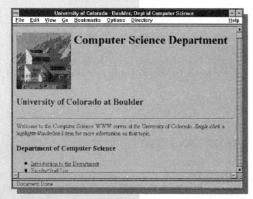

http://www.cs.colorado.edu/
Education; University of Colorado at Boulder

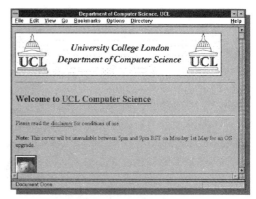

http://www.cs.ucl.ac.uk/
Education; University College London

http://www.cs.wisc.edu/
Education; University of Wisconsin Madison

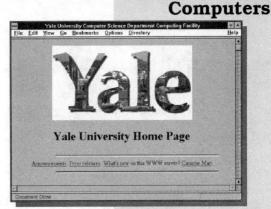

http://www.cs.yale.edu/HTML/YaleCSCFHome.html
Computer science; Education; Yale University

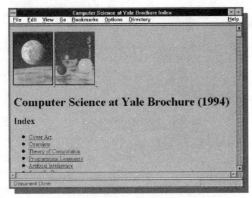

http://www.cs.yale.edu/HTML/YALE/CS/Brochure/brochure.html
Computer science; Programming languages; Theory; Yale

http://www.csd.uu.se/
Computing Science Department; Education; Uppsala University

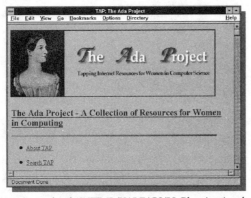

http://www.cs.yale.edu/HTML/YALE/CS/HyPlans/tap/tap.html
Ada Project; Computing; Women in Computer Science

http://www.csh.rit.edu/welcome.html
Computer Science; Hardware; Software

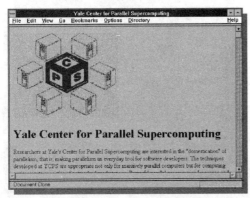

http://www.cs.yale.edu/HTML/YALE/YCPS/FrontDoor.html
Parallel supercomputing; Software; Yale

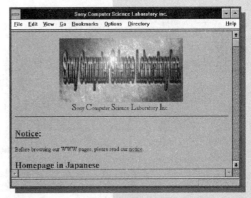

http://www.csl.sony.co.jp/
Computer Science; Japan; Japanese; Sony computer

Computers

http://www.dbai.tuwien.ac.at/
AI; Austria; Computers; Information; Fuzzy logic; Vienna

http://www.dstc.edu.au/
Distributed systems; Networks; Software

http://www.decus.org/
DEC; Digital Equipment Computer Users Society

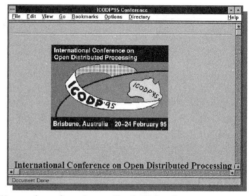

http://www.dstc.edu.au/events/icodp95.html
Australia; Brisbane; Computers; Conferences; Open systems

http://www.digital.com/pub/doc/bcs/bcshome.htm
Boston Computer Society; Internet SIG

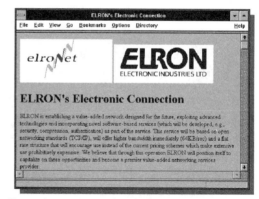

http://www.elron.net/www/elronet/elronet.html
Flat rate; Network; Networking services

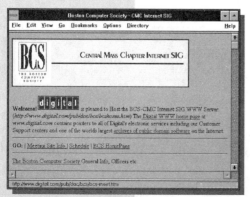

http://www.digital.com/pub/doc/bcs/bcshome.html
Boston Computer Society

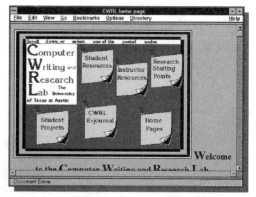

http://www.en.utexas.edu/
Austin; Computer Writing; Research; University of Texas

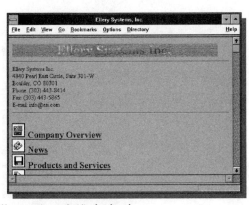

http://www.esi.com/esi/index.html
Ellery Systems; Products and services

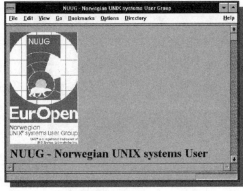

http://www.eunet.no/nuug/nuug.html
Computing; Norwegian; UNIX

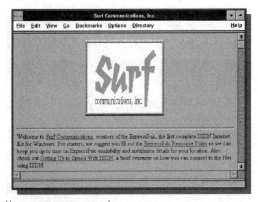

http://www.expressway.com/
ISDN; Networking; Surf Communications

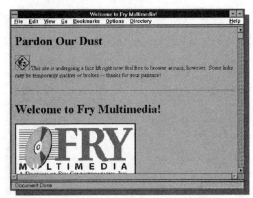

http://www.frymulti.com/
Communication; Fry Multimedia

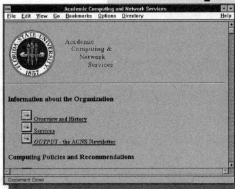

http://www.fsu.edu/ACNS/index.html
Florida State University

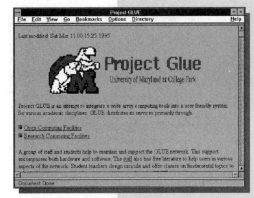

http://www.glue.umd.edu/
Computing; Integrated applications; Project Glue

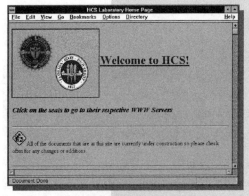

http://www.hcs.eng.fsu.edu/
High-performance Computing; Research; Simulation

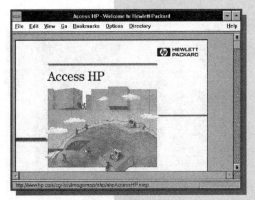

http://www.hp.com/
Hewlett Packard; Printers

93

Computers

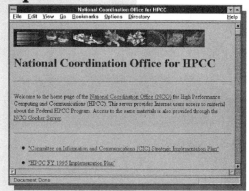

http://www.hpcc.gov/index.html
High performance computing; Parallel processing

http://www.infi.net/pilot/gateways/gateindex.html
Computers; Hardware; Internet; Pilot Online; Software

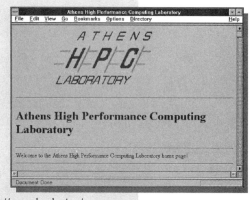

http://www.hpcl.cti.gr/
Athens; Greece; High performance computing; Networks

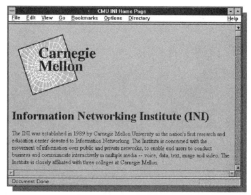

http://www.ini.cmu.edu/
Carnegie Mellon University; Information Networking

http://www.hut.fi/ATK/uTuki/uTuki_Home.html
Finnish universities; Microsystems support

http://www.intel.com/
Intel; Pentium; Processors; Products and services

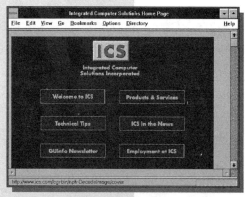

http://www.ics.com/Welcome.html
ICS; Integrated Computer Solutions Homepage; Products

http://www.internet-is.com/netguru/in-iis.html
Consulting; Net Guru Technologies; Research; Training

http://www.island.net/~teranet
AI; Teranet; Web server

http://www.jma.com/
Network Translation Inc.; PIX; Private Internet Exchange

http://www.kiae.su/www/wtr/
Relcom; Reliable communications; Russia

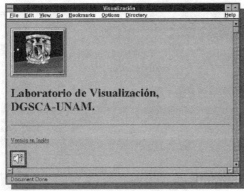

http://www.labvis.unam.mx/
Computer science; Spanish; Visualization

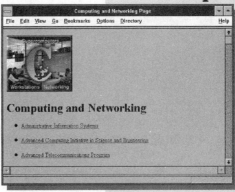

http://www.llnl.gov/comp/comp.html
Lawrence Livermore National Laboratory; Networking

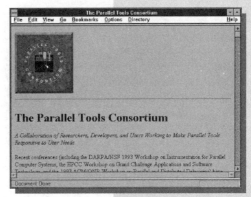

http://www.llnl.gov/ptools/ptools.html
Parallel tools; Programming

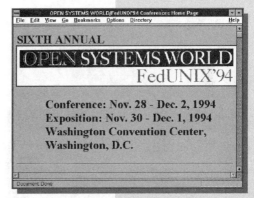

http://www.mcsp.com/OSW-FedUNIX.html
Computers; Open systems; UNIX; Washington DC

http://www.meiko.com:80/welcome.html
Meiko; Networks; Parallel computing

95

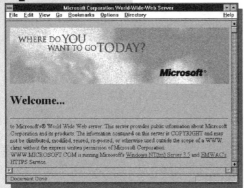

http://www.microsoft.com/
Computers; Manufacturer; Microsoft; Software

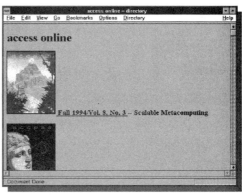

http://www.ncsa.uiuc.edu/Pubs/access/accessDir.html
Electronic magazine; Supercomputing

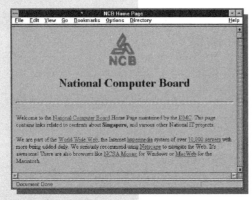

http://www.ncb.gov.sg/
Hypermedia; National Computer Board; Singapore

http://www.ncsa.uiuc.edu/SDG/IT94/IT94Info.html
Mosaic; WWW conferences

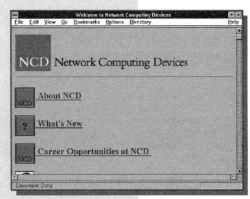

http://www.ncd.com/
Career opportunities; Computers; Networks; X Window

http://www.next.com/
NEXT Computer; Products and services; Technical support

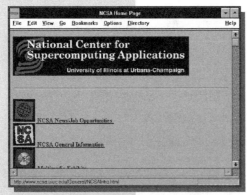

http://www.ncsa.uiuc.edu/General/NCSAHome.html
Supercomputing

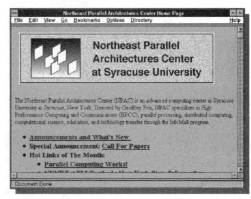

http://www.npac.syr.edu/
Communications; Parallel Architectures

http://www.nw.com/
Communications; Hardware; Networks; Software

http://www.organic.com/Ads/Xircom/index.html
Mobile networking; Xircom

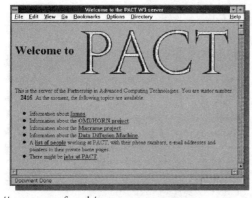

http://www.pact.srf.ac.uk/
PACT; Partnership in Advanced Computing Technologies

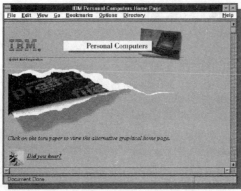

http://www.pc.ibm.com/
IBM; OS/2; Personal Computers; Warp

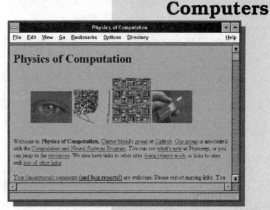

http://www.pcmp.caltech.edu:80/
Computation; Neural systems; Neuromorphic analog; Physics

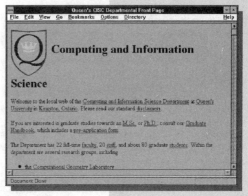

http://www.qucis.queensu.ca:1999/
Education; Queen's University in Kingston Ontario

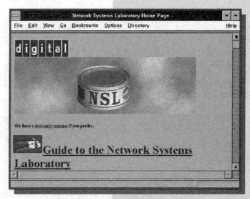

http://www.research.digital.com/nsl/home.html
Digital; Network Systems Laboratory; NSL

http://www.rnp.br/
Audio; Brazil; Portuguese; Web server

Computers

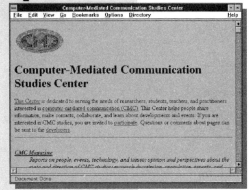

http://www.rpi.edu/~decemj/cmc/center.html
Communications; News media; Research

http://www.rsa.com/
Cryptography; Factoring; PGP; Security

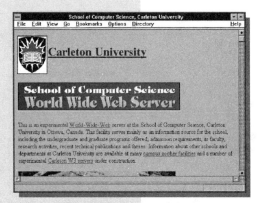

http://www.scs.carleton.ca/
Carleton University; School of Computer Science

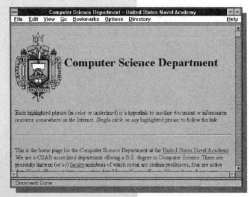

http://www.scs.usna.navy.mil/scs_home.html
Computer Science; Education; United States Naval Academy

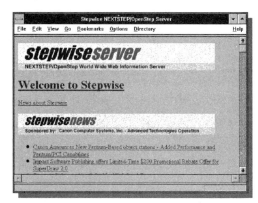

http://www.stepwise.com/
NEXTSTEP; Openstep; Stepwise

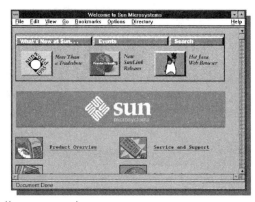

http://www.sun.com/
Product support; Servers; Workstations

http://www.super.unam.mx/
Spanish; Web server

http://www.tivoli.com/
Computer products; Distributed systems; Network management

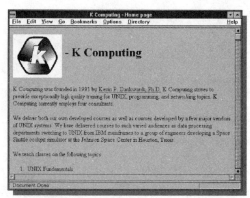

http://www.trinet.com/kcomputing/
Computers; Networks; Programming; Training; Unix

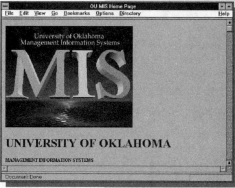

http://www.uoknor.edu/mis
Management Information Systems; University of Oklahoma

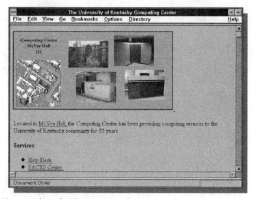

http://www.uky.edu/ComputingCenter/
Computing Center; University of Kentucky

http://www.us.dell.com/
Computers; Dell; Office equipment

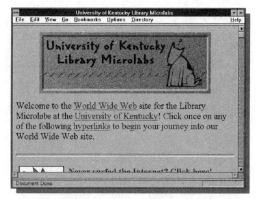

http://www.uky.edu/MicroLabs/microlab-homepage.html
Public Computing; University of Kentucky

http://www.vidya.com/
Electronic distribution; Multimedia design

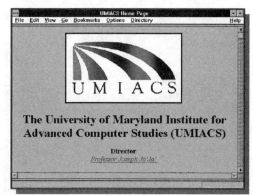

http://www.umiacs.umd.edu/
Advanced Computer Studies; Education; University of Maryland

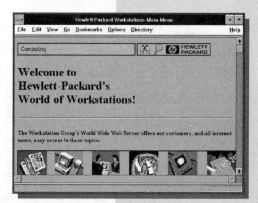

http://www.wsg.hp.com/wsg/index.html
Computing; Hewlett-Packard; Workstations

Corporations

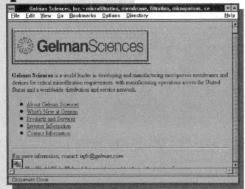

http://argus-inc.com/Gelman/Gelman.html
Gelman Sciences; Microfiltration; Microporous membranes

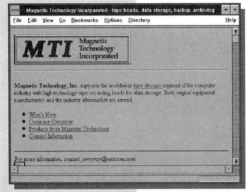

http://argus-inc.com/MagTech/MagTech.html
Backup; Data storage; Quarter inch cartridge; Tape drives

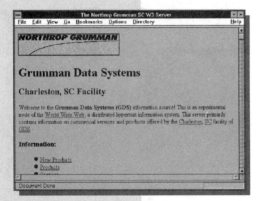

http://axon.scra.org/
Grumman; Hypertext information; Manufacturing

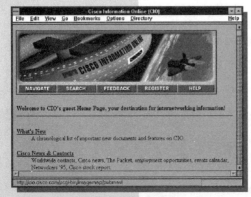

http://cio.cisco.com/public/guest_home.shtml
CIO; Cisco; Hardware; Internetworking; New documents

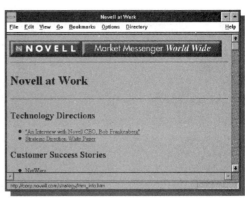

http://corp.novell.com/strategy/strategi.htm
Novell; Technology

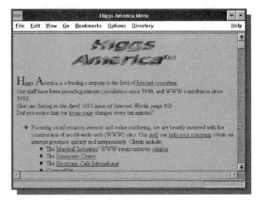

http://coupon.net/higgs.html
Higgs America; Internet consulting

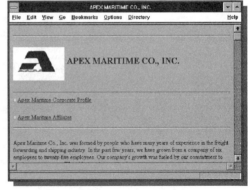

http://cyber.cclims.com/comp/apex/apex.html
Distribution; Shipping; Transportation; Warehousing

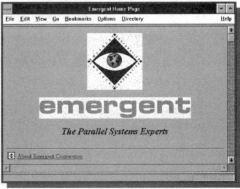

http://emergent.com/
Commercial Parallel Systems; Consultants; Implementation

http://end2.bedrock.com/
BedRock; Information solutions; Internet

http://fuji.stanford.edu/icenter/icenter.html
Bechtel International Center

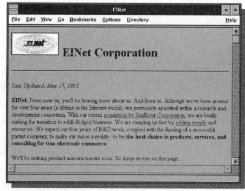

http://galaxy.einet.net/EINet/EINet.html
Consulting; EINet; Electronic commerce

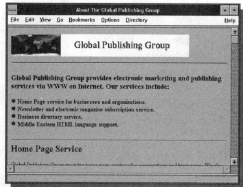

http://gpg.com/intro.html
Businesses; Home page services; Internet presence; Organizations

http://haskel.com//index.html
Haskel Corporation; Products

http://hawk.csd.harris.com/
Harris Computer Systems Corporation

http://health.mirical.com/site/Mirical/mirical.html
Health; Nutrition; Nutrition analysis; Software; Vitamins

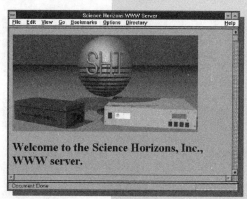

http://horizon.horizon.com/
Physics; Science; Science Horizons Inc.

Corporations

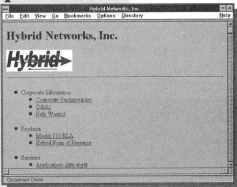

http://hybrid.com/HybridHomePage.html
Networking; Products; Services

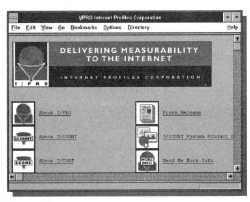

http://ipro.com/
Internet measurability; Internet Profiles Corporation

http://icemcfd.com/index.html
Computational fluid dynamics; Engineering; Software; Support

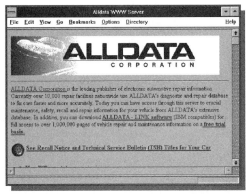

http://irsociety.com/
Diagnostic repair database; Automotive repair; Publisher

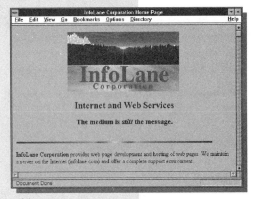

http://infolane.com/
Homepage development; InfoLane Corporation

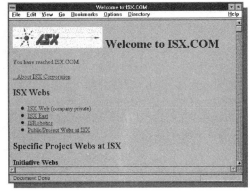

http://isx.com/
ISRobotic; ISX Web; Research projects; Robotics; Web

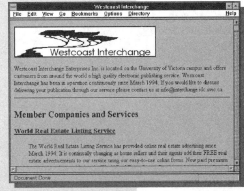

http://interchange.idc.uvic.ca/
Electronic publishing service; Real Estate

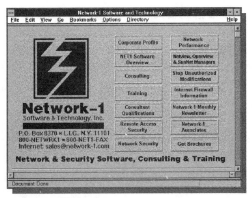

http://iu.net/n1/index.html
Corporate Profile; Network Performance; Remote Access Security

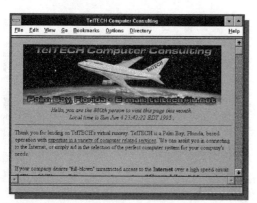

http://iu.net/teltech/index.html
Florida; Internet access; Palm Bay; TelTECH

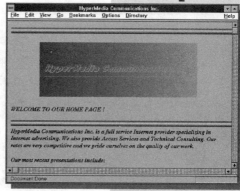

http://media1.hypernet.com/
Internet service provider; Marketing

http://jsasoc.com/keymexx.html
Marketing; Mexico; Product testing; Sales; TEM

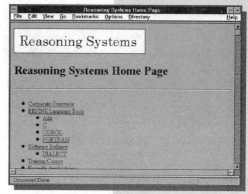

http://mosaic.reasoning.com/home.html
Products; Programming; Reasoning Systems; Services

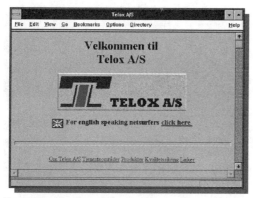

http://login.eunet.no/~rune/telox.html
Norway; Telox A/S

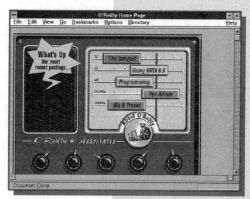

http://nearnet.gnn.com/gnn/bus/ora/
Books; Internet; Programming; UNIX

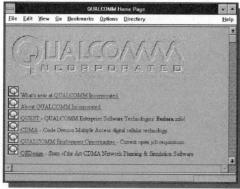

http://lorien.qualcomm.com/QualHome.html
E-mail; Eudora; QUALCOMM Incorporated; Software

http://netmedia.com/ims/IMS.html
Client software; IMS; Internet Media Services

Corporations

http://portola.com/TR/index.html
Company overview; Telepresence Research Inc.

http://sunnyside.com/
Quartermaster; Secure Netsite server; Software

http://rel.semi.harris.com/
Company services; Electronics; Harris Semiconductor

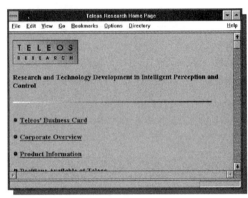

http://teleos.com/index.html
Intelligent Perception and Control; Teleos Research

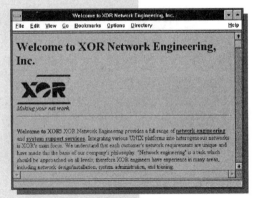

http://storefront.xor.com/xor/index.html
Network engineering; Products and services; UNIX

http://unidata.com/
Database management; Software; Spanish; Unidata

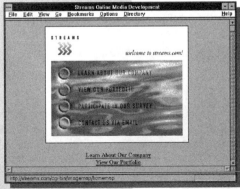

http://streams.com/
Advertising; Marketing; Streams Online Media Development

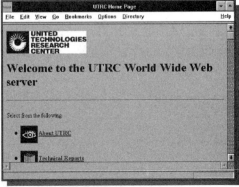

http://utrcwww.utc.com/
Company information; United Technologies

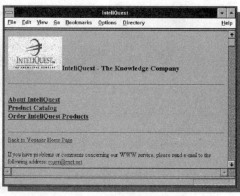

http://voyager.enet.net/iquest/index.html
Company information; InteliQuest; Product catalog

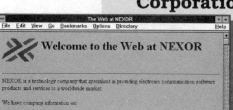

http://web.nexor.co.uk/
Electronic communication; Product; Services

http://wavefront.wti.com/
Press releases; Product information; Wavefront

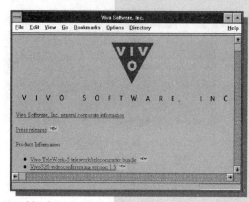

http://world.std.com/~vivo/
Vivo Software Inc.; Corporate Information

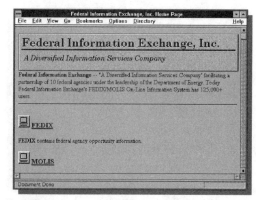

http://web.fie.com/
FEDIX; MOLIS; Online information

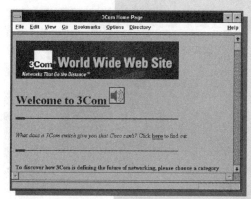

http://www.3com.com/
3Com; Audio; Networking; Networks

http://web.nec.com/
NEC; Product overview; Sales support and services

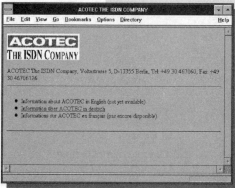

http://www.acotec.de/
ACOTEC; Berlin; Germany; ISDN; Products

Corporations

http://www.adobe.com/
Free Adobe software; Product information

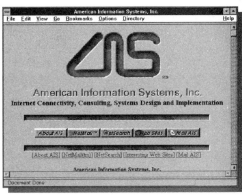

http://www.ais.net/
Consulting; Information systems; Internet Connectivity

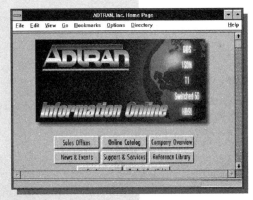

http://www.adtran.com/
Library; News; On-line catalog; Reference; Sales; Services

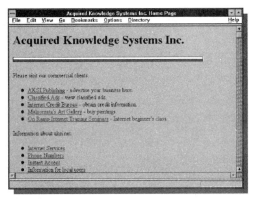

http://www.aksi.net/
Acquired Knowledge Systems Inc.; Internet services

http://www.aggroup.com/
Multiple protocol; Networks; Tools; Troubleshooting

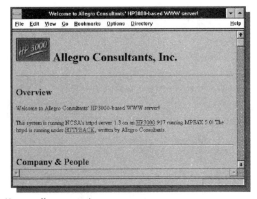

http://www.allegro.com/
Allegro Consultants; Products; Software

http://www.aimnet.com/
Aimnet; Access; Connectivity

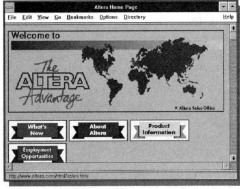

http://www.altera.com/index.html
Altera Corporation; Employment; News; Products; Sales

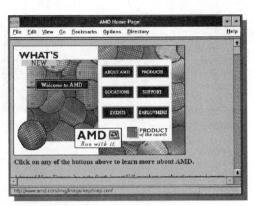

http://www.amd.com/
Embedded processors; IC; Integrated circuits; Microprocessors

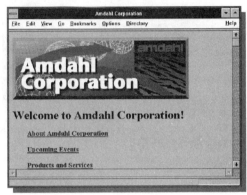

http://www.amdahl.com/
Amdahl Corporation; Employment; News; Products; Services

http://www.ameritech.com/
Ameritech; Communications; Products and services

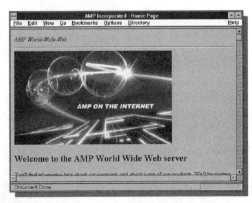

http://www.amp.com/
AMP; Products and services

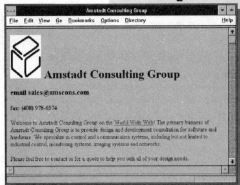

http://www.amscons.com/index.html
Consultation; Design; Hardware; Imaging; Software

http://www.amsinc.com/
Health care; Insurance; Pharmaceutical; Telecommunications

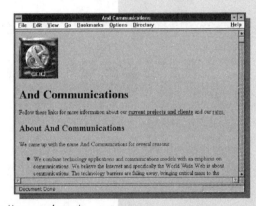

http://www.and.com/
And Communications; Consultants; Technology applications

107

http://www.andataco.com/
California; Client/server; Manufacture; Products; Services;

Corporations

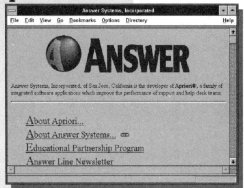

http://www.answer.com/
Apriori; Help desk; Integrated software; Technical support

http://www.arlington.com/~reckless/reckless.html
Photography; Print services; Sacramento; Typesetting

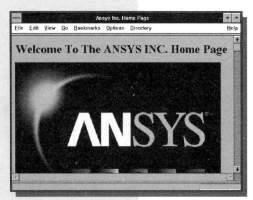

http://www.ansys.com/
Ansys; News; Products

http://www.asante.com/
News; Products; Sales; Technical support; Tradeshows

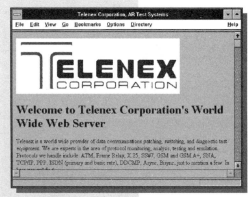

http://www.ar.telenex.com/
Data communication; Equipment; ISDN; Telenex

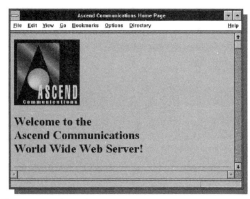

http://www.ascend.com/
Connectivity; Remote LAN; Video; Videoconferencing

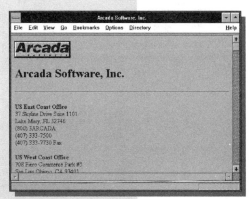

http://www.arcada.com/arcada.htm
Data protection; Software; Storage management

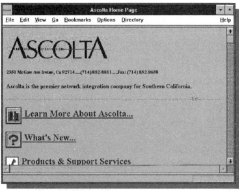

http://www.ascolta.com/
Network integration; News; Services; Southern California

Corporations

http://www.aspentec.com/index.html
Dynamic process modeling technology; Engineering tools

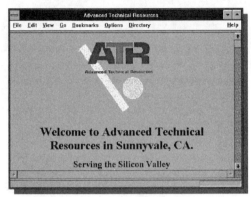

http://www.atr1.com/
Directories; Links; Silicon Valley; Technical Resources

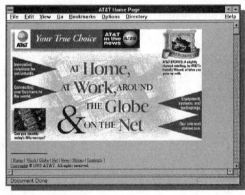

http://www.att.com/
AT&T; Products; Services

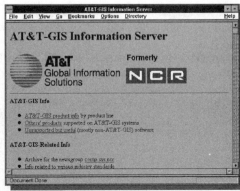

http://www.attgis.com/
AT&T; Newsgroup; Software

http://www.auspex.com/
Auspex Systems; Employment; News; Products; Services

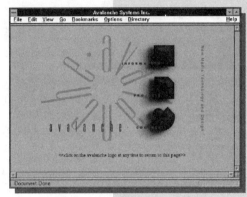

http://www.avsi.com/avalanche.html
Avalanche; Company information; Products; Services

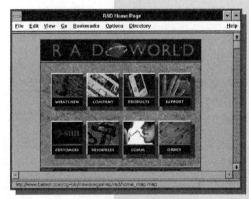

http://www.batnet.com/RAD/
News; Products; RAD Technologies

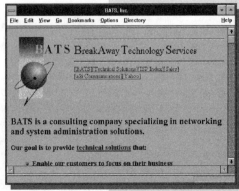

http://www.bats.com/bats/
Consulting; Networking; System administration

109

Corporations

http://www.bdt.com/
Business; News; Products; Services

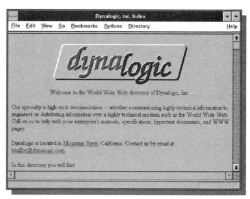

http://www.best.com/~lstaffor/
Distribution; Documentation; Publishing; Services; Writing

http://www.beckman.com/bkmnhome.htm
Bioresearch; Clinical diagnostics; Information; Services

http://www.biap.com/iconix/
CASE; Development; Tools; Training

http://www.best.com/
Internet service provider; San Francisco Bay Area

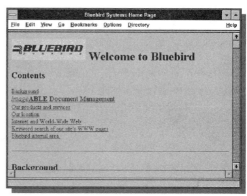

http://www.bluebird.com/
Document management; Services products; Software

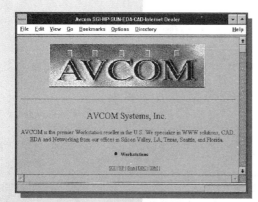

http://www.best.com/~avcom/avcom.htm
CAD; Networking; Workstation reseller

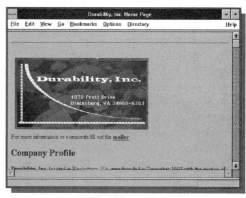

http://www.bnt.com/~durability/
Company profile; Products and services

http://www.bnt.com/~logical
Economic Projects; Health; Logical support; Virginia

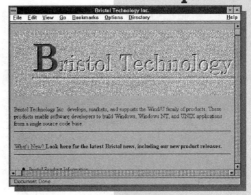

http://www.bristol.com/
Goods and services; Software developers; UNIX applications

http://www.bonsai.com/
California; Consulting; Livermore; Services; Software

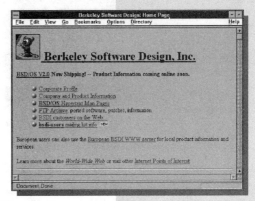

http://www.bsdi.com/
Berkeley Software Design Inc.; BSD/386; Product information

http://www.bookport.com/Fortuity/welcome.html
Knowledge management; Marketing consulting; Publishers

http://www.bseng.com/
Engineering; Services; Company Information

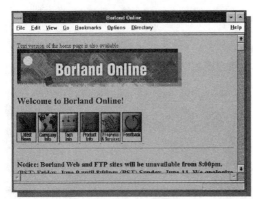

http://www.borland.com/
Borland; News; Products

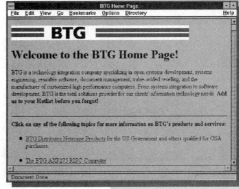

http://www.btg.com/
Computers; LAN; Networks; RISC; UNIX; WAN

Corporations

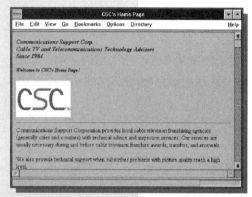

http://www.btg.com/techsys/
BTG; Business; Government; Netscape

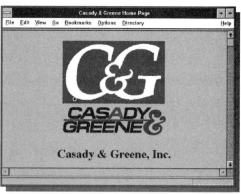

http://www.casadyg.com/
Macintosh; Software; Utilities

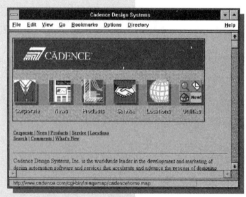

http://www.cabletv.com/
Advisors; Cable TV; Technology; Telecommunications

http://www.castles.com/comm/bcs/bcs.html
Consulting; Networks; PC; Training

http://www.cadence.com/
Automation software; Design; Marketing; Services

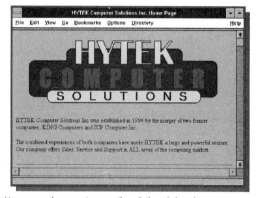

http://www.castles.com/comm/hytek/hytek.html
Computers; Sales; Service; Support

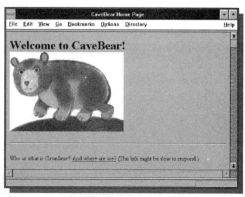

http://www.careermosaic.com/cm/readrite/rr1.html
Disk drives; Miniaturization; Technology; Thin film

http://www.cavebear.com/CaveBear/cavebear.html
CaveBear; Consulting; Internet; Product Development

http://www.cdinet.com/
CDInet; Communications; Networks

http://www.cli.com/index.html
Advanced research; Development; Modeling

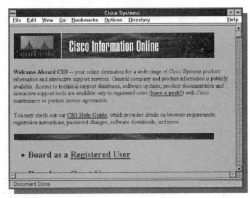

http://www.cdpd.pcsi.com/
Cirrus Logic family; Telecommunication; Wireless products

http://www.compatible.com/
Hardware; Internet; Internetworking products

http://www.cisco.com/
Cisco systems; Communications; Hardware; Software

http://www.consensus.com:8300/
Consensus Development Corporation

http://www.clark.net/pub/networx/networx.html
Autos; Cars; Current projects; NetWorX

http://www.creaf.com/
Creative Labs; Multimedia; Sound Blaster; Sound cards

Corporations

http://www.cris.com/
Communications; Concentric Network; Networking

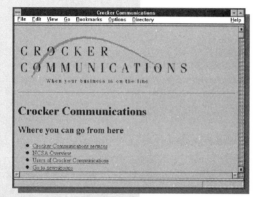

http://www.crocker.com/
Crocker Communications; NCSA; Telecommunications

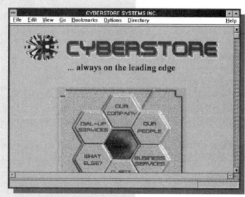

http://www.cyberstore.net/
Cyberstore; Products and services

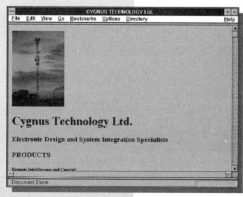

http://www.cygnus.nb.ca/cygnus/cygnus.html
Electronic design; Software; System Integration

http://www.delmarva.com/
ABUI; Delmarva; Electricity; Power plants

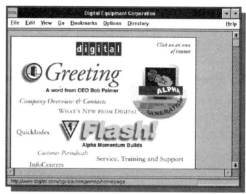

http://www.digital.com/
Computers; Digital Electronic Corp.; PC

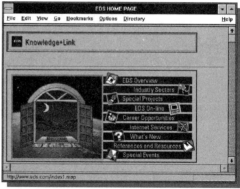

http://www.eds.com/
Career opportunities; EDS; Internet services

http://www.eit.com/
Information technology; R&D and consulting

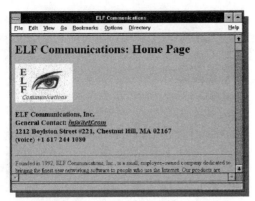

http://www.elf.com/elf/home.html
ELF Communications; Networking Software

http://www.eznet.net/memorandom/
Computing; Consulting; Internet; MemoRandom

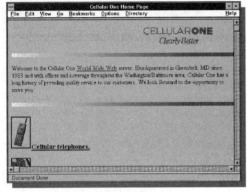

http://www.elpress.com:80/cellone/cellone.html
Cellular; Phones; Telecommunication

http://www.farallon.com/
Apple Talk; Farallon; Plug-and-play networking; TCP/IP

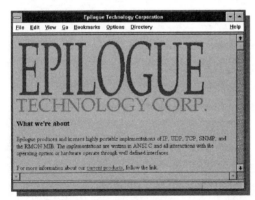

http://www.epilogue.com/Epilogue.html
ANSI C; Portable Software; SNMP; TCP/IP

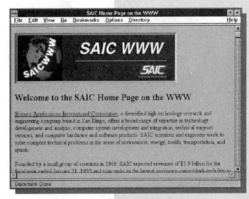

http://www.fed.org/
Energy; Environment; Health; Transportation

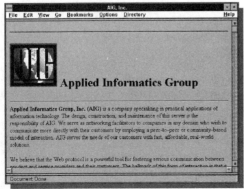

http://www.explore.com/aig.html
AIG Inc.; Design; Development; Information technology

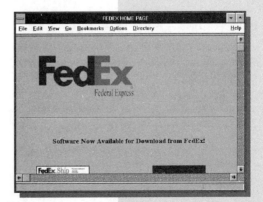

http://www.fedex.com/
Federal Express; FedEx; Software

Corporations

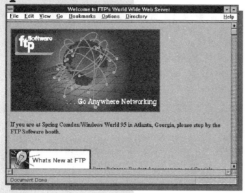

http://www.ftp.com/
FTP software; Internet; Networking

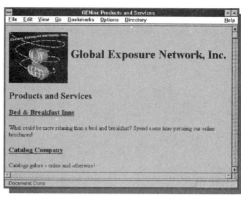

http://www.geninc.com/
Bed and Breakfast Inns; Catalog; Global Exposure Network

http://www.fujitsu.co.jp/
Electronics; Fujitsu; Japan

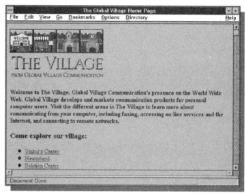

http://www.globalvillag.com/
Communication products; PCs; Remote access; Software

http://www.ge.com/
General Electric; Manufacturing; Products; Services

http://www.goodyear.com/
Blimp; Goodyear Tire and Rubber Company; Products; Services

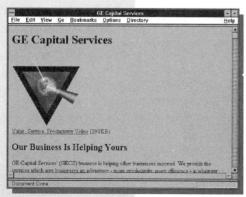

http://www.ge.com/gec/index.html
Business; Finance; Home insurance; Leasing; Renting

http://www.hal.com/
Company information; Computer

http://www.hitachi.co.jp/
Computer hardware; Electronics; Japan

http://www.hotngui.com/
Consultations; GUI design; Semi-custom Objects

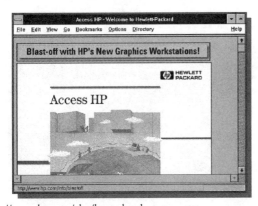

http://www.hp.com/ahp/home.html
Hewlett-Packard; Company Information

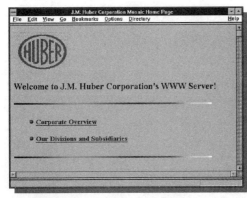

http://www.huber.com/
Directories; Indexes; J. M. Huber

http://www.human.com/mkt/westex/index.html
Westex Automotive; Company Information

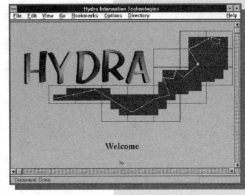

http://www.hydra.com/
Hydra; Information Technology; Networking

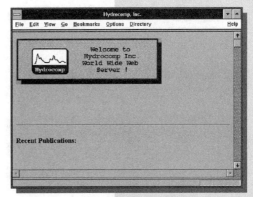

http://www.hydrocomp.com/
Hydrology; Reservoir Management; Water Resource

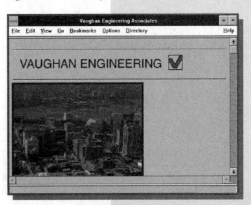

http://www.hypercomp.ns.ca/vaughan.html
Vaughan Engineering Associates

Corporations

http://www.hyperglot.com/
Knoxville; Tennessee; US Internet Inc

http://www.iambic.com/iambic
Design; Manufacture; Newton; PDA; Software

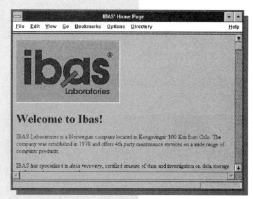

http://www.ibas.no/ibas/
Computers; IBAS Laboratories; Maintenance services; Norway

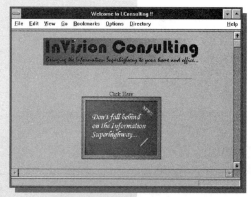

http://www.iconsulting.com/invision.html
Employment; Information; News; Services

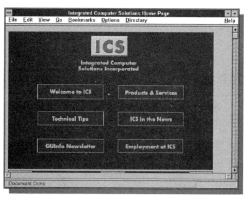

http://www.ics.com/
Company Information; Employment

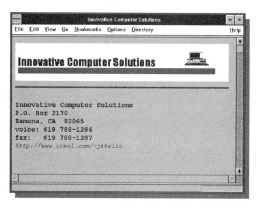

http://www.icsol.com/~jthelin
Innovative Computer Solutions

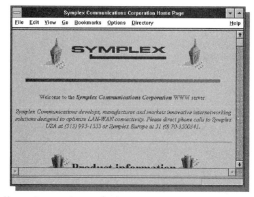

http://www.iea.com/~symplex/
Connectivity; Internetworking; LAN; Marketing; WAN

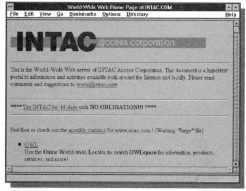

http://www.intac.com/
INTAC Access Corporation; Internet service provider

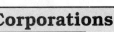

http://www.internet-is.com/cybermedia/in-iis.html
CyberMedia; Internet Products; Technical Support

http://www.iuma.com/iuma-bin/sgi.sh
Silicon Graphics; Surf; World Wide Web

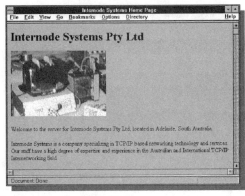

http://www.internode.com.au/
Internetworking; Networking; Protocols; TCP/IP

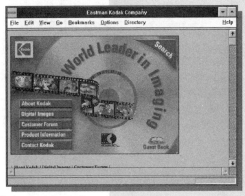

http://www.kodak.com/
Digital images; Products and services

119

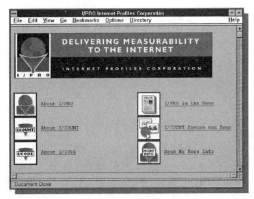

http://www.ipro.com/
Internet Profiles; Quantified Markets

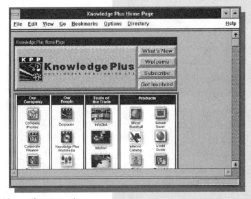

http://www.kpp.com/
Knowledge Plus; Multimedia Publishing; Products

http://www.iquest.com:80/~fairgate/
Macintosh consulting; Software development

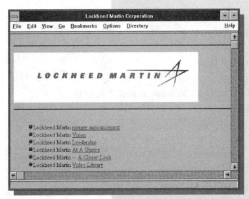

http://www.lockheed.com/
Airplanes; Lockheed Martin Corporation; Video library

Corporations

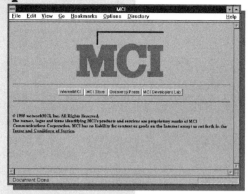

http://www.mci.com/
Gramercy Press; Internet; MCI

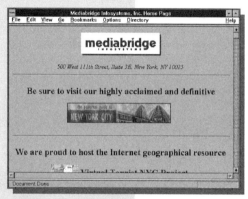

http://www.mediabridge.com/
Guide to New York; Mediabridge; Virtual tourist

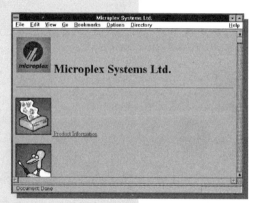

http://www.microplex.com/
Microplex Systems Ltd.; Product information; Services

http://www.microserve.net/index.html
Information services; MicroServe; MIS

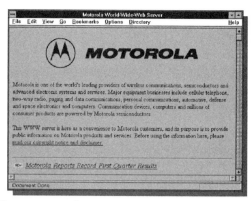

http://www.mot.com/
Electronics; Semiconductors; Wireless communications

http://www.music.sony.com/
Electronics; Music; Sony

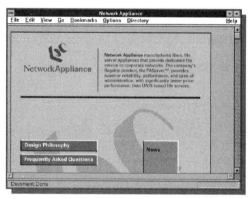

http://www.netapp.com/
NetworkAppliance; Products; Services

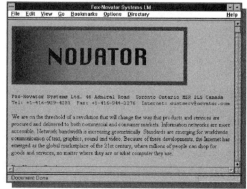

http://www.novator.com/
Consumer markets; Fox-Novator; Products and services

120

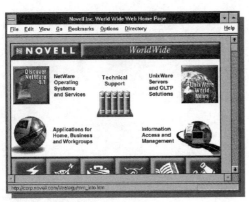

http://www.novell.com/
Novell; Network operating systems; Software

http://www.primenet.com/~jimb/tjind.html
TJ Industries; Company information

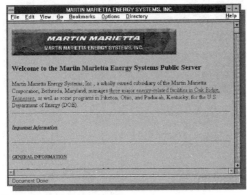

http://www.ornl.gov/mmes.html
Energy; Power production; Technology

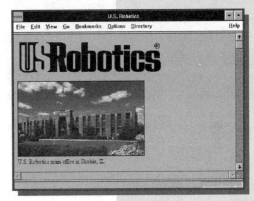

http://www.primenet.com/usr/
Communications; Hardware; US Robotics

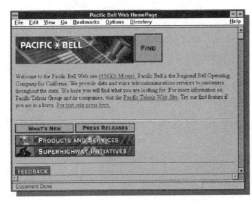

http://www.pacbell.com/
Pacific Bell; Products; Services; Telecommunications

http://www.qms.com/
Printers; Products; QMS; Services

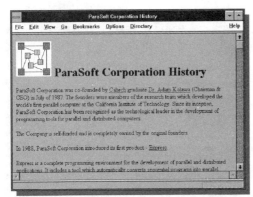

http://www.parasoft.com/company.html
Parallel and distributed computers; ParaSoft Corporation

http://www.quadralay.com/
Company information; Guest book; Quadralay

Corporations

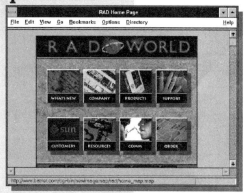

http://www.rad.com/
Data communications; Products and services

http://www.rand.org/
Fellowships; Publications; RAND; Research

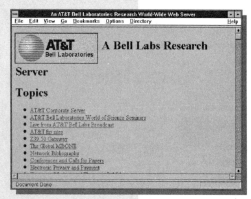

http://www.research.att.com/
Bell Labs Research; Hardware; Software; Telecommunications

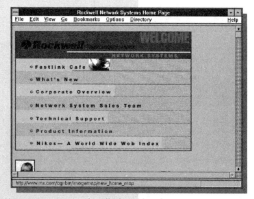

http://www.rns.com/rockwell/about.html
Product information; Rockwell Network Systems

http://www.rockwell.com/
Aerospace; Aviation; Defense; Telecommunications

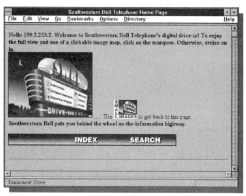

http://www.sbc.com/
Communications technology; Electronics; Telephone

http://www.sco.com/
Products; SCO Open Systems Software; Services

http://www.scubed.com/
Company information; Maxwell Labs; Web server

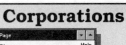

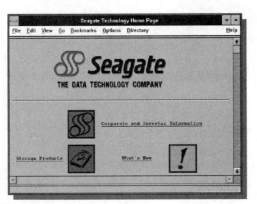

http://www.seagate.com/
Seagate Technology; Storage products

http://www.service.com/cm/uswest/home.html
Corporate background; Opportunities; US West Page 1

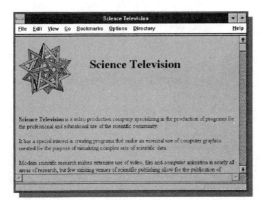

http://www.service.com/stv/home.html
Education; Television; Videos

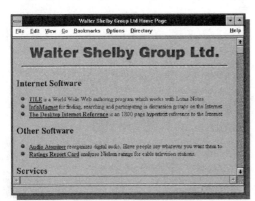

http://www.shelby.com/pub/listserv/wsg.html
Software; Walter Shelby Group Ltd

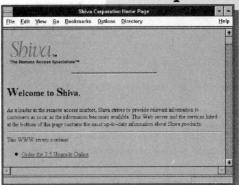

http://www.shiva.com/
Networks; Remote Access; Shiva

http://www.sprintlink.net/
Communications; Sprint; Technology

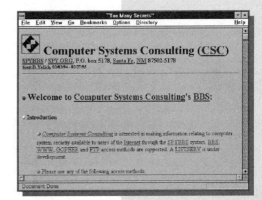

http://www.spy.org/
FTP; GOPHER; Internet; Security; WWW

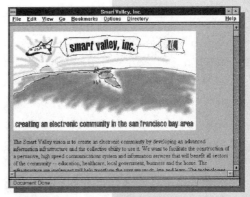

http://www.svi.org/
Electronic Community; San Francisco Bay Area

Corporations

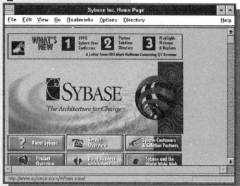

http://www.sybase.com/
Client/server software; Products and services; Sybase Inc.

http://www.tais.com/
Products and services; Toshiba America

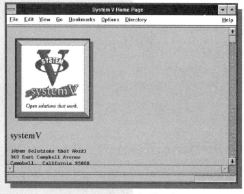

http://www.systemv.com/systemv/index.html
Software; System V; Open systems

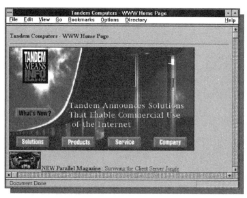

http://www.tandem.com/
Computing; Products; Services; Tandem Computers

124

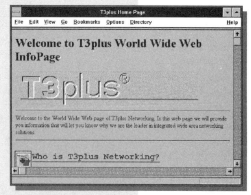

http://www.t3plus.com/
Integrated wide area networking; T3plus Networking

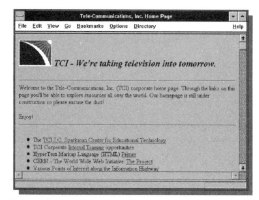

http://www.tcinc.com/
HTML; Internet; TCI; Tele-Communications Inc.

http://www.tach.net/
Internet Provider; Tachyon Communication

http://www.teleport.com/~crawford
Vulcan's Forge; WWW Homepage

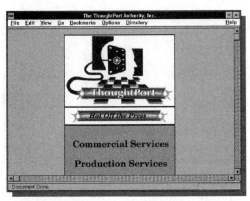

http://www.thoughtport.com/
Production services; ThoughtPort Authority; Web publishing

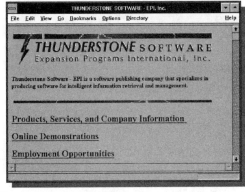

http://www.thunderstone.com/
Products and services; Thunderstone Software

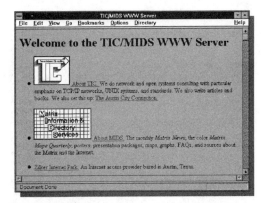

http://www.tic.com/
Open systems consulting; TCP/IP networks; TIC/MIDS

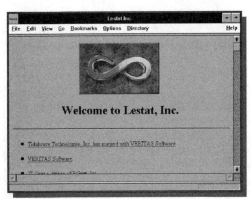

http://www.tidalwave.com/
Lestat Inc; Tidalwave Technologies

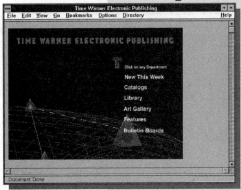

http://www.timeinc.com/twep/
Art; Catalogs; Library; Electronic publishing; Time Warner

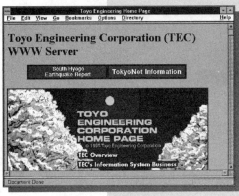

http://www.toyo-eng.co.jp/
Engineering; International; Japan; TokyoNet

http://www.triticom.com/
LAN management; Software tools; Triticom

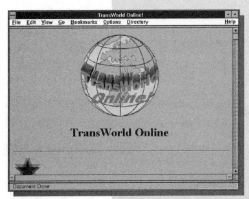

http://www.two.com/
Business presence; TransWorld Online; Web access

Corporations

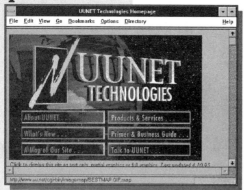

http://www.uu.net/
Business guide; Products and services; UUNET

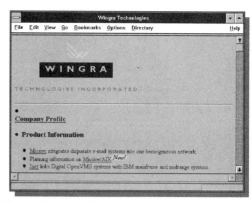

http://www.wingra.com/
Company profile; Wingra Technologies

http://www.verity.com/
Verity Inc.

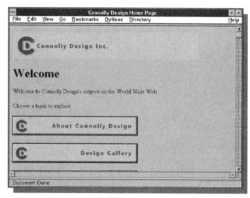

http://www.worldlinx.com/cdi
Company profile; Connolly Design; Design gallery

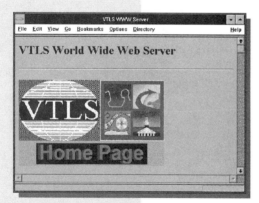

http://www.vtls.com/
Blacksburg; Virginia; VTLS; Web server

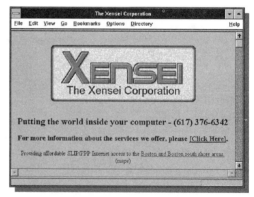

http://www.xensei.com/
Boston; Computers; PPP; SLIP; Xensei Corporation

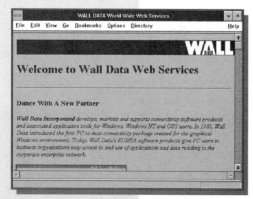

http://www.walldata.com/
OS/2; Wall Data World Wide Web Services; Windows

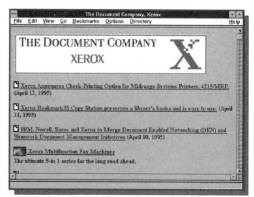

http://www.xerox.com/
Copiers; News; Printers; Products; Technology; Xerox

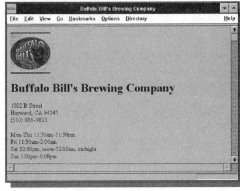

http://and.com/3rock/3rock.html
Ale; Beer; Brewing; Berkeley California

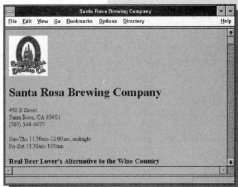

http://and.com/srbc/srbc.html
Beer; Santa Rosa Brewing Company

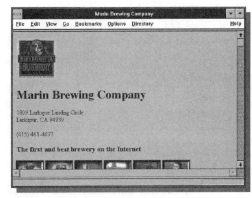

http://and.com/bb/bb.html
Beer; Buffalo Bill's Brewing Company; Newsletter

http://chile.ucdmc.ucdavis.edu:8000/www/chile.html
Chile peppers; Food; Spices

127

http://and.com/mbc/mbc.html
Beer; Marin Brewing Company

http://eMall.com/chile/
Chile; Gifts; Hot Tamales; Sauces

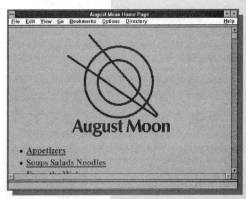

http://and.com/realbeer/rbp.html
Beer; Brewers; Homebrewing; Microbreweries

http://fentonnet.com/moon/august.html
Food; Oriental; Restaurants

Culinary

http://gsb.stanford.edu/goodlife/home.html
Restaurants; San Francisco Peninsula

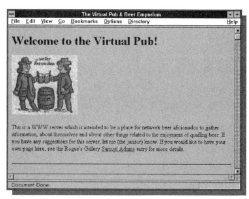

http://lager.geo.brown.edu:8080/virtual-pub/
Beer; Pub; Samuel Adams

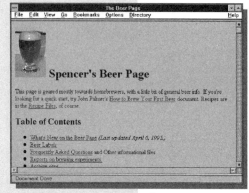

http://guraldi.itn.med.umich.edu/Beer/
Beer; Beer labels; Pilsner; Recipe files

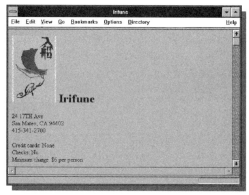

http://market.net/sfbay/dining/irifune/index.html
Banquet facilities; Dining; Irifune; On-line menu; San Mateo

http://icemcfd.com/sungate.html
Exotic; Salsa; Sauces

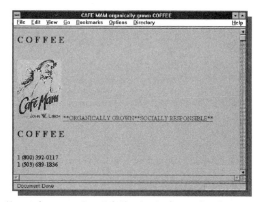

http://mmink.cts.com/mmink/dossiers/cafemam.html
Coffee; Gourmet foods

http://ificinfo.health.org/
International Food Information Council Foundation

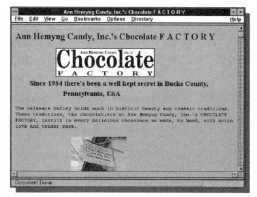

http://mmink.cts.com/mmink/dossiers/choco.html
Candy; Chocolate; Chocolatiers; Hand-made confections

http://netmedia.com/ims/rest/ADS/pollos/pollos.html
Burritos; Mexican Restaurant; Roasted Chicken

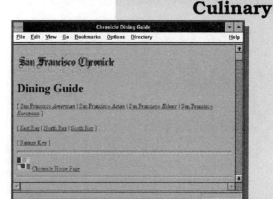

http://sfgate.com/new/schron/food/index.html
Dining Guide; San Francisco Chronicle

http://netmedia.com/ims/rest/ADS/scotts/scott_main_final.html
Scott's Seafood Grill & Bar

http://solano.community.net/community/solano/business/bnl.html
B&L Cattle Company; Black Angus Beef; Dining; Restaurant

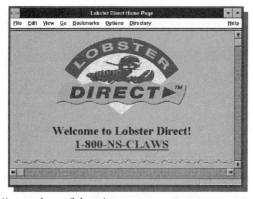

http://novaweb.com/lobster/
Canada; Lobster; Mail order; Nova Scotia; Orders; Sales

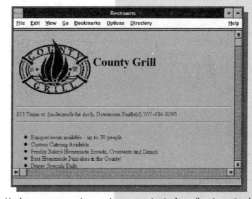

http://solano.community.net/community/solano/business/cg.html
Catering; County Grill; Croissants; Danish; Pancakes

http://sddtsun.sddt.com/files/lifestyles/eats.html
Dining Guide; Index; On-Line; San Diego

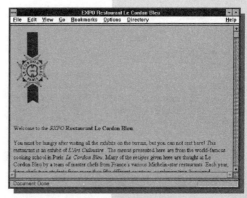

http://sunsite.unc.edu/expo/restaurant/restaurant.html
Food; Recipes; Restaurant

129

Culinary

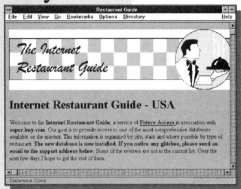

http://super.hwy.com/RestaurantGuide.html
City; Database; Restaurant Guide

http://systemv.systemv.com/pink/
European Taste; Fine American Chocolates

http://town.hall.org/food/deli.html
Digital Deli; Unusual foods; Wine specialists

http://town.hall.org/food/sage.html
Red Sage; Restaurant; Washington DC

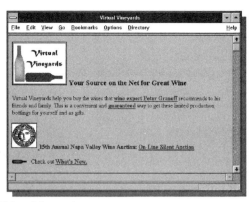

http://virtualvin.com/
News; On-line auctions; Virtual Vineyards; Wine

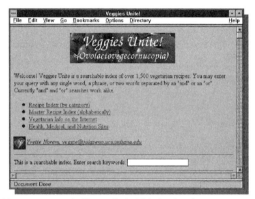

http://www-sc.ucssc.indiana.edu/cgi-bin/recipes/
Diet; Foods; Recipes; Vegetarian recipes

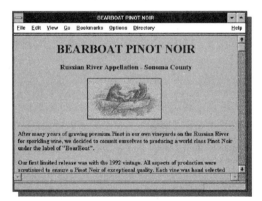

http://www.bearboat.com/
Pinot Noir; Sonoma County; Vineyards; Wine

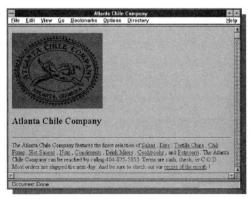

http://www.bizweb.com/chile.html
Chili; Food; Recipes; Salsa

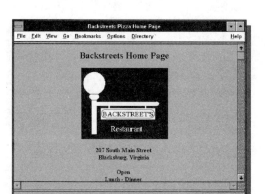

http://www.bnt.com/~backstreets/
Backstreets; Restaurants; Virginia

http://www.dcs.ed.ac.uk/staff/jhb/whisky/
Alcohol; Beverages; Distilleries; Malt whisky; Scotland

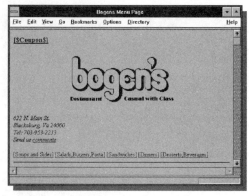

http://www.bnt.com/~bogens
Bogens; Restaurant; Virginia

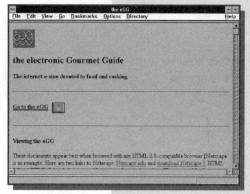

http://www.deltanet.com:80/2way/egg/
Gourmet food; Recipes

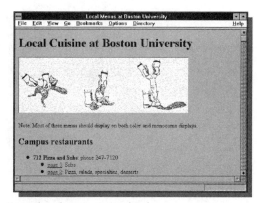

http://www.bu.edu/menu/menu.html
Boston University; Food; Menus

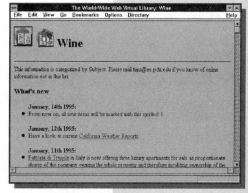

http://www.ee.pdx.edu/~timt/html/wine.html
Wine; Wine makers

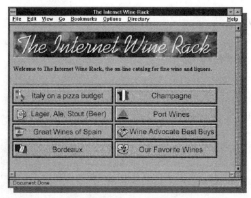

http://www.clark.net/pub/wine/home.html
Beer; Champagne; Italy; Travel; Wine

http://www.food.emporium.com/~finefood/
Catalogs; Gourmet food; Magazines

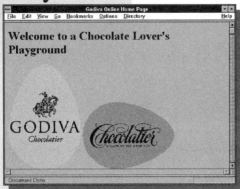

http://www.godiva.com/
Chocolate Lover's Playground; Godiva Chocolatier

http://www.ip.net/smithfield/home.html
Hams; Smithfield Farms; Virginia

http://www.hot.presence.com/g/p/H3/index.html
Cooking; Entertainment; Recipes

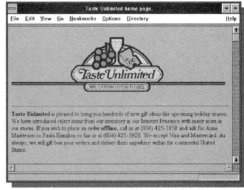

http://www.ip.net/tu/home.html
Catering; Gift; Special foods; Taste Unlimited; Wine

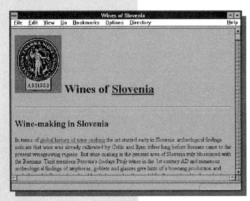

http://www.ijs.si/wine_uvod.html
Gourmet foods; Slovenia; Wines

http://www.novator.com/FOODWARE/FOODWARE.html
Food Gourmet; FOODWARE; Recipes

http://www.infonet.net/showcase/coffee
Beverages; Coffee; Online coffee community; Resources

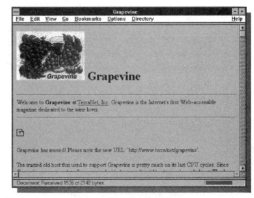

http://www.opal.com/grapevine
Gourmet Foods; Wines

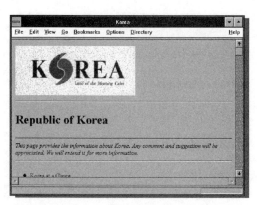

http://cair-archive.kaist.ac.kr/korea/index.html
Asia; Korea; People; Government

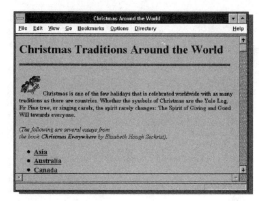

http://christmas.com/christmas.html
Christmas traditions; International

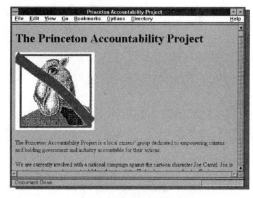

http://eno.princeton.edu/~jonathan/pap.html
Empowering citizens; Government; Princeton accountability

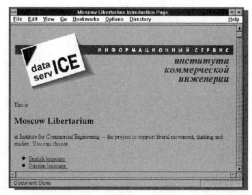

http://feast.fe.msk.ru/libertarium/
Engineering; Institute for Commercial Engineering; Russia

http://heiwww.unige.ch/switzerland/
Culture; Maps; Switzerland

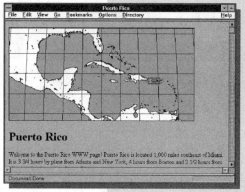

http://hpprdk01.prd.hp.com/
Culture; Puerto Rico; Travel

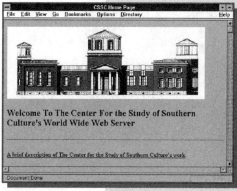

http://imp.cssc.olemiss.edu/
Social science; Sociology; Southern culture

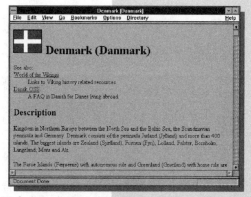

http://info.denet.dk/denmark.html
Culture; Danish; Denmark; Travel; Vikings

Culture

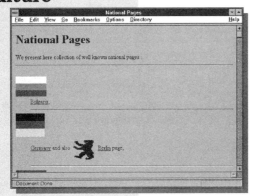

http://info.fuw.edu.pl/national.html
Bulgaria; Europe; Germany; National Pages

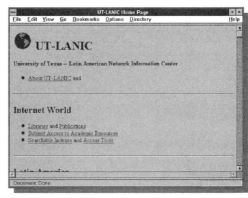

http://lanic.utexas.edu/
Austin; Latin America; University of Texas

http://info.fuw.edu.pl/pl/PolandHome.html
Government; Poland; Polish culture; Warsaw University

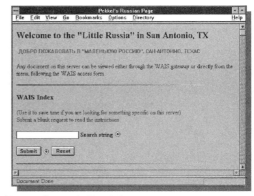

http://mars.uthscsa.edu/Russia/
Russia; San Antonio Texas; USSR

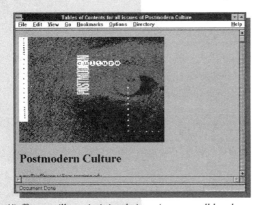

http://jefferson.village.virginia.edu/pmc/contents.all.html
Online magazine; Postmodern Culture

http://mirror.wwa.com/mirror/atlantis/millpop/homepage.htm
Culture; Pop commentary

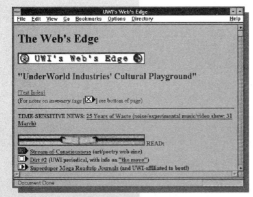

http://kzsu.stanford.edu/uwi.html
Art; Culture; Poetry; Web's Edge

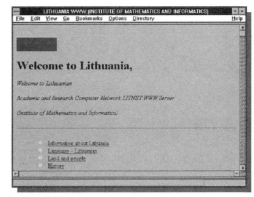

http://neris.mii.lt/
Lithuania; Web servers

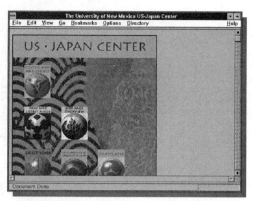

http://nobunaga.unm.edu:8001/
Events; Information; US-Japan Center

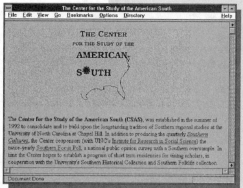

http://sunsite.unc.edu/doug_m/pages/south/center/center.html
Cultures; Social sciences; Study of the American South

http://s700.uminho.pt/cult-europ.html
Europe; Tourism; Vacations

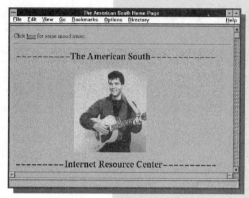

http://sunsite.unc.edu/doug_m/pages/south/south.html
American South; Country music; Music

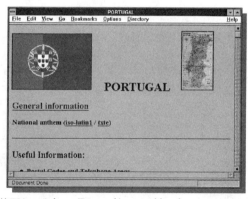

http://s700.uminho.pt/Portugal/portugal.html
Culture; National anthem; Portugal

http://tehran.stanford.edu/
Culture; Iran; Tehran

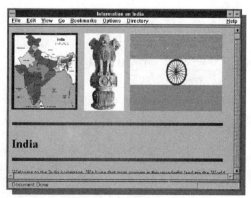

http://spiderman.bu.edu:80/misc/india
Business; Culture; India; Map

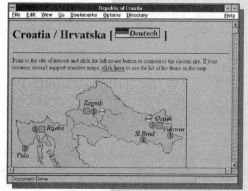

http://tjev.tel.etf.hr/hrvatska/HR.html
Croatia; German; Hrvatska; Maps

Culture

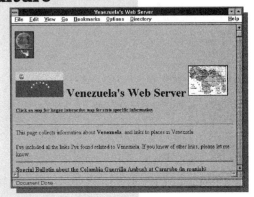

http://venezuela.mit.edu/
Venezuela; Web servers; Government

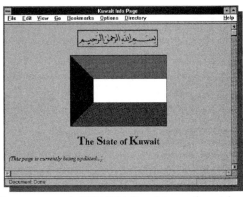

http://www.cs.cmu.edu:8001/Web/People/anwar/kuwait.html
Gulf; Kuwait; Middle East

http://web.msu.edu/mfest94/index.html
Celebration; Costumes; Foods; Michigan Festival; Music

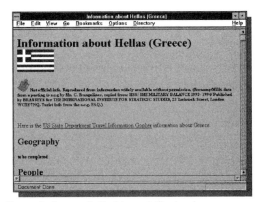

http://www.forthnet.gr/hellas/about_hellas.html
Culture; Geography; Greece; Greek; Travel

http://www.chemie.fu-berlin.de/adressen/brd.html
Culture; Geography; Germany; Government

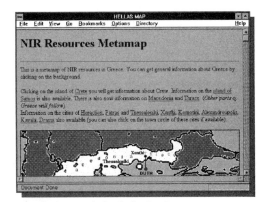

http://www.forthnet.gr/hellas/hellas.html
Crete; Culture; Greece; Maps

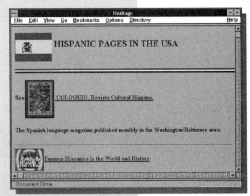

http://www.clark.net/pub/jgbustam/heritage/heritage.html
Hispanics; Online magazines; Spanish

http://www.fsz.bme.hu/hungary/homepage.html
Hungary; Map; Web sites

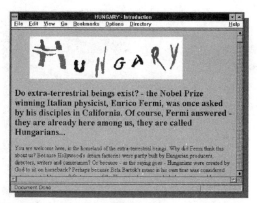

http://www.fsz.bme.hu/hungary/intro.html
Culture; History; Hungary

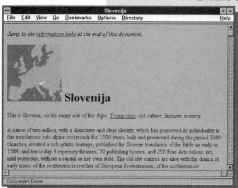

http://www.ijs.si/slo.html
Alps; Culture; Slovenija

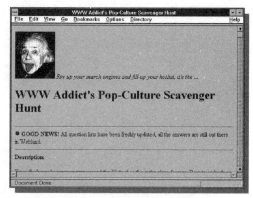

http://www.galcit.caltech.edu/~ta/hunt/wwwhunt.html
Cool stuff; Pop Culture; Webland

http://www.infopost.com/europe/germany/saxony/index.html
Culture; Sachsen; Saxony; Travel

137

http://www.human.com/Cultural/index.html
California; Santa Cruz County

http://www.mastercard.com/
Collection of stories; Cultural treasures; MasterCard

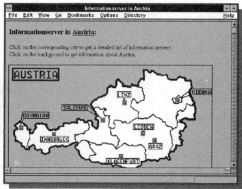

http://www.ifs.univie.ac.at/austria.html
Austria; Geography; Map

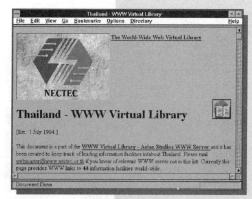

http://www.nectec.or.th/WWW-VL-Thailand.html
Asia; Asian studies; Asian studies; Library; Thailand

Databases

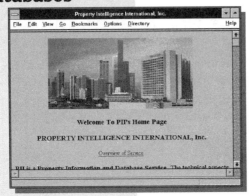

http://anshar.shadow.net/~pii/
Intelligence; Property information; Real estate database

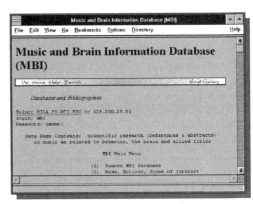

http://galaxy.einet.net/hytelnet/FUL063.html
Behavior; Brain; Database; Music; Research

http://biomed.nus.sg/PID/PID.html
Poison control; Poisons Information Database; Toxicology

http://galaxy.einet.net/hytelnet/FUL064.html
Database; Music; Research literature

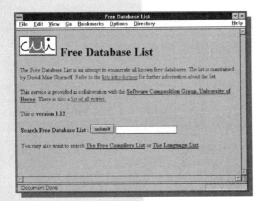

http://cuiwww.unige.ch/~scg/FreeDB
Compilers; Free databases; Software

http://gcmd.gsfc.nasa.gov/
Climate; Environment; Global change; Science

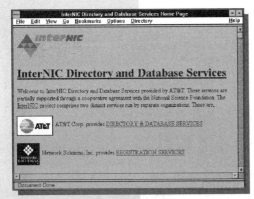

http://ds.internic.net/ds-home.html
AT&T database services; Network Solutions Inc.

http://gdbwww.gdb.org/
Demonstrations; DNA; Genome; WAIS

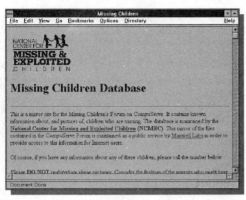

http://inept.scubed.com:8001/public_service/missing.html
Exploited children; Missing children; NCMEC

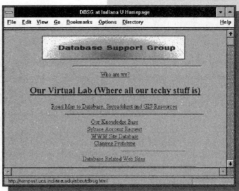

http://tempest.ucs.indiana.edu/
Indiana University; Knowledge Base; Virtual Lab

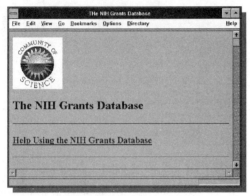

http://medoc.gdb.org/best/fedfund/nih-intro.html
Database; Grants; National Institutes of Health

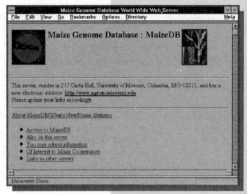

http://teosinte.agron.missouri.edu/top.html
Maize Genome Database; University of Missouri

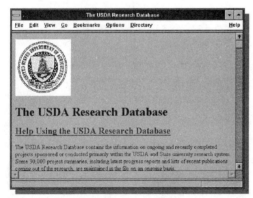

http://medoc.gdb.org/best/stc/usda-best.html
Database; Research; US Department of Agriculture

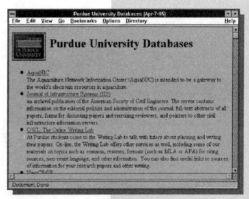

http://thorplus.lib.purdue.edu/databases/
Databases; Purdue University

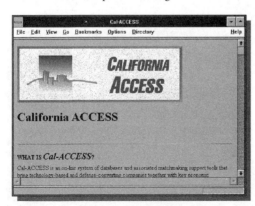

http://merkury.saic.com/calaccess/CalACCESS.html
On-line databases; Defense-converting companies; Tools

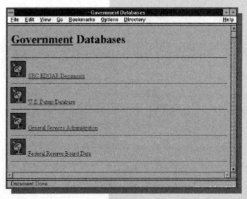

http://town.hall.org/govt/govt.html
Federal Reserve; Government databases; GSA; Patents

139

Databases

http://webcrawler.cs.washington.edu/cgi-bin/WebQuery
Frequently asked questions; Hints for searching

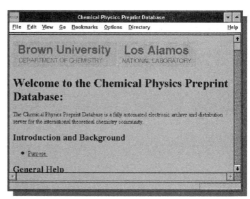

http://www.chem.brown.edu/chem-ph.html
Chemical Physics Preprint Database; Electronic archive

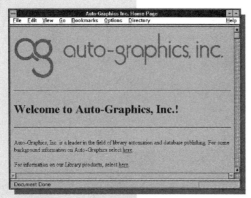

http://www.agfx.com/
Database publishing; Library automation

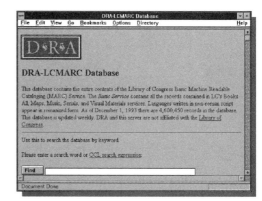

http://www.dra.com/lcmarc
LCMARC; Library of Congress Basic Machine Readable

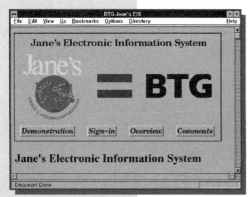

http://www.btg.com/janes/welcome.html
Aircraft; Jane's Electronic Information; Military equipment

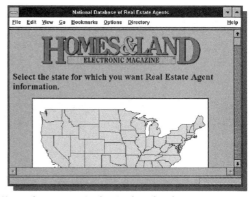

http://www.homes.com/realtor/realtors.html
Agents; Homes & Land; Magazine; Maps; Real estate

http://www.cgnet.com/
CGNET Services International; Databases

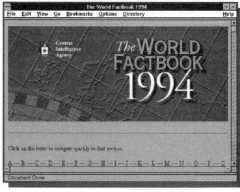

http://www.ic.gov/94fact/fb94toc/fb94toc.html
CIA; Factbook; Information; World information

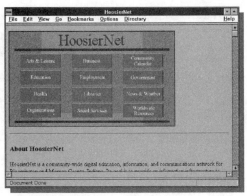

http://access.bloomington.in.us/
Community information; HoosierNet; Indiana University

http://artdirect.com/california/la/homepage
Art Galleries; Los Angeles; Museums; Performing Arts

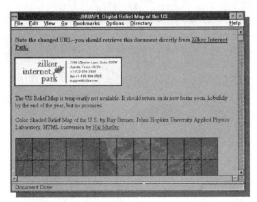

http://ageninfo.tamu.edu:80/apl-us/
Cartography; Maps; US

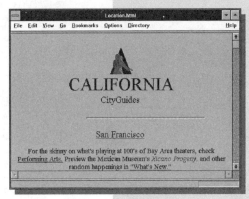

http://artdirect.com/california/location.html
California cities; Guides

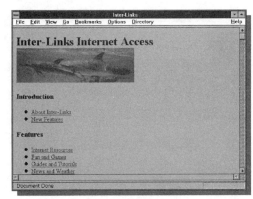

http://alpha.acast.nova.edu/start.html
Games; Guides; Internet access; Tutorials; Weather

http://artdirect.com/california/sacramento/homepage
California Cities; Guides; Sacramento

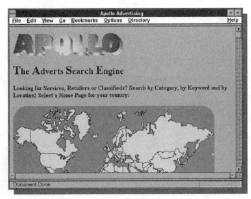

http://apollo.co.uk/
Advertisers; Retailers; Services

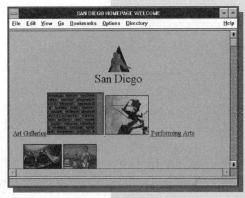

http://artdirect.com/california/san.diego/homepage
California cities; Guides; San Diego

Directories

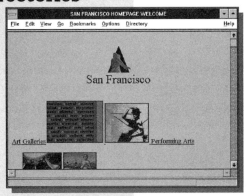

http://artdirect.com/california/san.francisco/homepage
California cities; Guides; San Francisco

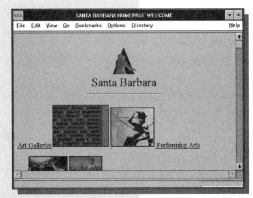

http://artdirect.com/california/sb/home.html
California cities; Guides; Santa Barbara

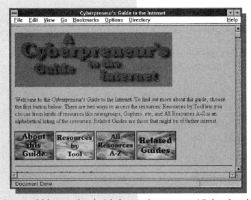

http://asa.ugl.lib.umich.edu/chdocs/cyberpreneur/Cyber.html
Guides; Internet; Resources; Tools

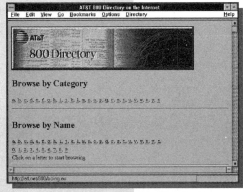

http://att.net/dir800
AT&T 800 Directory; Business; Toll-free number

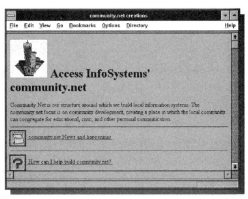

http://community.net/community/index.html
Civics; Community Net; Education

http://cos.gdb.org/maps/cos/exp/states/expstates.html
Map; Scientific expertise; Search

http://crusher.bev.net/index.html
Blacksburg; Community information; Virginia

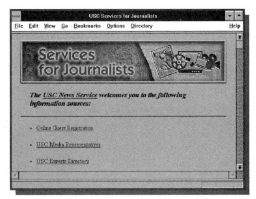

http://cwis.usc.edu/dept/News_Service/media_services.html
Journalists; USC; USC News Service

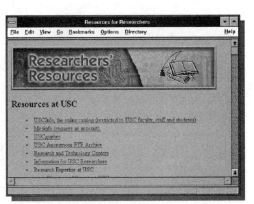

http://cwis.usc.edu/users/help/draft/Research_Resources.html
Researchers' Resources; USC

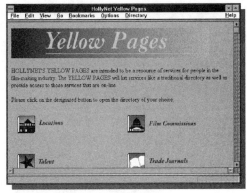

http://cwis.usc.edu:80/dept/etc/hollynet/yp/
Hollywood; Movie industry

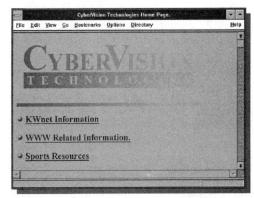

http://cybervision.kwnet.on.ca/
CyberVision Technologies; KWnet; Sports resources

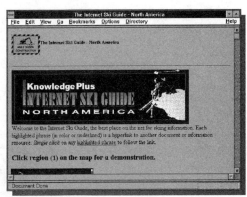

http://cybil.kplus.bc.ca/www/ski_net/ski_na.htm
Alpine; Nordic; Ski guide

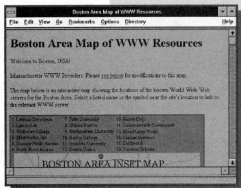

http://donald.phast.umass.edu/misc/boston.html
Boston; Cities; Massachusetts; New England; USA

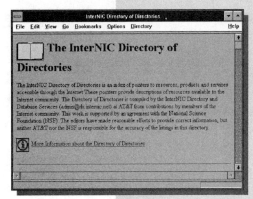

http://ds.internic.net/ds/dsdirofdirs.html
Directory of Directories; InterNIC

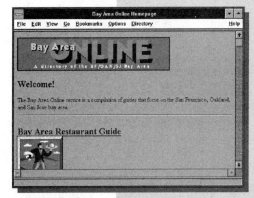

http://emerson.netmedia.com/IMS/bao/ba_online.html
California; Guides; Oakland; San Francisco; San Jose

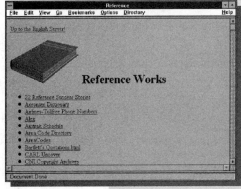

http://english-server.hss.cmu.edu/Reference.html
Acronym Dictionary; Amtrak schedule; Area codes; Reference

143

Directories

http://fentonnet.com/
Fentonnet; Jobs; Twin cities; Web resources

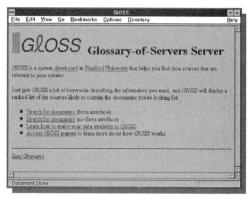

http://gloss.stanford.edu/
Gloss; Glossary-of-Servers Server; Search for documents

http://footbag.org/
Footbag Information Sources; Leagues; Organizations; Sports

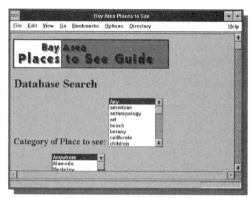

http://hamilton.netmedia.com/ims/pts/pts.html
Bay Area; California; Community information

144

http://gagme.wwa.com/~boba/pick.html
Links; Pick of the Day; Recommendations; Spider's Web

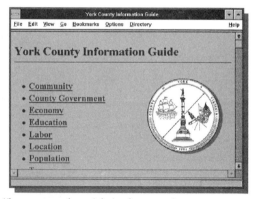

http://hampton.roads.net/nhr/york_county/
Community information; History; York County

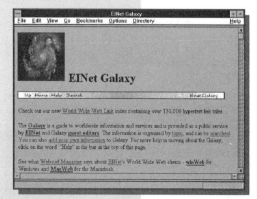

http://galaxy.einet.net/
Indexes; World Wide Web services

http://home.mcom.com/escapes/internet_search.html
Help; Internet Search; On-line search engines

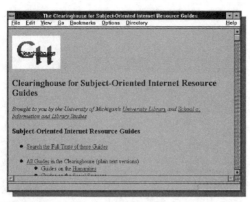

http://http2.sils.umich.edu/~lou/chhome.html
Internet resource guides

http://info.fuw.edu.pl/pl/PolandResourceMap.html
Map; Poland; Web servers

http://ibd.ar.com/
Business; Catalogs; Online sales; Shopping centers; Stores

http://info.pue.udlap.mx/www-mex-eng.html
Map; Mexico; WWW Servers

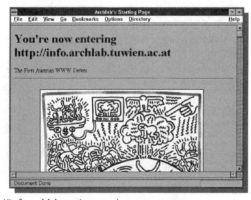

http://info.archlab.tuwien.ac.at/
Austria; Web server

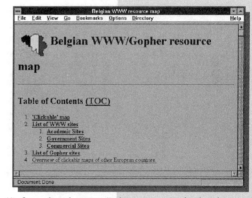

http://info1.vub.ac.be:8080/Belgium_map/index.html
Academic; Belgian; Belgium; Government; Map; Web sites

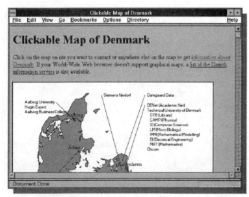

http://info.denet.dk/dkmap.html
Denmark; Maps

http://infopages.com/
Guides; Maximized On-line; Southern California

Directories

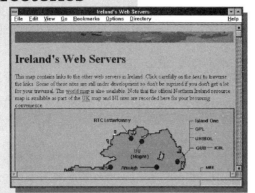

http://itdsrv1.ul.ie/Information/ServerMapIreland.html
Ireland; Maps; Web servers

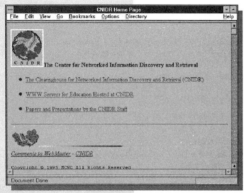

http://kudzu.cnidr.org/welcome.html
Networked information discovery and retrieval

http://kzsu.stanford.edu/uwi/reviews.html
Cool things; Underground Web sites; WWW

http://lemur.stanford.edu/
Directory; Internet sites; Web sites

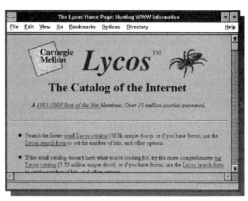

http://lycos.cs.cmu.edu/
Information; Research

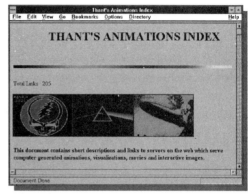

http://mambo.ucsc.edu/psl/thant/thant.html
Animations; Interactive images; Visualizations

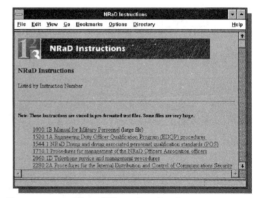

http://manta.nosc.mil/~ratliff/numbers.html
Manuals; NRaD Instructions; Publications; Regulations

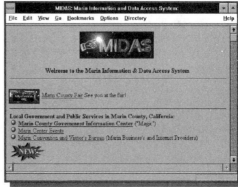

http://marin.org/
California; Community information; Marin County

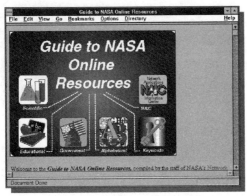

http://mofile.fi/base.htm
Finland; Magazine; On-line

http://nemo.ncsl.nist.gov/~sressler/hotvr.html
Directories; Links; Virtual reality

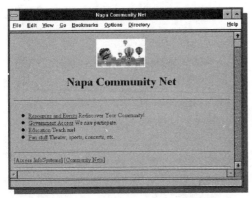

http://naic.nasa.gov/naic/guide/
Education; Guide to NASA online resources; Science

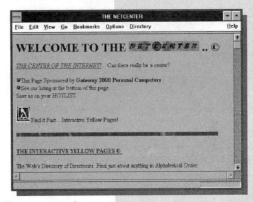

http://netcenter.com/
Directories; Netcenter; Yellow pages

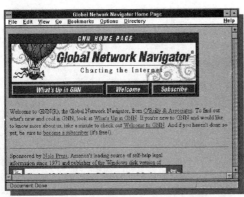

http://napa.community.net/community/napa/index.html
Internet; Napa Community Net

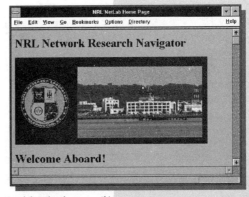

http://netlab.itd.nrl.navy.mil/
Naval research laboratory; Network research

http://nearnet.gnn.com/gnn/gnn.html
Global Network Navigator; GNN; O'Reilly and Associates

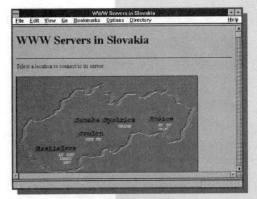

http://nic.uakom.sk/hypertext/homepage.html
Slovakia; Web servers

Directories

http://quiknet.com/
Internet access; Web server

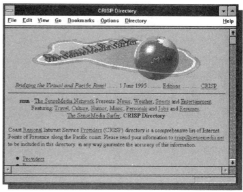

http://sensemedia.net/crisp
Coast Regional Internet Service Providers; Internet presence

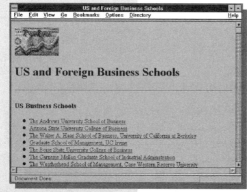

http://riskweb.bus.utexas.edu/bschool.html
Business schools; Graduate programs; Harvard University

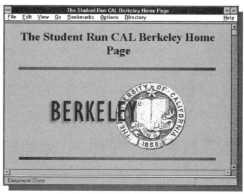

http://server.berkeley.edu/
Education; University of California Berkeley

http://s700.uminho.pt/europa.html
Europe; European Web servers

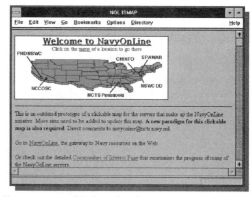

http://sneezy.nosc.mil/nolmap.html
Directory; Naval information online; NavyOnLine

http://s700.uminho.pt/homepage-pt.html
Maps; Portugal; Web servers

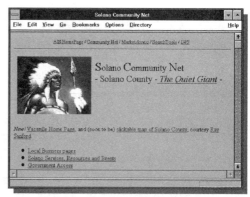

http://solano.community.net/community/solano/index.html
Local business; Solano Community Net; Solano County

http://spacelink.msfc.nasa.gov/
Education; NASA; News; Teachers

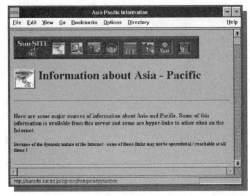

http://sunsite.sut.ac.jp/asia/asia.html
Asia-Pacific Information; Resources

http://tcomeng.com/cities/ssf/index.html
California; South San Francisco

http://teal.nosc.mil/planet_earth/california.html
California information; West Coast

http://teal.nosc.mil/planet_earth/states.html
Servers; United States of America

http://tonyt.galstar.com/
Community information; Oklahoma; Tulsa

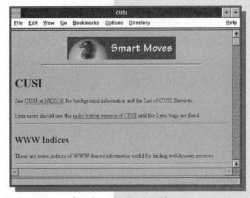

http://uranus.eng.auth.gr/new/moves/cusi/
CUSI; Directories; Index; Search

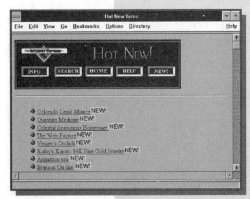

http://usa.net/home/hotnew.html
Directories; Hot New Items; Links

149

Directories

http://utkvx1.utk.edu/~xurs/china.html
China; Web sites

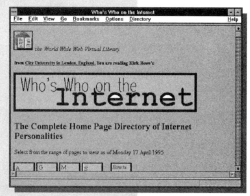

http://web.city.ac.uk/citylive/pages.html
Internet directory; Personal homepages

http://web.urec.fr/france/france.html
France servers; Information; Map

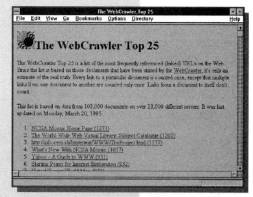

http://webcrawler.cs.washington.edu/WebCrawler/Top25.html
Index; Popular sites; Web sites

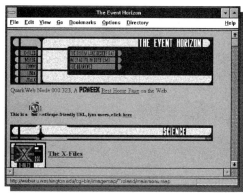

http://weber.u.washington.edu/~roland/
Best Homepage; Event Horizon; X-Files

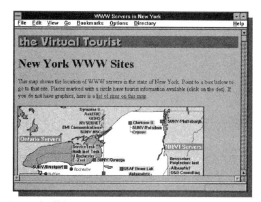

http://wings.buffalo.edu/world/nywww.html
Map; New York; Tourist

http://woi.com/woi/
Award winning site; Index; Links; World of Interest

http://www-ca.llnl.gov/california/servers.html
California World Wide Web Servers

http://www.abb.no/abb/pub/Homepage.html
Gas; Petrochemical market; International oil; Supplier; Systems

http://www.ais.net/findafriend
Friends; Information resources; Missing persons; Relatives

http://www.acoates.com/sjliving
Art; Entertainment; Museums; On-Line guide; Parks; San Jose

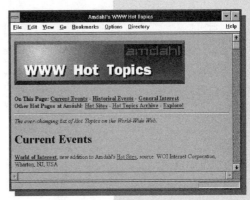

http://www.amdahl.com/internet/hot.html
Amdahl; Topics; Web sites

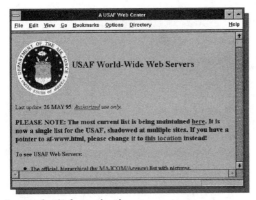

http://www.af.mil/af-www.html
Directories; Index; Internet server; List; U.S. Air Force

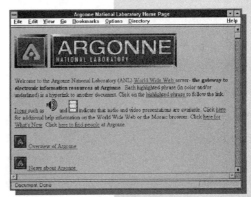

http://www.anl.gov/
Argonne National Laboratory; Audio; Video

http://www.ainet.com/
Internet resources; Links; Starting points

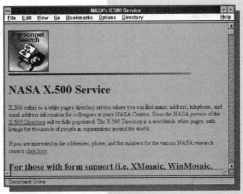

http://www.arc.nasa.gov/x500.html
NASA; White pages directory; X.500

151

Directories

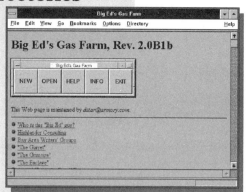

http://www.armory.com/~dstar/
Consulting; Directories; Links; Writers groups

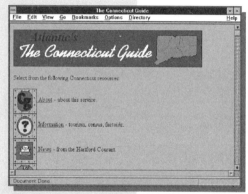

http://www.atlantic.com/ctguide/
Census; Connecticut; News; Tourism

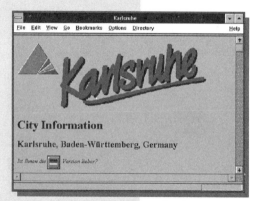

http://www.ba-karlsruhe.de/KA/KA_eng.html
Baden-Wurttemberg; Community information; Karlsruhe

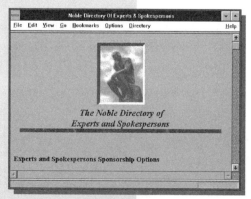

http://www.catalog.com/experts/
Internet presence; Site lists; Web

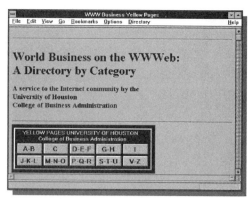

http://www.cba.uh.edu/ylowpges/ylowpges.html
Business; Shopping; University of Houston

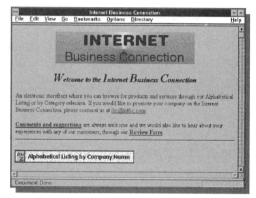

http://www.charm.net/~ibc/
Business; Web connection

http://www.charm.net/baltimore.html
Baltimore; Community information; Maryland

http://www.ci.chi.il.us/
Chicago; Community information; Illinois; Mosaic project

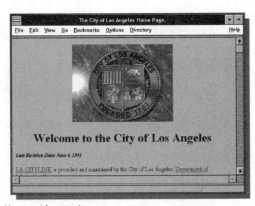

http://www.ci.la.ca.us/
California; Community information; Los Angeles

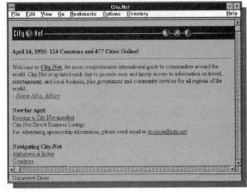

http://www.city.net/
Cities; City.Net; Communities; International guide

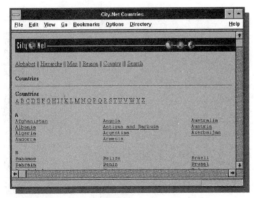

http://www.city.net/countries/
City Net; Countries; Directory

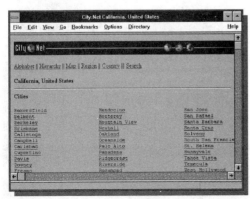

http://www.city.net/countries/united_states/california/
California; City Net; Directory

http://www.commerce.digital.com/oetc/home.html
Development; Directories; Export; Ohio

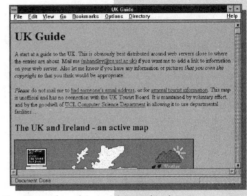

http://www.cs.ucl.ac.uk/misc/uk/intro.html
Ireland; Maps; United Kingdom

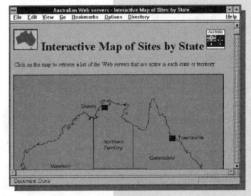

http://www.csu.edu.au/links/ozmap.html
Maps; Travel; Web servers

http://www.dcc.uchile.cl/chile/chile.html
Chile; Culture; Map; News; Spanish; Tourism

Directories

http://www.destek.net/
Internet Access Services and Consulting; New England

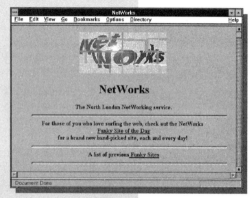

http://www.dircon.co.uk/networks/
Funky sites; NetWorks; North London

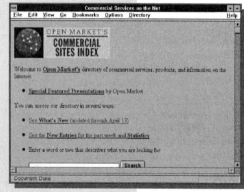

http://www.directory.net/
Business; Commercial Sites Index; Web

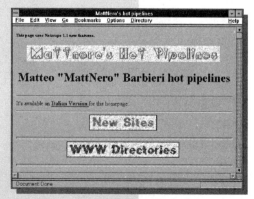

http://www.dsi.unimi.it/Users/Students/barbieri/home.html
Italian; Italy; Web servers

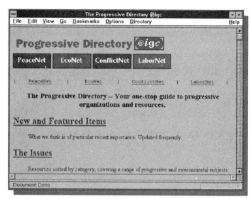

http://www.econet.apc.org/
Progressive subjects; Site directory

http://www.eeb.ele.tue.nl/map/netherlands.html
Danish; Dutch; Holland; Netherlands

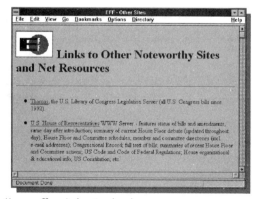

http://www.eff.org/othersites.html
Congress; Government agencies; Web links

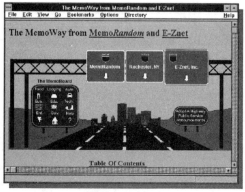

http://www.eznet.net/
E-Znet; East Coast; Internet Access

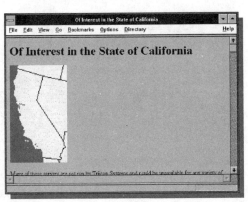

http://www.foundation.tricon.com/triicon_home/CA/index.html
California; Directories; Internet Servers

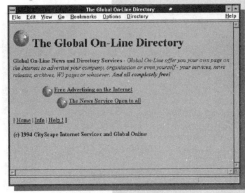

http://www.gold.net/gold/
Advertising; Directory; Global online news; News service

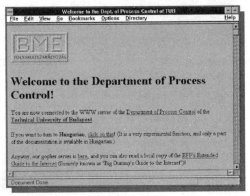

http://www.fsz.bme.hu/
Budapest; Hungarian; Internet guide; Process Control

http://www.gomedia.com/ol.welcome.html
Internet resources; Kansas; Tornado

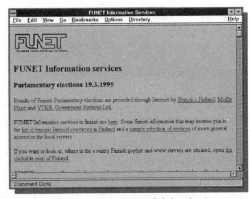

http://www.funet.fi/funet/FUNET-english.html
Finland; Finnish; FUNET; Government

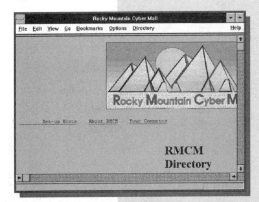

http://www.hardiman.com/malls/rmcm/
Cybermall; Online mall; Rocky Mountain

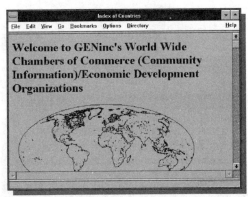

http://www.geninc.com/geni/maps/chamber_world_menu.html
Chamber of Commerce; Economic Development; GENinc

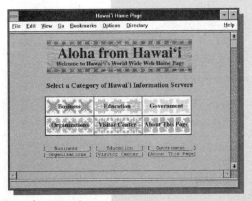

http://www.hawaii.net/
Business; Education; Government; Hawaii

Directories

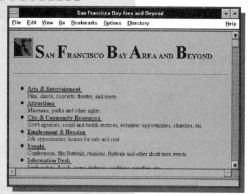

http://www.hyperion.com/ba/sfbay.html
Community information; San Francisco Bay Area

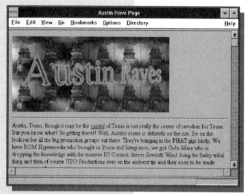

http://www.hyperreal.com/raves/texas/austin.html
Austin Raves; Directories; Entertainment; Links; Texas

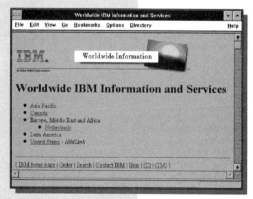

http://www.ibmlink.ibm.com/
IBM; Information; Services

http://www.ieunet.ie/
Eunet; Ieunet; Ireland

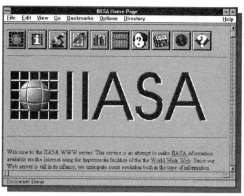

http://www.iiasa.ac.at/
IIASA; System analysis; Technology transfer

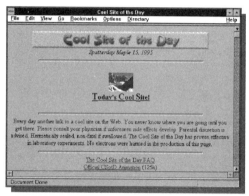

http://www.infi.net/cool.html
Cool sites; Links; Web sites

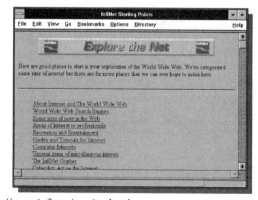

http://www.infi.net/starting.html
InfiNet; Links; Starting points

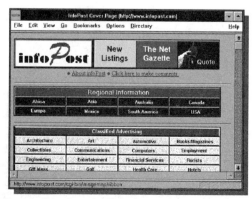

http://www.infopost.com/index.html
Advertising; InfoPost; International

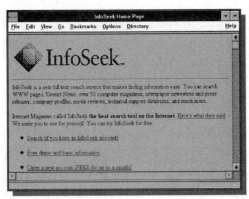

http://www.infoseek.com/
InfoSeek; Search service; Usenet news; WWW pages

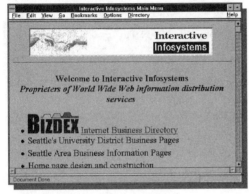

http://www.infosystems.com/interactive.html
Interactive Infosystems; Seattle area business

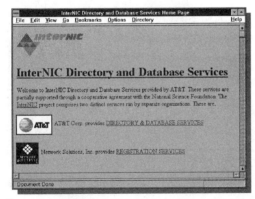

http://www.internic.net/
AT&T; Databases; InterNIC; Sites

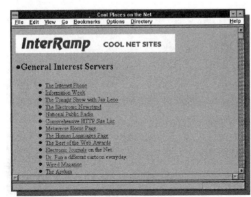

http://www.interramp.com/cool/cool.html/
Business; Cool Sites; Games; Museums; Shopping; Weather

http://www.ip.net/shops.html
Internet shops; Market; Online shopping

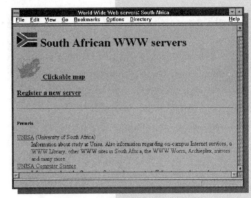

http://www.is.co.za/www-za.html
Map; South Africa; Web sites

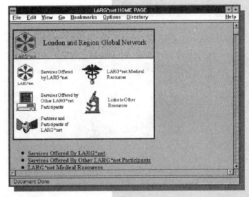

http://www.largnet.uwo.ca/
London and Region Global Network; Medical Resources

http://www.leo.org/info_muc/WWWother/demap.html
Geography; Germany; Maps; Web sites

157

Directories

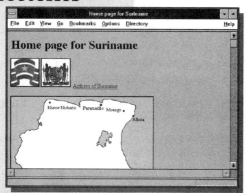

http://www.let.rug.nl/~erikt/.Suriname
South America; Suriname

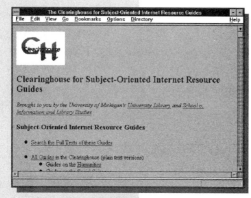

http://www.lib.umich.edu/chhome.html
Internet; Resource guides; Subject-oriented

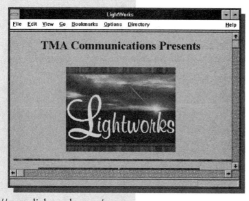

http://www.lightworks.com/
Art; Astro-Weather; Book and Music Stores; Cartoons; LightWorks

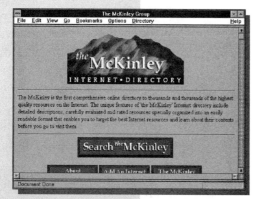

http://www.mckinley.com/
Directory; Internet Resources; Web sites

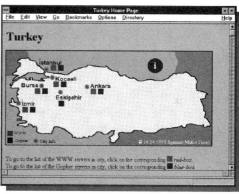

http://www.metu.edu.tr:80/Turkey/
Geography; Maps; Turkey

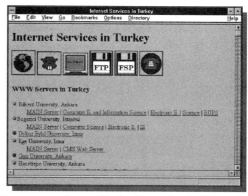

http://www.metu.edu.tr:80/Turkey/inet-turkey.html
Turkey; Universities; Web sites

http://www.mi.cnr.it/NIR-IT/NIR-map.html
Culture; Italy; Maps; Travel

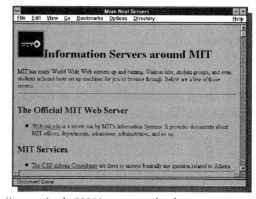

http://www.mit.edu:8001/server-pages.html
Information servers; Internet; MIT services

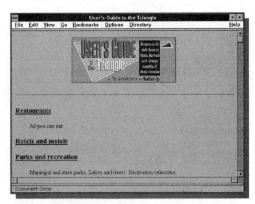

http://www.nando.net/triguide/
Hotels; North Carolina; Parks; Restaurants

http://www.nectec.or.th/
National Electronics and Computer Technology Center; NECTEC

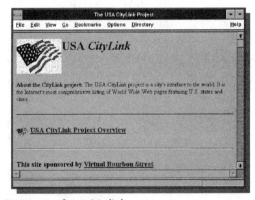

http://www.neosoft.com/citylink
Cities; USA CityLink; Virtual Bourbon Street

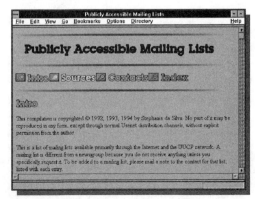

http://www.neosoft.com/internet/paml
Mail; Mailing lists; Publicity

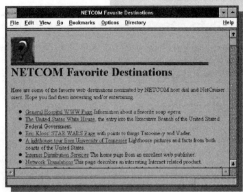

http://www.netcom.com/netcom/fav.html
Favorite destinations; Links; NETCOM

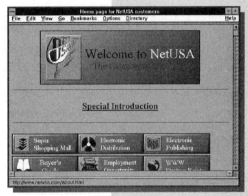

http://www.netusa.com/
Electronic distribution; NetUSA; Online mall

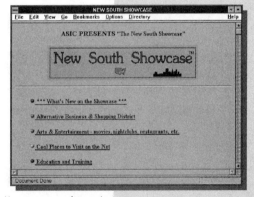

http://www.newsouth.com/
Arts; Cool net sites; New South Showcase; Nightclubs

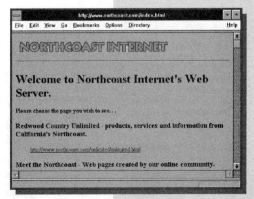

http://www.northcoast.com/index.html
California; Directory; Northcoast Internet

Directories

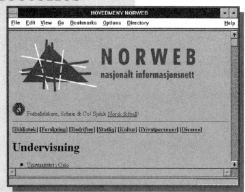

http://www.nta.no/uninett/norweb.html
Norway; NORWEB; Olympics

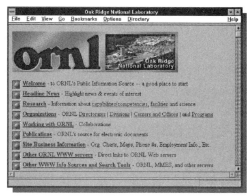

http://www.ornl.gov/
Laboratories; Oak Ridge

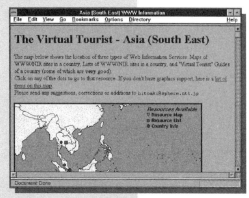

http://www.ntt.jp/AP/asia-SE.html
Guides; Map; Southeast Asia; Tourist

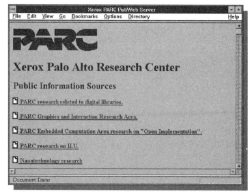

http://www.parc.xerox.com/PARC/default.html
Information sources; PARC; Xerox Palo Alto Research Center

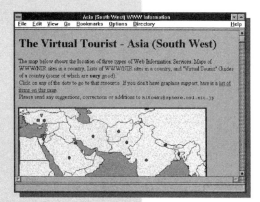

http://www.ntt.jp/AP/asia-SW.html
South West Asia; Tourist

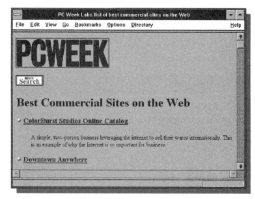

http://www.pcweek.ziff.com/~pcweek/best_comm_sites.html
Best commercial sites; Directories; PC Week

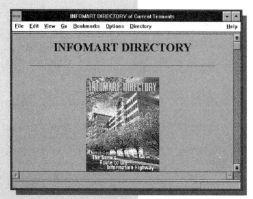

http://www.onramp.net//infomart/directory/director.html
Current tenants; Informart Directory

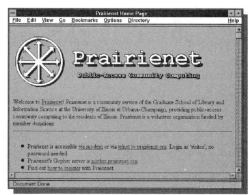

http://www.prairienet.org/index.html
Community service; Prairienet; Public access computing

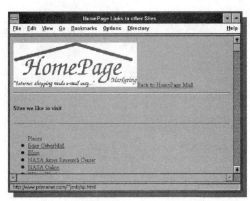

http://www.primenet.com/~jimb/sites.html
Homepage marketing; Online shopping

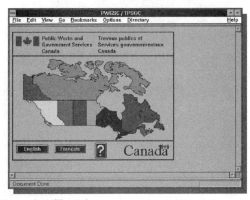

http://www.Pwc-Tpc.ca/
Canada; Government; Maps

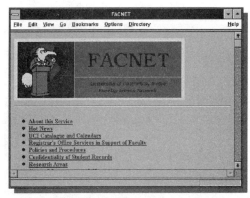

http://www.reg.uci.edu/FACNET/
Education; Faculty; University of California Irvine

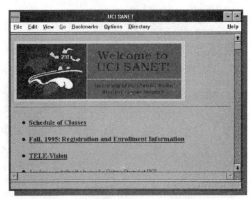

http://www.reg.uci.edu/SANET/
Student information; University of California Irvine

http://www.resort.com/index.html
Geek House; The Resort; UC Santa Cruz

http://www.review.com/
Education; Princeton Review

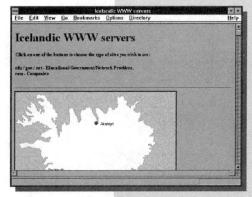

http://www.rfisk.is/english/sites.html
Iceland; Maps; Web servers

http://www.riv.nl/
Business; Netherlands; Publishing; Riverland

Directories

http://www.sal.ists.ca/services/w3_can/www_index.html
Canada; North America; Space; Astrophysics

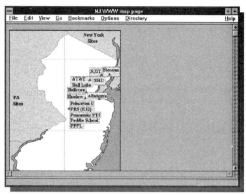

http://www.stevens-tech.edu/nj.html
East coast; New Jersey; Web sites

http://www.service.uit.no/homepage-no
Geography; Map; Norway

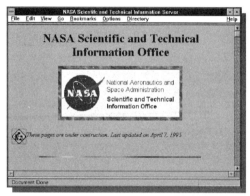

http://www.sti.nasa.gov/STI-homepage.html
NASA; Scientific and Technical Information Office

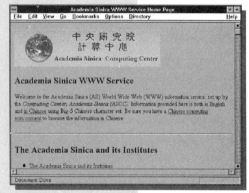

http://www.sinica.edu.tw/
China; Chinese; Web server

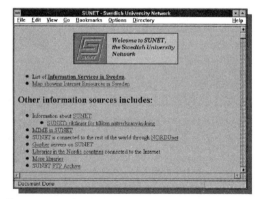

http://www.sunet.se/
Inernet resources; Maps; Scandinavia; Sweden; Swedish universities

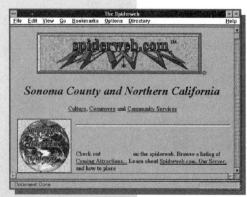

http://www.spiderweb.com/
Community; Culture; Sonoma County; Spiderweb

http://www.tasc.com/
Entertainment; News; Sports; Weather

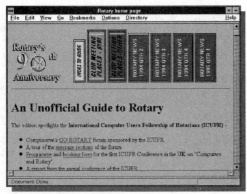

http://www.tecc.co.uk/public/PaulHarris/
Fellowship of Rotarians; Philanthropy; Rotary

http://www.tvnet.com/ITVG/itvg.html
TV listings; Polls; Review

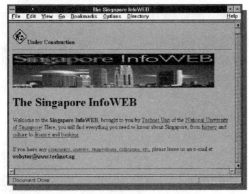

http://www.technet.sg/InfoWEB
Asia; Culture; Finance and banking; History; Singapore

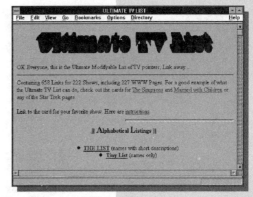

http://www.tvnet.com/UTVL/utvl.html
Program descriptions; TV listings

163

http://www.telepost.no/
Business; Magazines; News; Norway; Recreation; Scandinavia

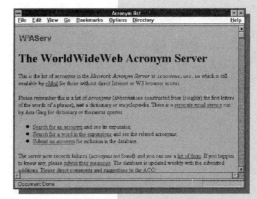

http://www.ucc.ie/info/net/acronyms/acro.html
Acronym server; Search for an acronym

http://www.tue.nl/maps.html
Country maps; Europe; Web servers

http://www.uji.es/spain_www.html
Internet; Maps; Spain

Directories

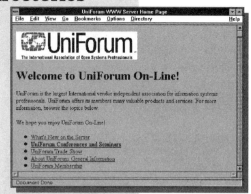

http://www.uniforum.org/
Association of Open Systems Professionals; Information systems

http://www.well.com/
Virtual community; Well

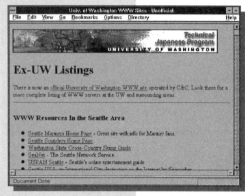

http://www.uwtc.washington.edu/uwhome.html
Mariners; Seattle area Web sites; Skiing guide

http://www.wincorp.com/windata/
One World Plaza

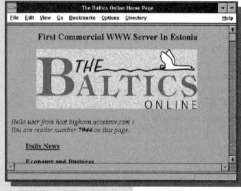

http://www.viabalt.ee/
Baltic; Estonia; WWW server

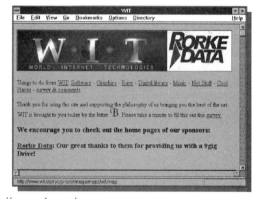

http://www.wit.com/
Cool places; Digital library; Graphics; Music; Software; WIT

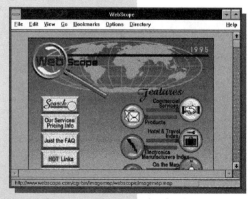

http://www.webscope.com/homepage.html
Electronics manufacturers index; Hotel and travel index

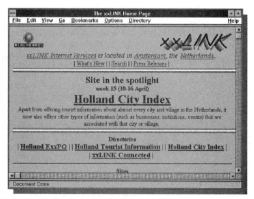

http://www.xxlink.nl/
City Index; Holland; Netherlands

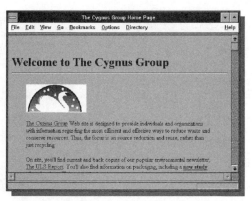

http://cygnus-group.com/
Environment; Newsletter; Recycling; Waste reduction

http://envirolink.org/FSCR/FSCR.html
Non-profit; Public interest; Santa Clara River

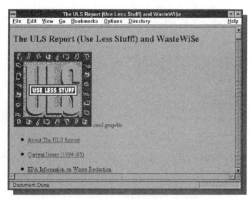

http://garnet.msen.com:70/1/vendor/cygnus/ULS
EPA Information; Use less stuff; Waste reduction

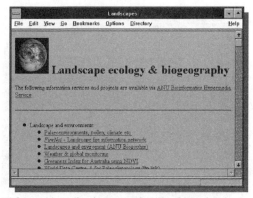

http://life.anu.edu.au/landscape_ecology/landscape.html
Biogeography; Landscape ecology; Pollen; Weather

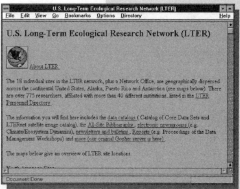

http://LTERnet.edu/
Ecological Research; University of Washington

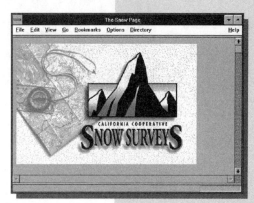

http://snow.water.ca.gov/
California; Snow surveys

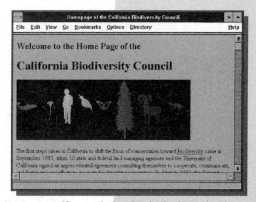

http://spp-www.cdf.ca.gov/htdocs/biodiv/bechome.html
Biodiversity; California

http://town.hall.org/environment/wild_soc/wilderness.html
Protection; Public lands; Wilderness Society

Economics

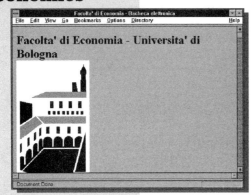

http://ecn01.cineca.it/
Economics; Italy; University of Bologna

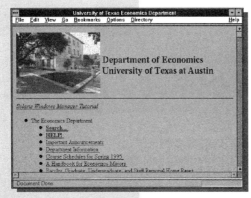

http://mundo.eco.utexas.edu/
Austin; Economics; University of Texas

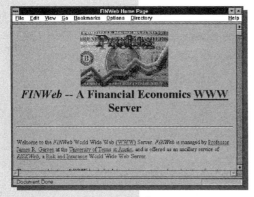

http://riskweb.bus.utexas.edu/finweb.htm
Austin; Financial Economics; University of Texas

http://sol.uvic.ca/econ
Department of Economics; Education; University of Victoria

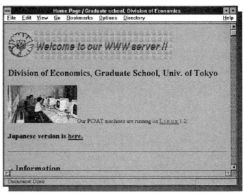

http://steven.e.u-tokyo.ac.jp/
Economics Japan; Graduate School; University of Tokyo

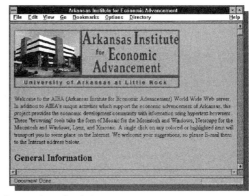

http://www.aiea.ualr.edu/
Economics; Little Rock; University of Arkansas

http://www.e.u-tokyo.ac.jp/
Economics; Japan; University of Tokyo

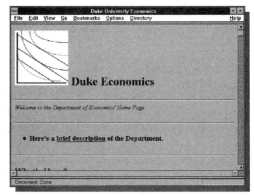

http://www.econ.duke.edu/
Duke University; Economics

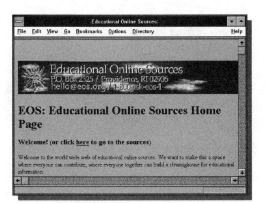

http://archive.phish.net/eos1/main_image.html
Links; On-line Education Resources

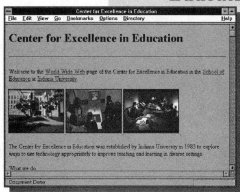

http://cee.indiana.edu/
Education; Indiana University

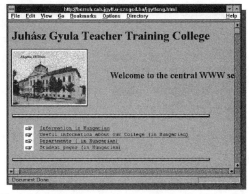

http://berreh.cab.jgytf.u-szeged.hu/jgytfeng.html
Hungary; Juhasz Gyula Teacher Training College

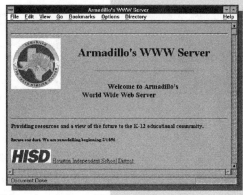

http://chico.rice.edu/armadillo/
Computers; Grade school; High school; Houston; K-12

http://caosun.unica.it/asf/HomePage.html
Education; Italy; UNICA

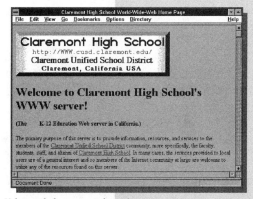

http://chs.cusd.claremont.edu:80/
High schools; K-12; School district

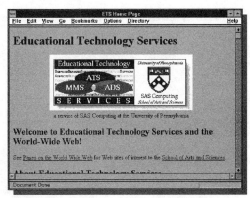

http://ccat.sas.upenn.edu/
Arts & Sciences; University of Pennsylvania

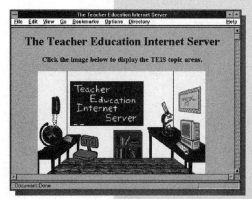

http://curry.edschool.virginia.edu/teis
Grants; Resources; Teacher education; Teaching

167

Education

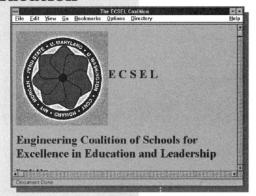

http://echo.umd.edu/
Engineering Coalition of Schools

http://fuji.stanford.edu/
Information Infrastructure; Technical Japanese

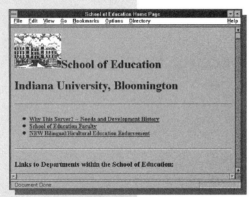

http://education.indiana.edu/
Education; Indiana University

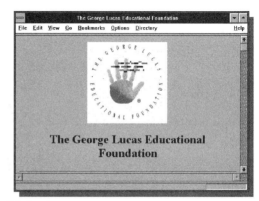

http://glef.org/
The George Lucas Educational Foundation

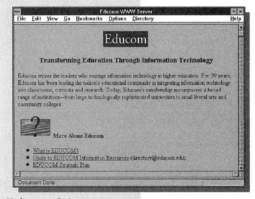

http://educom.edu/
Communications; Curriculum; Educom; Research

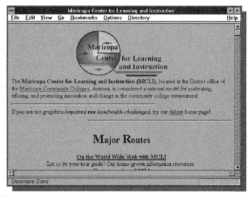

http://hakatai.mcli.dist.maricopa.edu/
Community colleges; Resources; Teaching; Technology

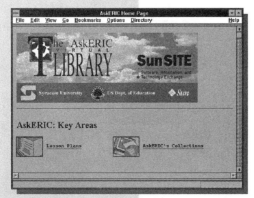

http://ericir.syr.edu/
AskERIC; Education; Lesson Plans; Teaching

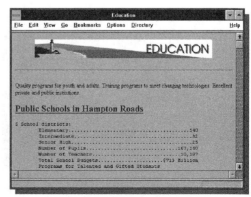

http://hampton.roads.net/nhr/education.html
Education; Hampton Roads; Virginia

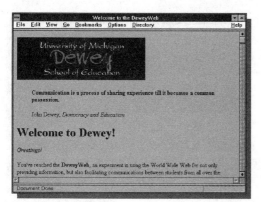

http://ics.soe.umich.edu/
Communications; Experiments; Michigan; Science; Teaching

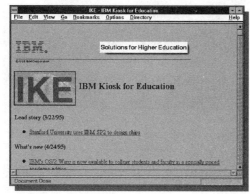

http://ike.engr.washington.edu/
Higher Education; IBM; Warp

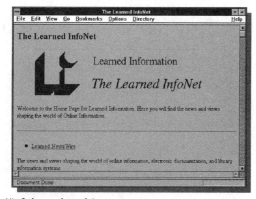

http://info.learned.co.uk/
Electronic documentation; InfoNet; Information systems;

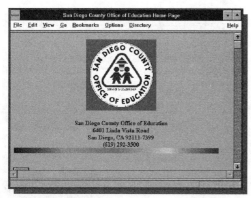

http://intergate.sdcoe.k12.ca.us/
Education; San Diego County

http://k12.cnidr.org/gsh/gshwelcome.html
Global Schoolhouse Project; Schools; Students; Teachers

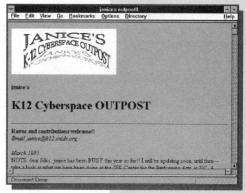

http://k12.cnidr.org/janice_k12/k12menu.html
K-12; Maps; Resources; Teaching; Tools

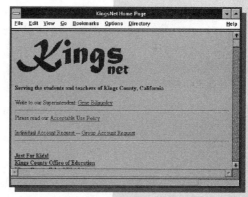

http://kings.k12.ca.us/
California; Kings County; Students; Teachers

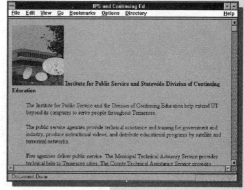

http://loki.ur.utk.edu/campus/ips.html
Continuing Education; Public Service; University of Tennessee

169

Education

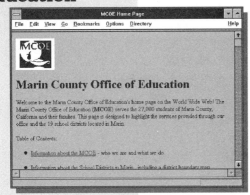

http://marin.k12.ca.us/
California; Education; Marin County

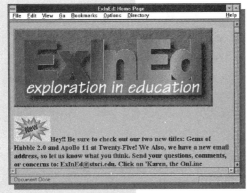

http://marvel.stsci.edu/exined-html/exined-home.html
Astrophysics; Geography; Planetary science; Rockets; Space

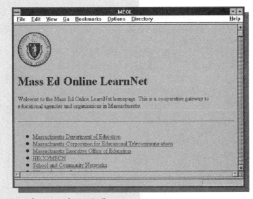

http://meol.mass.edu:70/0/home
Educational agencies; Massachusetts

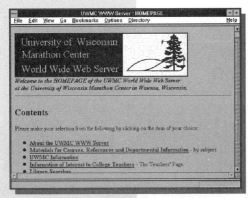

http://mthwww.uwc.edu/wwwmahes/homepage.htm
Education; University of Wisconsin Marathon Center

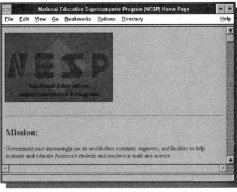

http://nebbs.nersc.gov/
Engineers; Scientists; Students; Supercomputer; Teachers

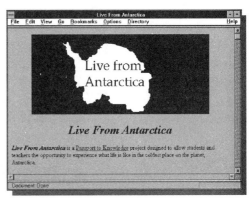

http://quest.arc.nasa.gov/livefrom/livefrom.html
Antarctica; Life; Multimedia field trip

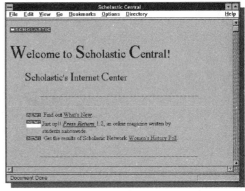

http://scholastic.com:2005/
Curriculum; Scholastic; Schools; Teaching materials

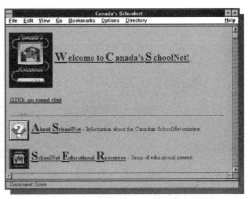

http://schoolnet.carleton.ca/schoolnet/english/schlnet.html
Canada; Education; SchoolNet

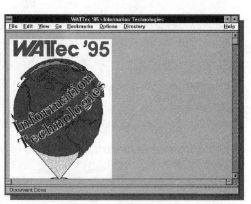

http://solar.rtd.utk.edu/orawww/Wattec/default.html
Electronic commerce; Healthcare; Technology

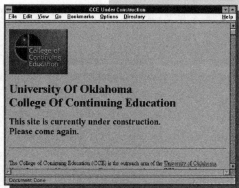

http://tel.occe.uoknor.edu/cce.html
Continuing Education; University of Oklahoma

http://sunsite.unc.edu/cisco/cisco-home.html
Education; Research

http://twine.cis.brown.edu:80/
Communications; Information technology; Universities

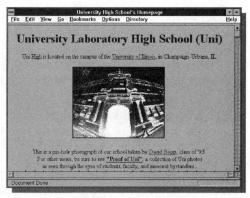

http://superdec.uni.uiuc.edu/
High School; Photos; University Laboratory High School

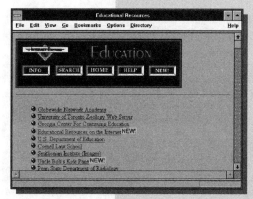

http://usa.net/home/educ.html
Directories; Educational Resources; Links

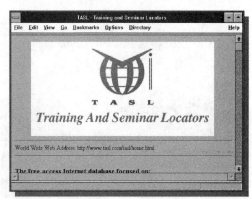

http://tasl.com/tasl/home.html
Database; Training and Seminar Locators

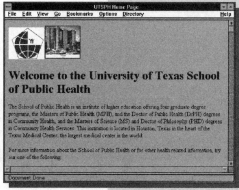

http://utsph.sph.uth.tmc.edu/
Education; University of Texas School of Public Health

Education

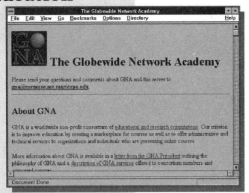

http://uu-gna.mit.edu:8001/uu-gna/
Educational and research organizations; GNA

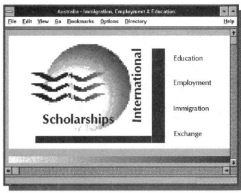

http://www.access.digex.net/~int-opp/
Australia; Education; Employment; FAQ; Immigration

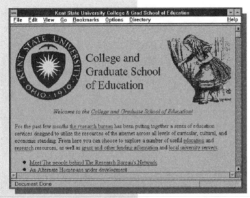

http://vishnu.educ.kent.edu/
Education; Graduate School; Kent State University; Research

http://www.acsu.buffalo.edu/~naras-r/gurukul.html
Housing; India; Literacy; Teaching; Third World

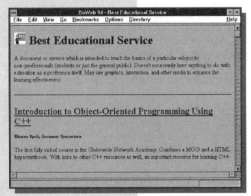

http://wings.buffalo.edu/contest/awards/educate.html
C++; Object-Oriented Programming

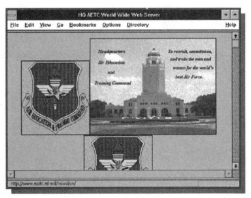

http://www.aetc.af.mil/
Air Education and Training Command; U.S. Air Force

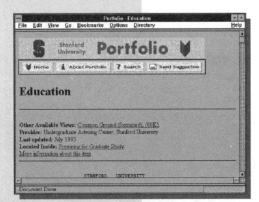

http://www-portfolio.stanford.edu/100084
Education; Stanford University

http://www.bev.net/education/SeaWorld/homepage.html
Animals; Busch Gardens; Sea World; Shamu; Zoology

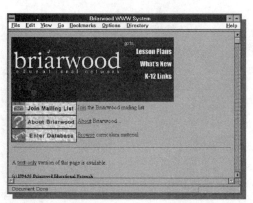

http://www.briarwood.com/
Education networks; K-12; Lesson Plans

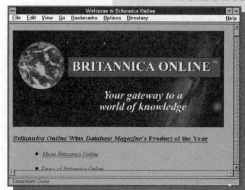

http://www.eb.com/
Britannica; Encyclopedia; Reference

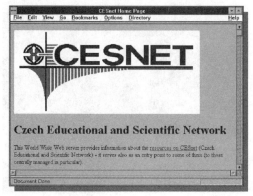

http://www.cesnet.cz:80/
Czechoslovakia; Education; Education; Science; Scientific

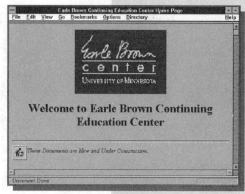

http://www.ebcec.cee.umn.edu:80/homepage/ebcec.htm
Earle Brown Continuing Education; University of Minnesota

173

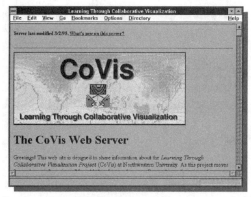

http://www.covis.nwu.edu/
Collaborative Visualization; Learning; Northwestern University

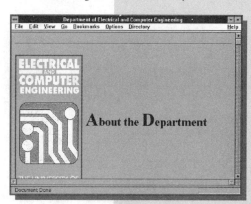

http://www.ece.scarolina.edu/
Electrical engineering; Computers; Pulsed power lasers

http://www.crs4.it/HTML/homecrs4.html
Center for Advanced Studies Research and Development; Italy

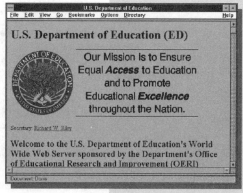

http://www.ed.gov/
Education; Government; Research

Education

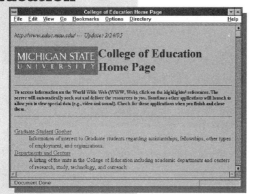

http://www.educ.msu.edu/
Education; Michigan State University

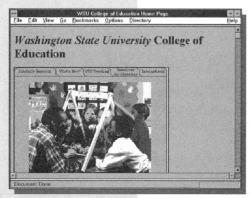

http://www.educ.wsu.edu/
Education; Washington State Univeristy

http://www.ehhs.cmich.edu/
Education; Education sites; Teachers

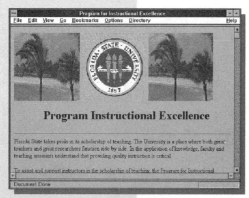

http://www.fsu.edu:80/CS-projects/pie/
Florida State University; Instructional

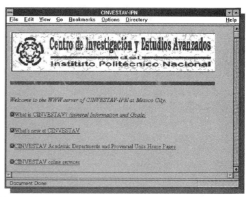

http://www.gene.cinvestav.mx/ciea.html
Mexico; Politics; Spanish

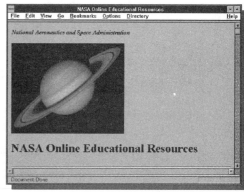

http://www.gsfc.nasa.gov/nasa_online_education.html
Aeronautics; NASA; Online educational resources

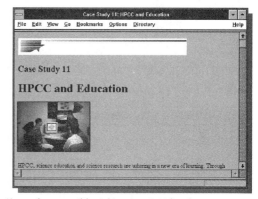

http://www.hpcc.gov/blue94/section.5.11.html
Case study; Education; HPCC; Schools; Technology

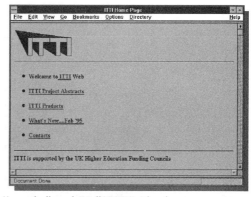

http://www.hull.ac.uk/Hull/ITTI/itti.html
Abstracts; Education; Information technology; United Kingdom

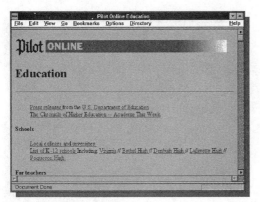

http://www.infi.net/pilot/edu.html
Education; K-12; US Department of Education

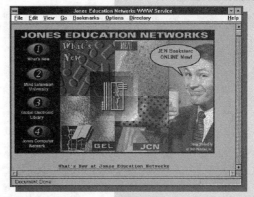

http://www.meu.edu/
Books; Electronic Library; Jones Education Networks

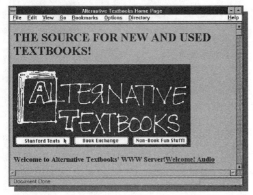

http://www.internex.net/TEXTBOOKS/home.html
Book exchange; Books; Textbooks

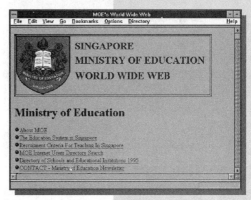

http://www.moe.ac.sg/
Education; Ministry of Education; Singapore

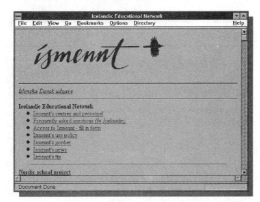

http://www.ismennt.is/ismennt/grunn_uk.html
Iceland; Nordic schools

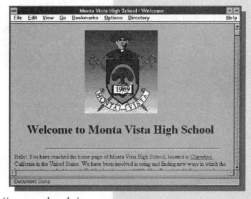

http://www.mvhs.edu/
Cupertino; California; High school; Internet

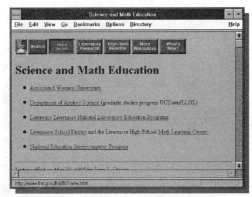

http://www.llnl.gov/sci_educ/sci_ed.html
Lawrence Livermore National Laboratory; Science; Math

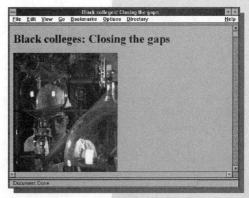

http://www.nando.net/sproject/colleges/index.html
Black colleges; Education

175

Education

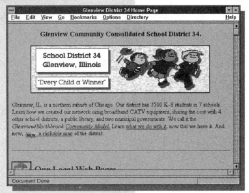

http://www.ncook.k12.il.us/dist34_home_page.html
Chicago; Illinois; K-8; Schools; Teaching

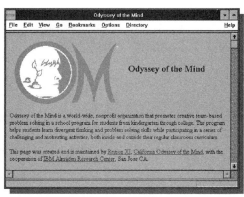

http://www.odyssey.org/odyssey/
College; Kindergarten; Odyssey of the Mind; Problem solving

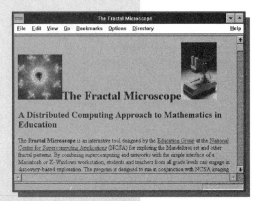

http://www.ncsa.uiuc.edu/Edu/Fractal/Fractal_Home.html
Fractal Microscope; Mandelbrot; Mathematics

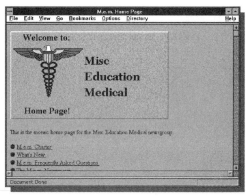

http://www.primenet.com/~gwa/med.ed/memhome.html
Education; Misc Educational Medical

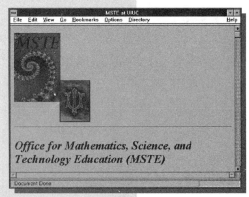

http://www.ncsa.uiuc.edu/Edu/MSTE
Mathematics; MSTE; Science; Technology; Universities

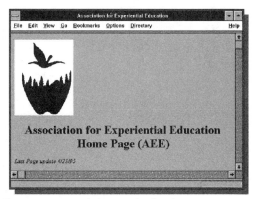

http://www.princeton.edu/~rcurtis/aee.html
AEE; Association for Experiential Education

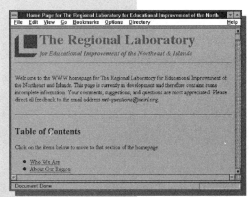

http://www.neirl.org/
Educational improvement; Laboratories; Research

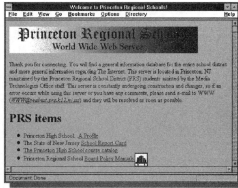

http://www.prs.k12.nj.us/
High school; New Jersey; Princeton High School; Students

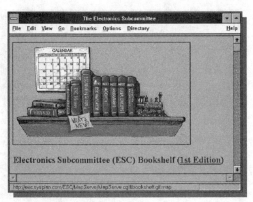

http://esc.sysplan.com/esc/index.html
Books; Electronics; News

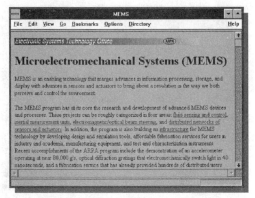

http://esto.sysplan.com/ESTO/MEMS/
Development; Microelectromechanical Systems; Research

http://joyce.eng.yale.edu/
Electrical engineering; IEEE; Yale College

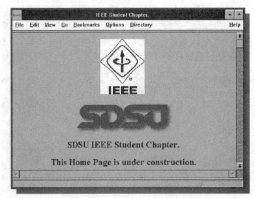

http://rohan.sdsu.edu/ieee/
IEEE; San Diego State University

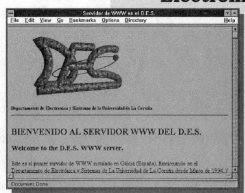

http://sol.des.fi.udc.es/
Education; La Universidad de La Coruna; Spanish

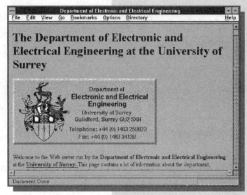

http://www.ee.surrey.ac.uk/
Engineering; Education; University of Surrey

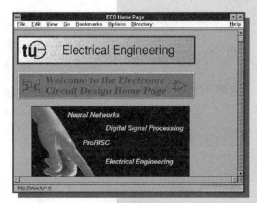

http://www.eeb.ele.tue.nl/index.html
Electrical engineering; Networks; Processors

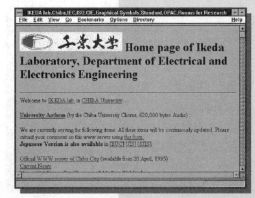

http://www.hike.te.chiba-u.ac.jp/
CHIBA University; Electronics Engineering

Engineering

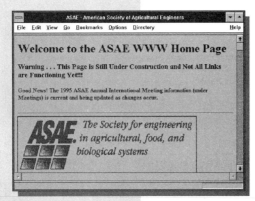

http://apscts.pclab.apsc.ubc.ca/engineering.html
Applied Science; University of British Columbia

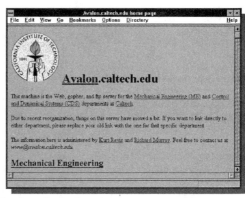

http://avalon.caltech.edu:80/
Control and Dynamical Systems; Mechanical engineering

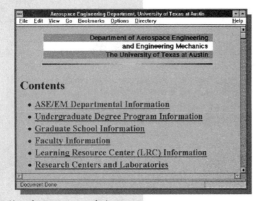

http://asae.org/
American Society of Agricultural Engineers

http://concrete.t.u-tokyo.ac.jp/
Civil Engineering; Concrete Engineering; University of Tokyo

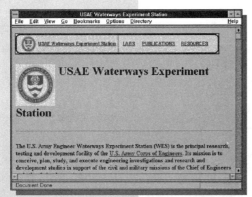

http://asecls1.ae.utexas.edu/
Aerospace Engineering; Austin; Mechanics; University of Texas

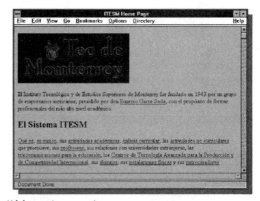

http://dch.mty.itesm.mx/
El Instituto Technologico y de Estudios Superiores de Monterrey

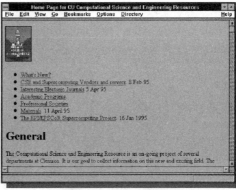

http://athena.wes.army.mil/
Disease registry; Toxic substances

http://diogenes.cs.clemson.edu/CSE/homepage.html
Clemson; Computational Science; Engineering

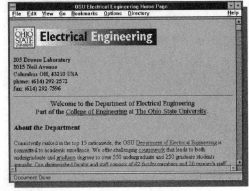

http://eec.psu.edu/
Engineering Education; Penn State University

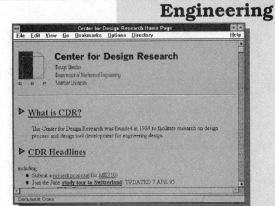

http://gummo.stanford.edu/
Design Research; Stanford University

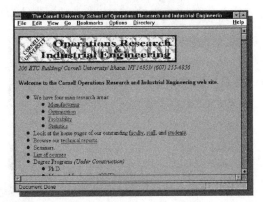

http://eewww.eng.ohio-state.edu/
Electrical Engineering; Ohio State University

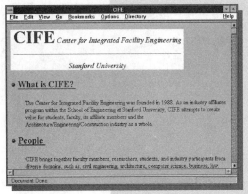

http://gummo.stanford.edu/html/ICM/CIFE.html
Integrated Facility Engineering; Stanford University

http://ftp.orie.cornell.edu/
Cornell University; Industrial Engineering; Operations Research

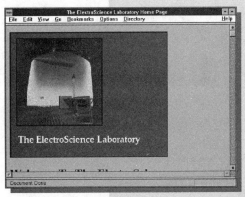

http://hertz.eng.ohio-state.edu/
Electrical Engineering; ElectroScience; Ohio State University

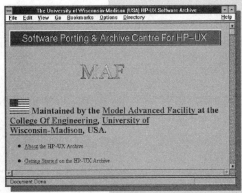

http://goddard.eng.ohio-state.edu/
Engineering; Ohio State University

http://hpux.cae.wisc.edu/
Computer Aided Engineering; Madison; University of Wisconsin

Engineering

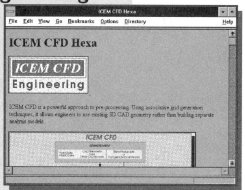

http://icemcfd.com/hexa.html
3D; Computational fluid dynamics; Software

http://irwin.t.u-tokyo.ac.jp/index.html
Japan; Mechanical Engineering; University of Tokyo

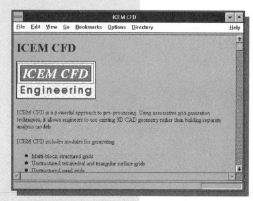

http://icemcfd.com/icemcfd.html
3D; CAD; Engineering; Models

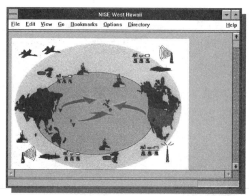

http://lono.nosc.mil/
Platform integration; System engineering; Testing; Validation

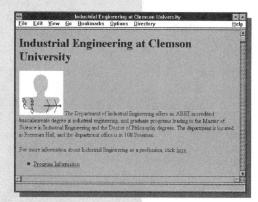

http://ie.eng.clemson.edu:80/
Clemson University; Education; Industrial Engineering

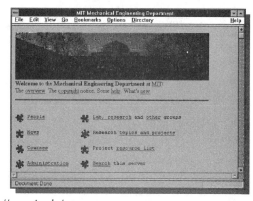

http://me.mit.edu/
Massachusetts Institute of Technology; Mechanical Engineering

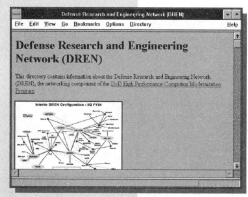

http://info.arl.army.mil/ACIS/ACD/DREN/index.html
Defense Research and Engineering Network

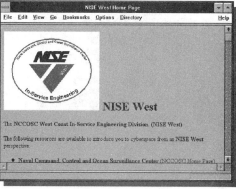

http://mork.nosc.mil/
Naval Command Control and Ocean Surveillance Center

http://pni.engr.udayton.edu/orgs/swe
Society of Woman Engineers; SWE

http://prairienet.org/community/health/prairie/readme.html
Concrete; Materials; Structures

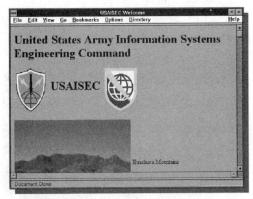

http://rogue.cec.army.mil/
Army; Engineering; Technology; USAISEC

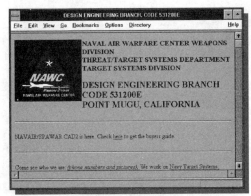

http://salmon.mugu.navy.mil/
Engineering; Naval Air Warfare Center Weapons Division

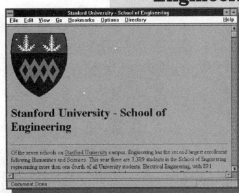

http://sierra.stanford.edu/soe.html
Engineering; Stanford University

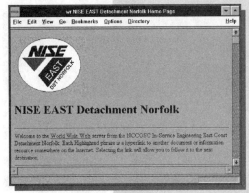

http://silk.nosc.mil/index.html
In-Service Engineering East Coast Detachment Norfolk

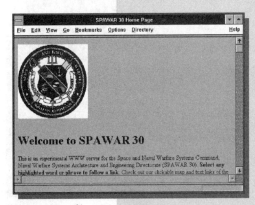

http://sneezy.nosc.mil/
Engineering; Naval; Space; Warfare

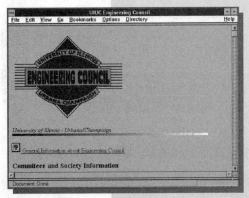

http://stimpy.cen.uiuc.edu/
Engineering council

Engineering

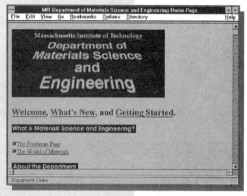

http://svr-www.eng.cam.ac.uk/
Cambridge University; Robotics; Speech; United Kingdom; Vision

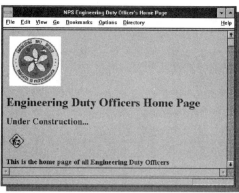

http://vislab-www.nps.navy.mil/~edo
Engineering Duty Officer; Naval Postgraduate School

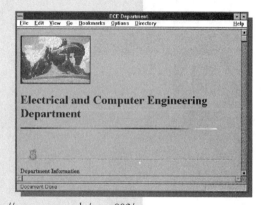

http://tantalum.mit.edu/
Massachusetts Institute of Technology; Materials Science

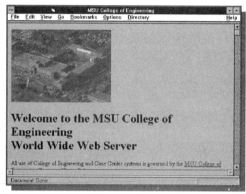

http://web.egr.msu.edu/
Engineering; Michigan State University

http://uts.cc.utexas.edu/~czvr002/
Austin; Electrical & Computer Engineering; University of Texas

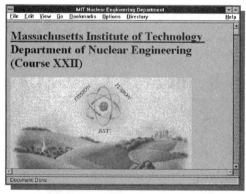

http://web.mit.edu/afs/athena/activity/a/ans/www/NED.html
Massachusetts Institute of Technology; Nuclear Engineering

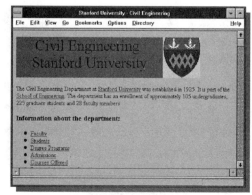

http://venus.hanyang.ac.kr/
Electronic Engineering; Hanyang University; Korea

http://www-ce.stanford.edu/cive.html
Civil engineering; Stanford University

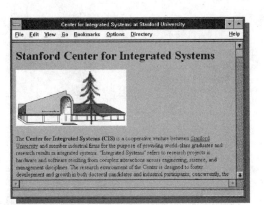

http://www-cis.stanford.edu/cis/
Integrated Systems; Stanford

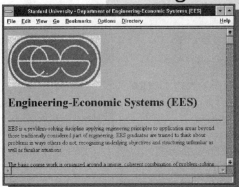

http://www-soe.stanford.edu/ees.html
Economic Systems; Engineering

http://www-dsed.llnl.gov/
Defense Sciences; Electronics; National security

http://www.abe.msstate.edu/
Agricultural; Biological Engineering; Mississippi State University

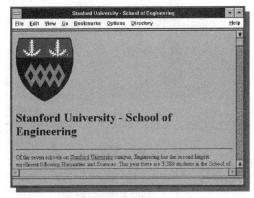

http://www-ee.stanford.edu/soe.html
School of Engineering; Stanford University

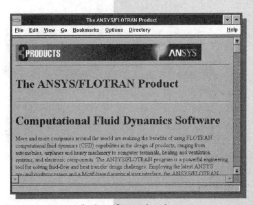

http://www.ansys.com/htdocs/flotran.html
CFD; Computational Fluid Dynamics; Products; Software

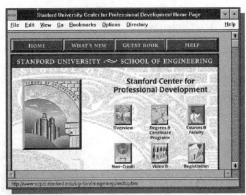

http://www-sitn.stanford.edu/sitn.html
Engineering; Professional Development; Stanford University

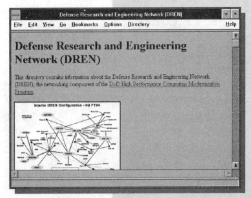

http://www.arl.mil/HPCMP/DREN/index.html
Defense Research; High performance computing

Engineering

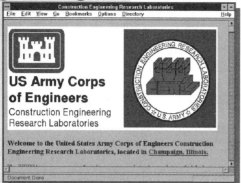

http://www.cecer.army.mil/welcome.html
Construction Engineering; US Army Corps of Engineers

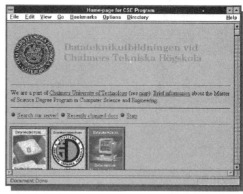

http://www.dtek.chalmers.se/
Chalmers University of Technology; Education

http://www.ceintl.com/
Computational Analysis and Simulation; Software; Visualization

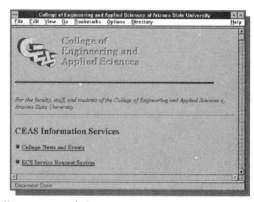

http://www.eas.asu.edu/
Arizona State University; College of Engineering; Applied Sciences

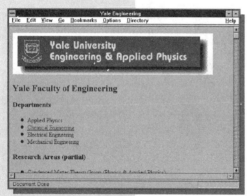

http://www.cis.yale.edu/council/engineering.html
Chemical; Electrical; Engineering; Mechanical; Yale University

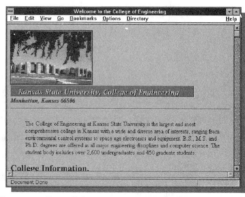

http://www.ecc.ksu.edu/
Engineering Computing; Kansas State University; Manhattan

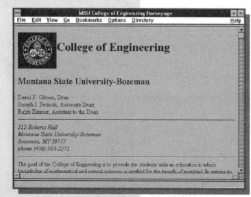

http://www.coe.montana.edu/
College of Engineering; Montana State University-Bozeman

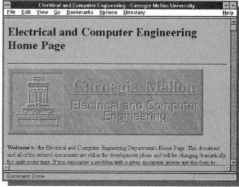

http://www.ece.cmu.edu/Home-Page.html
Carnegie Mellon University; Computer Engineering; Electrical

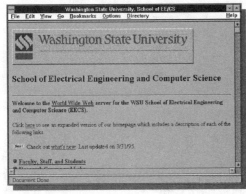

http://www.ece.jhu.edu/
Baltimore; Electrical; Johns Hopkins University; Maryland

http://www.ecl.wustl.edu/seas/
Applied Science; Engineering; Washington University

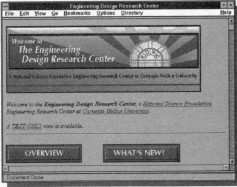

http://www.ecn.purdue.edu/
Engineering; Purdue University

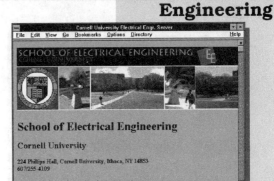

http://www.ee.cornell.edu/
Cornell University; Electrical Engineering

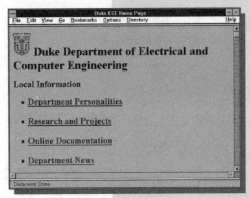

http://www.ee.duke.edu/
Duke University; Electrical Engineering

http://www.ee.hun.edu.tr/
Electrical; Electronics; Engineering; Hacettepe University; Turkey

Engineering Design Research Center

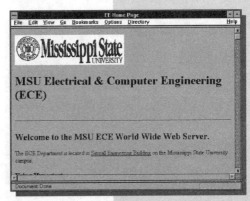

http://www.edrc.cmu.edu:8080/
Carnegie Mellon University; Engineering Design; Research

http://www.ee.msstate.edu/
Computer Engineering; Electrical; Mississippi State University

Engineering

http://www.ee.washington.edu/ee.html
Electrical Engineering; University of Washington

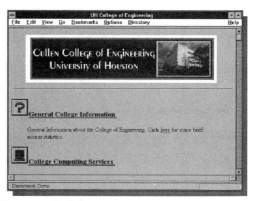

http://www.egr.uh.edu/
Cullen College; Engineering; University of Houston

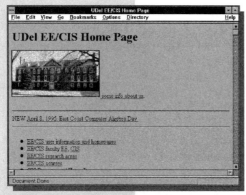

http://www.eecis.udel.edu/
Computer Information Sciences; University of Delaware

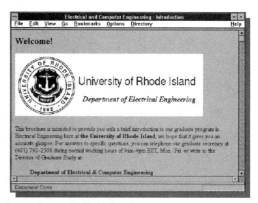

http://www.ele.uri.edu/index.html
Electrical Engineering; University of Rhode Island

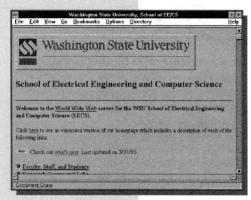

http://www.eecs.wsu.edu/
Computer Science; Electrical; Washington State Univeristy

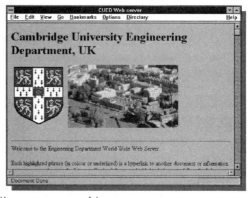

http://www.eng.cam.ac.uk/
Cambridge University; Engineering; United Kingdom

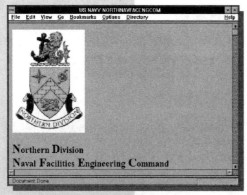

http://www.efdnorth.navfac.navy.mil/
Military; Naval Facilities Engineering Command; US Navy

http://www.eng.fsu.edu/
Engineering; Florida State University; Tallahassee

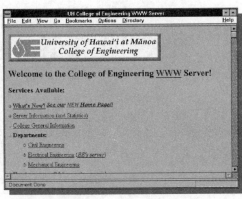

http://www.eng.hawaii.edu/
Engineering; University of Hawaii

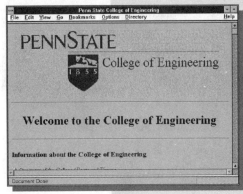

http://www.engr.mun.ca/
Applied Science; Canada; Memorial University of Newfoundland

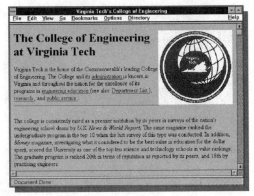

http://www.eng.vt.edu/
Engineering; Virginia Tech

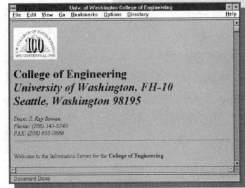

http://www.engr.psu.edu/
Engineering; Penn State University

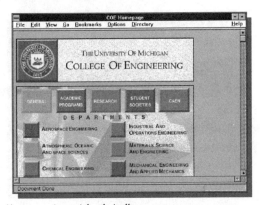

http://www.engin.umich.edu/college
Education; Engineering; University of Michigan

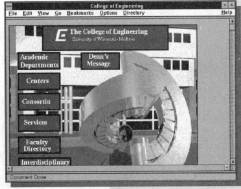

http://www.engr.washington.edu/
Engineering; University of Washington

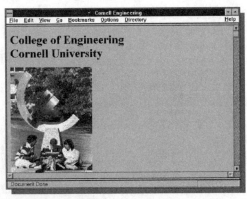

http://www.engr.cornell.edu/
Cornell University; Engineering

http://www.engr.wisc.edu/
Engineering; Madison; University of Wisconsin

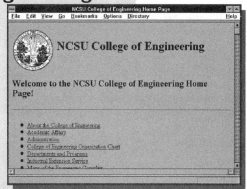

http://www.eos.ncsu.edu/coe/coe.html
College of Engineering; North Carolina State University

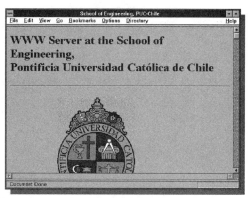

http://www.ing.puc.cl/index-english.html
Pontifica Universidad Catoalica de Chile

http://www.erc.msstate.edu/
Mississippi State University; NSF Engineering Research

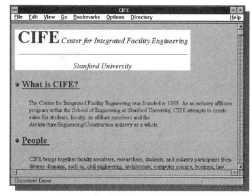

http://www.ipn.mx/main.htm
CIFE; Integrated Facility Engineering; Stanford University

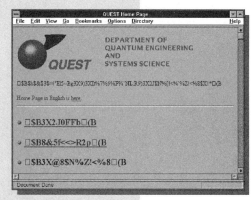

http://www.gen.u-tokyo.ac.jp/
Japan; Quantum Engineering; Science; University of Tokyo

http://www.iscas.pe.u-tokyo.ac.jp/lab.html
Japan; Precision Machinery Engineering; University of Tokyo

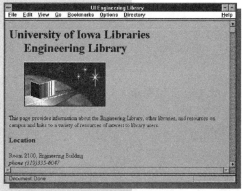

http://www.icaen.uiowa.edu/eng.info/englib.html
Engineering Library; University of Iowa

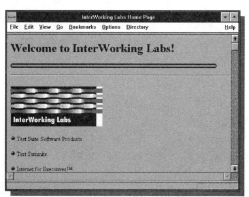

http://www.iwl.com/IWL/HomePage.html
InterWorking Labs; Test Suite Software Products

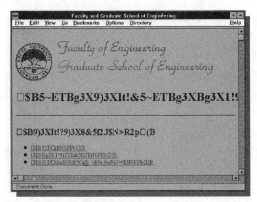

http://www.kogaku.kyoto-u.ac.jp/
Engineering; Japan; Kyoto University

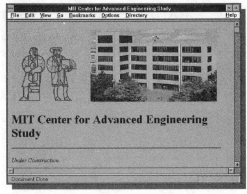

http://www.nmis.org/AboutNMIS/CAES/Html/caes.html
Engineering; Massachusetts Institute of Technology

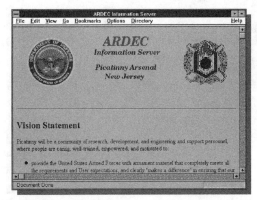

http://www.pica.army.mil/
Armament material; Armed Forces; Engineering

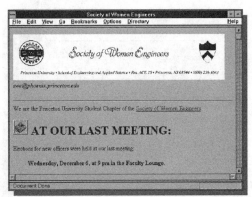

http://www.princeton.edu/~swe
Events; Meetings; Princeton; Society of Woman Engineers

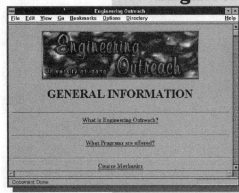

http://www.uidaho.edu/evo
Engineering; University of Idaho

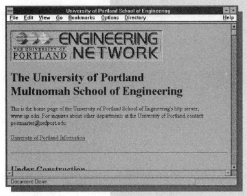

http://www.up.edu/
Engineering; University of Portland

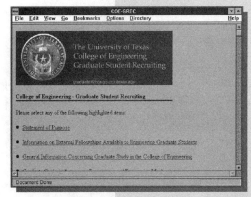

http://www.utexas.edu/depts/coe-grec/.html/main.html
Austin; Engineering; Graduate Student; University of Texas

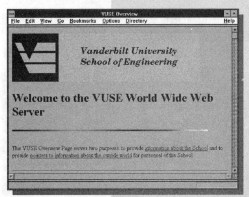

http://www.vuse.vanderbilt.edu/
School of Engineering; Vanderbilt University

189

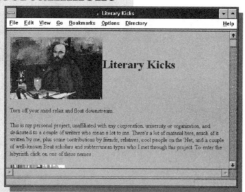

http://199.0.70.23/~brooklyn/LitKicks.html
Entertainment; Literature

http://cyborganic.com/~justin/astrol
Astrology; Entertainment

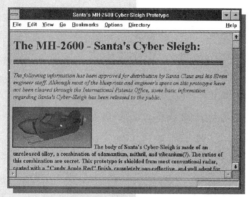

http://christmas.com/sleigh-stats.html
Entertainment; Humor; Santa Claus; Sleigh

http://deeptht.armory.com/~bsc/
Spock; Star Trek; Starfleet

http://christmas.com/xmas/
Feliz Navidad; Merry Christmas; Santa

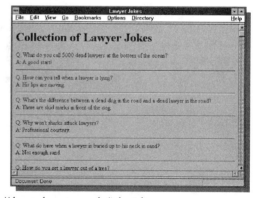

http://deputy.law.utexas.edu/jokes1.htm
Entertainment; Humor; Jokes; Lawyers

http://christmas.com/xmas/mail-santa.html
E-Mail; Entertainment; Humor; Santa Claus; Sleigh

http://disserv.stu.umn.edu/~thingles/PoundMac/
Chat; Mac; Macintosh; IRC

Entertainment

http://fishwrap.mit.edu/Hacks/Gallery.html
Computers; Hackers; MIT

http://force.stwing.upenn.edu:8001/~jruspini/starwars.html
Lucas; Science fiction; Star Wars

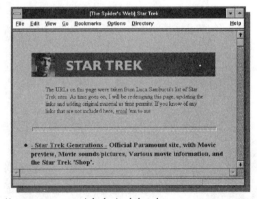

http://gagme.wwa.com/~boba/trek.html
Movie previews; Spider's Web; Star Trek

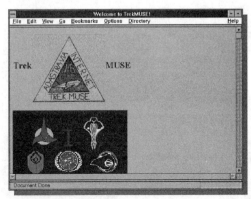

http://grimmy.cnidr.org/
Internet; Muse; Trek

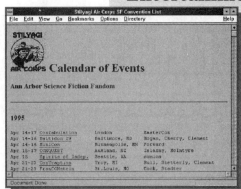

http://grimmy.cnidr.org/con.list.html
Calendar of events; Science fiction

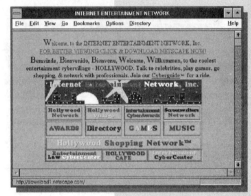

http://hollywoodnetwork.com/
Directories; Games; Links; Music

191

http://iglou.com/lou/kyfair.html
Bluegrass; Kentucky; Louisville; State fairs

http://interserve.com/Savoyards.html
Light operas; Musicals; Stanford Savoyards; Theater company

Entertainment

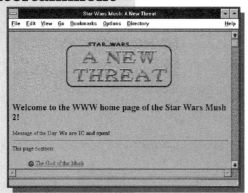

http://ix.urz.uni-heidelberg.de/~jradelef/swmush.html
Science fiction; Star Wars Mush 2

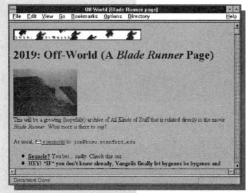

http://kzsu.stanford.edu/uwi/br/off-world.html
Blade Runner; Off-World; Science fiction

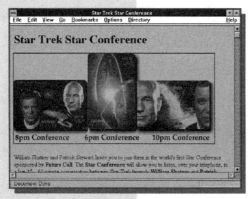

http://metaverse.com/startrek/
Kirk; McCoy; Spock; Star Trek

http://mistral.enst.fr/
Art; Entertainment; Museums

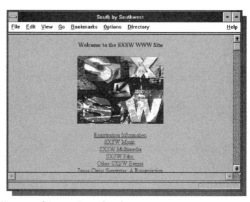

http://monsterbit.com/sxsw.html
Fun; Multimedia; Music; South by Southwest

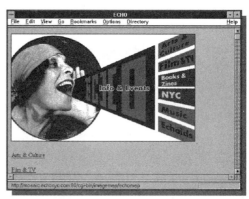

http://mosaic.echonyc.com:80/
Art; Books; Conferences; Magazines; News; New York

http://net101.com/Goldhil/index.html
Adventure; Education; Fun; Metaphysical; Videos

http://net23.com/0/max/main.html
Full motion video; Max Headroom

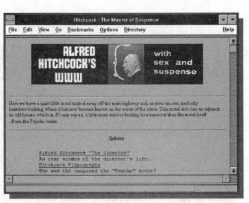

http://nextdch.mty.itesm.mx/~plopezg/Kaplan/Hitchcock.html
Hitchcock; Movies; Suspense; Trivia

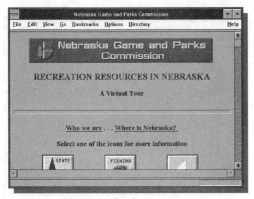

http://ngp.ngpc.state.ne.us/gp.html
Hunting; Fishing; Nebraska; Recreation; Wildlife

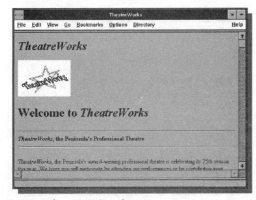

http://none.coolware.com/tworks
Performing arts; Professional theatre

http://northpole.net/santa.html
Children; Entertainment; Fun; Northpole; Santa Claus

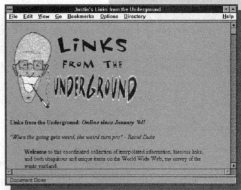

http://raptor.sccs.swarthmore.edu/jahall/
Electronic media; Underground Web links

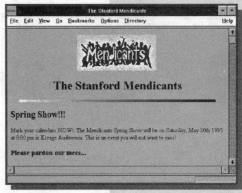

http://rescomp.stanford.edu/~pweston/mendicants.html
Mendicants; Stanford

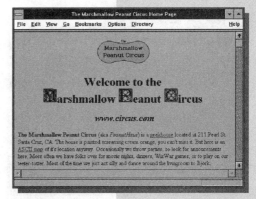

http://samsara.circus.com/
Entertainment; Marshmallow Peanut Circus; Santa Cruz

http://seachange.com/highlander
Highlander; Science fiction; The Gathering

193

Entertainment

http://sfm.com/ppl/sara/bats.html
Bay Area; Improv; Theater company

http://touchstone.power.net/galaxy/
Business opportunities; Entertainment; Show business

http://stwing.resnet.upenn.edu:8001/~jruspini/starwars.html
Galaxy; Science fiction; Star Wars

http://turnpike.net/metro/mirsky/Worst.html
Entertainment; Humor; Worst of the Web

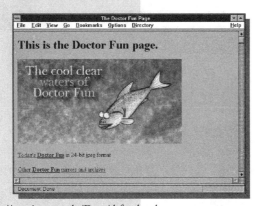

http://sunsite.unc.edu/Dave/drfun.html
Archives; Doctor Fun; Images; JPEG

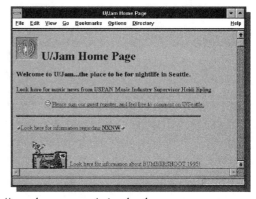

http://useattle.uspan.com/u-jam.html
Seattle nightlife; U/Jam

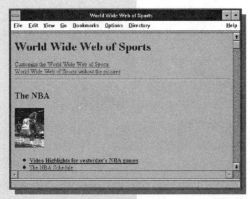

http://tns-www.lcs.mit.edu/cgi-bin/sports
Basketball; NBA highlights; Sports

http://web.cs.ualberta.ca/~davidw/MegRyan/meg.cgi
Actress; Meg Ryan; Tribute

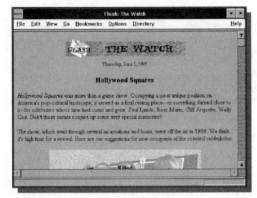

http://web3.starwave.com/showbiz/
Links; Mr. Showbiz; News

http://web3.starwave.com/showbiz/flash/thewatch/
American pop-culture; Hollywood Squares

http://www-leland.stanford.edu/group/rams-head/
Ram's Head Theatrical Society

http://www.armory.com/comics/
Comics; Gallery; Images

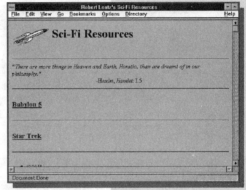

http://www.astro.nwu.edu/lentz/sci-fi/home-sci-fi.html
Babylon 5; Science fiction; Star Trek

http://www.cbs.com/lateshow/lateshow.html
The Late Show with David Letterman; Top Ten lists; TV

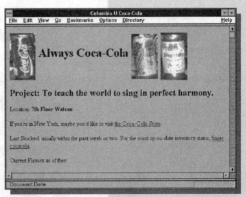

http://www.cc.columbia.edu/~cocacola/
Coca-Cola; Coke; Soda

http://www.armory.com/~crisper/
Ellsworth Air Force Base; South Dakota; UFO Landing

Entertainment

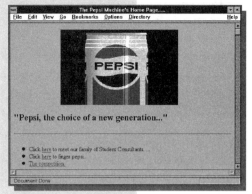

http://www.cc.columbia.edu/~pepsi/
Pepsi; Soda; Student soda check

http://www.csh.rit.edu/proj/drink.html
Coca-Cola; Coke Machine; Computer Science

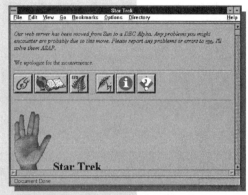

http://www.cosy.sbg.ac.at/rec/startrek/index.html
Entertainment; Kirk; Spock; Star Trek

http://www.cybermalls.com/cymont/speeder/speeder.htm
Caffeine; Coffee; Java

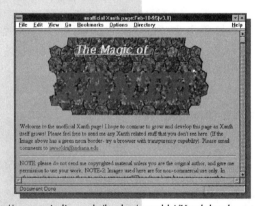

http://www.cs.indiana.edu/hyplan/awooldri/Xanth.html
Fantasy; Science fiction; Xanth

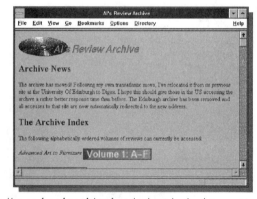

http://www.dcs.ed.ac.uk/students/pg/awrc/review/
Archives; Art; Reviews

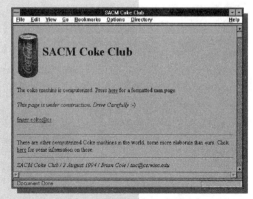

http://www.cs.wisc.edu/~sacmuse/coke/coke.html
Coca-Cola Classic; Coke

http://www.ee.pdx.edu/~caseyh/horror/horror.html
Fiction; Horror stories; Horror Web Page

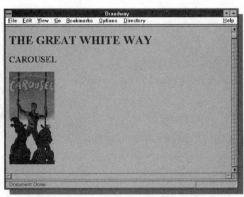

http://www.escape.com/eMall/exploreny/broadway/carousel.html
Broadway; Carousel; Musical

http://www.escape.com/eMall/exploreny/broadway/cats.html
Andrew Lloyd Webber; Broadway; Cats; Felines; Musicals

http://www.escape.com/eMall/exploreny/broadway/phantom.html
Broadway; Musicals; Phantom of the Opera

http://www.escape.com/eMall/exploreny/broadway/saigon.html
Broadway; Musical; Vietnam

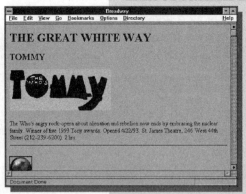

http://www.escape.com/eMall/exploreny/broadway/tommy.html
Broadway; Musicals; The Who

http://www.galcit.caltech.edu/~ta/cgi-bin/asylhome-ta
Art; Discussion; Entertainment

http://www.infi.net/pilot/ent.html
Entertainment; Movie theater guide; Pilot Online

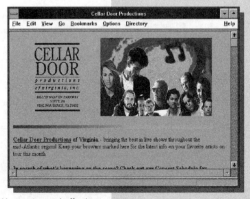

http://www.ip.net/cellar/
Cellar Door Productions; Live shows; Virginia

Entertainment

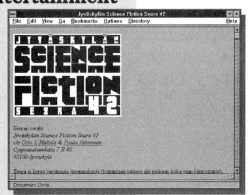

http://www.jyu.fi/~otto/42.html
International sites; Science fiction

http://www.matisse.net/files/bytebar.menu
ICON Byte Bar & Grill

198

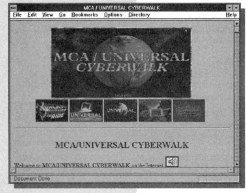

http://www.mca.com/
Entertainment; Game shows; TV shows

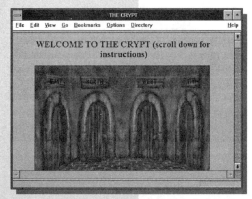

http://www.mca.com/universal_pictures/tales/crypt.html
Entertainment; Horror

http://www.mit.edu:8001/people/jcb/BCE/bce.html
Boston; Chamber Music

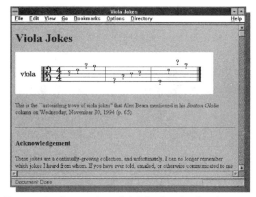

http://www.mit.edu:8001/people/jcb/viola-jokes.html
Humor; Jokes; Music; Viola

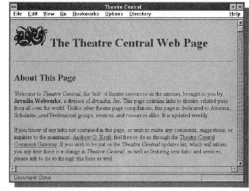

http://www.mit.edu:8001/people/quijote/theatre-central.html
Arcadia Webworks; Theatre

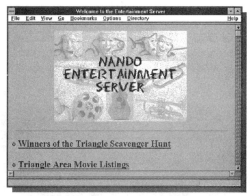

http://www.nando.net/epage/nao/nao.html
Movie listings; Scavenger hunt

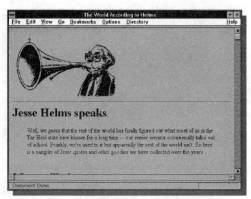

http://www.nando.net/sproject/jesse/helms.html
Jesse Helms speaks; North Carolina

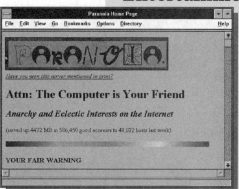

http://www.paranoia.com/
Computers; FAQs; Paranoia; Software

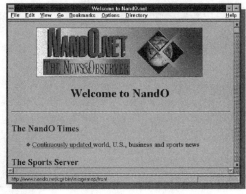

http://www.nando.net/welcome.html
Business; News; Sports

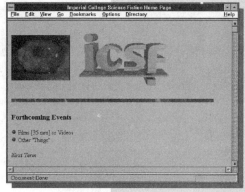

http://www.ph.ic.ac.uk/moontg/
Films; Science fiction; Videos

http://www.ncsa.uiuc.edu/Edu/StateFair
4-H; Farm animals; Illinois; State fairs

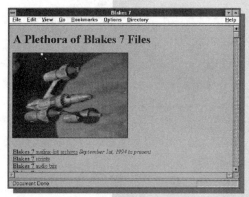

http://www.phlab.missouri.edu/c621052_www/Blakes7/
Audio; Blakes 7; Science fiction; Scripts

http://www.ot.com/skew
Arts; Entertainment; Magazines; Short stories

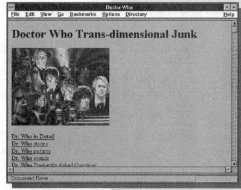

http://www.phlab.missouri.edu/c621052_www/Dr.Who/
Audio; Dr. Who; Pictures; Stories

Entertainment

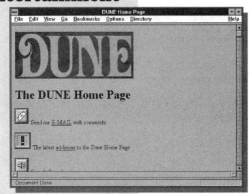

http://www.princeton.edu/~cgilmore/dune/dune.html
Audio; Discussions; DUNE; Science fiction

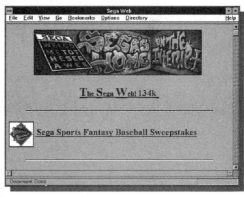

http://www.segaoa.com/
Kids; Sega Sports; Video games

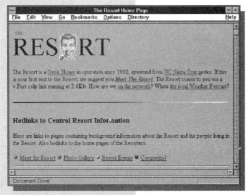

http://www.resort.com/
Geek House; Photo Gallery; UC Santa Cruz

http://www.stack.urc.tue.nl/~remy/
Archive; Jack Vance; Stories

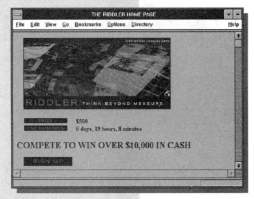

http://www.riddler.com/
Interactive imagination; RIDDLER

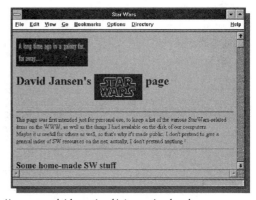

http://www.strw.leidenuniv.nl/~jansen/sw.html
Entertainment; Star Wars

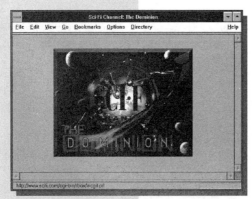

http://www.scifi.com/
Sci-Fi; Science fiction

http://www.ten-io.com/index.html
Shopping bargains; Travel and Entertainment Network

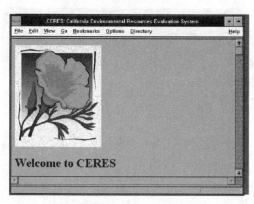

http://agency.resource.ca.gov/
California Environmental Resources Evaluation System

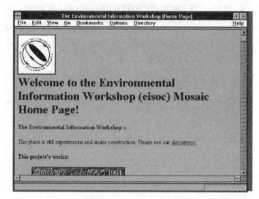

http://andro.sfc.keio.ac.jp/
Ecology; Environment; Information workshop

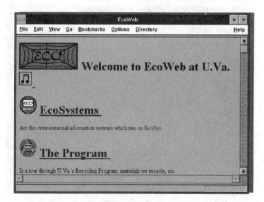

http://ecosys.drdr.virginia.edu/EcoWeb.html
Ecology; Ecosystems; Environment

http://envirolink.org/
Conservation; Earth; Environment; Recycling

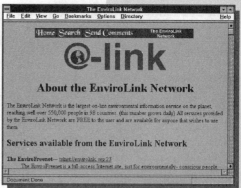

http://envirolink.org/about.html
Environmental information; The EnviroLink Network

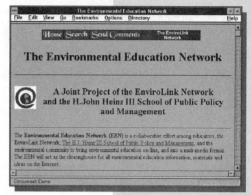

http://envirolink.org/enviroed/
Educators; Environmental Education Network

http://envirolink.org/start_web.html
Environment; Green products; Research

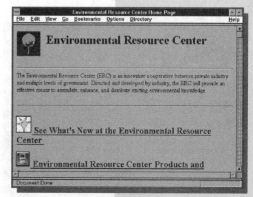

http://ftp.clearlake.ibm.com/ERC/main.html
Ecology; Environmental Resource Center

201

Environment

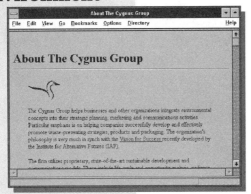

http://garnet.msen.com:70/0h/vendor/cygnus/About-Cygnus.html
Environmental concepts; Waste-preventing strategies

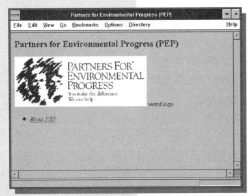

http://garnet.msen.com:70/1/vendor/cygnus/PEP
Partners for Environmental Progress; PEP

http://gcmd.gsfc.nasa.gov:80/
Earth science; Environmental; Global change; Goddard; NASA

http://grn.com/grn/
Earth; Ecology; Environment; Recycling

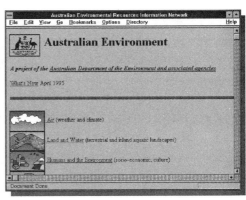

http://homechheese.eas.asu.edu/info/sso/cry.html
Air; Aquatic landscapes; Australia; Socio-economic

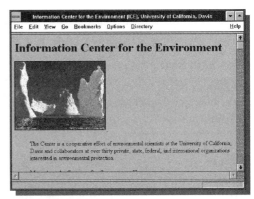

http://ice.ucdavis.edu/
Ecology; Environment; Science

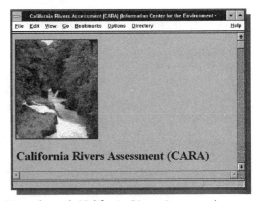

http://ice.ucdavis.edu/California_Rivers_Assessment/
California Rivers Assessment; CARA; Environment

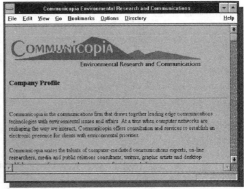

http://interchange.idc.uvic.ca/communicopia/index.html
Communicopia; Environmental Research and Communications

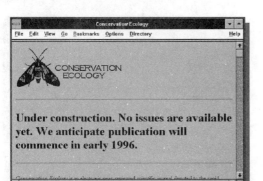

http://journal.biology.carleton.ca/
Conservation; Ecology; Ecosystems

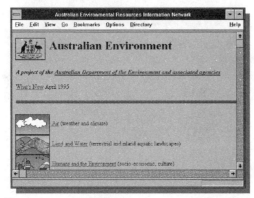

http://kaos.erin.gov.au/erin.html
Air; Australian environment; Climate; Ecology; Land and water

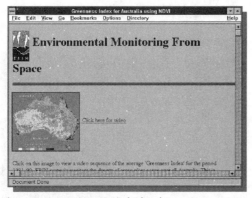

http://kaos.erin.gov.au/sat_pics/ndvi.html
Environment; Images; Space; Video

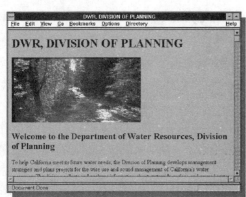

http://locke.water.ca.gov:80/
Management; Planning; Water resources

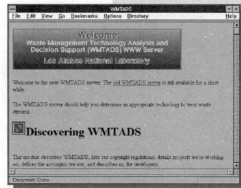

http://mwir.lanl.gov:80/
Los Alamos; Waste management; Waste streams

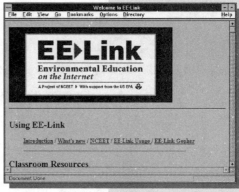

http://nceet.snre.umich.edu/
Ecology; Environmental education; Information services

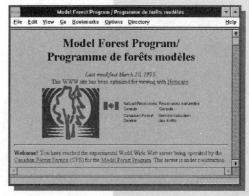

http://NCR157.NCR.Forestry.CA/MF.HTM
Canada; Ecology; Environment; Forests; Natural resources

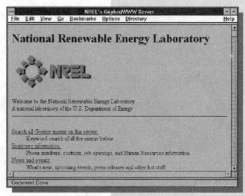

http://nrelinfo.nrel.gov:70/
News; Renewable energy; US Department of Energy

Environment

http://ns.noaa.gov/NESDIS/NESDIS_Home.html
NESDIS; Satellite; Space

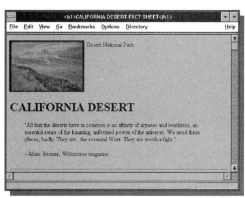

http://town.hall.org/environment/wild_soc/ca-fact.html
California desert information

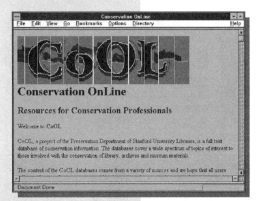

http://palimpsest.stanford.edu/
Conservation; Preservation; Stanford University libraries

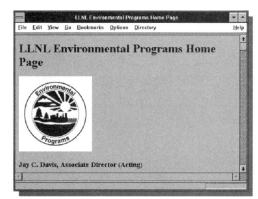

http://www-ep.es.llnl.gov/www-ep/ep-home.html
Programs; Lawrence Livermore National Laboratory

http://solstice.crest.org/
Alternative energy; Policy; Renewable energy; Science

http://www.ciesin.org/TG/HDP/HDP-home.html
Earth studies; Environment; Global change

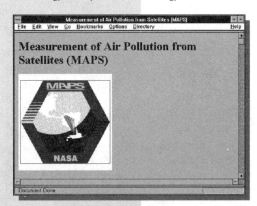

http://stormy.larc.nasa.gov/press.html
Air pollution; Environment; Measurement

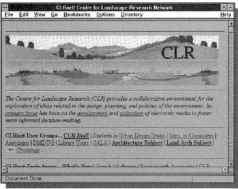

http://www.clr.toronto.edu/
Center for Landscape Research; Design; Planning; Policies

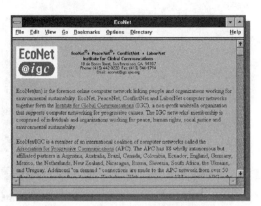

http://www.econet.apc.org/lcv/econet_info.html
EcoNet; Institute for Global Communications; Progressive causes

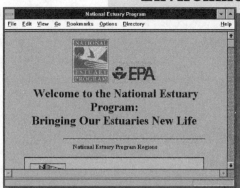

http://www.epa.gov/nep/nep.html
Birds; EPA; National Estuary Program

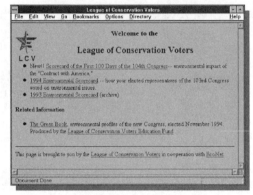

http://www.econet.apc.org/lcv/scorecard.html
Ecology; League of Conservation Voters; Green Book

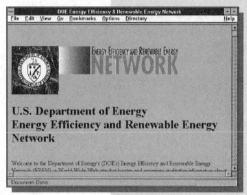

http://www.eren.doe.gov/
Energy efficiency; Renewable energy; US Department of Energy

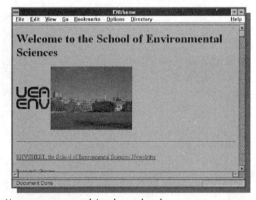

http://www.env.uea.ac.uk/envhome.html
Climate; Ecology; Environment; Environmental Sciences

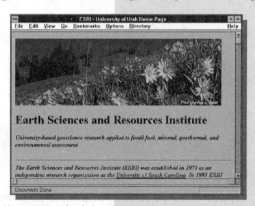

http://www.esri.utah.edu/
Earth Sciences; University of Utah

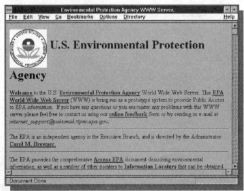

http://www.epa.gov/
Environmental Protection; EPA Government

http://www.foe.co.uk/
Earth; Environment; Resources

Games

http://aloha.com/~irwins/pog/milk_hunt.html
Great Hawaiian Milkcap Hunt; Online game

http://coyote.csusm.edu/cwis/winworld/games.html
Games; Shareware; Video

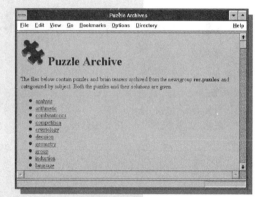

http://alpha.acast.nova.edu/puzzles.html
Games; Logic; Puzzles

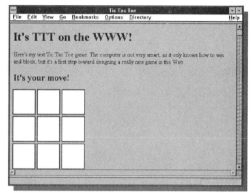

http://csugrad.cs.vt.edu/~jfink/ttt.html
Tic Tac Toe

http://btech.netaxs.com/
BattleTech; Role-playing games; War games

http://cybersight.com/cgi-bin/cs/idic/joe/
Multi-author stories; Writing

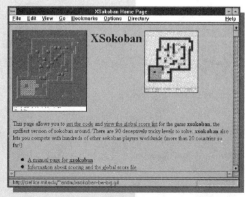

http://clef.lcs.mit.edu/~andru/xsokoban.html
Multi-user games; Puzzles

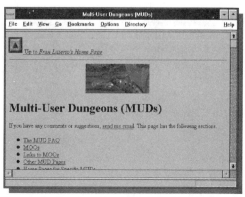

http://draco.centerline.com:8080/~franl/mud.html
MOOs; MUDs; Role-playing games; Social games

http://einstein.et.tudelft.nl/~arlet/slide.cgi
Puzzles

http://legowww.homepages.com/
Kids; Legos; Toys

http://einstein.et.tudelft.nl/~mvdlaan/WebMind/WM_intro.html
Interactive games; WebMind

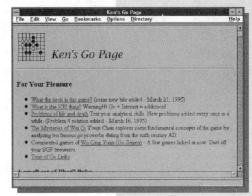

http://ltiwww.epfl.ch/~warkent/go/
Board games; Go; Strategy

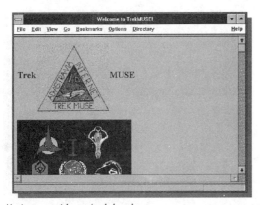

http://grimmy.cnidr.org/trek.html
Computer games; Games; Star Trek

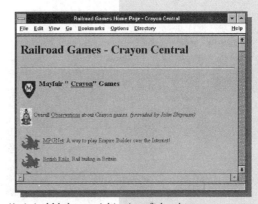

http://ntia.its.bldrdoc.gov/~bing/mayf1.html
Crayon Central; Hobbies; Railroad games

http://helios.acm.rpi.edu/addventure/
Adventure; Adventure game; Kids

http://ntia.its.bldrdoc.gov/~bing/mayfair.html
Crayon; Railroad games

Games

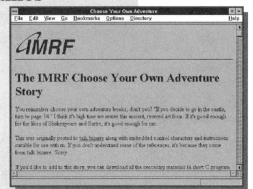

http://physics.purdue.edu/~sho/choose_main.html
Adventure; Multi-line stories

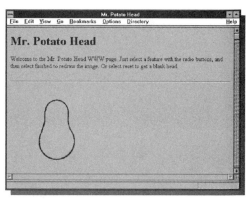

http://www.acsu.buffalo.edu/cgi-bin/potato
Mr. Potato Head; Puzzles

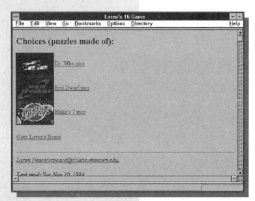

http://sgi1.phlab.missouri.edu/c621052_www/game/
Puzzles

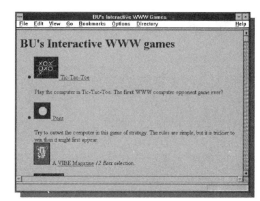

http://www.bu.edu/Games/games.html
Interactive games; Tic Tac Toe; Pegs

http://wcl-rs.bham.ac.uk/~djh/
Games related information

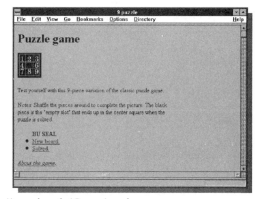

http://www.bu.edu/Games/puzzle
Puzzle games

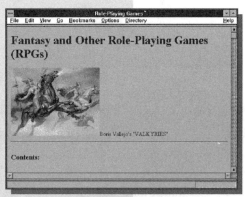

http://www.acm.uiuc.edu/duff/index.html
Dungeons & Dragons; Fantasy; Games; Role playing

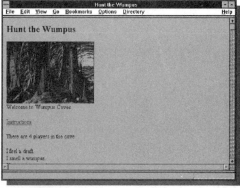

http://www.bu.edu/htbin/wcl
Interactive games; Text-based games

Games

http://www.charm.net/~dagorhir
Acting; Dark ages; Role-playing games

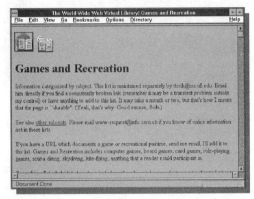

http://www.cis.ufl.edu/~thoth/library/recreation.html
Card games; Kite-flying; Scuba diving

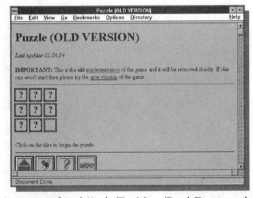

http://www.cm.cf.ac.uk/AndysTestMenu/PuzzleDocument.html
Games; Puzzle

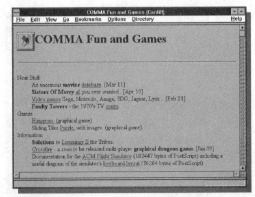

http://www.cm.cf.ac.uk/Fun/
Game solutions; Hangman; Puzzles

http://www.cm.cf.ac.uk/Games/
Doom; Games; Online Hints

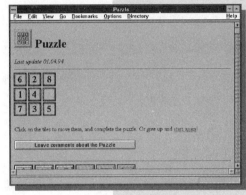

http://www.cm.cf.ac.uk/htbin/AndrewW/Puzzle/puzzle.p
Puzzle games

209

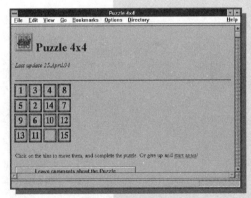

http://www.cm.cf.ac.uk/htbin/AndrewW/Puzzle/puzzle4x4.p
Puzzle games

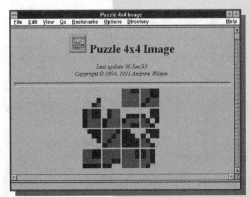

http://www.cm.cf.ac.uk/htbin/AndrewW/Puzzle/puzzle4x4image
Puzzle games

Games

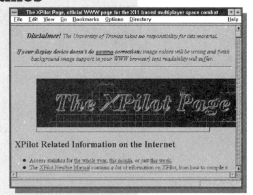

http://www.cs.uit.no/XPilot/
Airplanes; Flight simulators

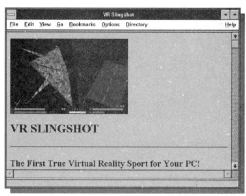

http://www.cts.com/~vrman
3D; Dogfight Simulation; Games; VR Slingshot

http://www.cs.umd.edu/users/fms/GameBoy/
Gameboy; Secrets; Video games

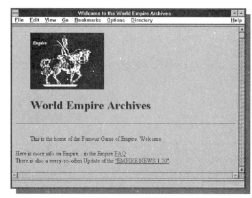

http://www.engg.ksu.edu/empire/
Role-playing; War games

http://www.cs.umu.se/cgi-bin/scripts/jackpot
Electronic slot machine; Jackpot

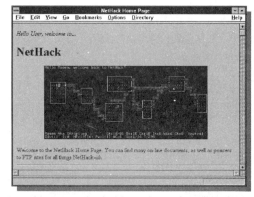

http://www.engin.umich.edu/labs/mel/mneylon/nh/nethack.html
Mazes; Strategy games

http://www.cs.utah.edu/~driskill/highlander.html
Fantasy; Role-playing games

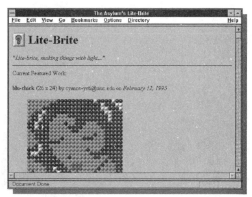

http://www.galcit.caltech.edu/~ta/lb/lb.html
Art; Images; Lite-Brite

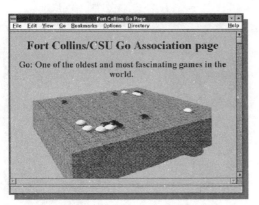

http://www.lance.colostate.edu/~chriso/go.html
Board games; Go

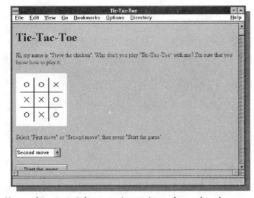

http://www.linc.or.jp/~hamano/game/crossword.html
Crossword puzzles; Word games

http://www.linc.or.jp/~hamano/game/marubatsu.html
Logic games; Tic Tac Toe

http://www.lm.com/users/peterb/angband/angband.html
Fantasy; Role-playing games

http://www.lysator.liu.se/pinball/expo/
Games; Pinball exposition; Recreation

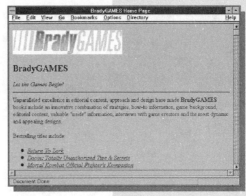

http://www.mcp.com:80/brady/
BradyGAMES; Documentation; Game books; Games

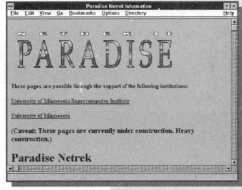

http://www.msi.umn.edu/paradise/
Graphical space combat; Multi-player; Star Trek

http://www.nada.kth.se/~nv91-asa/mage.html
Fantasy; Role-playing games

Genetics

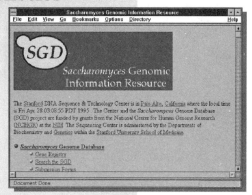

http://genome-www.stanford.edu/
Medicine; Saccharomyces Genomic Information Resource

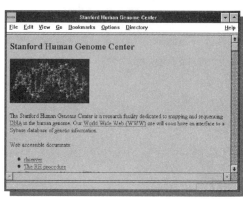

http://shgc.stanford.edu/
DNA; Genetic; Human genome; Information; Stanford

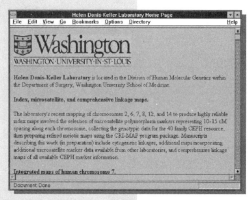

http://hdklab.wustl.edu/
Helen Donis-Keller; Molecular Genetics; Washington University

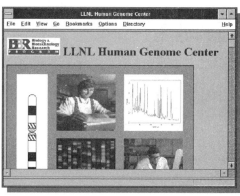

http://www-bio.llnl.gov/bbrp/genome/genome.html
Human Genome Center; Lawrence Livermore National Laboratory

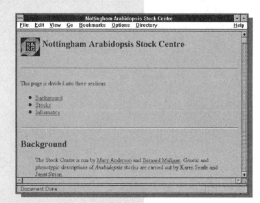

http://nasc.life.nott.ac.uk/description.html
Genetics; Nottingham Arabidopsis Stock Centre; Phenotypic

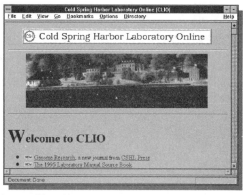

http://www.cshl.org/
DNA; Genetics; Genome research

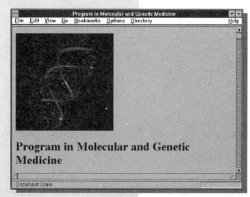

http://pmgm-www.stanford.edu/
Molecular and Genetic Medicine; Stanford University

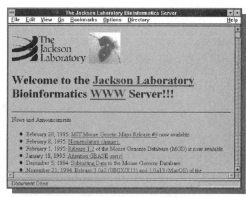

http://www.informatics.jax.org/
Bioinformatics; Genetic; Genomy Database

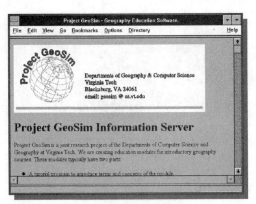

http://geosim.cs.vt.edu/index.html
Earth; Geography; Migration; Population; World

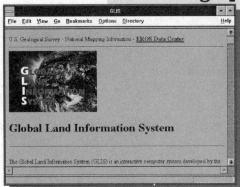

http://sun1.cr.usgs.gov/glis/glis.html
Earth; Geography; Geology; Maps; Science

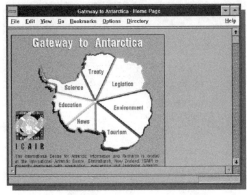

http://icair.iac.org.nz/
Antarctica; Climate; Geography; Geology; NSF

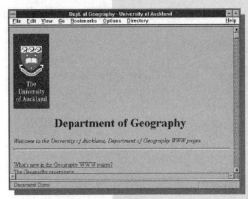

http://www.auckland.ac.nz/geog/
New Zealand; University of Auckland; Geography

213

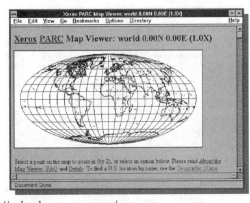

http://pubweb.parc.xerox.com/map
Maps; US location; Xerox PARC Map Viewer

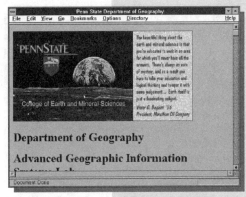

http://www.gis.psu.edu/
Department of Geography; Penn State University

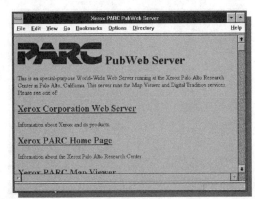

http://pubweb.parc.xerox.com:80/
Cartography; Geography; Maps; Palo Alto; PARC

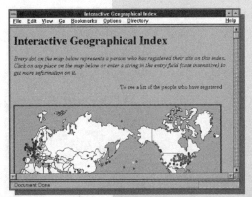

http://www.hcc.hawaii.edu/htbin/plotd
Geography; Index; Map; World

Geology

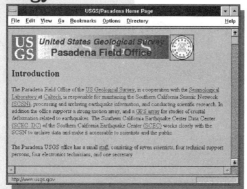

http://aladdin.gps.caltech.edu/usgs-pas.html
Pasadena; US Geological Survey

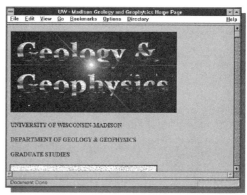

http://geology.wisc.edu/
Geology & Geophysics; Madison; University of Wisconsin

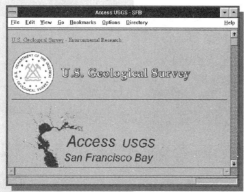

http://bard.wr.usgs.gov/access/access_sfb.html
Environmental Research; San Francisco; Geological Survey

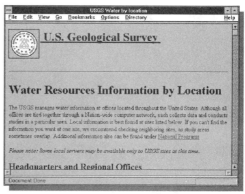

http://h2o.er.usgs.gov/public/wrd002.html
By location; US Geological Survey; Water resources

http://chem.iupui.edu/DinoFest.html
Dinosaurs; Indiana University-Purdue University; Jurassic Park

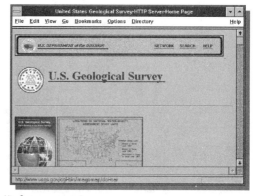

http://info.er.usgs.gov/
Cartography; Department of the Interior; Geology; Maps

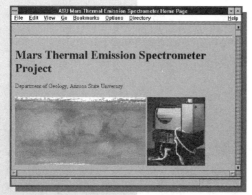

http://esther.la.asu.edu/asu_tes/
Arizona State University; Mars; Thermal Emission Spectrometer

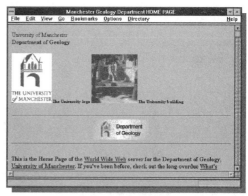

http://info.mcc.ac.uk/Geology/home-page.html
Geology; Science; Education

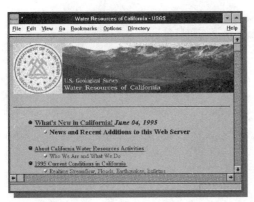

http://s101dcascr.wr.usgs.gov/ca_gen.html
California; US Geology Survey; Water resources

http://vulcan.wr.usgs.gov/Vhp/cvo.html
Cascades Volcano Observatory; Geology

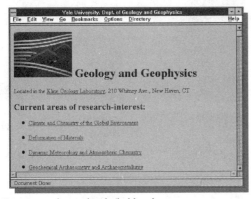

http://stormy.geology.yale.edu/kgl.html
Chemistry; Climate; Geology; Geophysics

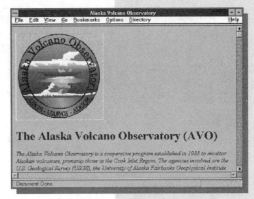

http://www.avo.alaska.edu/
Alaska Volcano Observatory; Geology

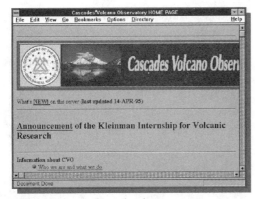

http://vulcan.wr.usgs.gov/home.html
Cascades; Pacific Northwest; Volcanoes

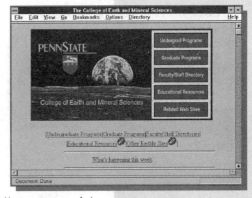

http://www.ems.psu.edu/
Earth; Mineral Sciences; Penn State University

http://vulcan.wr.usgs.gov/Projects/Emissions/framework.html
Global change; Volcanic emissions; Volcanoes

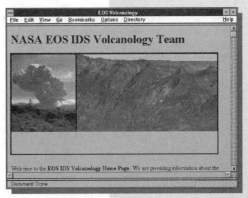

http://www.geo.mtu.edu/eos
Geography; NASA; Volcanoes; Volcanology

Goods and Services

http://199.35.37.1/pink/
Candy; Chocolates; European taste; Sweets

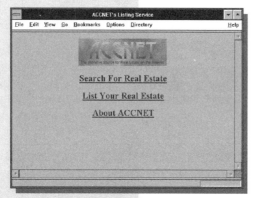

http://accnet.com/homes/index.html
ACCNET; Listing Service; Real estate

http://adware.com/mall/neovideo/welcome.html
Glow in the Dark; Light sensitive ink; Novelty item; Shirts

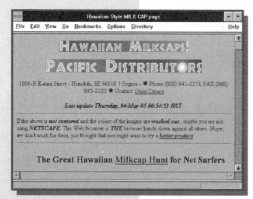

http://aloha.com/~irwins/pog/pog.html
Hawaii; Milk cap hunt

http://arganet.tenagra.com/Racquet_Workshop/Tennis.html
Equipment; Tennis; Tournament

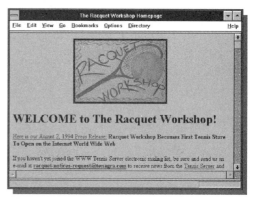

http://arganet.tenagra.com/Racquet_Workshop/Workshop.html
Racquets; Racquet sports; Tennis equipment

http://awinc.com/Lyle/lylehome.html
British Columbia; Canada; Lyle Little; Real estate

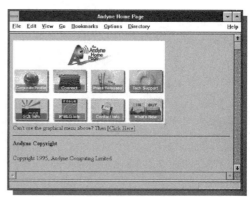

http://bbs.andyne.on.ca/main.html
Products and services; Technical support

http://bookport.com/source/albion9508.html
Albion Books; Electronic media; Publisher; San Francisco

http://branch.com/milne/Milne01.html
Milne Jewelry; Online catalog

http://branch.com/
Goods and Services; Marketing; Shopping

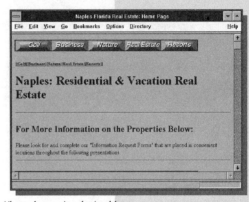

http://branch.com/naples/real.htm
Business; Golf; Naples; Real estate; Vacation properties

http://branch.com/cdexpress/index.html
CD; CD; Commerce; Gifts; Music

http://branch.com/netsurfer/netsurfr.html
Clothing; Computer products; Electronic Catalog; Leather

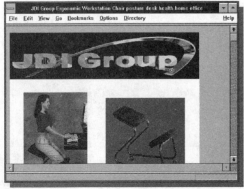

http://branch.com/jdi
Desk; Ergonomic workstation chair; Home office; Posture

http://branch.com/orfila/orfila.html
Gift boxes; Gifts; Gourmet cooking oils; Sauces; Vinegars; Wine

Goods and Services

http://branch.com/pagers/
Communications; Pagers

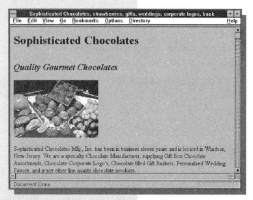

http://branch.com/sophisticated/
Candy; Gifts; Gourmet chocolates

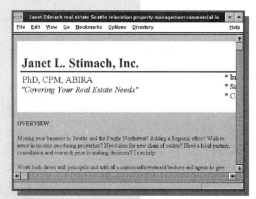

http://branch.com/stimach
Commercial investments; Real estate; Relocation; Seattle

http://branch.com/toucan/toucan.html
Foods; Rainforests; Sweets; Toucan Chocolates

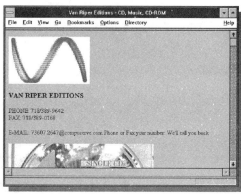

http://branch.com/vanriper/vanriper.html
CD; CD-ROM; Music

http://branch.com:1080/enrico/enrico.html
Advertising; Illustration; Photography; Portraits

http://branch.com:1080/united/united.html
AIDS; Charities; Clothes; Shirts

http://catalog.com/wincorp/dd/ddindex.html
Dance; Dress; Fashion

http://catalog.florida.com/cchome.htm
Catalogs; Gifts; Mail-order merchandise

http://cdnow.com/
Gifts; Internet Music Store; Magazine Warehouse

http://catalog.savvy.com/
Catalogs; Cybermart; Free stuff; Presents

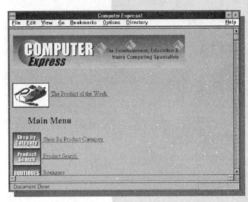

http://cexpress.com:2700/
Computers; Education; Entertainment; Sales; Software

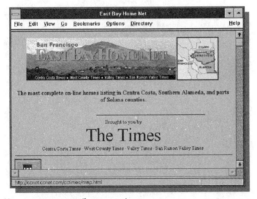

http://ccnet.ccnet.com/homenet/
Contra Costa; Real estate; Solano counties; Southern Alameda

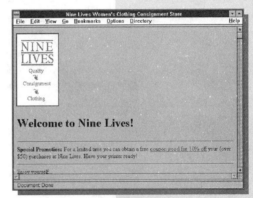

http://chezhal.slip.netcom.com/index.html
Cat food; Cats; Felines; Nine Lives

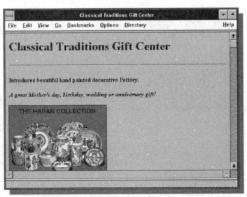

http://ccnet.com/products/traditions/welcome.html
Gifts; Hand painted; Pottery

http://chili.rt66.com/cyspacemalls/
Internet; Mall; Online; Shopping

219

Goods and Services

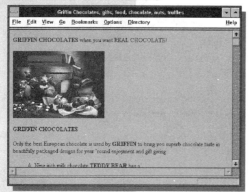

http://chocolate.com/chocolate/griffin.html
Chocolate; Chocolates; Food; Gifts; Nuts; Truffles

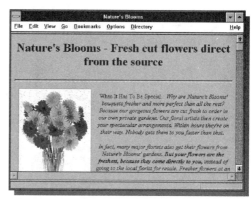

http://cybermart.com/nb/
Florist; Flowers; Gifts

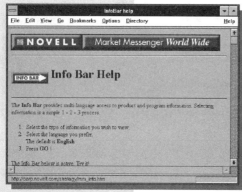

http://corp.novell.com/infohelp.htm
Help; Multi-language; Novell; Products; Program information

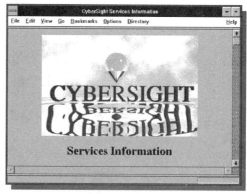

http://cybersight.com/cgi-bin/imi/s?main.gmml
CyberSight; Products and services

http://coupon.com/coupon.html
CouponNet; Coupons

http://cyberzine.org/html/Waves/wavepage.html
Makin' Waves Studios; Multimedia; Video

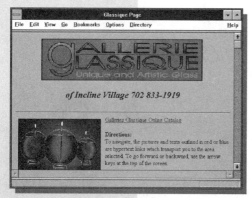

http://cybermart.com/glass/
Artistic Glass; Gifts; Pictures

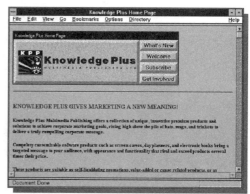

http://cybil.kplus.bc.ca/
Marketing goals; Planners; Screen savers; Software products

http://da.awa.com/cm/
Books; Clothing; Rods; Fishing tackle; Lures; Optics

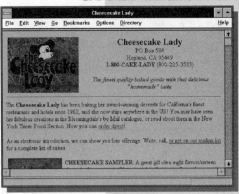

http://dol.meer.net/catalogs/cheesecake/index.html
Baked goods; Cheesecake

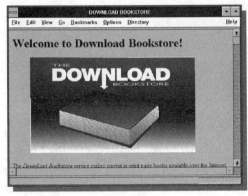

http://dab.psi.net/DownloadBookstore/
Books; Entertainment; Shopping

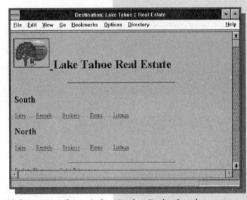

http://dol.meer.net/locns/tahoe/realest/index.html
Lake Tahoe; Real Estate

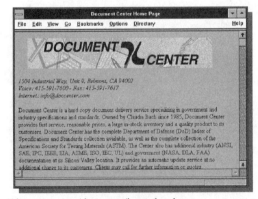

http://doccenter.com/doccenter/home.html
Hard copy document delivery service

http://emall.com/Harvest/Harvest1.html
Diet; Food; Gifts; Harvest burger sampler

http://dol.meer.net/catalogs/casa/index.html
Catalogs; Chocolate; Fruit; Nuts; Online orders

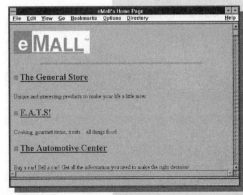

http://eMall.com/Home.html
Shopping; Variety

Goods and Services

http://end2.bedrock.com/mall/attache/home.html
ACI Micro Systems Inc.; Jumpstart II; Product information

http://funstuff.com/
CD-ROM; Laser discs; Web Intertainment

http://execpc.com/~donbah
Artist; Goldsmith; Jewelry; Jewelry designer

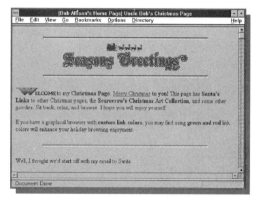

http://gagme.wwa.com/~boba/christmas.html
Art collection; Christmas; Santa

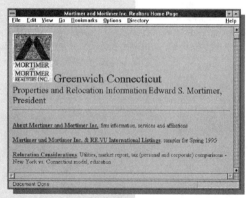

http://found.cs.nyu.edu/CAT/affiliates/mortimer/mortimer.html
Connecticut; Real estate; Relocation information

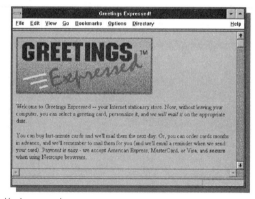

http://gei.na.com/
Delivery; Mail order; Stationery store

http://ftp.cdrom.com/
CD; CD-ROM Electronic Catalog; Products

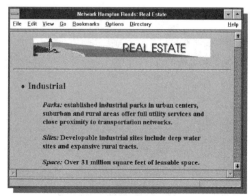

http://hampton.roads.net/nhr/realestate.html
Hampton Roads; Real estate; Virginia

http://hisurf.aloha.com/Harpers/HG.html
Accessories; Electric guitars; Products

http://incorporate.com/tcc/home.html
Business; Corporate services; Incorporation

http://hoohana.aloha.net/~bec/
Espresso; Hawaii; Kona coffee; Products

http://inetstore.com/
Computer assessories; Online ordering

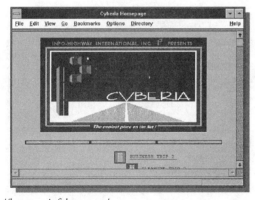

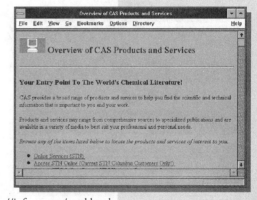

http://houston.infohwy.com/
Gifts; Necessities; Online malls

http://info.cas.org/prod.html
CAS; Chemical literature; Products and services

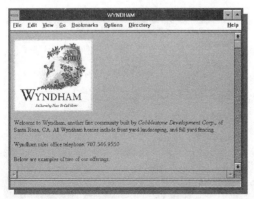

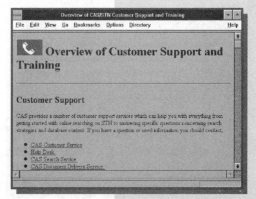

http://ig.dca.hybrid.com/igmkplc/wyndham/wyndham.html
California; Fencing; Landscaping; Santa Rosa; Wyndham

http://info.cas.org/supp.html
CAS; Chemical abstracts; Customer support and training

Goods and Services

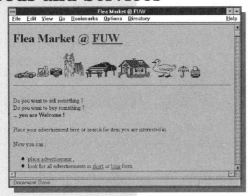

http://info.fuw.edu.pl/market/market.html
Advertisement; Flea Market; Online garage sale

http://intergal.com/shopping.htm
Directories; Internet Shopping Galleria; Links; Products

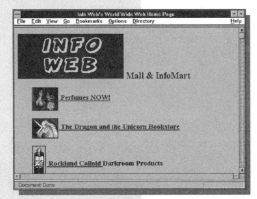

http://infoweb.net/
Books; Gifts; Mall; Online shopping

http://iquest.com/~topcycle/
Bicycle; Biking; Shopping; Sporting goods

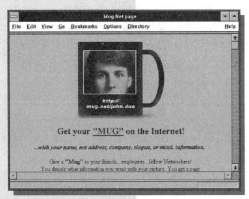

http://innovation.com/mug/index.html
Entertainment; Mugs; Personal; Products

http://isms.com/
Gifts; Internet Shopping Mall; Japanese

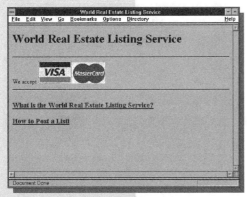

http://interchange.idc.uvic.ca/wrels/index.html
Real estate; Westcoast Interchange

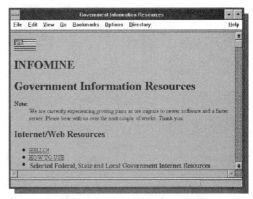

http://lib-www.ucr.edu/govpub/
Government; Research

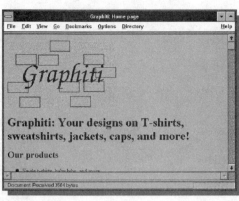

http://libertynet.org/~graphiti
Caps; Clothing; Custom design; Jackets; Personalized design

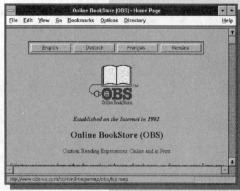

http://marketplace.com:80/obs/obshome.html
Books; Gifts; Online Bookstore

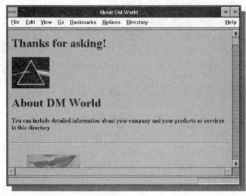

http://mainsail.com/dminfo.html
DM World; Marketing; Web advertising

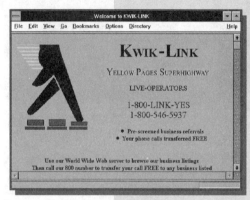

http://meer.net/kwik-link
Pre-screened business referrals; Yellow Pages

http://mainsail.com/safety/index.htm
Safety Products International

http://micromedia.com/index.htm
Micro Media online storefronts

http://marketplace.com/
Cyberspace; Online market; TCP/IP; UNIX

http://mls.saic.com/mls.coffee.html
Directories; Global coffeehouses

225

Goods and Services

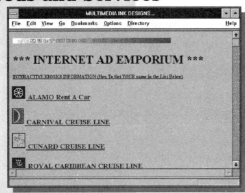

http://mmink.com/mmink/dossiers/techstd/techstd.html
Advertising; Cruises; Rental cars; Travel

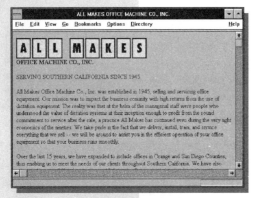

http://mmink.cts.com/mmink/dossiers/allmakes.html
Machines; Office equipment; Sales; Services

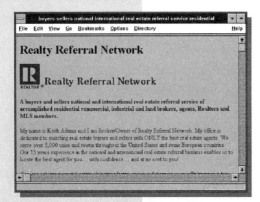

http://mmink.cts.com/mmink/dossiers/rrn.html
Real estate; Realty Referral Network

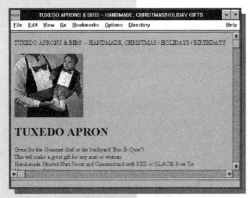

http://mmink.cts.com/mmink/dossiers/tuxedo.html
Gifts; Handmade clothing; Humorous clothing

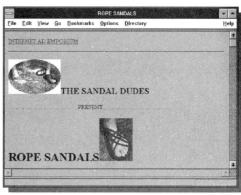

http://mmink.cts.com/mmink/kiosks/sandals/ropesandals.html
Clothes; Feet; Footwear; Sandals; Shoes

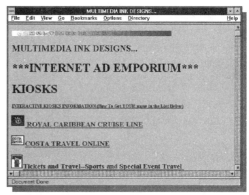

http://mmink.cts.com/mmink/mmi.html
Cruises; Multimedia; Special events; Travel

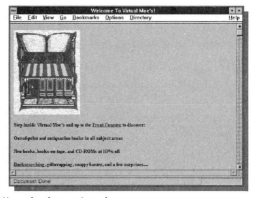

http://moesbooks.com/moe.htm
Books; CD-ROM; Gifts; Online shopping; Virtual Moe's

http://net101.com/index.html
Consultation; Electronic Publishing; Internet Training

http://netmarket.com/
Cybermart; Gifts; Online malls

http://netmart.com/
Gifts; Net-Mart; Shopping Mall

http://netmedia.com/ims/ssc/ssc.html
California; Palo Alto; Stanford Shopping

http://netmedia.com/ims/STORES/Phileas/Phileas.html
Books; Maps; Sports; Travel

http://newton.uiowa.edu/
Archive; Newton; University of Iowa

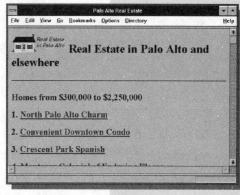

http://none.coolware.com/real/realestate.html
Homes; Palo Alto; Real estate

http://nw.com/bahnware/
Advertising; BAHNWARE; Consultation; Internet services

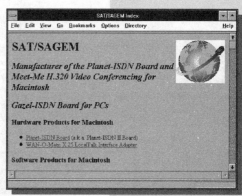

http://nw.com/satusa/
Hardware; Products Macintosh; Software

227

Goods and Services

http://nyweb.com/toaa/
Advertising; Online advertising

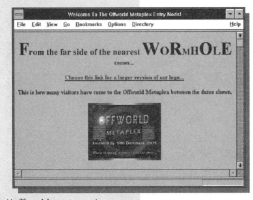

http://offworld.wwa.com/
Artwork; Experiments; Points of interest

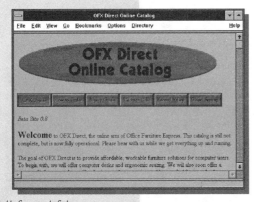

http://ofx.com/ofx/
Chairs; Desks; Ergonomic; Online catalog

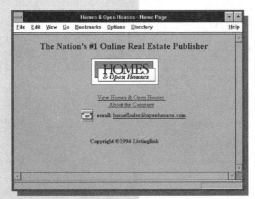

http://openhouses.com/
Online; Publisher; Real estate

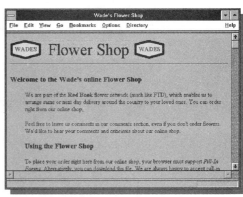

http://oscar.biznet.com.blacksburg.va.us/~wades/flower.html
Florist; Flower shop; Gifts

http://planetreebok.com/
Clothing; Reebok; Shoes; Sports

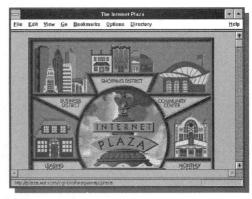

http://plaza.xor.com/
Business; Shopping

http://plaza.xor.com/stores/outlets.html
Books; Deadwear; Florists; Online shopping

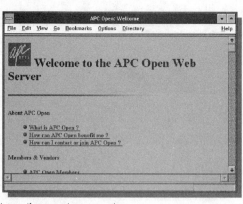

http://pogo.jkcg.com/apc_open/
Membership; Products and services; Vendors

http://rainer.bnt.com/vvv.html
Store software; Versatile virtual vending

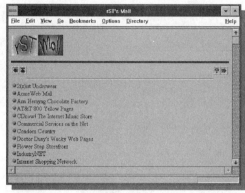

http://polaris.net/~trexcom/shop.html
Directories; Online shopping

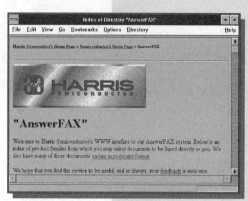

http://rel.semi.harris.com/docs/AnswerFAX/
Fax; Harris Corporation; Product information

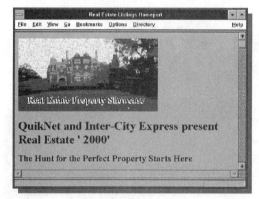

http://quiknet.com/realshow.html
Homes; Listings; Real estate; Shopping

http://reol.com/welcome.html
Online; Real estate

http://rainer.bnt.com/htbin/wa
Food; Grocery Store; Online

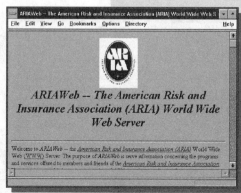

http://riskweb.bus.utexas.edu/aria.html
Insurance; Services

Goods and Services

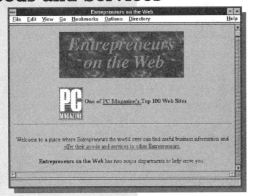

http://sashimi.wwa.com/~notime/eotw/EOTW.html
Entrepreneur; Goods and services

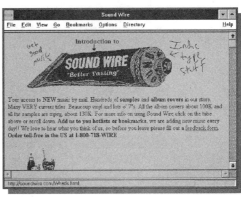

http://soundwire.com/
Entertainment; Graphics; Mail order; Music

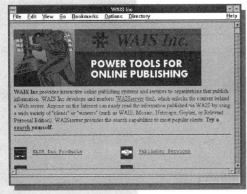

http://server.wais.com/
Electronic publishing; Publisher services; WAIS

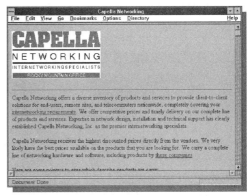

http://storefront.xor.com/capella/index.html
Hardware; Internetworking; Software; Telecommuters

http://simon.com/
Institutional accessories; Online sales; Simon

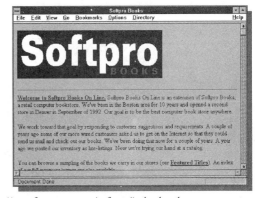

http://storefront.xor.com/softpro/index.html
Bookstores; Computer books; Gifts

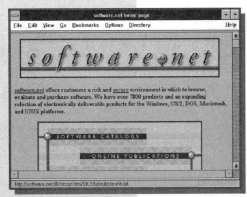

http://software.net/
Catalogs; Software store

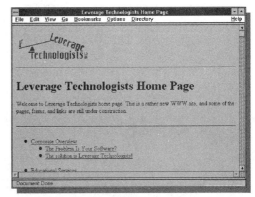

http://stout.levtech.com/home.html
Consulting; Educational; Software engineering

http://teamate.mmb.com/
Bulletin; Internet service; TEAMate Software; UNIX

http://usa.net/home/shopping.html
Consumer information; Directories; Market Place; Shopping

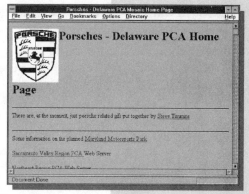

http://tig.com/Imaginarium/
Catalog; Coupons; Gifts; Imaginarium

http://warthog.us.udel.edu:80/porsches.html/
Automobiles; Cars; Gifts; Porshes

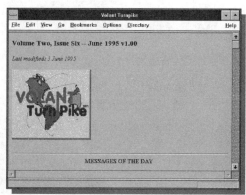

http://town.hall.org/places/city_lights/
Books; Booksellers; Gifts; Publishing

http://wave.intellisoft.com/salondirect/
Professional quality hair care products

http://turnpike.net/
Internet goods and services; Volant Turnpike

http://webnet.pic.net/ucs
Carpet sales; Flooring mills

Goods and Services

http://www.abmall.com/fil/fil.html
Babydolls; Bras; Fantasies; Garterbelts; Hosiery; Lace; Wigs

http://www.adnetsol.com//frststp/frststp.html
Computers; New; Repairs; Sales; Service; Used

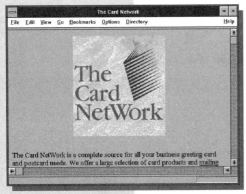

http://www.abmall.com/tcn/hp.html
Business; Greeting card; Mailing service; Postcard

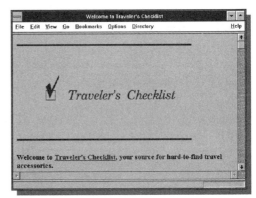

http://www.ag.com/Travelers/Checklist
Travel tips; Vacations

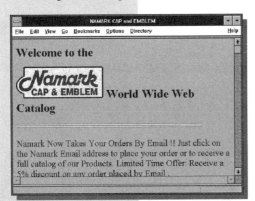

http://www.accessnv.com/namark
Catalog; Namark Cap and Emblem; Online sales

http://www.ais.net/netmall/
Gifts; Online shopping; Virtual Mall

http://www.acmeweb.com/mi
Artists; Gallery; Mirror Images

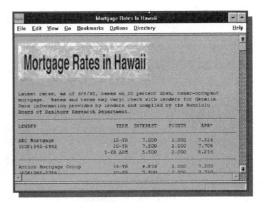

http://www.aloha.net/hol/mall/hbr/rates.html
Hawaii; Lenders; Mortgage rates; Real estate; Real estate

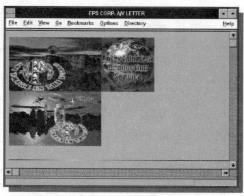

http://www.amug.org/~eps/eps3p.html
Entertainment Production Services; Products and services

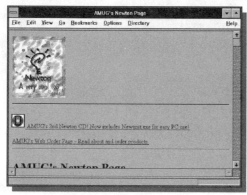

http://www.amug.org/amug_newton.html
AMUG; Information; News; Newton

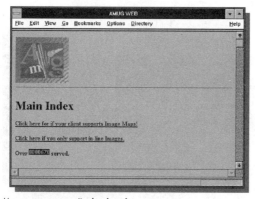

http://www.amug.org/index.html
AMUG web; Images; Maps

http://www.apk.net/cdrom
CD; CD-ROM reviews; Online ordering

http://www.aus.xanadu.com/GlassWings/arcade/myers/mgp.html
Food; Gourmet; Popcorn

http://www.aus.xanadu.com/GlassWings/welcome.html
Australia; Gifts; Online malls

233

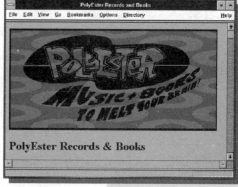

http://www.aus.xanadu.com/PolyEster/polyester.html
Books; Catalogs; Music

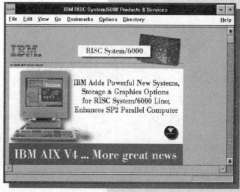

http://www.austin.ibm.com/
AIX V4; IBM; RISC

Goods and Services

http://www.austin.ibm.com/software/OpenGL/
IBM; Information; Links; OpenGL; Products

http://www.austinre.com/dhall/dhall.htm
Austin; Homes; New; Real estate

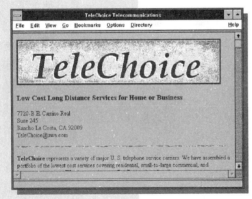

http://www.awa.com/tc/
Business; Home; Long distance services

http://www.aztec.com/pub/aztec/hans/
Hans Christian; News; Products; Recreation; Travel; Yachts

http://www.baynet.com/cc/cchome.html
Palo Alto; Properties; Real estate

http://www.baynet.com/hgi/hgi.html
Brokerage; Loan programs; Loan rates; Mortgages

http://www.baynet.com/homeline.html
Guides; Homes; Real estate

http://www.baynet.com/homes/index.html
Homes; Northern California; Real estate; San Francisco

http://www.baynet.com/summerhill/index.html
Homebuyer's newsletter; Houses; SummerHill Homes

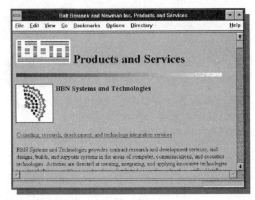

http://www.bbn.com/products.html
Bolt Beranek and Newman; Products and services

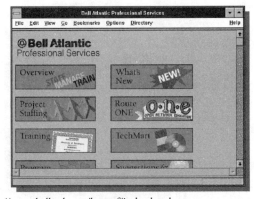

http://www.bell-atl.com/baprof/index.html
Bell Atlantic; Services; Training

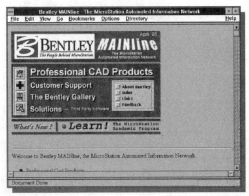

http://www.bentley.com/
Bentley MAINline; CAD products; Design

http://www.berkeleyic.com/
Custom; Design; Home pages; Multimedia; Presence; Web

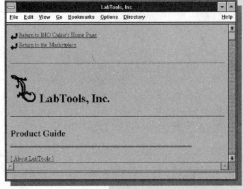

http://www.best.com/~aurora/anita.html
Design; Home page creation; Services; Web

http://www.bio.com/bio/labtools/labtools_toc.html
Laboratory equipment; News; Products

http://www.bitcon.no/
Bergen IT Consult AS - BITCon; Norway

235

Goods and Services

http://www.biznet.com.blacksburg.va.us/~wades
Delivery; Food; Online shopping

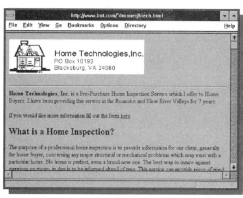

http://www.bnt.com/~dmauer/htech.html
Home Technologies; Pre-Purchase Home Inspection Service

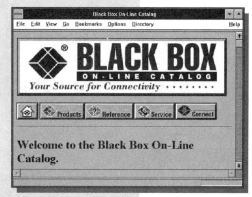

http://www.blackbox.com/
Black box; Online catalog; Products

http://www.bnt.com/~rfrazier/
Computer disposal; Old PCs

http://www.blowfish.com/
Arts; Books; Comics; Crafts; Erotic; Magazines; Mail-order

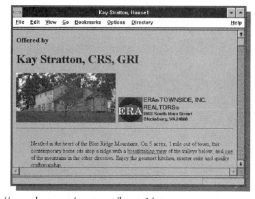

http://www.bnt.com/~stratton/house1/
Blue Ridge Mountains; Real estate

http://www.bnt.com/~anderson/
Anderson and Associates; Newsletter; Technology

http://www.bnt.com/~techbook/
Catalog; Software; Tech bookstore; Virginia

http://www.bnt.com/netdiamonds/
Fine jewelry; Loose diamonds; Products; Services

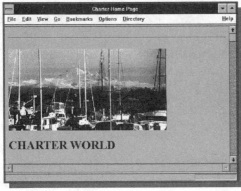

http://www.boatnet.com/~boatnet/charter/chartop.html
Boats; Charters; Recreation

http://www.boatnet.com/~boatnet/index.html
Boats; Charters; Marine; Online catalog; Yachts; Sailboats

http://www.books.com/
Books; Book stores; Online book sales

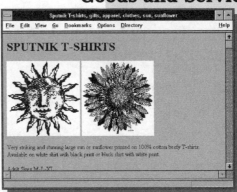

http://www.branch.com/sputnik/sputnik.html
Clothing; Online malls; T-shirts

http://www.bravo.com/bravo/Phonecards/phone.html
Business; Finance; Phonecards

http://www.btg.com/spencer
Online shopping; Spencer Gifts

http://www.btw.com/corporate/toc.html
Books That Work; Corporate overview; Software

Goods and Services

http://www.bytes.com/
Books; Bookstore; GIFs

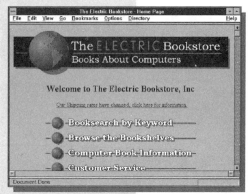

http://www.cadvision.com/bookstore/electric.html
Books; Bookstore; Electronic Bookstore Inc.; Gifts

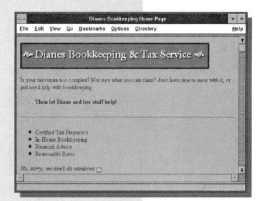

http://www.castles.com/comm/dianes/dianes.html
Bookkeeping; Tax returns

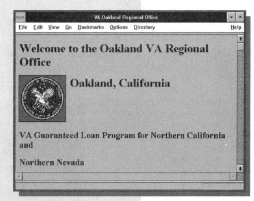

http://www.ccnet.com/services/va/welcome.html
California; Oakland; VA; Veterans Administration

http://www.ceainc.com/TransAm
Online sports clothing catalog; TransAmerica

http://www.center.org/csd/home.html
Programming; Research; Software; Software development

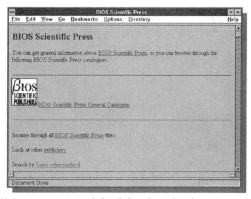

http://www.cityscape.co.uk/bookshop/bicat.html
BIOS Scientific Press; General Catalogue; Publishers

http://www.cityscape.co.uk/bookshop/bwcat.html
Blackwell Publishers; Books; Catalog; Geography

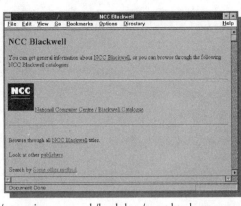

http://www.cityscape.co.uk/bookshop/nccat.html
Blackwell Catalogue; National Computer Centre; Publishers

http://www.clbooks.com/
Books; Bookstore; Gifts; Multimedia

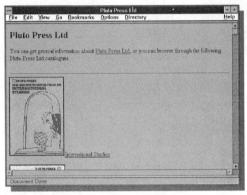

http://www.cityscape.co.uk/bookshop/plcat.html
Catalogues; International studies; Pluto Press Ltd.

http://www.clickshop.com/
Catalog; Internet programming; Talking products

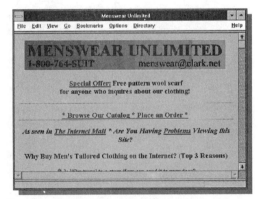

http://www.clark.net/pub/menswear/suits.html
Clothing; Men's clothing; Online store

http://www.clickshop.com:80/speak/
Audio; Malls; Online malls; Sound

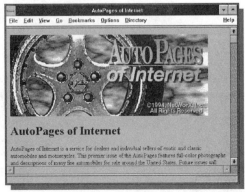

http://www.clark.net/pub/networx/autopage/autopage.html
Automobiles; Cars; Exotic autos

http://www.coat.com/
Clothing; Coats; Online stores

Goods and Services

http://www.crocker.com/~densmore/
Media products; Newshare Corp.; Supplier

http://www.cts.com/
CTS Network Services

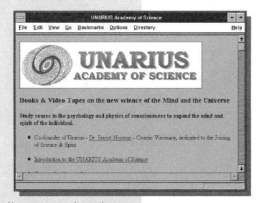

http://www.cts.com/~unarius
Books; Mind; New science; UNARIUS; Universe; Video tapes

http://www.cts.com:80/~flowers
Flowers; Novelties; Online florists; Plants

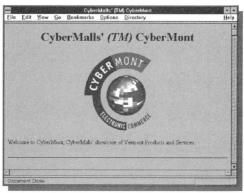

http://www.cybermalls.com/cymont/cymonmal.htm
CyberMont; Online shopping; Vermont Products and Services

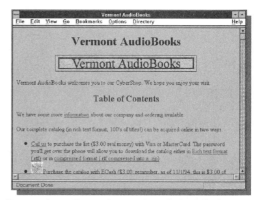

http://www.cybermalls.com/cymont/vtaudio/vtaudio.htm
CDs; Gifts; Online shopping; Vermont AudioBooks

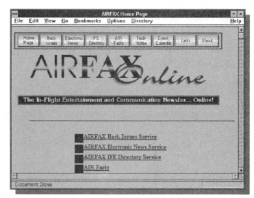

http://www.cyberspace.com/airfax
AIRFAX; Electronic news; In-flight entertainment

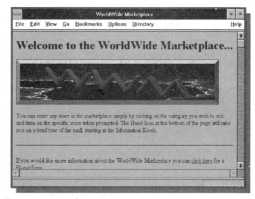

http://www.cygnus.nb.ca/
Online kiosk; Online malls

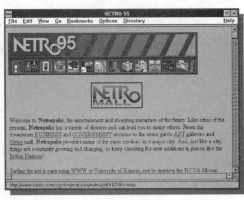

http://www.dash.com/
Art; Business; Education; Games; Online mall

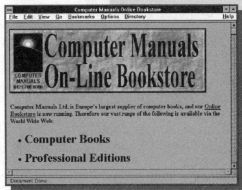

http://www.demon.co.uk/compman/
Computer books; Europe; Magazines

http://www.dealernet.com/
Automobiles; Boats; Exotic autos; Trailers

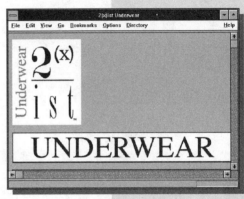

http://www.digex.net/2xist.html
Men's clothing; Online undies; Underwear

http://www.deepspace.com/deepspace.html
Online shopping; Sites; Virtual Mall

http://www.digimark.net/
Marketing; Music; Shopping

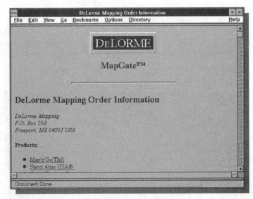

http://www.delorme.com/orders/orders.htm
Atlases; CD-ROM; MapGate; Maps; Software

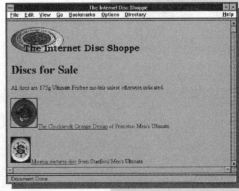

http://www.digimark.net/disc/
Recreation; Sports; Ultimate Frisbee

241

Goods and Services

http://www.digiplanet.com/DP/
Digital Planet; Products and services

http://www.dnai.com/~sotd
Berkeley Integration Group Inc.; Hardware; Network

http://www.easynet.co.uk/compbook.htm
Books; Computer Bookshops; Multimedia; UK; Europe

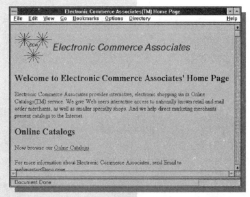

http://www.eca.com/
Electronic shopping; Online catalogs

http://www.echi.com/
Art; Electric Chicago; Fashion; Online shopping

http://www.Echi.com/SQJ.html
Custom jewelry; Diamonds; Gifts; Jewelry; Online jeweler

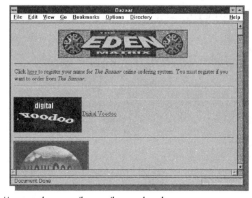

http://www.eden.com/bazaar/bazaar.html
Digital Voodoo; Online ordering; The Bazaar

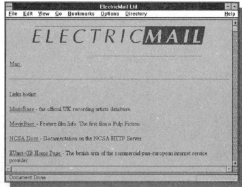

http://www.elmail.co.uk/
Cambridge University; ElectricMail; United Kingdom

Goods and Services

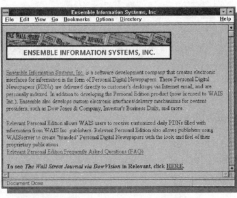

http://www.ensemble.com/
E-Mail; Newspapers; Personal digital newspapers; Software

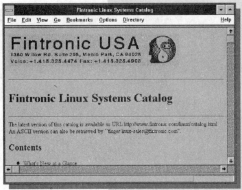

http://www.fintronic.com/linux/catalog.html
Computer products; Linux; Unix workstations; Workstations

http://www.eunet.no/eunet/books.html
Books; EUnet; Internet service provider; Norway

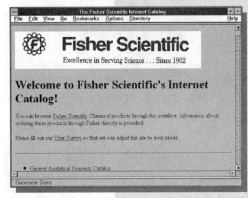

http://www.fisher1.com/
Catalog; Chemical products; Fisher Scientific

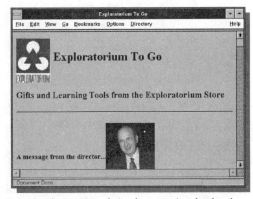

http://www.exploratorium.edu/explo_to_go/catalog.html
Games; Gifts; Online stores; Toys

http://www.floathe.com/
Advertising; Public relations

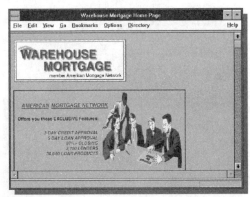

http://www.financing.com/warehouse/
Credit; Lenders; Loan; Mortgage; Warehouse

http://www.flowerstop.com/fstop/fstopmain.html
Flowers; FTD; Gifts

243

Goods and Services

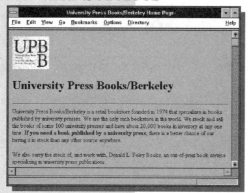

http://www.fractals.com/upb/html/upb_intro.html
Berkeley; Bookstore; University Press Books

http://www.gate.net/~dmusic/aim.html
Gifts; Online shopping; Virtual Mall

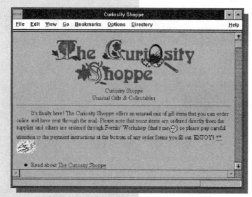

http://www.gate.net/curiosity/
Collectibles; Curiosity Shoppe; Gifts

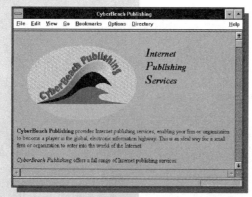

http://www.gate.net/cyberbeach/
CyberBeach; Internet publishing

http://www.gate.net/flowermarket/
Flowers; Jennie's Flower Shop; Tampa

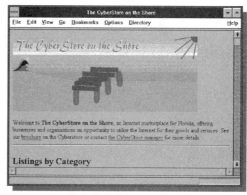

http://www.gate.net/marketplace/
Businesses; CyberStore; Florida

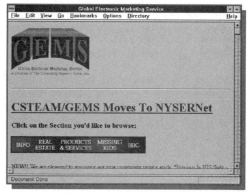

http://www.gems.com/
Products; Real Estate; Services

http://www.gems.com:80/ppd/
Phone; Teleconferencing; Videoconferencing; Videophone

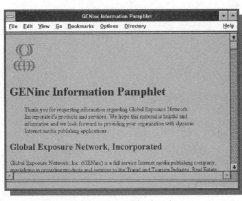

http://www.geninc.com/geni/pamphlet.html
Advertising; GENinc

http://www.gomedia.com/
Go Media; Products and services

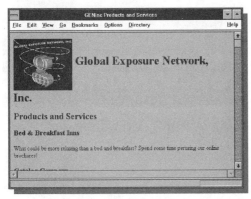

http://www.geninc.com/geni/products.html
Bed and breakfast inns; GENinc

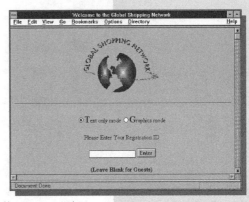

http://www.gsn.com/
Cybermart; Gifts; Online shopping

http://www.geo.net:8240/
CD-ROM; Macintosh; Online catalogs; Software

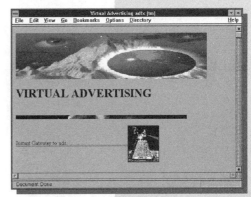

http://www.halcyon.com/zz/top.html
Advertising; Virtual advertising

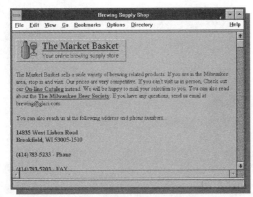

http://www.glaci.com/market/brewing/homepage.html
Beer; Brewing; Catalogs; Online market

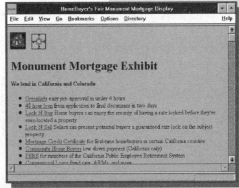

http://www.homefair.com/homefair/monument.html
Loans; Mortgage; Real estate

245

Goods and Services

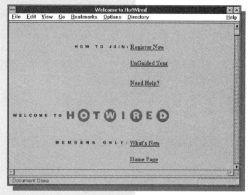

http://www.hotwired.com/
Electronic media; Members only

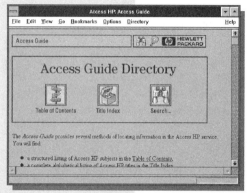

http://www.hp.com/AccessGuide/AccessGuide.html
Books; Guides; Online catalog; Publishing program

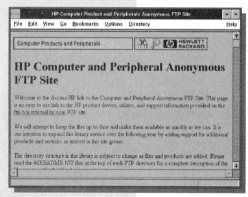

http://www.hp.com/go/ftp-sites
Anonymous FTP; Computers; Peripherals; Products

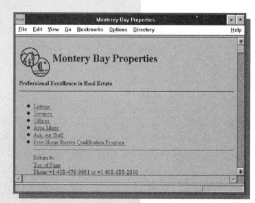

http://www.human.com/mbprop/
Listings; Monterey Bay Properties; Real estate; Services

http://www.human.com/mkt/ddist/
Home brew kit; Premier Mini-Brewery

http://www.human.com/mkt/fsbo/fsbo.html
FSBO; House sales; Northern California; Real estate

http://www.human.com/sonic/sonic.html
Computer burglar alarms; Security

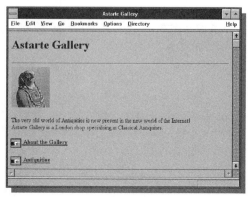

http://www.icl.co.uk/Astarte/
Antiquities; Classical

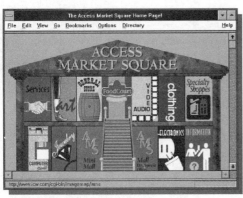

http://www.icw.com/ams.html
Art; Computers; Jewelry; Products; Services

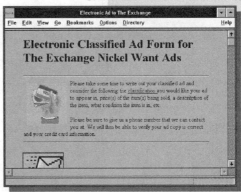

http://www.iea.com/~adlinkex/Exchange/ex-ad.html
Advertising; Classified ad; Want ads

http://www.icw.com/global/startrek.html
Holographic T-shirts

http://www.iea.com/~adlinkex/index.html
Advertising; Classifieds; Nickel Want Ads; Publications

http://www.icw.com/netsweat/netsweat.html
Gifts; Online shopping; Sweatshirts; T-shirts

http://www.iihe.ac.be/
Education; University of Brussels

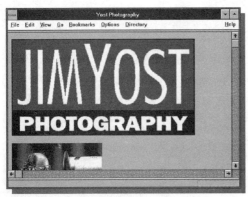

http://www.icw.com/yost/yost.html
Jim Yost; Yost Photography

http://www.iis.com/
Internet consulting; Outsourcing; Web presence

247

Goods and Services

http://www.imall.com/homepage.html
Free classifieds; IMall; Mall directory; Online shopping

http://www.industry.net/
Employment; Engineering; Industrial equipment

http://www.industry.net/cgi-bin/prog/menu/guest/main
IndustryNet Online Marketplace

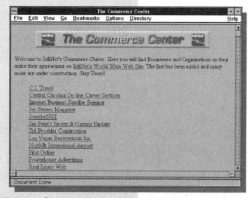

http://www.infi.net/commerce.html
Commerce; InfiNet; Malls; Online malls; Shopping

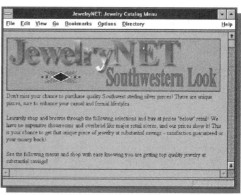

http://www.infi.net/jewel/
Catalogs; Handmade; Jewelry; Online jeweler; Southwest

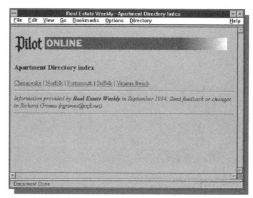

http://www.infi.net/pilot/apartments/index.html
Apartment directory; Pilot Online; Southeastern Virginia

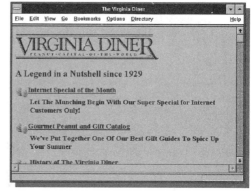

http://www.infi.net/vadiner/
Gourmet; Peanut; The Virginia Diner

http://www.infohaus.fv.com/infohaus.html
First Virtual InfoHaus; Information mall

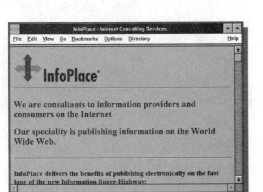

http://www.infoplace.com/infoplace/infoplace-home.html
Consulting; InfoPlace; Internet

http://www.internet-is.com/re/city.html
Four Circles Realty; Real estate

http://www.infopost.com/sandiego/architects/resdesign.html
Hermann Zillgens Associates; Residential design

http://www.internet-is.com/skornia/index.html
Law services; Virtual Law Firm

http://www.informix.com/
Informix; Products; Services

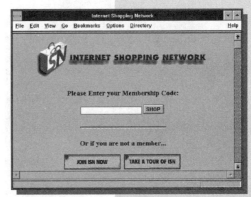

http://www.internet.net/
Membership Stores; Shopping

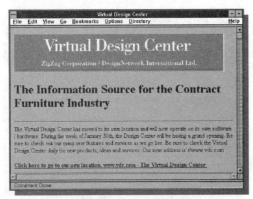

http://www.interaccess.com/users/mmqb
Furniture Industry; Virtual Design Center

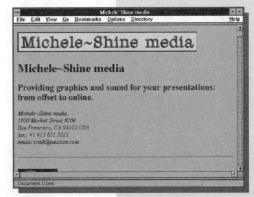

http://www.internex.com/MSM/home.html
Graphic design; Multimedia; Presentations; Sound

http://www.internex.net/epen/index.html
Digital design; Electronic Pen; Web publishing

http://www.ip.net/
Merchandise; Online publishing

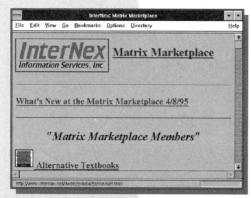

http://www.internex.net/market.html
Goods and Services; InterNex

http://www.ip.net/cgi-bin/shopkeeper
Internet Shopkeeper; Mall

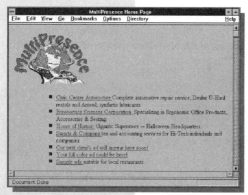

http://www.internex.net/multipresence/
Automotive repair; Ergonomic Office Products; Online resources

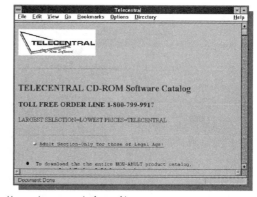

http://www.iquest.net/~tlcental/
CD-ROM Software Catalog; Multimedia; Online shopping

http://www.intertel.com/
Homes; Homebuying; New York; New Jersey; Real estate

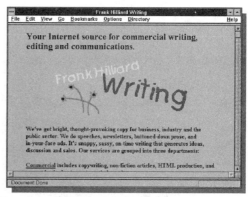

http://www.islandnet.com/~hilliard/frank.html
Business; Commercial; Communications; Editing; Writing

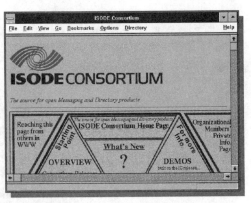

http://www.isode.com/
Directory; ISODE Consortium; Open messaging

http://www.iuma.com/Warner/
Entertainment; Music; Records

http://www.jewelquest.com/
Crystal; Jewelry; Online jeweler

http://www.jkcg.com/Webmaster/Ispy/index.html
Investigations; Investigative consultants; Private investigators

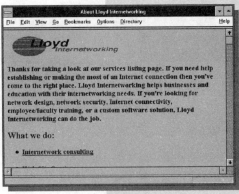

http://www.lloyd.com/what.we.do.html
Business; Connectivity; Software; Design; Security; Training

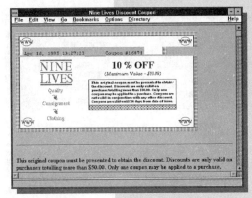

http://www.los-gatos.scruznet.com/cgi-bin/ninelives_coupon
Discounts; Shopping

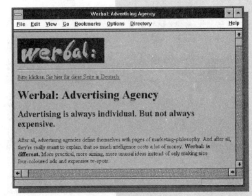

http://www.marktplatz.ch/werbal/index.html
Advertising agency; Werbal

http://www.mbnet.mb.ca:80/flatland/mall/discreet/
Clothing; Lingerie; Online boutique

Goods and Services

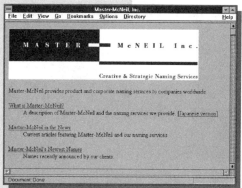

http://www.naming.com/naming.html
Business services; Naming services; Trademarks

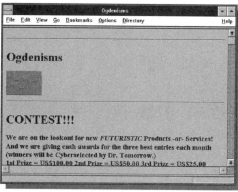

http://www.nas.com/~drtom/gems.html
Contest; Futuristic; Ogdenisms; Products and services

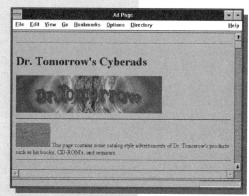

http://www.nas.com/~drtom/ads.html
Advertisements; Catalog; Dr. Tomorrow

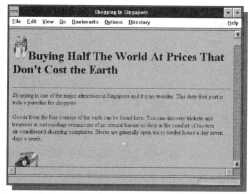

http://www.ncb.gov.sg/sog/6.shop.html
Clothing; Electronics; Furniture; Oriental art; Singapore

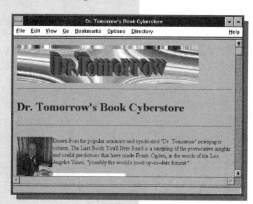

http://www.nas.com/~drtom/books.html
Books; Cyberstore; Dr. Tomorrow

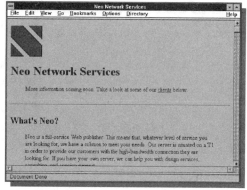

http://www.neo.com/
HTML; Neo Network; Web publishing

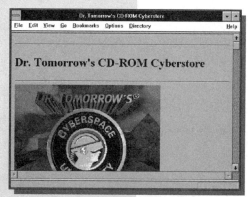

http://www.nas.com/~drtom/cd_rom.html
Dr. Tomorrow's CD-ROM Cyberstore

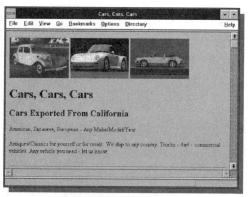

http://www.netpart.com:80/jacob/
Automobiles; Antique cars; Classic cars; Online autos

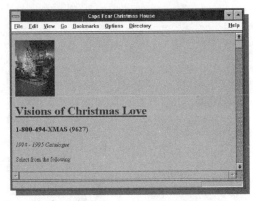

http://www.netweb.com/mall/collegepro/
College; Employment; Home painters; Painting

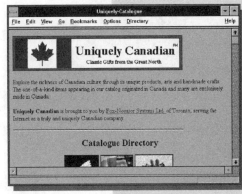

http://www.novator.com/UC-Catalog/UC-Internet.html
Canadian; Gifts; Great North; Uniquely-Catalogue

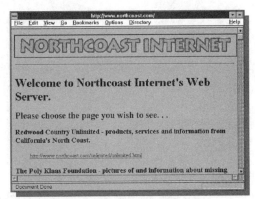

http://www.noel.com/xmas
Christmas gifts; Gifts; Presents; Toys

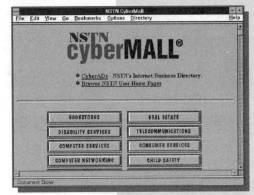

http://www.nstn.ca/cybermall/first.html
Bookstore; Cybermall; Gifts; Real Estate

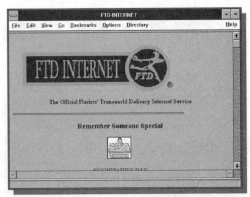

http://www.northcoast.com/
California's North Coast; Information; Products; Services

http://www.nstn.ns.ca/
Canada; Online kiosks; Online malls

http://www.novator.com/FTD-Catalog/FTD-Internet.html
Flowers; FTD; Online florists

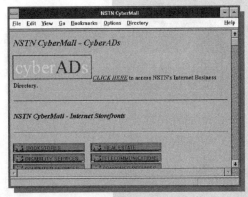

http://www.nstn.ns.ca/cybermall/cybermall.html
Bookstores; Disabilities; Real estate; Telecommunications

Goods and Services

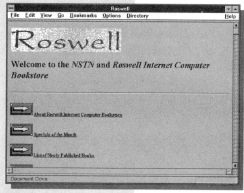

http://www.nstn.ns.ca/cybermall/roswell/roswell.html
Bookstore; Computer books; Gift

http://www.ocm.com/
Consultants; Hardware; Resellers; Software companies

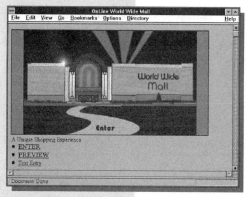

http://www.olworld.com/olworld/
Cybermall; Gifts; Online shopping

http://www.omix.com/
AMI news; Financial news; Online Marketspace; Ski conditions

http://www.onramp.net//infomart/infomart.html
Information services; Multimedia; Networking

http://www.onramp.net/imagemaker/
Dogs; Online pet stores; Pets

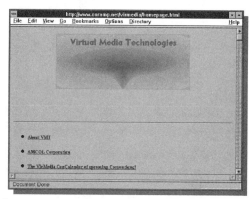

http://www.onramp.net/virmedia/homepage.html
Products and services; Virtual Media Technologies

http://www.openmarket.com/stores/directory.shtml
Demonstration stores; Information stores; Open Marketplace

http://www.organic.com/
Internet services; Organic Online

http://www.owl.net/
Advertising; OWL.net; Search for products or services

http://www.os2.iaccess.za/pgp/
Pam Golding Properties; PGP services; Real estate

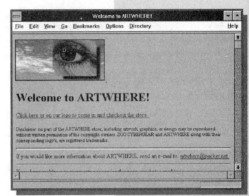

http://www.packet.net/business/artwhere/Welcome.html
Clothing; Fashion; Fashion accessories; Online gallery

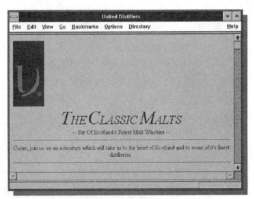

http://www.os2.iaccess.za/ud/
Online liquor; Scotland; Whiskey

http://www.packet.net/business/nge/Welcome.html
Gold; Online coin shop; Rare coins; Silver

http://www.oslonett.no/html/adv/advertisers.html
Lubricants; Metals; Norway

http://www.primenet.com/~jimb/hpimage.html
E-Mail; Homepage Imaging; Online shopping

255

Goods and Services

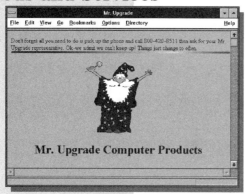

http://www.primenet.com/~jimb/mrupgrad.html
Computer products; Mr. Upgrade

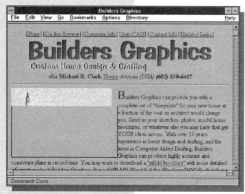

http://www.primenet.com/~mrclark/builders.html
Blueprints; Construction; Home building

http://www.primenet.com/art-rom/
Art-ROM; Digital communications; Marketing; Publishing

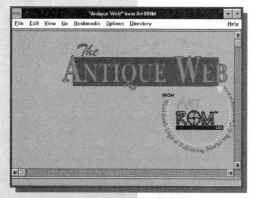

http://www.primenet.com/art-rom/antiqueweb/
Antique Web; Antiques; Art-ROM

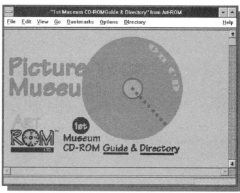

http://www.primenet.com/art-rom/cdromweb/
Art-ROM; CD-ROM guide; Directory; Museum

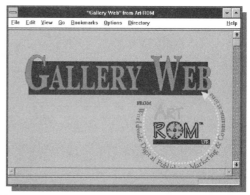

http://www.primenet.com/art-rom/galleryweb/
Art-ROM; Gallery Web

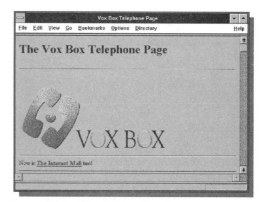

http://www.pubnix.net/~evan/
Internet mall; Telephone page; Vox Box

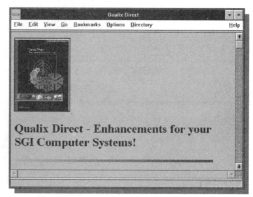

http://www.qualix.com/product/sgi/Welcome.html
Enhancements; Qualix Direct; SGI computer

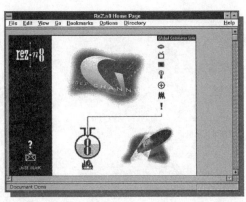

http://www.rezn8.com/
Advertising; Animation; Graphics; Images

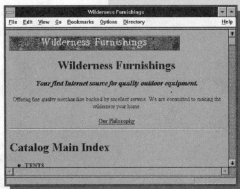

http://www.sccsi.com/Wilderness/wilderness.html
Hunting; Outdoor equipment; Sporting goods; Wilderness

http://www.saturncars.com/
Automobiles; Cars; Products and services; Saturn

http://www.sco.COM/Third/third.html
Santa Cruz Operations; SCO; Services; Third party products

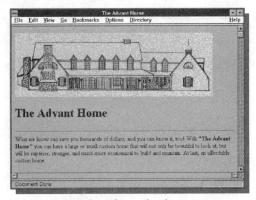

http://www.sccsi.com/Advant/homes.html
Architecture; Custom home

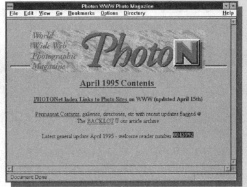

http://www.scotborders.co.uk/photon/
Images; Online photographic magazines; Photo sites

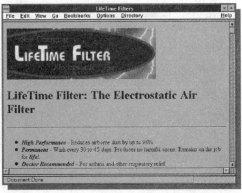

http://www.sccsi.com/LifeTime/lifetime_welcome.html
Air filters; Airborne dust; Asthma

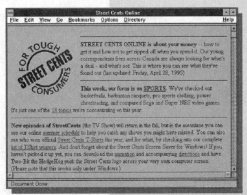

http://www.screen.com/streetcents.html
Buyer protection; Consumer information; Street Cents

257

Goods and Services

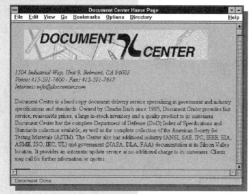

http://www.service.com/doccenter/home.html
Document delivery; Government standards; Hard copy

http://www.service.digital.com/html/emall.html
DEC; Future Fantasy Bookstore; Gifts

258

http://www.shopkeeper.com/shops/Ujamaa_Fashions/
African clothing; Batik; Online fashions; Women's clothing

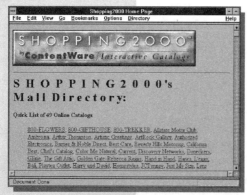

http://www.shopping2000.com/
800-Flowers; Gifts; Interactive Catalog; Online shopping

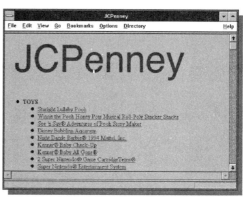

http://www.shopping2000.com/shopping2000/jcp/
Department stores; JCPenney; Online malls

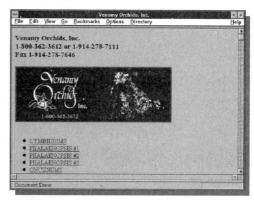

http://www.shopping2000.com/shopping2000/venamy/
Florist; Flowers; Online shopping; Venamy Orchids

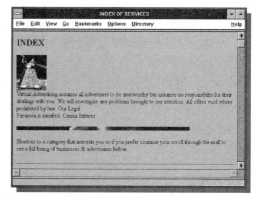

http://www.shore.net/~adfx/1.html
Catalogs; Food; Online advertising; Travel

http://www.sigma.unb.ca/
InterAd; Internet advertising; Marketing

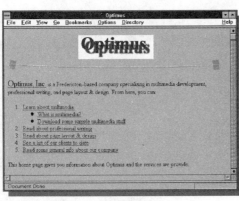

http://www.sigma.unb.ca/optimus/optimus.htm
Multimedia; Multimedia services; Page layout; Writing

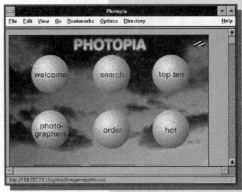

http://www.solutionsrc.com/PHOTOPIA/
Cameras; Pictures; Photography; Stock photos

http://www.sii.com/products/prodinfo.html
Product information; System Integrators

http://www.spectracom.com/designstudio/
Design studio; Jewelry; Picture frames

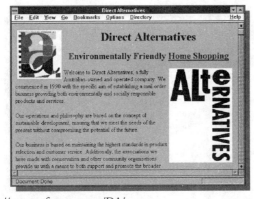

http://www.sofcom.com.au/DA/
Australia; Home shopping; Online shopping

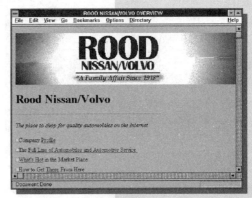

http://www.spry.com/rood/disc.html
Automobiles; Cars sales; Nissan; Volvo

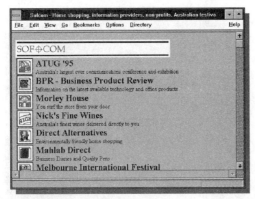

http://www.sofcom.com.au/Welcome.html
Australia; Melbourne; Tourism

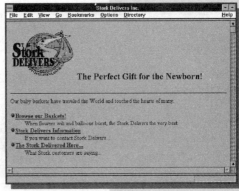

http://www.stork.com/sd.html
Gifts; Shopping; Presents for babies

Goods and Services

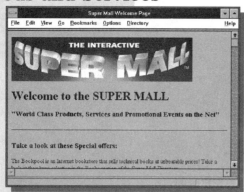

http://www.supermall.com/
CD-ROM; Employment; Publications; Software

http://www.tagsys.com/
Business services; Personal services; Retail; Travel

http://www.tagsys.com/Ads/TedJacobsen/
Real estate; Ted Burton Jacobsen; The Prudential

http://www.techimage.com/techimage
Public relations; Tech Image

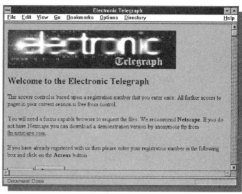

http://www.telegraph.co.uk/
Electronic telegraph; News; Periodicals

http://www.teleport.com/~codpiece/
Men's clothing; Online clothiers

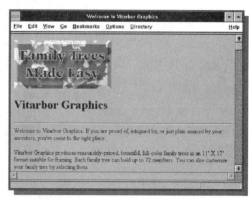

http://www.teleport.com/~jcrunch/vitarbor.html
Family trees; Vitarbor Graphics

http://www.teleport.com/~paulec/catalog.html
Accessories; Fashion; Jewelry

http://www.thegroup.net/impala/imphome.htm
Arts; Crafts; Impala Gallery; International

http://www.toystore.com/~wrt/
Ann Arbor; Gifts; Michigan; White Rabbit Toys

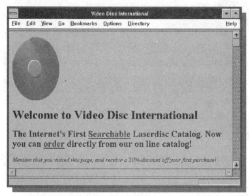

http://www.thesphere.com/VDI/
Catalog; Laserdisc; Video Disc International

http://www.trinet.com/allen.html
Advertising; Communications; Interactive marketing

http://www.tiac.net/users/visitech/home.html
High-tech gifts; Online store; Presents

http://www.tvisions.com/
Demos; Electronic books; Software; TeleVisions Inc.

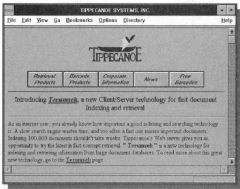

http://www.tippecanoe.com/
Client/server technology; Tecumseh; TIPPECANOE Systems

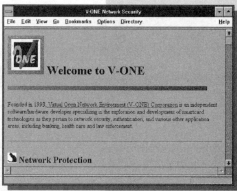

http://www.v-one.com/
Hardware; Smartcard; Software; V-ONE Network Security

Goods and Services

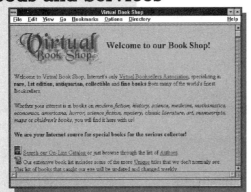

http://www.virtual.bookshop.com/
First editions; Online bookstores; Rare books

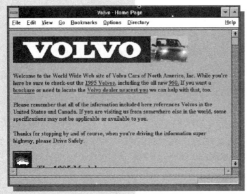

http://www.volvocars.com/
Automobiles; Cars; Dealers; Volvo

http://www.w2.com/
Online shopping; Products and services; World Square

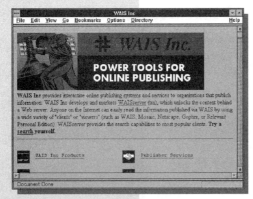

http://www.wais.com/
Electronic publishing; WAIS

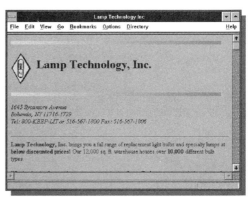

http://www.webscope.com/lamptech/info.html
Light bulbs; Online lighting stores

http://www.webscope.com/magnacom/homepage.html
Computer products; Hardware; Online stores; Supplies

http://www.wilder.com/eureka.html
Clothing; Food; Online stores; Shopping; Software

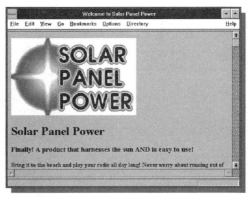

http://www.wilder.com/solar.html
Electricity; Energy conservation; High-tech gifts; Solar energy

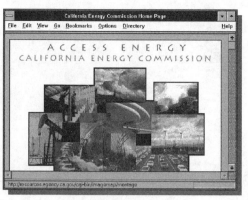

http://agency.resource.ca.gov/cechomepage.html
California; Energy; Environment

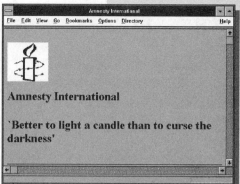

http://cyberzine.org/html/Amnesty/aihomepage.html
Amnesty International; Civil rights; Political prisoners

http://agency.resource.ca.gov/doc.html
California; Department of Conservation

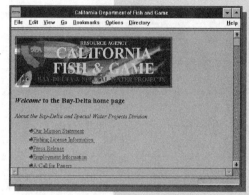

http://darkstar.delta.dfg.ca.gov/
Department of Fish and Game; Special Water Projects

263

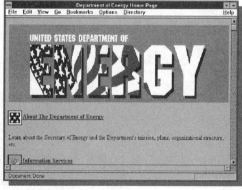

http://apollo.osti.gov/home.html
Department of Energy; Government; Mission; Plans

http://debra.dgbt.doc.ca/opengov
Business; Canada; Government

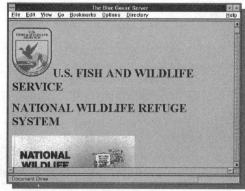

http://bluegoose.arw.r9.fws.gov/
Fish; Wildlife; Wildlife refuge

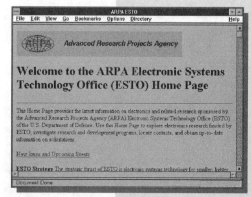

http://esto.sysplan.com/ESTO/
Advanced projects; ARPA; Government; Research

Government

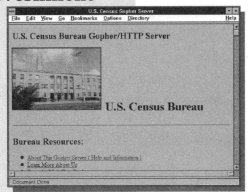

http://gopher.census.gov:70/
Census Bureau; Gopher server

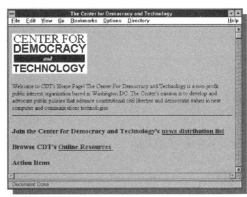

http://manning.cais.com/
Center for Democracy and Technology; Civil liberties

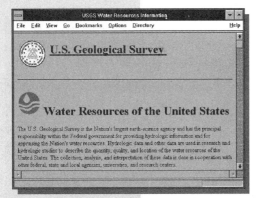

http://h2o.er.usgs.gov/
US Geological Survey; Water resources

http://math.nps.navy.mil/~mike/or.html
Department of Operations Research; Naval Postgraduate School

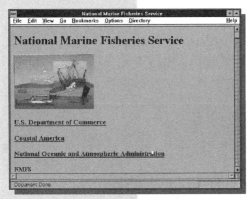

http://kingfish.ssp.nmfs.gov/home-page.html
Commerce; Fisheries; Marine; NOAA

http://munex.arme.cornell.edu/welcome.html
Cornell University; Local government

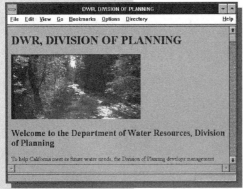

http://locke.water.ca.gov/
California; Department of Water Resources; Government

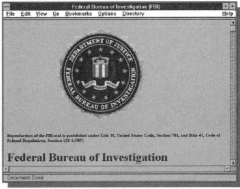

http://naic.nasa.gov/fbi/
Crime; FBI; Justice

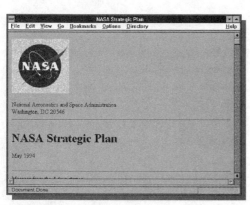

http://nctn.hq.nasa.gov/nsp/nsp.html
NASA; Space; Strategic plan

http://newproducts.jpl.nasa.gov/calendar
Events; NASA; Space calendar

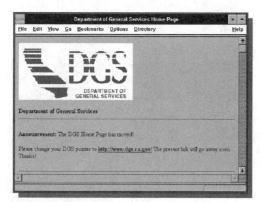

http://ois.dgs.ca.gov/dgs.html
California; Department of General Services

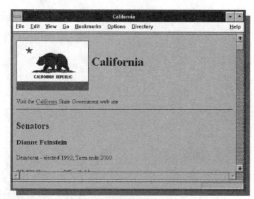

http://policy.net/capweb/States/CA/CA.html
California; Government; Politics

http://procure.msfc.nasa.gov/
Business; NASA; Procurement; Purchasing

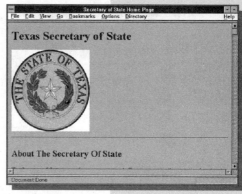

http://register.sos.texas.gov:80/
Secretary of State; Texas

265

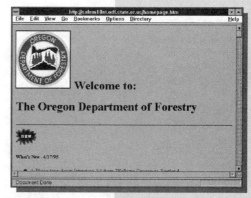

http://salem10nt.odf.state.or.us/homepage.htm
Forestry; Renewable resources; Trees

http://shango.harvard.edu/
Harvard University; JFK School of Government

Government

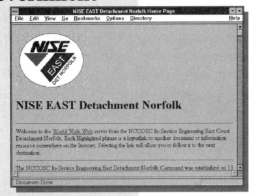

http://silk.nosc.mil/
Engineering; Government; NCCOSC

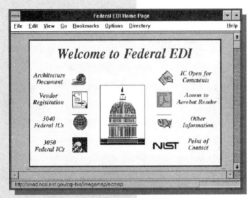

http://snad.ncsl.nist.gov/dartg/edi/fededi.html
Federal EDI

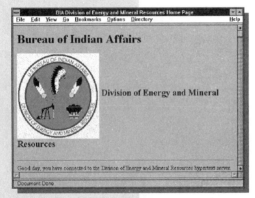

http://snake2.cr.usgs.gov:80/
Energy resources; Indian affairs; Mineral resources

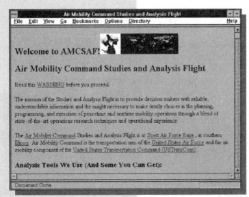

http://spartan.safb.af.mil/
Air Mobility Command; Scott Air Force Base

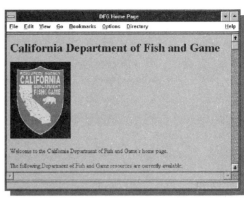

http://spock.dfg.ca.gov/
California; Fish and game

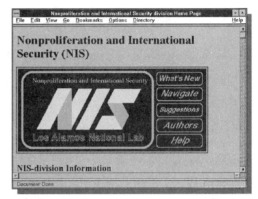

http://sst.lanl.gov:80/
Los Alamos National Laboratory; NIS

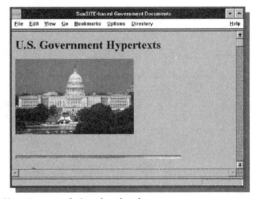

http://sunsite.unc.edu/govdocs.html
Contacts; Documents; Information; US Government

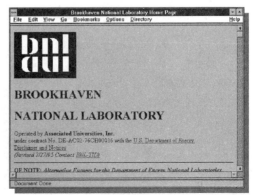

http://suntid.bnl.gov:8080/bnl.html
Alternative energy; Department of energy

http://tcomeng.com/cities/ssf/fire/index.html
South San Francisco Fire Department

http://tcomeng.com/cities/ssf/police/index.html
South San Francisco Police Department

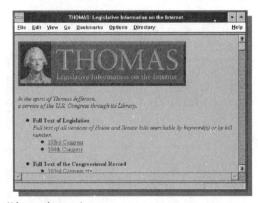

http://thomas.loc.gov/
Congress; Thomas Jefferson; Legislation

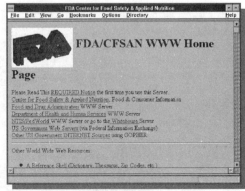

http://vm.cfsan.fda.gov/index.html
Food and consumer information; FDA

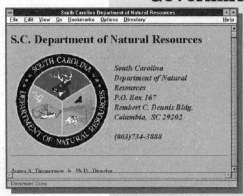

http://water.dnr.state.sc.us/www/dnr/dnr.html
Fish; Game; Natural resources; South Carolina; Wildlife

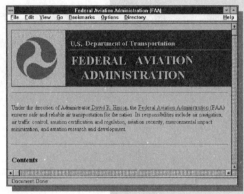

http://web.fie.com:80/web/fed/faa/
Air traffic control; Aviation; Aviation security; FAA

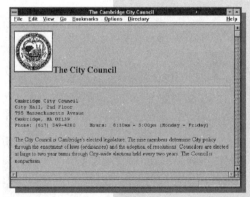

http://web.mit.edu/user/l/a/laszlo/cambridge/council.html
Cambridge; Local government

http://web.msu.edu/debate/debate.html
1992 Presidential debate; Bill Clinton; George Bush

Government

http://www.abag.ca.gov/
Bay area governement; Information services

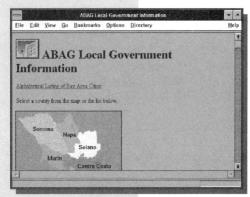

http://www.abag.ca.gov/abag/local_gov/local_gov.html
Bay Area; California; Local Government Information

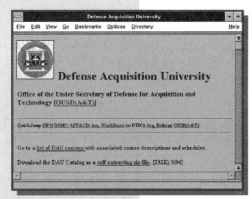

http://www.acq.osd.mil/dau/dau.html
Course descriptions; Defense acquisition; Government

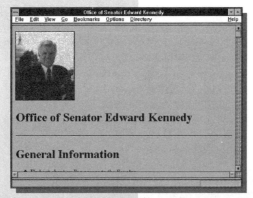

http://www.ai.mit.edu/projects/iiip/Kennedy/homepage.html
Kennedy; Politics; Senate

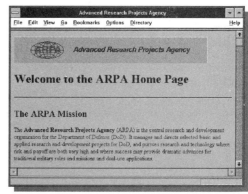

http://www.arpa.mil/
Advanced Research Projects Agency; Department of Defense

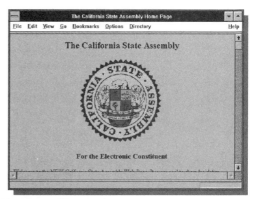

http://www.assembly.ca.gov/
California; Online news; State Assembly

http://www.bna.com/
Business; Government; Labor; Publisher

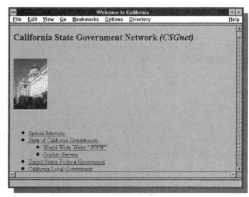

http://www.ca.gov/
California; State governments; Web sites

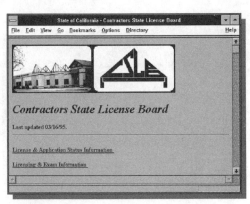

http://www.ca.gov/cslb/home.html
California; Contractors State License Board

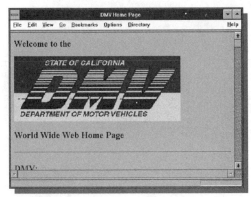

http://www.ca.gov/dmv/dmv.html
California; Department of Motor Vehicles

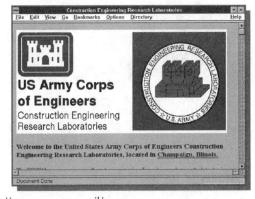

http://www.cecer.army.mil/
Government; US Army Corps of Engineering

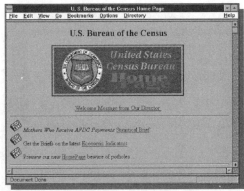

http://www.census.gov/
Census Bureau; Economic indicators; Population

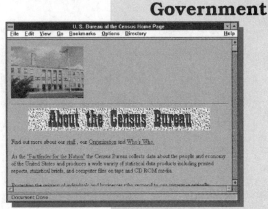

http://www.census.gov/About.html
Census Bureau; Information server

http://www.census.gov/dev/devcor.html
Electronic documents; HTML; Web

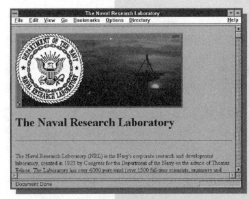

http://www.cmf.nrl.navy.mil/
Government; Naval Research Laboratory

http://www.doc.gov/
Commerce; Trade

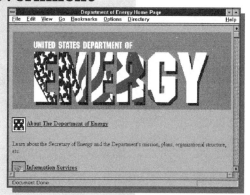

http://www.doe.gov/
Department of Energy; Mission; Organizational

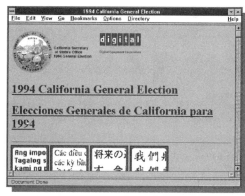

http://www.election.ca.gov/
California General Elections; DEC; Digital Equipment Group

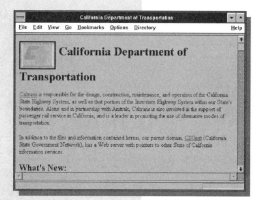

http://www.dot.ca.gov/
California Department of Transportation

http://www.fedworld.gov/
Government; Federal

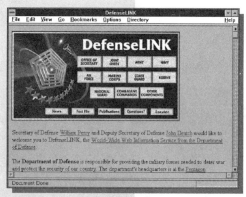

http://www.dtic.dla.mil/defenselink/
Defense; DefenseLINK; Military forces; Security

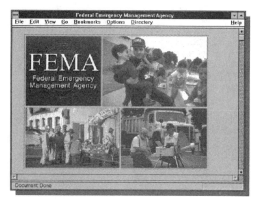

http://www.fema.gov/
Emergency Management Relief; FEMA

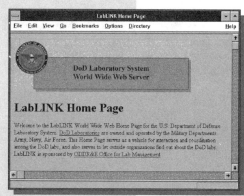

http://www.dtic.dla.mil/lablink
Department of Defense Laboratory System; LabLINK

http://www.fws.gov/
Government; US Fish and Wildlife Service

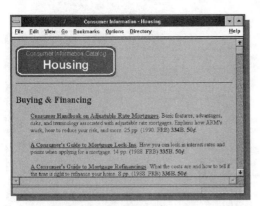

http://www.gsa.gov/staff/pa/cic/housing.htm
Consumer; Guide; Handbook; Housing; Mortgage

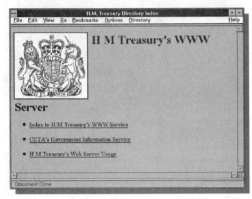

http://www.hm-treasury.gov.uk/
Treasury; United Kingdom

http://www.house.gov/
Congress; House of Representatives; Legislation

http://www.ic.gov/
CIA; Counterintelligence; Foreign intelligence; National security

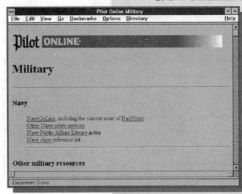

http://www.infi.net/pilot/military.html
Military; Navy ships; NavyOnline

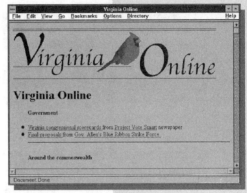

http://www.infi.net/vaonline.html
Around the commonwealth; Government; Virginia Online

271

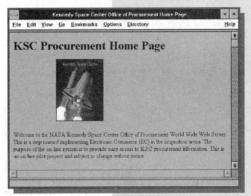

http://www.ksc.nasa.gov/procurement/procurement.html
NASA Kennedy Space Center; Procurement

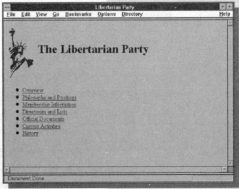

http://www.lp.org/lp/
History; Libertarian Party; Official documents; Philosophy

Government

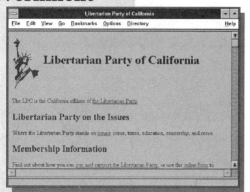

http://www.lp.org/lp/ca/lpc.html
California; Libertarian Party; Politics

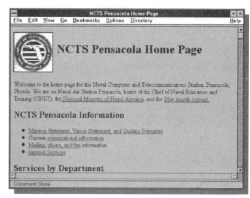

http://www.ncts.navy.mil/ncts/index.html
Blue Angels; Computers; Naval aviation; Telecommunications

http://www.nasa.gov/hqpao/hqpao_home.html
Events; History; Library; NASA

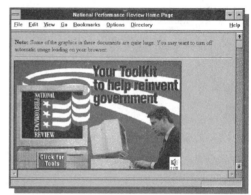

http://www.npr.gov/
Discussion; Government

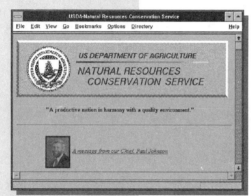

http://www.ncg.scs.ag.gov/
Agriculture; National Resources Conservation Service

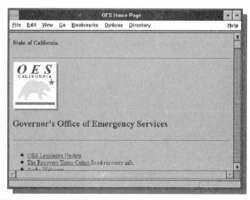

http://www.oes.ca.gov:8001/
California; Office of Emergency Services

http://www.ncts.navy.mil/
Defense; Military; Navy

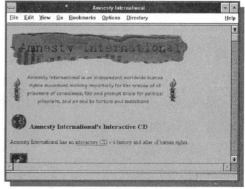

http://www.organic.com/Non.profits/Amnesty/index.html
Amnesty International; Human rights

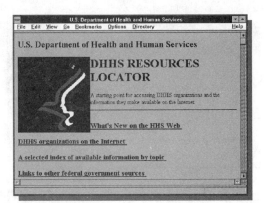

http://www.os.dhhs.gov/
Health and Human Services

http://www.pbs.org/
National programming; PBS; PBStore

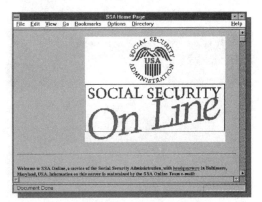

http://www.ssa.gov/
Government; Social Security Administration; SSA

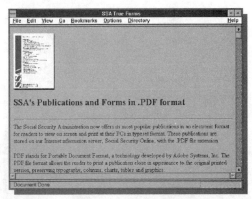

http://www.ssa.gov/OPA_Home/OPA_OI/pdffiles.html
Forms; Publications; Social Security Administration

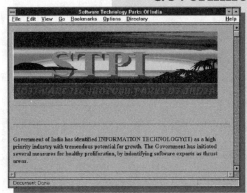

http://www.stph.net/
India; Information technology

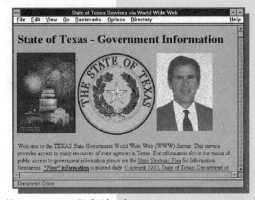

http://www.texas.gov/index.html
State; Texas; State Stragetic Plan

273

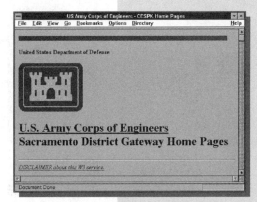

http://www.usace.mil/usace.html
Corps of Engineers; Department of Defense; US Army

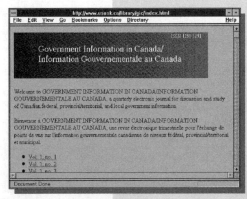

http://www.usask.ca/library/gic/index.html
Canada; Electronic journal; Government information

Graduate schools

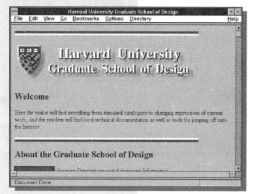

http://gsd.harvard.edu/
Design; Graduate school; Harvard University

http://heiwww.unige.ch/
Graduate Institute of International Studies; Switzerland

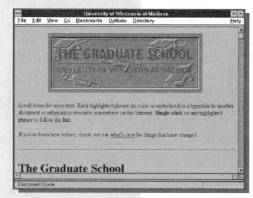

http://info.gradsch.wisc.edu/
Graduate school; Madison; University of Wisconsin

http://milieu.grads.vt.edu/
Virginia Polytechnic Institute and State University

http://minko.hyg.med.kyoto-u.ac.jp/
Japan; Kyoto University; Social and Preventive Medicine

http://www.agsm.unsw.edu.au/Welcome.html
Australian Graduate School of Management; Education

http://www.grad.uiuc.edu/
Graduate College; University of Illinois

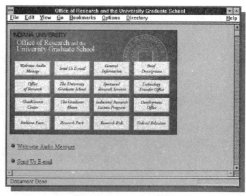

http://www.indiana.edu/~rugs/index.html
Indiana University; Small business grants; Technology

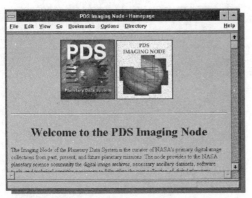

http://cdwings.jpl.nasa.gov/PDS/
NASA digital images; Planetary Data System

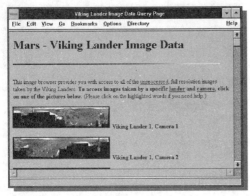

http://cdwings.jpl.nasa.gov/PDS/public/vikingl/vl_images.html
Mars; NASA digital images; Planetary Data System; Viking

http://colargol.edb.tih.no/~geirme/gizmos/gizmo.html
Icons; Images; Mosaic

http://cybermart.com/demars/demars.html
Images; Photo gallery

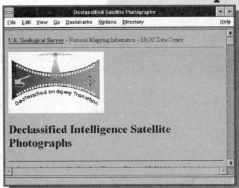

http://edcwww.cr.usgs.gov/dclass/dclass.html
Declassified; Images; Intelligence; Satellite Photographs

http://iguana.images.com/
Digital imagery; Display; Graphics; Production; Transmission

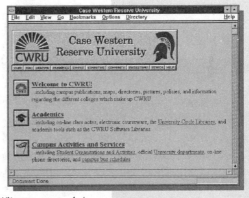

http://litwww.cwru.edu/
Case Western Reserve University; Graphics

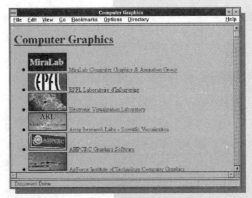

http://mambo.ucsc.edu/psl/cg.html
Animation; Computer graphics; Visualization

Graphics

http://mmm.wwa.com/tab/alibrary.htm
Art book; Graphics; Image

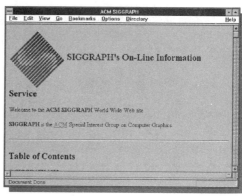

http://siggraph.org/
ACM; Computer graphics; SIGGRAPH

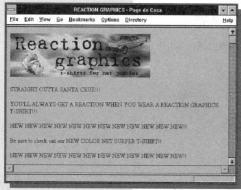

http://olt.et.tudelft.nl/fun/pictures/pictures.html
Digital picture archive; GIF; JPEG

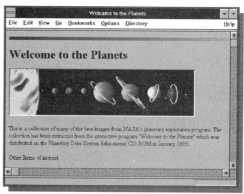

http://stardust.jpl.nasa.gov/planets/
Education; Images; NASA; Planetary exploration; Planets

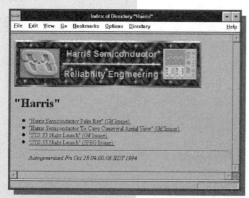

http://reaction.scruznet.com/
Graphics; Online shopping; T-shirts

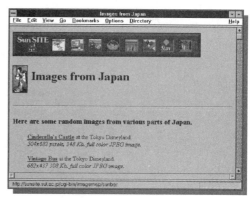

http://sunsite.sut.ac.jp/asia/japan/jpics.html
Images; Japan; Tokyo

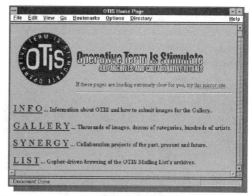

http://rel.semi.harris.com/ftp/pub/images/Harris/
Images; Reliability engineering; Semiconductor

http://sunsite.unc.edu/otis/otis.html
Artists; Gallery; Images; OTIS

276

http://turnpike.net/emporium/S/socal/index.html
Desktop publishing; Printing; Services; So Cal Graphics

http://www.awa.com/sfff/sfff.html
Fractals; San Francisco

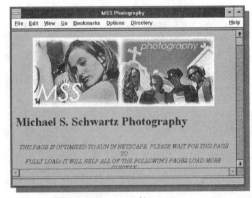

http://web.msu.edu/gallery/index.html
Campus beauty; Michigan State University; Photo gallery

http://www.graphics.cornell.edu/
Computer Graphics; Cornell University

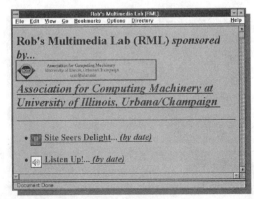

http://web.sirius.com/%7Emeatyard/
Photography services; Images

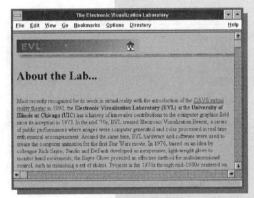

http://www.ncsa.uiuc.edu/EVL/docs/html/EVL.LAB.html
Animation; Electronic Visualization Laboratory

http://www.acm.uiuc.edu/rml/
Audio; Images; Multimedia Lab

http://www.ntua.gr/mandel/mandel.html
Fractals; Graphics

Health care

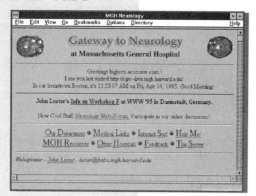

http://132.183.145.103/
Massachusetts General Hospital; Neurology

http://beach.silcom.com/~campbell/
Consultants; Managed health care

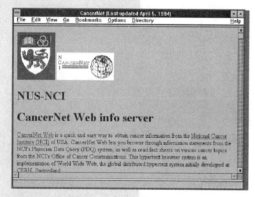

http://biomed.nus.sg/Cancer/welcome.html
Cancer; National Cancer Institute; Oncology

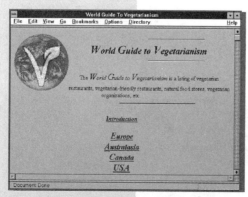

http://catless.ncl.ac.uk/Vegetarian/Guide/index.html
Food; Natural recipes; Restaurants; Vegetables

http://cipr-diva.mgh.harvard.edu/
Imaging; Pharmaceutical research

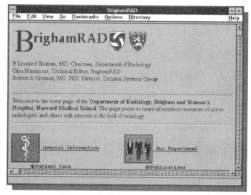

http://count51.med.harvard.edu/BWH/BWHRad.html
Harvard Medical School; Radiology

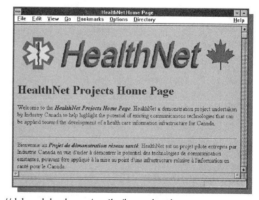

http://debra.dgbt.doc.ca/~mike/home.html
Canada; HealthNet; Medicine

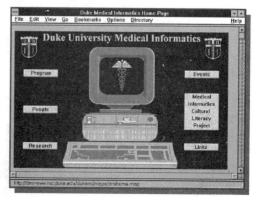

http://dmi-www.mc.duke.edu/
Duke University; Medical informatics

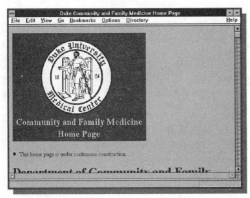

http://dmi-www.mc.duke.edu/cfm/cfmhome.html
Community medicine; Family medicine

http://fscn1.fsci.umn.edu/
Department of Food Science and Nutrition; Education

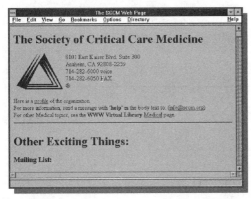

http://execpc.com/sccm
Critical care; Support groups

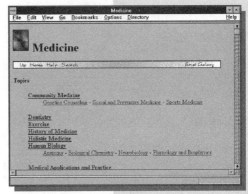

http://galaxy.einet.net/galaxy/Medicine.html
Community medicine; Dentistry; Exercise; Holistic

http://fohnix.metronet.com/~thearc/welcome.html
Arc of the United States; Mental retardation; National organization

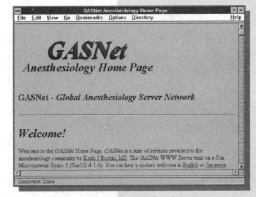

http://gasnet.med.nyu.edu/HomePage.html
Anesthesiology; Physicians

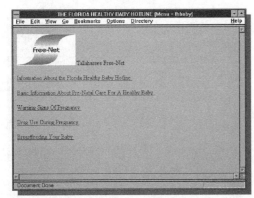

http://freenet3.scri.fsu.edu:81/ht-free/fhbaby.html
Birth; Breast feeding; Infants; Parenting; Pregnancy

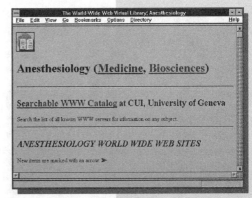

http://gasnet.med.nyu.edu/index.html
Anesthesiology; Biosciences; Medicine

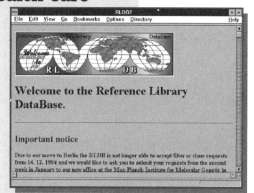

http://gea.lif.icnet.uk/
Molecular genetics; Reference database

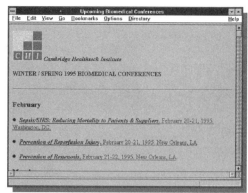

http://id.wing.net/~chi/upcoming.html
Biomedical conferences; Cambridge Healthtech

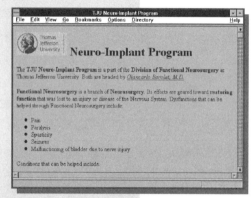

http://he1.uns.tju.edu/~doctorb/bppp.html
Functional neurosurgery; Neuro-implantation

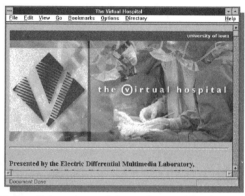

http://indy.radiology.uiowa.edu/VirtualHospital.html
Multimedia; Virtual Hospital

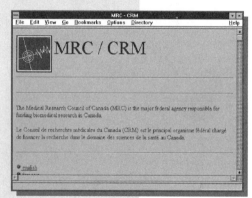

http://hpb1.hwc.ca:8100/
Biomedical research; Canada; French

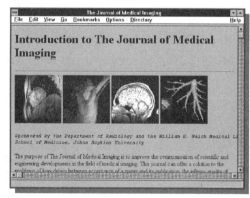

http://jmi.gdb.org/JMI/ejourn.html
Johns Hopkins University; Medical imaging

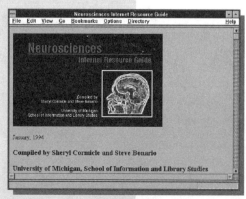

http://http2.sils.umich.edu/Public/nirg/nirg1.html
Neurosciences; University of Michigan

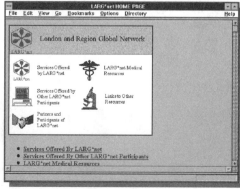

http://johns.largnet.uwo.ca/
LARG*net; London and region; Medical services

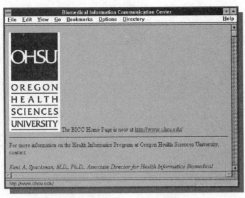

http://main.ohsu.edu/
Health informatics; Oregon Health Sciences

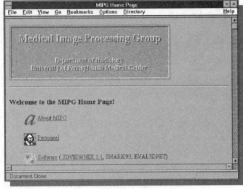

http://mipgsun.mipg.upenn.edu/
Medical Image Processing; University of Pennsylvania

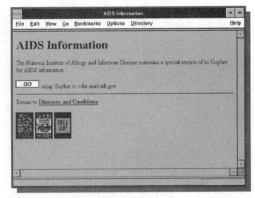

http://nearnet.gnn.com/wic/health.03.html
AIDS; National Institute of Allergy and Infectious Diseases

http://nightingale.con.utk.edu:70/0/homepage.html
Nursing; University of Tennessee; Web sites

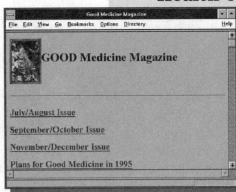

http://none.coolware.com/health/good_med/ThisIssue.html
Good Medicine Magazine; Health care; Publications

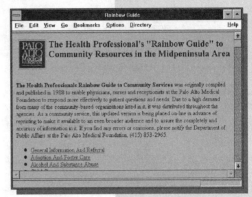

http://none.coolware.com/health/pamf/rg/RG.html
Health professionals; Nurses; Physicians; Receptionists

281

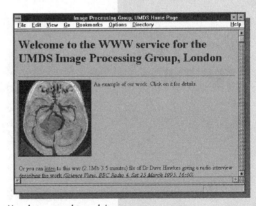

http://nothung.umds.ac.uk/
Image processing; Medicine

http://nysernet.org/bcic/
Breast cancer; Oncology

Health care

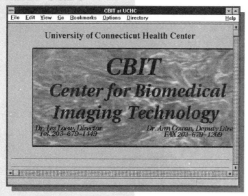

http://panda.uchc.edu/htbit/
Biomedical imaging

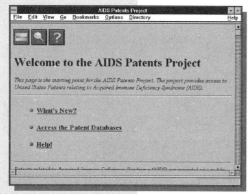

http://patents.cnidr.org/welcome.html
AIDS; Patent databases

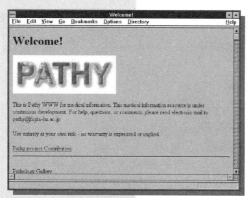

http://pathy.fujita-hu.ac.jp/pathy.html
Medicine; Pathology; Gallery

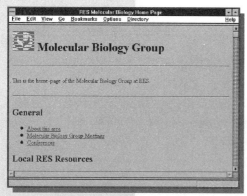

http://resc9.res.bbsrc.ac.uk/plantpath/molbio/
Molecular biology; Group events

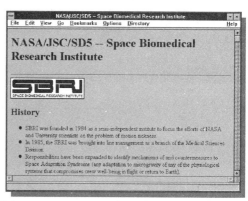

http://sd-www.jsc.nasa.gov/orgchart/sd5.html
Biomedical research; NASA; Space

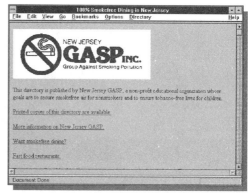

http://sunsite.unc.edu/boutell/infact/gasp/gasp.html
GASP; Group Against Smoking Pollution; New Jersey

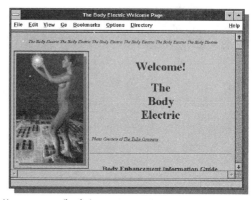

http://surgery.com/body/
Beautification; Body Electric

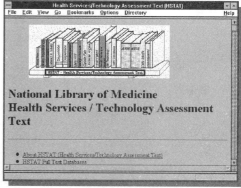

http://text.nlm.nih.gov/
Health services; National Library of Medicine

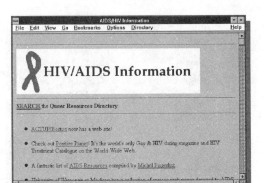

http://vector.casti.com/QRD/.html/AIDS.html
AIDS; AIDS resources; HIV

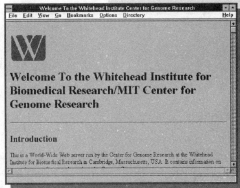

http://www-genome.wi.mit.edu/
Biomedical research; Genome research

http://vvv.com/HealthNews/
Blood pressure; International news; Vasectomy

http://www.acupuncture.com/acupuncture/
Acupuncture; Chinese; Herbology; Massage

http://web.fie.com/web/fed/nih/
National Institute of Allergy and Infectious Diseases; NIAID

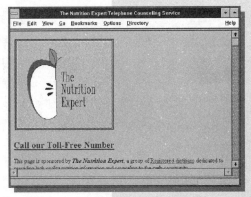

http://www.alaska.net/~tne/
Counseling; Dietitians; Information; Nutrition

http://www-busph.bu.edu/
Boston University; Public health

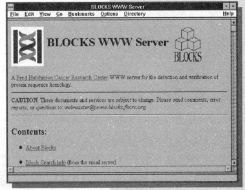

http://www.blocks.fhcrc.org/
Cancer; Protein sequence homology

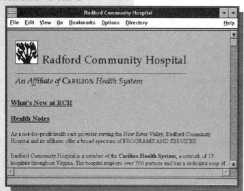

http://www.bnt.com/~rch
Health notes; Radford Community Hospital; Virginia

http://www.c3.lanl.gov/cic3/projects/Medical/main.html
Los Alamos National Laboratory; Medical data

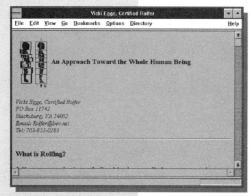

http://www.bnt.com/~rolfer/
Health; Massage; Rolfing

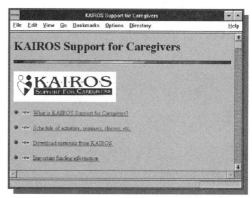

http://www.catalog.com/kairos/welcome.htm
AIDS; Caregivers; Education; KAIROS; Support group

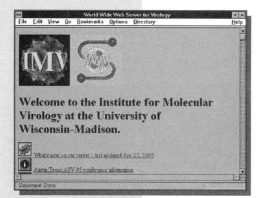

http://www.bocklabs.wisc.edu/
Science; Virology; Virus; Wisconsin

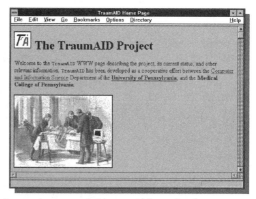

http://www.cis.upenn.edu/~traumaid/home.html
Trauma; University of Pennsylvania

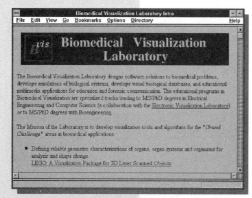

http://www.bvis.uic.edu/
Biomedical software; Biomedical visualization

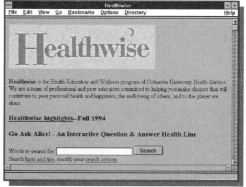

http://www.columbia.edu/cu/healthwise/
Health education; Interactive question and answer

http://www.cpmc.columbia.edu/
Degree programs; Medical informatics

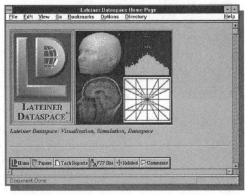

http://www.dataspace.com/
Computing; Simulation; Visualization

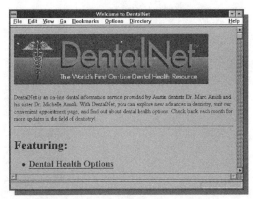

http://www.dentalnet.com/dentalnet/
Dental health; Dentistry

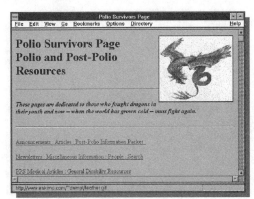

http://www.eskimo.com/~dempt/polio.html
Polio; Polio survivors; Post-Polio resources

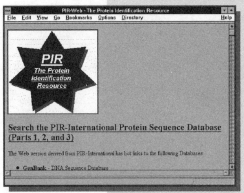

http://www.gdb.org/Dan/proteins/pir.html
Protein identification; Protein sequence database

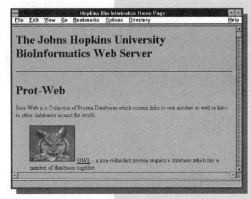

http://www.gdb.org/hopkins.html
Bioinformatics; Protein database; Protein sequence

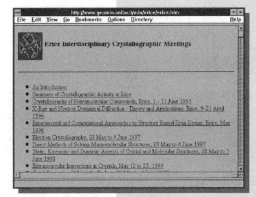

http://www.geomin.unibo.it/min/erice/erice.htm
Crystals; Drug design; Supramolecular compounds

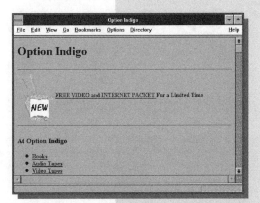

http://www.human.com/mkt/option/indigo/index.html
Audio; Books; Couples; Families; Tapes; Video

285

Health care

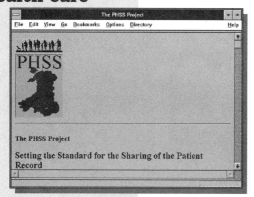

http://www.ihi.aber.ac.uk/IHI/phss.html
Health; Patient records

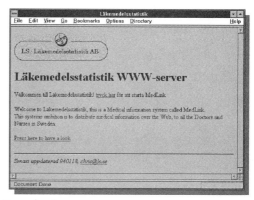

http://www.ls.se/
Medical information; MedLink; Sweden

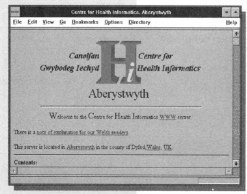

http://www.ihi.aber.ac.uk/index.html
Centre for Health Informatics; University of Wales; Welsh

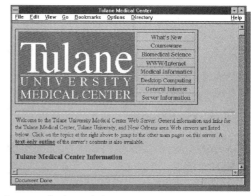

http://www.mcl.tulane.edu/
Education; Tulane University Medical Center

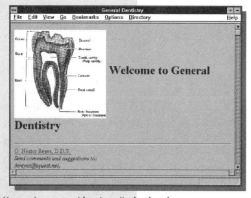

http://www.iquest.net/dentistry/index.html
General Dentistry resources

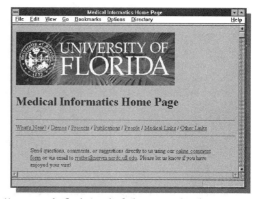

http://www.med.ufl.edu/medinfo/homepage.html
Medical informatics; University of Florida

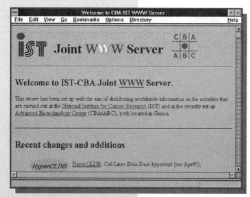

http://www.ist.unige.it/
Advanced biotechnology; Cancer research

http://www.nih.gov/
Health; Medicine; National Institute of Health

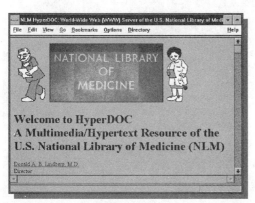

http://www.nlm.nih.gov/
Health; Multimedia; US National Library of Medicine

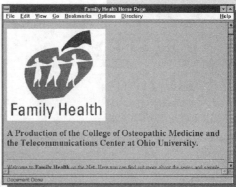

http://www.tcom.ohiou.edu/family-health.html
Audio; Osteopathy; Telecommunications

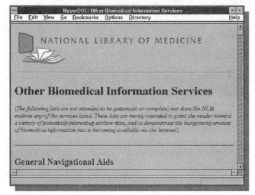

http://www.nlm.nih.gov/current_news.dir/biomed.html
Biomedical; National Library of Medicine

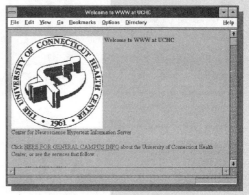

http://www.uchc.edu/
Medicine; Neuroscience; University of Connecticut

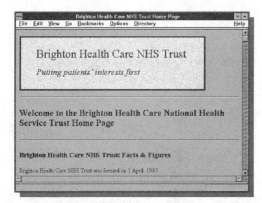

http://www.pavilion.co.uk/HealthServices/BrightonHealthCare/
Brighton; Health care; Medicine

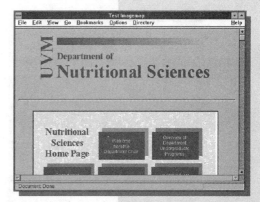

http://www.uvm.edu/nusc/intro.html
Department of Nutritional Sciences; Education

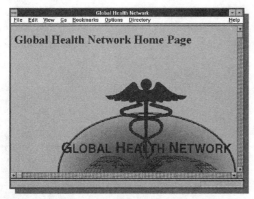

http://www.pitt.edu/~amy/ghn/ghn.html
Global Health Network

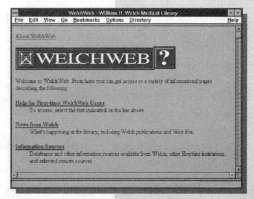

http://www.welch.jhu.edu/
Medical library; Medical resources

History

http://arcweb.sos.state.or.us/osuhomepage.html
Farmers; Oregon; Oregon State University; World War II

http://eMall.Com/ExploreNY/NY1.html
Battery Park; Dutch; Manhattan; New York

http://hampton.roads.net/nhr/williamsburg/
Community information; History; Williamsburg

http://http2.sils.umich.edu/HCHS/
Health sciences; Medicine

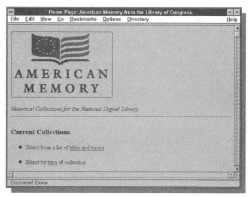

http://lcweb2.loc.gov/amhome.html
Collections; Library of Congress; Recordings

http://sunsite.unc.edu/expo/1492.exhibit/Intro.html
Christopher Columbus; Discovery; New World

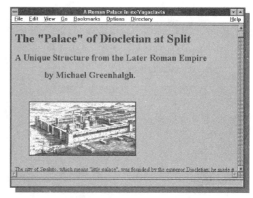

http://sunsite.unc.edu/expo/palace.exhibit/intro.html
Architecture; Roman Empire

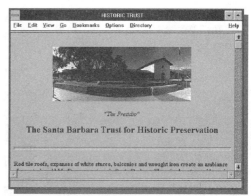

http://www.artdirect.com/sbthp/
Historic preservation; Santa Barbara Trust

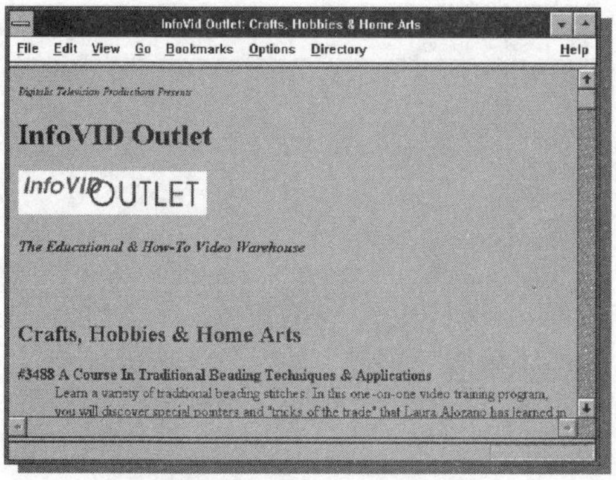

http://branch.com:1080/infovid/c313.html
Arts; Crafts; Education; Hobbies

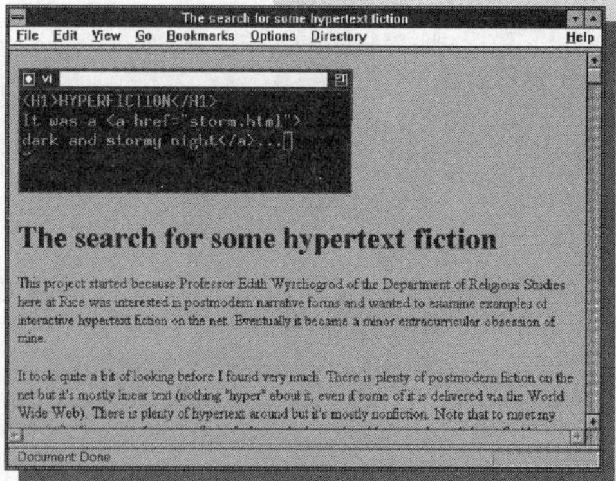

http://is.rice.edu/~riddle/hyperfiction.html
Hypertext fiction; Search

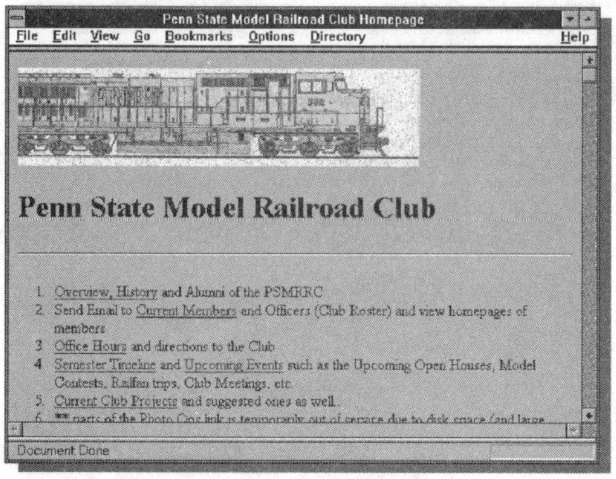

http://cac.psu.edu/~jha105/psmrrc.html
Model Railroad Club; Penn State University

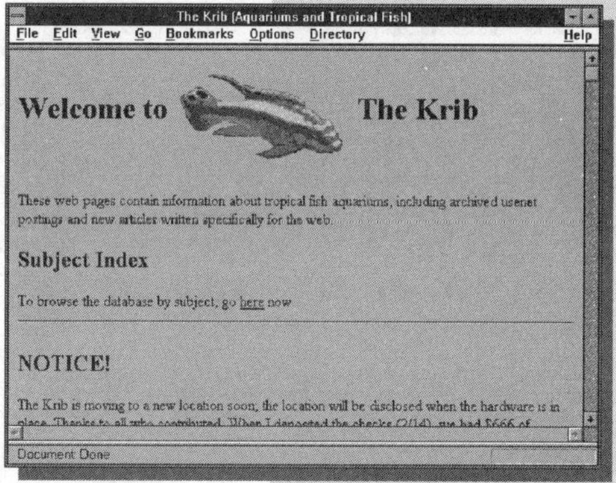

http://marge.phys.washington.edu/fish/index.html
Aquariums; Tropical fish

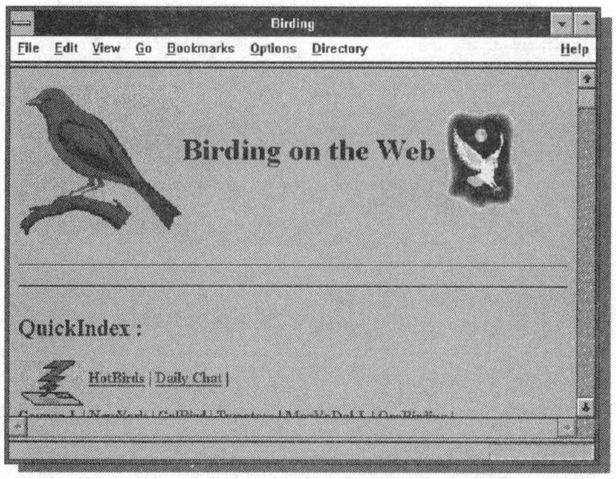

http://compstat.wharton.upenn.edu:8001/~siler/birding.html
Bird watching; Hobbies; Ornithology

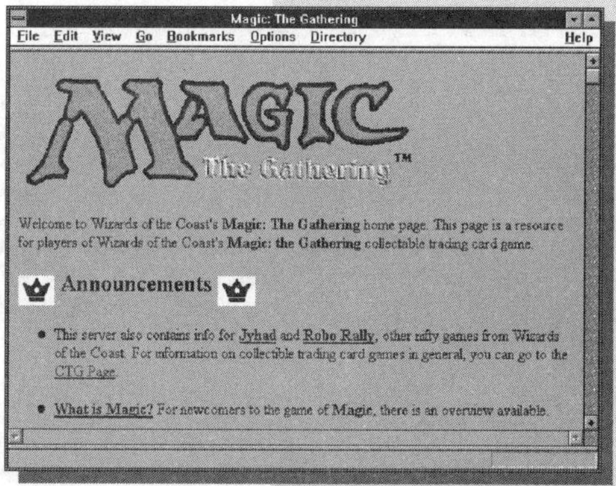

http://marvin.macc.wisc.edu/deckmaster/magic
Collecting; Trading cards

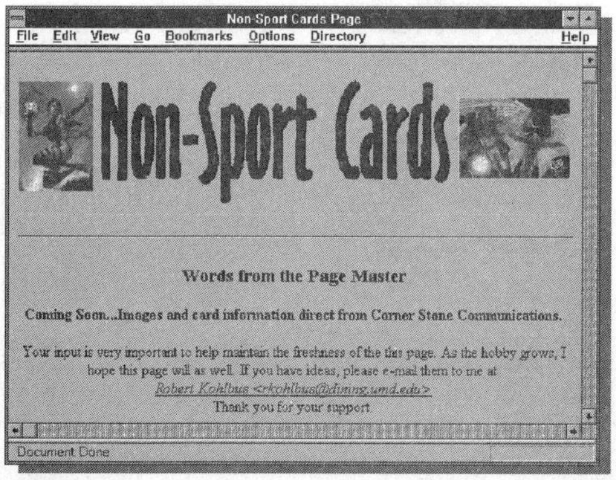

http://empire.umd.edu/
Collections; Electronic images; Hobbies

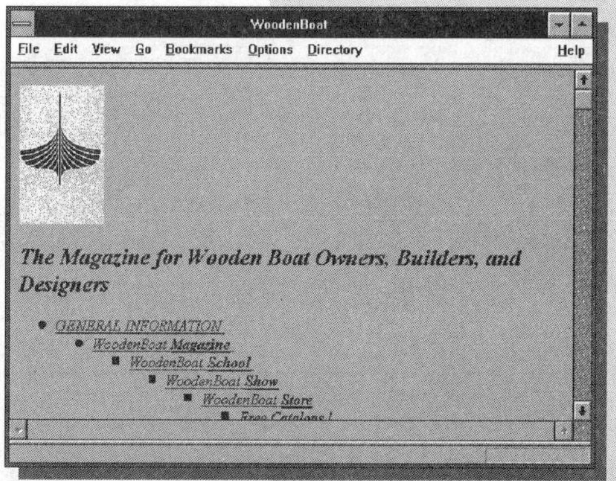

http://media1.hypernet.com/WoodenBoat.html
Boats; Hobbies; Marine; Ships

Hobbies

http://motorcycle.com/motorcycle.html
Bikes; Motorcycle Online; Resources

http://ttsw.com/MainQuiltingPage.html
Sewing; Stitching

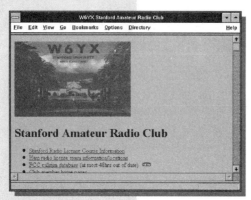

http://w6yx.stanford.edu/w6yx.html
Amateur Radio Club; Ham radio; Stanford

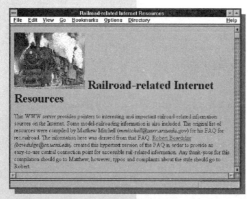

http://www-cse.ucsd.edu/users/bowdidge/railroad/rail-home.html
Collecting; Modeling; Railroads

http://www.abmall.com/kk/dolls.html
Girl's clothes; Handmade doll clothes; Handsewn

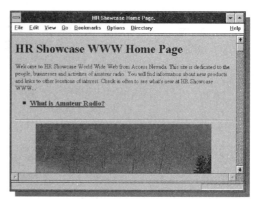

http://www.accessnv.com/hrshow
Amateur radio; HAM radio; Hobbies

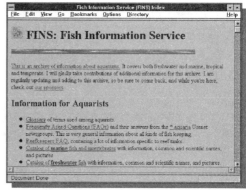

http://www.actwin.com/fish/
Aquaria; Fish Information service; Marine fish and invertebrates

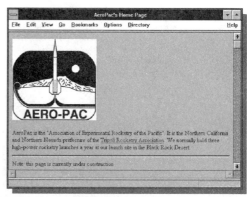

http://www.aeropac.org/aeropac/
Experimental rocketry; Models; Rockets

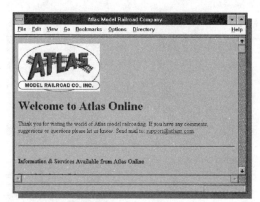

http://www.atlasrr.com/atlasrr/
Models; Railroad; Railroading

http://www.atlasrr.com/atlasrr/layouts/web.layouts/sandiego.html
Models; Museum; Railroad; Railroading; San Diego

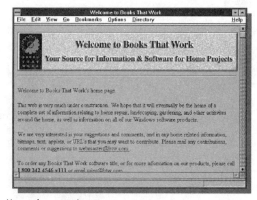

http://www.btw.com/
Gardening; Home repair; Landscaping

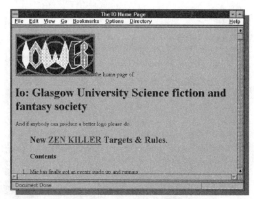

http://www.dcs.gla.ac.uk/~pageth/IO/Ioweb.html
Fantasy; Science fiction

http://www.elpress.com:80/staunton/ANTQS.HTML
Antiques; Collectibles; Furniture; Hobbies; Virginia

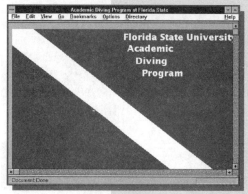

http://www.fsu.edu:80/CS-projects/diving/
Diving; Florida State University

http://www.hal.com/services/juggle/
Hobbies; Juggling; Recreation

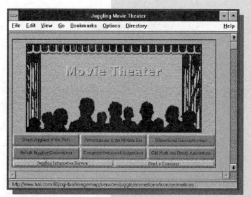

http://www.hal.com/services/juggle/animations
Entertainers; Hobbies; Juggling

Humor

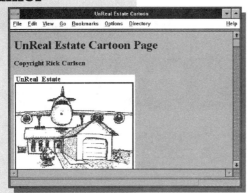

http://mindlink.net/Rick_Carlsen/unreal.htm
Cartoons; Humor

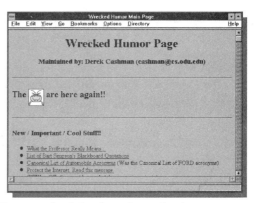

http://www.cs.odu.edu/~cashman/humor.html
Humor; Jokes

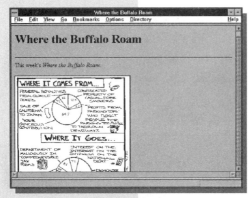

http://plaza.xor.com/wtbr/index.html
Cartoons; Jokes; Parodies

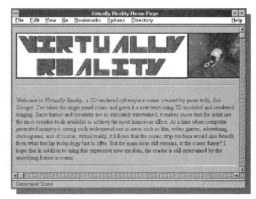

http://www.onramp.net/~scroger/vreality.html
3D graphics; Comics; Humor

http://sunsite.unc.edu/Dave/archive.html
Cartoons; Comics

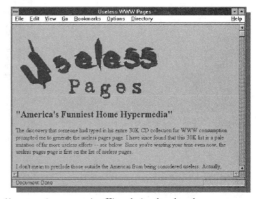

http://www.primus.com/staff/paulp/useless.html
Humor; Hypermedia; Useless

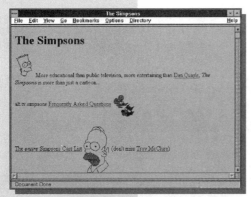

http://turtle.ncsa.uiuc.edu/alan/simpsons.html
Bart; Homer; The Simpsons

http://zeb.nysaes.cornell.edu/CGI/ctoons.cgi
Cartoons; Comics

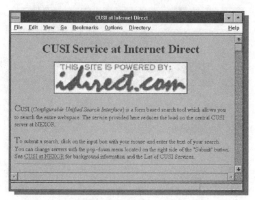

http://abyss.idirect.com/cusi.html
CUSI; Internet Direct; Web Search

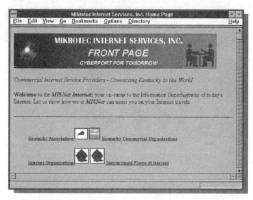

http://andromeda.mis.net/
Internet service provider; Kentucky

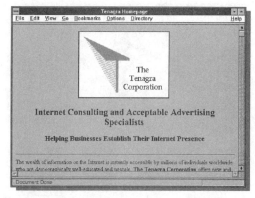

http://arganet.tenagra.com/
Advertising; Consulting; Internet

http://aun.uninett.no/
Information server; Norway; Web server

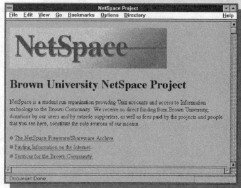

http://baldrick.cecer.army.mil/hyplans/burnett/MDB/
Brown University; Information sources; Internet

http://barrnet.net/
BARRNET; Internet Services Corporation

293

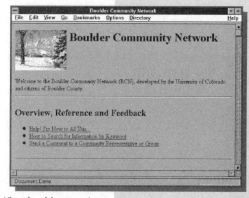

http://bcn.boulder.co.us/
Boulder Colorado; Community; Culture

http://bud.peinet.pe.ca/
Digital gallery; Internet road trips; Tips

Internet/WWW services

http://catalog.com/aaart/
Business services; Design; Installation; Management

http://community.net/ais/index.html
Electronic publishing; Internet; Telecommunications

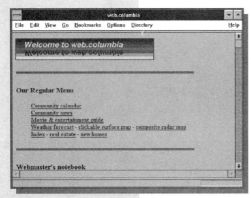

http://catalog.com/columbia/
Community; Entertainment; News; Real estate; Weather

http://crash.cts.com/
Business presence; CTS; Network Services

http://chiba.picosof.com:7777/
Multimedia; Sprawl; Web access

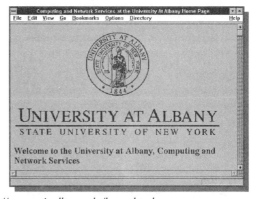

http://cscmosaic.albany.edu/home.html
Education; University of Albany

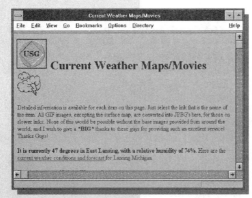

http://clunix.cl.msu.edu:80/weather
Forecasts; Meteorology; Weather maps

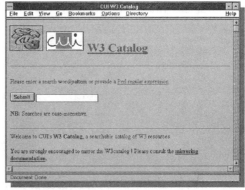

http://cuiwww.unige.ch/w3catalog
Perl; Searching; Web sites; WWW Resources

294

http://curry.edschool.virginia.edu/murray/tutorial/Tutorial.html
Browsers; Mosaic; Networks; Teaching

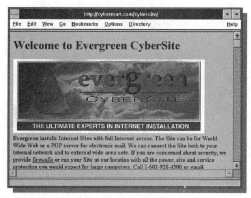

http://cybermart.com/
Evergreen Internet; Internet service provider

http://cybermart.com/cybersite/
Arizona; Evergreen; Internet access

http://daneel.sds.no/htdocs/sds/SDS-hoved-n.html
Norway; Statens Datasentral a.s; Web server

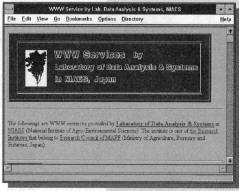

http://das.niaes.affrc.go.jp/WWW/index.html
Japan; NIAES; WWW Services

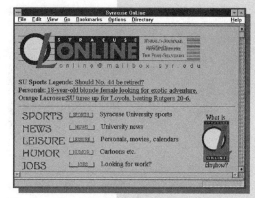

http://dataserver.syr.edu:8080/HTTPB/syronline.html
News; Newspapers; Syracuse University

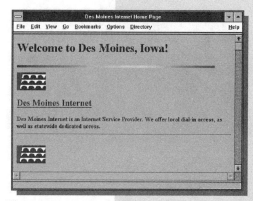

http://dsm6.dsmnet.com/welcome.html
Des Moines; Internet access; Iowa

http://enemy.gsfc.nasa.gov/sswg/SSWG.html
Information resources; Space science; Web

295

Internet/WWW services

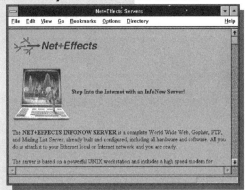

http://energetic.com/net-effects/infonow_server.html
FTP; Gopher; Hardware; Mailing list; Software; Web

http://fuzine.mt.cs.cmu.edu/mlm/lycos-all.html
Lycos; Web searching; WWW information

http://espresso.cafe.net/
Cafe; Espresso; Java

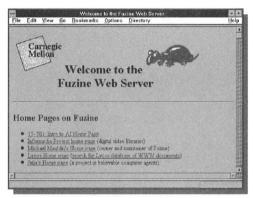

http://fuzine.mt.cs.cmu.edu/Welcome.html
Carnegie Mellon; Computer agents; Fuzine; Introduction to AI

http://fender.onramp.net/
Internet access; OnRamp Online; Web site

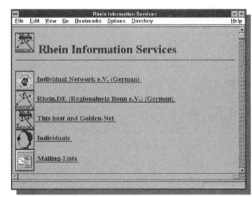

http://gak.rhein.de:80/
German; Mailing lists; Rhein information services

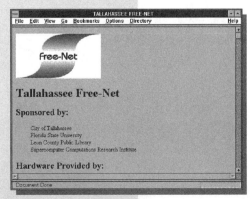

http://freenet3.scri.fsu.edu:81/
Florida State University; Tallahassee Free-Net

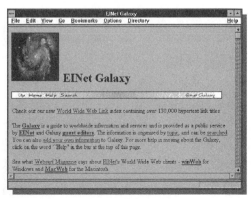

http://galaxy.einet.net/galaxy.html
Browsers; Information services

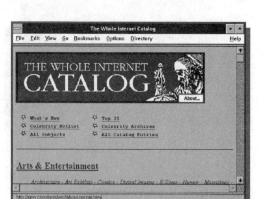

http://gnn.com/gnn/wic/index.html
Directories; Links; News; The Whole Internet Catalog; Web

http://harvest.cs.colorado.edu/
Harvest Information Discovery and Access System; Internet tools

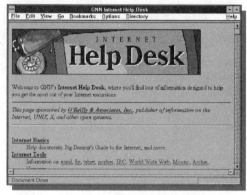

http://gnn.interpath.net/gnn/helpdesk/index.html
Guide; Internet help desk; Tools

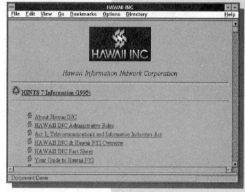

http://hinc.hinc.hawaii.gov/hinc/hawaii_inc.html
Guide; Hawaii; Information services

http://gnofn.org/
Community information; New Orleans

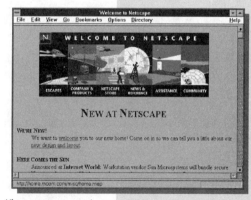

http://home.mcom.com/
Netscape; Services; Web browsers

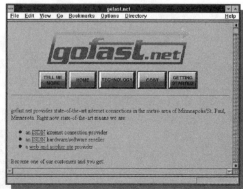

http://gofast.net/
Internet service provider; ISDN; Minneapolis/St. Paul

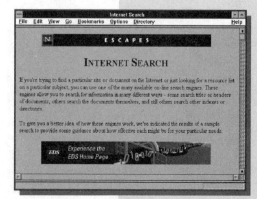

http://home.mcom.com/home/internet-search.html
Internet search; Resource list; Search engines

Internet/WWW services

http://hyperg.tu-graz.ac.at/6C950B/Cjargon
Collection; Hacker's Jargon; Help

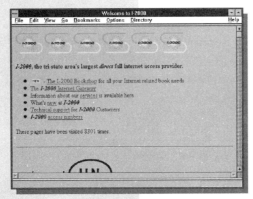

http://i-2000.com/
Books; I-2000 Bookshop; Internet

http://idom-www.informatik.uni-hamburg.de:80/
IDOM; Information service; Multimedia

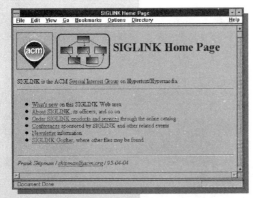

http://info.acm.org/siglink/
ACM; Hypertext/Hypermedia; Special Internet Group

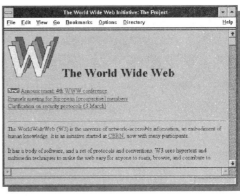

http://info.cern.ch/
CERN; Protocols; Research

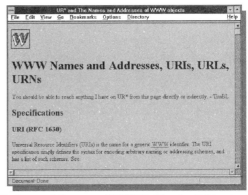

http://info.cern.ch/hypertext/WWW/Addressing/Addressing.html
URIs; URLs; URNs; WWW Names and Address

http://info.cern.ch/hypertext/WWW/FAQ/Bootstrap.html
Getting started; W3; World Wide Web

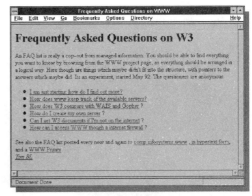

http://info.cern.ch/hypertext/WWW/FAQ/List.html
Frequently asked questions; Internet; Web

298

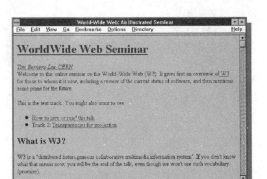

http://info.cern.ch/hypertext/WWW/Talks/General.html
W3; Web Seminar; WWW

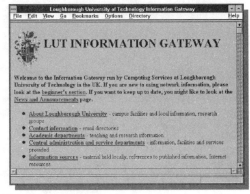

http://info.lut.ac.uk/home.html
Education; Loughborough University of Technology; UK

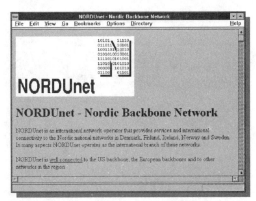

http://info.nordu.net/
Denmark Finland Iceland Norway and Sweden; Internet access

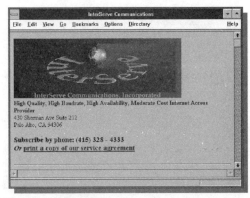

http://interserve.com/is.html
Internet service provider; InterServe Communications

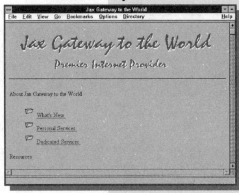

http://jax.gttw.com/Jax-GTTW/index.html
Florida; Internet service provider

http://jwflorencecomm.com/~the/Place.html
JW Florence Communications; Web links

http://lafn.org/
California; Canada; Education resources; Libraries; Medical

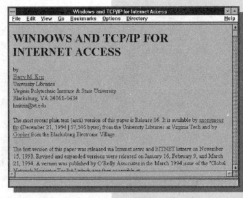

http://learning.lib.vt.edu/wintcpip/wintcpip.html
Internet access; TCP/IP; University libraries

Internet/WWW services

http://leonardo.net/
Computer graphics; Internet access; Programming

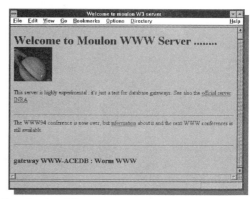

http://moulon.inra.fr/
Database gateways; WWW94 conference

http://login.eunet.no/~presno/index.html
Global communication; Online World

http://netmedia.com/
Communication; Internet Media Services; Product and services

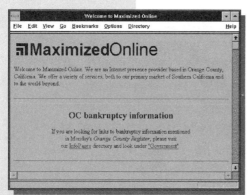

http://maxonline.com/maxonline/
Bankruptcy; California; Internet provider; Orange County

http://netwings.com/
Internet presence; Macintosh; NetWings; Software

http://metaverse.com/vibe/onramp/onramp.html
Internet access; On Ramp Inc.

http://none.coolware.com/
Coolware; Graphics; Internet resources

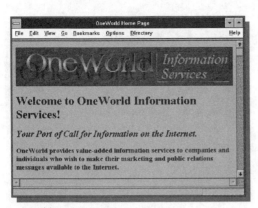

http://oneworld.wa.com/
Business; Informations; Northeast US

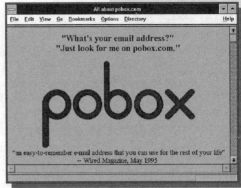

http://pobox.com/pobox/frommenghome.html
E-Mail address services

http://onr.com/
Financial; Internet access; News; Provider

http://pubweb.parc.xerox.com/
Palo Alto Research Center; Xerox PARC

301

http://pacificrim.com/
Internet connectivity; Pacific Rim Network

http://quiknet.com/quiknet.html
Internet service provider; World Wide Web Service

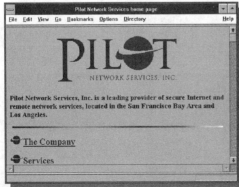

http://pilot.net/
Los Angeles; Remote network; San Francisco; Secure Internet

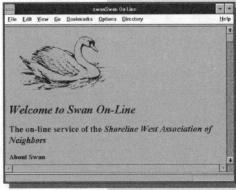

http://reality.sgi.com/csp/swan/
California; Community services; Mountain View; Online

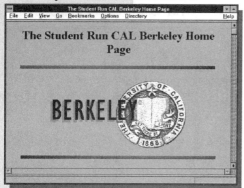

http://server.berkeley.edu:80/
Education; University of California Berkeley

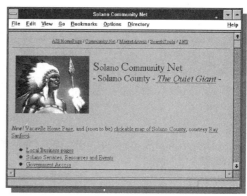

http://solano.community.net/community/solano/index2.html
Local businesses; Solano Community services

http://sjcpl.lib.in.us/MFNet/MFNetMainMenu.html
Community information; Indiana; Michiana; Services

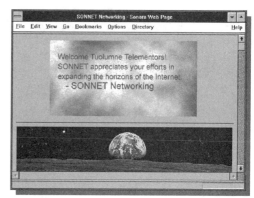

http://sonnet.com/
Internet service provider; Sonora

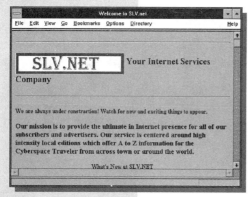

http://slv.net/
Advertising; Internet services; News

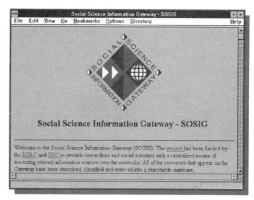

http://sosig.esrc.bris.ac.uk/
Social science; SOSIG; Welfare

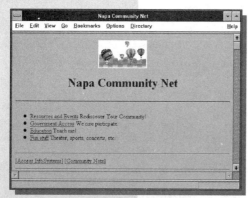

http://solano.community.net/community/napa/index.html
Education; Fun stuff; Napa Community services

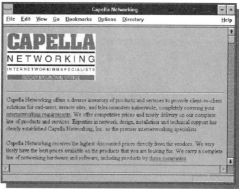

http://storefront.xor.com/capella
End-users; Products; Remote sites; Services; Telecommuters

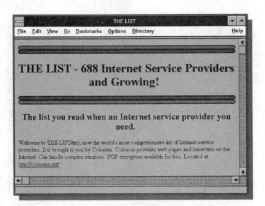

http://thelist.com/
Directory; Index; Internet service providers

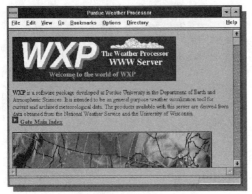

http://thunder.atms.purdue.edu/
Forecasts; Purdue University; Weather

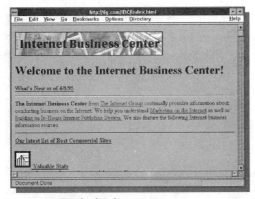

http://tig.com/IBC/index.html
Internet business; Internet marketing; Marketing; Publishing

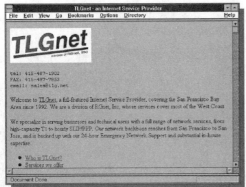

http://tlg.org/
Internet service provider; San Francisco; TLGnet

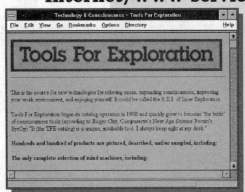

http://tools.willow.com/
Catalog; Consciousness; Enjoyment; Stress relief; Technology

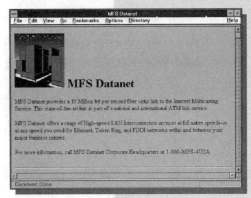

http://town.hall.org/sponsors/mfs.html
ATM link; High-speed networks; Internet Multicasting Service

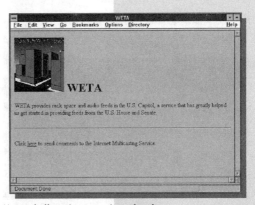

http://town.hall.org/sponsors/weta.html
Audio feeds; US Capitol; WETA

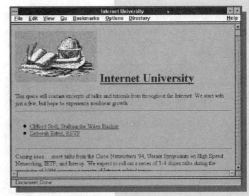

http://town.hall.org/university/index.html
High speed networking; Internet University; Interop

Internet/WWW services

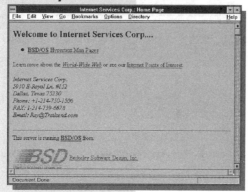

http://trailsend.trailsend.com/
Internet Services Corp.; Points of Internet; Web

http://web.telepost.no/KapitalData/94nr9/52eunet.html
EUnet; Europe; Internet

http://trinet.com/
Consulting; Marketing; Web specialists

http://where.com/
Information searching; Web sites; WHERE.COM

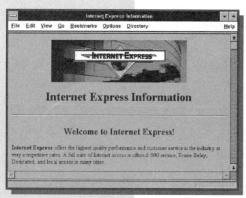

http://usa.net/home/inxinfo.html
Frame relay; Internet service provider

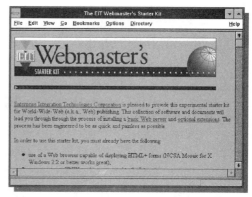

http://wsk.eit.com/wsk/doc/
Getting started; HTML; Web publishing

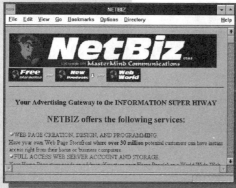

http://voyager.via.net/netbiz/netbiz.html
Advertising; Business; Internet; Programming; Web page design

http://wwa.com/
Chicago; Information; Internet Provider; Superhighway

http://www.3pco.net/
Internet services; Links; Resources

http://www.accesscom.com/
Directories; Internet services; Links; Resources

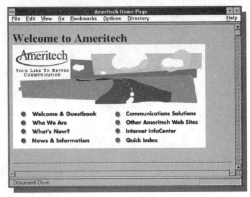

http://www.aads.net/
Interactive services; News; Telecommunications

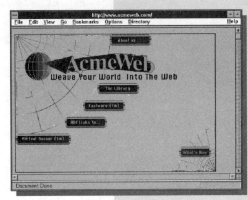

http://www.acmeweb.com/
Online shopping; Web resources

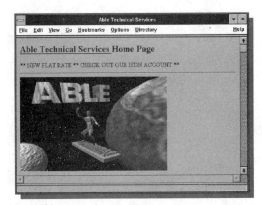

http://www.ablecom.net/
Flat rates; ISDN; Technical services

http://www.active.co.za/
Active access; South Africa's latest Internet provider

305

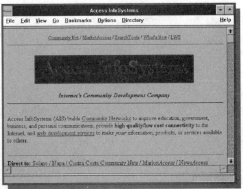

http://www.access-info.com/
Business; Communications; Education; Government; Personal

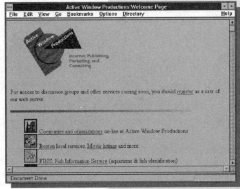

http://www.actwin.com/
Aquariums; Boston; Fish; Movie listings

Internet/WWW services

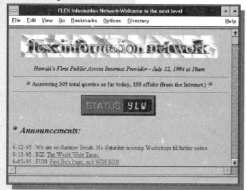

http://www.aloha.com/
Hawaii; Internet service provider; Public access

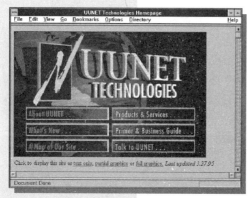

http://www.alter.net/
Products; Services; UUNET Technologies

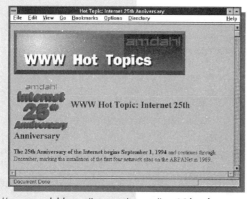

http://www.amdahl.com/internet/events/inet25.html
Internet 25th Anniversary; Web; WWW Hot Topics

http://www.amug.org/~eps/onsite1.html
InterNet Computer Services; Services; Training

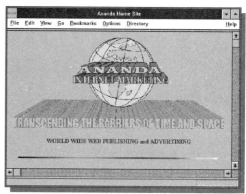

http://www.ananda.com/plg/ananda/
Advertising; Custom design; Internet marketing; Publishing

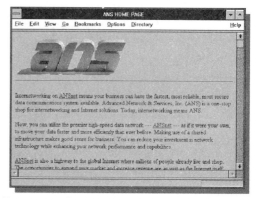

http://www.ans.net/
Data communications; Internetworking

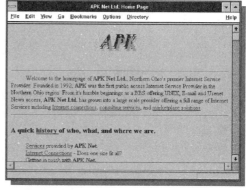

http://www.apk.net/apk
Consulting; Internet service provider; Northern Ohio; Services

http://www.aplatform.com/
APlatform; Internet services

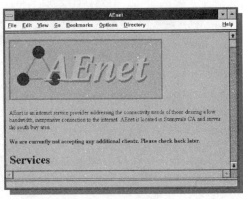

http://www.arasmith.com/aenet/index.html
Connectivity; Inexpensive; Low bandwidth; Sunnyvale

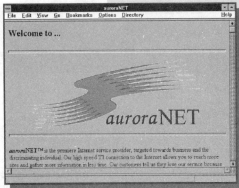

http://www.aurora.net/
AuroraNET; Internet service provider; T1

http://www.ark.com/
Arkansas; Gopher; Regional news

http://www.bahnware.com/bahnware/
BAHNWARE; Products; Services; Travel

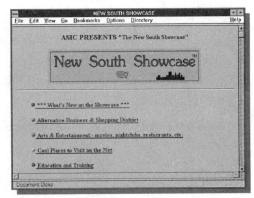

http://www.asa-net.com/nss/
Atlanta; Business; Entertainment; Shopping; Southeast

http://www.batnet.com/
Directories; Links; Services; Wombat Internet Guild

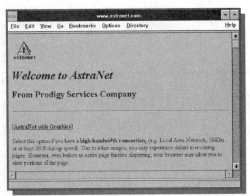

http://www.astranet.com/
AstraNet; Online services; Prodigy services

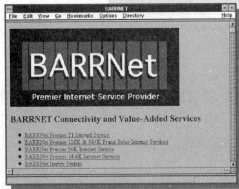

http://www.bbn.com/barrnet.html
BARRNET; Internet service provider; T1

Internet/WWW services

http://www.bbnplanet.com/
BBN Planet; Information service; Services

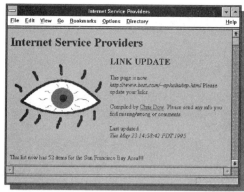

http://www.best.com/~ophelia/internet.html
Directories; Information; Internet providers; San Francisco

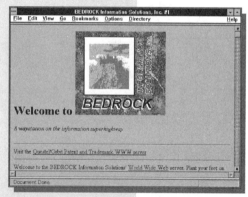

http://www.bedrock.com/
Questel/Orbit Patent and Trademark

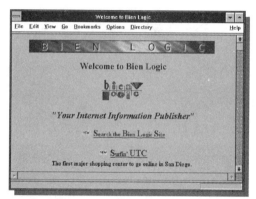

http://www.bienlogic.com/
Information; Internet; Publisher

http://www.belmont.gov/belmont
Belmont; California; Community information; Services

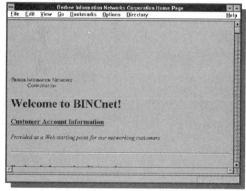

http://www.binc.net/
Networking; Products and services

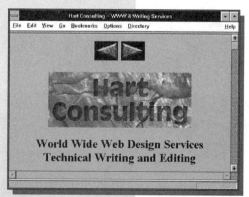

http://www.best.com/~hart/
Editing; Services; Technical; Writing

http://www.biz.net/
BizNet; Internet access; Small business

http://www.bsis.com/
Financial services; Information technology; Mosaic

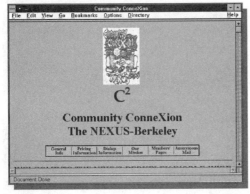

http://www.c2.org/
Company information; Products; Services

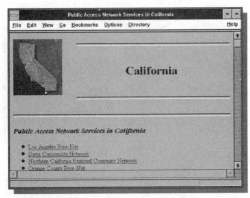

http://www.cais.com/morino/htdocs/states/ca.htm
California; Networks; Public access; Services

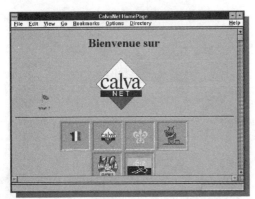

http://www.calvacom.fr/
France; Information service; News

http://www.calweb.com/
California; Internet service provider; News; Sacramento

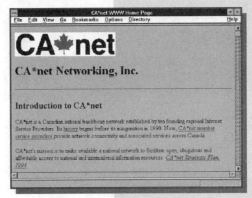

http://www.canet.ca/canet/index.html
CA*net; Canada; Internet service provider

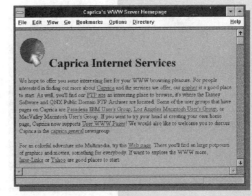

http://www.caprica.com/
Directories; Disney; FTP; Links; QNX Public Domain

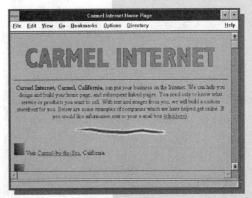

http://www.carmelnet.com/
California; Carmel; Community information

Internet/WWW services

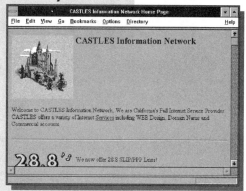

http://www.castles.com/
Business; Commercial accounts; Domain Name; WEB Design

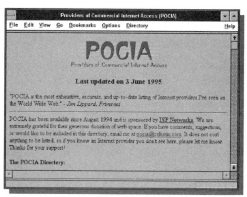

http://www.celestin.com/pocia/index.html
Directories; Internet service providers; Links; Listings

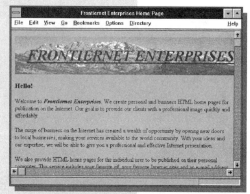

http://www.castles.com/frontier/frontier.html
Business; Home pages; HTML; Internet publication; Personal

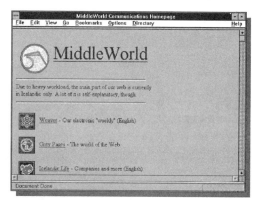

http://www.centrum.is/english/index.html
Icelandic Life; Internet access; Web resources

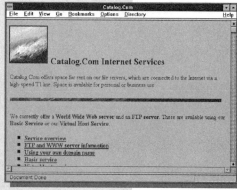

http://www.catalog.com/catalog/top.html
Catalog.Com; Internet services; Internet space for rent; T1 line

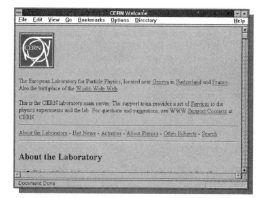

http://www.cern.ch/
CERN; European Laboratory for Particle Physics; Physics

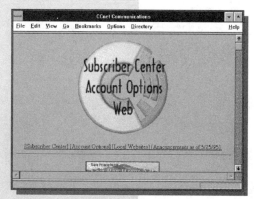

http://www.ccnet.com/
CCnet Communications; Internet services; News

http://www.charm.net/~web/
Making WWW pages; URL database; WWW development

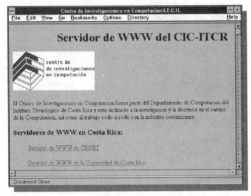

http://www.charm.net/ppp.html
Charm Net; Communications; Connectivity; Internet software

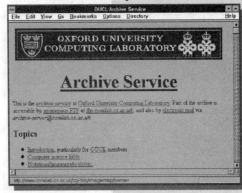

http://www.comlab.ox.ac.uk/archive/
Art galleries; Image archives; Museums; Oxford University

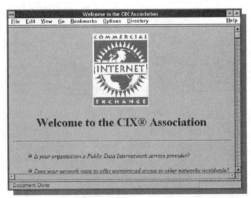

http://www.cic.itcr.ac.cr/cic.html
Education; Instituto Technologico de Costa Rica; Spanish

http://www.community.net/marketplace.html
HTML; Paperless publishing; Style guide; Web development

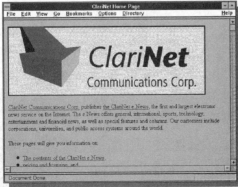

http://www.cix.org/CIXhome.html
Access; CIX; Internet; Provider

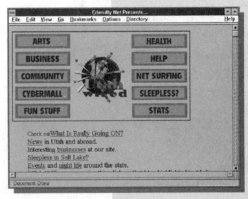

http://www.comnet.com/
Friendly Net; Internet access; Utah; Web resources

http://www.clarinet.com/
Entertainment; Financial news; Newspapers; News; Sports

http://www.compuserve.com/
CIS; CompuServe; Web server

Internet/WWW services

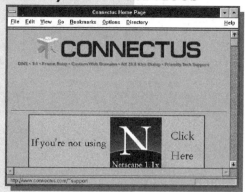

http://www.connectus.com/
Internet service provider; Web development

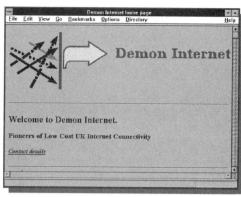

http://www.demon.co.uk/
UK Internet service provider

http://www.cs.yale.edu/HTML/WorldWideWebTop.html
Indexes; NCSA; Search engines; WWW

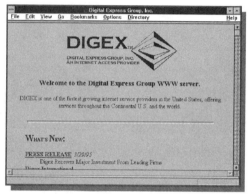

http://www.digex.net/
Digital Express Group; Internet service provider

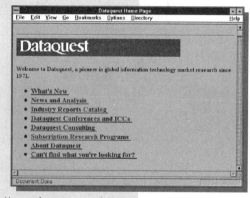

http://www.dataquest.com/
Analysis; Consulting; Market research; News

http://www.digital.com/gnn/wic/index.html
News; Online catalog; Search

http://www.datawave.net/
Document retrieval; Fax

http://www.dkrz.de:80/
Europe; Germany; Web server

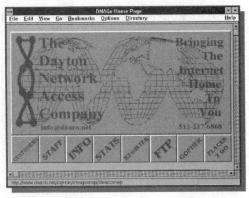

http://www.dnaco.net/
Dayton; FTP; Gopher; Internet service provider

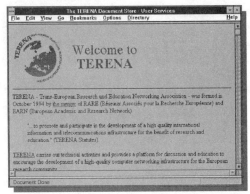

http://www.earn.net/
Telecommunications; European; Research; Education

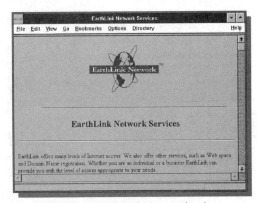

http://www.earthlink.net/EarthLink_Services.html
EarthLink; Internet service provider

http://www.eicon.com/
Eicon Technology; Technology; Web server

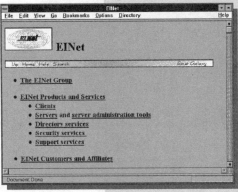

http://www.einet.net/EINet/EINet.html
EINet; Internet access; Products and services; Security

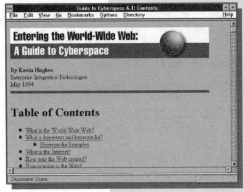

http://www.eit.com/web/www.guide/
A Guide to Cyberspace; Hypermedia; Hypermedia; WWW

313

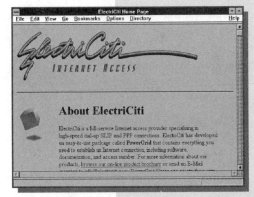

http://www.electriciti.com/
ElectriCiti; Internet service provider; San Diego

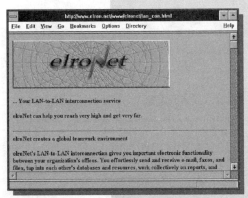

http://www.elron.net/www/elronet/lan_con.html
Elronet; LAN to LAN interconnection service

Internet/WWW services

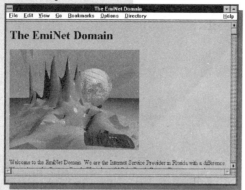

http://www.emi.net/
EmiNet; Florida; Internet service provider

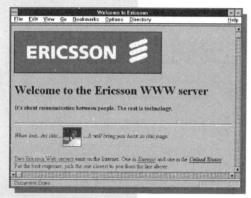

http://www.ericsson.nl/
Ericsson; Technology; Telecommunications

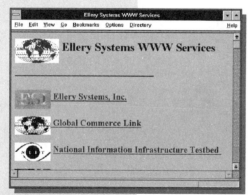

http://www.esi.com/
Ellery Systems; Links; Commerce

http://www.EU.net/
Europe; French; German; Internet access

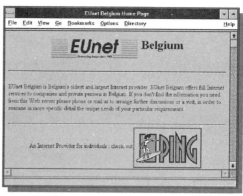

http://www.eunet.be/
Belgium; EUnet; Internet service provider

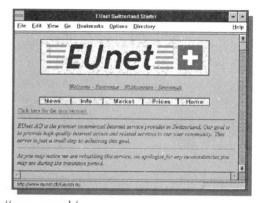

http://www.eunet.ch/
EUnet; Internet service provider; Switzerland

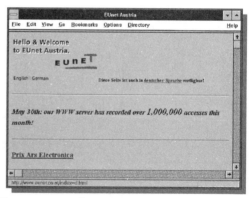

http://www.eunet.co.at/
Austria; EUnet; Internet service provider

http://www.eunet.es/
Education; EUnet; Internet provider

http://www.eunet.no/EUnet-Norge/EUnet-Norge-AS.html
EUnet; Internet service provider; Norway

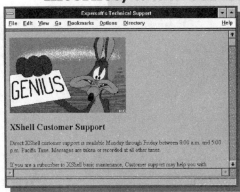

http://www.expersoft.com/techsupport/
Expersoft; Technical support; XShell

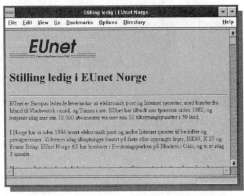

http://www.eunet.no/EUnet-Norge/stilling.html
EUnet; Internet service provider; Norway

http://www.flightpath.com/
Access; Individuals; Small business

http://www.eunet.no/kunder/
EUnet; Internet service provider; Norway

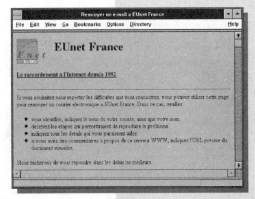

http://www.fnet.fr/f-readmail.html
EUnet; France; Internet service provider

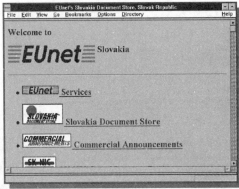

http://www.eunet.sk/
EUnet; Europe; Internet access; Commercial sites

http://www.forum.net/
Business presence; ForumNet; Internet; Marketing services

Internet/WWW services

http://www.foundation.tricon.com/
Internet Services Provider; Second Foundation Internet Services

http://www.garlic.com/
California; Internet Services Provider; Santa Clara Valley

http://www.fractals.com/
FractalNet; Graphics; Information services

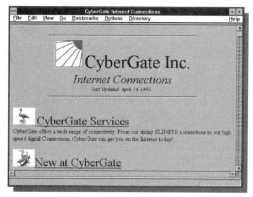

http://www.gate.net/
CyberGate Inc.; Florida; Internet service provider

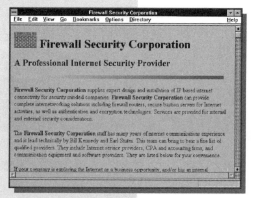

http://www.frus.com/
Firewall Security Corporation; Internet

http://www.gbn.com/
Business services; Communication; Global Commerce Link

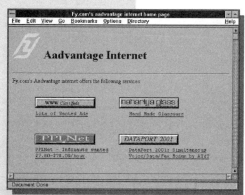

http://www.fy.com/
Fy.com; Internet service provider; Classifieds

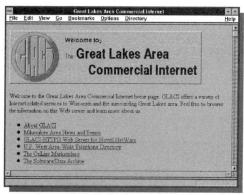

http://www.glaci.com/Welcome.html
Great Lakes Area Commercial Internet; Internet provider

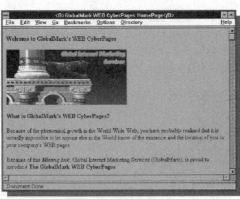

http://www.globalmark.com/globalmark/
Internet presence; Marketing services; Web

http://www.hiway.co.uk/index.html
HIWAY; Internet service provider; United Kingdom

http://www.gsu.edu/dept/gsucc/cs/home.html
Georgia State University; Web tour

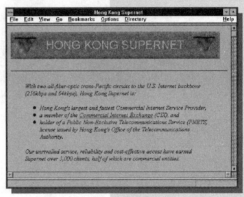

http://www.hk.super.net/
Hong Kong Supernet; Internet service provider

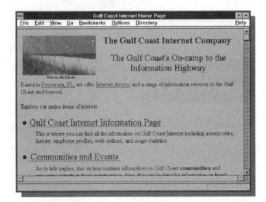

http://www.gulf.net/
Florida; Gulf Coast; Internet service provider

http://www.human.com/
Free Pages; Human Factor; Internet Help

http://www.hillside.co.uk/
Hillside server; Hillside Systems; United Kingdom

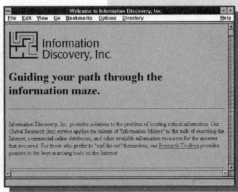

http://www.i-discover.com/
Information Discovery Inc.; Internet searching; Tools

Internet/WWW services

http://www.I2020.net/
Information superhighway; Internet access

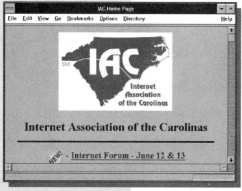

http://www.iac.org/iac/
Information; Internet Association of the Carolinas; News

http://www.iat.com/
Canada; Mac software; Macintosh; Puerto Rico; US

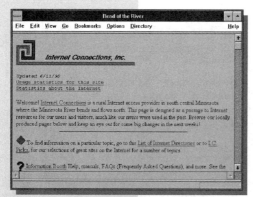

http://www.ic.mankato.mn.us/
Internet service provider; South-central Minnesota

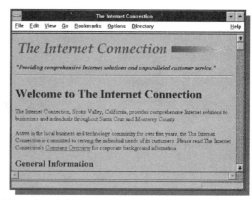

http://www.ico.net/
Businesses; California; Internet service provider; Scotts Valley

http://www.ids.net/
East Coast; Intelecom Data Systems; Internet service provider

http://www.iglou.com/iglou/iglou_main.html
IgLou Internet Services; Internet access; PPP; SLIP

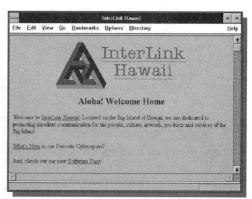

http://www.ilhawaii.net/
Art; Culture; Interlink Hawaii; Products; Services; Software

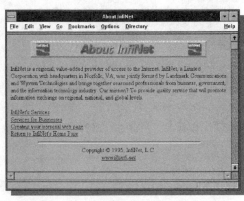

http://www.infi.net/about.html
InfiNet; Norfolk; Virginia; Wyvern Technologies

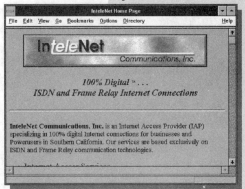

http://www.intelenet.com/welcome.html
Frame relay; Internet services provider; ISDN

http://www.infi.net:80/vegas/
Cool sites; InfiNet; Internet; Vegas; Web

http://www.intelli.com/
Intelli.com; Internet resources

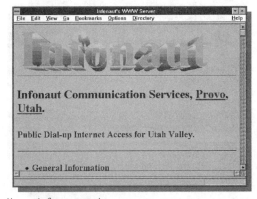

http://www.infonaut.com/
Internet service provider; Provo; Utah

http://www.interaccess.com/Guest/Guest.html
Chicagoland; InterAccess; Internet service provider

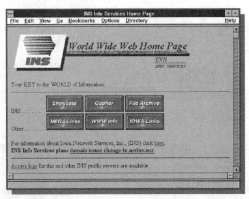

http://www.infonet.net/
Internet services; Iowa Network Services Inc.

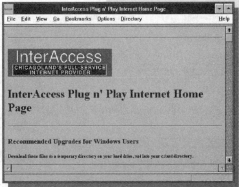

http://www.interaccess.com/iainfo/pnp.html
Chicago; InterAccess; Plug and play

Internet/WWW services

http://www.interaccess.com/index.html
Access; Chicago; HTML; Seminars

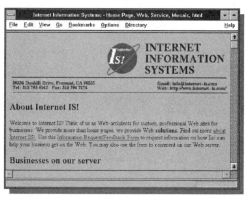

http://www.internet-is.com/index.html
Business; Custom; Professional; Web Sites

http://www.interaccess.com/survey/survey.htm
Chicago; InterAccess; Survey

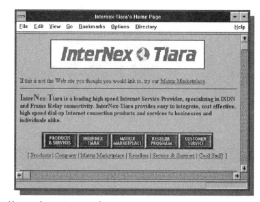

http://www.internex.com/
Frame Relay; Internet service provider; InterNex-Tiara; ISDN

http://www.intermind.net/
InterMind; Internet service provider; Las Vegas

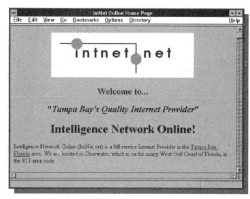

http://www.intnet.net/
Intelligence Network Online; Internet provider; Tampa Bay

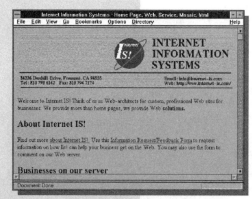

http://www.internet-is.com/
Business sites; Internet information services; Web solutions

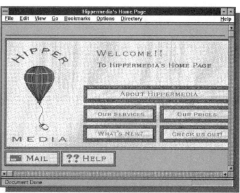

http://www.io.org/~farellc/hipper.html
Access; Marketing; Provider

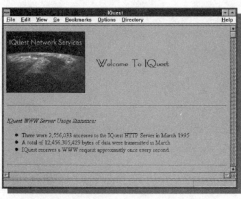

http://www.iquest.net/
Indianapolis; IQuest Network Services; Web server

http://www.is.co.za/
Internet provider; Popular Internet resources; South Africa

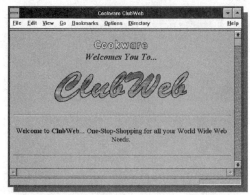

http://www.iquest.net/cw/cookware.html
ClubWeb; Cookware

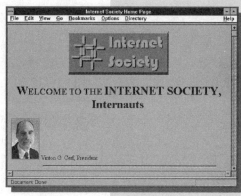

http://www.isoc.org/
Cerf; Internauts; Internet Society; Surfing

321

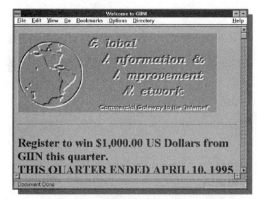

http://www.iquest.net/giin/
Global Information and Improvement; Internet services

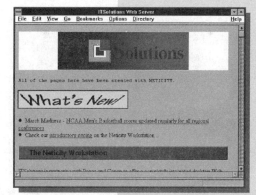

http://www.its.com/
Internet services; ITSolutions

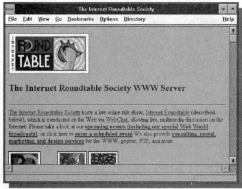

http://www.IRsociety.com/
Events; Discussion; Marketing; Roundtable

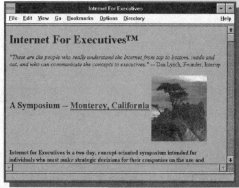

http://www.iwl.com/I4E/i4e.html
Internet for Executives; Symposium

Internet/WWW services

http://www.lanka.net/
Internet service provider; Sri Lanka

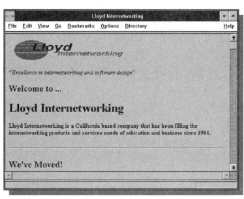

http://www.lloyd.com/
Business; Education; Internetworking; Services

http://www.lava.net/
Businesses; LavaNet; Web sites

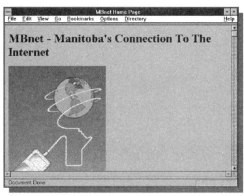

http://www.mbnet.mb.ca/
Canada; Internet connections; Web sites

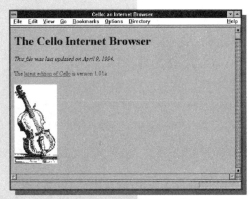

http://www.law.cornell.edu/cello/cellotop.html
Browsers; Cello; Internet tools; Internet utilities

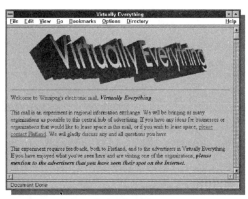

http://www.mbnet.mb.ca/flatland/mall/
Canada; Flatland; Online mall; Winnipeg

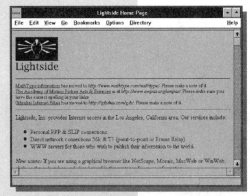

http://www.lightside.com/
Internet service provider; Lightside

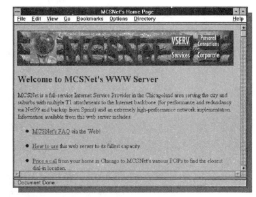

http://www.mcs.net/
Chicagoland; Internet service provider; Web

http://babel.uoregon.edu/yamada.html
University of Oregon; Yamada Language Center

http://csli-www.stanford.edu/
Language; Stanford University

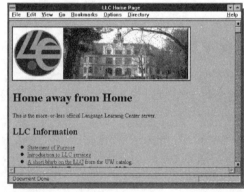

http://d9.llc.washington.edu/
Language; University of Washington

http://ling.ohio-state.edu/
Linguistics; Ohio State University

http://logos.svenska.gu.se/lbeng.html
Language; Lexicons; Reading; Swedish

http://meena.cc.uregina.ca/~liushus/pub/read-chn.html
Applications; Chinese; Reading; Text

http://netmedia.com/chinese/summer.html
Chinese; Japanese; Language program; Stanford

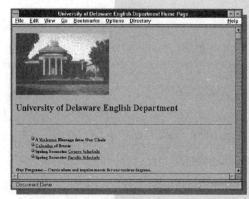

http://odin.english.udel.edu/
English; University of Delaware

Languages

http://tuna.uchicago.edu/
ARTFL; France; French Language

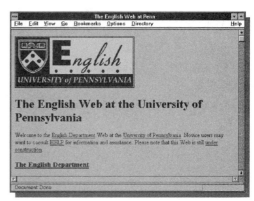

http://www.english.upenn.edu/
English; University of Pennsylvania

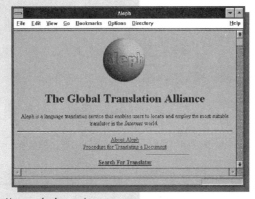

http://www.aleph.com/
Language translation service; Translators

http://www.internet-is.com/linguatec/in-iis.html
Language and Intercultural Training; Multicultural

http://www.cogsci.ed.ac.uk/elsnet/home.html
Europe; Language; Speech

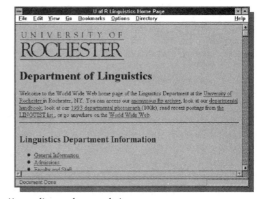

http://www.ling.rochester.edu/
Linguistics; New York; University of Rochester

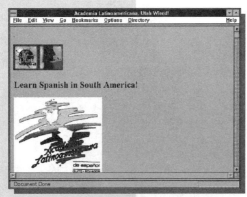

http://www.comnet.com/ecuador/learnSpanish.html
Education; South America; Spanish language

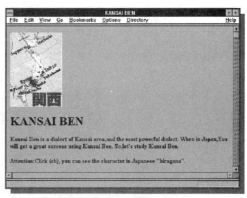

http://www.twics.com/~TOKUMARU/Osaka.html
Japanese; Kansai Ben

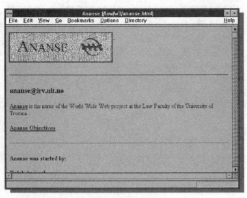

http://ananse.irv.uit.no/law/w3/ananse.html
Law; Universities; Ananse

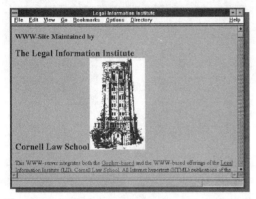

http://fatty.law.cornell.edu/
Cornell Law School; Internet tool; Legal Information Institute

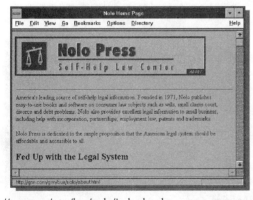

http://gnn.com/gnn/bus/nolo/index.html
Books; Legal information; Publishing; Self-help

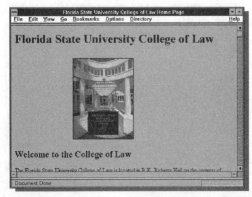

http://law.fsu.edu:80/
Florida State University; Law

http://law.net/
Internet services; Legal

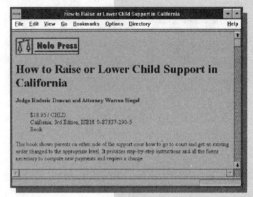

http://nearnet.gnn.com/gnn/bus/nolo/item/chld.html
California; Child support; Legal advice

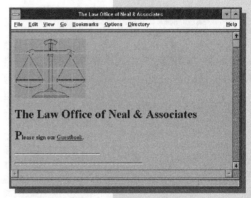

http://seamless.com/hdn/hdn.html
Law office; Legal advice

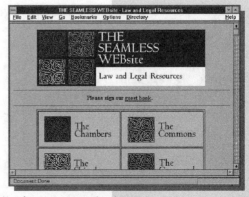

http://starbase.ingress.com/tsw/
Law; Legal resources

Law

http://sunsite.unc.edu/patents/intropat.html
Internet Patent Research System; Laws; Patents

http://tsw.ingress.com/tsw/qj/qj.html
Lawyers; Research; Services; Writing

http://tsw.ingress.com/tsw/cj/cj.html
Copyrights; Trademarks; Intellectual property; Legal advice

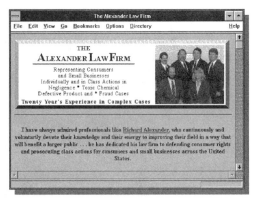

http://tsw.ingress.com/tsw/talf/talf.html
Consumer rights; Law Firm

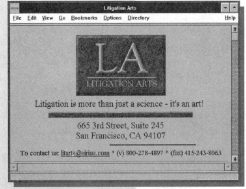

http://tsw.ingress.com/tsw/ds/ds.html
Law office; Technology

http://venable.com/
Attorneys; Baltimore; Business; Law

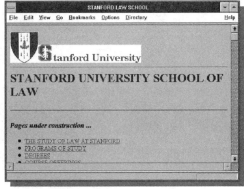

http://tsw.ingress.com/tsw/litarts/lahome.html
Law office; Legal advice; Litigation

http://www-leland.stanford.edu/group/law/
Law; Stanford University

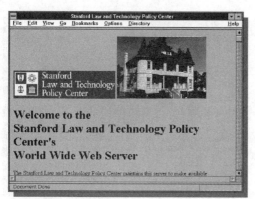

http://www-techlaw.stanford.edu/
Education; Stanford Law and Technology Policy Center

http://www.5010geary.com/
Licensed tax professionals; Tax laws

http://www.ai.mit.edu/people/ellens/PLN/pln.html
Human rights; Laws; Prison Legal News

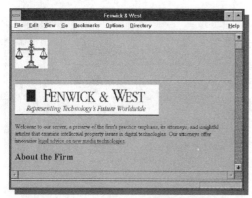

http://www.batnet.com/oikoumene/FWHome.html
Law firm; Legal advice; New media technologies

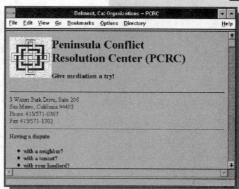

http://www.belmont.gov/orgs/pcrc/
Legal; Mediation; Peninsula Conflict Resolution Center

http://www.benedict.com/index.html
Copyright information; Information technology; Legal

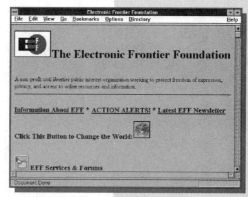

http://www.eff.org/
Civil liberties; Freedom of expression; Privacy; Public interest

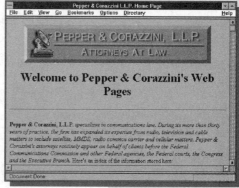

http://www.iis.com/p-and-c/
Executive Branch; Law firms; Legal; Media

327

Law

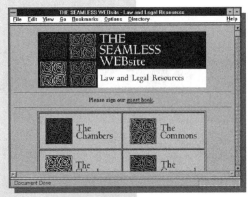

http://www.infi.net/pilot/law.html
Law; Legal Documents; US Constitution

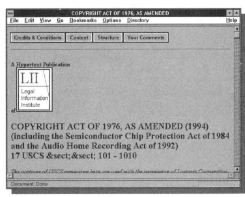

http://www.law.cornell.edu//usc/17/overview.html
Copyright; Legal information; Legal Information Institute

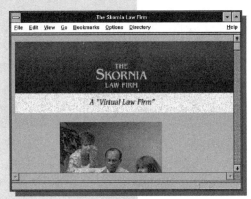

http://www.ingress.com/tsw/
Law; Legal resources; Web resources

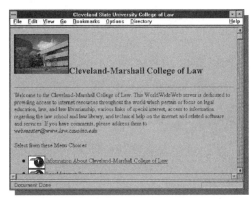

http://www.law.csuohio.edu/
Law; Law libraries; Legal education

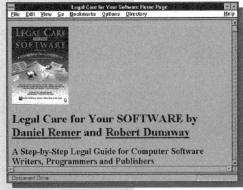

http://www.internet-is.com/skornia/in-iis.html
Skornia Law Firm

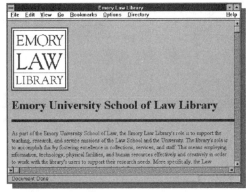

http://www.law.emory.edu/LAW/law.html
Emory University; Law Library

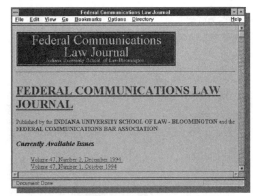

http://www.island.com/LegalCare/welcome.html
Law; Legal; Software

http://www.law.indiana.edu/fclj/fclj.html
Federal Communications Law Journal; Indiana University

http://cdtelnet1.ucr.edu/
Riverside; Science libraries; University of California

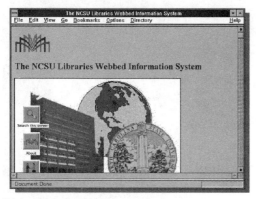

http://dewey.lib.ncsu.edu/
Education; North Carolina State University

http://dpls.dacc.wisc.edu/
Data and Program Library; Madison; University of Wisconsin

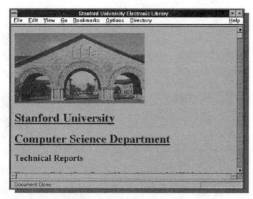

http://elib.stanford.edu/
Electronic Library; Stanford University

http://galaxy.einet.net/hytelnet/DK002.html
Humanities; Royal Danish Library; Social sciences; Theology

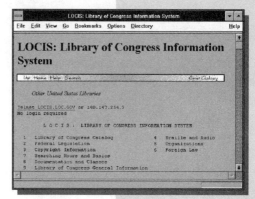

http://galaxy.einet.net/hytelnet/US373.html
Library of Congress Information System

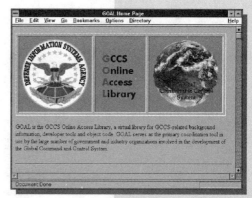

http://hakita.nosc.mil/gccs/goal.html
Global Command and Control System; Library; Online

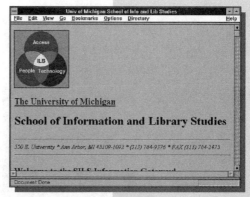

http://http2.sils.umich.edu/
Education; University of Michigan

Libraries

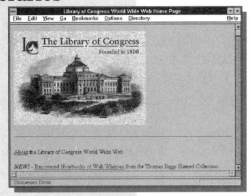

http://lcweb.loc.gov/homepage
Books; ISBN; Library of Congress

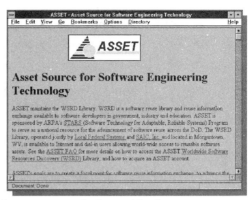

http://source.asset.com/background.html
Reliable systems; Reusable software; Software engineering

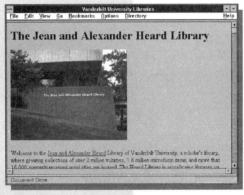

http://libdev1.lib.vanderbilt.edu/
Jean and Alexander Heard Library; Vanderbilt University

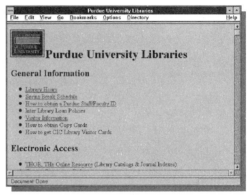

http://thorplus.lib.purdue.edu/library_info/index.html
Libraries; Purdue University

http://milkyway.wils.wisc.edu/
Library; Madison; University of Wisconsin

http://ulispsn.ulis.ac.jp:8001/html/ENG_homepage.html
Japan; University of Library and Information Science

http://sjcpl.lib.in.us/
Indiana; Public libraries

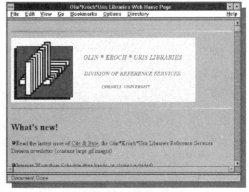

http://urisref.library.cornell.edu/olinref.html
Cornell University; Library; Olin/Uris Reference

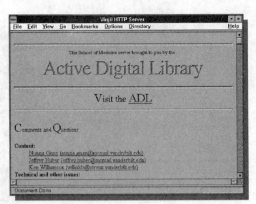

http://virgil.mc.vanderbilt.edu/
Digital libraries; Medicine; Vanderbilt University

http://web.msu.edu/vincent/
Interviews; Lectures; Performances; Speeches; Vincent Voice

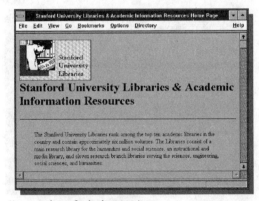

http://www-sul.stanford.edu:8000/
Academic Information; Libraries; Stanford

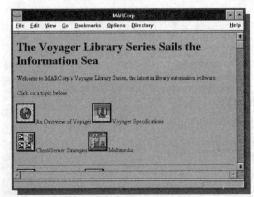

http://www.aimnet.com/voyager/home.html
Library automation software

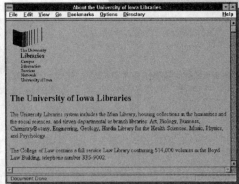

http://www.arcade.uiowa.edu/arcade/www/libraries/index.html
Libraries; University of Iowa

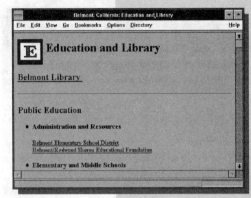

http://www.belmont.gov/educ/index.html
Belmont; California; Education; Library; Schools

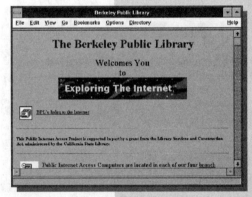

http://www.ci.berkeley.ca.us/bpl/
Berkeley Public Library

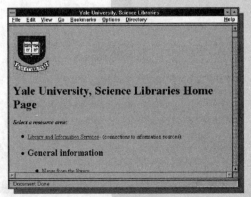

http://www.cis.yale.edu/~dstern/top.html
Science libraries; Topic search; Yale University

331

Libraries

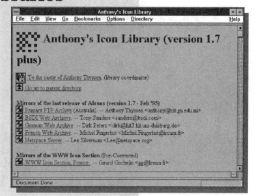

http://www.cit.gu.edu.au/~anthony/icons/
Archive; Icons; Web servers

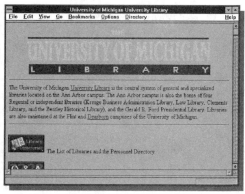

http://www.lib.umich.edu/
Business administration; Law; University of Michigan

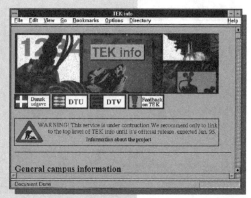

http://www.dtb.dk/
Campus information; Denmark; Technical libraries

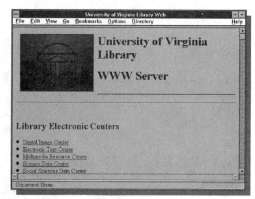

http://www.lib.virginia.edu/
Libraries; University of Virginia

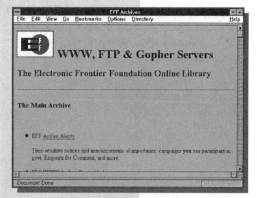

http://www.eff.org/archives.html
FTP; Gopher; Servers; WWW

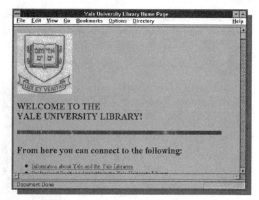

http://www.library.yale.edu/
Libraries; Yale University

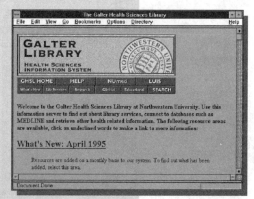

http://www.ghsl.nwu.edu/
Health; Health sciences; Libraries; Medicine; MEDLINE

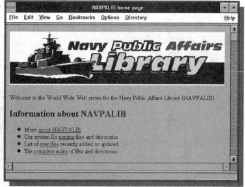

http://www.navy.mil/navpalib/.www/welcome.html
NAVPALIB; Navy Public Affairs Library

Literature

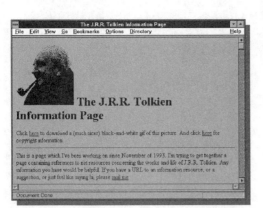

http://csclub.uwaterloo.ca/u/relipper/tolkien/rootpage.html
Authors; J.R.R. Tolkien; Writers

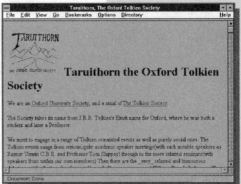

http://sable.ox.ac.uk/~tolksoc/
Author; Science fiction; The Tolkien Society; Writing

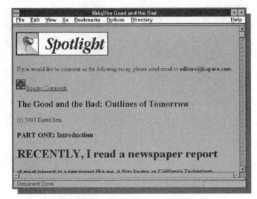

http://kspace.com/KM/spot.sys/Brin/pages/piece1.html
Essays; Feedback; Reviews; Writing

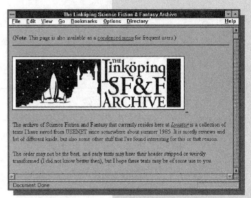

http://sf.www.lysator.liu.se/sf_archive/sf_main.html
Archives; Fantasy; Science fiction

333

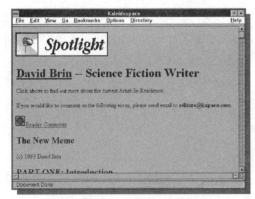

http://kspace.com/KM/spot.sys/Brin/pages/piece7.html
Feedback; Science fiction; Writing

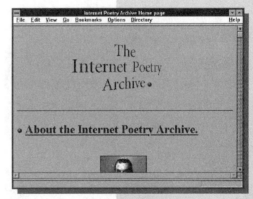

http://sunsite.unc.edu/dykki/poetry/home.html
Poems; Poetry; Literature

http://marketplace.com/0/alt.x/althome.html
Essays; Interviews; Pop fiction

http://sunsite.unc.edu/dykki/poetry/milosz/milcov.html
Czeslaw Milosz; Lithuania; Poetry; Poland

Literature

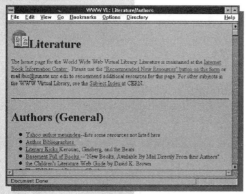

http://sunsite.unc.edu/ibic/IBIC-Authors.html
Author bibliographies; Literature; Virtual library

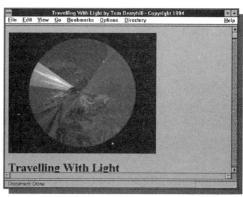

http://wimsey.com/anima/NEXUS/TomStuff/Travelling.html
Poetry; Poets; Tom Berryhill

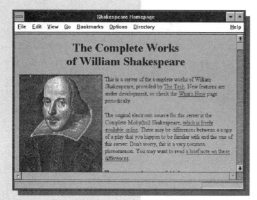

http://the-tech.mit.edu/Shakespeare/works.html
Complete Works; Literature; William Shakespeare

http://www.charm.net/~brooklyn/LitKicks.html
Literature; Reading; Writers

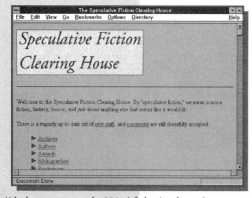

http://thule.mt.cs.cmu.edu:8001/sf-clearing-house/
Clearing House; Horror; Speculative

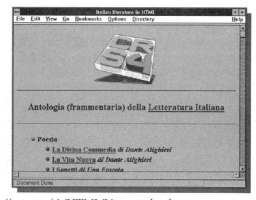

http://www.crs4.it/HTML/Literature.html
Italian literature; Italy

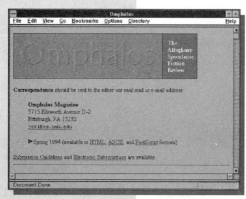

http://thule.mt.cs.cmu.edu:8001/sf-clearing-house/zines/omphalos/
Online magazine; Reviews; Science fiction

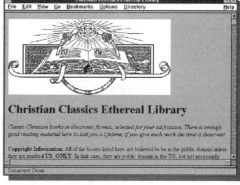

http://www.cs.pitt.edu/~planting/books/
Books; Christian Classics; Ethereal library

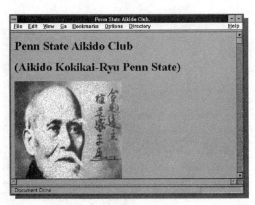

http://cac.psu.edu/~santoro/aikido.html
Aikido Club; Penn State University

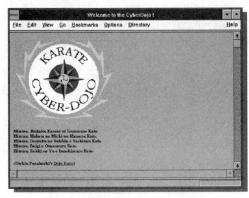

http://cswww2.essex.ac.uk/Web/karate/CyberDojo/
Education; Karate; Martial arts

http://gpu.srv.ualberta.ca/~lfowler/home2.html
Martial arts; Philosophy

http://smartone.svi.org/~nates/judo.html
Judo; Kodokan; Palo Alto

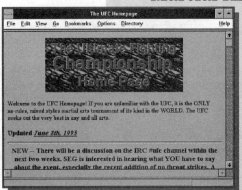

http://thelair.zynet.com/~ufc/
Martial arts; Mixed styles; No-rules; Tournament

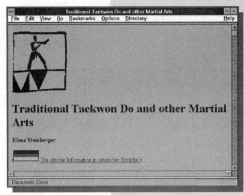

http://www.bl.physik.tu-muenchen.de/~k2/budo_english/
Karate; Martial arts; Taekwon Do

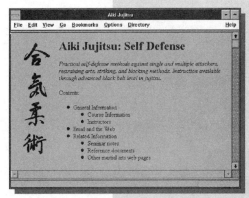

http://www.stanford.edu/group/jujitsu/
Aiki Jujitsu; Martial arts; Self defense

http://www.ugcs.caltech.edu/~rachel/bamm.html
Abuse; Assault; Martial arts; Self defense

335

Mathematics

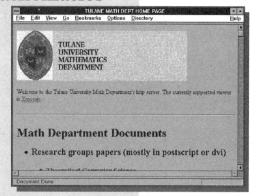

http://bach.math.tulane.edu/
Mathematics; Tulane University

http://hub.terc.edu/
Mathematics; Resources; Science; TERC

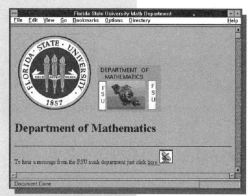

http://euclid.math.fsu.edu:80/
Florida State University; Mathematics

http://imag.fr/
France; Institut des Mathematiques Appliquees de Grenoble

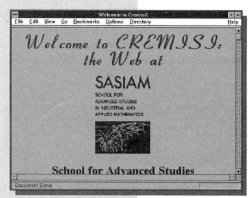

http://fourier.csata.it/
Applied mathematics; CREMISI; Education

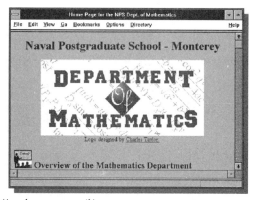

http://math.nps.navy.mil/
Mathematics; Naval Postgraduate School

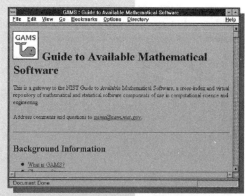

http://gams.cam.nist.gov:80/
Engineering; Mathematical software; Statistical software

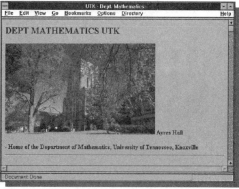

http://mathsun1.math.utk.edu/
Knoxville; Mathematics; University of Tennessee

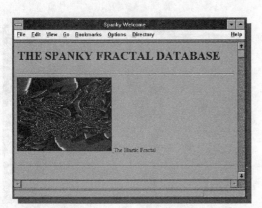

http://spanky.triumf.ca/
Engineering; Fractal; Graphics; Software

http://www.cs.wesleyan.edu/
Mathematics; Computer Science; Wesleyan University

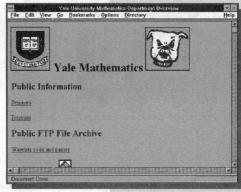

http://taygeta.oc.nps.navy.mil/random.html
Random Number Generation

http://www.cs.yale.edu/HTML/YALE/MATH/FrontDoor.html
Mathematics; Seminars

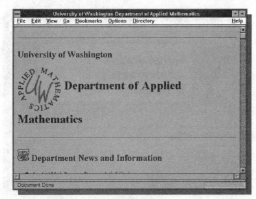

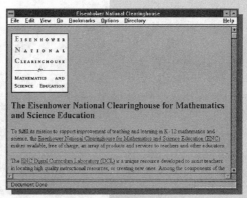

http://www.amath.washington.edu/
Applied Mathematics; University of Washington

http://www.enc.org/
Mathematics; Ohio State University; Science

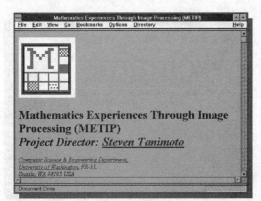

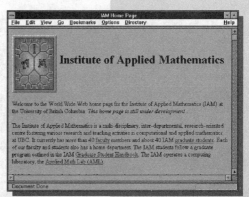

http://www.cs.washington.edu/research/metip/metip.html
Computer science; Engineering; Math; METIP

http://www.iam.ubc.ca/home
Applied Mathematics; Canada; University of British Columbia

Mathematics

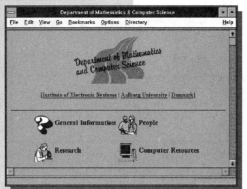

http://www.iesd.auc.dk/
Aalborg University; Computer Science; Denmark; Mathematics

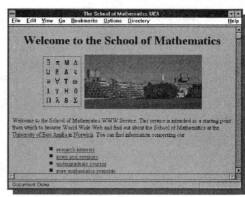

http://www.mth.uea.ac.uk/welcome.html
Education; School of Mathematics

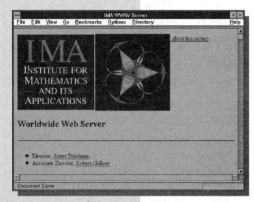

http://www.ima.umn.edu/
Mathematics; University of Minnesota

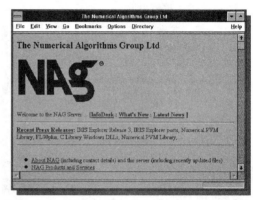

http://www.nag.co.uk:70/
Mathematical software; Numerical analysis; Scientific software

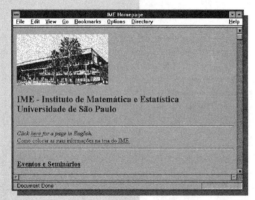

http://www.ime.usp.br/
Brazil; Mathematics; Statistics; University of Sao Paulo

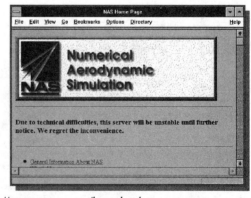

http://www.nas.nasa.gov/home.html
Mathematics; Numerical Aerodynamic Simulation

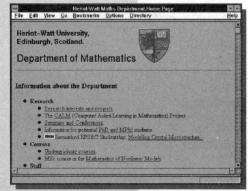

http://www.ma.hw.ac.uk/maths.html
Mathematics in medicine; Mathematics research; Scotland

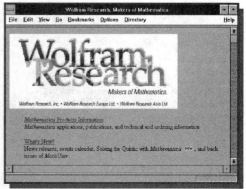

http://www.wri.com/
Wolfram Research; Mathematica

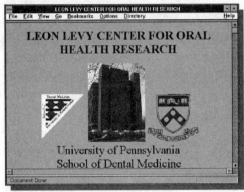

http://atsdr1.atsdr.cdc.gov:8080/atsdrhome.html
Disease registry; Toxic substances

http://biochem.dental.upenn.edu/
Dental; Health Research; Leon Levy; University of Pennsylvania

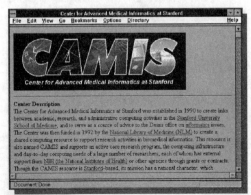

http://bms200.med.navy.mil/
Bureau of Medicine and Surgery; US Navy

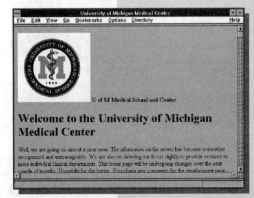

http://camis.Stanford.EDU/
Advanced Medical Informatics; Stanford; Library;

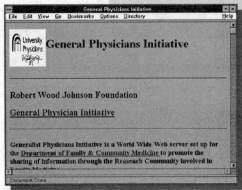

http://charlotte.hsc.missouri.edu/
Family and Community Medicine; University of Missouri

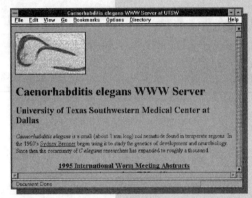

http://eatworms.swmed.edu/
Caenorhabditis elegans; Medicine; Soil nematode

http://gamma.wustl.edu/home.html
Nuclear Medicine; Washington University

http://ganglion.anes.med.umich.edu/
Medicine; University of Michigan

Medicine

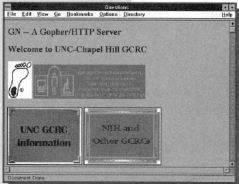

http://gcrc.med.unc.edu:70/
Clinical Research; Medicine; University of North Carolina

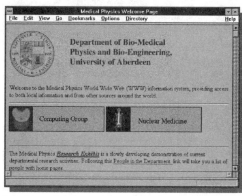

http://info.biomed.abdn.ac.uk/
Aberdeen ; Bio-medical physics; Nuclear medicine

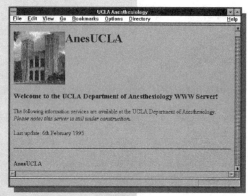

http://hypnos.anes.ucla.edu/index.html
Anesthesiology; UCLA

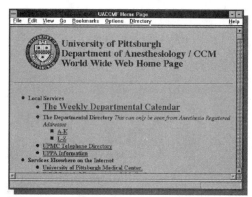

http://info.pitt.edu/~anes/
Anesthesiology; University of Pittsburgh

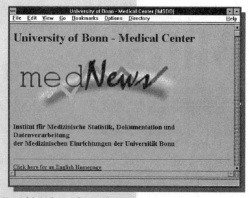

http://imsdd.meb.uni-bonn.de/
Medicine; University of Bonn

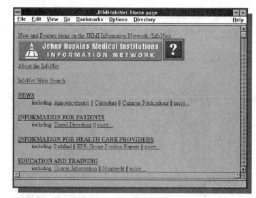

http://infonet.welch.jhu.edu/
Johns Hopkins University; Medicine

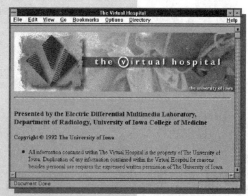

http://indy.radiology.uiowa.edu/
Medicine; Radiology; Virtual hospital

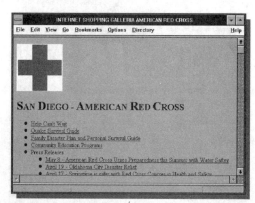

http://intergal.com/Amerredc.html
American Red Cross; Emergency services; San Diego

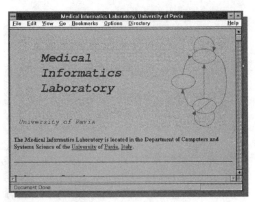

http://ipvaimed9.unipv.it/
Information system; Italy; Medicine; University of Pavia

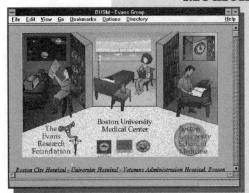

http://med-med1.bu.edu/busm.html
Boston University; Medicine

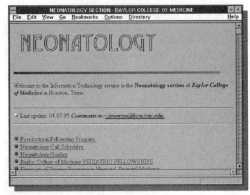

http://l.neo.tch.tmc.edu/neo.html
Baylor College of Medicine; Neonatology

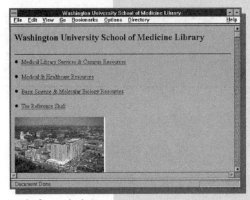

http://medinfo.wustl.edu/
Medical Library; Washington University

http://lenti.med.umn.edu/
Computational biology; University of Minnesota

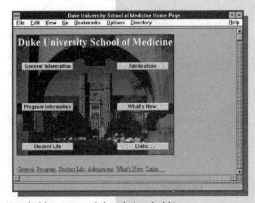

http://medschl-www.mc.duke.edu/medschl/
Duke University; Medicine

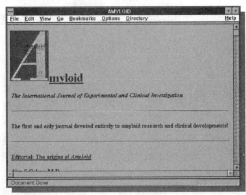

http://med-med1.bu.edu/amyloid/amyloid.html
Amyloid research; International journal; Clinical investigation

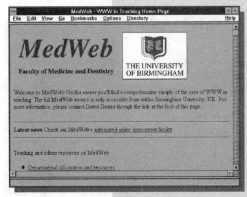

http://medweb.bham.ac.uk/
Birmingham University; U.K.; Dentistry; Medicine

Medicine

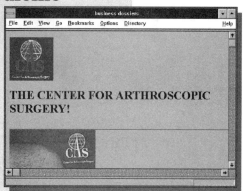

http://mmink.cts.com/mmink/dossiers/cas.html
Arthroscopic surgery; Knee injuries

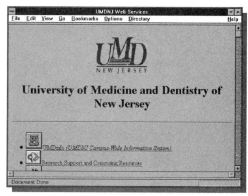

http://njmsa.umdnj.edu/umdnj.html
University of Medicine and Dentistry of New Jersey

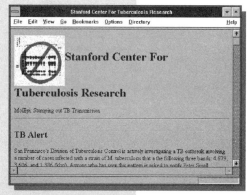

http://molepi.stanford.edu/tb.www.html
Stanford Center; Tuberculosis Research

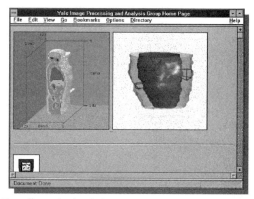

http://noodle.med.yale.edu/
Image processing; Yale University

http://musom.mu.wvnet.edu/
Marshall University; Medicine

http://planetree1.utmem.edu/
Health sciences; University of Tennessee Memphis

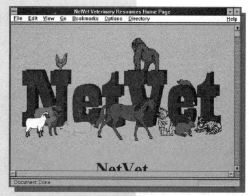

http://netvet.wustl.edu/
Cats; Dogs; Veterinarian medicine; Vets

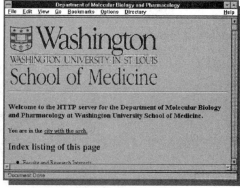

http://quapaw.astate.edu/
Molecular Biology; Pharmacology; Washington University

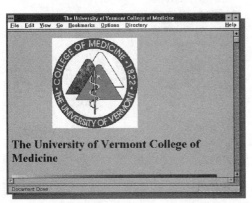

http://salus.uvm.edu/
Education; University of Vermont College of Medicine

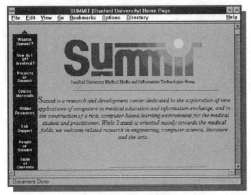

http://summit.stanford.edu/welcome.html
Information Technologies; Medical Media; Stanford University

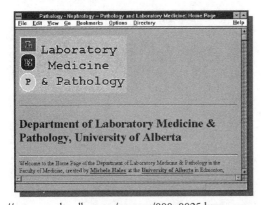

http://synapse.uah.ualberta.ca/synapse/000p0025.htm
Alberta; Laboratory medicine; Pathology

http://turnpike.net/emporium/C/CAPNET/index.htm
Biofeedback; Health care; Interactive multimedia applications

http://vet.purdue.edu/
Purdue University; Veterinary Medicine

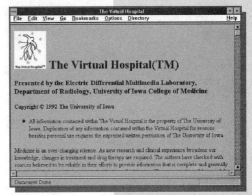

http://vh.radiology.uiowa.edu/
Medicine; Radiology; University of Iowa; Virtual Hospital

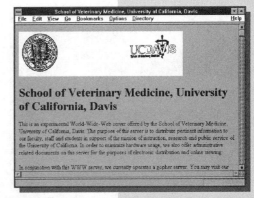

http://vmgopher.ucdavis.edu/
University of Cal. at Davis; Veterinary medicine

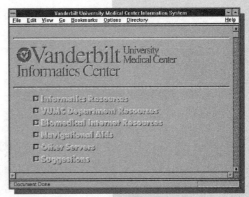

http://vumclib.mc.vanderbilt.edu/main.html
Medical Center; Vanderbilt University

Medicine

http://weber.u.washington.edu/~anesth/
Anesthesiology; University of Washington

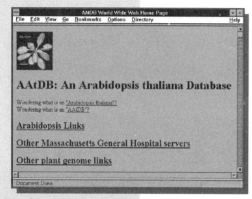

http://weeds.mgh.harvard.edu/
Arabidopsis thaliana; Massachusetts General Hospital

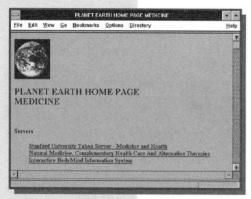

http://white.nosc.mil/med.html
Alternative therapies; Medicine and health; Natural medicine

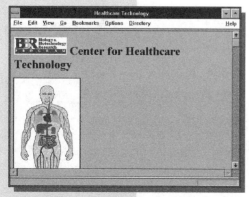

http://www-bio.llnl.gov/bbrp/healthcare/healthcare.html
Health care; Technology; Lawrence Livermore Laboratory

http://www-camis.stanford.edu/
Advanced medical informatics; Stanford

http://www-med.stanford.edu/
Health Care; Stanford University Medical Center

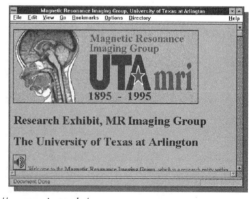

http://www-mri.uta.edu/
Magnetic resonance imaging; University of Texas at Arlington

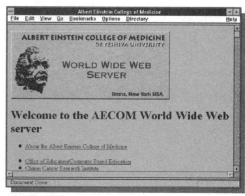

http://www.aecom.yu.edu/
Albert Einstein; Medicine; Yeshiva University

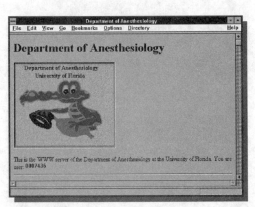

http://www.anest.ufl.edu/
Anesthesiology; University of Florida

http://www.atc.olivetti.com/red-cross/homepage.html
Emergency medical; Palo Alto; Red Cross

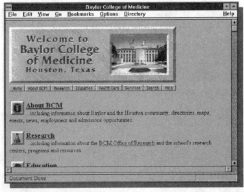

http://www.bcm.tmc.edu/
Baylor College; Houston; Medicine; Texas

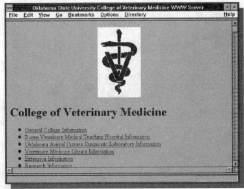

http://www.cvm.okstate.edu/
Oklahoma State University; Veterinary medicine

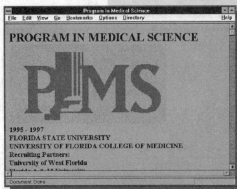

http://www.fsu.edu/~ntessel/pims.html
Florida State University; Medical Science

http://www.mco.edu/
Education; Medical College of Ohio

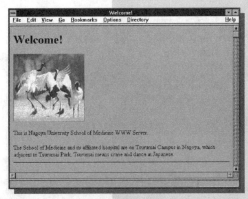

http://www.med.nagoya-u.ac.jp/
Medicine; Nagoya University; Japan

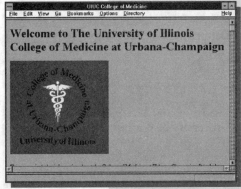

http://www.med.uiuc.edu/
Medicine; University of Illinois

Medicine

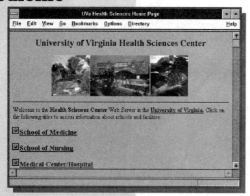

http://www.med.virginia.edu/
Education; University of Virginia

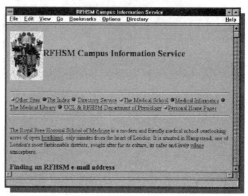

http://www.rfhsm.ac.uk/
Medicine; Royal Free Hospital School of Medicine

http://www.meddean.luc.edu/lumen/
Loyola University; Medicine

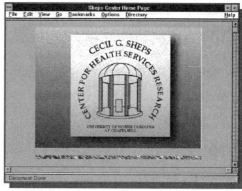

http://www.schsr.unc.edu/
Medicine; Rural medicine; University of North Carolina

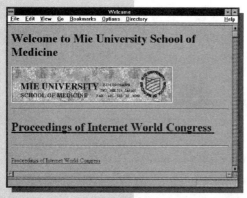

http://www.medic.mie-u.ac.jp/
Medicine; Mie University

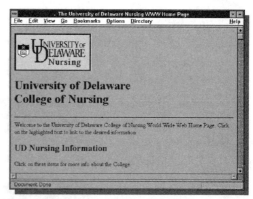

http://www.udel.edu/brentt/UD_Nursing.html
Nursing; University of Delware

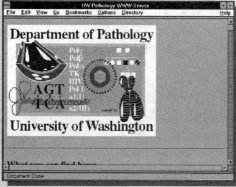

http://www.pathology.washington.edu/
Department of Pathology; Education; University of Washington

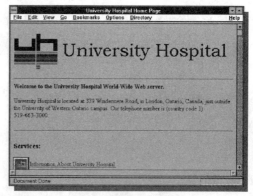

http://www.uh.london.on.ca/
Canada; Education; Ontario; University Hospital

http://bazaar.com/Worlddom/worlddom.html
Artists; Mail order catalog; Music; News; World Domination

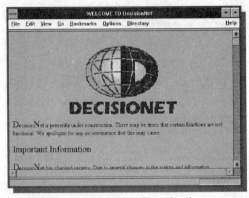

http://bhargava.as.nps.navy.mil/dNethome.html
Decision support services; Modeling

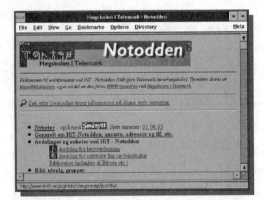

http://bjorn.tmlh.no/
Hogskolen i Telemark; Norway; Notodden

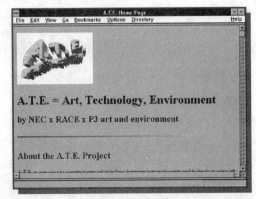

http://brains.race.u-tokyo.ac.jp/ATE.html
A.T.E.; A.T.E. Project; Art; Environment; Technology

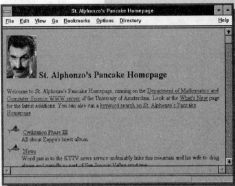

http://carol.fwi.uva.nl/~heederik/zappa/
Albums; Frank Zappa; Mothers Of Invention; Music

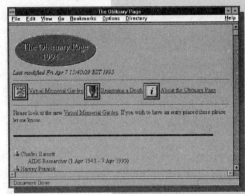

http://catless.ncl.ac.uk/Obituary/README.html
Obituary Page; Registering a Death; Virtual Memorial Garden

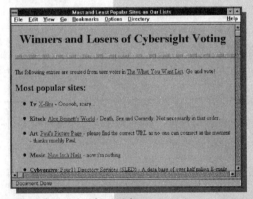

http://cybersight.com/cgi-bin/cs/nlists
Art; Media; Music; TV

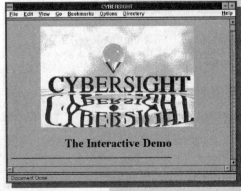

http://cybersight.com/cgi-bin/cs/s?main.gmml
Cybersight; Demo; Internet

Miscellaneous

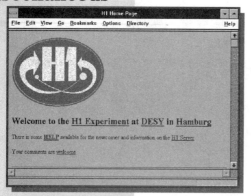

http://dice2.desy.de/
Germany; H1 Experiment; Hamburg

http://dvts.dvts.com/
DaVinci Time & Space; Links; News; Publications

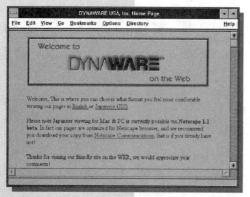

http://dynaware.com/~dynaware/index.html
Dynaware USA; English; Japanese

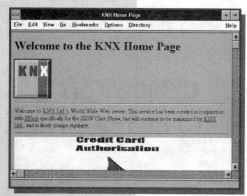

http://fleet.britain.eu.net/~knx/
KNX Ltd; United Kingdom; West Yorkshire

http://freenet.vancouver.bc.ca/
Canada; Vancouver Regional FreeNet; World Wide Web

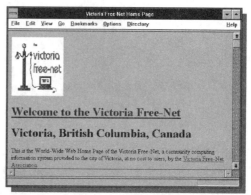

http://freenet.victoria.bc.ca/vifa.html
Canada; Victoria FreeNet; World Wide Web

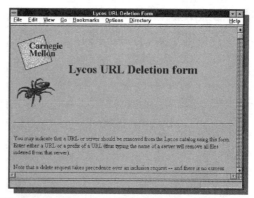

http://fuzine.mt.cs.cmu.edu/mlm/lycos-delete.html
Carnegie Mellon; Lycos; URL deletion

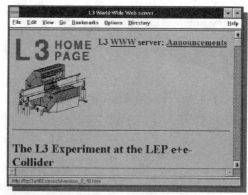

http://hpl3sn02.cern.ch/
L3 Experiment at the LEP e+e- Collider

348

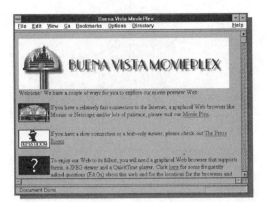

http://bvp.wdp.com/BVI/index.html
Buena Vista; Movies; Theatres

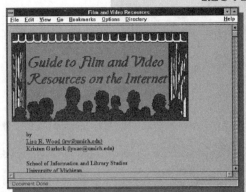

http://http2.sils.umich.edu/Public/fvl/film.html
Film; Guide; Video

http://bvp.wdp.com/BVPM/MooVPlex.html
Buena Park; Entertainment; Movies; Theatre

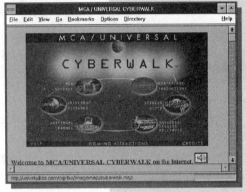

http://univstudios.com/
Entertainment industry; MCA/Universal; Movies

http://digiplanet.com/STARGATE/index.html
MGM; Motion picture; StarGate

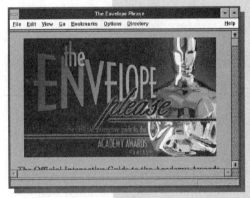

http://visualize.pacopost.com/
Academy Awards; Interactive Guide

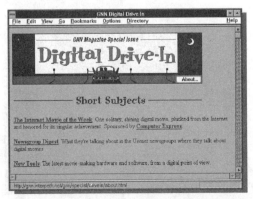

http://gnn.interpath.net/gnn/special/drivein/index.html
Digital movies; Movie reviews; Multimedia

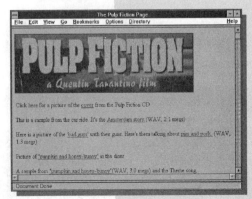

http://wolf.cso.uiuc.edu/pulpfict.html
Audio; Pulp Fiction; Tarantino

Movies

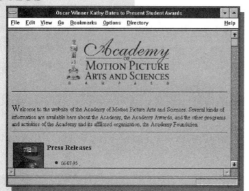

http://www.ampas.org/ampas/
Academy of Motion Picture Arts and Sciences; News

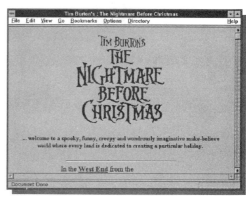

http://www.musicbase.co.uk/movie/night/
Animation; Imagination; Movies

http://www.hollywood.com/
Hollywood Online; Movie information; Previews; Sound clips

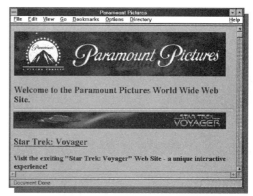

http://www.paramount.com/
Interactive; Paramount Pictures; Star Trek; Voyager

http://www.ios.com/~jbonne/qt/
Film; Movies; Tarantino

http://www.uspan.com:80/miramar/
Catalog; Films; Movies

http://www.mdstud.chalmers.se/hkmovie/
Hong Kong; Movies; Previews

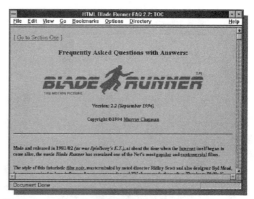

http://www.vir.com/VideoFilm/Blade/brfaq_0.html
Blade Runner; FAQs; Film; Movies

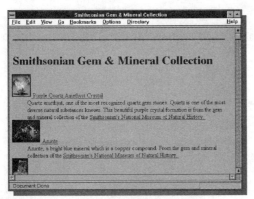

http://galaxy.einet.net/images/gems/gems-icons.html
Azurite; Gems; Minerals; Quartz amethyst; Smithsonian

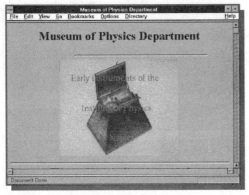

http://hpl33.na.infn.it/Museum/Museum.html
Italy; Museums; Naples; Physics

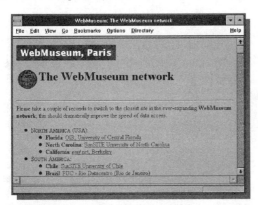

http://mistral.enst.fr/~pioch/louvre/louvre.html
Museums; Online

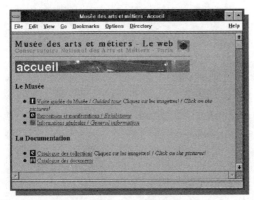

http://web.cs.nott.ac.uk/~nlc/pratchett.html
Arts; France; French; Museums

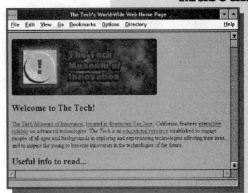

http://whyanext.com/thetech.html
Interactive exhibits; Museum of Innovation; San Jose

http://www.crs4.it/HTML/RUGGIERO/MUSEO/mus_ind.html
Archaeology; Exhibits; Italy; Museums

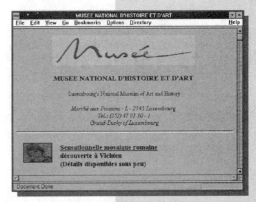

http://www.men.lu/~fumanti/LuxMusee.html
Art; Art exhibits; Art work; History; Museums

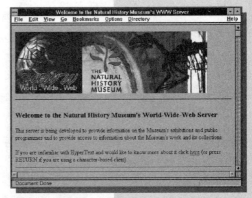

http://www.nhm.ac.uk/
Exhibitions; Great Britain; Natural history museum

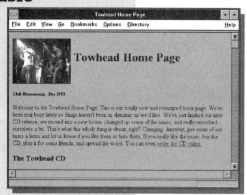

http://36.8.0.205/umbra/Towhead/Towhead.html
Music; Towhead

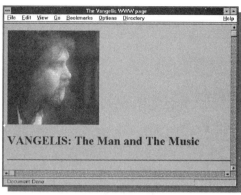

http://bau2.uibk.ac.at/perki/Vangelis.html
Performer; Songs; Vangelis

http://actor.cs.vt.edu/~wentz/index.html
Elvis Costello; Enigma; Singers; Songwriters

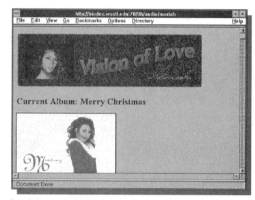

http://biodec.wustl.edu:70/0h/audio/mariah
Pop music; Singers

http://american.recordings.com/
American Recordings

http://biogopher.wustl.edu:70/1/audio/bmg
Columbia House; Compact disc; Music clubs

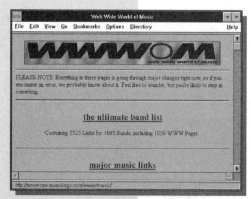

http://american.recordings.com/wwwofmusic/index.html
Band list; Music links

http://bmi.com/
BMI; Songs; Songwriters

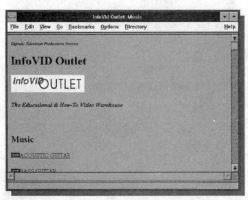

http://branch.com/infovid/c325.html
Education; InfoVid Outlet; Music; Video

http://breakfast.com:2500/Default.html
Indie recording labels; Orbit; Pop music

http://ccrma-www.stanford.edu/
Acoustics; Computer research; Music

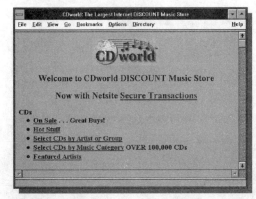

http://cdworld.com/
CD; Discounts; Music store

http://christian-death.acc.brad.ac.uk:/
Alternative; Gothic; Industrial; Rock

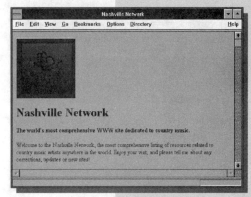

http://club.eng.cam.ac.uk/~94mab/country/
Country music; Nashville

353

http://coos.dartmouth.edu/~joeh/
Heavy metal; Rock

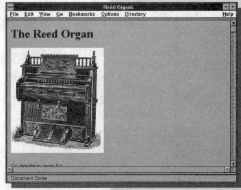

http://cse.utoledo.edu/userhomes/estell/organs/home.html
Keyboards; Music; Reed Organ

Music

http://datura.cerl.uiuc.edu/
CERL; Sound group

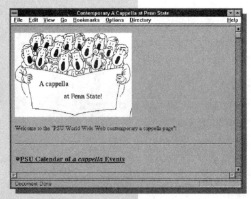

http://east.isx.com/~schnitzi/elvis.html
Guitar tablature; Pop music; Rock

http://eec.psu.edu/~panulla/harmony/
A cappella music; Penn State University

http://fallon.com/mattj/vh/vhpage.html
Hard Rock; Heavy metal; Rock

http://fuzine.mt.cs.cmu.edu/mlm/lycos-home.html
Catalog; Lycos

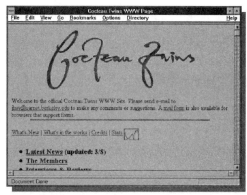

http://garnet.berkeley.edu:8080/
Alternative music; Pop music

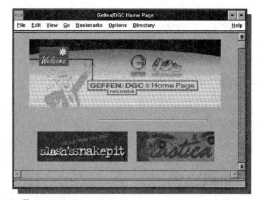

http://geffen.com/
Geffen/DGC Records

http://gemm.com/
Collectibles; Global Electronic Music Marketplace

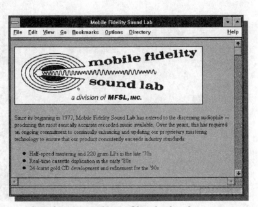

http://gnn.digital.com/gnn/bus/mfsl/index.html
Audio technology; Mastering; Recording; Sound

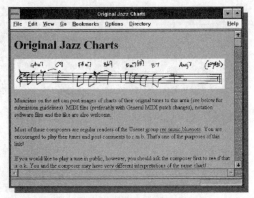

http://hokin.physics.wisc.edu/jazz/charts.html
Jazz; MIDI; Museums

http://hostname.pencom.com/subdirs/rmc/home.html
Artists; Concert reviews; rec.music.christian

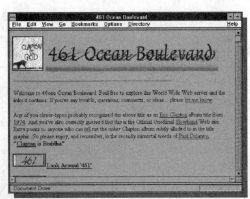

http://http.bsd.uchicago.edu/~d-hillman/welcome.html
Blues music; Eric Clapton; Rock

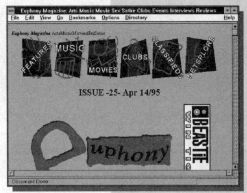

http://imagineer.com/euphony
Magazine; Movies; News

http://iris3.carb.nist.gov:8000/pub/ram/music/primus/primus.html
Funk; Progressive; Rock

355

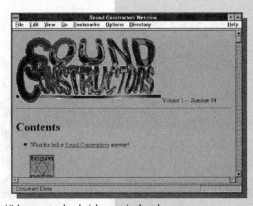

http://isl-garnet.uah.edu/claassen/sc.html
Electronic; Equipment

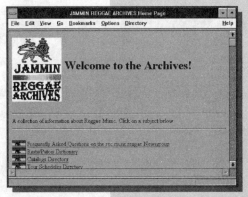

http://jammin.nosc.mil/jammin.html
Newsgroups; Reggae

Music

http://jrusby.uoregon.edu/obf/obfhome.html
Bach; Oregon

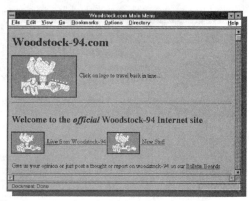

http://metaverse.com/woodstock/index.html
Music; Rock; Woodstock 94

http://kspace.com/KM/music.sys/musiclist.html
Directory; Index; Music

http://mothra.nts.uci.edu:80/~dhwalker/dixie/
England; Ireland; Scotland; Traditional music

http://lecaine.music.mcgill.ca/
Artists; Library; Music database

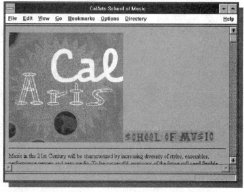

http://music.calarts.edu/
CalArts School of Music; Music

http://metaverse.com/vibe/
Music; On Ramp Inc.; VIBE; Vibrations

http://muspe1.cirfid.unibo.it/welcome.htm
Italy; Music; Performing Arts; University of Bologna

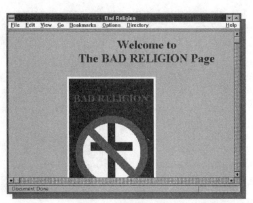

http://nebuleuse.enst-bretagne.fr:80/~lepoulti/BAD.RELIGION/
Alternative music; Punk rock; Rock

http://nyx10.cs.du.edu:8001/~gsherwin/jehu.html
Alternative music; Punk rock; Rock

http://netspace.org/gsw/sounds.html
God Street Sound Clips; Lyrics; Music

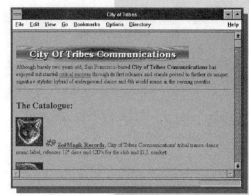

http://organic.com/Music/City.o.tribes/index.html
4th World music; City of Tribes Communications; Dance

http://newalbion.com/
Index; Music; New Albion Records

http://organic.com/Music/GAMH/
Entertainment; Fine food; Nightclub; San Francisco

http://none.coolware.com/entmt/smileyface/smileyface.html
Bands; Music; Smileyface

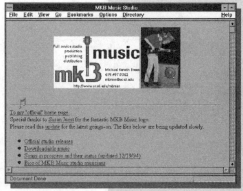

http://orpheus.ucsd.edu/mbreen/mkb_music/index.html
MKB; Music; Studio

News

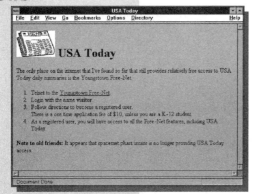

http://alpha.acast.nova.edu/usatoday.html
K-12; Online newspaper; Periodical; USA Today

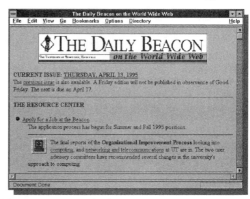

http://beacon-www.asa.utk.edu/
Student paper; The Daily Beacon

http://avion.db.erau.edu/
Aviation/Aerospace Newspaper; Avion Online

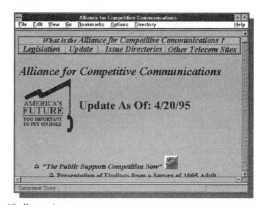

http://bell.com/
Competitive communications; Legislation; Telecommunications

http://azstarnet.com/
Arizona Daily Star; News; Online newspaper; StarNet

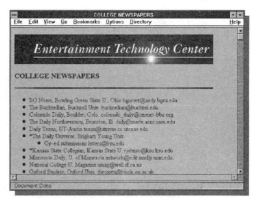

http://cwis.usc.edu/dept/etc/media/cnews.html
College newspapers; Student paper

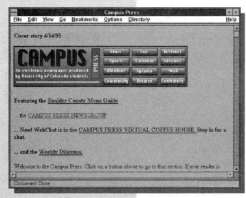

http://bcn.boulder.co.us/campuspress/Presshome.html
Campus Press; Student paper; University of Colorado

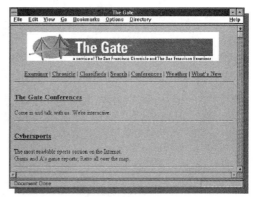

http://cyber.sfgate.com/
Bay Area; News; Periodicals; San Francisco

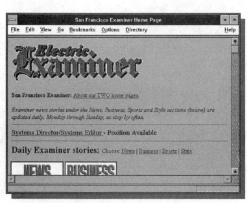

http://cyber.sfgate.com/examiner/
Business; News; San Francisco Examiner; Sports

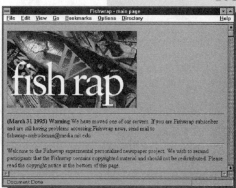

http://fishwrap.mit.edu/
Fishwrap; News; Online newspaper

http://cyber.sfgate.com/examiner/49ers/49ershome.html
49ers; News; San Francisco Examiner; Sports

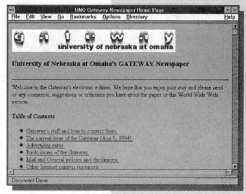

http://gateway-news.unomaha.edu/gateway/gateway.html
Student paper; University of Nebraska at Omaha; Newspaper

http://cybermart.com/bonanza/LTNN.html
Community information; Lake Tahoe; News; Recreation

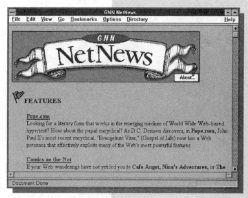

http://gnn.com/news/index.html
GNN NetNews; Hypertext; Online news

http://enews.com/
Electronic newsstands; News; Periodicals

http://gopher.det-freepress.com:9002/
Detroit Free Press; Online newspaper

359

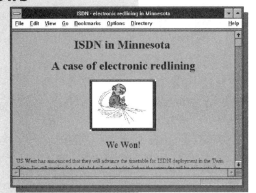

http://haven.com/isdn.html
ISDN; Minnesota; News; Redlining; US West

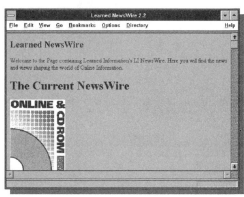

http://info.learned.co.uk/1s/newswire
Learned NewsWire; Online information

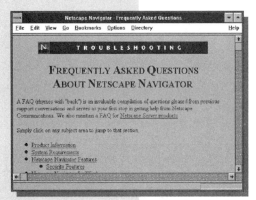

http://home.mcom.com/home/faq_docs/faq_client.html
FAQ; Netscape Navigator; News; Software

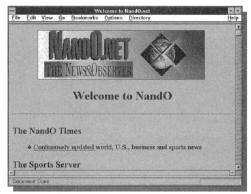

http://merlin.nando.net/
Business; News; Sports

http://home.mcom.com/home/whatsnew/whats_new.html
Articles; Monkeys; Photos

http://metaverse.com/vibe/sleaze/index.shtml
Adam Curry; Entertainment news

http://info.fuw.edu.pl/gw/0/gazeta.htm
Gazeta Online; Online newspaper; Poland

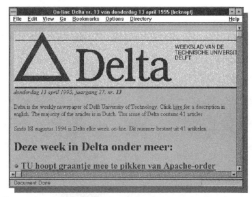

http://muresh.et.tudelft.nl/delta/laatste/voorpagina.html
Delta; Delta University of Technology; Student paper

http://newproducts.jpl.nasa.gov/
Health care; Public safety; Telecommunications

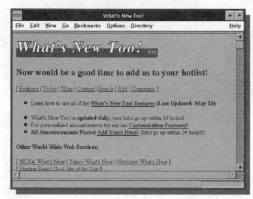

http://newtoo.manifest.com/WhatsNewToo/index.html
Directories; Links; News; Search

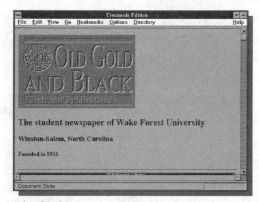

http://ogb.wfu.edu/
Electronic publications; Student paper; Wake Forest University

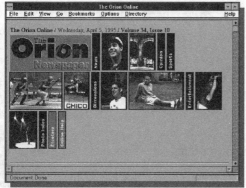

http://orion.csuchico.edu/
Chico State University; Student paper; The Orion

http://sfgate.com/examiner/
Business; News; San Francisco Examiner; Sports

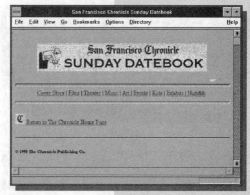

http://sfgate.com/new/schron/datebook/index.html
Art; Exhibits; Films; Kids; Music; Nightlife; Theater

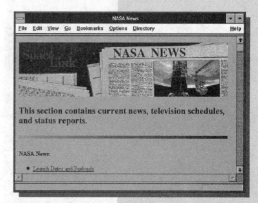

http://spacelink.msfc.nasa.gov/html/NASA.News.html
Events; NASA News; Space

http://the-tech.mit.edu/
News service; Online media; Periodical

News

http://town.hall.org/places/npc/
Broadcast; Communications media; National Press Club

http://www.baynet.com/smtimes.html
Online newspaper; San Mateo Times

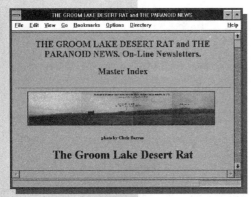

http://weber.u.washington.edu/~roland/rat
Aliens; ET; Groom Lake

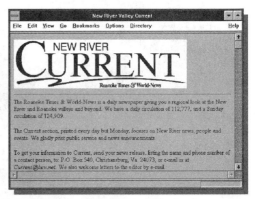

http://www.bev.net/mall/NRCurrent/index.html
New River Current; Online newspaper

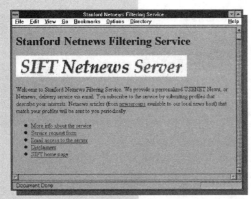

http://woodstock.stanford.edu:2000/
Netnews filtering; Stanford; USENET

http://www.bucknell.edu/bucknellian/
Bucknell University; Student paper; The Bucknellian

http://www.amdahl.com/doc/texture/Docs/whats-new.html
Amdahl Corporation; News

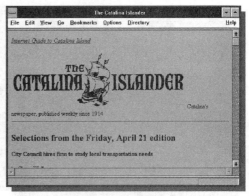

http://www.catalina-island.com/guide/islander.html
Catalina Island; Guide; Information; News; Publication; Vacation

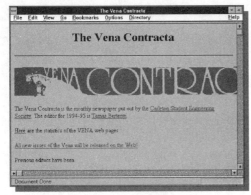

http://www.ccnet.com/SF_Free_Press/welcome.html
Bay Area; Online newspaper; The San Francisco Free Press

http://www.cnd.org:80/CNDservices.html
China News Digest; Services

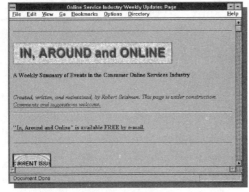

http://www.civeng.carleton.ca/CSES/VENA/
Carleton; Student paper; The Vena Contracta

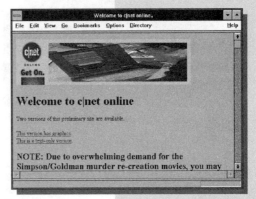

http://www.cnet.com/
Graphics; Kato; News; OJ

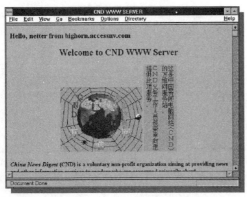

http://www.clark.net/pub/robert/home.html
Events; Newsletters; Online business news

http://www.crs4.it/~ruggiero/unione.html
Italy; Online newspaper

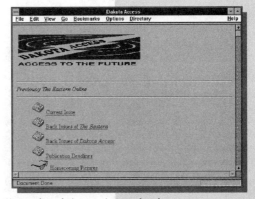

http://www.cnd.org/
China News Digest; Chinese

http://www.dsu.edu/eastern/eastern.html
Dakota Access; Student paper; The Eastern

Oceanography

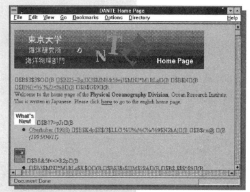

http://aqua.ucsd.edu/
Aquarium; Oceanography; San Diego

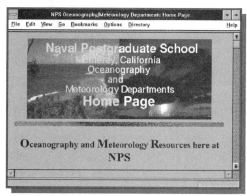

http://heron.met.nps.navy.mil/
Meteorology; Naval Postgraduate School; Oceanography

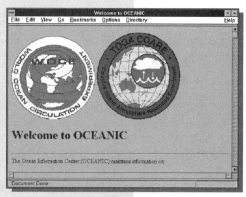

http://dante.ori.u-tokyo.ac.jp/
Japanese; Oceanography; Research

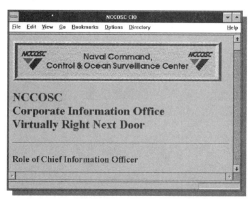

http://nrad00sv.nosc.mil/~mole/CIO_HomePage/CIO.html
Chief Information Officer; Control and ocean surveillance

http://diu.cms.udel.edu/
Marine biology; Oceanic; Oceanography

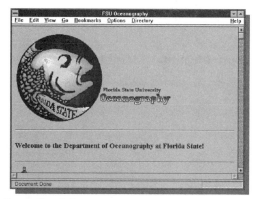

http://ocean.fsu.edu/
Florida State University; Oceanography

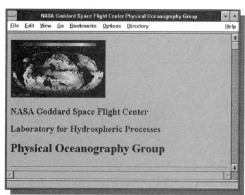

http://helium.nrlmry.navy.mil/neons_home.html
Naval Environmental Operational Nowcasting System

http://oraac.gsfc.nasa.gov/
NASA Goddard Space Flight Center; Physical Oceanography

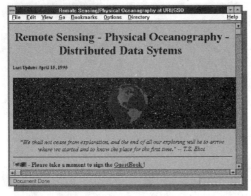

http://sapphire.cse.ucsc.edu/MosaicMet/top-view.html
Meteorological; Oceanographic science; REINAS Project

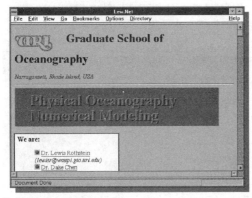

http://satori.gso.uri.edu/
Oceanography; University of Rhode Island

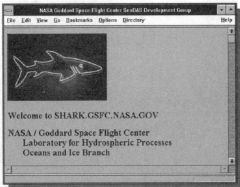

http://seip.gso.uri.edu/
Graduate school; Oceanography; University of Rhode Island

http://shark.gsfc.nasa.gov/
Goddard Space Flight Center; SeaDAS Development Group

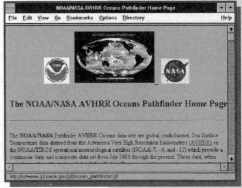

http://sst-www.jpl.nasa.gov/
NOAA/NASA AVHRR Oceans Pathfinder

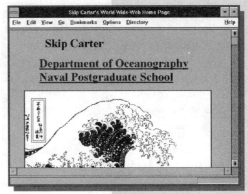

http://taygeta.oc.nps.navy.mil/skips_home.html
Naval Postgraduate School; Oceanography

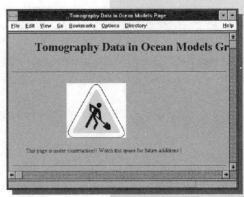

http://taygeta.oc.nps.navy.mil/tomography.html
Tomography Data in Ocean Models

http://underwater.iis.u-tokyo.ac.jp/Welcome-e.html
Naval Architecture & Ocean Engineering; University of Tokyo

Personal

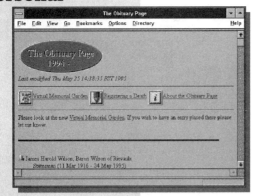

http://catless.ncl.ac.uk/Obituary/
Death; Memorials; Obituaries

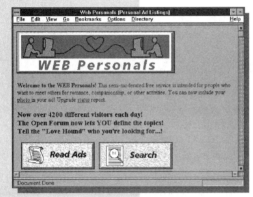

http://hamilton.netmedia.com:80/date/
Companionship; Cybersex; Romance; Web personals

http://match.com/
Dating service; Fun; Love; Marriage; Personals; Romance; Sex

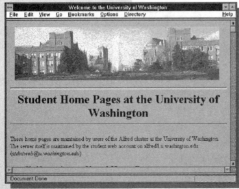

http://weber.u.washington.edu:80/stdntweb/
Personal; Student pages; University of Washington

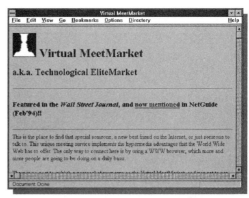

http://wwa.com:1111/
Cybersex; Romance; Virtual MeetMarket

http://www-leland.stanford.edu/group/bridge/
Peer Counseling; The Bridge

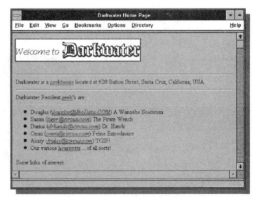

http://www.biodata.com/douglas/darkwater.html
California; Darkwater; Geekhouse; Santa Cruz

http://www.infi.net/pilot/personals.html
Dating; Romance; The Meeting Place

366

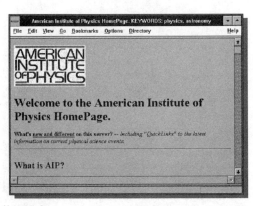

http://aip.org/
American Institute; Astronomy; Physics

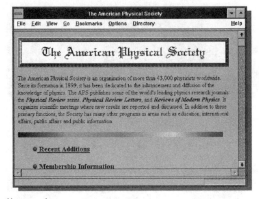

http://aps.org/
Education; Physical society; Physics; Publications

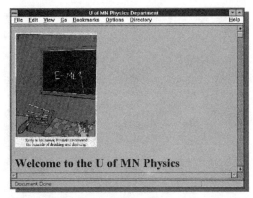

http://cedar.spa.umn.edu/
Physics; University of Minnesota

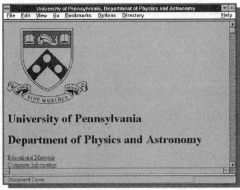

http://dept.physics.upenn.edu/
Physics; University of Pennsylvania

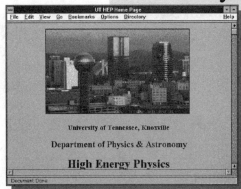

http://enigma.phys.utk.edu/
Knoxville; Physics; University of Tennessee

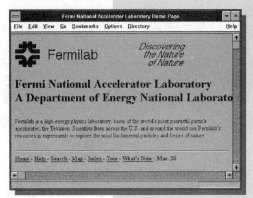

http://fnnews.fnal.gov/
Accelerator; Physics; Science

http://heplibw3.slac.stanford.edu/FIND/FHMAIN.HTML
Physics; Science; Software

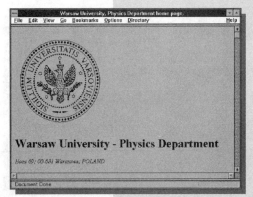

http://info.fuw.edu.pl/
Poland; Warsaw University

Physics

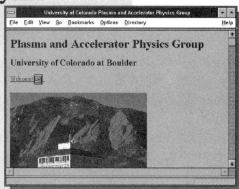

http://jove.colorado.edu/homepage.html
Physics; Plasma; Science; University of Colorado

http://pgsa.rice.edu/home.html
Physics; Rice University

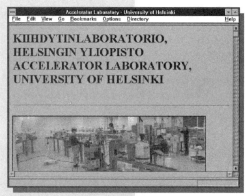

http://kl-linux.helsinki.fi/
Accelerator Laboratory; University of Helsinki

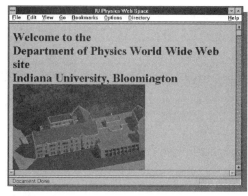

http://physics.indiana.edu/
Indiana University; Physics

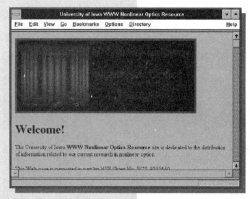

http://marv.eng.uiowa.edu/
Light; Optics; Physics; Science; University of Iowa

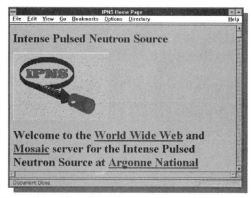

http://pnsjph.pns.anl.gov:80/
Argonne; Intense pulsed neutron; Physics

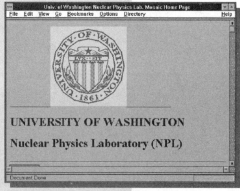

http://mist.npl.washington.edu/home.html
Nuclear Physics; University of Washington

http://slacvm.slac.stanford.edu/find/explist.html
Energy; Physics; Science; Stanford University

http://bug.village.virginia.edu/
Modeling; Programming; Virtual Reality

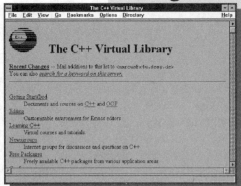

http://info.desy.de/user/projects/C++.html
C++; Learning C++; Library; OOP

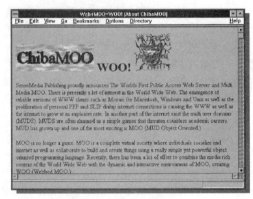

http://chiba.picosof.com/about
Mac; Objects; MOO; MUD; Windows; WOO

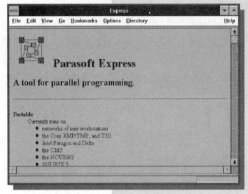

http://ivory.nosc.mil/htdocs/express/express.html
Parallel programming; Parasoft Express; Software tools

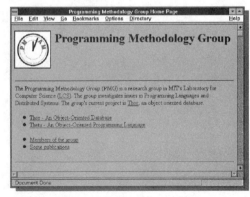

http://clef.lcs.mit.edu/
Massachusetts Institute of Technology; Programming

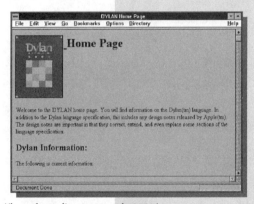

http://legend.gwydion.cs.cmu.edu:8001/
DYLAN; Language specification; Programming

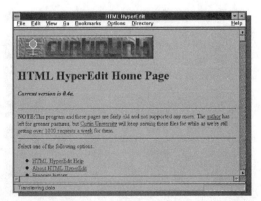

http://info.curtin.edu.au/computing/packages/htmledit/home.htm
HTML; HTTP; HyperEdit; Web pages

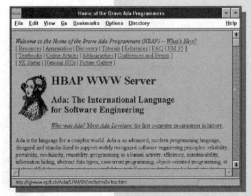

http://lglwww.epfl.ch/Ada/
Ada; Language; Programming; Software Engineering

369

Programming

http://oneworld.wa.com/htmldev/devpage/dev-page.html
HTML development; HTTP; Web documents

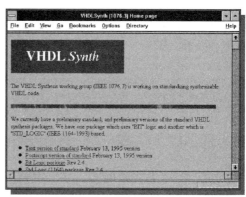

http://vhdl.org/vi/vhdlsynth/vhdlsynth.html
IEEE; Synthesis; VHDL

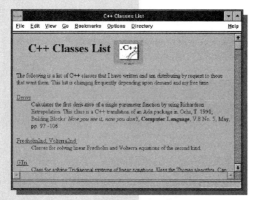

http://taygeta.oc.nps.navy.mil/ada.html
Ada; Computer programming languages; Software

http://web.kaleida.com/
Media player; Programming language for multimedia

http://taygeta.oc.nps.navy.mil/Classes.html
C++ Classes List

http://web.nexor.co.uk/perl/perl.html
Languages; Perl; Programming

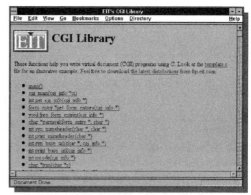

Forth Interest Group Home Page

http://taygeta.oc.nps.navy.mil/fig_home.html
Forth Interest Group

http://wsk.eit.com/wsk/dist/doc/libcgi/libcgi.html
C programming; CGI Library; Computing

http://www.best.com/~imagine/sentek/
Consulting; Object-oriented programming; Programmers

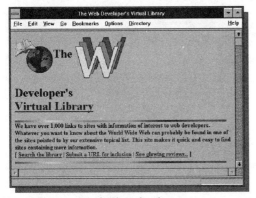

http://www.charm.net/~web/About.html
Virtual library; Web; Web developers

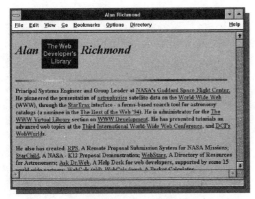

http://www.charm.net/~web/Alan/Richmond.html
HTML; Web Developer's Library

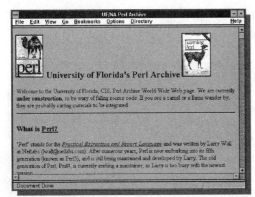

http://www.cis.ufl.edu/perl/
Perl archive; Practical Extraction and Report Language

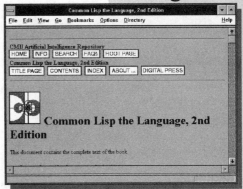

http://www.cs.cmu.edu:8001/Web/Groups/AI/html/cltl/cltl2.html
Common Lisp; Programming Language

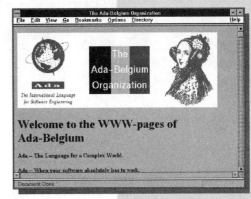

http://www.cs.kuleuven.ac.be/~dirk/ada-belgium/
Ada; Compilers; Programming languages

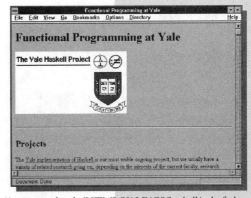

http://www.cs.yale.edu/HTML/YALE/CS/haskell/yale-fp.html
Functional programming; Haskell Project; Yale

http://www.cs.yale.edu/HTML/YALE/CS/Linda/linda.html
Linda; Programming languages; Software systems; Yale

Psychology

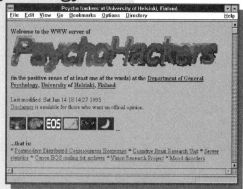

http://avocado.pc.helsinki.fi/
Psychology; University of Helsinki; Finland

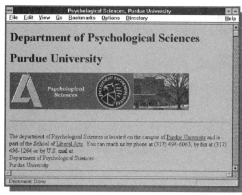

http://wizard.psych.purdue.edu/
Psychological sciences; Purdue University

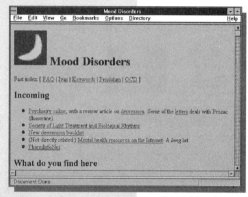

http://avocado.pc.helsinki.fi/~janne/mood/mood.html
Depression; Mood disorders; Psychology; Therapy

http://www.cc.utexas.edu/psycgrad/psycgrad.html
PSYCGRAD; Psychology forums; Scientific journals

http://ctipsych.york.ac.uk/ctipsych.html
Computers; Psychology; Teaching; University of York

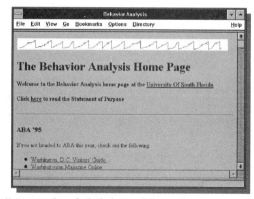

http://www.coedu.usf.edu/behavior/behavior.html
Behavior analysis; University of South Florida

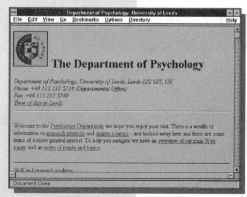

http://lethe.leeds.ac.uk/
Department of Psychology; Education

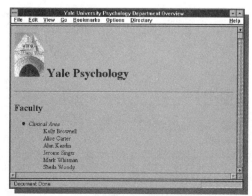

http://www.cs.yale.edu/HTML/YALE/PSYCH/FrontDoor.html
Clinical; Psychology; Yale

http://apollo.co.uk/a/annettem/
Annette Martin; Book; Discovering Your Psychic World

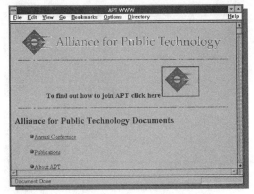

http://apt.org/apt.html
Alliance for Public Technology; Documents; Publications

http://axxon.fcaglp.unlp.edu.ar/axxon.html
Fiction; Multimedia; Spanish

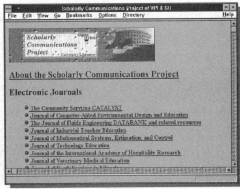

http://borg.lib.vt.edu/
Electronic journals; Scholarly Communications Project

http://ccnet.com/SF_Free_Press/
Free Press; News; San Francisco

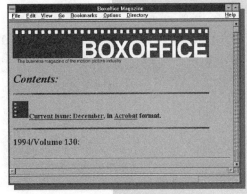

http://cwis.usc.edu/dept/etc/boxoffice/boxoffice.html
Magazines; Movie industry

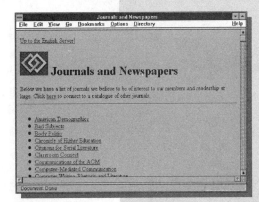

http://english-server.hss.cmu.edu/Journals.html
Electronic periodicals; Journals; Magazines; Newspapers

http://enternet.iuma.com/
Enternet Communications; Influx magazine

Publications

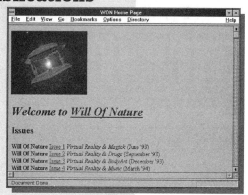

http://erg.ucd.ie/won.html
BodyArt; Drugs; Music; Virtual reality; Will of Nature

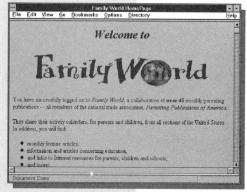

http://family.com/homepage.html
Event calendars; Family World; Online publications; Parenting

http://ftp.etext.org/Zines/InterText/intertext.html
Fantasy; Fiction; Horror; Online magazine; Short stories

http://gate.globalx.net/monitor/
Canada; Global Monitor; News; Online magazine

http://inept.scubed.com:8001/tax/tax.html
Information services; Taxes; Taxing Times

http://life.anu.edu.au/ci/ci.html
Electronic Journal of Complex Systems Research

http://mmnewsstand.com/
Magazine subscriptions; Multimedia; Products; Videotapes

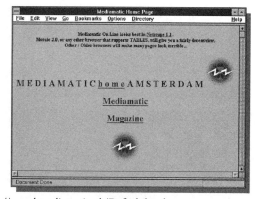

http://mmol.mediamatic.nl:/Default.html
Amsterdam; Electronic media; Periodicals

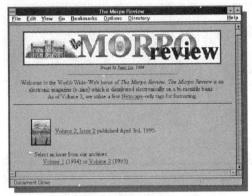

http://mojones.com/motherjones.html
Independent thinking; Online Magazine; Periodical; Politics

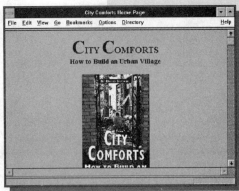

http://nwlink.com/~dsucher/comfort/
Book; City Comforts; Pleasant urban life

http://morpo.creighton.edu/morpo
E-zine; Fiction; Nonfiction; Online magazine; Poetry

http://pathfinder.com/
Entertainment; News magazines

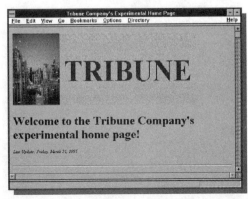

http://newton.otago.ac.nz:808/trol/Rolhome.html
Journal of research; New Zealand; Radioscientist Online

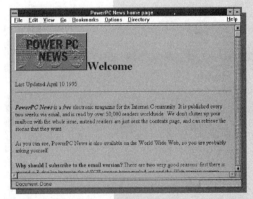

http://power.globalnews.com/
Computers; Mac; Online magazine; PowerPC News

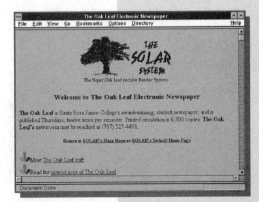

http://none.coolware.com/tribune/tcohtml.html
Daily newspapers; News; Newspapers

http://quercas.santarosa.edu/mainmenu/issues/oakLeafIssues
Santa Rose Junior College; Student paper

Publications

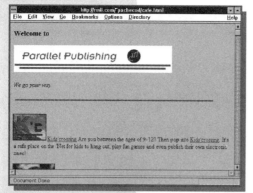

http://rmii.com/~pachecod/cafe.html
Games; K-12; Kids; Parallel Publishing

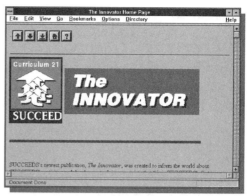

http://succeed.che.ufl.edu/SUCCEED/pubs/innovator/
Conferences; Engineering; Publications; SUCCEED

http://rubicon.water.ca.gov/
California; Department of Water Resources; Reports

http://sunsite.unc.edu/martin/gonzo.html
Georgetown University; Satire; Student publication

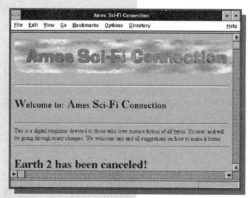

http://scifitoys.com/ames
Digital magazine; Sci-Fi; Science fiction

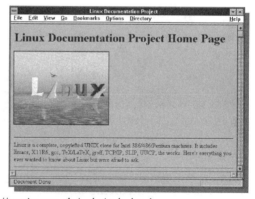

http://sunsite.unc.edu/mdw/mdw.html
Linux documentation; SLIP; TCP/IP; UUCP

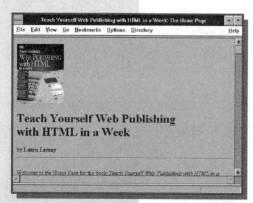

http://slack.lne.com/lemay/theBook/
Book; Teach Yourself Web Publishing; HTML

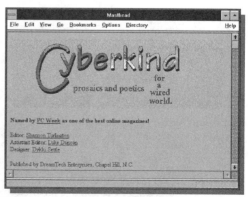

http://sunsite.unc.edu/shannon/ckind/title.html
Online magazine; Poems; Poetry

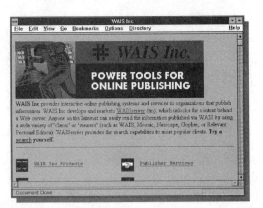

http://techweb.cmp.com/
Online publishing; Tools; WAIS

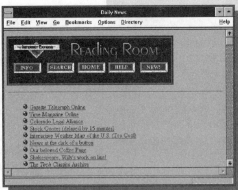

http://usa.net/home/daily.html
Directories; Links; News

http://the-tech.mit.edu:80/The-Tech
Academic paper; MIT; Newsletters

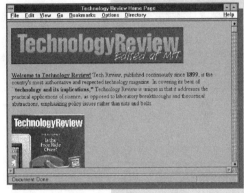

http://web.mit.edu/afs/athena/org/t/techreview/www/tr.html
Online magazine; Science; Technology Review

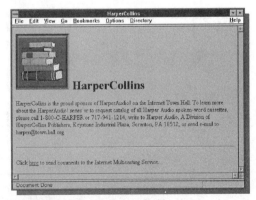

http://town.hall.org/sponsors/harper.html
Catalog; HarperCollins; Publishing

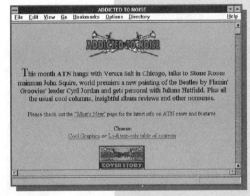

http://www.addict.com/ATN/
Album reviews; Columns; Graphics; Online magazine

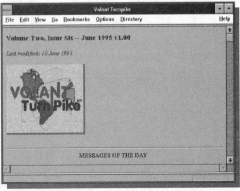

http://turnpike.net/turnpike/index.html
Internet resources; Volant Turnpike

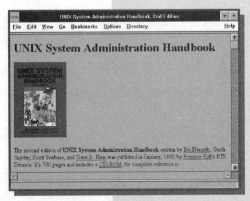

http://www.admin.com/
CD-ROM; Handbook; System Administration; UNIX

Publications

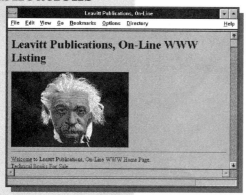

http://www.armory.com/~leavitt/
Ancient; Gnosis; Modern; Technical books

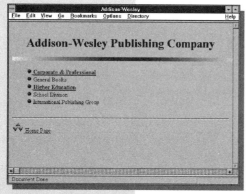

http://www.aw.com/awpc.html
Addison-Wesley Publishing Company; Books; Publisher

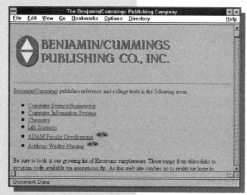

http://www.aw.com/bc/home.html
Benjamin/Cummings Publishing Company; Books; Publishers

http://www.batnet.com/taugher/
Black literature; Collecting; Detective; Fiction; Mysteries

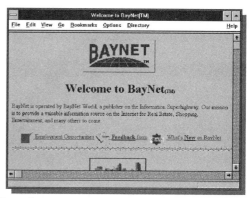

http://www.baynet.com/
Entertainment; Information; Publisher; Real estate; Shopping

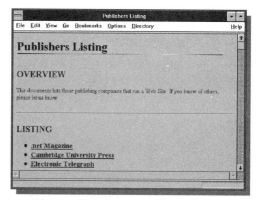

http://www.bham.ac.uk/documents/publishers.html
Directories; Index; Links; Listing; Publishers

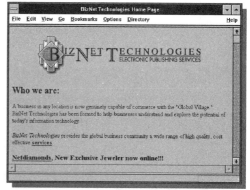

http://www.bnt.com/
BizNet Technologies; Electronic publishing

http://www.boardwatch.com/
BBS; Electronic bulletin boards; Information; Magazine

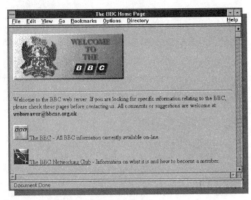

http://aragorn.solutionsrc.com:80/KMPS/
Country music; Radio stations; Seattle

http://auntie.bbcnc.org.uk/
BBC; British Broadcasting Company

http://fbwww.epfl.ch/
Campus life; FERUE; Radio; Switzerland; Universities

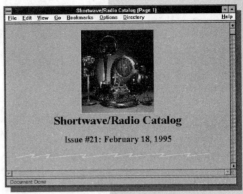

http://itre.uncecs.edu/radio/
Catalog; HAM; Radio; Shortwave

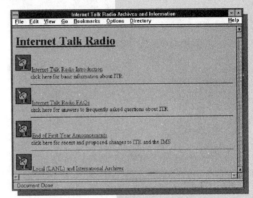

http://juggler.lanl.gov/itr.html
FAQs; Internet Talk Radio; News

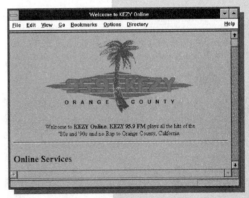

http://kezy.com/kezy/index.htm
'80s and '90s music; KEZY 95.9 FM; No Rap

SAREX - Shuttle Amateur Radio
Experiment

http://hypatia.gsfc.nasa.gov/sarex_mainpage.html
Amateur radio experiment; SAREX; Shuttle

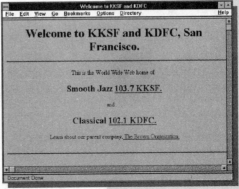

http://kksf.tbo.com/
Classical; KDFC; KKSF; Radio; San Francisco; Smooth Jazz

Radio

http://kzsu.stanford.edu/
KZSU; Radio; Stanford University

http://www.accessnv.com/knpr
FM Radio; KNPR; Nevada

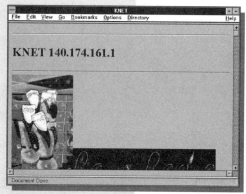

http://metaverse.com/knet/
KNET; Music; Radio

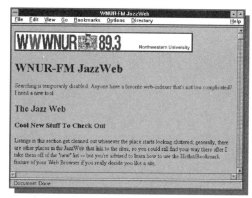

http://www.acns.nwu.edu/WNUR/jazzbase/
Blue Note; Improvisation; Jazz

http://spacsun.rice.edu/~vek/ktru.html
FM radio; Jazz; KTRU

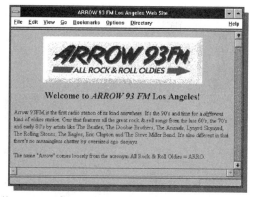

http://www.arrowfm.com/
60's; 70's; 80's; ARROW 93 FM; Los Angeles; Rock

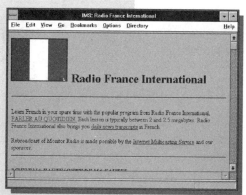

http://town.hall.org/travel/france/rfi.html
Internet Multicasting Service; Radio France International

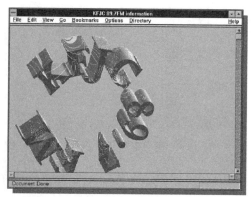

http://www.cygnus.com/misc/kfjc.html
KFJC; Music; Radio

http://agency.resource.ca.gov/parks/dpr.html
California; Parks; Recreation

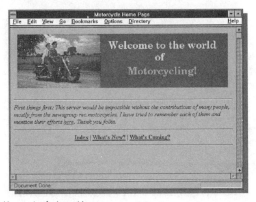

http://cs.wpi.edu/~ravi/
Cycling; Harley; Hogs; Motorcycles

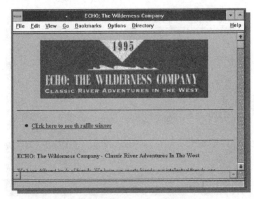

http://cyber.cclims.com/comp/echo/echo.html
Adventure; Recreation; River trips; Sports; Wilderness

http://deeptht.armory.com/~zap/adverts/flightschool.html
Aviation; Fly airplanes; Learning; Recreation; Training

http://deeptht.armory.com/~zap/adverts/wop.html
Antique; Aviation; Biplanes; Open-cockpit; Recreation

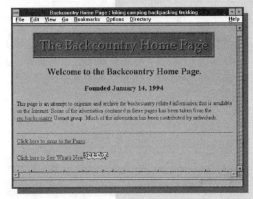

http://io.datasys.swri.edu/
Camping; Hiking; Recreation

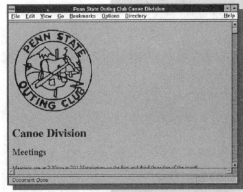

http://random.chem.psu.edu/psoc/
Outing Club - Canoe Division; Penn State University

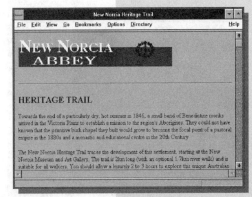

http://stour.iinet.com.au/Heritage/1_INTRO.html
Australia; Hiking; Norcia; Walking

381

Recreation

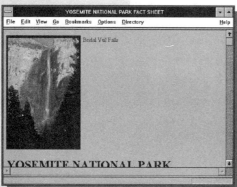

http://town.hall.org/environment/wild_soc/yosemite.html
Camping; Hiking; Yosemite National Park

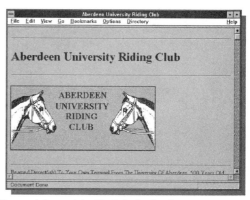

http://www.abdn.ac.uk/~u02pda/index.html
Aberdeen University Riding Club; Equestrian; Horse

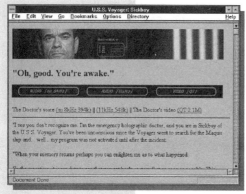

http://voyager.paramount.com/
Audio; Games; Video; Voyager

http://www.best.com/~dijon/disneyland/
Anaheim California; Disneyland Park; Travel; Vacation

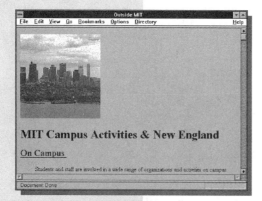

http://web.mit.edu/outandabout.html
Education; MIT campus activities; New England

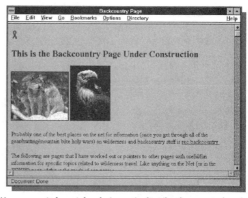

http://www.css.itd.umich.edu/users/colinj/backcountry.html
Backpacking; Camping; Hiking

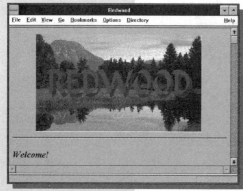

http://www-leland.stanford.edu/group/redwood/
Outdoor Recreation; Redwood; Stanford

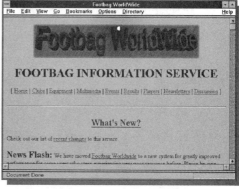

http://www.cup.hp.com/~footbag/
Footbag Information Service; Newsletters; Players

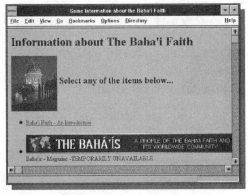

http://ccat.sas.upenn.edu/rs/rs.html
Religious Studies; University of Pennsylvania

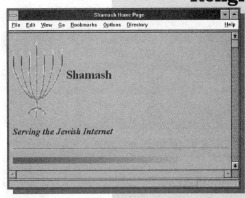

http://shamash.nysernet.org/
Israel; Jewish Internet; Judaism; Shamash

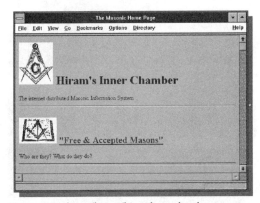

http://herald.usask.ca/~maton/bahai.html
Bahá'ís; Faith; Spirituality; Worship

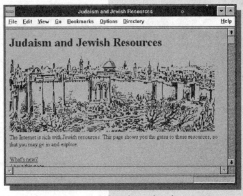

http://shamash.nysernet.org/trb/judaism.html
Faith; Judaism; Jewish resources

http://international.com/hiram/hiramhome.html
Free & Accepted Masons; Masonic

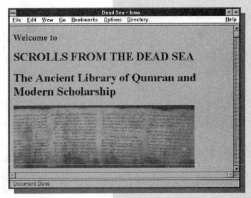

http://sunsite.unc.edu/expo/deadsea.scrolls.exhibit/intro.html
Dead Sea Scrolls; Library; Qumran

http://rain.org/~kfa/
Index; Krishnamurti Foundation of America

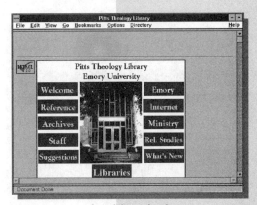

http://sys1.pitts.emory.edu/ptl_home.html
Emory University; Pitts Theology Library

Religion

http://www.best.com/~ferneau/pao-www/pao.top.html
Community information; Jewish; Orthodox; Palo Alto; Resources

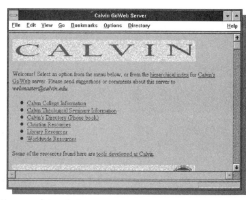

http://www.calvin.edu/
Calvin; Faith; Religion; Seminary; Theology

http://www.bethany.org/
Christian services; Religion

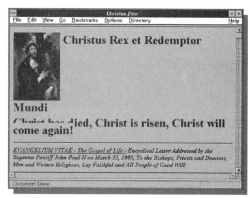

http://www.christusrex.org/
Christianity; Religion

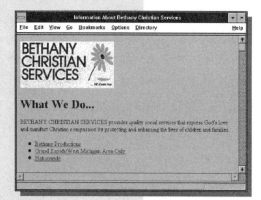

http://www.bethany.org/bethany/what_we_do.html
Beliefs; Christianity; Religion; Social services

http://www.khouse.org/khouse/index.html
Bible; Christianity; Ministry

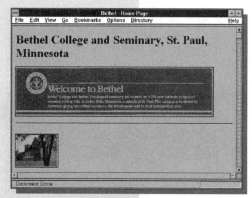

http://www.bethel.org/
Bethel College and Seminary; Bible; Religion

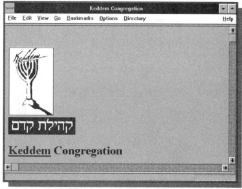

http://www.NeXT.COM/~amarcum/Keddem.html
Judaism; Keddem Congregation; Religion

Schools

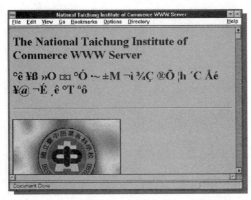

http://alpha.ntcic.edu.tw/
National Taichung Institute of Commerce; Taiwan

http://cdc8g5.cdc.polimi.it/
Italy; Politecnico de Milano

http://cronos.sgia.imp.mx/General.html
Education; Instituto Mexicano del Petroleo

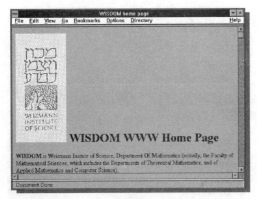

http://eris.wisdom.weizmann.ac.il/
Israel; Weizmann Institute of Science

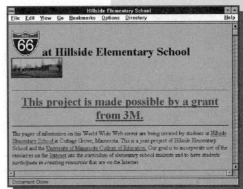

http://hillside.coled.umn.edu/
3M; Hillside Elementary School; Internet; Students

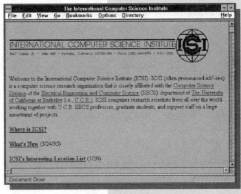

http://http.icsi.berkeley.edu/
Computer science; Electrical engineering; International

385

http://itre.uncecs.edu/
Institute for Transportation Research and Education

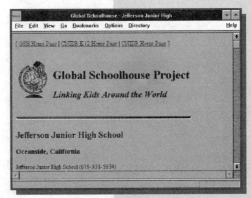

http://k12.cnidr.org/gsh/schools/ca/jjh/jjh.html
California; Jefferson Junior High; Oceanside

Schools

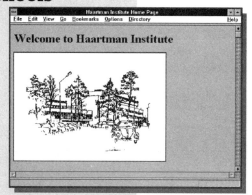

http://kirke.helsinki.fi/
Haartman Institute; Helsinki; Finland

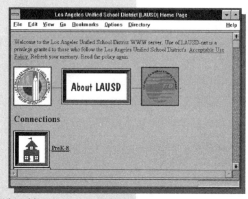

http://lausd.k12.ca.us/
Education; Los Angeles Unified School District

http://mac94.ralphbunche.rbs.edu/
Academics; Elementary school; Ralph Bunche School; Students

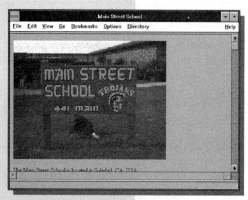

http://monterey.k12.ca.us/mainst/mainst.html
California; Main Street School; Soledad

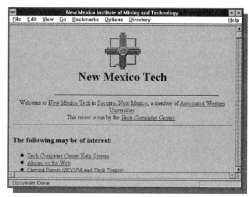

http://nmt.edu/
Education; New Mexico Tech

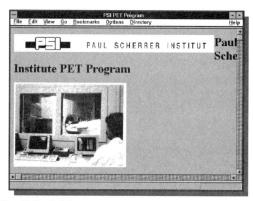

http://pss023.psi.ch/
Paul Scherrer Institute; PET program

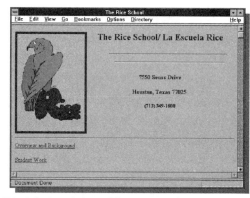

http://riceinfo.rice.edu/armadillo/Rice/Rice_home.html
K-8 School; Rice University

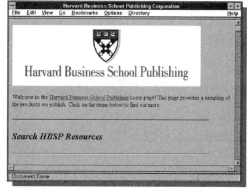

http://rosy.harvard.edu/
Harvard Business School Publishing; Harvard University

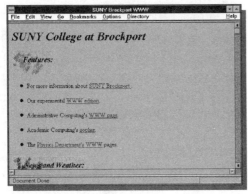

http://santafe.edu/
Education; New Mexico; Santa Fe Institute

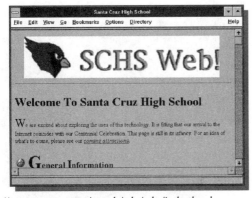

http://www.acs.brockport.edu/
Brockport; State University of New York

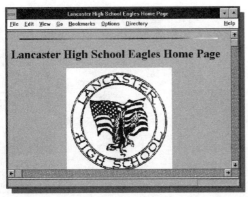

http://www.armory.com/~cards/edu/schs/index.html
Santa Cruz High School

http://www.av.qnet.com/~dickc/lnhs1.html
Antelope Valley; California; Eagles; Lancaster High School

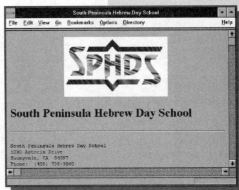

http://www.best.com/~ferneau/pao-www/pao.sphds.html
Children; Education; Jewish; Hebrew Day School

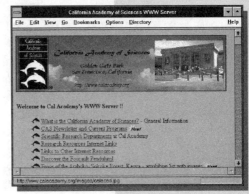

http://www.calacademy.org/
California Academy of Sciences; Information

http://www.caltech.edu:80/
California Institute of Technology; Education

http://www.ccnet.com/~campo/
California; Campolindo High School; Education; Moraga

Schools

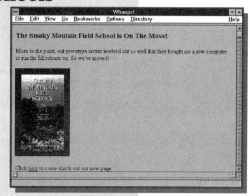

http://www.ce.utk.edu/smoky.html
Culture; Smoky Mountain Field School

http://www.chalmers.se/
Chalmers tekniska hogskola

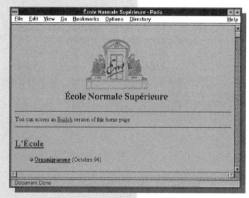

http://www.ens.fr/
École Normale Supérieure; France

http://www.ensta.fr/
École Nationale Supérieure de Techniques Avancées; France

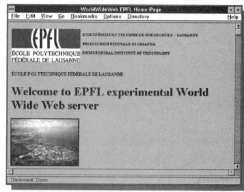

http://www.epfl.ch/
Polytechnique Federale de Lausanne; Switzerland

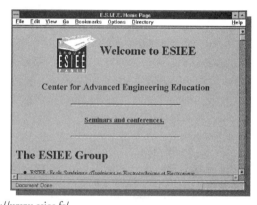

http://www.esiee.fr/
France; Suprieure D'Ingnieur en lectronique et lectrotechnique

http://www.ethz.ch/
Swiss Federal Institute of Technology; Switzerland; Zurich

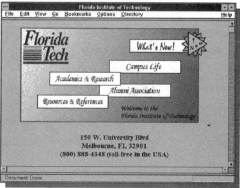

http://www.fit.edu/
Florida Institute of Technology; Florida Tech; Melbourne

http://asp1.sbs.ohio-state.edu/
Atmospheric Sciences; Ohio State University

http://best.gdb.org/
Community of science; Web sites

http://best.gdb.org/best.html
Community of Science; Science databases

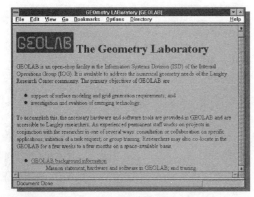

http://cabsparc.larc.nasa.gov:80/GEOLAB/
Geometry laboratory; Grid generation; Surface modeling

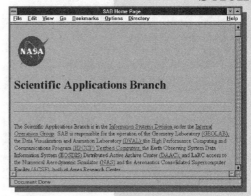

http://cabsparc.larc.nasa.gov:80/SAB/
Geometry laboratory; NASA; Scientific applications

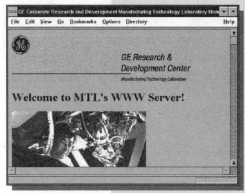

http://ce-toolkit.crd.ge.com/
GE; Manufacturing; Networks; Research; Science

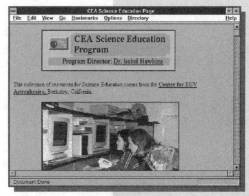

http://cea-ftp.cea.berkeley.edu/Education/
Astrophysics; CEA; Outreach; Teaching; Tools

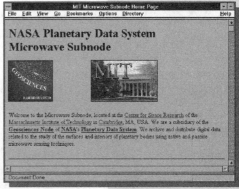

http://delcano.mit.edu/
Massachusetts Institute of Technology; Space Research

Science

http://esther.la.asu.edu/sas
Conference; Events; Society for Applied Spectroscopy

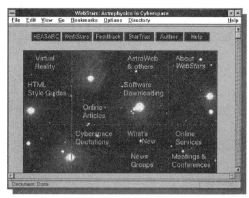

http://guinan.gsfc.nasa.gov:80/
Cyberspace; Software; Virtual reality

http://freedom.larc.nasa.gov:80/
Space concepts; Space systems

http://hagar.ph.utexas.edu/
Engineering; Fusion plasmas; Fusion research

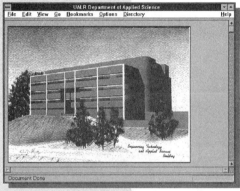

http://giles.ualr.edu/git.html
Applied Science; Little Rock; University of Arkansas

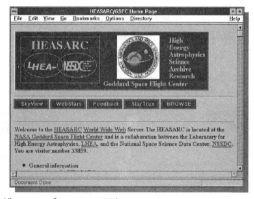

http://heasarc.gsfc.nasa.gov:80/
Astrophysics; Goddard; NASA; Space science

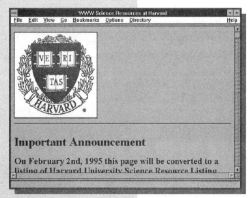

http://golgi.harvard.edu/harvard.html
Harvard University; Science resources

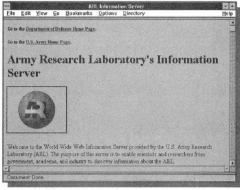

http://info.arl.army.mil/
Army Research Lab; Government; Information server

http://lancet.mit.edu/decavitator
Boats; Cycling; Human-powered vehicles

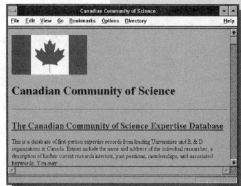

http://medoc.gdb.org/work/best-dbs-canada.html
Canada; Community of Science; Expertise Database

http://maas-neotek.arc.nasa.gov/dante/
Ames research group; Intelligent mechanisms; NASA

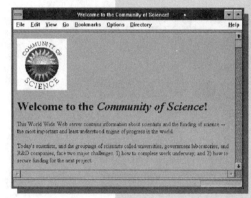

http://medoc.gdb.org/work/info/cosinfo.html
Community of Science; Research

http://maas-neotek.arc.nasa.gov:80/
AI; Intelligent mechanisms; NASA

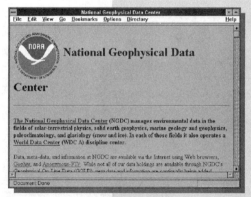

http://meridian.ngdc.noaa.gov:80/
Marine geology; Solar-terrestrial physics; Solid earth geophysics

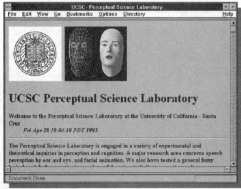

http://mambo.ucsc.edu/
Cognition; Learning; University of California-Santa Cruz

http://meteor.atms.purdue.edu/
Earth and Atmospheric Sciences; Purdue University

Science

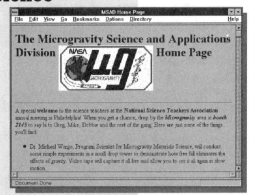

http://microgravity.msad.hq.nasa.gov:80/
Free fall; Gravity; Microgravity; NASA

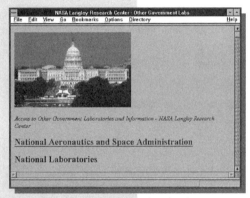

http://mosaic.larc.nasa.gov/nasaonline/gov.html
Government; Laboratories; NASA; National laboratories

392

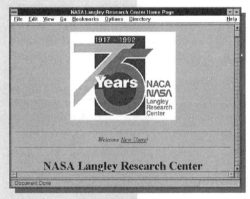

http://mosaic.larc.nasa.gov:80/
Langley Research Center; NASA

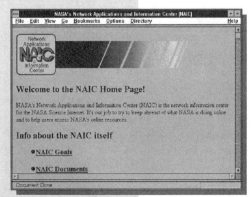

http://naic.nasa.gov/naic/
NAIC; Network Applications and Information Center

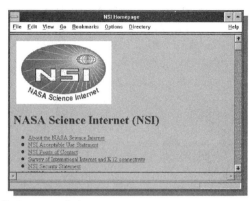

http://naic.nasa.gov/nsi
NASA Science Internet; NSI; Space

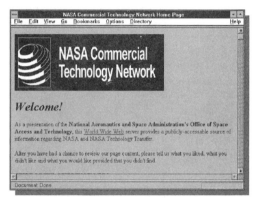

http://nctn.oact.hq.nasa.gov:80/
NASA; Technology transfer

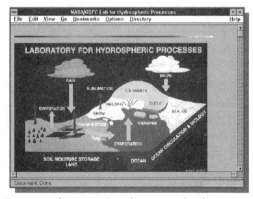

http://neptune.gsfc.nasa.gov/970_home_page.html
Climate; Geography; Hydrospheric science

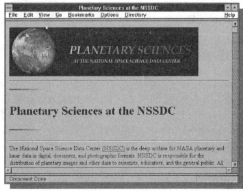

http://nssdc.gsfc.nasa.gov/planetary/planetary_home.html
Lunar data; NSSDC; Planetary sciences

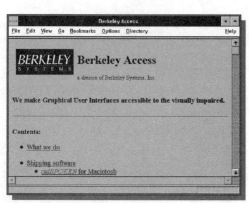

http://access.berksys.com/
Graphical User Interfaces; GUI; Visually impaired

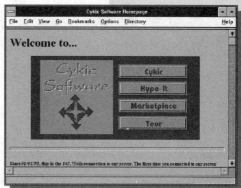

http://cykic.com/
Internet; Software; World Wide Web servers

http://artos.larc.nasa.gov/se/html/se_home.html
Design; Lockheed; Reuse; Software engineering

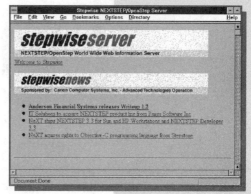

http://digifix.digifix.com/
Next; Nextstep; Software; Solution

http://coyote.csusm.edu/cwis/winworld/winsock.html
California State University-San Marcos; Windows shareware

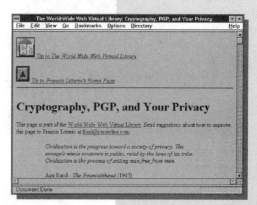

http://draco.centerline.com:8080/~franl/crypto.html
Cryptography; PGP; Privacy; Security

http://coyote.csusm.edu/cwis/winworld/winworld.html
Freeware; PKZIP; Windows Shareware

http://freedom.larc.nasa.gov/spqr/spqr.html
Aeronautics; Design; Software productivity

Software

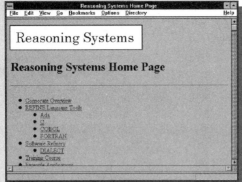

http://ftp.reasoning.com/
Language tools; Reasoning Systems; Software; Source code

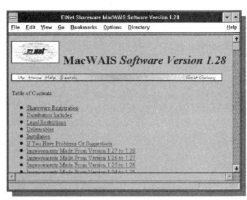

http://galaxy.einet.net/EINet/MacWAIS.html
Macintosh; MacWAIS; Shareware

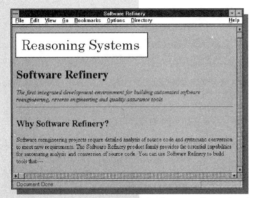

http://ftp.reasoning.com/pub/mosaic/Software-Refinery.html
Software reengineering; Software refinery; Source code

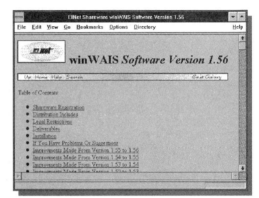

http://galaxy.einet.net/EINet/winWAIS.html
Browser; Windows; WinWAIS

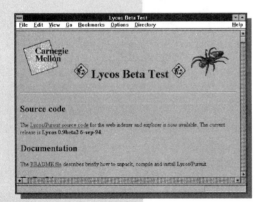

http://fuzine.mt.cs.cmu.edu/mlm/lycos-beta.html
Carnegie Mellon; Lycos beta; Source code

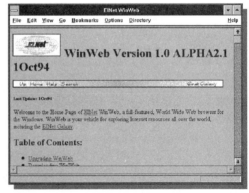

http://galaxy.einet.net/EINet/WinWeb/WinWebHome.html
Browser; Windows; WinWeb

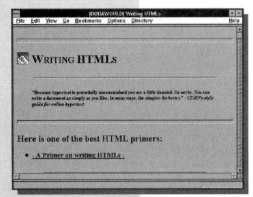

http://gagme.wwa.com/~boba/primer.html
HTML; Home page development; Text mark-up

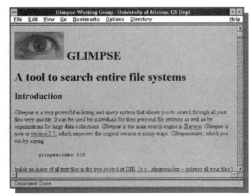

http://glimpse.cs.arizona.edu:1994/
Glimpse; Query system; Tools for searching

http://hamilton.netmedia.com/adobe
Acrobat; Adobe Photoshop; Sun

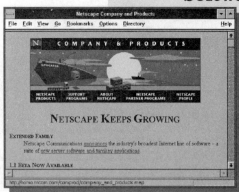

http://home.mcom.com/info/how-to-get-it.html
Server software; Turnkey applications

http://home.mcom.com/home/
Internet; Netscape; Web software

http://home.netscape.com/
Browser; Information; Netscape; News; Software

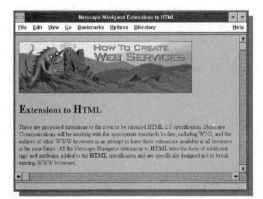

http://home.mcom.com/home/services_docs/html-extensions.html
HTML Extensions; Netscape Navigator

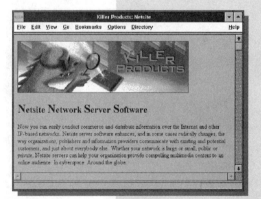

http://home.netscape.com/MCOM/products_docs/server.html
Multimedia; Netsite Network Server Software

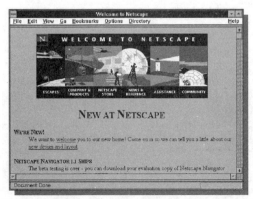

http://home.mcom.com/home/welcome.html
Company and products; Navigator; Netscape

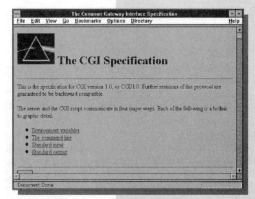

http://hoohoo.ncsa.uiuc.edu/cgi/interface.html
CGI scripts; CGI Specification; Common Gateway Interface

Software

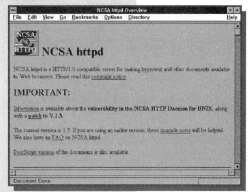

http://hoohoo.ncsa.uiuc.edu/docs/
HTTP Daemon for UNIX; NCSA httpd; Web browser

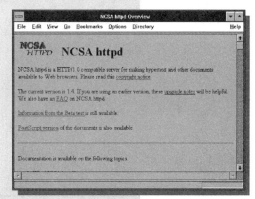

http://hoohoo.ncsa.uiuc.edu/docs/Overview.html
HTML; Httpd; NCSA; Web

http://iamwww.unibe.ch/~scg/Src/
Perl scripts; Software Archive; Software Composition Group

http://idris.com/IDRIShome.html
Information visualization; Intelligent agents; Market research

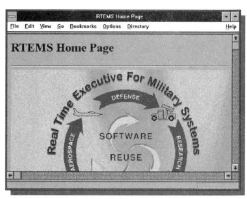

http://lancelot.gcs.redstone.army.mil/rg4/rtems.html
Real-Time Executive for Military Systems; RTEMS

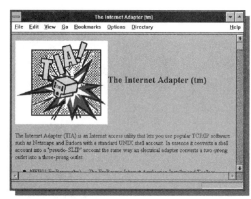

http://marketplace.com:80/tia/tiahome.html
Internet adapter; Netscape; TCP/IP; UNIX

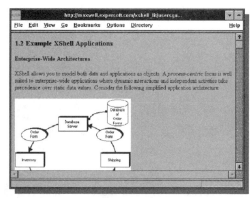

http://maxwell.expersoft.com/xshell_lit/usersguide/ch1.2.html
Data; Object-oriented modeling; XShell applications

http://mirror.wwa.com/mirror/spike/94/browsers.htm
Cello; Mosaic; Netscape; Tapestry; Web Browsers; WinWeb

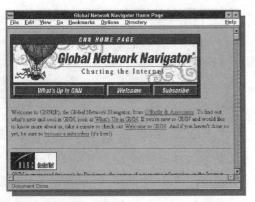

http://nearnet.gnn.com/gnn.html
GNN; Internet sources; News

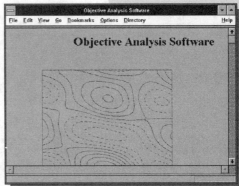

http://taygeta.oc.nps.navy.mil/objan.html
C; Fortran; Objective Analysis Software

http://riwww.osf.org:8001/
Interoperability; Portability; Scalability; Usability

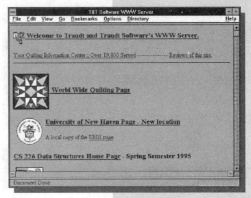

http://ttsw.com/
Data structures; Quilting; University of New Haven

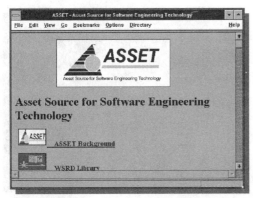

http://source.asset.com/
Asset Source for Software Engineering Technology

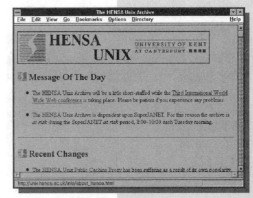

http://unix.hensa.ac.uk/hensa.unix.html
HENSA UNIX Archive; University of Kent at Canterbury

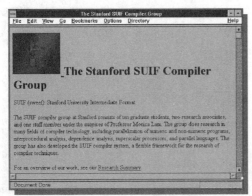

http://suif.stanford.edu/
Compiler; Languages; Stanford University

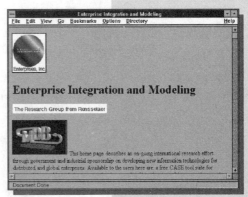

http://viu.eng.rpi.edu/
CASE tools; Software Engineering

Software

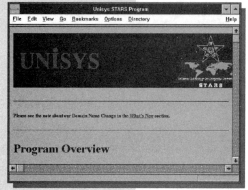

http://vulture.stars.reston.paramax.com/
Reliable Systems; Adaptable Software Technology; Unisys

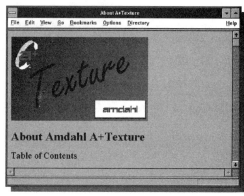

http://www.amdahl.com/doc/texture/AboutTexture.html
Client/Server; Software; TCP/IP

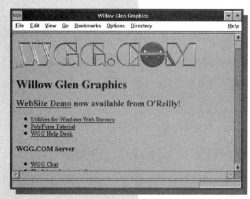

http://wgg.com/
Willow Glen Graphics; Windows Web Servers

http://www.answer.com/apriori/apriori.html
Answer Systems; Apriori; Software

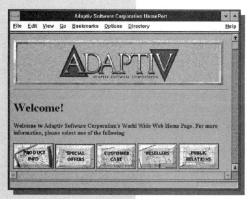

http://www.adaptiv.com/
Products; Resellers; Software

http://www.atext.com/
Plug and play; Text information management; Web servers

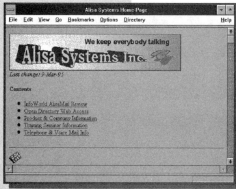

http://www.alisa.com/
E-Mail; Products; Services; Telephone; Training; Voice mail

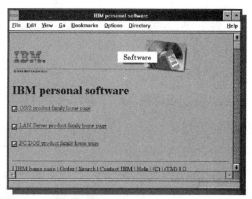

http://www.austin.ibm.com/pspinfo/
Software; OS/2; LAN; PC DOS

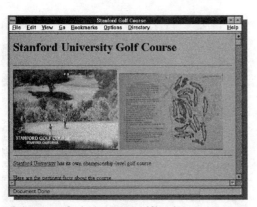

http://akebono.stanford.edu/~jerry/golf.html
Course facts; Stanford University Golf Course

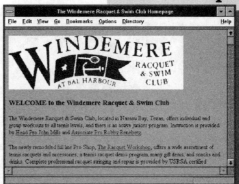

http://arganet.tenagra.com/Racquet_Workshop/Windemere.html
Nassau Bay; Pro shop; Texas

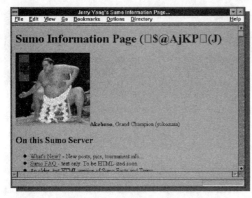

http://akebono.stanford.edu/~jerry/sumo/
Sports; Sumo wrestling

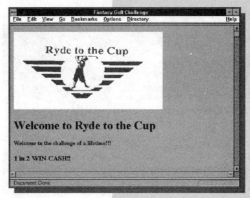

http://caligari.dartmouth.edu/~ryde/ryde.html
Fantasy Golf Challenge; Golf; Ryder Cup

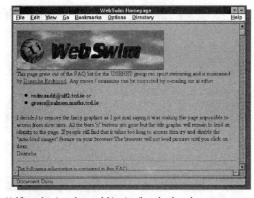

http://alf2.tcd.ie/~redmondd/swim/header.html
Aquatic sports; Diving; Swimming

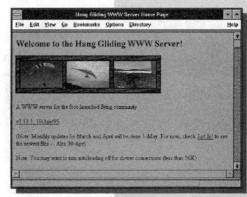

http://cougar.stanford.edu:7878/HGMPSHomePage.html
Aviator; Free-fall; Hang gliding; Para sailing

http://allsports.questtech.com/nfl/nfl.html
All sports; Basketball; Football

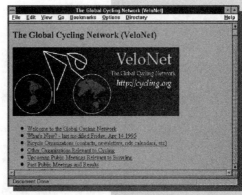

http://cycling.org/
Bicycling; Global Cycling Network; Organizations

Sports

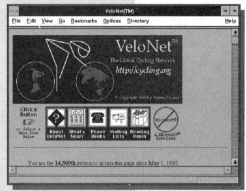

http://cycling.org:80/
The Global Cycling Network; VeloNet

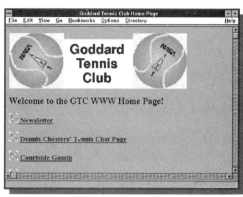

http://epims1.gsfc.nasa.gov/tennis/GTC_homepage.html
Goddard; NASA; Tennis

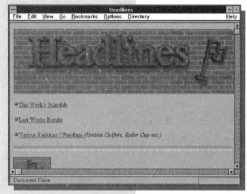

http://dallas.nmhu.edu/golf/headlines.htm
Golf; Rankings; Results; Schedule; Standings

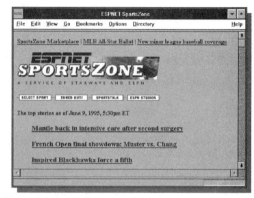

http://espnet.sportszone.com/
ESPN; News; Sports

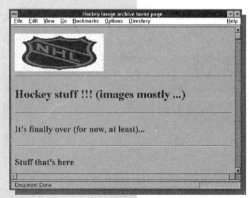

http://deathstar.rutgers.edu/people/jimg/nhl/nhlhome.html
Hockey; Images; NFL; Stanley Cup

http://fun.com/sports/
Baseball; Hockey; Soccer; Virtual shops

http://dfw.net/~bnc/mda.html
Anaheim; California; Hockey; Mighty Ducks

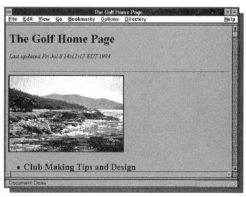

http://geminga.dartmouth.edu:80/~pete/golf/
Course design; Golf; Trips

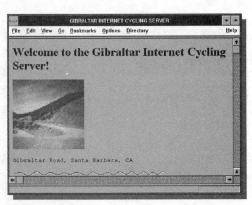

http://gibikes.com/gib/
Bikes; Cycling; Racing; Ride announcements

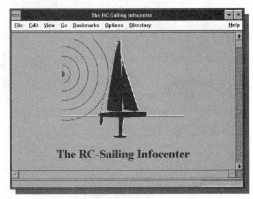

http://honeybee.helsinki.fi/surcp/rcsail.htm
Hobbies; Radio-control; Sailing

http://info.mcc.ac.uk/UMIST_Sport/bssh.html
British; History; Sports

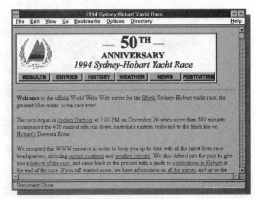

http://info.tas.gov.au/shyr/index.html
Boats; Sports; Sydney Australia; Yachting

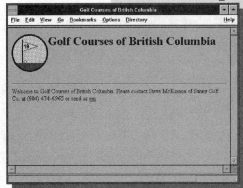

http://interchange.idc.uvic.ca/~golf/golfbc.html
British Columbia; Canada; Games; Golf; Recreation; Sports

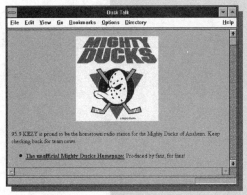

http://kezy.com/kezy/ducks.htm
Anaheim; California; Hockey; Mighty Ducks

http://maxwell.uhh.hawaii.edu/hockey/hockey.html
Games; Hockey; NHL; Sports

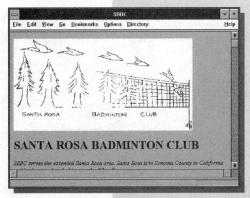

http://mid1.external.hp.com/stanb/srbc.html
Badminton club; California; Santa Rosa; Sonoma County

http://mirach.cs.buffalo.edu/~khoub-s/WC94.html
Pictures; Soccer; Teams; World Cup

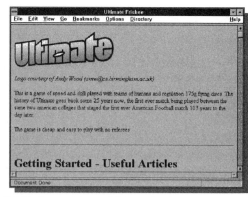

http://pipkin.lut.ac.uk/~scott/ultimate.html
Clubs; Frisbee; Getting started; Ultimate

http://nyweb.com/marathon.html
Marathon; New York City; Recreation; Running; Sports

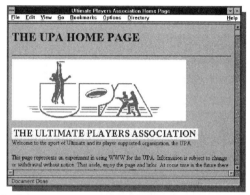

http://radon.gas.uug.arizona.edu/~hko/upa/home.html
Frisbee; Ultimate; Ultimate Payers Association

http://oasis.efn.org/novasrc/fp.html
Discounts; Fishing; Hobbies; Products; Sports; Supplies

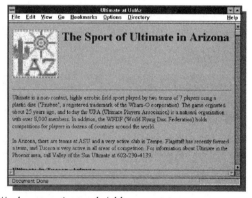

http://radon.uug.arizona.edu/~hko
Frisbee; Ultimate in Arizona; World Flying Disc Federation

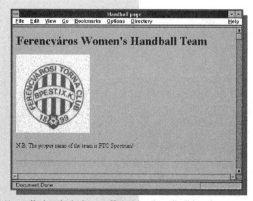

http://ogyalla.konkoly.hu/staff/zsoldos/handball.html
Clubs; Rules; Team Handball

http://rmd-www.mr.ic.ac.uk/snow/snowpage.html
Outdoors; Recreation; Skiing; Snow; Weather

http://rschp2.anu.edu.au:8080/cave/cave.html
Caves; Spelunking sites

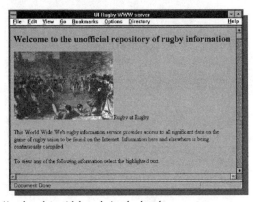

http://rugby.phys.uidaho.edu/rugby.html
Clubs; Rugby; Rules

http://sal.cs.uiuc.edu/rec.guns/
Crime; Guns; Gun safety; Hobbies; NRA

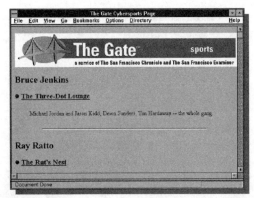

http://sfgate.com/sports/
Baseball; Basketball; Hockey; San Francisco

http://tbone.biol.scarolina.edu/~dan/swim/usc.swim.html
Diving; South Carolina; Swimming

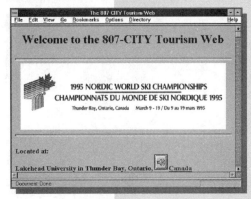

http://tourism.807-city.on.ca/
Multimedia; Nordic skiing; Winter sports

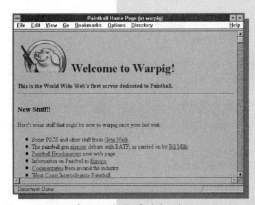

http://warpig.cati.csufresno.edu/Default.html
Europe; Information; Paintball

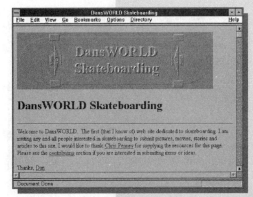

http://web.cps.msu.edu/~dunhamda/dw/dansworld.html
Pictures; Skateboarding; Stones

Sports

http://web.msu.edu/turf/index.html
Silverdome; Soccer; World Cup

http://weber.u.washington.edu/~finch/HWShome.html
Husky Winter Sports; University of Washington

http://www-hal.cs.uiuc.edu/~laff/Sotg/sotg.html
SOTG Committee; Ultimate

http://www-leland.stanford.edu/group/cycling/
Stanford Cycling Club

http://www.ac95.org/
America's Cup '95; Boating; Sailing

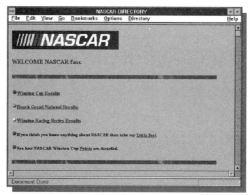

http://www.acpub.duke.edu/~jwcarp/nascarhome.html
Car racing; NASCAR; Winston Cup results

http://www.aladdin.co.uk/cpy/
Yacht brokerage; Yachting

http://www.armory.com/~deadslug/candlestick_park.html
Baseball; Candlestick Park; Giants; San Francisco

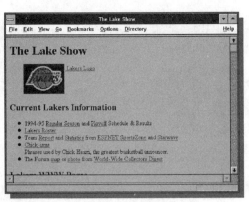

http://www.armory.com/~lew/sports/basketball/
Basketball; Information; Lakers; Los Angeles; News

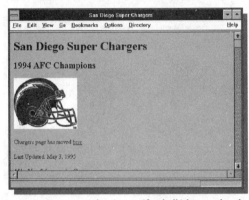

http://www.armory.com/~lew/sports/football/chargers.html
Chargers; Football; Information; News; San Diego

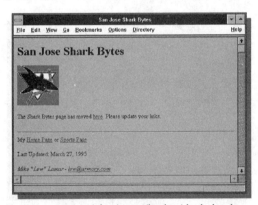

http://www.armory.com/~lew/sports/hockey/sharks.html
Hockey; Information; News; San Jose; Sharks

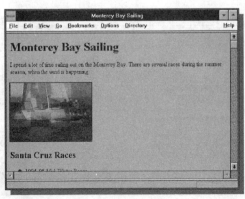

http://www.armory.com/~lew/sports/sailing/
Monterey Bay; Races; Recreation; Sailing

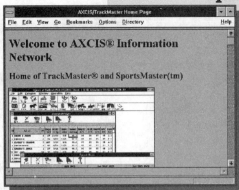

http://www.axcis.com/
Handicapping system; Thoroughbred horse racing

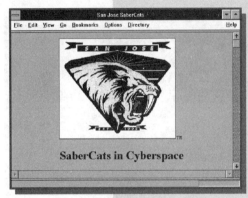

http://www.best.com/~bmason/SaberCats/index.htm
Arena Football League; SaberCats; San Jose

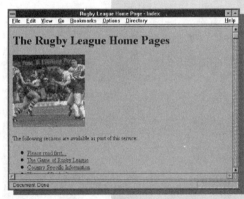

http://www.brad.ac.uk/~cgrussel/
Clubs; Pain; Rugby; Sports

http://www.brad.ac.uk:80/~msbraith/S/s.html
Fantasy Golf Challenge

Sports

http://www.cdf.toronto.edu/personal/chris/tennis/edberg.html
FAQs; Stefan Edberg; Tennis

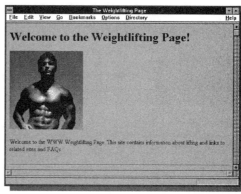

http://www.cs.odu.edu/~ksw/weights.html
Bodybuilding; Weightlifting

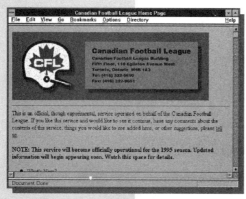

http://www.CFL.ca/
Canadian Football League; CFL

http://www.cs.rochester.edu/u/ferguson/ultimate/
Frisbee; Recreation; Ultimate

 406

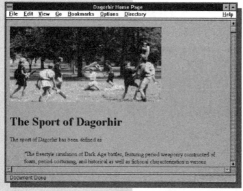

http://www.charm.net:80/~dagorhir
Dagorhir; Recreation; Sports

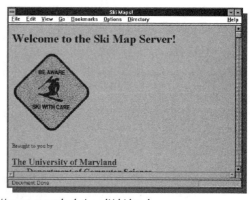

http://www.cs.umd.edu/~regli/ski.html
Resorts; Ski; Weather

http://www.cis.ufl.edu/skydive
Airplanes; Free-fall; Skydiving

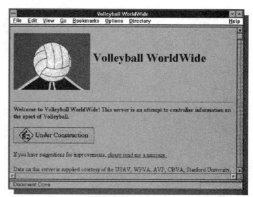

http://www.cup.hp.com/~vball/
Recreation; Sports; Volleyball

http://ig.dca.hybrid.com/
Data transfer technology

http://ike.engr.washington.edu/iat/
Technology; University of North Carolina

http://info.main.conacyt.mx/
Science; Spanish; Technology

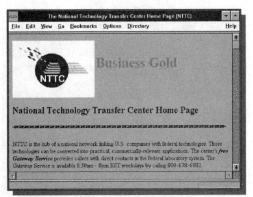

http://iridium.nttc.edu/nttc.html
Federal technologies; National Technology Transfer Center

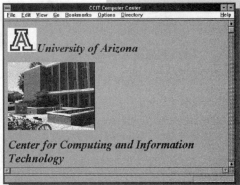

http://lion.ccit.arizona.edu:80/
Computing and Information Technology; University of Arizona

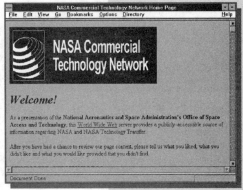

http://nctn.hq.nasa.gov/nctnHome.html
Aeronautics; NASA; Space; Technology; Technology transfer

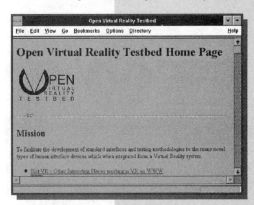

http://nemo.ncsl.nist.gov/~sressler/OVRThome.html
Open Virtual Reality Testbed; Testing methodologies

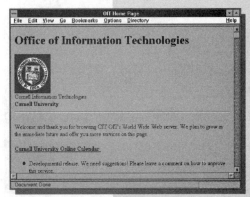

http://oitnext.cit.cornell.edu/
Cornell University; Information Technologies

Technology

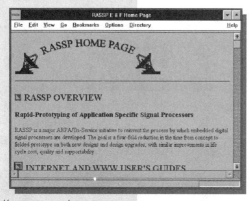

http://peewee.chinalake.navy.mil/computational_sciences/cs.html
China Lake; Computational sciences; Signal processing

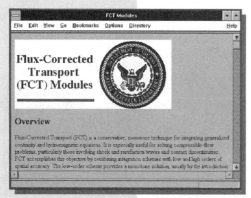

http://rassp.scra.org/
Rapid-prototyping of application specific signal processors

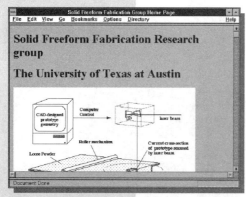

http://sdcd.gsfc.nasa.gov/ESS/exchange/contrib/gardner/FCT.html
FCT; Flux-Corrected Transport; Navy

http://tag-fileserver.larc.nasa.gov/
Aerospace; NASA; Projects; Success

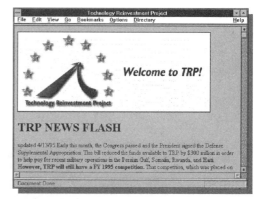

http://trp.ida.org/TRP.Home_Page.html
Congress; President; Technology reinvestment

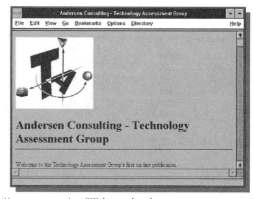

http://www.ac.com/tag/Welcome.html
Andersen Consulting; Technology assessment

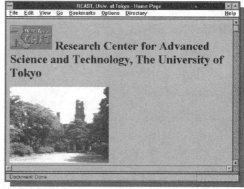

http://www.ai.rcast.u-tokyo.ac.jp/RCAST/RCAST.html
Japan; Research; Science; Technology; University of Tokyo

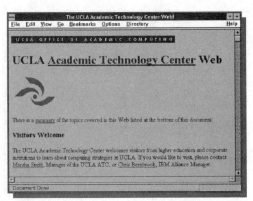

http://www.atc.ucla.edu/
Los Angeles; Technology; UCLA; University of California

http://www.careermosaic.com/cm/witi
Membership; WITI; Women in Technology

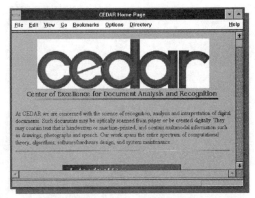

http://www.cedar.buffalo.edu:80/
Character recognition; Document Analysis; OCR

http://www.dyit.edu.tw/
Da-Yeh Institute of Technology; Taiwan

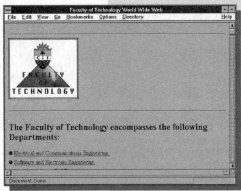

http://www.ee.cit.ac.nz/
Education; New Zealand

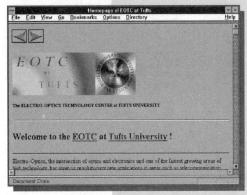

http://www.eotc.tufts.edu/
Electro-Optics Technology; Tufts University

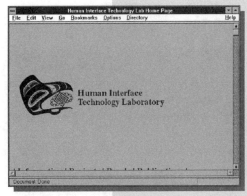

http://www.hitl.washington.edu/
Human Interface Technology; University of Washington

http://www.larc.nasa.gov/org/isd/security/sub/its.html
Firewalls; Information technology; Security

Technology

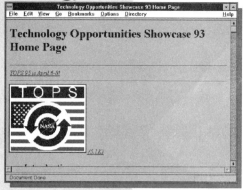

http://www.larc.nasa.gov/tops/tops.html
Aerospace; Opportunities; Technology

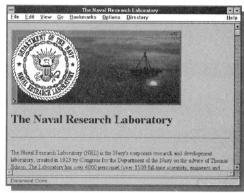

http://www.nrl.navy.mil/
Military; Naval Research Laboratory; Technology

http://www.llnl.gov/vision/vision.html
Goals; Lawrence Livermore National Laboratory; Vision

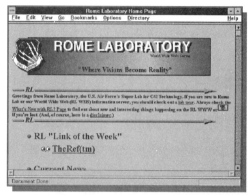

http://www.rl.af.mil:8001/
Air Force; Rome Laboratory; Technology; USAF

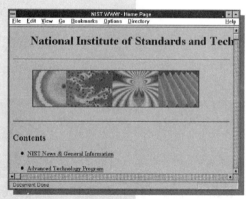

http://www.nist.gov/welcome.html
NIST; Standards; Technology

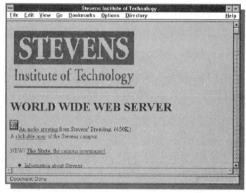

http://www.stevens-tech.edu/
New Jersey; Stevens Institute of Technology; Technology institutes

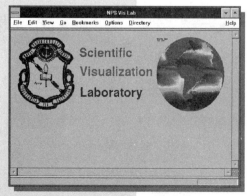

http://www.nps.navy.mil/VisLab/home.html
Naval Postgraduate School; Scientific Visualization Laboratory

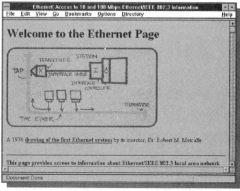

http://wwwhost.ots.utexas.edu/ethernet/ethernet-home.html
Dr. Robert M. Metcalfe; Ethernet; Networks

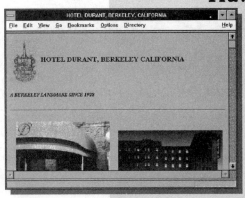

http://alaskan.com/
Alaska; Outdoor Adventures; Recreation; Shopping

http://cyber.cclims.com/comp/hdur/hdur.html
Accommodations; Berkeley; California; Hotel Durant; Lodging

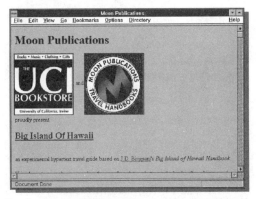

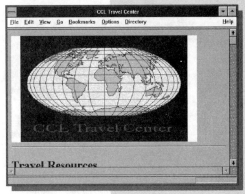

http://aton.hypercomp.ns.ca/pix/halifax.html
Canada; Halifax Nova Scotia

http://cyber.cclims.com/mall/travel/travel.html
Business; Links; Travel directory

http://bookweb.cwis.uci.edu:8042/Books/Moon/moon.html
Books; Bookstore; Travel guide

http://cyber.cclims.com/waterfront/
California; Lodging; Oakland; Waterfront Plaza Hotel

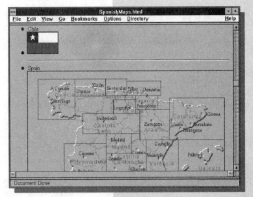

http://cyber.cclims.com/comp/ftg/ftg.html
Catalog; Family; Travel guides

http://edb518ea.edb.utexas.edu/html/spanishmaps.html#Chile
Spain; Spanish maps; Travel

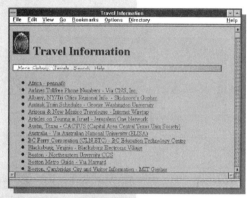

http://edb518ea.edb.utexas.edu/html/spanishmaps.html#Mexico
Mexico; Web servers; Culture

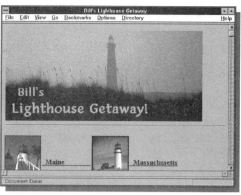

http://gopher.lib.utk.edu:70/lights.html
Lighthouses; Maine; Massachusetts

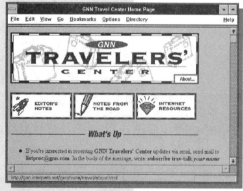

http://galaxy.einet.net/GJ/travel.html
City information; Tourism; Travel

http://heiwww.unige.ch:80/switzerland/
Europe; Swiss; Switzerland

http://gnn.interpath.net/gnn/meta/travel/index.html
Tourism; Vacations; Web sites

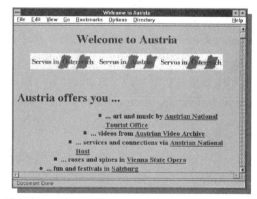

http://hirsch.cosy.sbg.ac.at/
Austria; Culture; Germany; History

http://godric.nosc.mil/planet_earth/sandiego.html
Community information; San Diego

http://http2.sils.umich.edu/Antarctica/Story.html
Antarctica; Snow; South Pole

http://infaut.e-technik.tu-magdeburg.de/md/city_info.html
Germany; Hotels; Maps; Sights; Tourism

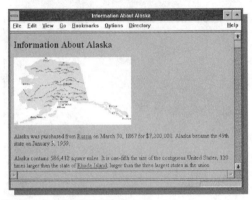

http://info.alaska.edu:70/1s/Alaska
Alaska; Northwest; USA

http://infoguide.com/
Beaches; Florida; South; USA

http://iquest.com/~cvb/
Alabama; Community information; Huntsville

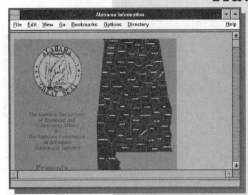

http://isl-garnet.uah.edu/alhome.html
Alabama; South; USA

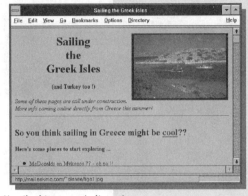

http://mail.eskimo.com/~dianee/
Greece; Greek isles; Mykonos; Sailing; Turkey

413

http://market.net/travel/tc/index.html
Brochures; Cruises; Mailing list; San Mateo; Travelcraft

http://maui.net/
Hawaii; Maui; Scuba; Travel; Whales

Travel

http://meteora.ucsd.edu:80/~norman/paris/Accueil/
France; Louvre; Paris; Restaurants; Travel

http://net101.com/BBCA/
Bed & Breakfast; California; Directories; Index

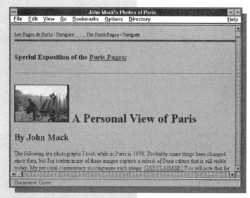

http://meteora.ucsd.edu:80/~norman/paris/Expos/PersonalView/
Images; Paris; Photos; Travel

http://nyweb.com/mainmenu.html
Big Apple; New York City; Northeast; USA

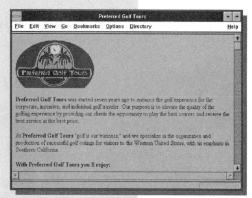

http://mmink.cts.com/mmink/dossiers/prefgolf.html
Corporate; Golf Tours; Individual; Personal; Travel

http://redwood.northcoast.com/~bknotts/Eureka.html
California; Community information; Eureka

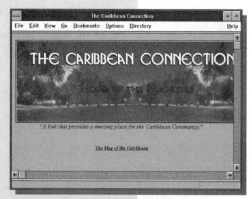

http://mrlxp2.mrl.uiuc.edu/~stuart/caribbean.html
Caribbean; Islands; Tourism; Vacations

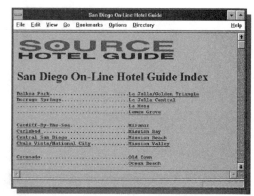

http://sddtsun.sddt.com/files/lifestyles/hotels.html
Hotel Guide; Online; San Diego

http://www.hotspots.hawaii.com/
Community information; Directories; Hawaii; Index

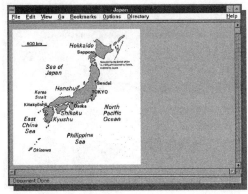

http://www.ic.gov/94fact/country/122.html
Culture; Japan; Japanese; Map

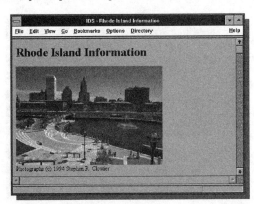

http://www.ids.net/ri/ri.html
Community information; Directories; Links; Rhode Island

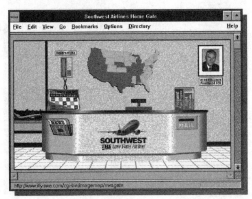

http://www.iflyswa.com/
Flights; No frills; Southwest Airlines

http://www.iglou.com/louisville.html
Kentucky; Louisville; Visitor center

http://www.infi.net/vegas/vlv/index.html
Elvis; Gaming; Tourism; Virtual Las Vegas

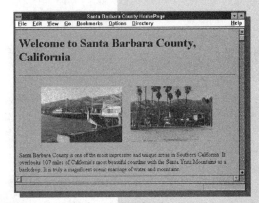

http://www.internet-cafe.com/sb/sb.html
California; Santa Barbara; Tourism

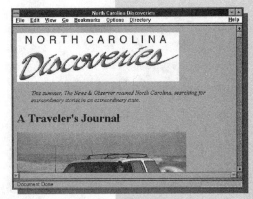

http://www.nando.net/ncd/week16/final.html
Extraordinary stories; North Carolina; Tar Heels

http://www.nando.net/pctravel.html
Airline tickets; Plane; Reservations

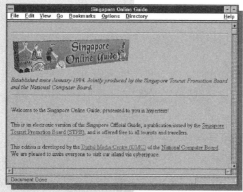

http://www.ncb.gov.sg/sog/sog.html
Singapore; Tourists; Travel

http://www.ncsa.uiuc.edu/SDG/IT94/Venue.html
Chicago; Restaurants; Travel

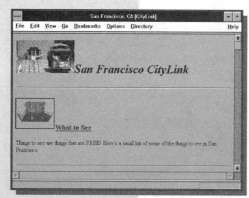

http://www.neosoft.com/citylink/san-francisco/default.html
Bay Area; San Francisco CityLink

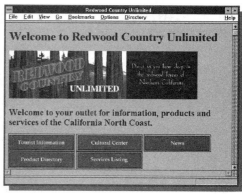

http://www.northcoast.com/unlimited/unlimited.html
California; Redwood country; Tourism

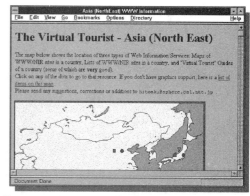

http://www.ntt.jp/AP/asia-NE.html
Asia; Far East; Guides; Maps; Tourists

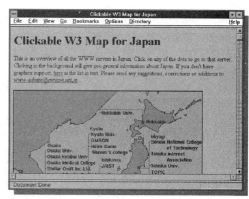

http://www.ntt.jp/japan/map/
Culture; Japan; Map; Schools

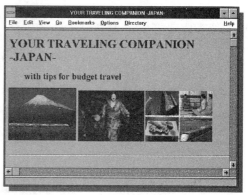

http://www.ntt.jp:80/japan/TCJ/TC.html
Asia; Far East; Japan; Oriental; Tourism

http://www.oslonett.no/data/adv/AA/AA.html
Arctic; Norway; Scandinavia

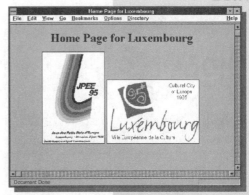

http://www.restena.lu/luxembourg/lux_welcome.html
Culture; Luxembourg; Travel

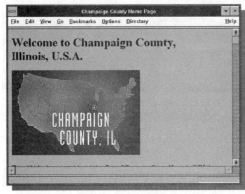

http://www.prairienet.org/SiliconPrairie/ccnet.html
Champaign County Illinois; Local government; Tourism

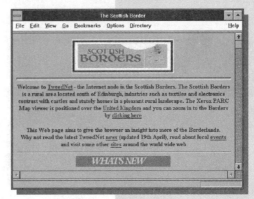

http://www.scotborders.co.uk/
Edinburgh; Europe; Scotland; Tourism

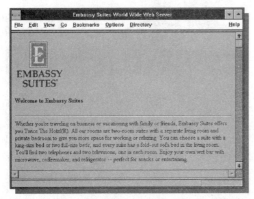

http://www.promus.com/embassy.html
Embassy Suites; Hotel; Lodging

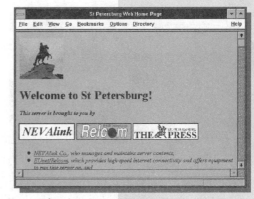

http://www.spb.su/
Russia; Soviet Union; St Petersburg

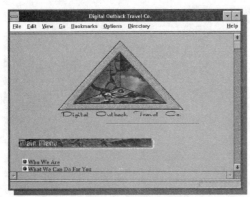

http://www.realtime.net/~lthumper/
Travel; Trip planning; Vacations

http://www.st-louis.mo.us/
Missouri; St. Louis; Tourism

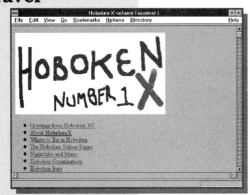

http://www.stevens-tech.edu/hobokenx/hobokenx.html
Hoboken; New Jersey; Travel

http://www.vegas.com/
City; Gambling; Las Vegas; Nevada; Tourism; USA

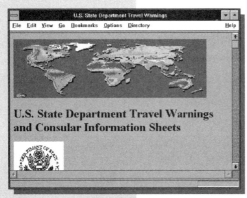

http://www.stolaf.edu/network/travel-advisories.html
Foreign advisories; Tourism; US State Department

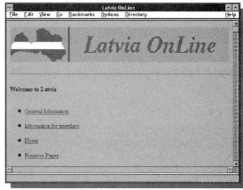

http://www.vernet.lv/
Business; General information; Latvia; Tourism; Travel

http://www.tcs.co.at/fvp.html
Austria; Salzburg; Travel

http://www.virtualvegas.com/
Gambling; Las Vegas; Shows

http://www.traveller.com/
News; Trade; Traveler Information Services

http://www.viva.com/nm/nmhome.html
Almanac; Culture; New Mexico; VIVA

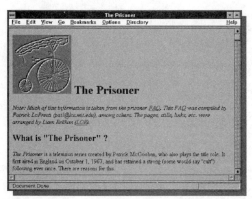

http://itdsrv1.ul.ie/Entertainment/Prisoner/the-prisoner.html
Television series; The Prisoner

http://metaverse.com/vibe/tvtonite/tonite.html
Cable TV; Listings; Network TV; TV Tonite

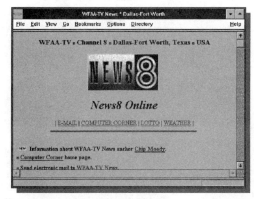

http://rampages.onramp.net/~news8/
Dallas-Fort Worth; Texas; TV News; WFAA

http://tvnet.com/
Descriptions; Images; Show listings; TV

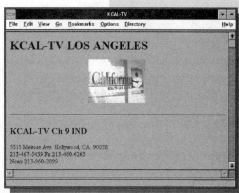

http://tvnet.com/TV/CAtv/KCAL.html
KCAL-TV; Los Angeles

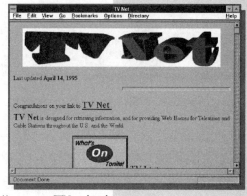

http://tvnet.com/TVnet.html
Cable stations; Listings; Television; TV Net

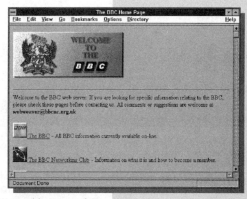

http://www.bbcnc.org.uk/
BBC; Networking Club; Programs

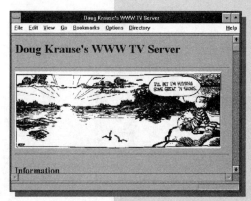

http://www.best.com/~dijon/tv/
Directories; Information; TV

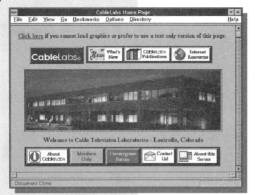

http://www.cablelabs.com/
Cable television laboratories; Products and services

http://www.ftms.com/vidiot/upn.html
Star Trek; Voyager; UPN

http://www.carleton.edu:80/BG/
Battlestar Galactica; Science fiction

http://www.hu.mtu.edu/~gjwalli/fktoc.html
Forever Knight; Show background

http://www.cbs.com/
CBS News; CBS Television; Dan Rather; Letterman

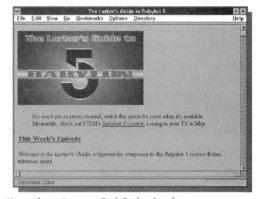

http://www.hyperion.com/lurk/lurker.html
Babylon 5; Entertainment; Science fiction; TV

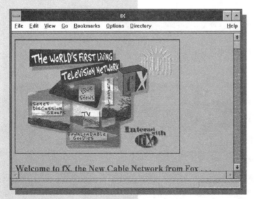

http://www.delphi.com/fx/fxtop.html
Cable; FX; Television; TV

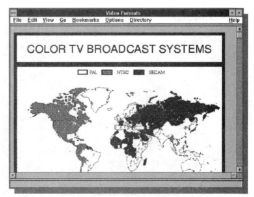

http://www.sdsc.edu/0/SDSC/Geninfo/Fun/format.html
Map; NTSC; PAL; SECAM; TV Broadcasting Systems

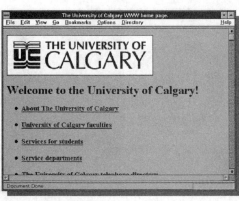

http://acs6.acs.ucalgary.ca/
Canada; University of Calgary

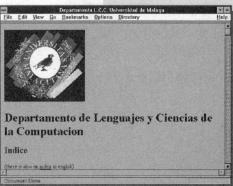

http://apolo.uma.es/
Education; Spanish; Universidad de Malaga

http://aguila.dpi.udec.cl/www/udec.html
Education; Spanish; Universidad de Concepcion

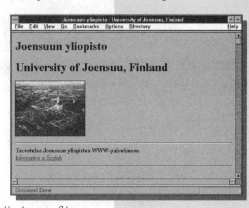

http://cc.joensuu.fi/
Finland; University of Joensuu

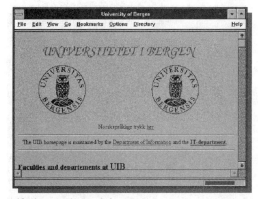

http://alf.uib.no/index.english
Norway; University of Bergen

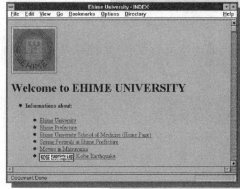

http://ccs42.dpc.ehime-u.ac.jp:8000/
Ehime University; Japan

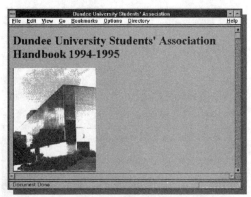

http://alpha.mic.dundee.ac.uk/dusa/dusa.html
Dundee University; United Kingdom

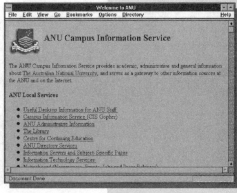

http://cis.anu.edu.au/
Education; The Australian National University

Universities—Non US

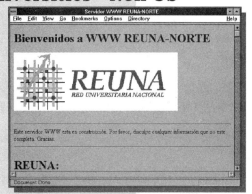

http://cobre.reuna.cl/
Chile; University of Reuna

http://gopher.ku.dk/
Denmark; Education; Kobenhavns Universitet

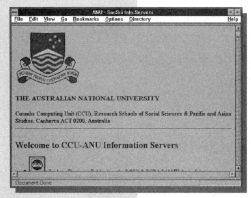

http://coombs.anu.edu.au/
Australian National University; Education

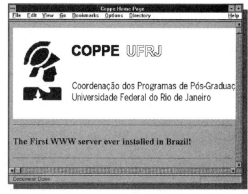

http://guarani.cos.ufrj.br:8000/HOME.html
Education; Portuguese; Universidade Federal do Rio de Janeiro

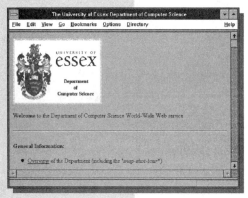

http://cswww.essex.ac.uk/
Computer Science; United Kingdom; University of Essex

http://hcrl.open.ac.uk/ou/ouhome.html
Education; Open University

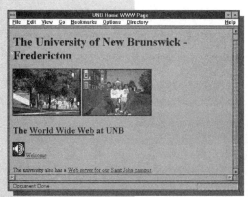

http://degaulle.hil.unb.ca/
Education; University of New Brunswick

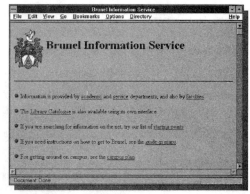

http://http1.brunel.ac.uk:8080/
Brunel University; United Kingdom

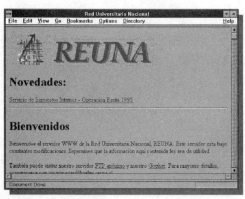

http://huelen.reuna.cl/
Education; Red Universitaria Nacional; Spanish

http://info.queensu.ca/index.html
Canada; Kingston; Ontario; Queen's University

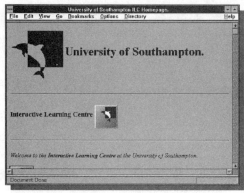

http://ilc.ecs.soton.ac.uk/welcome.html
United Kingdom; University of Southampton

http://kin.cieamer.conacyt.mx/
Education; Universidad de Merida

423

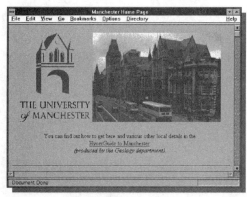

http://info.mcc.ac.uk/UofM.html
Manchester University; United Kingdom

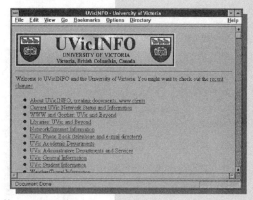

http://www.uvic.ca/
Canada; University of Victoria

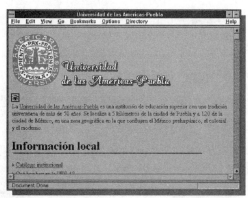

http://info.pue.udlap.mx/
Mexico; University of the Americas

http://kritios.uni-muenster.de/share/mosaic/share/DOCS/root.html
Germany; Munster; Westfalische Wilhelms University

Universities—Non US

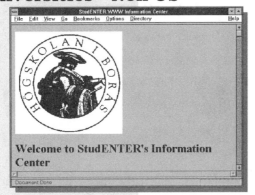

http://lestat.shv.hb.se/
Sweden; University of Boras

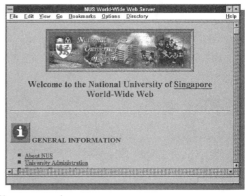

http://nuscc.nus.sg/
Education; National University of Singapore

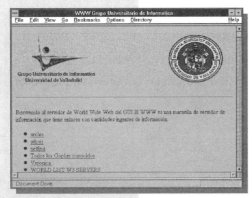

http://luna.gui.uva.es/
Education; Spanish; Universidad de Valladolid

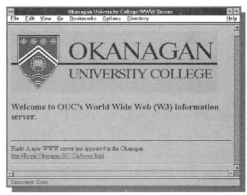

http://oksw01.okanagan.bc.ca/home.html
Canada; Okanagan University College

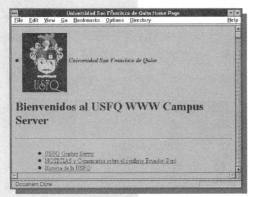

http://mail.usfq.edu.ec/root.htm
Education; Spanish; Universidad San Francisco de Quito

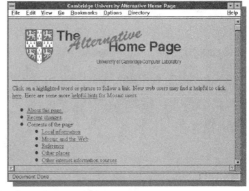

http://pelican.cl.cam.ac.uk/
Cambridge University; Computer

http://muresh.et.tudelft.nl/dimes/index.html
Delft Institute of MicroElectronics and Submicron Technology

http://s700.uminho.pt/
Departamento de Informatica da Universidade do Minho

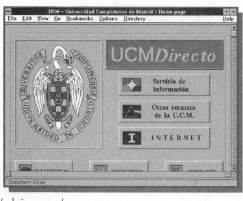

http://sol.sis.ucm.es/
Education; Spanish; Universidad Complutense de Madrid

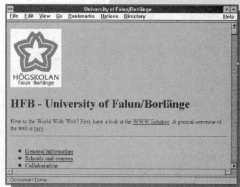

http://txfs1.hfb.se/
Sweden; University of Falun/Borlange

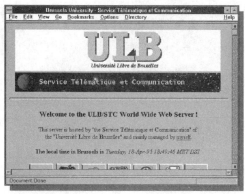

http://sun4.iihe.ac.be/
Belgium; Brussels University

http://ulima.edu.pe/
Education; Spanish; Universidad de Lima

http://trasporti.cineca.it/
Institute of Transport; Italy; University of Bologna

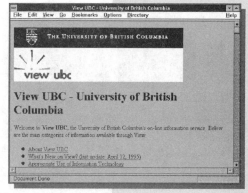

http://view.ubc.ca/
Canada; University of British Columbia

425

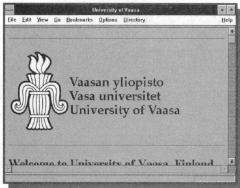

http://www.uwasa.fi/
Europe; Finland; Schools; University; Vaasa

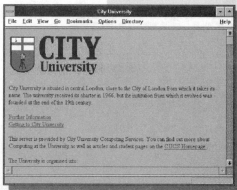

http://web.city.ac.uk/city/city.html
City University; England; London

Universities—Non US

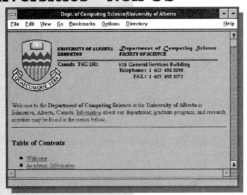

http://web.cs.ualberta.ca/
Canada; Computing Science; University of Alberta

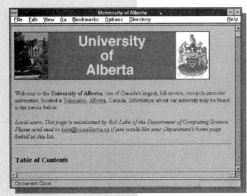

http://web.cs.ualberta.ca/UAlberta.html
Canada; University of Alberta

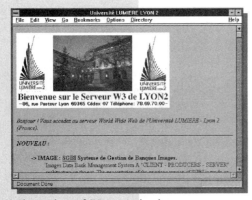

http://web.univ-lyon2.fr/Universite.html
France; Universite Lumiere Lyon

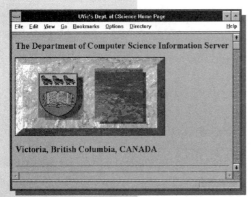

http://www-csc.uvic.ca/welcome.html
Computer Science; University of Victoria

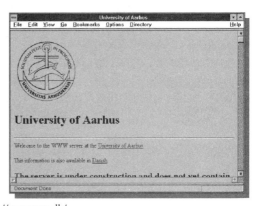

http://www.aau.dk/
Denmark; University of Aarhus

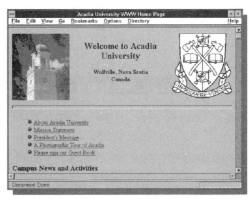

http://www.acadiau.ca/
Acadia University; Canada; Nova Scotia; Wolfville

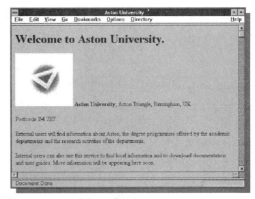

http://www.aston.ac.uk/home.html
United Kingdom; University of Aston

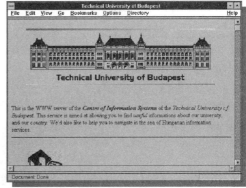

http://www.bme.hu/
Hungary; Technical University of Budapest

http://acad.udallas.edu/
University of Dallas

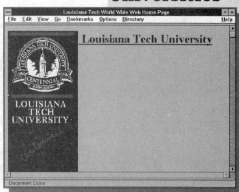

http://aurora.latech.edu/
Louisiana Tech University

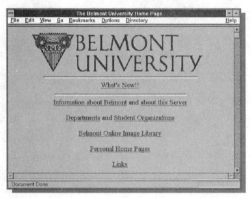

http://acklen.belmont.edu/
Belmont University; Tennessee

http://bluejay.creighton.edu/
Creighton University; Jesuits; Nebraska; Catholic; Omaha

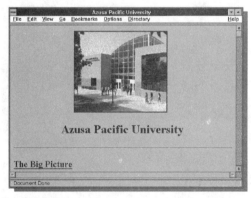

http://apu.edu/
Azusa Pacific University

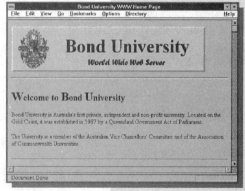

http://bond.edu.au/
Australia; Bond University

http://athena.lib.csufresno.edu/csuf.htm
California State University; Fresno

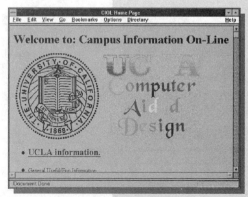

http://cad.ucla.edu/Welcome
Los Angeles; UCLA; University of California

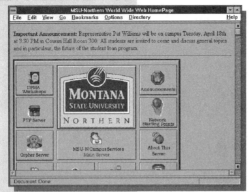

http://cis.nmclites.edu/
Montana State University; Northern Havre

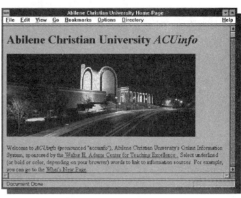

http://cteserver.acu.edu/
Abilene Christian University

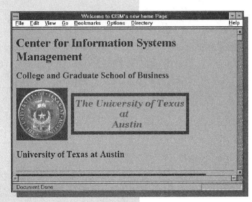

http://cism.bus.utexas.edu/
Austin; Information Systems Management; University of Texas

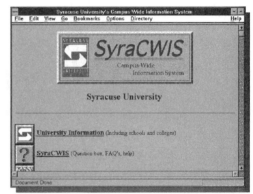

http://cwis.syr.edu/
Syracuse University

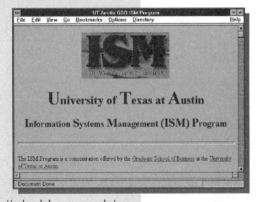

http://cobweb.bus.utexas.edu/
Austin; Information Systems Management; University of Texas

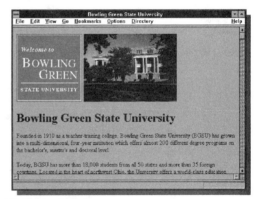

http://dad.bgsu.edu:80/
Bowling Green State University; Education

http://coyote.csusm.edu/
California State University; San Marcos

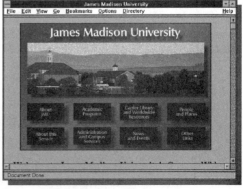

http://doc.jmu.edu/
James Madison University

http://dolphin.upenn.edu/
Small Schools; University of Pennsylvania

http://gateway.cis.ysu.edu/
Youngstown State University

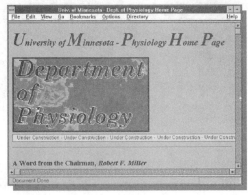

http://enlil.med.umn.edu:/physlhp/
Physiology; University of Minnesota

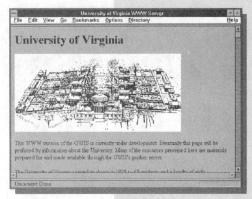

http://gwis.virginia.edu/
Charlottesville; University of Virginia

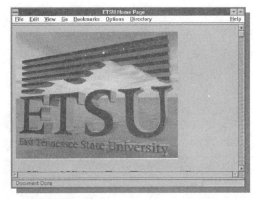

http://etsu.east-tenn-st.edu/
Eastern Tennessee State University; Education

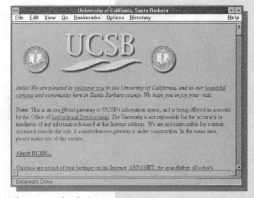

http://id-www.ucsb.edu/
Santa Barbara; University of California

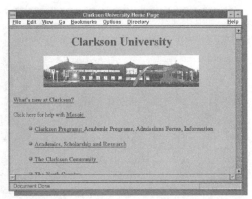

http://fire.clarkson.edu/
Clarkson University

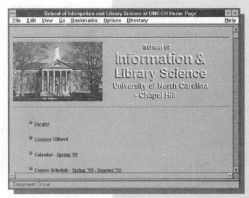

http://ils.unc.edu/ilshome.html
Information and Library Science; University of North Carolina

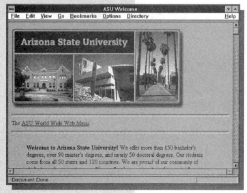

http://info.asu.edu:80/
Arizona State University; Education

http://lead.csustan.edu/
California State University; Stanislaus

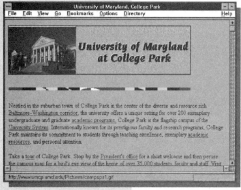

http://inform.umd.edu/
Education; University of Maryland at College Park

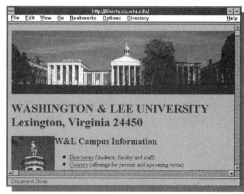

http://liberty.uc.wlu.edu/
Lexington; Virginia; Washington & Lee University

http://jsucc.jsu.edu/welcome.html
Jacksonville State University

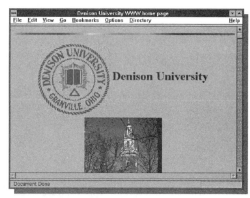

http://louie.cc.denison.edu/
Denison University; Granville; Ohio

http://kuhttp.cc.ukans.edu/cwis/UDK/KUhome/KUHome.html
University of Kansas

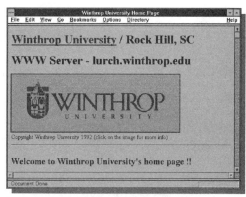

http://lurch.winthrop.edu/WinthropHomePage.html
Winthrop University

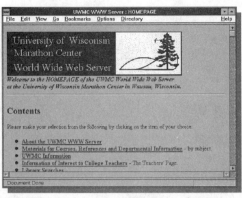

http://mthwww.uwc.edu/wwwmahes/homepage.html
Marathon Center; University of Wisconsin

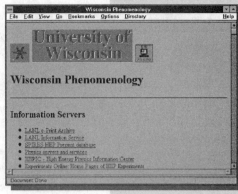

http://phenom.physics.wisc.edu/
Madison; Phenomenology; University of Wisconsin

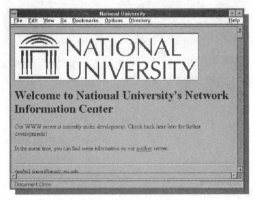

http://nunic.nu.edu/
National University

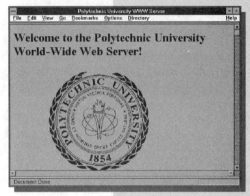

http://rama.poly.edu/
Polytechnic University of New York

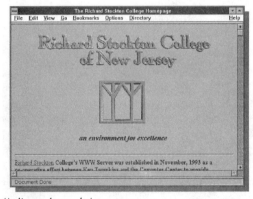

http://odin.stockton.edu/
Richard Stockton University

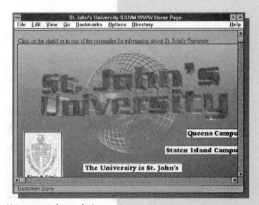

http://sjuvm.stjohns.edu/
St. John's University

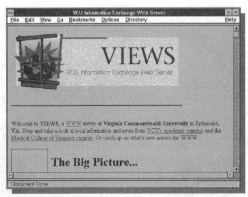

http://opal.vcu.edu/
Virginia Commonwealth University

http://toons.cc.ndsu.nodak.edu/ndsu/Home.html
North Dakota State University

431

Universities—US

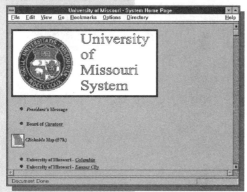

http://um.ics.missouri.edu/
University Extension; University of Missouri

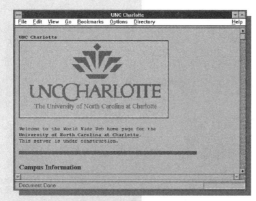

http://unccvm.uncc.edu/
Charlotte; University of North Carolina

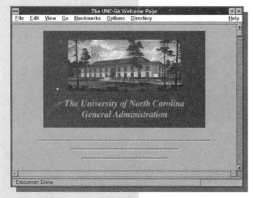

http://uncecs.edu/
General Administration; University of North Carolina

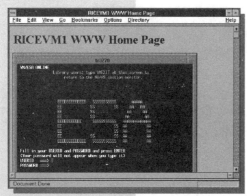

http://vm.rice.edu/
Rice University

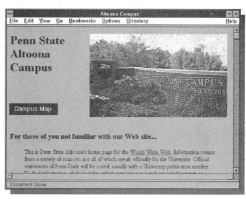

http://www.aa.psu.edu/
Altoona; Penn State University

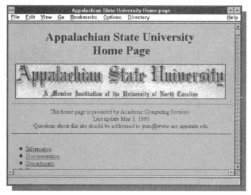

http://www.acs.appstate.edu:80/
Appalachian State University; Education

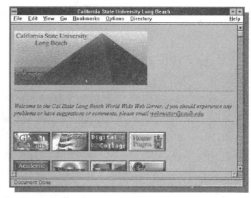

http://www.acs.csulb.edu/
California State University; Long Beach

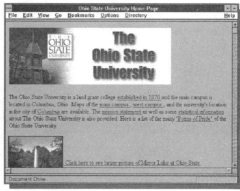

http://www.acs.ohio-state.edu/index.html
Education; Ohio State University

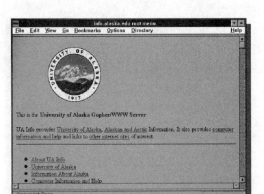

http://www.alaska.edu/
University of Alaska

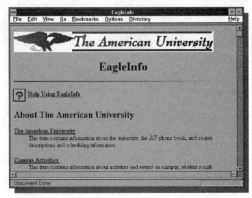

http://www.american.edu/
American University

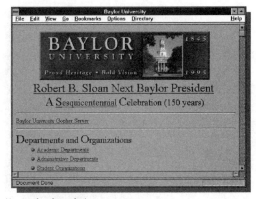

http://www.baylor.edu/
Baylor University; Houston; Texas

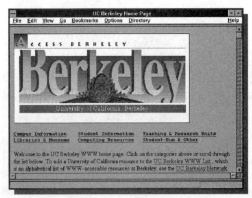

http://www.berkeley.edu:80/
Education; University of California Berkeley

http://www.binghamton.edu/
Binghamton; State University of New York

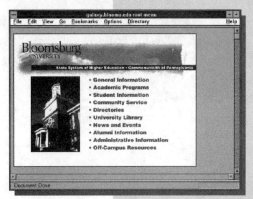

http://www.bloomu.edu/
Bloomsburg University; Pennsylvania

http://www.bradley.edu/
Bradley University

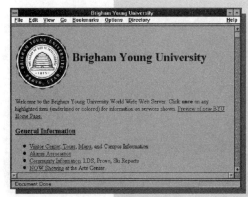

http://www.byu.edu/
Brigham Young University; LDS; Mormon

http://www.calpoly.edu/
California; Education

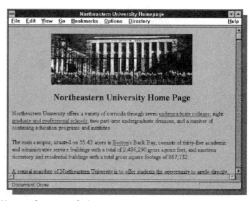

http://www.dac.neu.edu/
Boston; Massachusetts; Northeastern University

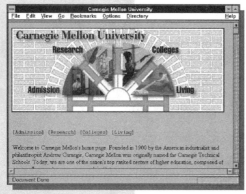

http://www.cmu.edu/
Carnegie Mellon University; Educational

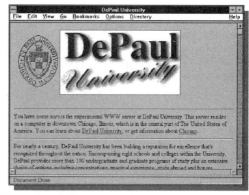

http://www.depaul.edu/
Chicago; DePaul University; Illinois

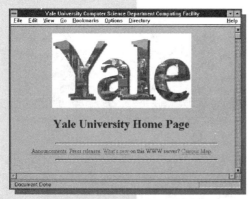

http://www.cs.yale.edu/HTML/YALE/Home.html
Education; Yale University

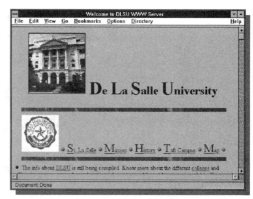

http://www.dlsu.edu.ph/
De La Salle University; Phillipines

http://www.csuohio.edu/
Cleveland State University; Education

http://www.drexel.edu/
Drexel University

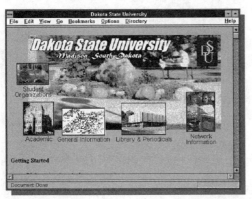

http://www.dsu.edu/
Dakota State University; Madison; South Dakota

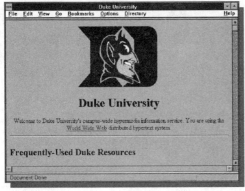

http://www.duke.edu/
Duke University

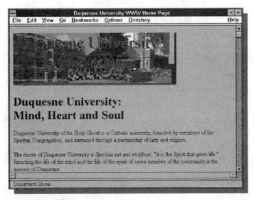

http://www.duq.edu/
Catholic; Duquesne University

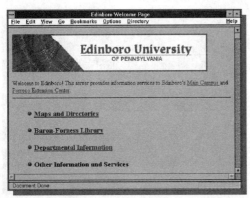

http://www.edinboro.edu/
Edinboro University of Pennsylvania

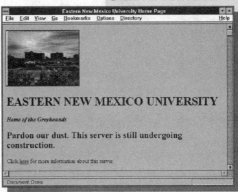

http://www.enmu.edu/
Eastern New Mexico University

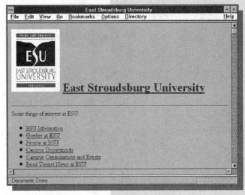

http://www.esu.edu/
East Stroudsburg State University

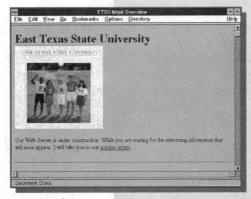

http://www.etsu.edu/
East Texas State University

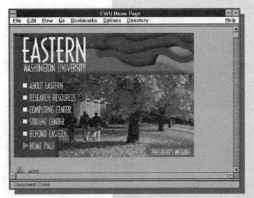

http://www.ewu.edu/
Eastern Washington University

Universities—US

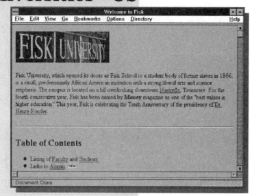

http://www.fisk.edu/
Fisk University; Nashville; Tennessee

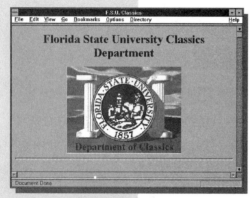

http://www.fsu.edu:80/~cgatlin/
Classics; Florida State University

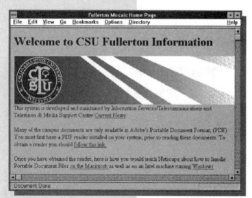

http://www.fullerton.edu/
California State University; Fullerton

http://www.furman.edu/
Furman University

http://www.gallaudet.edu/
Deaf; Gallaudet University; Hearing

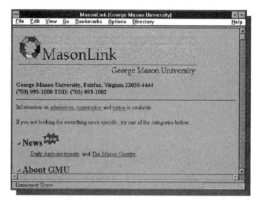

http://www.gmu.edu/
George Mason University

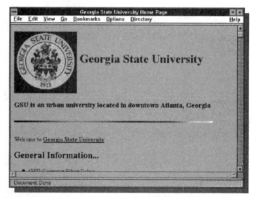

http://www.gsu.edu/
Atlanta; Georgia State University

http://www.harvard.edu/
Harvard University; Massachusetts

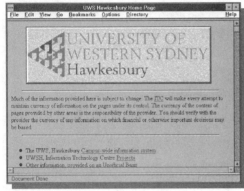

http://www.hawaii.edu/uhinfo.html
Manoa; University of Hawaii

http://www.indiana.edu/
Bloomington; Indiana University

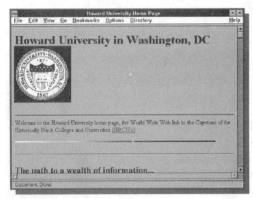

http://www.hawkesbury.uws.edu.au/HEART/
Australia; Hawkesbury; University of Western Sydney

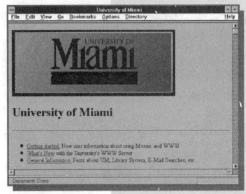

http://www.ir.miami.edu/
University of Miami

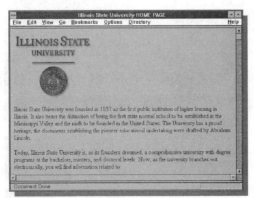

http://www.howard.edu/
Education; Howard University

http://www.jhu.edu/
Baltimore; Johns Hopkins University; Maryland

http://www.ilstu.edu/
Illinois State University

http://www.lehigh.edu/
Lehigh University

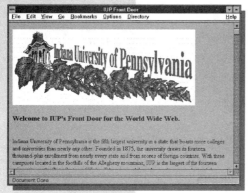

http://www.lib.iup.edu/
Indiana University of Pennsylvania

http://www.reg.uci.edu/SANET/ucb.html
Education; University of California Berkeley

http://www.louisville.edu/
Kentucky; University of Louisville

http://www.reg.uci.edu/SANET/ucd.html
Education; University of California Davis

438

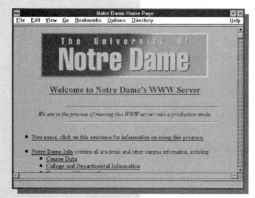

http://www.nd.edu/
Education; University of Notre Dame

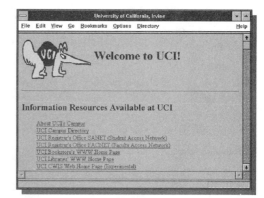

http://www.reg.uci.edu/SANET/uci.html
Education; University of California Irvine

http://www.okstate.edu/
Education; Oklahoma State University

http://www.reg.uci.edu/SANET/ucla.html
Education; UCLA; University of California Los Angeles

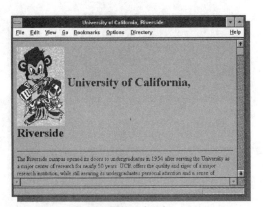

http://www.reg.uci.edu/SANET/ucr.html
Education; University of California Riverside

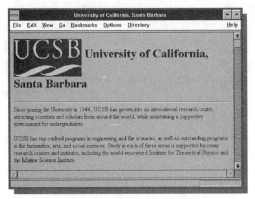

http://www.reg.uci.edu/SANET/ucsb.html
Education; University of California Santa Barbara

http://www.reg.uci.edu/SANET/ucsc.html
Education; University of California Santa Cruz

http://www.reg.uci.edu/SANET/ucsd.html
Education; University of California San Diego

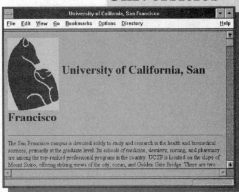

http://www.reg.uci.edu/SANET/ucsf.html
Education; University of California San Francisco

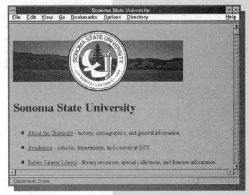

http://www.sonoma.edu/default.html
Education; Sonoma State University

439

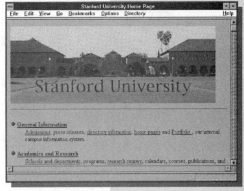

http://www.stanford.edu/
Education; Stanford University

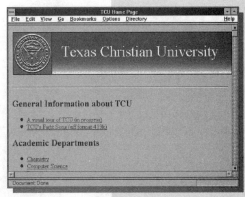

http://www.tcu.edu/
Business schools; Physics; Texas Christian University

http://www.uc.edu/
Ohio; University of Cincinnati

http://www.uconn.edu/
University of Connecticut

http://www.ucdavis.edu/
Davis; University of California

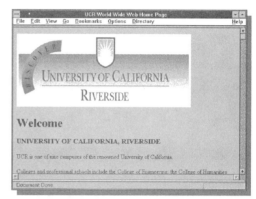

http://www.ucr.edu/
University of California Riverside

440

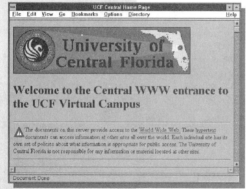

http://www.ucf.edu/
University of Central Florida

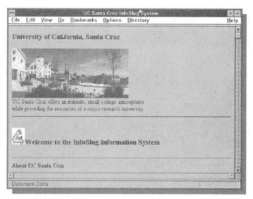

http://www.ucsc.edu/index.html
Education; University of California Santa Cruz

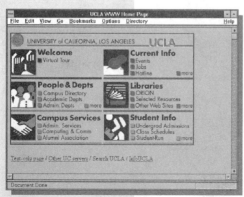

http://www.ucla.edu/
Los Angeles; UCLA; University of California

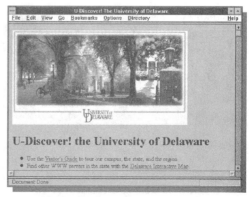

http://www.udel.edu/
University of Delaware

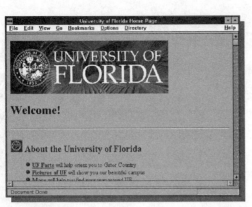

http://www.ufl.edu/
University of Florida

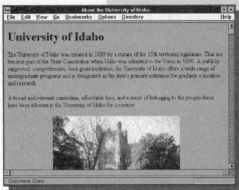

http://www.uidaho.edu/about-ui.html
University of Idaho

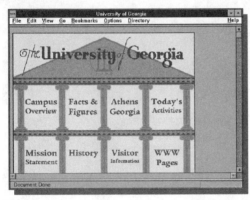

http://www.uga.edu/
University of Georgia

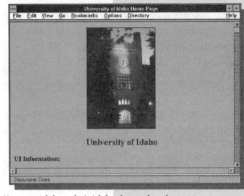

http://www.uidaho.edu/uidaho-home.html
University of Idaho

441

http://www.uh.edu/
University of Houston

http://www.uindy.edu/
University of Indianapolis

http://www.uic.edu/
Chicago; University of Illinois

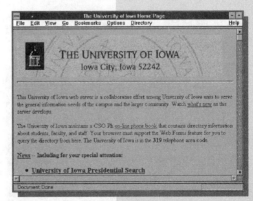

http://www.uiowa.edu/
University of Iowa

Universities—US

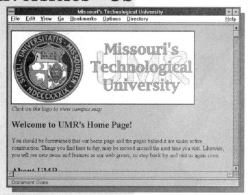

http://www.umr.edu/
Rolla; University of Missouri

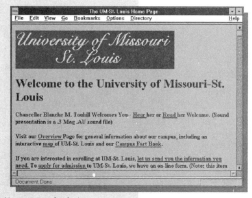

http://www.umsl.edu/
St. Louis; University of Missouri

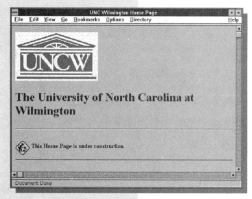

http://www.uncwil.edu/
University of North Carolina; Wilmington

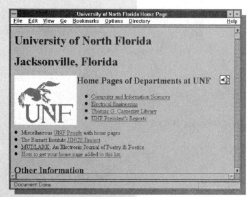

http://www.unf.edu/
Jacksonville; University of North Florida

http://www.unlv.edu/
Education; University of Nevada Las Vegas

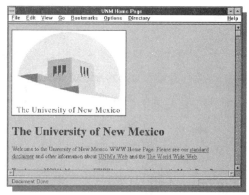

http://www.unm.edu/
University of New Mexico

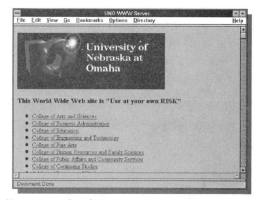

http://www.unomaha.edu/
Omaha; University of Nebraska

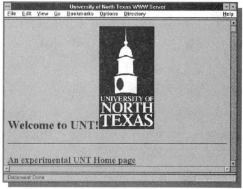

http://www.unt.edu/
University of North Texas

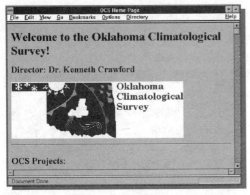

http://cougarxp.princeton.edu:2112/bpd/webweather.html
By state; Forecasts; US weather conditions

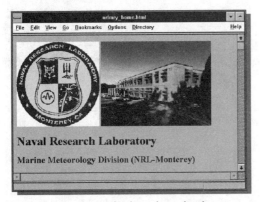

http://geowww.gcn.uoknor.edu/WWW/OCS/OCS.html
Climate Survey; University of Oklahoma

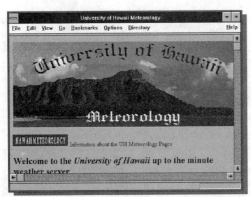

http://helium.nrlmry.navy.mil/nrlmry_home.html
Marine Meteorology Division; Naval Research Laboratory

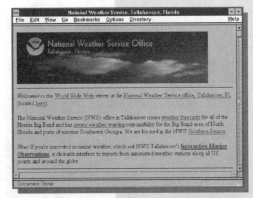

http://lumahai.soest.hawaii.edu/
Meteorology; University of Hawaii; Weather

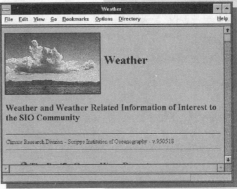

http://meteora.ucsd.edu/weather.html
Scripps Institution of Oceanography; Weather

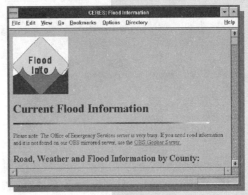

http://resources.agency.ca.gov/flood2.html
California Environmental Resources Evaluation System; Floods

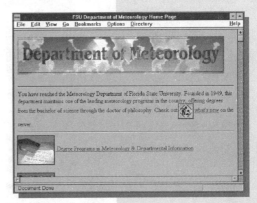

http://thunder.met.fsu.edu/
Florida State University; Meteorology

http://thunder.met.fsu.edu/nws/public_html/index.html
Marine observation; National Weather Service; NWS

443

Weather

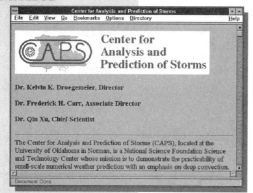

http://tornado.gcn.uoknor.edu/
Analysis and Prediction of Storms; University of Oklahoma

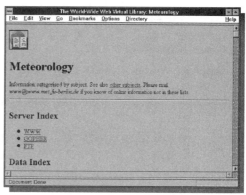

http://www.met.fu-berlin.de/DataSources/MetIndex.html
Internet sites; Meteorology

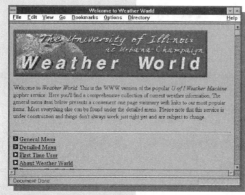

http://www.atmos.uiuc.edu/wxworld/html/top.html
Climate; Weather information; Weather World

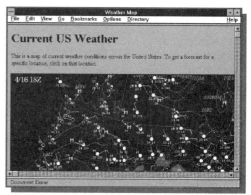

http://www.mit.edu:8001/usa.html
Current US Weather; United States; Weather conditions

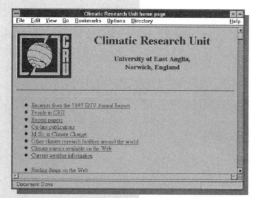

http://www.cru.uea.ac.uk/
Climate research; Research facilities; Weather

http://www.ncdc.noaa.gov/
Climate data; Meteorology; National Climatic Data Center

http://www.infi.net/pilot/weather.html
Hurricane updates; Local forecast; Pilot Online; Weather

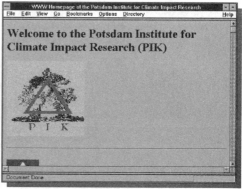

http://www.pik-potsdam.de:80/
Climate; Global warming;; Potsdam Institute; Research

Aeronautics

Department of Aeronautics and Astronautics
Aeronautics Consolidated Supercomputing Facility (ACSF)
Stanford Satellite Systems Development Laboratory Home Page
NSSDC Photo Gallery
NASA Technical Report Server (NTRS) FAQ
Desktop Aeronautics Index Page

http://aero.stanford.edu/aeroastro.html
http://cabsparc.larc.nasa.gov/ACSF/acsf.html
http://mastodon.arc.nasa.gov/SSDL.html
http://nssdc.gsfc.nasa.gov/photo_gallery/PhotoGallery.html
http://techreports.larc.nasa.gov/ntrs/ntrs-faq.html
http://www.batnet.com/dai/

Aerospace

The World Wide Web Aerospace Business Development Center
The SWAPRA Internet Survey
Magellan Image Server
Overview — Space
NASA Langley Colloquium and Sigma Series Lectures
Apollo-13
Project ASTP
NASA Langley Research Center Fact Sheet
What's New at LaRC
The NASA Vision Mission and Goals
TELS (Technology Experts Locator Service)
NASA Langley Research Center Home Page

http://arganet.tenagra.com/Tenagra/aero_bd.html
http://arganet.tenagra.com/Tenagra/swapras.html
http://delcano.mit.edu/cgi-bin/midr-query
http://info.cern.ch/Space/Overview.html
http://wmkpc.larc.nasa.gov/lectures.htm
http://www.ksc.nasa.gov/history/apollo/apollo-13/apollo-13.html
http://www.ksc.nasa.gov/history/astp/astp.html
http://www.larc.nasa.gov/facts/factsheet.html
http://www.larc.nasa.gov/facts/new.html
http://www.larc.nasa.gov/facts/vision.html
http://www.larc.nasa.gov/t2/tels.html
http://www.larc.nasa.gov/tour/tourpage.html

Agriculture

Ohio State Ag Engineering
Prescription Farming
The Agricultural Genome Information Server
Faculty of Agricultural Sciences
University of Maryland at College Park inforM system
Arboricultural Stuff

http://goddard.eng.ohio-state.edu/age-home.html
http://ma.itd.com:8000/p-farming.html
http://probe.nalusda.gov:8000/index.html
http://view.ubc.ca:80/1/acad-units/ag-sci
http://www.cen.uiuc.edu/cgi-bin/ryl
http://www.sccs.swarthmore.edu/~justin/Docs/arbor.html

Architecture

MSU School of Architecture Home Page
Architecture Home Page

http://sarc.msstate.edu/
http://www.sbu.ac.uk/Architecture/home.html

Art

Art:Exhibits
Art on the web
Drama
just outside the place
BELINDA Di Leo MFA PROJECT
The Heard Museum
David Voth's Home Page
Artists and Works
PARIS.ARCHIVE.LOUVRE
ANU Art History Top Level Menu Page
HypArt - The Project
The UNC Virtual Museum
EXPO Book Store
Guild Exhibit
Cloud Gallery: CDROM with stock photography
The Electric Gallery
THE PALACE OF FINE ARTS - a brief history
Art Artists and Galleries
The Jayhawk series by Mary K. Kuhner
FineArt Forum Gallery Page
Who's Got the Body?
The Andy Warhol Museum Home Page
ArtWorld: HomePage
Welcome to Pixel Pushers

http://akebono.stanford.edu/yahoo/Art/Exhibits/
http://altair.stmarys-ca.edu:70/1s/art
http://english-server.hss.cmu.edu/Drama.html
http://gertrude.art.uiuc.edu/ludgate/the/place.html
http://gort.ucsd.edu/mw/bdl.html
http://hanksville.phast.umass.edu/defs/independent/Heard/Heard.html
http://haven.uniserve.com/~dvoth
http://lydia.bradley.edu/exhibit/artists.html
http://meteora.ucsd.edu:80/~norman/paris/Musees/Louvre/Treasures/gifs
http://rubens.anu.edu.au/index.html
http://rzsun01.rrz.uni-hamburg.de/cgi-bin/HypArt.sh
http://sunsite.unc.edu/exhibits/vmuseum/vmuseumhome.html
http://sunsite.unc.edu/expo/expo/bookstore.html
http://www.bradley.edu/exhibit/index.html
http://www.commerce.digital.com/palo-alto/CloudGallery/home.html
http://www.egallery.com/egallery/
http://www.exploratorium.edu/Palace_History/Palace_History.html
http://www.infopost.com/sandiego/art/index.html
http://www.klab.caltech.edu/~flowers/jayhawk/
http://www.msstate.edu/Fineart_Online/gallery.html
http://www.sva.edu/WGTB/flypaper.html
http://www.warhol.org/warhol
http://www.wimsey.com/anima/ARTWORLDhome.html
http://www.wimsey.com/Pixel_Pushers

Artificial Intelligence

Computational Intelligence Research Laboratory
Neural Net Stuff
UIUC AI WWW Library
Journal of Artificial Intelligence Research
UCI Machine Learning Group
Institut Dalle Molle d'Intelligence Artificelle Perceptive (IDIAP)

http://cirl.uoregon.edu/
http://taygeta.oc.nps.navy.mil/nnet.html
http://www-ilg.cs.uiuc.edu/info/
http://www.cs.washington.edu/research/jair/home.html
http://www.ics.uci.edu/AI/ML/Machine-Learning.html
http://www.idiap.ch/

Astronomy

NASA Astrophysics Data System (ADS) Abstract Service
STARCAT
Department of Astronomy Cornell University Home Page
Exhibit
CTIO Home Page
DSN Solar System Menu
Mars Surveyor MENU
Planetary image finders

http://adswww.harvard.edu/abs_doc/abstract_service.html
http://arch-http.hq.eso.org/starcat.html
http://astrosun.tn.cornell.edu/Home.html
http://blazing.sunspot.noao.edu/Exhibit/Exhibit.html
http://ctios2.ctio.noao.edu/ctio.html
http://esther.la.asu.edu/asu_tes/TES_Editor/dsn_solarsyst.html
http://esther.la.asu.edu/asu_tes/TES_Editor/MsurveyorMENU.html
http://fi-www.arc.nasa.goV/fia/projects/bayes-group/Atlas

Additional Sites

The WWW Virtual Library: Astronomy and Astrophysics	http://info.cern.ch/hypertext/DataSources/bySubject/astro/astro.html
NRAO Green Bank	http://info.gb.nrao.edu/
What's New with Project BAMBI	http://irsociety.com/0c:/sara/bambinew.htm|
Inter University Center for Astronomy and Astrophysics	http://iucaa.iucaa.ernet.in/welcome.html
Comet Shoemaker-Levy Home Page (JPL)	http://newproducts.jpl.nasa.gov/sl9/sl9.html
SL9 Observations in Massachusetts	http://scruffy.phast.umass.edu/Whately/sl9.html
SEDS Messier Database	http://seds.lpl.arizona.edu/messier/Messier.html
The Nine Planets	http://seds.lpl.arizona.edu/nineplanets/nineplanets/nineplanets.html
The Morehead Planetarium's WWW Page!	http://tfnet.ils.unc.edu/~dataman
WARSAW UNIVERSITY ASTRONOMICAL OBSERVATORY	http://www.astrouw.edu.pl/index.html
Views Of The Solar System	http://www.c3.lanl.gov/~cjhamil/SolarSystem/homepage.html
CFHT Home Page	http://www.cfht.hawaii.edu/
Book Reviews	http://www.cnde.iastate.edu/staff/swormley/bkr.html
UC Santa Barbara Astrophysics Home Page	http://www.deepspace.ucsb.edu/
Earth and Universe	http://www.eia.brad.ac.uk/btl/
Mount Wilson Observatory	http://www.mtwilson.edu/index.html
Earth and Sky Radio Scripts	http://www.tpoint.net:70/1s/earthandsky

Biology

Candida albicans information	http://alces.med.umn.edu/Candida.html
The BioMolecular Engineering Research Center	http://bmerc-www.bu.edu/
NetFrog Title Page	http://curry.edschool.Virginia.EDU:80/~insttech/frog/
TAMU Department of Plant Pathology	http://cygnus.tamu.edu/
Virtual Frog Dissection Kit Info Page	http://george.lbl.gov/ITG.hm.pg.docs/dissect/info.html
The World-Wide Web Virtual Library: Biosciences	http://golgi.harvard.edu/biopages.html
The WWW VL Biosciences: Index	http://golgi.harvard.edu/htbin/biopages
Biology	http://info.er.usgs.gov/network/science/biology/index.html
KBS Home Page	http://kbs.msu.edu/
Biological Agricultural and Medical Resources	http://lib-www.ucr.edu/bioag/
The Graduate College	http://mole.uvm.edu/Biology
Biology	http://nearnet.gnn.com/wic/bio.toc.html
Department of Biological Sciences	http://simon.kent.edu/Biology/BiologyHP.html
Tree Physiology	http://sol.uvic.ca/treephys
Entomology at Colorado State University	http://www.colostate.edu/Depts/Entomology/ent.html
The National Center for Biotechnology Information	http://www.ncbi.nlm.nih.gov:80/
NCGR: Home Page	http://www.ncgr.org/
The NIH Molecular Modeling Home Page	http://www.nih.gov/molecular_modeling/mmhome.html
Instituut voor Moleculaire Biologie en Biotechnologie	http://www.vub.ac.be/IMOL/IMOL.html

Business and finance

GSU RMI Home Page	http://131.96.94.5/gsuweb.htm
Business	http://akebono.stanford.edu/yahoo/Business/
Economy:Markets and Investments	http://akebono.stanford.edu/yahoo/Economy/Markets_and_Investments
Trade Law Library - Internet sites for Law Economics and Commerce	http://ananse.irv.uit.no/law/nav/law_ref.html
Print Publications Related to Business Use of the Internet	http://arganet.tenagra.com/Tenagra/books.html
Branch Business Center	http://branch.com/business.htm#business
Marcus Associates	http://branch.com/marcus
Making Money on Internet	http://cism.bus.utexas.edu/ravi/making_money.html
Literal Research : Internet Transactions	http://com.primenet.com/research/
Cardservice International	http://cyberzine.org/html/Credit/morganpage.html
NYU EDGAR Development Site	http://edgar.stern.nyu.edu/edgar.html
Fast EDGAR Mutual Funds Reporting	http://edgar.stern.nyu.edu/mutual.html
EDGAR Prospectus Report	http://edgar.stern.nyu.edu/prospectus.html
Strategyweb - The Central Forum of the Business Strategy Community	http://fender.onramp.net/~atw_dhw/precom.htm
ABOUT HOME BASED BUSINESSES	http://freenet3.scri.fsu.edu:81/ht-free/hbb1.html
Network Money: The Future of Banking and Commerce on the Internet	http://gnn.com/meta/finance/feat/emoney.home.html
Personal Finance Center	http://gnn.interpath.net/gnn/meta/finance/index.html
CICNet Home Page	http://gopher.cic.net/
Hampton Roads: Economy	http://hampton.roads.net/nhr/economy.html
Internet Business Systems Home Page	http://InetBSystems.us.com/IBS/IBS.html
Consejo Nacional de Promocion de Inversiones	http://lanic.utexas.edu/la/venezuela/conapri/conapri.html
MarketPlace.com - The Internet Information Mall	http://marketplace.com:80/csd/development.html
Prices at Marketplace.com	http://marketplace.com:80/csd/prices.html
Marketplace.com Storefront	http://marketplace.com:80/csd/store.html
The Insider: Public Companies	http://networth.galt.com/www/home/insider/publicco.htm
NETworth by GALT Technologies	http://networth.galt.com:80/
James R. Garven's Home Page	http://riskweb.bus.utexas.edu/
FINWeb Home Page	http://riskweb.bus.utexas.edu/finweb.html
About The Journal of Risk and Insurance...	http://riskweb.bus.utexas.edu/jri.htm
About ARIA's Meetings...	http://riskweb.bus.utexas.edu/meeting.htm
What is Risk Management and Insurance?	http://riskweb.bus.utexas.edu/riskmgmt.htm
About the World Wide Web...	http://riskweb.bus.utexas.edu/www.htm
DIE Industry Group WWW Home Page	http://vhdl.org/pub/die/
GOLD MOUNTAIN LAND HOMEPAGE	http://www.aimnet.com/~ayl/antelope.htm
R.M.C. - Home Page	http://www.aimnet.com/forecast/home.html
Visitor Information: All about Downtown Anywhere	http://www.awa.com/info.html
Questel/Orbit: Patent and Trademark Welcome Page	http://www.bedrock.com/mall/OQ/welcome.html
BizWeb Company Information Form	http://www.bizweb.com/InfoForm/infoform.html
BankAmerica Home Page	http://www.bofa.com/
Master Mind Network	http://www.catalog.com/rmg/mm_net.htm

The Professional Fiduciary Association of San DiegoCounty	http://www.catalog.com/rmg/pfa.htm
Richard M. Greenwood MBA	http://www.catalog.com/rmg/rmg.htm
Checkfree Home Page	http://www.checkfree.com/
CTSNET Business & Finance Center	http://www.cts.com/cts/biz/
DigiCash home page	http://www.digicash.com/
Personal Finance Center	http://www.digital.com/gnn/meta/finance/index.html
Foreign Exchange Rates	http://www.dna.lth.se/cgi-bin/rates
Washington Trade Center	http://www.eskimo.com/~bwest
Russian Security Market News (Russian)	http://www.fe.msk.ru/infomarket/
GENinc Products and Services	http://www.geninc.com/welcome.html
Clients	http://www.iaccess.za/ecoserv/clients.html
Enterprise Mortgage Corporation	http://www.infi.net/REWeb/enterprise/
J. M. Froehler Construction	http://www.infi.net/REWeb/JMFroehler/
The Westgate Hotel	http://www.infopost.com/sandiego/hotels/westgate/index.html
Urban Planning	http://www.infopost.com/urban/index.html
Welcome!	http://www.intercon.com/
HomeOwners Finance:	http://www.internet-is.com/homeowners/
The Indus Entrepreneurs	http://www.internet-is.com/tie/index.html
Swarts & Company	http://www.internex.com/multipresence/swarts.html
Nelson Capital Management	http://www.internex.com/NCM/home.html
Franchise Opportunities Report	http://www.ip.net/hayes-fin/newsletter0704.html
Cookware Web Demographics	http://www.iquest.net/cw/web/demograph.html
Somers & Associates	http://www.jkcg.com/Webmaster/Ispy/
Vanguard Capital	http://www.kern.com/~cwmarket/biz/vanguard/vguard.html
C & W MARKETING BUSINESS PAGE	http://www.kern.com/~cwmarket/index.html
Dainamic Consulting Projects	http://www.netpart.com/dai/projects.html
Opal Web Server	http://www.opal.com/
QuoteCom BusinessWire Info	http://www.quote.com/info/bwire.html
QuoteCom Quick Quotes	http://www.quote.com/quot.html
IBM Networking Home Page	http://www.raleigh.ibm.com/nethome.html
Internet Credit Bureau Customer Application	http://www.satelnet.org/credit/application.html
Credit Information	http://www.satelnet.org/credit/credit-info.html
TCC Introduction	http://www.service.com/tcc/corp12.html
Internet Business Center	http://www.tig.com/IBC/
Thomson-Shore's Book Manufacturing Home Page	http://www.tshore.com/
PacifiCorp WWW Home Page	http://www.upl.com/
Home Page	http://www.usbanksl.com
Xenitec Home Page	http://www.xenitec.on.ca/
Gastown Webspace - A virtual town	http://gastown.xmission.com/~gastown/

447

Careers

JOBS	http://ageninfo.tamu.edu/jobs.html
Business:Employment:Jobs	http://akebono.stanford.edu/yahoo/Business/Employment/Jobs/
Employment Resources	http://alpha.acast.nova.edu/employment.html
ACM SIGMOD's Database Jobs Listings	http://bunny.cs.uiuc.edu/jobs/
Usenet News Job Browser	http://fire.clarkson.edu/cgi-bin/news/newssearch
Job Center	http://mainsail.com/jobsinfo.html
Job Search Welcome Page	http://www.adnetsol.com/jsearch/jshome1.html
Job Opportunities	http://www.bristol.com/Company/jobs.html
E-Span Database Search	http://www.espan.com/cgi-bin/wwwais
FAQ	http://www.espan.com/faq.html
Interactive Employment Network	http://www.espan.com/ienhome.html
E-Span Employment Database Search	http://www.espan.com/js/library/srch.html
Welcome to helpwanted.com	http://www.helpwanted.com/
Central Carolina On-Line Career Services	http://www.infi.net/ccocs
IntelliMatch(tm) On-Line Job & Career Services	http://www.intellimatch.com/intellimatch/
SkillSearch	http://www.internet-is.com/skillsearch/
TKO Personnel Inc.	http://www.internet-is.com/tko/in-iis.html
Msen Home Page	http://www.msen.com/
NCSA Job Announcments	http://www.ncsa.uiuc.edu/General/Jobs/00Jobs.html
Contact College Pro	http://www.netweb.com/mall/collegepro/contact.html
Join College Pro	http://www.netweb.com/mall/collegepro/form.html
Search College Pro	http://www.netweb.com/mall/collegepro/search.html
College Pro	http://www.netweb.com/mall/collegepro/Welcome.html
OSA OpticsNet Employment	http://www.osa.org/osapage/employ/employnet.html
Jobs.Offered Database	http://www.service.com/cm/usenet.html
SIPA Home Page	http://www.sipa.org/sipa/
Professional Development Home Page	http://www.tcom.ohiou.edu/training.html
Job Search and Employment Opportunities: Best Bets from the Net	http://www.umich.edu/~philray/job-guide/
Big Dreams	http://www.wimsey.com/~duncans/

Children

Rudyard Kipling's The Jungle Book	http://bvp.wdp.com/BVPM/PressRoom/JungleBook/JungleBook.html
The Lion King	http://bvp.wdp.com/BVPM/PressRoom/LionKing/LionKing.html
Buckman Kindergarten Spanish Counting Book	http://davinci.vancouver.wsu.edu/buckman/SpanishBook.html
Explorer Post 500 Home Page	http://erda.rl.af.mil/~gurecki
PPO HOME Page	http://fmatdds01.tu-graz.ac.at/guertl/scout/ppoe_eng.html
Circle 10 Council	http://seton.cor.net/scouts/c10.html
BSA Troop 117	http://seton.cor.net/scouts/t117.html
Explorer Post 512 Santa Clara County Council BSA	http://www.almaden.ibm.com/scouting/post512.html

Additional Sites

Boy Scout Troop 204 Lafayette CA	http://www.ccnet.com/~jecairn/t204/troop204.htm
Interesting Places for Kids	http://www.crc.ricoh.com/people/steve/kids.html
Yep It's Barney's Page	http://www.galcit.caltech.edu/~ta/barney/barney.html
GEMS - Missing Kids	http://www.gems.com/kids/index.html
Polly Klaas Foundation	http://www.northcoast.com/klaas/klaas.html
Parents Helping Parents	http://www.portal.com/~cbntmkr/php.html
Boy Scouts of America	http://www.scouting.org/scouting/

Colleges

Augsburg College Main Menu	http://bbs.augsburg.edu/augsburg.html
Chemistry at Harvey Mudd College	http://nmrws.chem.hmc.edu/
Neptune Home Page	http://sun.cc.westga.edu/localhome.html
Assumption College Home Page	http://www.assumption.edu/
Department of Computing Imperial College London.	http://www.doc.ic.ac.uk/
Estrella Mountain Community College Center's WWW Server	http://www.emc.maricopa.edu/
ReZun Interactive Concepts Inc.	http://www.kciLink.com/rezun/
LVCC Home Page	http://www.longview.cc.mo.us/
Loyola College Home Page	http://www.loyola.edu/
History of Santa Barbara City College	http://www.sbcc.cc.ca.us/sbcc/history.html
Santa Barbara City College	http://www.sbcc.cc.ca.us/sbcc_home.html
Partnerships and Collaborations	http://www.sdsc.edu/1/Parts_Collabs/parts_collabs.html
General Information at SDSC	http://www.sdsc.edu/1/SDSC/Geninfo/geninfo.html
St. Olaf WWW Server	http://www.stolaf.edu:80/welcome.html
Trinity Home Page	http://www.trincoll.edu/homepage.html
North Carolina State University College of Textiles	http://www.tx.ncsu.edu/
University of Kentucky - Colleges	http://www.uky.edu/colleges.html
Wellesley College Campus-Wide Information System	http://www.wellesley.edu/

Communications

Dan Kegel's ISDN Page	http://alumni.caltech.edu/~dank/isdn/
Branch Business Center	http://branch.com/business.htm#communications
International Association of Business Communicators	http://ccnet.com/~shel/iabc.html
LAN2LAN Personal Office for ISDN	http://cio.cisco.com/warp/public/558/45.html
PCS_Auctions	http://fcc.gov:70/1/PCS_Auctions
EII Concept Paper	http://human.com/mkt/island/
Books on ISDN	http://igwe.vub.ac.be/~svendk/books.html
Suppliers by name	http://igwe.vub.ac.be/~svendk/suppliers_by_name.html
Gazel1.html	http://nw.com/satusa/Gazel1.html
SatelNET Communications	http://satelnet.org/
The CallAmerica Nexus	http://slonet.org/
The LLNL Advanced Telecommunications Program	http://www-atp.llnl.gov/atp/
Computer and Communication Companies	http://www-atp.llnl.gov/atp/companies.html
California ISDN User Group	http://www.almaden.ibm.com/ciug/ciug.html
Ameritech - Solutions Guide - Ameritech DataServices	http://www.ameritech.com/solutions/business/asg-data_services.html
Pipeline 50 ISDN	http://www.ascend.com/prodinfo/pipeline/P50ISDN.html
Telecommunication Sites	http://www.ba.com/sites.html
Bell Atlantic Home Page	http://www.bell-atl.com/
The BellSouth Telecommunications Homepage	http://www.bst.bls.com/
The CallAmerica Nexus	http://www.callamer.com/
LAMG Article	http://www.caprica.com/~dginsberg/article.html
David Ginsberg's ISDN Web Page	http://www.caprica.com/~dginsberg/isdn.html
Bell Atlantic Residence Customer Information	http://www.cnm.bell-atl.com/customer/consumer/home.html
HOME page of Depts. of EEICE	http://www.ee.t.u-tokyo.ac.jp/
Welcome to the FCC Web Server	http://www.fcc.gov/
NTT ISDN HOME PAGE	http://www.info.hqs.cae.ntt.jp/SER/ISDN/ISDN.html
ISDN Systems Inc: FX-PRI ISDN/Frame Relay PC Adapter	http://www.infoanalytic.com/isc/fxpri.htm
...New York ISDN Users Group...	http://www.interport.net/~digital/index.html
Janal Communications Home Page	http://www.janal-communications.com/janal.html
Journalism: Environment Science	http://www.lehigh.edu/injrl/public/www-data/s&emenu.html
NTT Home Page	http://www.ntt.jp/index.html
ISDN	http://www.pacbell.com/isdn/isdn_home.html
Telecommunications Center Home Page	http://www.tcom.ohiou.edu/
ITC Home Page	http://www.telematrix.com/
Tahlequah Telecommunications	http://www.tq.com/
UIUC College of Communications Home Page	http://www.uiuc.edu/colleges/comm/
Technical Communication Dept. at U of W	http://www.uwtc.washington.edu/TC/TCwelcome.html

Computers

Computer Science Department	http://a.cs.okstate.edu/welcome.html
UNIX Security Topics	http://ausg.dartmouth.edu/security.html
Branch Business Center	http://branch.com/business.htm#computer
ACM SIGMOD Information Server Home Page	http://bunny.cs.uiuc.edu/README.html
Langley Computer Users Committee (LCUC)	http://cabsparc.larc.nasa.gov/LCUC/lcuc.html
SAT/SAGEM Index	http://catalog.com/satusa
LANL Information Servers	http://cnls-www.lanl.gov/is.html
CPSR	http://cpsr.org/cpsr/cpsr_membership_info/cpsr.html
Center for Research in Computing and the Arts (CRCA)	http://crca-www.ucsd.edu/
University of Bonn CS Department V	http://cs.uni-bonn.de/
UTEP Welcome (CS Dept)	http://cs.utep.edu/
Harvard University Computer Science	http://das-www.harvard.edu/aiken.html

Harvard University Computer Science	http://decaxp.harvard.edu/
NYU Center for Digital Multimedia	http://found.cs.nyu.edu/
The DECnet Phase IV Specifications	http://gatekeeper.dec.com/pub/DEC/DECnet/PhaseIV/index.html
ICE WWW Server	http://ice-www.larc.nasa.gov:80/
David Singer's page of pointers at the IBM Almaden ResearchCenter	http://index.almaden.ibm.com/
Distributed Object Computing	http://info.gte.com/ftp/doc/doc.html
HQ AFC4A World Wide Web Server	http://infosphere.safb.af.mil/
Kestrel Institute	http://kestrel.edu/www/kestrel.html
OSU PC User Group	http://krumsee-pc.acs.ohio-state.edu/
NRaD HPC Fellowship	http://manta.nosc.mil/~kevork/hpc_fellowship
PlanetBoard.html	http://nw.com/satusa/Planet1.html
Server Contents	http://pclt.cis.yale.edu/
ISCR Home Page	http://redhook.llnl.gov:80/
The Well Connected Mac	http://rever.nmsu.edu/~elharo/faq/Macintosh.html
MSU/UCG Home Page	http://rs560.cl.msu.edu/
HUT / Digital Systems Laboratory	http://saturn.hut.fi/
Wit: A System for Wireless/Mobile Handheld Computing	http://snapple.cs.washington.edu:600/wit/wit.html
The WWW Virtual Library: Computing	http://src.doc.ic.ac.uk/bySubject/Computing/Overview.html
Telemedia Networks and Systems Group	http://tns-www.lcs.mit.edu/tns-www-home.html
Unix Workstation Support Group Home Page	http://uwsg.ucs.indiana.edu/
VIUF Internet Services WWW Home Page	http://vhdl.org/
VIUF Internet Services WWW Home Page	http://vhdl.org/Welcome.html
WWW Home Page for comp.home.automation	http://web.cs.ualberta.ca/~wade/HyperHome
Computing Dictionary	http://wombat.doc.ic.ac.uk/
ACC Amazon	http://www.acc.com/Descriptions/amazon.html
ACC Danube	http://www.acc.com/Descriptions/danube.html
ACC Nile	http://www.acc.com/Descriptions/nile.html
LANL ACL Home Page	http://www.acl.lanl.gov/
ACM - The First Society in Computing	http://www.acm.org/
Network Hardware Suppliers List	http://www.ai.mit.edu/datawave/hardware.html
The ATM Forum	http://www.atmforum.com/
Boston Computer Society Home Page	http://www.bcs.org/bcs/general_info.html
The Center for Advanced Computer Studies	http://www.cacs.usl.edu:80/Departments/CACS/
Display Tech Multimedia (computers to video)	http://www.ccnet.com/~dtmi/
College of CS at Northeastern University	http://www.ccs.neu.edu/
Trojan Room Coffee Machine	http://www.cl.cam.ac.uk/coffee/coffee.html
Digital Equipment Corporation - Commercial Services Demonstrations	http://www.commerce.digital.com/
Compaq Computer Corporation Graphic/Text Split	http://www.compaq.com/
Info about this Web Server	http://www.cosy.sbg.ac.at/www-doku/info.html
Cray Research Home Page	http://www.cray.com/
WWW VL: Human-Computer Interaction	http://www.cs.bgsu.edu/HCI/
Computer Science Department Front Doors and Gophers	http://www.cs.cmu.edu:8001/Web/People/anwar/CS-departments.html
The Beginners Pages	http://www.cs.stir.ac.uk/~jsd/beginners.html
UBC Computer Science Home Page	http://www.cs.ubc.ca/home
Univ. of Washington Computer Science & Engineering	http://www.cs.washington.edu/
Yale CS CF HI - Top	http://www.cs.yale.edu/HTML/YALE/CS/CF/HI/Top.html
ACM SIGCOMM	http://www.digital.com/pub/doc/sigcomm/ccr/overview.html
ELRON Electronic Industries	http://www.elron.net/www/elronet/elron.html
Archetypes 'Electronic Textbook' Table ofContents	http://www.etext.caltech.edu:80/
National Coordination Office for HPCC	http://www.hpcc.gov/index.html
The IBM home page	http://www.ibm.com/
Finding your way around IBM	http://www.ibm.com/Finding/
GRIDS	http://www.informatik.uni-stuttgart.de/ipvr/as/grids/grids-e.html
INRIA - HOME PAGE	http://www.inria.fr/welcome-eng.html
HI-TECH Homepage	http://www.internet-cafe.com/hi-tech/
ENS: Systems Integration	http://www.ip.net/ENS/si.html
Keele Computer Science - Home Page	http://www.keele.ac.uk/depts/cs/cshome.html
MIT Laboratory for Computer Science	http://www.lcs.mit.edu/
MetaCenter Home Page	http://www.ncsa.uiuc.edu/General/MetaCenter/MetaCenterHome.html
INFORMATION PROCESSING	http://www.osa.org/osapage/ipd.html
Computer Science Department	http://www.sbcc.cc.ca.us/comsc/comsc_home.html
San Diego Supercomputer Center	http://www.sdsc.edu/
Copyright Statement	http://www.sdsc.edu/0/SDSC/Geninfo/copyright.html
High Performance Computing Resources	http://www.sdsc.edu/0/SDSC/HPC.html
Apple Computer World Wide Technical Support Home Page	http://www.support.apple.com/
Policy for Responsible Computing at the University of Delaware	http://www.udel.edu/eileen/Ecce/policy.approved.html
CAEME Home Page	http://www.utah.edu/HTML_Docs/caeme/caemehp.html
Z-Connect Magazine	http://www.zds.com/
Experimental Computing Facility Home Page	http://xcf.berkeley.edu:80/

Corporations

Welcome to Apple Networking Products	http://abs.apple.com/
And Communications Glad To Have You Here	http://and.com/and.html
Comit Systems Inc. Home Page	http://comit.com/
SGO Technologies Home Page	http://cruzio.com/bus/computers/sgo/sgo.html
Internet Business Directory v.0.9	http://ibd.ar.com/IBD/Artecon_Inc.html
ICEM CFD Engineering	http://icemcfd.com/index.html
The Advanced Research Corporation Home Page	http://info.arc.com/
About CAS (Chemical Abstracts Service)	http://info.cas.org/about.html
Babel Press home page	http://market.net/literary/Production/babel/
What is Wavefront Technologies ?	http://wavefront.wti.com/whatis.html

449

Additional Sites

IBM Almaden Web Farm	http://www-i.almaden.ibm.com/
Action Systems Incorporated Home Page	http://www.actioninc.com/
American Management Systems	http://www.amsinc.com/default.htm
About Answer Systems...	http://www.answer.com/answer/answer.html
Corporate Background	http://www.answer.com/answer/corp.html
Answer Systems Contacts	http://www.answer.com/answer/people/people.html
Arasmith Engineering	http://www.arasmith.com/
NEVAlink Company Profile	http://www.arcom.spb.su/
The Aspen Technology Inc. Home Page	http://www.aspentec.com/welcome.html
HiLink Communications	http://www.aus.net/
Overview of Bolt Beranek and Newman Inc.	http://www.bbn.com/overview.html
Company Profile	http://www.beyond2000.com/reza/html/comprof.htm
Bristol Overview	http://www.bristol.com/Company/company.html
Consensus Development Home Page	http://www.consensus.com:8300/
Sunnyside Computing Inc.	http://www.cpsr.org/
Welcome to Cybersmith Inc.	http://www.csi.nb.ca/
Cybersmith Inc. / Home Page	http://www.csi.nb.ca/home.html
Dell Computer Home Page	http://www.dell.com/
Digital Equipment Corporation	http://www.digital.com/home.html
W3-Design HomePage	http://www.earthlink.net/w3/index.html
GE Plastics Home Page	http://www.ge.com/gep/homepage.html
HaL Computer Systems Inc.	http://www.hal.com/index.html
Hitachi Instruments Inc. Hitachi America Ltd. Information	http://www.hii.hitachi.com/hal2.html
Access HP - Welcome to Hewlett-Packard	http://www.hp.com/ahp/home.html
ADAK-200/400/600 Terminal Adapter Page	http://www.icus.com/adak200.html
Inference Corporation	http://www.inference.com/
Electrical Outlet Inc	http://www.infi.net/el-out/
NTT DYNAMIC LOOP INFORMATION	http://www.info.hqs.cae.ntt.jp/
Infonet Products and Services	http://www.info.net/Public/Infonet-toc.html
Hermann Zillgens Associates (http://www.infopost.com/hza)	http://www.infopost.com/sandiego/architects/index.html
Innosoft International Inc	http://www.innosoft.com/
NSI Home Page	http://www.inow.com/
NEW GENISYS Internet Consulting	http://www.intellisoft.com/newgenisys/
CyberMedia's WWW Home Page	http://www.internet-is.com/cybermedia/index.html
Digital Data Express	http://www.internet-is.com/dde/
Infinite Access Inc. Home Page	http://www.internex.com/infinite/index.html
Ascend Communications Home Page	http://www.internex.net/ascend/
International Communications Corporation (ICC)	http://www.ip.net/ICC/home.html
Kapor Enterprises Inc. WWW Server	http://www.kei.com/
Legato Systems Inc	http://www.legato.com/
Digital Planet	http://www.mgmua.com/
Quick Reference or Index to www.mips.com	http://www.mips.com/HTMLs/Quik_Ref.html
Motorola World-Wide-Web Server	http://www.mot.com/
NEC Home Page	http://www.nec.com/
NETCOM On-Line Communication Services Inc	http://www.netcom.com/netcom/homepage.html
NTT Home Page	http://www.ntt.jp/
IXI Limited Home Page has moved	http://www.sco.com/IXI/ixi.html
Silicon Graphics' Silicon Surf	http://www.sgi.com/
Sony Online	http://www.sony.com/
Who is T3plus?	http://www.t3plus.com/who.html
Tekelec Corporate Information	http://www.tekelec.com/corp/corp.html
Wentworth Worldwide Media	http://www.wentworth.com/wentworth/
Novell Inc. World Wide Web Home Page	http://www.wordperfect.com/
XVT SOFTWARE INC.	http://www.xvt.com/xvt

Culinary

Wine Home Page	http://augustus.csscr.washington.edu/personal/bigstar-mosaic/wine.html
Miniature Wine Grapevines of California	http://branch.com/dutch/dutch.htm
wine Forest Hill Vineyard chardonnay Napa Valley	http://branch.com/wine/wine.html
Destination: Lake Tahoe :: Dining	http://dol.meer.net/locns/tahoe/dining/index.html
Chile Today Hot Tamale	http://eMall.Com/Chile/Chile1.html
The Recipes Folder!	http://english-server.hss.cmu.edu/Recipes.html
Metroplex Reviews of Health-Conscious Restaurants	http://gopher.metronet.com:70/1/North-Texas-Free-Net/Directs/Rests
The Beer Page	http://guraldi.itn.med.umich.edu:80/Beer
WWW Vegetarian Sites	http://jalapeno.ucs.indiana.edu/~nazhuret/Fact/recipes-other.html
Chicago Area Restaurant Guide	http://netmedia.com/IMS/chicago/ca_rest_guide.html
Bay Area Restaurants	http://sfgate.com/~sfchron/dining/dining.html
Santa Cruz Area Wineries	http://slv.net/scarea/wineries.htm
Wine.Com	http://wine.com/wine/index.html
Peninsula Restaurants Guide	http://www-gsb.stanford.edu/goodlife/home.html
The Real Beer Page	http://www.and.com/realbeer/rbp.html
Anderson Valley Brewing Company Home Page	http://www.avbc.com/avbc/home.html
Eating out	http://www.ce.cmu.edu:8000/karim/pittsburgh/indian/eating.html
Kebab Vans of The World Item 10	http://www.cs.colorado.edu/homes/mcbryan/public_html/bb/28/10.html
A Malt Whisky Tour	http://www.dcs.ed.ac.uk/staff/jhb/whiskey
Datorforeningen vid Lunds Universitet och Lunds Tekniska Hogskola	http://WWW.DF.LTH.SE/
Hot Hot Hot Welcome	http://www.hot.presence.com/hot
Reviews	http://www.infi.net/journal/restaurants/reviews.html
Smithfield_Farms	http://www.ip.net/shops/Smithfield_Farms/home.html
Boston Restaurant List	http://www.osf.org:8001/boston-food/boston-food.html
Welcome to Pizza Hut!	http://www.pizzahut.com/

Pizza Hut User Comments	http://www.PizzaHut.COM/comments.html
Japanese Cuisine	http://www.rerf.or.jp/Outside/ENG/Hiroshima/Dining/Contents.html
Cuisine Bourgeoise	http://www.twics.com/~JEREMY/natto.html
Tokyo Food Page	http://www.twics.com/~robbs/tokyofood.html
WEIRD RECIPES	http://www.twics.com/~SABU/roadkill.html
Places to Eat	http://www.twics.com/~TIM/restaurants.html
LA COMIDA MEXICANA.	http://www.udg.mx/Cocina/menu.html
Creole/Cajun/etc. Recipe Page	http://www.webcom.com/~gumbo/recipe-page.html
WF.HP.html	http://www.wholefoods.com/wf.html
Wines on the Internet	http://www.wines.com/
Zima home page	http://www.zima.com/

Culture

CERN/ANU - Asian Studies WWW VL	http://coombs.anu.edu.au/WWWVL-AsianStudies.html
Cyber: Technology and Culture	http://english-server.hss.cmu.edu/Cyber.html
Japan - WWW Virtual Library	http://fuji.stanford.edu/VL/WWW-VL-Japan.html
LICC — Louisville (Unofficial Test Page)	http://iglou.com/MeersWorld/LICCHome
Academia de Arte Yepes	http://nw.com/bahnware/community-outreach/Academia/academia.html
DJG Karlsruhe - Welcome Page (eng)	http://phdrw3.kfk.de:8080/DJG/Welcome.eng.html
Federal Information Exchange Inc. - MOLIS Home Page	http://web.fie.com/web/mol/
Pointers to Internet Services in Turkey	http://www.bilkent.edu.tr/turkiye.html
Celebrating the Spirit	http://www.crc.ricoh.com:80/~rowanf/CTS/cts.html
The beauty of INDIA—Unity in Diversity	http://www.cs.clemson.edu/~nandu/india.html
WWW in Slovenia - Table of Contents	http://www.fagg.uni-lj.si/toc-si.htm
China Home Page	http://www.ihep.ac.cn/
Japanese Information	http://www.ntt.jp/japan/index.html
RED CIENTIFICA PERUANA - Servidor WWW	http://www.rcp.net.pe/rcp.html

Databases

Biorhythm	http://cad.ucla.edu:8001/biorhythm
E. coli Genetic Stock Center	http://cgsc.biology.yale.edu/
Australian Computer Science Academics Database	http://coral.cs.jcu.edu.au/acsadb/
Free Database List	http://cuiwww.unige.ch/cgi-bin/freedatabase
Environmental/Educational Databases & Resources	http://garnet.msen.com:70/1/vendor/cygnus/other-gophers
ISDN informationbase	http://igwe.vub.ac.be/~svendk/
Using CAS Databases on STN	http://info.cas.org/ACAD/cover.html
About STN International	http://info.cas.org/stn.html
WAIS sources	http://info.cern.ch/hypertext/Products/WAIS/Sources/Overview.html
The NSF Grants Database	http://medoc.gdb.org/best/fedfund/nsf-intro.html
Canadian Community of Science	http://medoc.gdb.org/work/expertise-canada.html
Community of Science	http://medoc.gdb.org/work/expertise.html
Canadian Community of Science - Facilities	http://medoc.gdb.org/work/facil-canada.html
RBSE's URL database	http://rbse.jsc.nasa.gov/eichmann/urlsearch.html
DA-CLOD: DA-CLOD Top Level Category	http://schiller.wustl.edu/DACLOD/daclod
Signal Processing Information Base (SPIB)	http://spib.rice.edu/spib.html
Digital Tradition Folk Song Full Text Search	http://web2.xerox.com/digitrad
WebCrawler Searching	http://webcrawler.cs.washington.edu/WebCrawler/WebQuery.html
Musi-Cal	http://www.automatrix.com/concerts/
Books That Work Garden Encyclopedia	http://www.btw.com/garden_archive/toc.html
Planetary Information Browser	http://www.c3.lanl.gov/~cjhamil/SolarSystem/query.html
Caltech World Wide Web Database	http://www.caltech.edu/cgi-bin/searchdatabase
DATABASE RESEARCH AT PENN	http://www.cis.upenn.edu/~wfan/DBHOME.html
COMMA Hotlist Database - Subject Search	http://www.cm.cf.ac.uk/htbin/AndrewW/Hotlist/hot_list_search.csh
Madame D.	http://www.fagg.uni-lj.si/ICARIS/madame_d.htm
NASA RECON DISCLAIMER	http://www.larc.nasa.gov/org/library/recon-disc.html
Databases available at this server	http://www.research.att.com/cgi-wald/dbaccess/
NIKOS Gateway	http://www.rns.com/cgi-bin/nikos
UUCC Image Database Search	http://www.utah.edu/HTML_Docs/Image_Database.html
University of Utah Computer Services	http://www.utah.edu/HTML_Docs/Services.html#Image_Database
World-Wide Profile Registry	http://www.wizard.com/wwpr.html

Directories

Government:States:California	http://akebono.stanford.edu/yahoo/Government/States/California/
Yahoo Search	http://akebono.stanford.edu/yahoo/search.html
Personal Pages	http://Backfence.Lightside.Com/Personal_Page.html
Killer Links	http://bazaar.com/Links/links.html
Arts & Sciences College Web Server	http://bones.asic.csuohio.edu/default.html
Other Malls and Storefronts Listing	http://branch.com/links.htm
Subjective Electronic Information Repository	http://cbl.leeds.ac.uk/nikos/doc/repository.html
Contra Costa Community Net	http://coco.community.net/community/coco/index.html
Welcome to Boardwalk Consulting	http://consulting.com/edu.html
Coombsweb Server Usage	http://coombs.anu.edu.au/usage/index.html
The Electronic Guide to Santa Cruz County	http://cruzio.com/
CSUnet Home Page	http://csu-server.calstate.edu/CSUnet/CSUnetHome.html
The Internic Directory of Directories WAIS Search	http://ds.internic.net/cgi-bin/wais.pl/dirofdirs
LaRC Hotlist	http://dval-www.larc.nasa.gov/larc_hotlist/larc_hotlist.cgi
Things Latin America/Spanish Speaking Countries WWW at EgoWeb	http://edb518ea.edb.utexas.edu/html/latinamerica.html#Argentina
Index to Multimedia Information Sources	http://fourier.dur.ac.uk:8000/mm.html
Internet Search Engines	http://free-net.mpls-stpaul.mn.us:8000/search.html

Additional Sites

Music References	http://freeabel.geom.umn.edu:8000/music.html
Business and Commerce	http://galaxy.einet.net/galaxy/Business-and-Commerce.html
Colorado (US States)	http://galaxy.einet.net/galaxy/Community/US-States/Colorado.html
Gopher Jewels	http://galaxy.einet.net/GJ/index.html
Search Gopher Space	http://galaxy.einet.net/gopher/gopher.html
Search All HyTelnet Entries	http://galaxy.einet.net/hytelnet/HYTELNET.html
Search the World-wide Web	http://galaxy.einet.net/www/www.html
Msen Information Services	http://garnet.msen.com:70/
W3 Search Engines	http://golgi.harvard.edu/meta-index.html
Directory Services (Phonebooks and Email)	http://gopher.bcm.tmc.edu:70/1/directories
World Wide Web Locator Guide	http://groucho.gsfc.nasa.gov/Code_520/locator/locator.html
Bay Area Restaurant Guide	http://hamilton.netmedia.com/ims/rest/ba_rest_guide.html
Network Hampton Roads Search Form	http://hampton.roads.net/cgi-bin/search-nhr
Cool Hypermedia (and other) servers	http://helpdesk-www.cit.cornell.edu/More_Docs/otherserv.html
Internet Directory	http://home.mcom.com/home/internet-directory.html
What's Cool?	http://home.mcom.com/home/whats-cool.html
Ireland Online Resources List	http://http.hq.eso.org/~fmurtagh/ireland-resources.html
IBD Catalogs	http://ibd.ar.com/Catalogs.html
Search Today's Usenet News	http://ibd.ar.com/News/About.html
PC Index	http://ici.proper.com/1/pc
List of Worldwide CAS and STN Representatives	http://info.cas.org/Support/agents.html
World-Wide Web Servers: Summary	http://info.cern.ch/hypertext/DataSources/WWW/Servers.html
An Overview of Hypertext and IR systems and applications	http://info.cern.ch/hypertext/Products/Overview.html
Overview — /WAIS	http://info.cern.ch/hypertext/Products/WAIS/Overview.html
COMPUTER SCIENCE DEPARTMENT - HOME PAGE	http://info.cs.pub.ro/
Danish Information Servers	http://info.denet.dk/dk-infoservers.html
List of Multimedia Servers in Poland	http://info.fuw.edu.pl/pl/servers-list.html
Internet Notes including RFCs FYIs STDs and IMRs.	http://info.internet.isi.edu/1/in-notes
WWW Servers in Mexico: List By State	http://info.pue.udlap.mx/mexico-geo.html
Campusinfo Innsbruck	http://info.uibk.ac.at:80/
Addresses and Contacts for Interfinance	http://intergroup.com/interfinance/addresses.html
Cornell University - CIT/Information Resources	http://ir-www.cit.cornell.edu/
Ireland: The Internet Collection	http://itdsrv1.ul.ie/Information/Ireland.html
Telerama Public Access Internet Lobby	http://ivory.lm.com/
EdWeb Home Page	http://k12.cnidr.org:90/
Useful Information Servers	http://kogwy.cc.keio.ac.jp:70/0/html/infoserver-gateway.html#ftp
ECN Home Page	http://lightlink.satcom.net/ECN/index.html
Web Information	http://loanstar.tamu.edu/~rjsparks/www.html
Los Angeles Webstation	http://losangeles.com/
Lycos Search Form	http://lycos.cs.cmu.edu/lycos-form.html
Mailing Lists Categories	http://mainsail.com/categor.html
Welcome to Direct Marketing World	http://mainsail.com/dmworld.htm
Other WWW Servers related to the MEMS field	http://mems.isi.edu/70/0/archives/otherWWWsites.html
SAIC Security - Wateridge	http://mls.saic.com/directions.html
WWW WAIS Gateway to NASA Online Resources	http://naic.nasa.gov/cgi-bin/guide-wwwwais
Government	http://nearnet.gnn.com/gnn/wic/govt.toc.html#us
Computer Images & Art	http://nearnet.gnn.com/gnn/wic/visart.05.html
Indexes of Online Books	http://nearnet.gnn.com/wic/lit.18.html
AT&T 800 Directory on the Internet	http://netlib.att.com/dir800
Bay Area Shopping Guide	http://netmedia.com/ims/shopping/ba_shopping_center_guide.html
Internet Multicasting Service	http://north.pole.org/
CRNet: Servidores WWW de Costa Rica	http://ns.cr:80/
NORTH TEXAS FREE-NET	http://ntfn.dccd.edu:70/1/North-Texas-Free-Net
Canadian Publications	http://pmax.dymaxion.ns.ca/~kc/iglbrd/canada/pubs.htm
Stanford Dorm Home Pages	http://rescomp.stanford.edu/dorms.html
Residential Education	http://rescomp.stanford.edu/resed.html
Current Weather Maps/Movies	http://rs560.cl.msu.edu/weather/
UK Sensitive Map - Academic	http://scitsc.wlv.ac.uk/ukinfo/uk.map.html
San Jose CA	http://sensemedia.net/san.jose
Students Improving Campus Online Services	http://server.berkeley.edu/SICOS.html
New Features/Updates	http://sfgate.com/~sfchron/standing/whatsnew.html
Classified Ads Directory	http://sfgate.com/classifieds/index.html
ResortNet Tahoe list	http://sierra.net/ResortNet/tahoe.html
COI Home Page	http://sneezy.nosc.mil/coi.html
United Kingdom Based WWW Servers.	http://src.doc.ic.ac.uk/all-uk.html
World-Wide Web sites: Massachusetts	http://sturtevant.com/wwwlist/mas.html
Adrian's Hotlist	http://sun1.bham.ac.uk/~mooreaj/docs/hotty.html
US www sites	http://sun1.bham.ac.uk/A.J.Moore/docs/hotter.html
CUSI	http://sunsite.doc.ic.ac.uk/cusi
World Wide Web FAQ	http://sunsite.unc.edu/boutell/faq/www_faq.html#www-hypertext
The Academic South	http://sunsite.unc.edu/doug_m/pages/south/academic.html
Text Based Home Page	http://usa.net/home/text.html
QRD: Home	http://vector.casti.com/QRD/.html/QRD-home-page.html
New on CVO's webserver	http://vulcan.wr.usgs.gov/News/new.html
Bay Area Restaurant Guide	http://w3.com/bayfood/ba_rest_guide_text.html
Listing by City	http://w3.com/bayfood/city_listing.html
Alphabetical Listing	http://w3.com/bayfood/rest_listing.html
List of Reviewed Restaurants	http://w3.com/bayfood/reviewed.html
Bay Area Restaurant Guide - Text Search	http://w3.com/bayfood/search_text.html
CUSI	http://www.biophys.uni-duesseldorf.de/gateways/cusi.html
The Biznet Yellow Pages	http://www.bnt.com/htbin/vmall.pl

452

Northwest Brokers	http://www.boatnet.com/boatnet/brokers/nwbroks/top.html
NW Boats	http://www.boatnet.com/boatnet/forsale/nwboats.html
UK Boats	http://www.boatnet.com/boatnet/forsale/ukboats/ukboats.html
Boatnet info	http://www.boatnet.com/boatnet/info.html
Internet Points-of-Interest	http://www.bsdi.com/points-of-interest.html
GBC TechConnect Directory	http://www.butterfly.net/baltimore/techdirectory/techindex.html
Exploring the Internet	http://www.cco.caltech.edu/~rich/web.html
Supercomputing Servers	http://www.ccsf.caltech.edu/other_sites.html
Other WWW Music Resources	http://www.cecer.army.mil/~burnett/MDB/musicResources.html
Joel's Hierarchical Subject Index	http://www.cen.uiuc.edu/~jj9544/
WWW-Server in Deutschland (Germany)	http://www.chemie.fu-berlin.de/outerspace/www-german.html
WWW Servers in Thailand	http://www.chiangmai.ac.th/Servers-th.html
Thailand WWW Information	http://www.chiangmai.ac.th/thmap.html
inBerkeley: City of Berkeley Home Page	http://www.ci.berkeley.ca.us/
Santa Cruz WWW Whitepages	http://www.circus.com/whitepages.html
Internet Request For Comments (RFC)	http://www.cis.ohio-state.edu/hypertext/information/rfc.html
Florida WWW Servers	http://www.cis.ufl.edu/home-page/fl-servers/
The Almost-Complete List of MUSHes	http://www.cis.upenn.edu/~lwl/muds.html
CompuNet Berlin Mainpage	http://www.cnb.compunet.de/
WWW in and outside of China	http://www.cnd.org/Other/Chinese.html
Academic/Educational Material	http://www.cnd.org/Other/misc.html
Other Chinese-related home pages	http://www.cnd.org/Other/rec.html
Maps at CMU	http://cs.cmu.edu:8001/Web/maps.html
Collected New Zealand / Aotearoa Information	http://cs.cmu.edu:8001/Web/People/mjw/NZ/MainPage.html
Top URLs 1 Mar - 7 Mar	http://cs.cmu.edu:8001/Web/People/spok/stats/top-latest-titles.html
On-line Reference Works	http://cs.cmu.edu:8001/Web/references.html
The Mother-of-all BBS	http://www.cs.colorado.edu/~mcbryan/bb/summary.html
WWWW - WORLD WIDE WEB WORM	http://www.cs.colorado.edu/home/mcbryan/WWWW.html
Australian WWW servers ..	http://www.csu.edu.au/links/ozweb.html
The Guide to Network Resource Tools	http://www.cuhk.hk/guides/earn/notice.html
Vermont/New Hampshire Map of WWW Resources	http://www.destek.net/Maps/VT-NH.html
WWW Servers in Korea	http://www.dongguk.ac.kr/
Cool Web Links	http://www.earthlink.net/Links.html
The EDEN MATRIX	http://www.eden.com/altindex.html
EDEN MATRIX Information	http://www.eden.com/eden/eden.html
MORE Eden Matrix	http://www.eden.com/more.html
Big Dummy's Guide to the Internet - Music	http://www.edv.agrar.tu-muenchen.de/cip/big-dummy/bdg_159.html
Sites with audio clips	http://www.eecs.nwu.edu/~jmyers/other-sounds.html
EFF's (Extended) Guide to the Internet	http://www.eff.org/papers/eegtti/eegttitop.html
Internet Resources List	http://www.eit.com/web/netservices.html
World Wide Web Servers	http://www.eit.com/web/www.servers/www.servers.html
Web.Word.Homepage	http://www.euro.net/innovation/Web_Word_Base/Web.WordHP.html
List of Servers (USA - District of Columbia)	http://www.fie.com/www/district.htm
List of WWW Servers (USA - Federal Government)	http://www.fie.com/www/us_gov.htm
NIR in Greece	http://www.forthnet.gr/hellas/nir-list.html
Four11 Directory Services (SLED)	http://www.Four11.com/
World-Wide Web Servers (Spain)	http://www.gae.unican.es/general/es-servers.html
GEMS - USA	http://www.gems.com/realestate/stview/usa/r.ca.usa.html
Index of Countries	http://www.geninc.com/geni/maps/chamber_world_menu.html
Seattle S/M Resources List	http://www.halcyon.com/elf/seattle.html
Journalism on the Web	http://www.halcyon.com/marcm/JournWeb.html
Indexes of the Internet	http://www.hmc.edu/www/info-resources/index.html
HTML Consultants Directory	http://www.holonet.net/holonet/consultants.html
About the World Wide Yellow Pages (tm)	http://www.homepages.com/info/AboutWWYP.html
WWW Servers in Norway	http://www.ii.uib.no/~magnus/norway.html
All IUB Departments Units and Divisions	http://www.indiana.edu/iub/alldepts.html
Triad Online	http://www.infi.net/nr/triad.html
Internet Products Inc.	http://www.ipinc.com/
Telecom Information Resources	http://www.ipps.lsa.umich.edu/telecom-info.html
A Collection of Computer Science Bibliographies	http://www.ira.uka.de/ftp/ira/bibliography/index.html
WWW Servers in Iceland	http://www.isnet.is/WWW/servers.html
Indiana University Southeast at New Albany	http://www.ius.indiana.edu/
LaRC Organizations	http://www.larc.nasa.gov/orgs/orgs.html
General Info about LLNL	http://www.llnl.gov/llnl/general.html
Lists of lists	http://www.llnl.gov/llnl/lists/listsl.html
California World Wide Web Servers	http://www.llnl.gov/ptools/california.servers.html
Switzerland-Based WWW Servers	http://www.math.ethz.ch/~zari/admin/chw3.html
College and University Home Pages	http://www.mit.edu:8001/people/cdemello/univ.html
Msen Interesting Servers	http://www.msen.com/interesting.html
Monta Vista High School - Resources	http://www.mvhs.edu/rsrcmenu.html
CLIO — National Archives Gopher/WWW	http://www.nara.gov/
New Internauts	http://www.navy.mil/new.internauts.html
NAVYONLINE WORKING GROUP	http://www.navy.mil/nolwg/
WHAT'S NEW WITH NAVYONLINE	http://www.navy.mil/whats.new.html
Online Coolie	http://www.ncb.gov.sg:1080/cgi-bin/coolie?query=asiaonline
Internet Resources Meta-Index	http://www.ncsa.uiuc.edu/SDG/Software/Mosaic/MetaIndex.html
The USA CityLink Project	http://www.NeoSoft.com:80/citylink/
Publicly Accessible Mailing Lists	http://www.NeoSoft.com:80/internet/paml/
Computer Currents	http://www.netusa.com/newsletters/computer-currents/compcurr.html
CUSI Services	http://www.nexor.co.uk/public/cusi/cusi.html
WWW Servers in Japan	http://www.ntt.jp/japan/internet/www-in-JP.html

Additional Sites

HyperMedia Zines on the Net	http://www.nwu.edu/ezines/
DCI's Trade Shows	http://www.ocm.com/dci
California Yellow Pages	http://www.research.digital.com/SRC/virtual-tourist/CaliforniaYP.html
Rhein Information Services	http://www.rhein.de/
Information Servers in Brazil	http://www.rnp.br/cern.html
NIKOS Gateway	http://www.rns.com/cgi-bin/nomad
Internet Tools Summary	http://www.rpi.edu/Internet/Guides/decemj/itools/top.html
World-Wide Web servers: New York	http://www.rpi.edu/NewYork/List.html
WWW.AU Index of Australian Sites	http://www.sofcom.com.au/cgi-bin/search.cgi?WWW.AUDB/URL.db
Newspapers and Journalism Links	http://www.spub.ksu.edu/other/journ.html
NASA Scientifc and Technical Information Server	http://www.sti.nasa.gov/STI-homepage.html
The JumpStation ISINDEX TITLE Search Page	http://www.stir.ac.uk/jsbin/title_js
WWPing Form Page	http://www.stir.ac.uk/jsbin/wwping
Telephone industry information	http://www.sunbelt.net/hypervision/ind.htm
SV-PAL Local Information	http://www.svpal.org/local.html
Rotary home page	http://www.tecc.co.uk/public/PaulHarris/
Scandinavia Online	http://www.telepost.no/Welcome.html
FTP servers	http://www.unisa.ac.za/0/docs/ftp.html
South African WWW servers	http://www.unisa.ac.za/0/docs/SA-servers.html
Colombia WWW Servers	http://www.univalle.edu.co/Colombia.html
PH Query	http://www.utah.edu/cgi-bin/phf
University of Utah Computer Services	http://www.utah.edu/HTML_Docs/Services.html#PH
Campus Map	http://www.utah.edu/Scripts/Campus_Map.acgi
Form for UTK Directory query	http://www.utk.edu/cgi-bin/phf
Data sources classified by access protocol	http://www.w3.org/hypertext/DataSources/ByAccess.html
Project Galactic Guide for the Web	http://www.willamette.edu/pgg
Nettwerk's NettWeb Home Page v2.04	http://www.wimsey.com/nettwerk/
Yale University World Wide Web Front Door	http://www.yale.edu/
World Wide Yellow Pages	http://www.yellow.com/

Education

Education	http://akebono.stanford.edu/yahoo/Education/
Educational Online Sources Front Door	http://archive.phish.net/eos1/
The World-Wide Web Virtual Library: Mechanical Engineering	http://CDR.stanford.edu/html/WWW-ME/home.html
Kids' Stuff	http://crusher.bev.net:70/1/Schoolhouse/kids
Hostelling International - AYH	http://cyber.cclims.com/comp/ayh/ayh.html
The English Server	http://english-server.hss.cmu.edu/
APA Web Server	http://enterzone.berkeley.edu/
AskERIC Home Page	http://eryx.syr.edu/
Children (The Family)	http://galaxy.einet.net/galaxy/Community/The-Family/Children.html
Infants (The Family)	http://galaxy.einet.net/galaxy/Community/The-Family/Infants.html
Educational Opportunities at Baylor College of Medicine	http://gopher.bcm.tmc.edu:70/1/localeinfo
Harvard National Model United Nations	http://hcs.harvard.edu/~hnmun/
The World-Wide Web Virtual Library: Civil Engineering	http://howe.ce.gatech.edu/WWW-CE/home.html
IKE - IBM Kiosk for Education	http://ike.engr.washington.edu/ike.html
The World-Wide Web Virtual Library: Subject Catalogue	http://info.cern.ch/hypertext/DataSources/bySubject/Overview.html
Liz Brigman's Public WWW Page	http://is.rice.edu:80/~liz
The World-Wide Web Virtual Library: Industrial Engineering	http://isye.gatech.edu/www-ie/
Teaching Parenting at McDonald's	http://joe.uwex.edu/joe/1993fall/iw5.html
Public Policy Education: A Path to PoliticalSupport	http://joe.uwex.edu/joe/1993winter/tp1.html
WWW Servers Hosted at CNIDR	http://k12.cnidr.org/
Educational Courses on the Web	http://lenti.med.umn.edu/~mwd/courses.html
ANU Educational resources	http://life.anu.edu.au/education.html
Home Page for Learning Resource Centers	http://lrc.nps.navy.mil:8080/
Monterey County Office of Education	http://netspace.students.brown.edu/eos/main_image.html
Educational Online Sources:	http://netspace.students.brown.edu/eos/main_image.html
The World-Wide Web Virtual Library: Nuclear Engineering	http://neutrino.nuc.berkeley.edu/NEadm.html
AWU HomePage	http://online.awu.org/homepage.html
Management Briefing Seminars	http://ott22.engin.umich.edu/mbs/mbsdoc.html
Water Resources Outreach and Education	http://s101dcascr.wr.usgs.gov/ca_outreach.html
EF STU Web	http://scwww.ctstateu.edu/
JASON Project	http://seawifs.gsfc.nasa.gov/JASON/JASON.html
BOY SCOUT TROOP 134	http://tcomeng.com/cities/brisbane/Comm/BSA.html
CUB SCOUT PACK 134	http://tcomeng.com/cities/brisbane/Comm/CubScts.html
The World-Wide Web Virtual Library: Educational Technology	http://tecfa.unige.ch/info-edu-comp.html
R & D Center for Information Technology in Education (TOTY)	http://toty.joensuu.fi/
Explorer Home Page	http://unite.tisl.ukans.edu/xmintro.html
The Globewide Network Academy	http://uu-nna.mit.edu:8001/uu-nna/index.html
Faculty of Education	http://view.ubc.ca:80/1/acad-units/education
http://www.adventure.com/spiel.html	http://www.adventure.com/spiel.html
MIT Artificial Intelligence Laboratory Home Page	http://www.ai.mit.edu/
Intelligent Information Infrastructure Project	http://www.ai.mit.edu/projects/iiip/home-page.html
Jon's Home-School Resource Page	http://www.armory.com/~jon/hs/HomeSchool.html
Educational resources	http://www.bbcnc.org.uk/education/index.html
Center for Rehabilitative Medicine Community Education Series	http://www.bnt.com/~rch/eduprgms.html
Mindful Education	http://www.callamer.com/itc/mindful.html
Welcome to Britannica Online	http://www.eb.com/eb.html
ECC Home Page	http://www.ecc.u-tokyo.ac.jp/
U.S. Department of Education	http://www.ed.gov:80/
University of Illinois Education Learning Resource Server	http://www.ed.uiuc.edu/
Educom WWW Server	http://www.educom.edu/

Computers and Academic Freedom	http://www.eff.org/CAF/cafhome.html
SciEd - Science and Mathematics Education Resources	http://www.halcyon.com/cairns/science.html
Interpedia Homepage	http://www.hmc.edu/www/interpedia/index.html
Low Temperature Laboratory Homepage	http://www.hut.fi/English/HUT/Units/Separate/LowTemperature/
Women's Resources @igc	http://www.igc.apc.org/igc/www.women.html
IIASA - Young Scientists Summer Program	http://www.iiasa.ac.at/docs/IIASA_YSSP.html
Internet Direct User Server II	http://www.indirect.com/user/sohail/442/index.html
Blue Heron Lodge WWW	http://www.infi.net/brickell
Library Solutions Institute and Press	http://www.internet-is.com/library/index.html
KANREN Info Main Menu	http://www.kanren.net/kanren/
Monta Vista High School - News	http://www.mvhs.edu/newsmenu.html
Educational Resources	http://www.nas.nasa.gov/HPCC/K12/edures.html
MetroBoston CWEIS	http://www.nda.com/mbcweis-homepage.html
Jim Breen's Ukiyo-E Gallery	http://www.rdt.monash.edu.au/~jwb/ukiyoe/ukiyoe.html
The WWW server of RESTENA	http://www.restena.lu/
WWW Home Page of the State Council of Higher Education (SCHEV)	http://www.schev.edu/
Education and Outreach at SDSC	http://www.sdsc.edu/1/SDSC/Educ_Outreach/educ_outreach.html
Sunergy Home Page	http://www.sun.com/sunergy/
Stony Brook Home Page	http://www.sunysb.edu/
HEMS Home Page	http://www.tcom.ohiou.edu/hems.html
Welcome Universitat Jaume I Spain	http://www.uji.es/
Study at Unisa	http://www.unisa.ac.za/0/docs/unisa.html
Faculdade de Educacao	http://www.usp.br/educacao/educacao.html
INSTRUCTIONAL AND RESEARCH COMPUTING	http://www.utirc.utoronto.ca/

Electronics

Branch Business Center	http://branch.com/business.htm#electronics
CAEDE	http://caede-www.larc.nasa.gov/caede.html
ESC Link Page	http://esc.sysplan.com/esc/navigator/link/index.html
The RASSP Program	http://esto.sysplan.com/ESTO/RASSP/
Icepak	http://icemcfd.com/icepak.html
iPOINT: Illinois Pulsar-based Optical Interconnect	http://ipoint.vlsi.uiuc.edu/
Electronic Research Administration	http://web.fie.com/web/era/
Stanford University - Electrical Engineering	http://www-ee.stanford.edu/ee.html
Stanford IEEE Home Page	http://www-soe.stanford.edu/soe/ieee/
IEEE Home Page	http://www.ieee.org/
Micromechanical Systems link	http://www.ieee.org/micromechanical/micromechanical.html
ETH Zurich Electronics Lab High Performance Computing Home Page	http://www.ife.ee.ethz.ch/music/hpc.html
ENS: Circuit Card Assembly and Repair (CCAR)	http://www.ip.net/ENS/ccar.html
EE Home Page	http://www.llnl.gov/eng/ee.html

455

Engineering

P & GE Alumni Reading Room	http://altona.pe.utexas.edu/
EDITEC home page	http://audrey.fagg.uni-lj.si:80/ICARIS/EDITEC/
Mechanical Engineering Department Home Page	http://cdr.stanford.edu/html/ME/home.html
Continuous Quality Improvement in Clemson Engineering	http://deming.eng.clemson.edu/
Engineering_Technology	http://fcc.gov:70/1/Engineering_Technology
Rice University Digital Signal Processing	http://jazz.rice.edu/
U.D. Mechanical Engineering	http://me.udel.edu/
SNL CA Center for Computational Engineering Home Page	http://midway.ca.sandia.gov/
SWE	http://stimpy.cen.uiuc.edu/soc/swe
Kalman Filter Information	http://taygeta.oc.nps.navy.mil/kalman.html
Center for Integrated Systems at Stanford University	http://www-cs.stanford.edu/
SC-CM Program Overview	http://www-sccm.stanford.edu/
Department of Engineering Science	http://www.auckland.ac.nz/esc/
Engineering Library - Cornell University	http://www.englib.cornell.edu/
Univ. of Washington College of Engineering	http://www.engr.washington.edu/
College of Engineering	http://www.engr.wisc.edu/
EPP's Home Page	http://www.epp.cmu.edu/
Engineering and Laboratory Notes	http://www.osa.org/osapage/engine/EngLabNotes.html
OPTICAL TECHNOLOGY DIVISION	http://www.osa.org/osapage/otd.html
Da Vinci Design Company	http://www.sccsi.com/DaVinci/davinci.html
SEAS Home Page	http://www.seas.upenn.edu/

Entertainment

Entertainment	http://akebono.stanford.edu/yahoo/Entertainment/
Events	http://akebono.stanford.edu/yahoo/Events/
Long Lawyer Jokers	http://deputy.law.utexas.edu/jokes2.htm
Digital Planet	http://digiplanet.com/DP/index.html
Recreation Sports & Hobbies	http://nearnet.gnn.com/wic/rec.toc.html
Mark Bennett's Star Wars Home Page	http://phymat.bham.ac.uk/BennetMN/starwars.html
Last Season's Shakespeare Santa Cruz	http://samsara.circus.com/~jasona/shakespearSantaCruz.html
What is a geek?	http://samsara.circus.com/~omni/geek.html
Chronicle Entertainment and Arts Page	http://sfgate.com/~sfchron/enter.html
Welcome to Condom Country	http://www.ag.com:104/Condom/Country/
Alberto's Nightclub	http://www.and.com/albertos/albertos.html
atom Co. Ltd. home page	http://www.atom.co.jp/
About Broadcasting Dataservices	http://www.bbcnc.org.uk/bbctv/sched/about_bds.html
Broadway	http://www.escape.com/eMall/exploreny/broadway/guysanddolls.html

Additional Sites

Adam's Star Wars Page	http://www.interaccess.com/users/jknorst/adam.html
INWO home page at Illuminati Online	http://www.io.com/sjgames/inwo/
Webchat	http://www.IRsociety.com/webchat.html
NandO Subscription	http://www.nando.net/subscribe/subscribe.html
The Ultimate Strip Club List	http://www.paranoia.com/~express/strip.html#toc
The World Sex Guide - a Prostitution FAQ List	http://www.paranoia.com/faq/prostitution/
Welcome to Penthouse	http://www.penthousemag.com/
Time Line	http://www.princeton.edu/~cgilmore/dune/docs/time_line.html
We are Celebrating Our 10th Anniversary!	http://www.trib.com/service/microv.html
Star Trek: The Next Generation (ST:TNG)	http://www.ugcs.caltech.edu/~werdna/sttng/
The Douglas Adams Worship Page	http://www.umd.umich.edu/~nhughes/dna/
ZZ9 Plural Z Alpha - Official DNA Fan Club	http://www.umd.umich.edu/~nhughes/dna/zz9/
Turun Science Fiction Seura ry.	http://www.utu.fi/org/yhd/tsfs/index.html
Science Fiction in Aotearoa	http://www.vuw.ac.nz/~thetroll/index.html
Vampyres Only	http://www.wimsey.com/~bmiddlet/vampyre/vampyre.html
Windham Hill Records	http://www.windham.com/

Environment

Environment and Nature	http://akebono.stanford.edu/yahoo/Environment_and_Nature/
REINAS Home Page	http://csl.cse.ucsc.edu/reinas.html
IAF Vision	http://cygnus-group.com/IAF.html
Other Newsletters	http://cygnus-group.com/other-gophers/Others.html
The EPA WASTEWI$E PROGRAM	http://cygnus-group.com/ULS/Waste/epa.html
The EnviroArts Gallery	http://envirolink.org/arts/
The Virtual Environmental Library	http://envirolink.org/elib/
All Environmental Web Resources	http://envirolink.org/envirowebs.html
Other Projects on the EnviroWeb	http://envirolink.org/projects.html
About the Information Center for the Environment (ICE)	http://ice.ucdavis.edu/about_ICE.html
Earth and Environmental Science	http://info.er.usgs.gov/network/science/earth/index.html
National Water Conditions	http://nwcwww.er.usgs.gov:8080/
CERES: California Environmental Resources Evaluation System	http://resources.agency.ca.gov/
EARTH COUNCIL'S WEB	http://terra.ecouncil.ac.cr/ecweb.htm
Energy Efficient Housing in Canada	http://web.cs.ualberta.ca/~art/house/
MIT ENERGY LAB Home Page	http://web.mit.edu/afs/athena/org/e/energylab/www/energylb.htm
Environmental Design Research Association	http://www.acs.ohio-state.edu/edra26/leadin.html
The EnviroWeb— A Project of the EnviroLink Network	http://www.envirolink.org/
SA Enviro Notes	http://www.iaccess.za/ecoserv/conf/calendar.html
ECOSERV Services	http://www.iaccess.za/ecoserv/services.html
Endangered Species	http://www.igc.apc.org/endangered/
Linkages Home Page	http://www.iisd.ca/linkages/index.html
NOAA Home Page	http://www.noaa.gov/
Environmental Recycling Hotline	http://www.primenet.com/erh.html
SEL INDEX Page	http://www.sel.bldrdoc.gov/index.html
Todays Space Weather	http://www.sel.bldrdoc.gov/today.html

Games

I-Ching	http://cad.ucla.edu/repository/useful/iching.html
Tarot	http://cad.ucla.edu/repository/useful/tarot.html
Welcome to Boardwalk Consulting	http://consulting.com/game.html
Welcome to Connect Four	http://csugrad.cs.vt.edu/htbin/Connect4.perl
CyberSight's Hangman!	http://cybersight.com/cgi-bin/cs/hangman
MasterWeb	http://dragon.aoc.nrao.edu/~casey/masterweb/masterweb.shtml
Web Puzzler	http://dragon.aoc.nrao.edu/~casey/puzzle/puzzle_top.shtml
Play by Mail (PBM) Games Homepage	http://fermi.clas.virginia.edu/~gl8f/pbm.html
The WWW Dungeon	http://hal.cling.gu.se/~cl0polau/wwwd/wwwdungeon.html
Welcome to JHM!	http://jhm.ccs.neu.edu:7043/
The Rules of Sprodzoom	http://myrddin.chu.cam.ac.uk/cusfs/sprodzoom.html
PSU Empire Page	http://random.chem.psu.edu/empire/
The Gateway to Othello	http://ronneby.hk-r.se/othello/othello.html
End of road	http://sensemedia.net/sprawl/7801
yow!	http://spider.navsses.navy.mil/www/mazeintro.html
Video Puzzle With Live Video Sources	http://tns-www.lcs.mit.edu/cgi-bin/vs/vspuzzle
Games Domain - Games related information site	http://wcl-rs.bham.ac.uk/~djh/index.html
GameBytes - WWW editions	http://wcl-rs.bham.ac.uk/GameBytes
The Guide To The Game of Othello	http://web.cs.ualberta.ca/~brock/othello.html
The Game Cabinet	http://web.kaleida.com/u/tidwell/GameCabinet.html
The Fascist Game	http://wombat.doc.ic.ac.uk/fascist/fascist.html
Role-Playing Games	http://www.acm.uiuc.edu:80/adnd
Doug's Myst Page	http://www.astro.washington.edu/ingram/myst/index.html
TIC TAC TOE	http://www.bu.edu/Games/tictactoe
Peg Game	http://www.bu.edu/htbin/pegs
Hunt the Wumpus	http://www.bu.edu/htbin/wcln
Othello - 60 moves left	http://www.cis.ohio-state.edu/htbin/othello
COMMA Fun and Games (Cardiff)	http://www.cm.cf.ac.uk/Fun/funmenu.html
surge's RPG archive and WWW references	http://www.cqs.washington.edu/~surge/rpg.html
Bridge on the Web	http://www.cs.vu.nl/~sater/bridge/bridge-on-the-web.html
Raj's WebStuff	http://www.cs.washington.edu:80/homes/raj/
The Dream Page	http://www.cs.washington.edu:80/homes/raj/dream.html
The Literature Page	http://www.cs.washington.edu:80/homes/raj/lit.html
The Psychology Page	http://www.cs.washington.edu:80/homes/raj/psych.html

Go an Addictive Game	http://www.cwi.nl/~jansteen/go/go.html
Dragonflight	http://www.eskimo.com/~graham/dragonflight.html
Fiction Therapy Group	http://www.galcit.caltech.edu/~ta/fiction/fiction.html
NFL Pool via the WWW	http://www.hal.com/~markg/NFL/
Max Blaster - Introduction	http://www.inmind.com/max/
Minesweeper	http://www.linc.or.jp/~hamano/game/minesweeper.html
Street Fighter	http://www.mca.com/universal_pictures/streetfighter/sf_homepage.html
Teaching Ladder Information Center	http://www.mcs.com/~whhosken/home.html
Madlibs	http://www.mit.edu:8001/madlib
John Conway's Game of Life	http://www.research.digital.com/nsl/projects/life/life.html
Raymond Interactive Theatre Ltd.	http://www.rit.com/
Great Minds Project	http://www.rpi.edu/~lambem/greatminds.html
Olli's Webory Game	http://www.rz.tu-clausthal.de/~inof/webory.html
AD&D at Stack	http://www.stack.urc.tue.nl/~nushae/
The WWW Backgammon Page	http://www.statslab.cam.ac.uk/~sret1/backgammon/main.html
Sundragon Games Home Page	http://www.sundragon.com/sundragon/home.html
UniPress Software Inc. — Win a Free UniPress T-Shirt	http://www.unipress.com/cgi-bin/tshirt.pl
Tic Tac Toe	http://www.willamette.edu/htbin/tic-tac-toe

Geography

CERN/ANU - Asian Studies WWW VL	http://eskinews.eskimo.com/nordic/
Live Access to Climate Data	http://ferret.wrc.noaa.gov/ferret/main-menu.html
GIS INSTITUTE UNIV OF IOWA	http://gort.ucsd.edu/mw/uoigis.html
MIT Radar Lab Home Page	http://graupel.mit.edu/Radar_Lab.html
by GEOGRAPHY	http://honor.uc.wlu.edu:1020/-ge
USGS - Education	http://info.er.usgs.gov/education/index.html
What Do Maps Show - Teacher background	http://info.er.usgs.gov/education/teacher/what-do-maps-show/index.html
Center for Seismic Studies Overview	http://www.css.gov/
DKRZ HomePage	http://www.dkrz.de/index-eng.html
GPS Division Home Page	http://www.gps.caltech.edu/
Kochi University Weather Index	http://www.is.kochi-u.ac.jp/weather/index.en.html
University NAVSTAR Consortium (UNAVCO)	http://www.unavco.ucar.edu/
Department of Geography University of Texas at Austin	http://www.utexas.edu/depts/grg/main.html

Geology

United States Geological Survey-HTTP Server-Home Page	http://info.er.usgs.gov/USGSHome.html
USGS CALIFORNIA ACTIVITIES	http://s101dcascr.wr.usgs.gov/activity.html
California District Archive	http://s101dcascr.wr.usgs.gov/ca_archive.html
Internet Tool Box	http://s101dcascr.wr.usgs.gov/ca_internet.html
USGS CALIFORNIA PROJECTS	http://s101dcascr.wr.usgs.gov/ca_project.html
Index of common Volcanic Hazards	http://vulcan.wr.usgs.gov/hazards.html
CVO Photo Archives	http://vulcan.wr.usgs.gov/photo_list.html
Volcano Disaster Assistance Program	http://vulcan.wr.usgs.gov/Vdap/vdap.html
The USGS Volcano Hazards Program	http://vulcan.wr.usgs.gov/Vhp/framework.html
Water Resources of Colorado	http://webserver.cr.usgs.gov/
Cornell University Geological Science Department	http://www.geo.cornell.edu/
MTU Volcanoes Page	http://www.geo.mtu.edu/volcanoes
Geological Sciences Home Page	http://www.geology.ubc.ca:80/
GPS Division Home Page	http://www.gps.caltech.edu:80/
Geological Survey of Finland	http://www.gsf.fi/
HOMEPAGE MINERALOGIE TU CLAUSTHAL	http://www.immr.tu-clausthal.de:80/
Brown University Planetary Geology	http://www.poppe.com:8400/
United States Geological Survey-HTTP Server-Home Page	http://www.usgs.gov/
VSC Home Page	http://www.vsc.washington.edu/

Goods and services

Business:Corporations:Real Estate	http://akebono.stanford.edu/yahoo/Business/Corporations/Real_Estate/
Branch Business Center	http://branch.com/business.htm#home
Edgewater Apartments	http://branch.com/edgewater/
First Federal Savings Bank of Indiana - mortages loans homes realestate	http://branch.com/first
Lama decorating interior design furniture	http://branch.com/lama/
Zimcom	http://branch.com/zimcom/
The Branch Mall	http://branch.com:1080/
Bigfoot page 1/1	http://ccnet.com/~crick/bigfoot.html
Display Tech Multimedia (computers to video)	http://ccnet.com/~dtmi/welcome.html
Dainamic Consulting	http://cnn.acsys.com:5050/~sims/kayak/kayak.html
Lerma Nagal Swartz Realtor	http://cruzio.com/bus/realestate/lermas/lermas.html
Mary Kay Cosmetics Cosmetics	http://cyberzine.org/html/Cosmetics/cosmetics2.html
Earth Spirit Designs Home Page	http://cyberzine.org/html/EarthSpirit/index.html
LGBT WWW Advertising Main Menu	http://cyberzine.org/html/LGBTADS/lgbtadspage.html
Travel & Tourism	http://cybil.kplus.bc.ca/www/tourism/tourism.htm
DigiCash home page	http://digicash.com/
Destination: Lake Tahoe :: Rental Services	http://dol.meer.net/¹ocns/tahoe/rentals/index.html
Earth Spirit Designs Home Page	http://envirolink.org/espirit/
Branch Mall by BRANCH INFORMATION SERVICES INC.	http://florist.com:1080/
Compact Disc Connection	http://galaxy.einet.net/hytelnet/OTH104.html
Compact Disc Europe	http://galaxy.einet.net/hytelnet/OTH131.html
PEP Information on Packaging	http://garnet.msen.com:70/1/vendor/cygnus/packaging
Internet Shopping Galleria San Diego County Real Estate	http://intergal.com/Realesta.html
UWI Shopping Maul	http://kzsu.stanford.edu/uwi/maul.html

457

Additional Sites

Graphiti: Home page	http://libertynet.org/~graphiti/link06.html
Advertising Agencies	http://mainsail.com/adverts.htm
List Brokers	http://mainsail.com/brokers.htm
Welcome to Global Catalogues	http://mainsail.com/catworld.htm
Computer Services	http://mainsail.com/comserve.htm
Direct Marketing Consultants	http://mainsail.com/consult.htm
Copy Writers	http://mainsail.com/copy.htm
DM Guide	http://mainsail.com/dmbook.html
DIRECT MAIL AND THE DYNAMICS OF RESPONSE	http://mainsail.com/dynindex.htm
Welcome aboard the Mainsail Server	http://mainsail.com/index.html
Mailing Lists by Categories	http://mainsail.com/intl.htm
About the Magazine section	http://mainsail.com/maginfo.html
Merge-Purge Services	http://mainsail.com/merge.htm
List Managers	http://mainsail.com/mgrs.htm
BAY & VALLEY HABITAT for HUMANITY Inc.	http://meer.net/users/taylor/habitat.htm
Gemlink	http://mindlink.net/dhiraj_raniga
CONROY'S FLORIST OF SAN DIEGO	http://mmink.com/mmink/dossiers/conroys/conroys.html
FREE HEALTH INSURANCE QUOTE HEALTH FREE	http://mmink.cts.com/mmink/dossiers/irn.html
MULTIMEDIA INK DESIGNS...	http://mmink.cts.com/mmink/dossiers/pi.html
scottsotheclown	http://mmink.cts.com/mmink/dossiers/scottso.html
MULTIMEDIA INK DESIGNS...	http://mmink.cts.com/mmink/dossiers/uve/uve.html
EARRINGS	http://mmink.cts.com/mmink/kiosks/earrings/earrings.html
Wade's Flower Shop	http://oscar.bnt.com/~wades/flower.html
Welcome to Softbank Exposition and Conference Company	http://programs.digitalworld.com/
Web/Net T-Shirts	http://sashimi.wwa.com/~notime/mdd/Index.html
seehomes.com 'The National Listing Service' (TEXT)	http://seehomes.com/HOMES/HTML/HMPGTXT.HTML
Internet Shopping Network	http://shop.internet.net/
Upbeat Inc. (Institutional Accessories)	http://simon.com/up
esj gregor	http://slv.net/esjhp2.htm
The WebScope Commercial Center - Current Tenants	http://stelcom.com/webscope/customers.html
Book Publishers and Retailers On-line	http://thule.mt.cs.cmu.edu:8001/jrrl-space/bookstores.html
Telemedia Networks and Systems Group	http://tns-www.lcs.mit.edu/
Computers At Large Saratoga California (Home Page)	http://www.aimnet.com/cal/
Even / Anna LTD.	http://www.ais.net:80/evenanna/
PRO CASE	http://www.allshop.com/mac/allshop/sia/mgcase/html/mgcase_hp.html
Applied Testing and Technology Home Page	http://www.aptest.com/
BayNet Real Estate	http://www.baynet.com/re.html
San Mateo Times Marketplace	http://www.baynet.com/smtimes/market/index.html
Access Stack Node (ASN)	http://www.baynetworks.com/Products/Routers/Systems/ASN.html
The Village Mall	http://www.bev.net/mall/index.html
Marine Marketplace	http://www.boatnet.com/~boatnet/market/marketop.html
Boatnet Home Page	http://www.boatnet.com/boatnet
Wilson Marine	http://www.boatnet.com/boatnet/market/wilson-marine/wilson.html
Anchiano Computer Eyewear	http://www.branch.com/eyewear/eyewear.html
HEIT VETERINARY SERVICES INC	http://www.castles.com/comm/hvs/hvs.html
VA Oakland Regional Office Property Sales Listing	http://www.ccnet.com/services/va/bbs-list.html
TransAmerica	http://www.ceainc.com/TransAm/index.html
The Entertainment & Media Professional Home Page	http://www.cenco.com/emp/
The Internet Book Shop	http://www.cityscape.co.uk/bookshop/ibsinf.html
Penguin Books Ltd	http://www.cityscape.co.uk/bookshop/pecat.html
Future Fantasy Bookstore - Home Page	http://www.commerce.digital.com/palo-alto/FutureFantasy/home.html
Java Byte On-Line Index	http://www.computek.net/jb
The Real Estate Network	http://www.csi.nb.ca/celerity
Response Form	http://www.cts.com/~karnobks/karnobks_form2.html
Cygnus Support Product Information Gallery	http://www.cygnus.com/data-dir.html
Cygnus Network Security	http://www.cygnus.com/data/cns.html
The Cygnus Support Developer's Kit	http://www.cygnus.com/data/toolkit.html
Cygnus Support Online Library	http://www.cygnus.com/library-dir.html
Shopping	http://www.dash.com/netro/sho/sho.html
Mail Today One-Stop Catalog Shop	http://www.flightpath.com/Clients/VHorizons/
Coldwell Banker Real Estate	http://www.garlic.com/cb/
Global Electronic Marketing Service	http://www.gems.com/index.html
GEMS - Realty Information Services	http://www.gems.com/realestate/index.html
Consumer Information Center	http://www.gsa.gov/staff/pa/cic/cic.htm
yperMedia Technologies	http://www.hmt.com/
HomeBuyer's Fair Welcome:	http://www.homefair.com/
Home Pages	http://www.homepages.com/
The Competitive Edge - Table of Contents	http://www.homes.com/services/compedge/TOC.html
HP Computer Product and Peripherals Anonymous FTP Site	http://www.hp.com/Misc/Peripherals.html
Sonic Computers Home Page	http://www.human.com/sonicc/index.html
Personal help from IBM	http://www.ibm.com/Orders/
Westminster Supply Home Page	http://www.icw.com/westminster/medical.html
Exchange Classified Headings	http://www.iea.com/~adlinkex/Exchange/class.html
PaperDirect - Home Page	http://www.imn.net/paperdirect/index.html
Electronic Safari	http://www.inct.com/es/
Powerhouse AdvertisingAdvertising	http://www.infi.net/powerhouse/
Real Estate Web	http://www.infi.net/REWeb/
The Virginia Diner Catalog	http://www.infi.net/vadiner/catalog.html
Krema Nut Company Home Page	http://www.infinet.com/~schapman/mwow/cmh/krema/homepage.html
Business Media Inc. Computer Products Catalog	http://www.infoanalytic.com/bmi/index.html
Welcome to the First Virtual InfoHaus!	http://www.infohaus.fv.com/

458

Designs by Margarita	http://www.infopost.com/margarita/index.html
Infowerks Homepage	http://www.infowerks.com/
Salon Direct Homepage	http://www.intellisoft.com/salondirect
The Famosa(TM) by Salvatore	http://www.internet-cafe.com/salvatore/
Myers Equity Express	http://www.internet-is.com:80/myers/mortform.html
Real Estate	http://www.iNTERspace.com/bus/realty/realty.html
Output Enablers	http://www.io.com/user/oe
The Internet Presence & Publishing Corporation	http://www.ip.net/
Welcome to the Internet Shopkeeper - a WWW based mall.	http://www.ip.net:80/shops.html
Nine Lives Consignment	http://www.los-gatos.scruznet.com/ninelives.html
The Internet Mall	http://www.mecklerweb.com/imall/
Telasar Computer Sales	http://www.Nashville.Net/telasar/
Dainamic Consulting	http://www.netpart.com/dai/home.html
Internet Reminder Service	http://www.novator.com/Remind/Remind.html
SHOPPING	http://www.ntt.jp/japan/TCJ/SHOPPING/00.html
Real Estate for Sale in and around Toronto Canada	http://www.onramp.ca/realestate/
Pam Golding Properties - Home Page	http://www.os2.iaccess.za/pgp/
HomePage Marketing	http://www.primenet.com/~jimb/hpinfo.html
Internet Credit Bureau Inc.	http://www.satelnet.org/credit/
Finder's Report	http://www.satelnet.org/credit/finders.html
Social Security Number Identification Search	http://www.satelnet.org/credit/ssn-search.html
Buning the Florist	http://www.satelnet.org/flowers/
Shopping2000 Home Page	http://www.shopping2000.com/shopping2000/shopping1.html
SII Company History / Backgrounder	http://www.sii.com/siiover.html
Charleston Real Estate	http://www.sims.net/places/charleston/real-estate.html
SmartWorks	http://www.smartworks.com/catalog/
THE PRINTER WORKS — Printers Service & Parts	http://www.stepwise.com/Vendors/ThePrinterWorks.htmld/index.html
STUFF.com's Home Page	http://www.stuff.com/
12.9 CPM LONG DISTANCE! FLAT RATE!	http://www.sunbelt.net/hypervision/car.htm
GUIDE TO SHOPPING FOR LONG DISTANCE	http://www.sunbelt.net/hypervision/plan.htm
Overview of the Long Distance Resellar Industry	http://www.sunbelt.net/hypervision/resel.htm
Customer Service	http://www.tekelec.com/service/customer.html
Product Information	http://www.tekelec.com/service/product.html
Tekelec Training	http://www.tekelec.com/training/index.html
The Telephone Customer's Corner	http://www.teleport.com/~mw/cc.html
Books On-line Listed by Title	http://www.thegroup.net/booktitl.htm
Internet Multicasting Service	http://www.town.hall.org/
Braille Translation Service	http://www.trib.com/service/braille.html
artCentric T-shirts	http://www.trinet.com/artc/
Internet College Exchange (ICX)	http://www.usmall.com/
Appellation Spring's Winery T-Shirt Display	http://www.wilder.com/winery.html
Wimsey Information Services	http://www.wimsey.com/index.html
The Internet Center for Arts and Crafts Specialty Gift Shops	http://www.xmission.com/~arts/
DECdirect Home Page	http://www2.service.digital.com/DECdirect/index.html
Digital SEWP. Home Page.	http://www2.service.digital.com/DECsewp/
The INRIA Videoconferencing System	http://zenon.inria.fr:8003/rodeo/personnel/Thierry.Turletti/ivs.html
The Corporate Mall	http://zeus.cybernetics.net/

Government

NW Region Home Page	http://198.238.212.10/regions/northwest/
Welcome to Boardwalk Consulting	http://consulting.com/gov.html
California Electronic Government Information	http://cpsr.org/dox/cegi.html
Blue Room	http://cyberzine.org/html/BlueRoom/bluehome.html
Ca. State Lands Commission Home Page	http://diablo.slc.ca.gov/
DOD's R&D CYCLE	http://dtic01.wpafb.af.mil/rdc.html
Events	http://fcc.gov:70/1/Events
City of Boulder Government	http://free-net.mpls stpaul.mn.us:8000/proto_top.html
Minnesota E-Democracy Project	http://free-net.mpls-stpaul.mn.us:8000/govt/e-democracy/
Government Agencies (Government)	http://galaxy.einet.net/galaxy/Government/Government-Agencies.html
U.S. and Michigan Politics	http://garnet.msen.com:70/1/vendor/freep/lookhere
Library of Congress World Wide Web Home Page	http://lcweb.loc.gov/homepage/lchp.html
Federal Bureau of Investigation (FBI)	http://naic.nasa.gov/fbi/index.html
DOD WWW Servers	http://navysgml.dt.navy.mil/dodsites.html
MIT Political Science	http://polisci-mac-2.mit.edu/
Federal Acquisition Jumpstation	http://procure.msfc.nasa.gov/fedproc/home.html
The Right To Keep and Bear Arms	http://sal.cs.uiuc.edu/rec.guns/rkba.html
US Army Corps of Engineers - CESPK Home Pages	http://spk41.usace.mil/
About the Library of Congress	http://sunsite.unc.edu/expo/expo/about.html
The National Performance Review	http://sunsite.unc.edu/npr/nptoc.html
Search U.S. Patent and Trademark Office Archives	http://town.hall.org/cgi-bin/srch-patent
COSMETICS in CFSAN	http://vm.cfsan.fda.gov/cosmetic.html
Center for Food Safety and Applied Nutrition (CFSAN)	http://vm.cfsan.fda.gov/list.html
The Origins of FEDIX/MOLIS	http://web.fie.com/history.htm
Federal Information Exchange Inc. - FEDIX Home Page	http://web.fie.com/web/fed/
DOE Office of Reconfiguration	http://web.fie.com/web/fed/doe/doeoor.htm
Federal Information Exchange Inc.	http://web.fie.com/web/fie/
Fedix/Molis User Registration	http://web.fie.com/web/login/register.htm
ABAG Homepage	http://www.abag.ca.gov/index.html
ARGENTINA's Ministry of Foreign Affairs	http://www.ar:70/
Solicitations	http://www.arpa.mil/Solicitations.html
State Government Agencies	http://www.assembly.ca.gov/StateGov.html

Additional Sites

Customer Registration Form	http://www.census.gov/ServSupp/register.html
Supreme Infotrainschedule	http://www.dorsai.org/~adamn/congress.html
The Canadian Consulate Trade Office	http://www.globalx.net/ccto/
U.S. General Services Administration(GSA)	http://www.gsa.gov/
U.S. House Of Representatives - Home Page	http://www.house.leg.state.mn.us/project/project.html
Member Directory - California	http://www.houssennet.nb.ca/dogworld.htm
U.S. Constitution - Table of Articles	http://www.law.cornell.edu/constitution/constitution.overview.html
Libertarian Party of Santa Clara County (CA)	http://www.lp.org/lp/ca/lpsc.html
LP of Santa Clara County - bylaws	http://www.lp.org/lp/ca/lpsc/lpsc-bylaws.html
Phillips Laboratory	http://www.plk.af.mil/
Libertarian Party	http://www.rahul.net/lp/
Jump-Off Page	http://www.saf.org/
U.S. Senate Gopher Server	http://www.senate.gov:70/
Ca. State Lands Commission Home Page	http://www.slc.ca.gov/
State of Utah WWW Server	http://www.state.ut.us/
United States Patent and Trademark Office	http://www.uspto.gov/
Welcome to the 21st Century Project	http://www.utexas.edu/depts/lbj-school/21cp/
Welcome to the White House	http://www.whitehouse.gov/
Window on State Government	http://www.window.texas.gov/window-on-state-gov.html

Graduate schools

MU Office of Research Home Page	http://sage.research.missouri.edu/
Faculty of Graduate Studies UBC	http://view.ubc.ca:80/1/acad-units/fogs
The Eli Broad College of Business & Graduate School ofManagement	http://www.bus.msu.edu/
UW Graduate School Webserver	http://www.grad.washington.edu/
GSIA Home Page	http://www.gsia.cmu.edu/
U. of Washington Graduate School of Public Affairs	http://www.gspa.washington.edu/
General Information	http://www.indiana.edu/~rugs/rugsdir.html
UVM Graduate College	http://www.uvm.edu/test/gradcoll.html

Graphics

On-line exhibitions images etc.	http://155.187.10.12/fun/exhibits.html
Aviation Image Archives	http://adswww.harvard.edu/GA/image_archives.html
PDS Imaging Node - Homepage	http://cdwings.jpl.nasa.gov/PDS/
On Line Catalog Information PDS Imaging Node	http://cdwings.jpl.nasa.gov/PDS/public/catalog_info.html
mandel	http://enigma.phys.utk.edu/mandel/
CURIOUS HOME PAGE	http://found.cs.nyu.edu/CAT/affiliates/curious/curioushp.html
GIF/JPEG Graphics	http://fourier.dur.ac.uk:8000/graphics.html
More pictures	http://fourier.dur.ac.uk:8000/taste.graphic.html
Pictures from Brazil	http://guarani.cos.ufrj.br:8000/Rio/Todas.html
gd 1.1.1	http://siva.cshl.org/gd/gd.html
Last files from alt.binaries.pictures.misc	http://web.cnam.fr/Images/Usenet/abpm/summaries/
Rutgers University Network Services WWW Icons and Logos	http://www-ns.rutgers.edu/doc-images
Fractal pictures & animations	http://www.cnam.fr/fractals.html
Standard Icons/Symbols	http://www.cs.indiana.edu/elisp/w3/icons.html
Dryden Research Aircraft Photo Archive	http://www.dfrf.nasa.gov/PhotoServer/photoServer.html
Video Colors	http://www.sdsc.edu/0/SDSC/Geninfo/Fun/color.html
Astronomical pictures & animations	http://www.univ-rennes1.fr/ASTRO/astro.english.html

Health care

Health	http://akebono.stanford.edu/yahoo/Health/
Health Resources	http://alpha.acast.nova.edu/medicine.html
HSPH Biostatistics Home Page	http://biosun1.harvard.edu/
BWH main entrance	http://bustoff.bwh.harvard.edu/
Department of Food Science & Nutrition	http://fscn1.fsci.umn.edu/fscn.htm
OMIM — Online Mendelian Inheritance in Man	http://gdbwww.gdb.org/omimdoc/omimtop.html
MycDB	http://kiev.physchem.kth.se/MycDB.html
Alcoholism Research Data Base	http://nearnet.gnn.com/wic/med.02.html
Health & Medicine	http://nearnet.gnn.com/wic/med.toc.html
Cholesterol	http://nearnet.gnn.com/wic/nutrit.02.html
Good Medicine Magazine	http://none.coolware.com:80/health/good_med/
The ABI/TBI Information Project	http://ns.sasquatch.com/tbi/
Breast Cancer Information	http://nysernet.org/breast/Default.html
ACUPUNCTURE.COM	http://www.acupuncture.com/acupuncture/
TruHealth Home Page	http://www.biz.net/truhealth/
Health Notes	http://www.bnt.com/~rch/healthno.html
M David Tilson Home Page	http://www.columbia.edu/~mdt1/
Department of Ophthalmology	http://www.columbia.edu/cu/ophthalmology/
The World-Wide Web Virtual Library: Pharmacy	http://www.cpb.uokhsc.edu/pharmacy/pharmint.html
University of Manchester Medical Informatics Group Home page	http://www.cs.man.ac.uk/mig/index.html
Fred Hutchinson Cancer Research Center	http://www.fhcrc.org/
Imaging & Visualization Laboratory	http://www.ge.com/crd/img_and_vis_lab.html
Three Dimensional Medical Reconstruction	http://www.ge.com/crd/ivl/three_dim_medical.html
Internet Health Resources - Home Page	http://www.ihr.com/
MACROSCOPIC PATTERNS OF LEUKEMIA MORTALITY	http://www.inel.gov/.research/.research_abstracts/.rb/index.html
AIDS and HIV - informations and resources	http://www.ircam.fr/solidarites/sida/index-e.html
Duke University Medical Center	http://www.mc.duke.edu/
PharmWeb - Pharmacy Information Resources	http://www.mcc.ac.uk/pharmacy/
Department of Neurological Surgery	http://www.med.nyu.edu/NeuroSurgery/HomePage.html
NIH GUIDE INDEX	http://www.med.nyu.edu/nih-guide.html

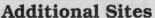

DEN-TEL-NET'S Home Page	http://www.onramp.net:80/Den-Tel-Net/
Occupational Safety and Health Administration Home Page	http://www.osha.gov/
Palo Alto Medical Foundation	http://www.service.com/PAMF/home.html
Clark County (Nevada) Pollen/Spore Reports	http://www.unlv.edu/CCHD/pollen/
UQ Anaesthesiology Home Page	http://www.uq.oz.au/anaesth/home.html
World Health Organization WWW Home Page	http://www.who.ch/
Internationl Travel and Health Page	http://www.who.ch/TravelAndHealth/TravelAndHealth_Home.html
World Health Organization Regional Office for Europe WWW	http://www.who.dk/
Educational Technology Branch	http://wwwetb.nlm.nih.gov/

History

Multicultural Cosmology Home Page	http://arcturus.pomona.claremont.edu/
James J. O'Donnell Home Page	http://ccat.sas.upenn.edu/jod/jod.html
The Viking Home Page	http://control.chalmers.se/vikings/viking.html
The World-Wide Web Virtual Library: History	http://history.cc.ukans.edu/history/WWW_history_main.html
POMPEII FORUM PROJECT	http://jefferson.village.virginia.edu/pompeii/page-1.html
WPA Life Histories—Home Page	http://lcweb2.loc.gov/wpaintro/wpahome.html
History of Science	http://nearnet.gnn.com:80/wic/histsci.toc.html
Home Page: American Memory from the Library of Congress	http://rs6.loc.gov/amhome.html
The Nation's Forum	http://rs6.loc.gov/nfhome.html
Berlin/Prague Cover Page	http://www-swiss.ai.mit.edu/philg/berlin-prague/book-cover.html
The Palo Alto Historical Association	http://www.commerce.digital.com/palo-alto/historical-assoc/home.html
Anne Frank WWW site	http://www.cs.washington.edu/homes/tdnguyen/Anne_Frank.html
All About Turkey	http://www.ege.edu.tr/Turkiye
AMS/HIS Home Page	http://www.gar.utexas.edu/
Labyrinth WWW Home Page	http://www.georgetown.edu/labyrinth/labyrinth-home.html
History of the Laboratory	http://www.llnl.gov/llnl/history/history.html
Jesuits and the Sciences: 1540-1995	http://www.luc.edu/~scilib/jessci.html
The Smoky Mountains	http://www.nando.net/smokies/smokies.html
A Roman Palace in ex-Yugoslavia	http://www.ncsa.uiuc.edu/SDG/Experimental/split/split1.html
HyperDOC: NLM History of Medicine Division	http://www.nlm.nih.gov/hmd.dir/hmd.html
Armenian Research Center Home Page	http://www.umd.umich.edu:80/dept/armenian/

Hobbies

Bradley University Amateur Radio Club	http://buarc.bradley.edu/
Unicycling Home Page	http://nimitz.mcs.kent.edu/~bkonarsk
Minolta Users' Group	http://tronic.rit.edu:80/minolta
Golden Mailing List Info	http://www-acs.ucsd.edu/home-pages/wade/golden.html
Fish Information Service (FINS) Index	http://www.actwin.com/fish/index.html
The World-Wide Web Virtual Library: Fish	http://www.actwin.com/WWWVL-Fish.html
cAVe Rock 100 Amateur Radio Repeater Home Page	http://www.ccnet.com/~rwilkins/
UK Student SF Societies Directory	http://www.cl.cam.ac.uk/users/gdr11/uk-sf-societies.html
World-Wide Web Access Statistics for the Kites pages	http://www.ensta.fr/~germond/data/kites_stat.html
Add a kite event to the list	http://www.ensta.fr/~germond/kites/event_add.html
The events page	http://www.ensta.fr/~germond/kites/events/
Pins for rec.kiters	http://www.ensta.fr/~germond/kites/pins.html
Kites & Computers	http://www.ensta.fr/~germond/kites/pointers.html
Introduction to Telephone Cards	http://www.funet.fi/pub/doc/telecom/phonecard/
Antiques	http://www.ic.mankato.mn.us/antiques/Antiques.html
Sports Cards and More	http://www.icw.com/sports/sports.html
Horse Previews Magazine	http://www.iea.com/~adlinkex/HP/index.html
Kite Flier's Site	http://www.kfs.org/kites
The Klingon Language Institute	http://www.kli.org/KLIhome.html
Jason's Kite Site	http://www.latrobe.edu.au/Glenn/KiteSite/Kites.html
Building a Library: A Collector's Guide	http://www.ncsa.uiuc.edu:80/SDG/People/marca/barker-beethoven.html

Humor

Upcoming Guests List	http://bingen.cs.csbsju.edu/letterman/guest-list.html
Late Show with David Letterman Episode Guide	http://bingen.cs.csbsju.edu/letterman/show-summary/LSsummary.html
WebWisdom	http://keck.tamu.edu/cgi/staff/webwisdom.html
Humorous Quotations	http://meta.stanford.edu/quotes.html
Jay's Comedy Club	http://paul.spu.edu/~zylstra/comedy/index.html
Taglines Galore!	http://www.brandonu.ca/~ennsnr/Tags/
Johann's Comics Page	http://www.cen.uiuc.edu/~jb2561/comic.html
Some stuff about COMICS	http://www.css.itd.umich.edu/users/kens/comics.html

Internet/WWW services

AHSL Public Health Guide	http://128.196.106.42/ph-hp.html
Actrix Information Exchange Home Page	http://actrix.gen.nz/
Search EFF's (Extended) Guide	http://alpha.acast.nova.edu/cgi-bin/srch.cgi/search/bigdummy/mylist
Finding People on the Internet	http://alpha.acast.nova.edu/phone.html
Tenagra Homepage	http://arganet.tenagra.com/Tenagra/tenagra.html
Contact Information in Europe	http://bb.eu.net/eunet-contacts.html
Worldwide Web Services	http://community.net/ais/web.html
Enterprise Services Home Page	http://crick.bcm.tmc.edu/ssc/HomePage.html
ArchiePlexForm	http://cuiwww.unige.ch/.archieplexform.html
Htgrep of unige-pages.html	http://cuiwww.unige.ch/cgi-bin/ugwww
Acronym and abbreviation list	http://curia.ucc.ie/info/net/acronyms/acro.html
ShareViews Video Tutor - New Internet Video	http://cyberzine.org/html/Video/video2.html

Additional Sites

InterNIC Internet Documentation (RFC's FYI's etc.)	http://ds.internic.net/ds/dspg1intdoc.html
InterNIC Directory Services	http://ds.internic.net/ds/dspgwp.html
Gateway to Free-Nets and Community Computer Networks	http://freenet.victoria.bc.ca/freenets.html
Search the Internet	http://garnet.msen.com:70/1/vendor/freep/search
Harvest Demonstration Brokers	http://harvest.cs.colorado.edu/harvest/demobrokers.html
Technical Discussion of the Harvest System	http://harvest.cs.colorado.edu/harvest/technical.html
Wisconsin Internet Service Gopher/HTTP Server	http://heather.wis.com/
CIT HelpDesk	http://helpdesk-www.cit.cornell.edu/
LaRC SNS EARS gateway	http://hercules.larc.nasa.gov:80/
Wide World Web Wonder Widget — Mozilla Printing	http://home.mcom.com/people/mtoy/cgi/www-print.cgi
Archie Request Form	http://hoohoo.ncsa.uiuc.edu/archie.html
FTP Interface	http://hoohoo.ncsa.uiuc.edu:80/ftp-interface.html
Form to Figure out a Domain Name	http://ibc.wustl.edu/domain_form.html
World-Wide Web proxies	http://info.cern.ch/hypertext/WWW/Proxies/
An executive summary of the World-Wide Web initiative	http://info.cern.ch/hypertext/WWW/Summary.html
The World Wide Web Initiative: The Project	http://info.cern.ch/hypertext/WWW/TheProject
InternetU - (407) 254-4901	http://iu.net/
ISS101 - Internet Survival Skills	http://kawika.hcc.hawaii.edu/iss101/iss101.html
Electronic Mail Using PINE	http://kawika.hcc.hawaii.edu/iss101/pine/pmast.html
LineX Communications	http://linex.com/
MarketPlace.com - The Internet Information Mall	http://marketplace.com:80/csd/FAQ.html
University of Utah Computer Center Help Desk Knowledge Base	http://mon.cc.utah.edu/
GNN Subscriber Information	http://nearnet.gnn.com/
The Whole Internet Catalog	http://nearnet.gnn.com/gnn/wic/newrescat.toc.html
Internet Media Services Inc.	http://netmedia.com/ims/rest/IMSrest.html
Oxford University Computing Services	http://pls.com/
RAINet Home Page	http://rain.psg.com/
CyberComm Online Services!	http://raven.cybercom.com/
Creating WWW Pages	http://riskweb.bus.utexas.edu/Creating.html
Interactive Weather Browser	http://rs560.cl.msu.edu/weather/interactive.html
USGS California - Internet Resources	http://s101dcascr.wr.usgs.gov/other.html
FUR.COM Home Page	http://snowfox.sj.scruznet.com/
Contra Costa Community Net	http://solano.community.net/community/coco/index.html
STOS WWW Server Home Page	http://stos-www.cit.cornell.edu/
Tezcatlipoca Inc. DBA Tezcat Communications	http://tezcat.com/
Leasing a Server	http://union.ncsa.uiuc.edu/HyperNews/get/www/leasing.html
ArchiePlexForm	http://web.doc.ic.ac.uk/archieplexform.html/
Welcome to ALIWEB	http://web.nexor.co.uk/aliweb/doc/aliweb.html
Welcome to NEXOR's Public Services	http://web.nexor.co.uk/public/welcome.html
The Willow Opportunity Center	http://willow.com/
Washington University FTP Archive	http://wuarchive.wustl.edu/
HOL Personal Accounts	http://www.aloha.net/hol/html/persact.html
San Jose Co-op	http://www.amscons.com/sj-coop.html
Atlantic's Home Page	http://www.atlantic.com/index.html
BBN/BARRNET Web Server	http://www.barrnet.net/
Basecamp Home Page	http://www.basecamp.com/
Internet Resources: Internet Guides	http://www.brandonu.ca/~ennsnr/Resources/guides.html
Information on WWW	http://www.bsdi.com/server/doc/web-info.html
California Software Incorporated	http://www.calsoft.com/
Archie Gateway	http://www.census.gov/cgi-bin/archie
CERFnet Home Page	http://www.cerf.net/
Ask Dr.Web	http://www.charm.net/~web/Email.html
CheckPoint Home Page	http://www.checkpoint.com/
On The Web Web Page Services	http://www.chiro.com/ontheweb/web/index.htm
More about WWW	http://www.cnd.org/Other/WWW.html
Internet Atlanta Home Page	http://www.com/atlanta/index.html
AIS - WEB Learning and Resource Page	http://www.community.net/community/all/webclass.html
Help - WWW für Anfänger	http://www.cosy.sbg.ac.at/www-doku/help.html
Canadian Domain Information Server	http://www.csi.nb.ca/domain/
DATABANK Inc	http://www.databank.com/
Performance Trouble Report	http://www.digital.com/hypertext/util/pathcheck.html
Commercial Services on the Net	http://www.directory.net/dir/directory.html
EarthLink Home Page	http://www.earthlink.net/
EdelWeb	http://www.edelweb.fr/EdelStuff/EdelWeb/EdelWeb.html
EINet Galaxy	http://www.einet.net/galaxy.html
Electric Press Inc.	http://www.elpress.com/homepage.html
LAN Dial up	http://www.elron.net/www/elronet/lan_dial.html
Profile: EUnet	http://www.EU.net/pr/Connexions.Nov93.html
EUnet Norge AS - Priser	http://www.eunet.no/EUnet-Norge/priser.html
EUnet NYTT	http://www.eunet.no/eunet-nytt/eunet-nytt.html
EuroNet Index	http://www.euro.net/
Infoboard Internet Services	http://www.garlic.com/infobord/
EUnet Germany Archive Services	http://www.Germany.EU.net/service/anonftp.html
WebTechs and HTML	http://www.hal.com/~markg/WebTechs/
Big Dummy's Guide to the Internet - Table of Contents	http://www.hcc.hawaii.edu/bdgtti/bdgtti-1.02_toc.html
A Brief Introduction to the World-Wide Web	http://www.hmc.edu/~codee/intro-www.html
The Wide Wide World of the Internet	http://www.hmc.edu/www/internet/index.html
Learning how to use the Internet	http://www.hmc.edu/www/internet/learning/index.html
The Human Factor Services	http://www.human.com/services.html
Idiom Consulting	http://www.idiom.com/
IIJ Home Page	http://www.iij.ad.jp/

Interleaf Inc.	http://www.ileaf.com/
Staff of UCS Network Information Services	http://www.indiana.edu/iu/nis-welcome.html
Internet Servers on all IU Campuses	http://www.indiana.edu/servers.html
Net Direct Inc.: Home Page	http://www.inetdirect.net/
The INFNet World Wide Web	http://www.infn.it/
InfoPlace - Internet Consulting Services	http://www.infoplace.com/infoplace/
InterAccess Guest Page	http://www.interaccess.com/Guest/Guest.html
Internet Cafe HomePage	http://www.internet-cafe.com/
Internet Trainers and Consultants	http://www.internet-cafe.com/itc/itc.html
Interse Corporation. Getting started.	http://www.interse.com/
IPAC Home Page	http://www.ipac.net/
ISnet Information	http://www.isnet.is/
Internet Conduct: Basic Reference Material	http://www.isoc.org/proceedings/conduct/conduct.html
ISP Home Page	http://www.isp.net/
Welcome to JovaNet Communications	http://www.jovanet.com/jovanet.html
WELCOME TO KAIWAN Internet WWW Page service	http://www.kaiwan.com/
Kern Internet Services WEB Server	http://www.kern.com/
Searching the Web	http://www.larc.nasa.gov/facts/search.html
Welcome to ArchiePlex	http://www.lerc.nasa.gov/Doc/archieplex.html
LLNL EMail Form	http://www.llnl.gov/llnl-bin/feedback/scoleman@llnl.gov
Newmarket Home Page	http://www.login.qc.ca/
Internet Literacy Consultants Home Page	http://www.matisse.net/
NEW YORK WEB HOME PAGE	http://www.mediaworks.com/
Texas Metronet	http://www.metronet.com/
MGL Systems Internet Home WWW Page	http://www.mgl.ca/
Web Street Mall	http://www.microserve.net:80/mall/
BisMark Internet Services Inc.	http://www.millcomm.com/
WWW.MIT.EDU Home Page	http://www.mit.edu/
WWW.MIT.EDU Home Page	http://www.mit.edu:8001/
The World Wide Web for Dummies	http://www.mit.edu:8001/people/rei/wwwintro.html
Welcome to MIS — Click on one of the five areas below.	http://www.mountain.net/
Elm - Electronic Mail for UNIX	http://www.myxa.com/elm.html
Welcome to The North Bay Network	http://www.nbn.com/
A Beginner's Guide to URLs	http://www.ncsa.uiuc.edu/demoweb/url-primer.html
A Beginner's Guide to HTML	http://www.ncsa.uiuc.edu/General/Internet/WWW/HTMLPrimer.html
What's New With NCSA Mosaic	http://www.ncsa.uiuc.edu/SDG/Software/Mosaic/Docs/whats-new.html
The Internet Service Company	http://www.net-serve.com/isc.html
Net+Effects Home Page	http://www.net.effects.com/
NETCOM — Internet Assistance and Information	http://www.netcom.com/netcom/assist.html
NETCOM's NetCruiser	http://www.netcom.com/netcom/numbers.html
NETCOM — Access to other Internet Services	http://www.netcom.com/netcom/waccess.html
net.Genesis Corporation Home Page	http://www.netgen.com/
NetPoint Communications' Home Page	http://www.netpoint.net/
NetRep Explorist Home	http://www.netrep.com/
Internet Services Corporation	http://www.netservices.com/
Network Intensive	http://www.ni.net/
NIIT Home Page	http://www.niit.org/niit/
NLnet	http://www.nl.net/nlnet/english/home.html
NLnet Internet Connections	http://www.nl.net/nlnet/english/nlnet-ip.html
WWW related Mailing-Lists in Japan(ese)	http://www.ntt.jp/japan/www-ml/index.html
Nuance Network Services	http://www.nuance.com/
Nucleus Information Service Home Page	http://www.nucleus.com/
ONRAMP Network Services Inc	http://www.onramp.ca/
COMPUSTAT - W3 Services - Home Page	http://www.os2.iaccess.za/index.htm
Welcome to PacketWorks	http://www.packet.net/
Welcome to OpenNet Technologies!	http://www.packet.net/business/garyh/Welcome.html
PEINet's Charted Crossings	http://www.peinet.pe.ca:2080/
PEM GmbH HTTP-SERVER	http://www.pem.com/english_index.html
The SenseMedia Surfer	http://www.picosof.com/
Pilot Network Services home page	http://www.pilot.net/
PING Homepage - Personal Internet Gate Austria	http://www.ping.at/
Pacific Information eXchange Inc. (PIXI)	http://www.pixi.com/
PlanetCom Home	http://www.planetcom.com/
Point of Presence Company	http://www.popco.com/
PSI HOME PAGE	http://www.psi.net/
Individual Services Page	http://www.psi.net/interramp/
QNSnet Home Page	http://www.qns.com/
United Kingdom and Ireland W3 Group	http://www.qub.ac.uk/sigweb/index.html
NetPress (Micromedium)	http://www.rahul.net/netpress/
Primenet Services for the Internet WWW	http://www.ramp.com/
onLine Home Page	http://www.red.net/
LvNet-Teleport Information Services	http://www.riga.lv/
EMI online	http://www.riv.nl/emi/default.htm
Route-One Multimedia Web services from IMC	http://www.route-one.co.uk/route-one/
The World Wide Web Unleashed Support Web	http://www.rpi.edu/~decemj/works/wwwu.html
Internet Tools Summary	http://www.rpi.edu/Internet/Guides/decemj/internet-tools.html
Internet Web Text	http://www.rpi.edu/Internet/Guides/decemj/text.html
South Coast Computing Services Inc.	http://www.sccsi.com/sccsi/home.html
Search the Internet	http://www.sdsc.edu/0/SDSC/Geninfo/Internet/search.html
Pointers of General Interest on the Internet	http://www.sdsc.edu/1/SDSC/Geninfo/Internet
Internet Distribution Services	http://www.service.com/

463

Additional Sites

SEVAnet's Home Page	http://www.seva.net/
North Shore Access Home Page	http://www.shore.net/
Sierra-Net	http://www.sierra.net/home.html
The 'Spiderweb (tm)' Serving the internet since August 1994	http://www.spiderweb.com/swhome.html
IMAGEnet	http://www.srv.net:8001/idi.html
JumpStation II Front Page	http://www.stir.ac.uk/jsbin/jsii
Welcome to Supernet	http://www.supernet.net/
SURAnet NIC Home Page	http://www.sura.net/
SV-PAL Home Page	http://www.svpal.org/
SWITCH Welcome Page	http://www.switch.ch/
Synergy Communications	http://www.synergy.net/synergy/synergy.html
TECH.NET	http://www.tech.net
TECHNET Singapore	http://www.technet.sg/
thenet.ch Home Page	http://www.thenet.ch/thenet.ch/
Welcome To The Sphere	http://www.thesphere.com/
TIAC's Home Page	http://www.tiac.net/index.html
Internet Starter Kit for Macintosh Internet Resources	http://www.tidbits.com/tidbits
The Internet Group	http://www.tig.com/
Turning Point Information Services home page	http://www.tpoint.net/
TriNet Services Inc. - Home Page	http://www.trinet.com/
TWICS	http://www.twics.com/www/home.html
TYRELL CORPORATION	http://www.tyrell.net/
U-NET 'Easy Internet Access' Home Page	http://www.u-net.com/
IRC channel #WWW	http://www.ugcs.caltech.edu/~kluster/ircwww.html
The Help Desk	http://www.uidaho.edu/helpdesk/helpdesk.html
HTML FAQ	http://www.umcc.umich.edu/~ec/www/html_faq.html
UniPress Software Inc. - (800) 222-0550	http://www.unipress.com/index.html
On-Campus Services	http://www.unisa.ac.za/0/docs/campus.html
Other services	http://www.unisa.ac.za/0/docs/other.html
United States Internet Home Page	http://www.usit.net/
Utopia Home Page	http://www.utopia.com/
The NEW and IMPROVED Utah Wired/The Friendly Net homepage	http://www.utw.com/
Willkommen bei VentureNET!	http://www.venture.net/
Internet Phone	http://www.vocaltec.com/
Technical Aspects of the World-Wide Web	http://www.w3.org/hypertext/WWW/Technical.html
The World Wide Web Initiative: The Project	http://www.w3.org/hypertext/WWW/TheProject
Techweb	http://www.wais.com:80/techweb/
The Internet Convention Center	http://www.wariat.org/
Welcome to Web Communications	http://www.webcom.com/
WilTel Home Page	http://www.wiltel.com/
BayWeb Home	http://www.woodwind.com/
WorldWide Access (SM) Home Page	http://www.wwa.com/
Welcome to wyoming.com LLC	http://www.wyoming.com/
Video: An Overview of the Internet and World-Wide Web	http://www.xerox.com/PARC/wwwvideo/wwwvideo.html
XMission Internet Access	http://www.xmission.com/
XS4ALL	http://www.xs4all.nl/
First Time Mosaic Users	http://www1.farallon.com/WWW/www1/First_Timers.html
WebPress Home Page	http://www2.interpath.net/
The World Lecture Hall	http://wwwhost.cc.utexas.edu/world/instruction/index.html

Languages

Hypertext Webster Interface	http://c.gp.cs.cmu.edu:5103/prog/webster
Middle English Search	http://etext.virginia.edu/Mideng.query.html
Dictionaries	http://math-www.uni-paderborn.de/HTML/Dictionaries.html
Webster's Dictionary	http://nimrod.mit.edu/common/reference/webster/
ARTFL Project: ROGET Form	http://tuna.uchicago.edu/forms_unrest/ROGET.html
WWW-server Elvis+ Page 0	http://www.elvis.ru/
English-German Dictionary	http://www.fmi.uni-passau.de/htbin/lt/lte/ltd
Lessons-Spanish	http://www.nas.com/~drtom/PRO3.html
Jim Breen's Japanese Page	http://www.rdt.monash.edu.au/~jwb/japanese.html
WORDNET Language Translation Service	http://www.ultranet.com/~wordnet/
Department of French and Italian	http://www.utexas.edu/depts/french/.web/main.html
Germanic Languages	http://www.utexas.edu/depts/german/main.html
Spanish and Portuguese	http://www.utexas.edu/depts/spn/
The Human-Languages Page	http://www.willamette.edu/~tjones/Language-Page.html
Say...	http://www.tios.cs.utwente.nl/say/form/

Law

GATT 1994	http://ananse.irv.uit.no/trade_law/gatt/nav/toc.html
Forensic Science	http://ash.lab.r1.fws.gov/
law.html	http://cavern.uark.edu/colleges/law.html
Government Law and Society has moved!	http://english-server.hss.cmu.edu/Govt.html
Heller Ehrman White & McAuliffe Resource Center	http://gnn.com/gnn/bus/hewm/index.html
Washington College of Law	http://sray.wcl.american.edu/pub/wcl.html
North American Free Trade Agreement	http://the-tech.mit.edu/Bulletins/nafta.html
Kevin Lee Thomason J.D. - Internet Consultant	http://tsw.ingress.com/tsw/train.html
Venable Home Page	http://venable.com/vbh.htm
Int'l Centre for Criminal Law Reform and Criminal Justice Policy	http://view.ubc.ca:80/1/acad-units/crim-justice
EFF ACTION ALERTS	http://www.eff.org/alerts.html
Trademarks of International Business Machines	http://www.ibm.com/trademarks.html

THE HACKER CRACKDOWN - Table of Contents	http://www.iesd.auc.dk/~amanda/crackdown/crackdown_toc.html
John P. Weil & Company - Law Practice Management Consultants	http://www.ingress.com/tsw/jpw/jpw.html
Jones Hall Hill & White	http://www.jhhw.com/
Legal Information Institute	http://www.law.cornell.edu/
U.C.C. - ARTICLES 1-9	http://www.law.cornell.edu/ucc/ucc.table.html
Indiana University School of Law - Bloomington	http://www.law.indiana.edu/
The Center for Corporate Law	http://www.law.uc.edu/CCL
UIUC Law	http://www.law.uiuc.edu/
University of Washington Law School WWW Home Page	http://www.law.washington.edu/CondonHome.html
General Information (University of Houston Law Center)	http://www.lawlib.uh.edu/LawCenter/law-info.html
University of Houston Law Libraries	http://www.lawlib.uh.edu/libraries/libinfo.html
Questel/Orbit: Patent and Trademark Welcome Page	http://www.questel.orbit.com/patents/
Hastings College of the Law	http://www.uchastings.edu/
Intellectual Property and the National Information Infrastructure	http://www.uspto.gov/niiip.html

Libraries

INFOMINE	http://coastal.udel.edu/
CUI Computer Science Library	http://cuiwww.unige.ch/cgi-bin/cuibib
Global Home Page	http://lcweb.loc.gov/global/globalhp.html
About the Library of Congress World Wide Web	http://lcweb.loc.gov/homepage/aboutlc.html
Library of Congress Exhibits	http://lcweb.loc.gov/homepage/exhibits.html
Reference Shelf	http://libdev1.lib.vanderbilt.edu/readyref.html
Washington University Archives - Home Page	http://library.wustl.edu/~spec/archives/
MIT Libraries	http://nimrod.mit.edu/
Britannica Online	http://nimrod.mit.edu/common/reference/britannica.html
MITosis - the MIT Libraries Gopher	http://nimrod.mit.edu/mitosis.html
Globewide Network Academy Meta-Library	http://uu-nna.mit.edu:8001/uu-nna/meta-library/index.html
MSU Vincent Voice Library	http://web.msu.edu/vincent/index.html
Cambridge City Hall — Library Commission	http://www.ai.mit.edu/projects/iiip/Cambridge/dir/library/library.html
Hardin Web Home Page	http://www.arcade.uiowa.edu/hardin-www/home.html
The UW Electronic Library	http://www.lib.uwaterloo.ca/
Library of Congress World Wide Web Home Page	http://www.loc.gov/
MITSFS Library Pinkdex	http://www.mit.edu:8001/pinkdex
NAVPALIB Latest News	http://www.navy.mil/navpalib/.www/latest.html
WELCOME TO THE NAVY PUBLIC AFFAIRS LIBRARY	http://www.ncts.navy.mil/navpalib/.www/welcome.html
HyperDOC: The Visible Human Project	http://www.nlm.nih.gov/extramural_research.dir/visible_human.html
NLM HyperDOC	http://www.nlm.nih.gov/welcome.html
OCLC Access Selection	http://www.oclc.org/
Rutgers University - Newark: Ackerson Law Library Home Page	http://www.rutgers.edu/lawschool.html
University of Kentucky Libraries	http://www.uky.edu/Libraries/
U of U Library Catalog	http://www.utah.edu/HTML_Docs/UofU_Lib.html
The World-Wide Web Virtual Library: Subject Catalogue	http://www.w3.org/hypertext/DataSources/bySubject/Overview.html
Digital Libraries and Xerox	http://www.xerox.com/PARC/dlbx/library.html

Literature

The Ohio Literacy Resource Center	http://archon.educ.kent.edu/index.html
Thesaurus Linguarum Hiberniae	http://curia.ucc.ie/curia/menu.html
The Good Reading Guide - Index	http://julmara.ce.chalmers.se/SF_archive/SFguide/
Search SF & Fantasy reviews	http://julmara.ce.chalmers.se/stefan/WWW/saifai_search.html
Cambridge University Science Fiction Society	http://myrddin.chu.cam.ac.uk/cusfs/
Charlie's Virtual Anthology	http://sf.www.lysator.liu.se/sf_archive/sub/Charles_Stross/index.html
The Commonplace Book	http://sunsite.unc.edu/ibic/Commonplace-Book.html
The WorldWideWeb Virtual Library: Literature	http://sunsite.unc.edu/ibic/IBIC-homepage.html
Arthur C. Clarke Award Winners	http://thule.mt.cs.cmu.edu:8001/sf-clearing-house/awards/acc.html
British Science Fiction Association Award Winners	http://thule.mt.cs.cmu.edu:8001/sf-clearing-house/awards/bsfa.html
Chesley Award Winners	http://thule.mt.cs.cmu.edu:8001/sf-clearing-house/awards/chesley.html
Locus Award Winners	http://thule.mt.cs.cmu.edu:8001/sf-clearing-house/awards/locus.html
Philip K. Dick Award Winners	http://thule.mt.cs.cmu.edu:8001/sf-clearing-house/awards/pkd.html
Bram Stoker Award Winners	http://thule.mt.cs.cmu.edu:8001/sf-clearing-house/awards/stoker.html
James Tiptree Jr. Award Winners	http://thule.mt.cs.cmu.edu:8001/sf-clearing-house/awards/tiptree.html
Conventions	http://thule.mt.cs.cmu.edu:8001/sf-clearing-house/conventions/
Speculative Fiction On-Line	http://thule.mt.cs.cmu.edu:8001/sf-clearing-house/fiction/
Short Fiction Market Response Times Surveys	http://thule.mt.cs.cmu.edu:8001/sf-clearing-house/writing/gregc/
Home Page for St Andrews University SF and Fantasy Society	http://www-theory.dcs.st-and.ac.uk/~aaa/SFFSoc.html
Nanotechnology in Science Fiction	http://www.arc.ab.ca/~morgan/N-SF.html
Cassidy's Tale	http://www.charm.net/~brooklyn/Topics/BarlowOnNeal.html
An annotated bibliography of science fiction criticism	http://www.cl.cam.ac.uk/users/gdr11/sf-bibliography.html
The On-line Books Page	http://www.cs.cmu.edu:8001/Web/books.html
19th-century German Lit Menu	http://www.fln.vcu.edu/menu.html
Search The Collected Works of Shakespeare	http://www.gh.cs.su.oz.au/Virtual/fsearch
Isaac Asimov FAQ	http://www.lightside.com/SpecialInterest/asimov/asimov-faq.html
Project Runeberg	http://www.lysator.liu.se/runeberg/Main.html
tkp: The Karoline von Gunderrode Pages	http://www.reed.edu/~ccampbel/KvG/
In the Pockets of the Night	http://www.sonoma.edu/Exhibits/EH/
Charles Deemer's Home Page	http://www.teleport.com/~cdeemer/index.html
Screenwriters/Playwrights Page	http://www.teleport.com/~cdeemer/scrwriter.html
Undergraduate Writing Center	http://www.utexas.edu/depts/uwc/.html/main.html
The Doomsday Brunette	http://zeb.nysaes.cornell.edu/CGI/ddb/demo.cgi

465

Additional Sites

Martial Arts

Entertainment:Sports:Martial Arts	http://akebono.stanford.edu/yahoo/Entertainment/Sports/Martial_Arts/
Rec.Martial-Arts FAQ	http://archie.ac.il/papers/rma/FAQ-rma.html
NTHI Tae Kwon-Do	http://www.stud.unit.no/studorg/nthitkd/english/etkdhome.html
Bay Area Wing Chun Associations	http://www.thesphere.com/SJWC/SJWC.html

Mathematics

Mathematics Archives WWW Server	http://archives.math.utk.edu/
GAMS : Guide to Available Mathematical Software	http://gams.nist.gov/
Technion Mathematics Department	http://gauss.Technion.AC.IL/
UT-Austin Math	http://henri.ma.utexas.edu/
MUNEX: QuickStart Page	http://math.duke.edu/
Vanderbilt University Department of Mathematics	http://math.vanderbilt.edu/
Faculty	http://math.vanderbilt.edu/faculty/faculty.html
Graduate Studies	http://math.vanderbilt.edu/gradprogram.html
UW Math Home Page	http://math.wisc.edu/
Laboratory for Computer Aided Mathematics - Helsinki	http://sophie.helsinki.fi/
GSU Mathematics and Computer Science Home Page	http://www.cs.gsu.edu/
The DAIMI WWW Server	http://www.daimi.aau.dk/
IMADA WWW home page	http://www.imada.ou.dk/
WWW server CIPRO Centra MFF UK	http://www.karlin.mff.cuni.cz:80/
Uni Hamburg Geomatikum Welcome	http://www.math.uni-hamburg.de:80/
Kent State Department of Math and Computer Science (MCS)	http://www.mcs.kent.edu/
College of Mathematical and Physical Sciences Ohio State	http://www.mps.ohio-state.edu/
Mathematics and Computing Science Eindhoven University	http://www.win.tue.nl/
FIZ Karlsruhe (Abt. Berlin) Home Page	http://www.zblmath.fiz-karlsruhe.de/

Medicine

UNC Chapel Hill School of Medicine	http://balsa.bme.unc.edu/med.html
Department of Neurological Surgery	http://frasier.c2tc.rl.af.mil/Campus/CampusCenter/CC217.html
Computer/Instrumentation Council SNM	http://gamma.wustl.edu/tf/caic.html
The World-Wide Web Virtual Library: Biosciences - Medicine	http://golgi.harvard.edu/biopages/medicine.html
Dept of Genetics & Molecular Medicine - EmoryUniversity	http://infinity.gen.emory.edu/
NYU-MC Hippocrates Home Page	http://mchip00.med.nyu.edu/HomePage.html
Information for Medicine	http://medstats.soton.ac.uk/0c:/medicine.htm|/
Univ. of Washington Immunology WWW Server	http://nucleus.immunol.washington.edu/
YCMI Home Page	http://paella.med.yale.edu/
The Medical Entities Dictionary (MED)	http://paella.med.yale.edu/medinf/med.html
CVM Home Page	http://pegasus.cvm.msstate.edu/
WWW serwer Akademii Medycznej w Gdansku	http://www.amg.gda.pl/
Radford Community Hospital What's New	http://www.bnt.com/~rch/whatsnew.html
International Network for Interfaith Health Practices	http://www.interaccess.com/ihpnet/
MCW International Travelers Clinic	http://www.intmed.mcw.edu/travel.html
Neurosciences on the Internet	http://www.lm.com/~nab
NYU Medical Center Home Page	http://www.med.nyu.edu/HomePage.html
Navy Psychiatry Information Services	http://www.navy.mil/navpsy/
UMDS ISD World Wide Web Service	http://www.umds.ac.uk/
HU - Hospital Universitario	http://www.usp.br/hospital/hu.html
Faculdade de Medicina - USP	http://www.usp.br/medicina/fm.html
UTMB Information Services	http://www.utmb.edu/
The Royal (Dick) School of Veterinary Studies	http://www.vet.ed.ac.uk/
University of Pensylvania School of Veterinary Medicine	http://www.vet.upenn.edu/
Auburn University College of Veterinary Medicine	http://www.vetmed.auburn.edu/
Auburn University College of Veterinary Medicine	http://www.vetmed.auburn.edu:80/
College of Vet Med Home Page	http://www.vetmed.ufl.edu/
VA-MD Regional College Home Page	http://www.vetmed.vt.edu/
UC Davis School of Veterinary Medicine	http://www.vetnet.ucdavis.edu/
USUHS Pathology	http://wwwpath.usuf2.usuhs.mil/
CERL - UNIVERSITY OF ARIZONA	http://zax.radiology.arizona.edu/
New York State College of Veterinary Medicine	http://zoo.vet.cornell.edu/

Miscellaneous

Input Section	http://alaskan.com/input.html
BlackMagic's Home Page	http://blackmagic.com/
Internet PCA Registration Authority Key Information	http://bs.mit.edu:8001/ipra.html
BPA-EDELWEB Cybershop	http://champagne.inria.fr/digishop/entrance.html
New User Registration	http://cio.cisco.com/public/newuser.html
Internet Font Browser: Font Name Search	http://cuiwww.unige.ch/parscan/-ul/OSG/Fonts/List/NameIndex.html
Liberty Hill Cyberwerks	http://cyberwerks.com/
The D0 Experiment	http://d0sgi0.fnal.gov/
Newman Council's Homepage	http://dolphin.upenn.edu/~newman/
Lycos URL Registration Form	http://fuzine.mt.cs.cmu.edu/mlm/lycos-register.html
Msen Home Page	http://garnet.msen.com/
Harvest Team Contact Information	http://harvest.cs.colorado.edu/harvest/teamcontact.html
Louisville Sister Cities	http://iglou.com/MeersWorld/SCLHome
ElectraCity Welcome	http://inforamp.net/electracity/index.html
National Integrated Pest Management Network - Home Page	http://ipm_www.ncsu.edu/
KBBS Online - Home Page	http://kbbs.kbbsnet.com/
Kvasir	http://kvasir.oslonett.no/kvasir/

LGI	http://lgi.imag.fr/
Sprakbanken	http://logos.svenska.gu.se/
David LaMacchia Defense Fund	http://martigny.ai.mit.edu/dldf/home.html
Expersoft Guest Registery	http://maxwell.expersoft.com/guestbook/
Welcome to the Metaverse	http://metaverse.com/
Cafe Renaissance	http://mls.saic.com/coffee/cafe_renaissance.html
Santa Claus home page	http://mofile.fi/rec/santa/santa.htm
Nanothinc Home Page	http://nanothinc.com/
SWAMIS NC Alternative Pop Menu Page	http://nether.net/~holden/html/swamis.htm
the n-dim project	http://paneer.ndim.edrc.cmu.edu:8888/
Stanford - Residential Computing	http://rescomp.stanford.edu/
The Resort Home Page	http://resort.com/
Ottawa Carleton Research Institute - Home Page	http://resudox.net/
Ranting Menu	http://samsara.circus.com/~jasona/ranting/menu.html
Sprawl Home Page	http://sensemedia.net/sprawl
THE COMMONWEALTH CLUB	http://sfgate.com/~common/
The Surface Navy Association Homepage - Monterey Bay Chapt	http://sm.nps.navy.mil/SNA/sna.html
Speleology Server Home Page	http://speleology.cs.yale.edu/
Data Distribution Laboratory (DDL)	http://stargate.jpl.nasa.gov/ddl
NII Cover Page	http://sunsite.unc.edu/nii/NII-Table-of-Contents.html
The SRMC SpiderWeb Home Page	http://sweb.srmc.com/
Miscellaneous Links	http://taygeta.oc.nps.navy.mil/misc_links.html
The Ballad of Ned Ludd	http://town.hall.org/places/ludd_land/index.html
New and Trendy Protocols	http://town.hall.org/trendy/trendy.html
GNA Personnel Form	http://uu-gna.mit.edu:8001/gna-forms/gna-form-personnel-01.pl
PLANET EARTH HOME PAGE	http://white.nosc.mil/info.html
Kennedy Kosher Co-op	http://www-leland.stanford.edu/group/kkc/
The Breeder's Registry	http://www.actwin.com/fish/br/index.html
AMUG WEB	http://www.amug.org/
Gateway to the anomoworld	http://www.armory.com/~anomie/
AstraNet — www.astranet.com	http://www.astranet.com/home1.html
Atlantis BBS	http://www.atlantis-bbs.com/main.htm
Glass Wings: Sensual Celebrations	http://www.aus.xanadu.com/GlassWings/sexual/celebrations.html
webfx Home Page	http://www.batnet.com/coredesign/
Golden Gate	http://www.best.com/~ggate/golden-gate.html
BUZZ ONLINE: The Talk of Los Angeles 6.07	http://www.buzzmag.com/buzz/
information emporium	http://www.catalog.com/ie/
Switched MultiMegaBit Data Service	http://www.cerf.net/smds.html
C-Group-Link Home Page	http://www.cgl.com/
Arrival: Emerald On The Matrix	http://www.charm.net/
CoSy Homepage	http://www.cosy.sbg.ac.at/home.html
Guest Book	http://www.cosy.sbg.ac.at/rec/guestbook/World.html
The Mentos FAQ v2.0	http://www.cs.hmc.edu/people/zbaker/mentos-faq.html
UCSTRI — Cover Page	http://www.cs.indiana.edu/cstr/
CATS PROGRAM Home Page	http://www.dcc.unicamp.br/cats
MGM/UA: The Lion's Den	http://www.digiplanet.com/MGM/
MGM: Tank Girl	http://www.digiplanet.com/tank_girl/tank.html
THE EDEN MATRIX	http://www.eden.com/
MBONE Information Web	http://www.eit.com/techinfo/mbone/
Elsevier Science - Home Page	http://www.elsevier.nl/
Statistiques sur www.eunet.fr	http://www.fnet.fr/www-stat/statistiques.html
FORWISS-Leitseite	http://www.forwiss.tu-muenchen.de:80/
Woman's Hospitality Exchange International Network	http://www.globalx.net/whein/
FRANK KROGER'S Home page	http://www.halcyon.com/fkroger/welcome.html
Welcome to Hyperion!	http://www.hyperion.com/
Funkopolis	http://www.hyperion.com/~funkster/
HomePage	http://www.i-link.net/200citys.html
PeaceNet Home Page	http://www.igc.apc.org/igc/pn.html
Illustra Home Page	http://www.illustra.com/
Message of the Day	http://www.infi.net/cgi-bin/motd.pl
Jetsetter Homepage	http://www.infi.net/jetsetters/
InfiNet's Media Partners	http://www.infi.net/partners.html
Feedback	http://www.infi.net/pilot/feedback.html
WWW-Server des Rechnerbetriebs Informatik RWTH Aachen	http://www.informatik.rwth-aachen.de/
Women's Leadership Network	http://www.interport.net/~asherman/wln.html
ICC: Programs we've been involved with..	http://www.ip.net/ICC/programs.html
Los Angeles County Museum of Art	http://www.lacma.org/
Welcome to LANIA	http://www.lania.mx/
NASA LaRC Visitor Count	http://www.larc.nasa.gov/stats/info/counter.html
Archive	http://www.llnl.gov/labsrc/archive.html
CARAL	http://www.matisse.net/politics/caral/caral.html
Dr. Tomorrow's CyberEmporium	http://www.nas.com/~drtom/tv.html
National Capital FreeNet/Libertel de la Capitale nationale	http://www.ncf.carleton.ca/
Welcome to NetCentral	http://www.netcentral.net/index.html
Kevin Savetz's page o' Stuff	http://www.northcoast.com/savetz/savetz.html
Akira Kurosawa's 'Dreams'	http://www.pitt.edu/~ddj/dreams/
Strange Ways' Home Page	http://www.pitt.edu/~zucker/strange-ways.html
HRS Home Page	http://www.psg.lcs.mit.edu/~carl/paige/HRS-home.html
Frequently Asked Questions (FAQ) on the Multicast Backbone	http://www.research.att.com/mbone-faq.html
The SIMS Internet Matrix Southeast WWW Server	http://www.sc.net/
Complex (Adaptive) Systems Information	http://www.seas.upenn.edu/~ale/cplxsys.html

Additional Sites

Digital-Cyberspace Mural page.	http://www.service.digital.com/html/dec_cspace.html
The Daphne Jackson Memorial Fellowships Trust	http://www.sst.ph.ic.ac.uk/trust/
TheWorld	http://www.theworld.com/
Telemedia Networks and Systems Group	http://www.tns.lcs.mit.edu/tns-www-home.html
TRIVR Home Page	http://www.trinet.com/trivr.html
UB Networks Home Page	http://www.ub.com/
Unisa: Examination results	http://www.unisa.ac.za/0/docs/exam.html
Wetware Services WWW Overview	http://www.wetware.com/
Xerox PARC Map Server Usage Graph	http://www.xerox.com/PARC/docs/usage.html
Gastown Webspace - A virtual town	http://www.xmission.com/~gastown/index.html
You Will	http://youwill.com/
Zstuff on the Web	http://zeb.nysaes.cornell.edu/

Movies

Entertainment:Movies and Films	http://akebono.stanford.edu/yahoo/Entertainment/Movies_and_Films/
Buena Vista MoviePlex	http://bvp.wdp.com/BVPM/index.html
Ed Wood	http://bvp.wdp.com/BVPM/PressRoom/EdWood/EdWood.html
Quiz Show	http://bvp.wdp.com/BVPM/PressRoom/QuizShow/QuizShow.html
Movie Review Query Engine	http://byron.sp.cs.cmu.edu:9086/movie
Sundance Home Page	http://cybermart.com/sundance/
MGM/StarGate	http://digiplanet.com/STARGATE/index.html
The University of Manchester CGU Movies	http://info.mcc.ac.uk/CGU/research/movies/
CinemaS p a c e	http://remarque.berkeley.edu:8001/~xcohen/
MPEG Movie Archive	http://w3.eeb.ele.tue.nl/mpeg/index.html
Boston Local Movie Listings	http://www.actwin.com/movies
Movies	http://www.cis.ohio-state.edu/hypertext/faq/usenet/movies/top.html
Internet Movie Database	http://www.cm.cf.ac.uk/Movies/moviequery.html
Oscars: The Internet Movie Database at Cardiff UK	http://www.cm.cf.ac.uk/Movies/Oscars.html
Main Page: The Internet Movie Database at Cardiff UK	http://www.cm.cf.ac.uk:80/Movies/
Internet Movie Database	http://www.cm.cf.ac.uk:80/Movies/moviequery.html
MGM/StarGate	http://www.earthlink.net/STARGATE/
MPEG Movie Archive	http://www.eeb.ele.tue.nl/mpeg/
RESERVOIR DOGS : HOME PAGE	http://www.foresight.co.uk/ents/dogs/dogin.html
Pilot Online Movie Guide	http://www.infi.net/pilot/movieguide.html
Festival	http://www.interport.net/festival
Main Page: The Internet Movie Database at Cardiff UK	http://www.leo.org/Movies/
Links to movie resources	http://www.maths.tcd.ie/pub/films/movie_hypdocs.html
The Internet Movie Database at Mississippi US	http://www.msstate.edu/M/on-this-day
Internet Movie Database	http://www.msstate.edu/Movies/moviequery.html
William Gibson's Alien III Script	http://www.umd.umich.edu/~nhughes/cyber/gibson/alien3.html
Space Movie Archive	http://www.univ-rennes1.fr/ASTRO/anim-e.html
'Professor Neon's TV & Movie Mania'	http://www.vortex.com/ProfNeon.htm

Museums

UCLA FOWLER MUSEUM OF CULTURAL HISTORY	http://artdirect.com/california/la/new/fowler
LAGUNA ART MUSEUM	http://artdirect.com/california/la/new/laguna
collection: Museum of New Zealand	http://hyperg.tu-graz.ac.at:80/B404BE8C/CNew_Zealand
Museum of Natural History & Cormack Planetarium	http://ids.net/~cormack_pl/rw.html
PARIS.MUSEES.LOUVRE	http://meteora.ucsd.edu:80/~norman/paris/Musees/Louvre/
PARIS.MUSEES.LOUVRE.TREASURES	http://meteora.ucsd.edu:80/~norman/paris/Musees/Louvre/Treasures/
Welcome to the University of California Museum of Paleontology	http://ucmp1.berkeley.edu/noinline.html
Carlos homepage	http://www.cc.emory.edu/CARLOS/carlos.html
WtR Virtual Exhibitions Catalogue	http://www.kiae.su/www/wtr/exhibits.html
La Trobe University Art Museum	http://www.latrobe.edu.au/Glenn/Museum/ArtMuseumHome.html
Leonardo da Vinci Museum	http://www.leonardo.net/main.html
Frederick R. Weisman Art Museum	http://www.micro.umn.edu/weisman/otherArt.html
RockWeb(TM) Interactive	http://www.rock.net/
Art.Online Home Page	http://www.terra.net/artonline/index.html
Huntsville Museum of Art	http://www.traveller.com/hma/
THE UNITED STATES HOLOCAUST MEMORIAL MUSEUM	http://www.ushmm.org/
Charlotte The Vermont Whale	http://www.uvm.edu/whale/whalehome.html
About the Digital Tradition Server	http://www.xerox.com/PARC/DigiTrad/AboutDigiTrad.html
Museums in the Netherlands	http://www.xxlink.nl/nbt/museums/

Music

the Alf Midi Site	http://alf.uib.no/People/midi/midi.html
Laurie Freelove/Gemma Cochran	http://atlantis.austin.apple.com/people.pages/cochran/Laurie.html
Ceolas celtic music archive	http://ceolas.stanford.edu/ceolas.html
The Catherine Wheel Home Page	http://gdbdoc.gdb.org/~patty/CW/CW_home_page.html
University of Michigan Music Library	http://http2.sils.umich.edu/~jpow/MusicLibrary.html
The Batish Institute of Indian Music and Fine Arts	http://hypatia.ucsc.edu:70/1/RELATED/Batish
Dolby/Home Page	http://kspace.com/KM/spot.sys/Dolby/pages/home.html
BMI HOMEPAGE	http://metaverse.com/bmi/index.html
Woodstock.com Main Menu	http://metaverse.com/woodstock/
Humanities	http://nearnet.gnn.com/wic/hum.toc.html#music
The MIT Music Library	http://nimrod.mit.edu/depts/music/music-top.html
MKB Music Harmony List	http://orpheus.ucsd.edu/mbreen/harmony.html
Michael's Interesting Music Network Locations	http://orpheus.ucsd.edu/mbreen/music.sites.html
UC San Diego Music Library	http://orpheus.ucsd.edu/music/
MOOSETONE RECORDS	http://pasture.ecn.purdue.edu/~stevensb/moose.html

Towhead Home Page	http://pcd.stanford.edu/umbra/Towhead/Towhead.html
VOCALIST Homepage	http://phoenix.oulu.fi/~mhotti/vocalist.html
Vergiftung Home Page	http://purgatory.ecn.purdue.edu:20002/JBC/david/vergiftung.html
The Jazz Butcher Conspiracy Home Page	http://purgatory.ecn.purdue.edu:20002/JBC/jbc.html
J. Feinstein's House O' Jazz	http://raptor.sccs.swarthmore.edu/~jbf/jazz.html
Rare Groove - WWW Tip Sheet	http://rg.media.mit.edu/RG/
The Boingo Page	http://rhino.harvard.edu/dan/boingo/boingo.html
Black Crowes home page	http://rock.net:80/fan-supported/black-crowes/
Severe Tire Damage — First Live Band on the Internet	http://sandbox.parc.xerox.com/hypertext/std/Band.html
Virginia Tech Music Department Home Page	http://server.music.vt.edu/
Higher Octave Music Home Page	http://smartworld.com/hioctave/hioct.html
Creative Musicians Coalition Home Page	http://spider.lloyd.com/~dragon/cmc.htm
The Rolling Stones Web Site	http://stones.com/
BEAST	http://sun1.bham.ac.uk/~mooreaj/docs/beast.html
Internet Underground Music Archive	http://sunsite.unc.edu/IUMA/index_graphic.html
IUMA Welcome to IUMA	http://sunsite.unc.edu/IUMA/index_text.html
Forward Progress: Progressive Rock Show & Music Archives	http://tam2000.tamu.edu/~mdb0213/index.html
Hammered Dulcimer	http://tfnet.ils.unc.edu/~gotwals/hd/dulcimer.html
Music from Croatia	http://tjev.tel.etf.hr/music/music.html
Trip 'n Spin Recordings	http://tripnspin.com/TNS/
Internet Underground Music Archive	http://uk.iuma.com/IUMA/index_graphic.html
San Diego Rocks	http://underground.net/Sdrocks/
WILMA	http://underground.net/Wilma
World Domination	http://underground.net/Worlddom
Led Zeppelin Home Page	http://uvacs.cs.virginia.edu/~jsw2y/zeppelin/zeppelin.html
Welcome to Musician's Web	http://valley.interact.nl/AV/MUSWEB/home.html
Misfits Central	http://watt.seas.Virginia.EDU:80/~msk4m/
CD shops	http://web.yl.is.s.u-tokyo.ac.jp/members/jeff/web/cd.html
The San Jose Symphony Home Port	http://webcom.com/%7Esjsympho/
Sacramento Master Singers	http://wheel.dcn.davis.ca.us/~jmcrowel/sms/
Woodstock '94 Home Page	http://woodstock94.com/album
The Fractal Music Project	http://www-ks.rus.uni-stuttgart.de/people/schulz/fmusic/
The Stanford Harmonics	http://www-leland.stanford.edu/group/harmonics/
LSJUMB Page 'O' Fun!	http://www-leland.stanford.edu/group/lsjumb/
Mixed Company	http://www-leland.stanford.edu/group/mixedco/
Stanford Symphony Orchestra	http://www-leland.stanford.edu/group/sso/
San Francisco Girls Chorus	http://www.3pco.net/orgs/sfgc/index.htm
Primarily A Cappella Home Page	http://www.accel.com/pac/index.htm
The (unofficial) EnoWeb	http://www.acns.nwu.edu/eno-l/
WNUR-FM JazzWeb	http://www.acns.nwu.edu/jazz/
Reviews Table of Contents	http://www.ai.mit.edu/~isbell/HFh/reviews/000-toc.html
ClubWeb Albany	http://www.albany.net/~mxr/clubweb/cw.html
Search Results	http://www.amug.org/~eps/musicsearch.html
The For Squirrels WWW site.	http://www.anest.ufl.edu/~chris/ForSquirrels.html
Carl Franklin - The Ballad Of Winston Harlen	http://www.apexsc.com/users/carlf/winston.html
PrettyBoy Records	http://www.apk.net/prettyboy
Leap the Gap	http://www.arc.org/
Nereid Cluster	http://www.armory.com/~zap/nc/nc.html
THE CAUER CALENDAR	http://www.artdirect.com/cauer/
IAMfree Sound	http://www.artnet.org/iamfree/IAMFREE/html/sound.html
The dat-heads mailing list archive	http://www.atd.ucar.edu/rdp/dat-heads
Japanese Independent Music Archive	http://www.atom.co.jp/INDIES/
Enya - Unofficial Home Page	http://www.bath.ac.uk/~ccsdra/enya/home.html
Sunnyvale Singers Home Page	http://www.best.com/~barbh/ssing/ssingers.html
D-Tox	http://www.binary9.com:80/~d-tox/
Genesis World Wide Web home page	http://www.brad.ac.uk/~agcatchp/gen_home.html
Breakfast Records	http://www.breakfast.com:2500/
CD Search	http://www.btg.com/~cknudsen/xmcd/query.html
Brave Combo	http://www.butterfly.net/obvious/bravecombo.html
The Ani DiFranco Home Page	http://www.cc.columbia.edu/~marg/ani/
ChuaSoundMusic	http://www.ccsr.uiuc.edu/People/gmk/Papers/ChuaSndRef.html
Erasure Welcome	http://www.cec.wustl.edu/~ccons/erasure/
On-Line Music Database	http://www.cecer.army.mil/~burnett/MDB/
YES HomePage	http://www.cen.uiuc.edu/~ea10735/yes.html
The Little Ol' Web Page from Texas	http://www.cen.uiuc.edu/~pz3900/zztop.html
FolkBook: An Online Acoustic Music Establishment.	http://www.cgrg.ohio-state.edu/folkbook/
The Depeche Mode Home Page	http://www.cis.ufl.edu/~sag/dm/
The Pierson Camerata Home Page	http://www.cis.yale.edu/~lbauer/camerata.html
Nadine Magazine Home Page	http://www.cis.yale.edu/~tpole/nadine/home_page.html
Buzzcocks	http://www.cityscape.co.uk/users/ac46/indbuzz.htm
Sisters Of Mercy Home Page	http://www.cm.cf.ac.uk/Sisters.Of.Mercy/
Acid Jazz	http://www.cmd.uu.se/AcidJazz/
A Succession of Repetitive Beats	http://www.crg.cs.nott.ac.uk/~mjr/Music/
Green Day	http://www.cs.caltech.edu/~adam/greenday.html
And Through The Wire - Peter Gabriel	http://www.cs.clemson.edu/~junderw/pg.html
John Mellencamp	http://www.cs.cmu.edu:8001/afs/andrew/usr/da2x/mosaic/
The Grateful Dead	http://www.cs.cmu.edu:8001/afs/cs.cmu.edu/user/mleone/web/dead.html
The Queensryche Page	http://www.cs.cmu.edu:8001/afs/cs/user/nkramer/ryche/ryche.html
Accordiana	http://www.cs.cmu.edu:8001/afs/cs/user/phoebe/mosaic/accordion.html
Blues Brothers FAQ Section 1	http://www.cs.monash.edu.au/~pringle/bluesbros/faq.html
Music	http://www.cs.tu-berlin.de/~eserte/music.html

Additional Sites

Iron Maiden Page	http://www.cs.tufts.edu/~stratton/maiden/maiden.html
The Drums and Percussion Page	http://www.cse.ogi.edu/Drum/
Into the Flood Again! - The Alice In Chains Homepage	http://www.csos.orst.edu/~mikec/aic.html
Information about Violet Arcana	http://www.csos.orst.edu/rfr/va/arcana.html
Music Instruction Software	http://www.cstp.umkc.edu/users/bhugh/musici.html
Jazz NET	http://www.dnai.com/~lmcohen/
Modulus Graphite Home Page	http://www.dnai.com/~modulus
The Mudkats Homepage	http://www.echo.com/mudkats/index.html
Deth Specula Homepage	http://www.echo.com/specula/index.html
Music Online	http://www.eden.com/music/music.html
MIDI Home Page	http://www.eeb.ele.tue.nl/midi/index.html
Mike Markowski's Beatles Page	http://www.eecis.udel.edu/~markowsk/beatles/
The Industrial Page	http://www.eecs.nwu.edu:80/~smishra/Industrial/
EFF & Aerosmith Rock the Net!	http://www.eff.org/virtour.html
Kylie Minogue	http://www.eia.brad.ac.uk/kylie/index.html
CAIRSS for Music database of music research literature	http://www.einet.net/hytelnet/FUL064.html
Folk Music Home Page	http://www.eit.com/web/folk/folkhome.html
Pearl Jam	http://www.engin.umich.edu/~galvin/pearljam.html
Cool Edit Home Page	http://www.ep.se/cool/
Bow Makers and Bowed Stringed Instrument Makers	http://www.eskimo.com/~dvz/violin-makers.html
The Opera Schedule Server	http://www.fsz.bme.hu/opera/main.html
St. Alphonzo's Pancake Homepage	http://www.fwi.uva.nl/~heederik/zappa/
THE KISS NETWORK - Los Angeles CA	http://www.galcit.caltech.edu/~aure/strwys.html
Bergen Jazz Forum informerer.	http://www.gfi.uib.no/~steingod/index.html
Redwood Symphony	http://www.globalvillag.com/~redwood
THE CANADIAN INTERNET MUSIC SOURCE Homepage	http://www.globalx.net/cims/
Go! Discs Title Page	http://www.godiscs.co.uk/godiscs
R.E.M. Home Page	http://www.halcyon.com/rem/index.html
Robert Todd's Chiefs Page	http://www.hcs.eng.fsu.edu/~todd/Chiefs.html
Renaissance Consort	http://www.hike.te.chiba-u.ac.jp/cons1/
Electronic Early Music	http://www.hike.te.chiba-u.ac.jp/eem/
History of Rock 'n' Roll	http://www.hollywood.com/rocknroll/
Rock & Roll Digital Gallery	http://www.hooked.net/julianne/index.html
GEMS main menu	http://www.hyperion.com/ftp/pub/gems/index.html
Chris Duarte Group	http://www.hyperweb.com/duarte/duarte.html
Roky Erickson	http://www.hyperweb.com/roky/roky.html
Piano Recordings by Jonathon Lee	http://www.icw.com/america/amerway/piano/piano.html
Front 242	http://www.ifi.uio.no/~terjesa/front242/main.html
The Electronic Bluegrass Magazine	http://www.info.net/BG
Abayudaya Jews in Uganda: Music	http://www.intac.com/PubService/uganda/music.html
E.R.M. Home Page	http://www.interaccess.com:80/users/numusic/
The Canadian Music Exchange	http://www.io.org/~cme/
Hidden Water	http://www.ipac.net/HW/hwhome.html
Amy Grant archive	http://www.ipc.uni-tuebingen.de/art
Serveur WWW de l'Ircam	http://www.ircam.fr/
IUMA Welcome to IUMA	http://www.iuma.com/
Santa Cruz Alternative Music (SCAM)	http://www.iuma.com/~scam/
Deth Specula	http://www.iuma.com/band_html/Deth_Specula.html
Bedazzled	http://www.iuma.com/Bedazzled/
Global Music Outlet	http://www.iuma.com/GMO/
Harbor Records	http://www.iuma.com/Harbor/
Heyday Records	http://www.iuma.com/Heyday/
House of Blues MBONE Events	http://www.iuma.com/HOB/
Internet Underground Music Archive	http://www.iuma.com/IUMA/index_text.html
Quagmire the label	http://www.iuma.com/Quagmire/
Reality Society Records	http://www.iuma.com/Reality_Society/
Relentless Pursuit Records	http://www.iuma.com/Relentless_Pursuit/
Silent Records	http://www.iuma.com/Silent/
STROBE MAGAZINE	http://www.iuma.com/strobe/
TeenBeat Records	http://www.iuma.com/TeenBeat/
Welcome to JAZZOnline!	http://www.jazzonln.com/JAZZ/
Leicester University RockSoc	http://www.le.ac.uk/CWIS/SU/SO/RSOC/rsoc.html
Leeds University Department of Music	http://www.leeds.ac.uk/music.html
The Csound Front Page	http://www.leeds.ac.uk/music/Man/c_front.html
LSI - Computer Music at LSI	http://www.lsi.usp.br/~musica/musica.html
Legionaires disease free since 1990	http://www.maires.co.uk:80/nw2n/
Hard Bop Cafe[tm] Jazz Home Page	http://www.mbnet.mb.ca/~mcgonig/hardbop.html
Planet StarChild	http://www.mcs.com/~bliss/starchild/home.html
Virtual Radio Home Page	http://www.microserve.net/vradio/
KITARO	http://www.mindspring.com/~shadow/kitaro/kitaro.html
Trombone-L Home Page	http://www.missouri.edu/~cceric/index.html
Janet Jackson Homepage	http://www.mit.edu:8001/people/agoyo1/janet.html
The Madonna Homepage	http://www.mit.edu:8001/people/jwb/Madonna.html
The Tori Amos Homepage	http://www.mit.edu:8001/people/nocturne/tori.html
Welcome to the Florida State University School of Music	http://www.music.fsu.edu/
Indiana University School of Music Home Page	http://www.music.indiana.edu/
Music Resources on the Internet	http://www.music.indiana.edu/misc/music_resources.html
Indigo Girls	http://www.music.sony.com/Music/ArtistInfo/IndigoGirls.html
Sony Music	http://www.music.sony.com/Music/MusicIndex.html
MusicBase	http://www.musicbase.co.uk/music/
Creation Records	http://www.musicbase.co.uk/music/creation/

470

The Motown Home Page	http://www.musicbase.co.uk/music/motown/
PWEI Home Page	http://www.musicbase.co.uk/music/pwei/
Mammoth Records Internet Center	http://www.nando.net/mammoth/
Beastie Boys Home Page	http://www.nando.net/music/gm/BeastieBoys/
Grand Royal	http://www.nando.net/music/gm/GrandRoyal/
Classical Music Reviews	http://www.ncsa.uiuc.edu/SDG/People/marca/music-reviews.html
Happy Bob Marley's 50th Birthday	http://www.netaxs.com/~aaron/Marley/Marley.html
Dead Can Dance	http://www.nets.com/dcd
Nashville Online	http://www.nol.com/nol/NOL_Home.html
NVG - ABBA	http://www.nvg.unit.no/moro/musikk/abba.html
Music	http://www.oulu.fi/music.html
The Bottom Line Archive	http://www.oulu.fi/tbl.html
Inter-Music	http://www.ozonline.com.au:80/TotalNode/AIMC/
Ballet Austin	http://www.pencom.com/arts/ballet/
Delta Snake Blues News	http://www.portal.com/~mojohand/delta_snake.html
The Princeton University Band	http://www.princeton.edu/~puband/
Tangerine Dream Home Page	http://www.public.iastate.edu/~hunter/TD/tngdrm.html
Austin Music	http://www.quadralay.com/www/Austin/AustinMusic/AustinMusic.html
RISM-US Home Page	http://www.rism.harvard.edu/RISM/
RockWeb(TM) Interactive	http://www.rock.net:80/
Schoolkids' Records	http://www.schoolkids.com/skr/
The UnOfficial NINE INCH NAILS Home Page	http://www.scri.fsu.edu/~patters/nin.html
Music	http://www.siba.fi/Kulttuuripalvelut/music.html
HILJAISET LEVYT	http://www.sjoki.uta.fi/~latvis/levyyht/hiljais.html
southern - iuma	http://www.southern.com/
Band Index	http://www.southern.com/Southern/bands.html
Australian Music World Wide Web Site	http://www.st.nepean.uws.edu.au/~ezsigri/ausmusic/index.html
The Rolling Stones Web Site	http://www.stones.com/
Deep Purple Home Page	http://www.tecc.co.uk/public/purple/Purple.html
Allegro	http://www.teleport.com/~allegro/
Violet Arcana	http://www.teleport.com/~arcana/
Guns n Roses Home Page	http://www.teleport.com/~boerio/gnr.html
The Classical Guitar Home Page	http://www.teleport.com/~jdimick/cg.html
The Mammoth Music Meta-List @ VIBE	http://www.timeinc.com/vibe/mmm/
The People of the South Wind	http://www.traveller.com/~rew/kansas.html
Classical Music Repertoire List	http://www.ugcs.caltech.edu/~werdna/repertoire.html
Shot of Rhythm - The John Hiatt Mailing List Archives	http://www.unicom.com/john-hiatt
HyperRust	http://www.uta.fi/~trkisa/hyperrust.html
Bogus Records pages	http://www.w2.com/bogus.html
Black Boot pages	http://www.w2.com/boot.html
Etiquette Records pages	http://www.w2.com/et.html
Go Kart Records pages	http://www.w2.com/gokart.html
Hands On Music Inc.	http://www.w2.com/hands.html
The San Jose Symphony Home Port	http://www.webcom.com/~sjsympho/
Grateful Dead Almanac	http://www.well.com/Community/Grateful.Dead.Almanac/
WELL Grateful Dead Conferences	http://www.well.com/Conferences/gd.html
Copyright Law	http://www.wimsey.com:80/tcp/Jan95/Elvis.html
Windham Hill. Kristen Hall.	http://www.windham.com/ourmusic/artist_pages/hall.empty.byartist.html
Jazz Improvisation	http://www.wisc.edu/jazz/
Virtual Audio - The Internet music source	http://www.xmission.com:80/~len/va/

471

News

CU-SeeMe Information from NCSU	http://152.1.57.56/Multimedia/CU-SeeMe/reflect_list.html
News:University Newspapers	http://akebono.stanford.edu/yahoo/News/University_Newspapers/
Campus Newspapers on the Internet	http://beacon-www.asa.utk.edu/resources/papers.html
What's New?	http://bristol.com/whats_new.html
The Network Observer	http://communication.ucsd.edu/pagre/tno.html
AIS - HOT NEWS!!	http://community.net/news.html
Welcome to Boardwalk Consulting	http://consulting.com/news.html
The Washington Weekly June 5	http://dolphin.gulf.net/
Gingrich Speeches	http://dolphin.gulf.net/Gingrich.html
The Inslaw Scandal	http://dolphin.gulf.net/inslawsc.html
The Mena Scandal	http://dolphin.gulf.net/menascandal.html
Presidential Primaries	http://dolphin.gulf.net/Primaries.html
The Whitewater Scandal	http://dolphin.gulf.net/whitew.html
White House Press Release Summaries Home Page (EXPERIMENTAL)	http://eos.esusda.gov/wh/whsum.html
News_Releases	http://fcc.gov:70/1/News_Releases
Speeches	http://fcc.gov:70/1/Speeches
Forum News Gateway	http://forum.swarthmore.edu/forum.news.gateway.html
Lycos: Frequently Asked Questions	http://fuzine.mt.cs.cmu.edu/mlm/lycos-faq.html
Fuzine Usage: Accesses per Day	http://fuzine.mt.cs.cmu.edu/usage-day.html
Welcome to the Detroit Free Press Gopher	http://garnet.msen.com:70/0/vendor/freep/about
Freedom of Information	http://garnet.msen.com:70/1/vendor/freep/foi
Behind Network Hampton Roads	http://hampton.roads.net/nhr/authors.html
Hampton Roads: Demographics	http://hampton.roads.net/nhr/demographics.html
Welcome To Newport News	http://hampton.roads.net/nhr/newportnews/
Frequently Asked Questions (and Answers) about Harvest	http://harvest.cs.colorado.edu/harvest/FAQ.html
Harvest Talks	http://harvest.cs.colorado.edu/harvest/talks.html
Netscape Communications News Release	http://home.netscape.com/info/newsrelease16.html
What's New From CAS	http://info.cas.org/newss.html
Internet Newsgroups	http://info.cern.ch/hypertext/DataSources/News/Groups/Overview.html

Additional Sites

** The SoCal-Raves Calendar **	http://infopages.com/socal-raves/calendar/
Newsletter Vol. 2 No. 3	http://intergroup.com/interfinance/newsletter.2.3.html
Online Newspaper Services main menu	http://marketplace.com/e-papers.list.www/e-papers.home.page.html
UNABOM Press Release	http://naic.nasa.gov/fbi/unabom.html
GNN NetNews	http://nearnet.gnn.com/gnn/news/index.html
What's New in the WIC	http://nearnet.gnn.com/wic/nunu.toc.html
News Online	http://nimrod.mit.edu/common/news_online.html
Ascend Frequently Asked Questions: Top	http://northshore.shore.net/%7Edreaming/ascend-faq/
TimesFax	http://nytimesfax.com/
Home Page Washington	http://olympus.dis.wa.gov/www/wahome.html
The USGS Today	http://quake.wr.usgs.gov/USGS/theusgs.html
The SOLAR System	http://quercas.santarosa.edu/
What's New in California	http://s101dcascr.wr.usgs.gov/new.html
The Virginian-Pilot	http://scholar.lib.vt.edu/VA-news/VA-Pilot/VA-Pilot.html
Sea Urchin Harvesters Association - California	http://seaurchin.org/
COLUMNS	http://sfgate.com/~sfchron/columns/colindex.html
Letters to the Editor	http://sfgate.com/~sfchron/edits/edits.html
Deaths in the Entertainment Business and Performing Arts	http://sfgate.com/~sfchron/obits/obcatdex.html
Obituaries (Chronological)	http://sfgate.com/~sfchron/obits/obchrono.html
Our Policy on Posting	http://sfgate.com/~sfchron/standing/policy.html
Top of the News	http://sfgate.com/~sfchron/topos/newsdex.html
GlasNews	http://solar.rtd.utk.edu/friends/news/glasnews/master.html
The Tech	http://the-tech.mit.edu/
To be Continued	http://thule.mt.cs.cmu.edu:8001/sf-clearing-house/zines/to-be-continued/
Support the Internet Multicasting Service	http://town.hall.org/sponsors/ims.html
Vanderbilt Television News Archive	http://tvnews.vanderbilt.edu/
Washington Telecom Newswire	http://wtn.com/wtn/wtn.html
MIT Planetary Science's Comet-Jupiter Impact Simulations	http://www-erl.mit.edu/flolab/csl9press/csl9hj.html
California Highway Conditions	http://www.amdahl.com/internet/general/travel/ca-highway.html
Arizona Daily Wildcat	http://www.arizona.edu/pubs/wildcat/wildcat.html
Armory Homepage Information And Updates	http://www.armory.com/info.html
The Hartford Courant	http://www.atlantic.com/ctguide/news/courant/news.html
AT&T makes ISDN more accessible and affordable from home	http://www.att.com/press/0294/940224.nsc.html
FAQ About This Server	http://www.austin.apple.com/aboutapple/faqaac.html
Bell Atlantic Media Relations	http://www.ba.com/
San Mateo Times	http://www.baynet.com/smtimes/home.html
BBN Press Releases	http://www.bbn.com/press.html
MacHTTP/WebSTAR Home Page	http://www.biap.com/
Bristol Technology licenses Microsoft Windows source code	http://www.bristol.com/Company/Announce/ms_source.html
The Daily News Worldwide	http://www.cfn.cs.dal.ca/Media/TodaysNews/TodaysNews.html
FAQ	http://www.cis.ohio-state.edu/hypertext/faq/usenet/sgi/faq/top.html
List of USENET FAQs	http://www.cis.ohio-state.edu/hypertext/faq/usenet/top.html
The Vena Contracta	http://www.civeng.carleton.ca/CSES/VENA/
Introduction To CINET	http://www.cnd.org:80/CINETintro.html
What's New with WWW and Mosaic at Yale?	http://www.cs.yale.edu/HTML/WhatsNew.html
Cygnus Support Press Releases	http://www.cygnus.com/pressrels-dir.html
What's New At Cygnus Support	http://www.cygnus.com/whatsnew.html
UCF InPrint: Home Page	http://www.digimark.net/inprint/index.html
WHAT'S NEW on Eden	http://www.eden.com/new/new.html
EFF - Usenet	http://www.eff.org/effusenet.html
News im Internet	http://www.eunet.ch/Services/newspoint-pr.html
ExperTalk	http://www.expersoft.com/ExperTalk/
Expersoft Press Releases	http://www.expersoft.com/pr/index.html
The NASA Newsroom	http://www.gsfc.nasa.gov/hqpao/newsroom.html
Mosaic Network News	http://www.hal.csuhayward.edu/
Seattle Hometown News	http://www.halcyon.com/normg/snews.html
CyberNews Home Page	http://www.hmc.edu/www/people/teverett/cybernews/Home.html
NASA Press Releases	http://www.hq.nasa.gov/office/pao/NewsRoom/releases.html
Today at NASA	http://www.hq.nasa.gov/office/pao/NewsRoom/today.html
What's New at The Human Factor	http://www.human.com/new.html
Cyberspace Report	http://www.ics.uci.edu/~ejw/csr/cyber.html
IIASA - Short History	http://www.iiasa.ac.at/docs/IIASA_History.html
Automation News Network	http://www.industry.net/ann.html
The Capital Home Page	http://www.infi.net/capital/
The Journal Online	http://www.infi.net/journal/
Welcome to Pilot Online	http://www.infi.net/pilot/
Classified Main Index	http://www.infi.net/pilot/classmain.html
EXTRA! EXTRA!	http://www.infi.net/pilot/extra.html
Roanoke Times Online	http://www.infi.net/roatimes/
Washingtonian Magazine Online	http://www.infi.net/washmag/
What's New at InfiNet L.C.	http://www.infi.net/whatsnew.html
NewTimes Index of Events	http://www.infi.net:80/vegas/newtimes
Crisis in Rwanda	http://www.intac.com/PubService/rwanda/
Interpath Home Page	http://www.interpath.net/
The Weekly Mail & Guardian	http://www.is.co.za/services/wmail/wmail.html
Commercial News Services on the Internet	http://www.jou.ufl.edu/commres/webjou.htm
Global Student News WWW site	http://www.jou.ufl.edu/forums/gsn/
LabSOURCE	http://www.llnl.gov/labsrc/
EXTRA	http://www.llnl.gov/labsrc/extra.html
NEWS HIGHLIGHTS	http://www.llnl.gov/labsrc/highlight.html
LEAD STORIES	http://www.llnl.gov/labsrc/lead.html

472

Lab News	http://www.llnl.gov/PAO/lab_news.html
USF Health Sciences NEWS	http://www.med.usf.edu/PUBAFF/news1.html
The Digital Missourian	http://www.missouri.edu/~jschool/digmo/index.html
What's new with the MV WWW server	http://www.mvhs.edu/new.html
On-Line Newspapers	http://www.nando.net/epage/htdocs/links/newspapers.html
The Nando Times	http://www.nando.net/newsroom/nt/nando.html
The Freedom Forum	http://www.nando.net/prof/freedom/1994/freedom.html
Newspaper	http://www.nas.com/~drtom/newspape.html
NAVY NEWS SERVICE	http://www.navy.mil/navpalib/news/navnews/.www/navnews.html
NewsPage Home Page	http://www.newspage.com/
NeXTanswers Document Retrieval System	http://www.next.com/NeXTanswers/
Global News: The NTT International Researcher's Newsletter	http://www.ntt.jp/GlobalNews/index.html
Providence Business News	http://www.pbn.com/
RNN Home Page	http://www.pencom.com/rru.html
PFM News & Mail - Xlink POP Mainz	http://www.PFM-Mainz.DE/
Callahan's Place Info	http://www.physics.su.oz.au/~mar/callahans.html
The Slant	http://www.rahul.net/tyler/slant.html
NewtNews	http://www.ridgecrest.ca.us/NewtNews/NN_top.html
The PC-Mac TCP/IP & NFS FAQ list by Rawn Shah	http://www.rtd.com/pcnfsfaq/faq.html
What's New at SCO	http://www.sco.com/new.html
Seattle Daily Journal of Commerce	http://www.seanet.com/Bazar/Publications/SDJC.html
Meta-List of What's New pages	http://www.seas.upenn.edu/~mengwong/whatsnew.list.html
ANSWERS Subscription Request	http://www.service.com/answers/answersorder.html
Palo Alto Weekly Home Page	http://www.service.com/PAW/home.html
SII Online News	http://www.sii.com/news.html
Mercury Center Home Page	http://www.sjmercury.com/
The St Petersburg Press Homepage	http://www.spb.su/sppress/
KSU Collegian Home Page	http://www.spub.ksu.edu/
The Vance Phile	http://www.stack.urc.tue.nl/~remy/vance/biblio/parm/phile.html
Press Releases & In the News	http://press.t3plus.com/press.html
Corporate Software's Technology Exchange	http://www.tech-board.com/tbot/home.html
Tekelec Press Releases	http://www.tekelec.com/press/index.html
News Page	http://www.trib.com/news/news.html
Welcome to The News Tribune	http://www.tribnet.com/
The Daily Tar Heel	http://www.unc.edu/dth/
News and other information from departments at Unisa	http://www.unisa.ac.za/0/docs/depts.html
Ideas DIGest ONLINE Home Page	http://www.wimsey.com/~idig/
NOS TeleTekst	http://www.win.tue.nl/teletext/nos/index.html
Technician's Home Page	http://www2.ncsu.edu/ncsu/stud_pubs/Technician/
Review Home Page	http://wwwhost.cc.utexas.edu/ftp/pub/review/ur.html

473

Oceanography

Sea Surface Temperature Satellite Images	http://dcz.gso.uri.edu/avhrr-archive/archive.html
Links to Oceanographic Information	http://oraac.gsfc.nasa.gov/~rienecke/po_others.html
Australian Oceanographic Data Centre - Home Page	http://www.AODC.gov.au/AODC.html
Bienvenido a CICESE	http://www.cicese.mx/DOCUMENTOS_CICESE/CICESE.html
University of Rhode Island/Graduate School of Oceanography	http://www.gso.uri.edu/
The Ocean Circulation and Climate Advanced Modelling Project	http://www.nwo.ac.uk/iosdl/iosdl/Rennell/occam/occam.html
ORI Home Page	http://www.ori.u-tokyo.ac.jp/
SACLANTCEN: Home Page	http://www.saclantc.nato.int/
SOEST WWW Services	http://www.soest.hawaii.edu/
IO - Instituto Oceanografico	http://www.usp.br/io/io.html
Woods Hole Oceanographic Institution http server	http://www.whoi.edu/

Personal

Positive Planet	http://cyberzine.org/html/HIV/mainpage.html
Friends of OSHO	http://earth.path.net/osho/
Michael Mauldin (Fuzzy) Home Page	http://fuzine.mt.cs.cmu.edu/mlm/home.html
Genealogy Online	http://genealogy.emcee.com/
Home Page for the Pegasus WWW Server	http://pegasus.cc.ucf.edu/
Rice University personal WWW pages	http://riceinfo.rice.edu/webshare_all.html
Food Family and Home	http://sfgate.com/~sfchron/homeplate/hoindex.html
Alpha Phi Alpha Fraternity Inc.	http://www-leland.stanford.edu/group/APhiA/
John Romkey	http://www.apocalypse.org/pub/u/romkey/home.html
Russ Jones Business Card	http://www.digital.com/info/rjones.html
EFF Homepages	http://www.eff.org/homes/homes.html
Jimen Ching's Web Page	http://www.eng.hawaii.edu/Contribs/jiching
About the SIPB Webmasters	http://www.mit.edu:8001/webmasters.html
SDSC Webmasters	http://www.sdsc.edu/0/SDSC/Webmaster/webmasters.html
Public Home Pages	http://www.uidaho.edu/public-pages.html

Physics

LLNL High Energy Physics Group	http://babar1.llnl.gov/
DFTUZ HyperText Archives	http://dftuz.unizar.es/
Instituto de Fisica - Facultad de Ciencias	http://fisica.edu.uy/
Physics (Science)	http://galaxy.einet.net/galaxy/Science/Physics.html
What's New Bob Park The American Physical Society	http://hq.aps.org/WN/wn95gen.html
Cecil H. and Ida M. Green Institute of Geophysics and Planetary Physics	http://igpp.ucsd.edu/
Overview on Lattice Field Theory	http://info.desy.de/user/projects/Lattice.html
IN2P3 HOME PAGE	http://info.in2p3.fr/

Additional Sites

UH HILO PHYSICS and ASTRONOMY	http://maxwell.uhh.hawaii.edu/index.html
LANL Physics Information Server	http://mentor.lanl.gov/
Yale Condensed Matter Theory	http://sachdev.physics.yale.edu/
SLAC Home Page	http://slacvm.slac.stanford.edu/FIND/slac.html
High Energy Physics Laboratory	http://squark.phys.washington.edu/
Harvard Physics Department	http://string.harvard.edu/
SLAC Home Page	http://www-slac.slac.stanford.edu/FIND/slac.html
Applied Physics Lab Univ. of Wash. Welcome Page	http://www.apl.washington.edu/
Northwestern University Physics & Astronomy	http://www.astro.nwu.edu/home.html
Accelerator Laboratory LMUand TUMunich	http://www.bl.physik.tu-muenchen.de/index_english/index_english.html
CEBAF Information	http://www.cebaf.gov:3000/cebaf.html
Physics Society Information	http://www.cern.ch/Physics/PhysSoc.html
High Alpha Electronic Workshop	http://www.dfrf.nasa.gov/Workshop/HighAlphaIV/highalpha.html
Fermi National Accelerator Laboratory Home Page	http://www.fnal.gov/
Dept. of Earth and Planetary Phys. Univ. of Tokyo	http://www.geoph.s.u-tokyo.ac.jp/
HEP Newsletters and Periodicals	http://www.hep.net/documents/newsletters/newsletters.html
Welcome to the Institute of Physics	http://www.ioppublishing.com/iopwelcome.html
Indiana University Cyclotron Facility Home Page	http://www.iucf.indiana.edu/
KEK Welcome	http://www.kek.jp/
LASSP Home Page	http://www.lassp.cornell.edu/
Laser Manufacturing Laboratory Home Page	http://www.ME.Berkeley.EDU:80/lml/
MPI-K Heidelberg Home Page	http://www.mpi-hd.mpg.de:80/
University of Cambridge Department of PhysicsCavendish Laboratory	http://www.phy.cam.ac.uk/www/physics.html
Auburn University Physics Department	http://www.physics.auburn.edu/
Research Institute for Theoretical Physics	http://www.physics.helsinki.fi/tft/tft.html
PL-Geophysics Directorate Home Page	http://www.plh.af.mil/
PPPL HOME PAGE	http://www.pppl.gov:80/
U. C. Irvine Department of Physics and Astronomy	http://www.ps.uci.edu/physics/
Fritz-Haber-Institut der MPG	http://www.rz-berlin.mpg.de:80/
SSC Page	http://www.ssc.gov/
Texas Center for Superconductivity at the Universityof Houston	http://www.tcs.uh.edu/
ZEBU: UO Physics WEB Server	http://zebu.uoregon.edu/
ZEUS Experiment Home Page	http://zow00.desy.de:8000/

Programming

ASIS WWW Server - Texinfo to HTML Translator	http://asis01.cern.ch/infohtml/texi2html.html
OO Bibliography	http://cuiwww.unige.ch/cgi-bin/bibrefs
Catalog of Free Compilers and Interpreters	http://cuiwww.unige.ch/freecomp
The Language List	http://cuiwww.unige.ch/langlist
HTML Editor for the Macintosh	http://dragon.acadiau.ca/~giles/HTML_Editor/Documentation.html
ISO Latin 1 Entities in HTML	http://info.cern.ch/hypertext/WWW/MarkUp/ISOlat1.html
HTTP: A protocol for networked information	http://info.cern.ch/hypertext/WWW/Protocols/HTTP/HTTP2.html
C++ Course Book Has Moved	http://info.desy.de/gna/html/cc/text/index.html
HTML: Hypertext Mark-up Language	http://lcweb.loc.gov/global/html.html
Intellectual Ammunition for Ada Programmers	http://lglwww.epfl.ch/Ada/Ammo/Ammunition.html
Genetically Programmed Music	http://nmt.edu/~jefu/notes/notes.html
PHIGS Validation Tests - Overview	http://speckle.ncsl.nist.gov/~cugini/pvt/hy-top.html
Simulated Annealing Information	http://taygeta.oc.nps.navy.mil/annealing/simanneal.html
Digital Filtering	http://taygeta.oc.nps.navy.mil/dfilter.html
Forth Information on Taygeta	http://taygeta.oc.nps.navy.mil/forth.html
Stochastic Differential Equation Information	http://taygeta.oc.nps.navy.mil/sdes.html
VIUF comp.lang.vhdl archive	http://vhdl.org/vi/comp.lang.vhdl/
IEEE DASC Shared Variable Working Group (VHDL)	http://vhdl.org/vi/svwg/
Virtual Reality Modeling Language (VRML) Forum	http://vrml.wired.com/
A Standard for Robot Exclusion	http://web.nexor.co.uk/mak/doc/robots/norobots.html
htMUD front door page	http://www.apocalypse.org/~phi/htmud.html
Collaborative Networked Communication: MUDs as Systems Tools	http://www.ccs.neu.edu/home/remy/documents/cncmast.html
CyberWeb SoftWare	http://www.charm.net/~web/CWSW.html
The MUD Resource Collection	http://www.cis.upenn.edu/~lwl/mudinfo.html
Gareth Rees: academic home page	http://www.cl.cam.ac.uk/users/gdr11
Python Language Home Page	http://www.cwi.nl/~guido/Python.html
HTML Fancy Stuff	http://www.hal.com/~barry/Links/html.html
HyperText Markup Language Specification Version 3.0	http://www.hpl.hp.co.uk/people/dsr/html/CoverPage.html
libwww-perl: Distribution Information	http://www.ics.uci.edu/WebSoft/libwww-perl/
Apple Developer Services and Products	http://info.apple.com/dev/developerservices.html
Sample Pages for Various Character Sets	http://www.ntt.jp/Mosaic-l10n/sample.html
Pages Software Inc Web Authoring Expressway	http://www.pages.com/
FORGE Introduction	http://www.qpsf.edu.au/workshop/forge/forge.html
Database tools and utilities	http://www.qualix.com/product/database/Welcome.html
Programming tools and libraries	http://www.qualix.com/product/programming/Welcome.html
SCO Developer Programs	http://www.sco.COM/Dev/Developers/developer.html
SGML Open Home Page	http://www.sgmlopen.org/

Psychology

Stanford Psychology	http://matia.stanford.edu/
Cognitive & Psychological Sciences	http://matia.stanford.edu/cogsci.html
E-Mail Directory	http://www.coedu.usf.edu/behavior/regist.html
Psychology General Information	http://www.psy.gla.ac.uk/
IU Cognitive Science program	http://www.psych.indiana.edu/
23ICAP Home Page	http://www.ucm.es/23ICAP/23icap.html

IP - Instituto de Psicologia	http://www.usp.br/ip/ip.html
Graduate Studies in Psychology	http://www.uvm.edu/~dhowell/PsychAtUVM/Department.html

Publications

ASIS WWW Server - HTML Info Manuals	http://asis01.cern.ch/infohtml/
The Miniatures Page: A WWW Magazine	http://biochem.dental.upenn.edu/Mosaic/bill/tmp.html
The Chronicle of Higher Education — Academe This Week	http://chronicle.merit.edu/
Welcome to Boardwalk Consulting	http://consulting.com/mag.html
UC Berkeley Technical Reports	http://cs-tr.cs.berkeley.edu:80/
Computer Science Technical Report Archive Sites (Searchable)	http://cuiwww.unige.ch/cgi-bin/cstr
Lycos: Documentation	http://fuzine.mt.cs.cmu.edu/mlm/lycos-docs.html
Journalism Resources	http://garnet.msen.com:70/1/vendor/freep/jresource
University of Idaho's Electronic Publications	http://gopher.uidaho.edu/11/e-pubs
Electronic Documents (includes E-Journals & E-Books)	http://gopher.uidaho.edu/11/libraries/e-texts
EJS Home Page	http://gpu.srv.ualberta.ca:8010/home1.htm
Harvest User's Manual	http://harvest.cs.colorado.edu/harvest/doc.html
Harvest Papers	http://harvest.cs.colorado.edu/harvest/papers.html
John C Dvorak's Great Operating System Quiz	http://icemcfd.com/wayne/osquiz.html
CAS Document Delivery Service	http://info.cas.org/Support/dds.html
CityLive! Contents Page [Editor: Kirk Bowe]	http://info.city.ac.uk/citylive/
Kaleidospace	http://kspace.com/KM/spot.sys/Brin/pages/piece9.html
Connectivity and complexity in landscapes and ecosystems	http://life.anu.edu.au/people/dgg/esa93.html
Complexity International	http://life.anu.edu.au:80/ci/ci.html
The Insight Knowledge Network	http://memec.com/
The Art Book - Price List	http://mmm.wwa.com/tab/tabsales.htm
Inquisitor Magazine	http://mosaic.echonyc.com/~xixax/Inquisitor/
Title to be Announced	http://myrddin.chu.cam.ac.uk/cusfs/ttba
Quanta Magazine	http://nearnet.gnn.com/wic/scifi.03.html
The RBSE Spider —Balancing Effective Search Against Web Load	http://rbse.jsc.nasa.gov/eichmann/www94/Spider/Spider.html
Book Reviews	http://sfgate.com/~sfchron/sunbooks/revindex.html
YSN archive	http://snorri.chem.washington.edu/ysarchive/index.html
Internet Standards	http://spird.jos.ec.lu.se/cgi-bin/DocServe-inet-stds
Verbiage Magazine	http://sunsite.unc.edu/boutell/verbiage/index.html
The IBIC Journal: Reviews of Current and Forthcoming Books	http://sunsite.unc.edu/ibic/IBIC-Journal.html
The Bottom Line Archive	http://syy.oulu.fi/tbl.html
NASA Technical Report Server Response Form	http://techreports.larc.nasa.gov/cgi-bin/ntrs-feedback
Welcome to Techweb	http://techweb.cmp.com/ia
Internet Drafts Overview	http://web.nexor.co.uk/public/internet-drafts/id.html
White House Electronic Access FAQ	http://www.acns.nwu.edu/us.gov.online.html
BOOKPORT: Access to Publishers	http://www.bookport.com/source/9505.html
BSDI Hypertext Man Pages	http://www.bsdi.com/bsdi-man/
Books That Work Corporate Overview	http://www.btw.com/corporate/corpback.html
Fashion Page	http://www.charm.net/~jakec/
The Chronicle of Higher Education — Academe This Week	http://www.chronicle.merit.edu/
The Third Eye	http://www.cimtegration.com/ent/multi/movie.htm
McGraw Hill	http://www.cityscape.co.uk/bookshop/mccat.html
The Jargon File 3.1.0	http://www.cnam.fr/Jargon/
HXWZ index	http://www.cnd.org/HXWZ/cm-all.hz.html
XIWT Documents	http://www.cnri.reston.va.us:3000/XIWT/documents/documents.html
CompuBooks Home Page	http://www.compubooks.com/books.html
CONNECT's World Wide Web Server	http://www.connect.org/connect/
Defrauding America	http://www.copi.com/defrauding_america/
IN SARDEGNA VIRTUAL	http://www.crs4.it/~cirio/ISV
Elephant Talk	http://www.cs.man.ac.uk/aig/staff/toby/discipline.html
Peter's E-Texts	http://www.cs.oberlin.edu/students/pjaques/etext/home.html
Fishnet	http://www.cs.washington.edu/homes/pauld/fishnet
Cambridge University Press	http://www.cup.cam.ac.uk/
Penguin Books Ltd	http://www.demon.co.uk/bookshop/pecat.html
Dryden Technical Report Server	http://www.dfrc.nasa.gov/ReportServer/dtrs.html
Elektra Home Page	http://www.digitas.org/
DIGITAL ASHCAN PREVIEWS	http://www.eden.com/comics/comics.html
Magical Blend Magazine Online	http://www.eden.com/magical/main.html
Magazines	http://www.eden.com/zines/zines.html
Other Pubs & Items - EFF	http://www.eff.org/papers/otherpapers.html
Samples of Electronic Publishing	http://www.elpress.com/samples/samples.html
The New Republic	http://www.enews.com:80/magazines/tnr/
The ETEXT Archives	http://www.etext.org/
InterText: The Online Fiction Magazine	http://www.etext.org/Zines/InterText/
Quanta Magazine	http://www.etext.org/Zines/Quanta/
Umneys Last Fall	http://www.eu.net/king/
FutureNet : .net - Subscribe!	http://www.futurenet.co.uk/netmag/Subscribe.html
Aimee'	http://www.halcyon.com/elf/other/Aimee-index.html
Fourth World Documentation Project Home Page	http://www.halcyon.com/FWDP/
HIP Webzine Cover Page	http://www.hip.com/
New Home Community Properties	http://www.homes.com/nhc/new.html
Existing Homes For Sale	http://www.homes.com/realestate/exist.html
Rental Properties	http://www.homes.com/rental/rent.html
Free Homes & Land Magazine	http://www.homes.com/services/hlmag.html
Homes and Land Welcome Page	http://www.homes.com/Welcome.html
RoundBook Publishing Inc.	http://www.human.com/roundbook/index.html
IEEE INSTITUTE Homepage	http://www.ieee.org/ti.html

Additional Sites

Campaign and Elections	http://www.infi.net/camelect/
eye — Toronto's Arts Newspaper	http://WWW.Interlog.COM/eye/
InfoWorld Home Page	http://www.internet.net/stores/infoworld/index.html
Axcess Magazine Home Page	http://www.internex.net/axcess/
Pixel Express Home	http://www.internex.net/pixel/Home.HTML
Realization Reports by Issue	http://www.itd.nrl.navy.mil/ONR/realization_report/rosenblum.toc.html
The Journalism List - new and improved (like cereal).	http://www.jou.ufl.edu/commres/jlist.htm
Journalism and Communications Academic WWW Sites	http://www.jou.ufl.edu/commres/jouwww.htm
Architronic	http://www.kent.edu/Architronic/homepage.html
Overview of the Scholarly Societies Project	http://www.lib.uwaterloo.ca/society/overview.html
MacUser On the World Wide Web	http://www.macuser.ziff.com/~macuser/
Welcome to Gramercy Press!	http://www.mci.com/gramercy/
Macmillan USA Information SuperLibrary (tm)	http://www.mcp.com/
New Riders Publishing Home Page	http://www.mcp.com:80/nrp/
Sams Home Page	http://www.mcp.com:80/sams/
Internet World Home Page	http://www.mecklerweb.com/mags/iw/iwhome.htm
VR World	http://www.mecklerweb.com/vr.htm
Miller Freeman Inc. Home Page	http://www.mfi.com/HomePage.html
Mother Jones	http://www.mojones.com/
Moon Travel Home Page	http://www.moon.com:7000/
Welcome to NandO.net	http://www.nando.net/
The NandO.net Bookstore	http://www.nando.net/bookstore/bookmain.html
Welcome to the News & Observer	http://www.nando.net/nando.html
WoWWW!	http://www.ncb.gov.sg/wired/WoWWW.html
WWW2 Electronic Proceedings	http://www.ncsa.uiuc.edu/SDG/IT94/Proceedings/
Netsurfer Digest Home Page	http://www.netsurf.com/nsd/index.html
O'Reilly Home Page	http://www.ora.com/
ORNL Review - The Lab's Research and Development Magazine	http://www.ornl.gov/ORNL/EINS_Reports/Review/text/home.html
Welcome to Pathfinder	http://www.pathfinder.com/pathfinder/Greet.html
Welcome to PC/Computing	http://www.pc-computing.ziff.com/~pccomp
Welcome to ZD net	http://www.pcweek.ziff.com/
Crash course on writing documents for the Web	http://www.pcweek.ziff.com/~eamonn/crash_course.html
HYPE Electrazine	http://www.phantom.com/~giant/hype.html
Computer Science Technical Reports Archive Sites	http://www.rdt.monash.edu.au/tr/siteslist.html
ANSWERS Cover Page	http://www.service.com/answers/cover.html
ANSI STANDARDS ACTION	http://www.service.com/doccenter/ansi_standards.html
Welcome to Computer Shopper	http://www.shopper.ziff.com/~cshopper/
Other news media on the net	http://www.sii.com/other.home.pages/papers.html
WAIS Access to NASA RECON	http://www.sti.nasa.gov/recon-wais.html
COMPLETE LIST OF SCAN TOPICS	http://www.sti.nasa.gov/scan.html
The Space Between	http://www.tagsys.com/Ads/SpaceBetween
The Net: Your Cyberspace Companion	http://www.thenet-usa.com/
Welcome to ENTERTAINMENT WEEKLY	http://www.timeinc.com/ew/
Inside Pathfinder	http://www.timeinc.com/pathfinder/
World Wide Home Page	http://www.timeinc.com/time/timehomepage.html
St. Pete Times Interactive Media	http://www.times.st-pete.fl.us/
trib.com Home Page	http://www.trib.com/
TRIANGLE ONLINE - Front Cover	http://www.trinet.com/online.html
UpClose Publishing Home Page	http://www.upclose.com/upclose/
VIBEonline V2	http://www.vibe.com/
Ventana Online Home Page...	http://www.vmedia.com/
Van Nostrand Reinhold	http://www.vnr.com/vnr.html
Welcome to Techweb	http://www.wais.com:80/win/
Friedman/Fairfax music book &CD publishers	http://www.webcom.com/~friedman/
Capacity Index	http://www.wimsey.com/Capacity/
The Computer Paper	http://www.wimsey.com/tcp/
International Teletimes Home Page	http://www.wimsey.com/teletimes.root/teletimes_home_page.html
Welcome To Windows Sources on the Web	http://www.winsources.ziff.com/~wsources/
Welcome to ZD net	http://www.ziff.com/
MacWEEK Home Page	http://www.ziff.com/~macweek/
PC MAGAZINE on the WEB	http://www.ziff.com/~pcmag/
PC Week	http://www.ziff.com/~pcweek/
Inter@ctive Week Home Page	http://zcias3.ziff.com/%7Eintweek/

Radio

The CBC Radio Trial	http://debra.dgbt.doc.ca/cbc/cbc.html
WUOT Program Guide	http://denali.cti-pet.com/WUOT_docs/DECEMBER.html
The KUCIA home page	http://kuhttp.cc.ukans.edu/cwis/organizations/kucia/kucia_home.html
Internet Talk Radio Travelling Circus	http://town.hall.org/circus/circus.html
Internet Talk Radio Anonymous FTP Archives	http://town.hall.org/radio/radio-sites.html
N0ARY/BBS	http://www.arasmith.com/n0ary/index.html
Laporte on Computers	http://www.ccnet.com/laporte/
Census Radio Broadcast Service	http://www.census.gov/org/pub_relations/pub_info/Radio/WOA.html
Internet Multicasting Service	http://www.cmf.nrl.navy.mil/radio/radio.html
Dr. Tomorrow Radio Show	http://www.nas.com/~drtom/radio.html
NPR Online	http://www.npr.org/
AM/FM	http://www.tecc.co.uk/public/tqm/amfm
Bailey Broadcasting	http://www.trib.com/bbs/bailey.html
RadioScope	http://www.trib.com/bbs/radioscope.html
The University of Kentucky - WUKY	http://www.uky.edu/WUKY/wuky.html
Welcome to the WVEC-TV home page.	http://www.wvec-tv13.com/wvec/

WZLX 100.7 Home Page   http://www.wzlx.com/wzlx/

Recreation

Mountain Biking   http://actlab.rtf.utexas.edu/~captain/mt.bike.html
Stanford University Footbag Club   http://gregorio.stanford.edu/footbag/
Upcoming Footbag Events   http://gregorio.stanford.edu/footbag/events.html
Stanford University Footbag Club   http://gregorio.stanford.edu/footbag/SUFC.html
Guide to the Gear   http://io.datasys.swri.edu/Gear.html
Cycling   http://sunwww.informatik.uni-tuebingen.de:8080/sport/rad/rad.html
Australian Scouting E-Mail Addresses   http://turnpike.net/metro/ahoneybu/emailadd.html
Adventuring/IGLOO Welcome Page   http://www.access.digex.net/~erewhon
Missouri Flyfishing Page   http://www.agron.missouri.edu/flyfishing
Footbag Clubs & Leagues   http://www.cup.hp.com/~footbag/clubs.html
Information on the Sport of Footbag   http://www.cup.hp.com/~footbag/info.html
Board? - The European Snowboarding Network   http://www.earth.ox.ac.uk/~andyc/
Cornell Organizational Recreational and Activities Web Servers   http://www.englib.cornell.edu/otherwww/raservers.html
Avid Explorer Home Page   http://www.explore.com/
THE ISFIT INTERNATIONAL WWW NODE   http://www.idt.unit.no:80/~isfit/
California Kayak Friends   http://www.intelenet.com/clubs/ckf/
Eco-Adventures Australia   http://www.internet-cafe.com/eco-adv-oz/
MGD Tap Room   http://www.mgdtaproom.com/
Canadian Himalayan Expeditions   http://www.netpart.com/che/brochure.html
Colorado Fishing   http://www.ofps.ucar.edu/~john/ff/co_ff.html
Arctic Adventours Inc.   http://www.oslonett.no/html/adv/AA/AA.html
Welcome to Wild Dunes   http://www.persimmon.com/WildDunes/
Outdoor Action Program Home Page   http://www.princeton.edu/~rcurtis/oa.html
Yellowstone Outdoorsman   http://www.srv.net:8001/outdoors.html
Starwave Corporation   http://www.starwave.com/
Pacific Offshore Divers Inc.   http://www.thesphere.com/PODI/
New Mexico Flyfishing   http://www.unm.edu/~datkins/flyfish/flyfish.html
Orienteering and Rogaining Home Page   http://www2.aos.princeton.edu/rdslater/orienteering/
Northern California Fly Fishing   http://www2.ecst.csuchico.edu:80/~jschlich/Flyfish/flyfish.html
Mountain Biking   http://xenon.stanford.edu/~rsf/mtn-bike.html
Human Powered Vehicle (HPV) archive   http://zippy.sonoma.edu:70/1/HPV/

Religion

CERN/ANU - Buddhist Studies WWW VL   http://coombs.anu.edu.au/WWWVL-Buddhism.html
Religion and Philosophy   http://dewey.lib.ncsu.edu/disciplines/religion.html
University of Virginia KJV Bible Search   http://etext.virginia.edu/kjv.query.html
The World-Wide Web Virtual Library: Secular Issues   http://freethought.tamu.edu/
Religion Page   http://hakatai.mcli.dist.maricopa.edu/smc/ml/religion.html
Christian Resource List   http://saturn.colorado.edu:8080/Christian/list.html
Dead Sea — Introduction   http://sunsite.unc.edu/expo/deadsea.scrolls.exhibit/world.scrolls.html
Judaism and Jewish Resources   http://www.acm.uiuc.edu/signet/JHSI/judaism.html
The WWW Bible Gateway   http://www.calvin.edu/cgi-bin/bible
Christian Resources on the Internet (1 of 3)   http://www.calvin.edu/christian-resources.html
Guide to Christian Literature on the Internet   http://www.calvin.edu/pw.html
Catholic Resources on the Net   http://www.cs.cmu.edu:8001/Web/People/spok/catholic.html
ICLnet Primer   http://www.iclnet.org/pub/resources/iclnet-primer.html
Pilot Online Religion   http://www.infi.net/pilot/religion.html
The Episcopal Church of St. Matthew   http://www.ior.com/~eeclarke/stmatts.html
Religion in England Overview   http://www.iris.brown.edu/iris/RIE/Religion_OV.html
Jews for Jesus Home Page   http://www.jews-for-jesus.org/
JBE Home Page   http://www.psu.edu/jbe/jbe.html
The Orthodox Christian Page in Europe   http://www.york.ac.uk/~em101/Orthodox.html

Schools

Frank J. Seiler Research Laboratory Web Server   http://aces.usafa.af.mil/
CSUWEB Index of Services   http://csugrad.cs.vt.edu/
Welcome to CUI   http://cuiwww.unige.ch/
Global Schoolhouse - La Costa Heights Elementary http://k12.cnidr.org/gsh/schools/ca/lch/lch.html
Brisbane Elementary School District   http://tcomeng.com/cities/brisbane/SchoolDist/SchoolsIndex.html
HotList of K-12 Internet School Sites   http://toons.cc.ndsu.nodak.edu/~sackmann/k12.html
African Studies WWW (U. Penn)   http://www.african.upenn.edu/African_Studies/AS.html
Documents of Interest   http://www.bev.net/education/schools/admin/interest.html
American Universities   http://www.clas.ufl.edu/CLAS/american-universities.html
Claremont Community Info Page   http://www.cusd.claremont.edu/www/academics/CUSD_info.html
FYI RFC #1578-Schools and Internet   http://www.cusd.claremont.edu/www/people/rmuir/rfc1578.html
Hogskolan i Karlskrona/Ronneby   http://www.hk-r.se/
Illinois Institute of Technology   http://www.iit.edu/
J. Stefan Institute Information System   http://www.ijs.si/
ILR School Home Page   http://www.ilr.cornell.edu/
IMSA Home Page   http://www.imsa.edu/
Pagina Principal de INBio   http://www.inbio.ac.cr/
Serveur WWW de l'INSA de Lyon   http://www.insa-lyon.fr/
Jackson Public School District   http://www.jackson.k12.ms.us/
Frazier Mountain High School   http://www.kern.com/frazier.html
Kyoto Institute of Technology Home Page   http://www.kit.ac.jp/
Valkommen till KTH   http://www.kth.se/
Kurume Home Page   http://www.kurume-it.ac.jp/kurume-it_home.html

477

Additional Sites

BAKA DOJYO KANNAI(Amiga IFF)	http://www.kyushu-id.ac.jp/kid/free/BAKADOU/Bakadou2.html
Kyutech Home Page	http://www.kyutech.ac.jp/
POLI Homepage	http://www.lsi.usp.br/poli/epoli.html
Lunds Tekniska Högskola	http://www.lth.se/
Monta Vista High School - Information	http://www.mvhs.edu/infomenu.html
The Internet Project at Monta Vista	http://www.mvhs.edu/tech/internet.html
Branson School	http://www.nbn.com/~branson
Nagoya Institute of Technology	http://www.nitech.ac.jp/index-e.html
Plugged In Home Page	http://www.pluggedin.org/
Penn State	http://www.psu.edu/
ULUDAG WWW Service	http://www.uludag.edu.tr/
Norges tekniske høgskole	http://www.unit.no/NTH
USAF Academy Home Page	http://www.usafa.af.mil/
Escola do Futuro	http://www.usp.br/futuro/futuro.html
Finger Gateway	http://www.utah.edu/cgi-bin/finger

Science

Flight Simulation at LaRC	http://bigben.larc.nasa.gov/fltsim/fltsim.html
FDA Approved Animal Drug Data Base	http://borg.lib.vt.edu/ejournals/vetfda.html
Aeronautics Consolidated Supercomputing Facility (ACSF)	http://cabsparc.larc.nasa.gov:80/ACSF/
ASAPWeb - ASAP Information and services	http://coombs.anu.edu.au/SpecialProj/ASAP/asap_information.html
Welcome to the Community of Science!	http://cos.gdb.org/work/info/cosinfo.html
What's new at CTIO	http://ctios2.ctio.noao.edu/neat/neat.html
The World-Wide Web Virtual Library: Electrical Engineering	http://epims1.gsfc.nasa.gov/engineering/ee.html
Collisions: When Two Tennis Balls Collide and a Bowling Ball Flies Out	http://fnnews.fnal.gov/collisions.html
LLNL High Energy Physics Group	http://gem1.llnl.gov:80/
OU College of Geosciences	http://geowww.gcn.uoknor.edu/
Yale University Center for Systems Science	http://giskard.eng.yale.edu/welcom.html
The Metaphysics Research Lab Home Page	http://mally.stanford.edu/
MIT-LNS Home Page	http://marie.mit.edu/
Federally-Funded Research in the U.S.	http://medoc.gdb.org/best/fed-fund.html
NAIC.NASA.GOV Web Information Available	http://naic.nasa.gov:80/
Archives Servies of the GSFC SSDOO	http://ndadsb.gsfc.nasa.gov:80/
MSTB Home Page	http://ndb1.larc.nasa.gov:80/
Science	http://nearnet.gnn.com/wic/sci.toc.html
NASA Ames Biocomputation Center	http://neuron.arc.nasa.gov:80/
MMRRCC Home Page	http://nmrsg.biophys.upenn.edu:8080/
Rapid Development Lab (RDL)	http://ollie.jsc.nasa.gov:80/
NASA Goddard Space Flight Center Physical OceanographyGroup	http://oraac.gsfc.nasa.gov:80/
University of Oregon Materials Science Institute	http://oregon.uoregon.edu/~lbiggs/msi.html
POC Lab MacHTTP Server	http://pekkel.uthscsa.edu/default.html
The Hopkins Ultraviolet Telescope	http://praxis.pha.jhu.edu/hut.html
MIT Computational Aerospace Sciences Laboratory	http://raphael.mit.edu/casl.html
SAVIAC	http://saviac.usae.bah.com/
NASA/GSFC Space Data and Computing Division	http://sdcd.gsfc.nasa.gov:80/
SeaWiFS Project	http://seawifs.gsfc.nasa.gov/scripts/SEAWIFS.html
Assessment Technology Branch	http://shemesh.larc.nasa.gov:80/
NASA Spacelink	http://spacelink.msfc.nasa.gov:80/
PROJECTS CONTROLS BRANCH	http://spocls.larc.nasa.gov:80/
NASA Space Shuttle Small Payloads Info	http://sspp.gsfc.nasa.gov:80/
National Science Foundation World Wide Web Server	http://stis.nsf.gov/
EROS home page	http://sun1.cr.usgs.gov:80/
Brookhaven National Laboratory Home Page	http://suntid.bnl.gov:8080/
The NASA JSC Automation Robotics and Simulation Division	http://tommy.jsc.nasa.gov:80/
Subway	http://ucmp1.berkeley.edu/subway.html
Center for Environmental Health Sciences	http://web.mit.edu/afs/athena/org/c/cehs/www/index.html
UT: Department of Information Science	http://web.yl.is.s.u-tokyo.ac.jp/is/is.html
WIS home page	http://wissgi.weizmann.ac.il/
Japanese Dairy Cattle Improvement Program	http://ws4.niai.affrc.go.jp/dairy/dairy.html
LLNL Energy Home Page	http://www-energy.llnl.gov/
NIF Home Page	http://www-phys.llnl.gov/X_Div/nif.html
Domestic Animal Endocrinology	http://www.ag.auburn.edu/dae/dae.html
Women and Minorities in Science and Engineering	http://www.ai.mit.edu/people/ellens/Gender/wom_and_min.html
Alberta Research Council	http://www.arc.ab.ca:80/
NASA Ames Research Center Home Page	http://www.arc.nasa.gov:80/
AOT Welcome	http://www.atdiv.lanl.gov:80/
AWI Welcome Page (External)	http://www.awi-bremerhaven.de/
Welcome to Sandia National Laboratories California Site	http://www.ca.sandia.gov/
Sleeping Solutions Homepage	http://www.catalog.com/sleep/joann
CEBAF Information	http://www.cebaf.gov:3000/
Page d'accueil du CERT ONERA	http://www.cert.fr/
The Kiosk - Home Page	http://WWW.ciesin.org/kiosk/home.html
Yale Science & Engineering Computing Facility	http://www.cis.yale.edu/secf-index.html
THE EARTH SYSTEM SCIENCE CENTER	http://www.essc.psu.edu/
Exploratorium Home Page	http://www.exploratorium.edu/
Instituto de Fisica - Facultad de Ciencias	http://www.fisica.edu.uy/
Purdue Food Science Home Page	http://www.foodsci.purdue.edu/
FSS HOME PAGE	http://www.fss.lanl.gov/
Newton Horace Winchell School of Earth Sciences WWW	http://www.geo.umn.edu/
DST Bologna	http://www.geomin.unibo.it/
GFDL's Home Page	http://www.gfdl.gov:80/

NOAA Geosciences Laboratory	http://www.grdl.noaa.gov:80/
NASA Information Services via World Wide Web	http://www.gsfc.nasa.gov/
GSI home page	http://www.gsi.de:80/
West Virginia University Information	http://www.hsc.wvu.edu/wvu.html
University of Washington Health Sciences Center	http://www.hslib.washington.edu/
ICASE Technical Report Server (ITRS)	http://www.icase.edu/docs/library/itrs.html
Institute for Photogrammetry / University of Stuttgart	http://www.ifp.uni-stuttgart.de:80/
IHPVA WWW server	http://www.ihpva.org/
Welcome to IIASA	http://www.iiasa.ac.at/Welcome.html
IIS Home Page	http://www.iis.u-tokyo.ac.jp/
ISPA Home Page	http://www.ispa.fsu.edu/
JAIST Home Page	http://www.jaist.ac.jp/
NASA Jet Propulsion Laboratory	http://www.jpl.nasa.gov:80/
NASA/Johnson Space Center Home Page	http://www.jsc.nasa.gov/jsc/home.html
NASA/Kennedy Space Center Home Page	http://www.ksc.nasa.gov/ksc.html
Los Alamos National Laboratory	http://www.lanl.gov/
LBL World Wide Web Home Page	http://www.lbl.gov/LBL.html
NASA Lewis Research Center Home Page	http://www.lerc.nasa.gov:80/
Eli Lilly and Company	http://www.lilly.com/
LLNL Home Page	http://www.llnl.gov/
LLNL Disclaimer	http://www.llnl.gov/disclaimer.html
Lockheed Missiles & Space Company Inc.	http://www.lmsc.lockheed.com/
University of Missouri-Columbia Health Sciences Services and Programs	http://www.miaims.missouri.edu/
NAS Home Page	http://www.nas.nasa.gov:80/
NCSA Digital Gallery CD-ROM- Science Theater	http://www.ncsa.uiuc.edu/SDG/DigitalGallery/DG_science_theater.html
NERSC WWW Home Page	http://www.nersc.gov:80/
Neuroscience FSU Home Page	http://www.neuro.fsu.edu/homepage.htm
NOAA National Oceanographic Data Center (NODC) Home Page	http://www.nodc.noaa.gov:80/
National Renewable Energy Laboratory	http://www.nrel.gov/
National Science Foundation World Wide Web Server	http://www.nsf.gov/
OPTICAL SCIENCES:	http://www.osa.org/osapage/osd.html
PHOTONICS	http://www.osa.org/osapage/phd.html
QUANTUM ELECTRONICS	http://www.osa.org/osapage/qed.html
Pacific Northwest Laboratory	http://www.pnl.gov:2080/
Gateway to NZ science	http://www.rsnz.govt.nz/
Sandia National Laboratories	http://www.sandia.gov/
SCI: Homepage	http://www.sci.kun.nl/
Space Environment Laboratory Index Page	http://www.sel.bldrdoc.gov:80/
SPIE HOME PAGE	http://www.spie.org/
Overview of the Cornell Theory Center	http://www.tc.cornell.edu/ctctour.html
U of Texas Houston	http://www.uth.tmc.edu/
UTIA's WWW home page	http://www.utia.cas.cz:80/
NCSU COLLEGE OF VETERINARY MEDICINE	http://www2.ncsu.edu/ncsu/cvm/cvmhome.html
Organizations Encouraging Women in Science and Engineering	http://xerxes.nas.edu:70/1/cwse

Software

UNIXhelp for users	http://alpha.acast.nova.edu/UNIXhelp/TOP_.html
Network Applications WWW Index	http://browneyes.ucs.indiana.edu/
Browser Requirements	http://cio.cisco.com/browser.html
Welcome to Boardwalk Consulting	http://consulting.com/software.html
DVAL Visualization Tools	http://dval-www.larc.nasa.gov/software/overview.html
EMWAC's Internet Toolchest for Windows NT	http://emwac.ed.ac.uk/html/internet_toolchest/top.html
EINet MacWeb	http://galaxy.einet.net/EINet/MacWeb/MacWebHome.html
Getting the Harvest Software	http://harvest.cs.colorado.edu/harvest/gettingsoftware.html
Netscape Navigator FTP and Mirror Sites	http://home.netscape.com/info/how-to-get-it.html
Server Scripts	http://hoohoo.ncsa.uiuc.edu/docs/info/Scripts.html
XRunner	http://ibd.ar.com/Catalogs/Mercury_Interactive/X-WinRunner.html
Word Processor Filters	http://info.cern.ch/hypertext/WWW/Tools/Word_proc_filters.html
Bridesmaid for Windows	http://infolane.com/infolane/simply/bride.html
SGML TagWizard	http://infolane.com/nice/nice.html
Mailing List Compilers	http://mainsail.com/lcompile.htm
rec.games.mud Frequently Asked/Answered Questions	http://math.okstate.edu/~jds/mudfaqs.html
XShell Evaluation Request Form	http://maxwell.expersoft.com/eval_request.html
Welcome to the world of Netscape 1.1 final release	http://mistral.enst.fr/netscape/
HelpDesk brochure	http://none.coolware.com/tech/bullseye.html
TinyMUD to HTML converter demo	http://pine.theory.cs.yale.edu:4201/mud2html/mud2html.html
Versatile Virtual Vending Specification Sheet	http://rainer.bnt.com/vvvspec.html
RBSE Program	http://rbse.jsc.nasa.gov/eichmann/rbse.html
WWW Virtual Library - Software Engineering	http://rbse.jsc.nasa.gov/virt-lib/soft-eng.html
RAFOS Float Setup Software V1.9	http://taygeta.oc.nps.navy.mil/setup.html
The DOS Internet Kit	http://tbone.biol.scarolina.edu/~dean/kit/kit.html
The XFree86-benchmarks Survey	http://thumbtack.bevc.blacksburg.va.us/xbench/
About CUSI	http://web.nexor.co.uk/public/cusi/doc/distribution
The Macintosh Software Catalog	http://web.nexor.co.uk/public/mac/archive/welcome.html
Microsoft Windows NT Users Group	http://www.actioninc.com/winntug.htm
Concurrent Versions System	http://www.aggregate.com/~zoo/cvs.html
Apriori Extensions & Add-On Products	http://www.answer.com/answer/consulting/extensions.html
AUGment Home Page	http://www.answer.com/augment/augment.html
ANSWER Educational Discount Program	http://www.answer.com/univ_program/program.html
Micro Star Software	http://www.awa.com/microstar
The BE Software Company Home Page	http://www.besoft.com/summary.html/

Additional Sites

I-Comm: Graphical Browser For Shell VAX & Freenet Account	http://www.best.com/~icomm/icomm.htm
Beverly Hills Software	http://www.bhs.com/
Blue Sky Software Corp. World Wide Web Home Page	http://www.blue-sky.com/
imageABLE Document Management Software	http://www.bluebird.com/imageable/
InternetWorks Home Page	http://www.booklink.com/
Cross-Platform Resources	http://www.bristol.com/Bibliography/bibliography.html
HyperHelp/Xprinter Demos	http://www.bristol.com/Products/demos.html
Books That Work Applets Table of Contents	http://www.btw.com/applets/toc.html
PROTEIN EXPERT	http://www.camsci.com/others/proteinexpert/proteinexpert.html
epsConverter 1.1	http://www.camsci.com/others/shareware/epsconverter.html
Intuit Page 1	http://www.careermosaic.com/cm/intuit/intuit1.html
hytelnet	http://www.cc.ukans.edu/hytelnet_html/START.TXT.html
Lynx Users Guide v2.3	http://www.cc.ukans.edu/lynx_help/Lynx_users_guide.html
Distributed Architecture	http://www.ceintl.com/EnSight/distibuted.html
EnSight	http://www.ceintl.com/EnSight/Overview.html
Welcome to ClarisWeb	http://www.claris.com/
REDO project archive	http://www.comlab.ox.ac.uk/archive/redo.html
DTP Internet Jumplist	http://www.cs.purdue.edu/homes/gwp/dtp/dtp.html
CU_HTML.DOT (Version 1.5.3)	http://www.cuhk.hk/csc/cu_html/cu_html.html
Cygnus Support Information Gallery	http://www.cygnus.com/
About Cygnus Support	http://www.cygnus.com/cygnus/about-cygnus.html
What's GNU? GNU's Not Unix!!	http://www.cygnus.com/cygnus/about-gnu.html
Sourceware Solutions	http://www.cygnus.com/cygnus/sourceware.html
Department of Computer Science: Icon Browser	http://www.di.unipi.it/iconbrowser/icons.html
DigiCash ecash - ecash home page	http://www.digicash.com/ecash/ecash-home.html
Getstats Documentation	http://www.eit.com/software/getstats/getstats.html
Lice - A Delegation Protocol	http://www.epilogue.com/~dab/delegation-protocol.html
Cica and Simtel Searches	http://www.fagg.uni-lj.si/cica.html
Shase Virtual Shareware Library	http://www.fagg.uni-lj.si/SHASE/
Folio Corporation Home Page	http://www.folio.com/
FreeBSD Home Page	http://www.freebsd.org/
Welcome to Fry Multimedia!	http://www.frymulti.com/
EURASE - European Associated Software Engeneering	http://www.germany.eu.net/EURASE/
Global Network Navigator Home Page	http://www.gnn.com/
Traveling Software's Home Page	http://www.halcyon.com/travsoft/homepage.html
MOMspider — Distribution Information	http://www.ics.uci.edu/WebSoft/MOMspider/
ISSI Home Page	http://www.issi.com/issi/issi-home_page.html
InterWorking Labs Home Page	http://www.IWL.com/IWL/
Jandel Scientific Software Home Page	http://www.jandel.com/
Welcome to the Linux Home Page	http://www.linux.org/
LabSOURCE	http://www.llnl.gov/labsrc/labsource.html
CVS INDEX	http://www.loria.fr/~molli/cvs-index.html
Lotus on the Web	http://www.lotus.com/
Maximized Software	http://www.maximized.com/
NETCOM On-Line Communication Services Inc	http://www.mcom.com/
Netscape Navigator FTP and Mirror Sites	http://www.mcom.com/info/how-to-get-it.html
Microsoft Windows NT Server	http://www.microsoft.com/pages/bussys/ntserver/nts10000.htm
NaviSoft's WWW Home Page	http://www.navisoft.com/
InfoNow Home Page	http://www.net.effects.com/InfoNow.html
NetCruiser Homeport	http://www.netcom.com/netcom/cruiser.html
NetManage World Wide Web Server	http://www.netmanage.com/
BorderWare Home Page	http://www.netpart.com/janus
Welcome to Netscape	http://www.netscape.com/
Multi-Localization enhancement of NCSA Mosaic for X 2.4	http://www.ntt.jp/Mosaic-l10n/README.html
Welcome To Oracle	http://www.oracle.com/
Pacific Animated Imaging	http://www.pai-west.com/
BenchWorks Home Page	http://www.parasoft.com/bws.html
Express Home Page	http://www.parasoft.com/express.html
F90 Home Page	http://www.parasoft.com/f90.html
Insure++ Home Page	http://www.parasoft.com/insure.html
Personal Library Software	http://www.pls.com/
Quarterdeck Home Page	http://www.qdeck.com/
Network/system administration products	http://www.qualix.com/product/network/Welcome.html
Productivity Application	http://www.qualix.com/product/productivity/Welcome.html
RealAudio Homepage	http://www.RealAudio.com/
Rocket Science Home Page	http://www.rocketsci.com/
html-helper-mode	http://www.santafe.edu/~nelson/tools
Applications Software	http://www.sdsc.edu/1/SDSC/Apps_SW/apps_sw.html
Software Engineering Institute Information Server	http://www.sei.cmu.edu/
Patch Services page.	http://www.service.digital.com/html/patch_service.html
software.net home page	http://www.software.net/
SPRY Home Page	http://www.spry.com/
Mosaic In A Box Home Page	http://www.spry.com/mbox/
Spyglass Home Page	http://www.spyglass.com/
SoftQuad Inc.'s Welcome Page	http://www.sq.com/
Getting HotMetaL by FTP	http://www.sq.com/hm-ftp.htm
ARPA STARS Program	http://www.stars.ballston.paramax.com/
Mindware: The Human Self Improvement Software: Home Page	http://www.systemv.com/mindware/index.html
Cornell Theory Center Overview	http://www.tc.cornell.edu/ctcIntro.html
Corporate Software's Technology Exchange	http://www.tech-board.com/tbot/
Banner Bits	http://www.uidaho.edu/banner

Chimera	http://www.unlv.edu/chimera
Public Hearings on Software Patents	http://www.uspto.gov/hearings.html
Vidya Media Ventures	http://vidya.com/
WWW Client Software products	http://www.w3.org/hypertext/WWW/Clients
World-Wide Web server software	http://www.w3.org/hypertext/WWW/Daemon/Overview.html
WINGate Technologies Home Page	http://www.wingate.com/
Winserve - Windows Internet Server	http://www.winserve.com/
Welcom Software Technology	http://www.wst.com/index.html
X Consortium welcome document	http://www.x.org/
Microlib/Mac Software Archive	http://wwwhost.cc.utexas.edu/cc/microlib-mac/main.html
Unix Resources	http://wwwhost.cc.utexas.edu/cc/services/unix/index.html

Sports

Men's Tennis Rankings and Results	http://access.digex.net/~jd/tennis.html
International Aerobatics Club Home Page	http://adswww.harvard.edu/IAC/iac_homepg.html
MITSA - Home Page	http://adswww.harvard.edu/MITSA/mitsa_homepg.html
Entertainment:Sports	http://akebono.stanford.edu/yahoo/Entertainment/Sports/
Entertainment:Sports:Golf	http://akebono.stanford.Edu/yahoo/Entertainment/Sports/Golf/
STRETCHING AND FLEXIBILITY - Table of Contents	http://archie.ac.il/papers/rma/stretching_toc.html
Welcome to Boardwalk Consulting	http://consulting.com/sports.html
Ski Web - Northern California & Nevada - Contents	http://diamond.sierra.net/SkiWeb/sierras/sw_reg01.html
Golf Archives	http://dunkin.princeton.edu/.golf
Enternet Skateboarding Table Of Contents	http://enternet.com/skate/skate.html
AMI News Recreation	http://garnet.msen.com:70/1/vendor/aminews/
Ski Reports	http://garnet.msen.com:70/11/vendor/aminews/ski-reports
Harvard Men's Swimming and Diving	http://hcs.harvard.edu/~menswim/
Soccer-Tables	http://iamwww.unibe.ch/~ftiwww/Sonstiges/Tabellen/Eindex.html
Climbing High	http://ike.engr.washington.edu/aixcell/climb.html
Ford Australian Open Information Page	http://insane.apana.org.au/~jsimmons/ozopen.html
PROFESSIONAL HOCKEY SERVER	http://maxwell.uhh.hawaii.edu/hockey/teams.html
Inline skating	http://morra.et.tudelft.nl/~bonzo/inline/inline.html
Cycling the Pacific Northwest	http://northcoast.com/~ebarnett/cyclepnw.htm
World Wide Web of Sports — Table Tennis (Ping-Pong)	http://peacock.tnjc.edu.tw/sports.html
Cricket	http://pipkin.lut.ac.uk/~ben/Cricket/index.html
The Running Page	http://polar.pica.army.mil/people/drears/running/running.html
View an Ultimate Pickup List	http://radon.gas.uug.arizona.edu/~hko/pickup/pickup1.html
rec.sport.disc FAQ (1/2)	http://radon.uug.arizona.edu/~hko/faq/faq1.html
The Frisbee Page	http://raptor.sccs.swarthmore.edu/~dalewis/frisbee.html
Southern Utah Golf Courses	http://sci.dixie.edu/StGeorge/Golf/golf.html
Northern California & Nevada Ski Conditions	http://sierra.net/SkiWeb/sierras/cond01.html
International Soccer Server	http://sotka.cs.tut.fi/riku/soccer.html
The Running Page	http://sunsite.unc.edu/drears/running/running.html
Steffi Graf FAQ	http://sunwww.informatik.uni-tuebingen.de:8080/sport/dtennis/graf.html
J-League Forum	http://syrinx.gen.u-tokyo.ac.jp/j-league/
Formula 1 Page off-line	http://www.abekrd.co.uk/Formula1/
America's Cup On-Line	http://www.ac95.org/
Aladdin Sailing Index	http://www.aladdin.co.uk/sihe/
Cleveland Sports	http://www.apk.net/sports
Go Dodger Blue	http://www.armory.com/~lew/sports/baseball/dodgers.html
Rec.Sports.Soccer - The WEB Page	http://www.atm.ch.cam.ac.uk/sports/
The World-Wide Web Virtual Library: Sport	http://www.atm.ch.cam.ac.uk/sports/sports.html
Saint-James Sportfishing Adventures	http://www.boatnet.com/boatnet/charter/Saint-James/STJames.html
NFL Playoff Races	http://www.cacs.usl.edu:80/~jkj/nfl/
Tennis Rankings	http://www.cdf.toronto.edu/DCS/FUN/ATP.html
ATP/WTA Doubles	http://www.cdf.toronto.edu/DCS/FUN/double.html
Tennis Rankings	http://www.cdf.toronto.edu/DCS/FUN/WTA.html
Boris Becker FAQ	http://www.cdf.toronto.edu/personal/chris/tennis/becker.html
GOODWILL GAMES	http://www.com/goodwill/index.html
The World Wide Web Virtual Library: Rowing	http://www.comlab.ox.ac.uk/archive/other/rowing.html
The Disc Golf Web Page	http://www.cqs.washington.edu/~josh/discgolf.html
BYU Sports	http://www.cs.byu.edu/sports/sports.html#basketball
The National Football League (NFL) Info Web	http://www.cs.cmu.edu:8001/afs/cs/user/vernon/www/nfl.html
World Skiing	http://www.cs.colorado.edu/homes/mcbryan/public_html/bb/ski/ski.html
Disc Golf informational sheet	http://www.cs.iastate.edu/~korver/discgolf.html
UPA Manual of Tournament Formats	http://www.cs.rochester.edu/u/ferguson/disc/upa-formats/
Sports Schedules As You Like 'Em	http://www.cs.rochester.edu/u/ferguson/schedules/
UPA Rules of Ultimate Ninth Edition	http://www.cs.rochester.edu/u/ferguson/ultimate/ultimate-rules.html
NHL Schedule	http://www.cs.ubc.ca/nhl
J. LEAGUE home page	http://www.dentsu.co.jp/J-LEAGUE/
DISCscribe Ltd. Home Page	http://www.discribe.ca/
Climbing Hardware	http://www.dtek.chalmers.se/Climbing/Hardware/index.html
The Climbing Archive!	http://www.dtek.chalmers.se/Climbing/index.html
REC.SPORT.SOCCER's guide to the FA Premiership	http://www.dur.ac.uk/~dma1jas/premiership.html
Korfball	http://www.earth.ox.ac.uk/~geoff/
The Racer Archive	http://www.eng.hawaii.edu/Contribs/carina/ra.home.page.html
The Controversial Salary Cap!	http://www.frymulti.com/thecap/
Palouse Parachute Club's Home Page	http://www.fsr.com/~bmoore/ppc.html
GolfData Web	http://www.gdol.com/
GEMS - IBIC	http://www.gems.com/ibic/
J.P.'s Fishing Page	http://www.geo.mtu.edu/~jsuchosk/fish/fishpage
NBA Pool via the WWW	http://www.hal.com/~markg/NBA/

481

Additional Sites

Rec.moto/DoD Home Page V2.1154f	http://www.halcyon.com/moto/rec_moto.html
The Referee's Page	http://www.iceonline.com/home/billc4/referee.html
Powder Hound Ski Report	http://www.icw.com/skireport.html
FENCING	http://www.ii.uib.no/~arild/fencing.html
Roadracing World & Motorcycle Technology	http://www.imat.com/rrwmt/index.html
Pilot Online Sports	http://www.infi.net/pilot/sports.html
Infosphere - Home Page	http://www.infosphere.com/
U.S.A. National Team Volleyball	http://www.jovanet.com/forum/vball/vball.html
WRC Infosystem	http://www.jyu.fi/~pakar/
Colorado's Front Range Cycling Home Page	http://www.lance.colostate.edu/~ja740467/bike/frbike.html
Laser WWW Information Server	http://www.law.indiana.edu/misc/laser.html
Nagano Olympic Winter Games	http://www.linc.or.jp/Nagano/index.html
Professional Wrestling Server	http://www.luc.edu/~mlong/wrestling.html
Seattle Mariners Home Plate	http://www.mariners.org/
The Tennis Server Homepage	http://www.mountain.net/Pinnacle/Racquet_Workshop/Tennis.html
The Baseball Server	http://www.nando.net/baseball/bbmain.html
Welcome to NandO X	http://www.nando.net/nandox.html
The Baseball Server	http://www.nando.net/newsroom/baseball/strike/george.html
Strike at a glance	http://www.nando.net/newsroom/baseball/strike/glance.html
The Baseball Server	http://www.nando.net/newsroom/baseball/strike/minors.html
The Sports Server	http://www.nando.net/sptsserv.html
The Internet Squash Federation	http://www.ncl.ac.uk/~npb/
Professional Basketball Server	http://www.netgen.com/sis/NBA/NBA.html
Professional Football Server	http://www.netgen.com/sis/NFL/NFL.html
Professional Hockey Server	http://www.netgen.com/sis/NHL/NHL.html
NRA-ILA Jump-off Page	http://www.nra.org/NRA-WWW-Server.html
Aquanaut	http://www.opal.com/aquanaut
Peter Yee's SCUBA archive at NASA-Ames	http://www.opal.com/aquanaut/pyee.html
Pittsburgh Vintage Grand Prix Association Electronic News	http://www.pitt.edu/~timq/
Club Mistral	http://www.sccsi.com/Club_Mistral/welcome.html
Mistral Welcome Page	http://www.sccsi.com/Mistral/mistral_welcome.html
Robby Naish	http://www.sccsi.com/Mistral/naish.html
Windsurfing Sports	http://www.sccsi.com/Windsurfing/shop.html
Sport: Skating lists	http://www.twi.tudelft.nl/Local/sports/skating.html
USL Basketball	http://www.usl.edu/Athletics/Basketball/
Las Vegas Sports Page	http://www.vegas.com/sports/sports.html
Dave Cheeseman's Windsurfing Page	http://www.vmark.co.uk/~dwc/windsurf/
Whistler resort on the World Wide Web	http://www.whistler.net/

482

Technology

NASA/MOD AIS Security Engineering Team	http://aset.rsoc.rockwell.com/
QUT World Wide Web Home Page	http://barley.qut.edu.au/qut_home_page.html
Backgrounds Data Center Home Page	http://bradbury.nrl.navy.mil/
IT Program	http://curry.edschool.Virginia.EDU:80/~insttech/ITpgm/
ENTERTAINMENT TECHNOLOGY CENTER HOME PAGE	http://cwis.usc.edu/dept/etc/
MINT WWW Server	http://dec2.cems.umn.edu/mint.htm
Delphi Welcome Page	http://delinfo.cern.ch/Delphi/Welcome.html
Welcome to Hashimoto Laboratory	http://dfs.iis.u-tokyo.ac.jp/
DoD Information Systems Technology Insertion	http://disa11.disa.atd.net/
Technology Education Home Page	http://ed1.eng.ohio-state.edu/
IST Home Page Indiana University	http://education.indiana.edu/isthome.html
The Asian Institute of Technology Home Page	http://emailhost.ait.ac.th/
Shock Wave Laboratory Stosswellenlabor	http://ernst.swl.rwth-aachen.de/
The Digital Information Infrastructure Guide	http://far.mit.edu/diig.html
FIRE - Fluid Dynamics Focused on Solution	http://firewww.avl.co.at/FIRE_home.html
Welcome to the Frame Relay Forum	http://frame-relay.indiana.edu/
Privacy in the Digital Age	http://garnet.msen.com:70/1/vendor/freep/privacy
SIGIR Information Server	http://info.sigir.acm.org/sigir/
collection: Information System Vienna University of Technology	http://info.tuwien.ac.at/ROOT
Welcome to JHM!	http://jh.ccs.neu.edu:7043/
Center for Information Technology	http://logic.stanford.edu/cit/cit.html
CIT Learning Technologies Center	http://ltc.cit.cornell.edu/
Design for Competitive Advantage Home Page	http://mijuno.larc.nasa.gov/
WMTADS	http://mwir.lanl.gov/
Navy CALS SGML DTD/FOSI Repository	http://navysgml.dt.navy.mil/
NASA Commercial Technology Network Home Page	http://nctn.hq.nasa.gov/nctnHome.html
Technology	http://nearnet.gnn.com/wic/tech.toc.html
System and Software Technology WWW Server	http://nemo.ncsl.nist.gov/
NetSpace Project	http://netspace.students.brown.edu/
ESPRIT NoEs Information Service	http://newcastle.cabernet.esprit.ec.org/
TLTL Home Page	http://pcfwww.ucs.indiana.edu/tltl/index.html
Cornell Video: 'CU-SeeMe'	http://pipkin.lut.ac.uk/~ben/video/cuseeme.html
Information Technology Management Home Page	http://sm.nps.navy.mil/sm/it.shtml
MIT RLE VLSI-CAD Web home page	http://sobolev.mit.edu/
CRPC Home Document	http://softlib.cs.rice.edu/CRPC.html
CIATEQ A.C. home page	http://sparc.ciateq.conacyt.mx/homeciateq.html
The Concurrent Systems Group	http://swarm.wustl.edu/
TNS Technology Demonstrations	http://tns-www.lcs.mit.edu/vs/demos.html
WAVES Home Page	http://vhdl.org/vi/waves/
ELF Introduction	http://vumclib.mc.vanderbilt.edu/elf/elf.html
Chinese Information and Networking Association	http://www.aimnet.com/cina/cina.html

Georgia High Tech Month	http://www.bie.net/hightech/homepage.html
Tec de Monterrey Campus Estado de Mexico - Pagina Hogar	http://www.cem.itesm.mx/
Center for Networked Multimedia	http://www.cnm.bell-atl.com/
XIWT Goals	http://www.cnri.reston.va.us:3000/XIWT/goals.html
Membership Agreement Draft	http://www.cnri.reston.va.us:3000/XIWT/membership/agreement.html
XIWT Members	http://www.cnri.reston.va.us:3000/XIWT/membership/members.html
Impress issue 1	http://www.demon.co.uk/setanta/
International Federation for Information Processing	http://www.dit.upm.es/~cdk/ifip.html
European Bioinformatics Institute (EBI)	http://www.ebi.ac.uk/
About EFF	http://www.eff.org/EFFdocs/about_eff.html
Join EFF!	http://www.eff.org/EFFdocs/join_eff.html
NanoNet: Penn State University	http://www.emprl.psu.edu/nnunpsu.html
Georgia Institute of Technology	http://www.gatech.edu/TechHome.html
GMD - German National Research Center for Information Technology	http://www.gmd.de:80/
Helsinki Univ. of Technology Computing Centre	http://www.hut.fi/ATK/cc_Home.html
Helsinki University of Technology	http://www.hut.fi/English/www.english.html
Teknillinen Korkeakoulu	http://www.hut.fi/index.html
IMW TU Clausthal Standardization	http://www.imw.tu-clausthal.de/imw/projects/step/stand.html
INPE's home page	http://www.inpe.br/
USC Information Sciences Institute	http://www.isi.edu/isi.html
Welcome to ITP!	http://www.itp.tsoa.nyu.edu/
Lappeenranta University of Technology	http://www.lut.fi/english.html
The Nieman Foundation	http://www.nando.net/nieman/may/confpage.html
NCSA Home Page	http://www.ncsa.uiuc.edu/
NSWC PHD World Wide Web HomePage (ex-NSWSES)	http://www.nswses.navy.mil/
Crane Division (NSWC)	http://www.nwscc.sea06.navy.mil/
Corporate Research	http://www.research.digital.com/home.html
Network/Computer Security Technology	http://www.tezcat.com/web/security/security_top_level.html
Internet Wire	http://www.trib.com/service/vw.html
THE FRENCH INSTITUTE HOME PAGE	http://www.upenn.edu/FI
Information Technology Initiatives Page	http://www.upenn.edu/ITI/it-initiatives.html
Welcome to the University of Technology Sydney	http://www.uts.edu.au/
Say...	http://www_tios.cs.utwente.nl/say/

Travel

State of Wisconsin Information Server	http://badger.state.wi.us/
Seaside California Home Page	http://bbs.ci.seaside.ca.us/
Beverly Hills California	http://bhs.com/Beverly.Hills/City.Information.html
Los Gatos The Town	http://chezhal.slip.netcom.com/los_gatos/los_gatos.html
Things Latin America/Spanish Speaking Countries WWW at EgoWeb	http://edb518ea.edb.utexas.edu/html/latinamerica.html#Mexico
Chesapeake Virginia's home page.	http://hampton.roads.net/nhr/chesapeake/
Hampton Virginia	http://hampton.roads.net/nhr/hampton/
The Norfolk Virginia home page.	http://hampton.roads.net/nhr/norfolk/
City of Portsmouth	http://hampton.roads.net/nhr/portsmouth/
City of Virginia Beach Information Guide	http://hampton.roads.net/nhr/vabeach/
Montclair Home Page	http://haven.ios.com/~armstron/montclair.html
STATE OF HAWAII	http://hinc.hinc.hawaii.gov/soh_home.html
Kuwait Sensitive Map	http://hsccwww.kuniv.edu.kw/
Louisville Visitor Center	http://iglou.com/lou/lou_main.html
World-Wide Web servers: Hawaii	http://info.cern.ch/hypertext/DataSources/WWW/haw.html
Guatemala	http://lanic.utexas.edu/la/ca/guatemala/
Panama	http://lanic.utexas.edu/la/ca/panama/
PARIS GUEST BOOK	http://meteora.ucsd.edu:80/~norman/paris/Guestbook/page330.html
Paris Pages - Electronic Mail	http://meteora.ucsd.edu:80/~norman/paris/Mailparis/
PARIS.POSTCARDS.FM.VISITORS	http://meteora.ucsd.edu:80/~norman/paris/Postcards/
Indicateur des métros / Subway navigator	http://metro.jussieu.fr:10001/
COSTA Table of Contents	http://mmink.cts.com/costa.html
MULTIMEDIA INK DESIGNS...	http://mmink.cts.com/costapackage.html
Go Hosteling	http://northcoast.com/~ebarnett/gohosteling.htm
SCOTTISH HIGHLANDS AND ISLANDS SERVER	http://nsa.bt.co.uk/nsa.html
German Railway Timetables and Information	http://rzstud1.rz.uni-karlsruhe.de/~ule3/info-trn.html
Cleveland Ohio	http://sauron.multiverse.com/cleveland/
Bay Area Transit Information	http://server.berkeley.edu/Transit/
Travel Store Home Page	http://smartworld.com/travel/travel.html
Brisbane index	http://tcomeng.com/cities/brisbane/index.html
Travel & Entertainment Network home page	http://ten-io.com/
France	http://town.hall.org/travel/france/france.html
Travel Sites	http://usa.net/home/travel.html
Welcome to U/Seattle	http://useattle.uspan.com/
CITY OF SAN DIEGO	http://white.nosc.mil/sandiego.html
Virtual Tourist World Map	http://wings.buffalo.edu/world/
Complete Guide to Galway	http://wombatix.physics.ucg.ie/galway/galway.html
Stanford Overseas Studies	http://www-osp.stanford.edu/
WELCOME TO THE CITY OF THOUSAND OAKS	http://www.adnetsol.com//chamber/tohome.html
City of Cambridge Massachusetts	http://www.ai.mit.edu/projects/iiip/Cambridge/homepage.html
Maps of Cambridge	http://www.ai.mit.edu/projects/iiip/Cambridge/mapmenu.html
Alaska Internet Travel Guide	http://www.alaska.net/~travel
The Alaskan Center	http://www.alaskan.com/
Hawaii OnLine Home Page	http://www.aloha.net/
The Connecticut Guide	http://www.atlantic.com/ct/intro.html
AU-System Weather Report	http://www.ausys.se/weather/weather.htm

Additional Sites

Bed & Breakfast Online Home Page	http://www.baynet.com/bb/list.html
Virtual Tourist Guide to Ireland	http://www.bess.tcd.ie/ireland.html
Business Information Exchange Travel Links	http://www.bie.net/travel.html
Carlsbad California USA	http://www.bluebird.com/carlsbad/
Multi-Scale Maps	http://www.c3.lanl.gov/~cjhamil/Browse/main.html
City of Albuquerque Home Page	http://www.cabq.gov/
CALIFORNIA TRAVEL PARKS ASSOCIATION	http://www.campgrounds.com/
Catalina Island Guide	http://www.catalina-island.com/guide/
Cathay Pacific (USA) Home Page	http://www.cathay-usa.com/
Canadian Airlines International Ltd.	http://www.CdnAir.CA/
Adventure crusing in the North-Atlantic	http://www.centrum.is/com/vinland.html
Instant Travel Home Page	http://www.cgl.com/~it/
AESU - Low-Cost Airfares & Tours to Europe	http://www.charm.net/~aesu/
Travel Sites in California	http://www.charm.net/~ken/catrav.html
COUNCIL TRAVEL	http://www.ciee.org/cts/ctshome.htm
City.Net Switzerland	http://www.city.net/countries/switzerland/
City of Palo Alto Home Page	http://www.city.palo-alto.ca.us/
Welcome to Sri Lanka	http://www.cm.cf.ac.uk/Sri_Lanka/
CND InfoBase — Scenery Pictures of China	http://www.cnd.org/Scenery/index.html
Arlington County Virginia Home Page	http://www.co.arlington.va.us/
Centro Regional de Sao Paulo	http://www.cr-sp.rnp.br/
The Electronic Guide to Santa Cruz County	http://www.cruzio.com/index.html
ROUTE 66	http://www.cs.kuleuven.ac.be/~swa/route66/main.html
Tube Main Index Page	http://www.cs.ucl.ac.uk/misc/uk/london/tube/index.html
Interactive Connecticut Map	http://www.cs.yale.edu/HTML/YALE/MAPS/connecticut.html
Guide to Australia ..	http://www.csu.edu.au/education/australia.html
Vermont Winter Guide	http://www.cybermalls.com/cymont/vermont/vermont.htm
Rec.Travel Library	http://www.digimark.net/rec-travel/
The definitive review of Dublin's watering holes	http://www.dsg.cs.tcd.ie/dsg_people/czimmerm/pubs.html
Des Moines Internet (DSMnet)	http://www.dsmnet.com/
Welcome to EENet ESTONIA!	http://www.eenet.ee/english.html
Edinburgh - Scotland's Capital City	http://www.efr.hw.ac.uk/EDC/Edinburgh.html
Staunton Virginia	http://www.elpress.com:80/staunton/
Explore New York	http://www.escape.com/eMall/exploreny/ny1.html
The Geneva International Guide / Le Guide International de Genève	http://www.eunet.ch/GenevaGuide
SLOVAKIA DOCUMENT STORE - Cover Page	http://www.eunet.sk/slovakia/slovakia.html
Travel Forums	http://www.explore.com/Explorer_forums.html
Matterhorn Home Page	http://www.explore.com/mat/matterhorn.html
Norwegian Cruise Line Home Page	http://www.explore.com/ncl/ncl.html
Welcome to Rochester	http://www.eznet.net/rochester/
A Napa Valley Virtual Visit	http://www.freerun.com/
NAPA VALLEY VIRTUAL VISIT	http://www.freerun.com/napavalley/homepag.html
Information resource map of Finland	http://www.funet.fi/resources/map.html
Atlanta! Home page	http://www.gatech.edu/3020/travelink/homepage.html
Welcome to the Great Lakes Region	http://www.great-lakes.net:2200/0/glinhome.html
Grand Rapids Free-Net	http://www.grfn.org/
Hello Holiday Inn	http://www.holiday-inn.com/
San Francisco Reservations	http://www.hotelres.com/
Mankato/North Mankato MN	http://www.ic.mankato.mn.us/reg9/city/cities.html
Tour in China	http://www.ihep.ac.cn/tour/china_tour.html
Province of Quebec Canada	http://www.iisys.com/quebec/quebec.htm
Specialized wine shops	http://www.ijs.si/vinoteke.html
C I Travel	http://www.infi.net/citravel/
Norfolk International Airport	http://www.infi.net/orf/
Pilot Online Travel	http://www.infi.net/pilot/travel.html
Las Vegas Reservations	http://www.infi.net/vegas/lvr/
Infolink Home Page	http://www.infolink.net/
Santa Barbara County lodging	http://www.internet-cafe.com/sb/lodging.html
Home Page of the Prime Minister's official residence of JAPAN	http://www.kantei.go.jp/
Hello Japan	http://www.kddlabs.co.jp/japan/
Moscow Kremlin On-line Excursion	http://www.kiae.su/www/wtr/kremlin/begin.html
Mir home page	http://www.kiss.com/fr/mir.html
Lincoln County Home Page	http://www.libby.org/
Telerama Public Access Internet Lobby	http://www.lm.com/
Los Gatos The Town	http://www.los-gatos.scruznet.com/los_gatos/los_gatos.html
Photo Tour of Maui and other parts of Hawaii	http://www.mhpcc.edu/tour/Tour.html
Milwaukee Marketplace	http://www.mixcom.com/index.html
Monterey Peninsula Home Page	http://www.monterey.com/california/
Virtual Tourism: Boston	http://www.pn.com/Services/Boston/
Virtual Tourist - California	http://www.research.digital.com/SRC/virtual-tourist/California.html
Icelandic Fisheries Laboratories WWW server	http://www.rfisk.is/
Iceland	http://www.rfisk.is/english/iceland/rest_of_iceland.html
Southern California Traffic Report	http://www.scubed.com:8001/caltrans/transnet.html
Seanet Home Page Seattle WA USA	http://www.seanet.com/
Aeroflot [Seanet]	http://www.seanet.com/Bazar/Aeroflot/Aeroflot.html
Discussion of 'A Tourist Expedition to Antarctica'	http://www.sils.umich.edu/HyperNews/get/Antarctica/Discussion.html
State of North Carolina	http://www.sips.state.nc.us/nchome.html
Boston Online	http://www.std.com/NE/boston.html
New England Online	http://www.std.com/NE/index.html
City of Sunnyvale California	http://www.svpal.org/sunnyvale/sunnyvale.html
Huntsville/Madison County Chamber of Commerce	http://www.traveller.com/hcc/

Guide to Huntsville Alabama	http://WWW.Traveller.COM:80/hcc/guide
About Winnipeg	http://www.umanitoba.ca/wpg/wpg.html
Las Vegas Events	http://www.unlv.edu/events/index.html
AOI Travel	http://www.xmission.com:80/~aoi/
Holland Tourist Information by subject	http://www.xxlink.nl/nbt
Palo Alto Airport Home Page (PAO)	http://xymox.palo-alto.ca.us/av/paohome.html

TV

Film and Television	http://english-server.hss.cmu.edu/Film&TV.html
Cable	http://fcc.gov:70/1/Cable
Blake's 7	http://hawks.ha.md.us/blake7/index.html
Cablevision Home Page 	http://tech.cmp.com/ai
CALIFORNIA TV STATIONS	http://tvnet.com/TV/CA.html
BBC TV and Radio programme schedules	http://www.bbcnc.org.uk/bbctv/sched.html
TV programme schedules	http://www.bbcnc.org.uk/bbctv/sched/prog_by_type.html
TV Listings Chronologically	http://www.bbcnc.org.uk/bbctv/sched/sched2.html
The BBC Home Page	http://www.bbcnc.org.uk/index.html
NewsChannel 5 Online	http://www.infi.net/nc5/nc5top.html
KGTV Home Page	http://www.kgtv.com/
KQED	http://www.kqed.org/
OU Public Television Home Page	http://www.tcom.ohiou.edu/tv.html

Universities-Non US

KUHP Hospital Information System Home Page	http://bigblue.kuhp.kyoto-u.ac.jp/kuhp/index.html
Centro de Operaciones REUNA Norte: Antofagasta	http://cobre.reuna.cl/Paginas/antofagasta.html
Faculty of Commerce WWW Server	http://commerce.ubc.ca/
The University of East Anglia (UEA)	http://cpca3.uea.ac.uk/welcome.html
The CCDC Home Page	http://csdvx2.ccdc.cam.ac.uk/
DCA - FEE - Unicamp Home Page	http://dca.fee.unicamp.br/
Dept of Computing Science U of Newcastle upon Tyne UK	http://dcs.www.ncl.ac.uk/
The University of Ulster WWW Server	http://dsets.ulst.ac.uk/index.html
University of British Columbia Faculty of Arts	http://edziza.arts.ubc.ca/0c:/cliocan/clionet.html
Hirose Lab. Home Page	http://ghidorah.t.u-tokyo.ac.jp/index.html
Universidad San Francisco de Quito Home Page	http://gopher.usfq.edu.ec/0c:/ecuador/guia.html
Campusinfo Innsbruck	http://info.uibk.ac.at/
Old UL Entry Point	http://itdsrv1.ul.ie/home-page.html
University of Delaware Expertise	http://medoc.gdb.org/work/fields/delaware.html
UAKOM Top^2 WWW Server in Slovakia	http://nic.uakom.sk/hypertext/home.html
Osaka Kyoiku Univ. Home page(E)	http://okumedia.cc.osaka-kyoiku.ac.jp/index_E.html
LUTCHI Research Centre	http://pipkin.lut.ac.uk/
Oxford University Computing Services	http://sable.ox.ac.uk/
University of Canberra WWW Information Service	http://services.canberra.edu.au/
Infodienste an der UdS	http://sparlast.phil15.uni-sb.de/uebersicht.html
EF STU Web	http://sun.sanet.sk/info/efstu-sl.html
SunSITE at Hong Kong (SunSITE.ust.hk)	http://sunsite.ust.hk/
Sakamura Laboratory Entrance Hall	http://tron.is.s.u-tokyo.ac.jp/
Count Floyd's 3-D House of the CSGSA...	http://web.cs.ualberta.ca/~csgsa/csgsa.cgi
Yonezawa Lab WWW Server	http://web.yl.is.s.u-tokyo.ac.jp/
IAI Home Page External	http://wmwap1.math.uni-wuppertal.de/
WiLAN - Top Home Page	http://wwwd85.wifak.uni-wuerzburg.de/
IWI Homepage	http://www-iwi.unisg.ch/
The World Wide Web	http://www.abdn.ac.uk/www_abdn/www_page.html
Analysys	http://www.analysys.co.uk/
Aalborg University: General information	http://www.auc.dk/
University of Auckland	http://www.auckland.ac.nz/
Uni-Bamberg Wirtschaftsinformatik	http://www.buva.sowi.uni-bamberg.de/
KOMABA Campus the University of Tokyo	http://www.c.u-tokyo.ac.jp/
Universidad Michoacana	http://www.ccu.umich.mx/
The School of Computing and Mathematical Sciences	http://www.cs.waikato.ac.nz/
University of the Witwatersrand Computer Science Dept. Home Page	http://www.cs.wits.ac.za/
University of Ottawa Department of Computer Science	http://www.csi.uottawa.ca/
Charles Sturt University ..	http://www.csu.edu.au/
Dalhousie University	http://www.dal.ca/
DCC-Imecc-Unicamp's Home Page	http://www.dcc.unicamp.br/
University of Hull Experimental Web Home Page	http://www.dcs.hull.ac.uk/
University of Abertay Dundee home page	http://www.dct.ac.uk/
Universidad Politecnica de Madrid	http://www.dit.upm.es/upm.html
De Montfort University UK - Home Page	http://www.dmu.ac.uk/
CRDP Home Page	http://www.droit.umontreal.ca/english.html
UNIVERSIDAD AUTONOMA DE NUEVO LEON	http://www.dsi.uanl.mx/
University of Durham Home Page	http://www.dur.ac.uk/
EDINFO - The University of Edinburgh's Information Service	http://www.ed.ac.uk/
Home Page - Informationssystem der Uni Salzburg	http://www.edvz.sbg.ac.at/home.html
Pag. Principal Enlaces	http://www.enlaces.ufro.cl/
University of Essex Home Page	http://www.essex.ac.uk/
HomePage Faculty of Electrical Engineering	http://www.et.tudelft.nl/
Univ. of Ljubljana FaGG	http://www.fagg.uni-lj.si/index.html
Uni Passau Home Page	http://www.fmi.uni-passau.de/welcome.html
Fisica Moderna-Univ. de Cantabria Home Page	http://www.gae.unican.es/
Hopkins Bio-Informatics Home Page	http://www.gdb.org/

Additional Sites

Griffith University Welcome Page	http://www.gu.edu.au/
Goteborg University	http://www.gu.se/
Helsingin yliopisto	http://www.helsinki.fi/
The HENSA Unix Archive	http://www.hensa.ac.uk/hensa.unix.html
Chiba University Overview	http://www.hike.te.chiba-u.ac.jp/chiba-u/
Hirosaki University Home Page	http://www.hirosaki-u.ac.jp/
Hiroshima City University	http://www.hiroshima-cu.ac.jp/
Hokkaido University Home Page	http://www.huie.hokudai.ac.jp/
Faculty of Arts and Humanities Göteborg University	http://www.hum.gu.se/humeng.html
Teknillinen Korkeakoulu	http://www.hut.fi/
IAIK ISDN DIAL UP	http://www.iaik.tu-graz.ac.at/ISDN/capipkt.html
INSTITUTO DE BIOTECNOLOGIA UNAM.	http://www.ibt.unam.mx/
Technical University of Wroclaw	http://www.ict.pwr.wroc.pl/
Universitetet i Trondheim (UNIT)	http://www.idt.unit.no/UNIT/unit.html
University of Ryukyus WWW Home Page.	http://www.ie.u-ryukyu.ac.jp/
Johannes Kepler University of Linz Home Page	http://www.ifs.uni-linz.ac.at/home.html
Peking University	http://www.ihep.ac.cn/uni/pku/pku.html
U.T.F.S.M. Home Page	http://www.inf.utfsm.cl/
Informationsanbieter an der RWTH Aachen	http://www.informatik.rwth-aachen.de/www_server_rwth.html
Uni-Bonn	http://www.informatik.uni-bonn.de/unibo.html
University of Erlangen-Nürnberg	http://www.informatik.uni-erlangen.de/tree/FAU
Home Page of the Faculty of Computer Science	http://www.informatik.uni-ulm.de/index.eng.html
Computer Science at the Vienna University of Technology	http://www.infosys.tuwien.ac.at/org/Fachgruppe.html
Escuela de Ingenieria Pontificia Universidad Catolica de Chile	http://www.ing.puc.cl/
Kyushu Sangyo University(KSU) Home Page	http://www.ip.kyusan-u.ac.jp/
IPL Home Page	http://www.ipl.t.u-tokyo.ac.jp/
Universite de Montreal - Departement IRO	http://www.iro.umontreal.ca/
Welcome Message (Kochi Univ — Dept Info Sci)	http://www.is.kochi-u.ac.jp/
József Attila University Home Page	http://www.jate.u-szeged.hu/
the JSK HOME page	http://www.jsk.t.u-tokyo.ac.jp/
Juristischer WWW-Server Saarbrucken	http://www.jura.uni-sb.de/
University of Jyvaskyla	http://www.jyu.fi/
Kagoshima University Home Page	http://www.kagoshima-u.ac.jp/
Chair of Knowledge Engineering	http://www.ke.ics.saitama-u.ac.jp/index_english.html
Kingston University Home Page	http://www.kingston.ac.uk/
KOBE University Home Page	http://www.kobe-u.ac.jp/
Katholieke Universiteit Leuven	http://www.kuleuven.ac.be/
KUN: Homepage	http://www.kun.nl/
Kyoto University Home Page	http://www.kyoto-u.ac.jp/English/
Kyushu University	http://www.kyushu-u.ac.jp/
Gunma Univ Home Page	http://www.la.gunma-u.ac.jp/
Lakehead University Home Page	http://www.lakeheadu.ca/menu.html
Lancaster University. UK (http://www.lancs.ac.uk/)	http://www.lancs.ac.uk/
La Trobe University Home Page	http://www.latrobe.edu.au/
The University of Leeds	http://www.leeds.ac.uk/
Lajos Kossuth University of Arts and Sciences	http://www.lib.klte.hu/index.english.html
Linköpings Universitet	http://www.liu.se/
Lund University Home Page	http://www.lu.se/
Lulea University	http://www.luth.se/
METU Campus Wide Information System	http://www.metu.edu.tr/
Mount Allison University's WWW Server	http://www.mta.ca/
Nagoya University Japan	http://www.nagoya-u.ac.jp/index-e.html
Nanyang Technological University Home Page	http://www.ntu.ac.sg/
University Of Otago	http://www.otago.ac.nz/
Universität Erlangen-Nürnberg	http://www.rrze.uni-erlangen.de:80/
Heinrich-Heine-Universitaet Duesseldorf	http://www.rz.uni-duesseldorf.de:80/
UPV/EHU WWW Home Page	http://www.sc.ehu.es/
Universitat Bielefeld - Home Page	http://www.techfak.uni-bielefeld.de:80/
TH Darmstadt Welcome Page	http://www.th-darmstadt.de:/
Home Page of the University of Aizu	http://www.u-aizu.ac.jp/
Universidad Autónoma de Madrid	http://www.uam.es/
Servidor de WWW de la Universidad Carlos III de Madrid	http://www.uc3m.es/
UCM — Universidad Complutense de Madrid — Home page	http://www.ucm.es/UCMD.html
Universidad de Cordoba Home Page	http://www.uco.es/
Mosaic de la Universidad de Colima	http://www.ucol.mx/
UCONN WWW Servers	http://www.uconn.edu/UCWWW/UCONNWWW.html
WWW de la Universidad de Costa Rica	http://www.ucr.ac.cr/
Universidad de Guadalajara	http://www.udg.mx/
UEC www Home page	http://www.uec.ac.jp/
Universitetet i Bergen	http://www.uib.no/
Universitetet i Oslo	http://www.uio.no/
KUOPION YLIOPISTO (uku.fi) home page	http://www.uku.fi/
ULCC WWW Visitor's Page	http://www.ulcc.ac.uk/
Home Page de l'Universite de Liege	http://www.ulg.ac.be/
ULPGC CWIS	http://www.ulpgc.es/
The University of Manitoba	http://www.umanitoba.ca/
The University of Manitoba	http://www.umanitoba.ca/UofM_homepage.html
Lublin Home Page	http://www.umcs.lublin.pl/
University of Minho Home Page	http://www.uminho.pt/
Umea universitet	http://www.umu.se/
UNB Home WWW Page	http://www.unb.ca/UNB.html

University of Bayreuth Mosaic Home Page	http://www.uni-bayreuth.de/homes/bayreuth.html
Universitat Dortmund	http://www.uni-dortmund.de/
Andere Services	http://www.uni-frankfurt.de/UNIadienste.html
Martin-Luther-Universitaet Halle-Wittenberg - HomePage	http://www.uni-halle.de/
Uni Hamburg Welcome	http://www.uni-hamburg.de/welcome_english.html
Uni Hamburg Welcome	http://www.uni-hamburg.de:80/
Welcome to Hohenheim	http://www.uni-hohenheim.de/
Friedrich-Schiller-Universitaet Jena	http://www.uni-jena.de/
Uni Kaiserslautern	http://www.uni-kl.de/
Home Page der Uni Konstanz	http://www.uni-konstanz.de/index.html
WWW-Server Universitaet Leipzig	http://www.uni-leipzig.de/
Startseite der Johannes Gutenberg-Universität	http://www.uni-mainz.de/Welcome.html
Homepage	http://www.uni-mannheim.de/
UMB Home Page	http://www.uni-mb.si/
Ludwig-Maximilians-University Munich	http://www.uni-muenchen.de/index-e.html
Ludwig-Maximilians-Universitat Munchen	http://www.uni-muenchen.de:80/
Universität-GH Paderborn	http://www.uni-paderborn.de/
Home Page Universitaet Stuttgart	http://www.uni-stuttgart.de/
Homepage des Informationssystems der Universitaet Tuebingen	http://www.uni-tuebingen.de/tue-home.html
Universitat der Bundeswehr Munchen	http://www.unibw-muenchen.de/
Universidade Estadual de Campinas	http://www.unicamp.br/
UNIVERSITE DE GENEVE	http://www.unige.ch/
Universite de Lausanne home page.	http://www.unil.ch/
Universidad de Oviedo - Home Page	http://www.uniovi.es/
Unipalm Group Welcome Page	http://www.unipalm.co.uk/unipalm/
Home Page of the University of Pisa	http://www.unipi.it/welcome.html
Universita' di Parma: Home Page	http://www.unipr.it/
LE CRI de l'Universite de Rennes 1	http://www.univ-rennes1.fr/
LE CRI de l'Universite de Rennes 1	http://www.univ-rennes1.fr/welcome.html
University of Zurich Home Page	http://www.unizh.ch/
UPEI Home Page	http://www.upei.ca/
Universitad Politecnica de Valencia (version castellana)	http://www.upv.es/
WWW de l'UQAM	http://www.uqam.ca/
URZ Heidelberg: Der WWW Informationsdienst	http://urz.uni-heidelberg.de/index.html
University of Saskatchewan	http://www.usask.ca/
USP - University ofSao Paulo	http://www.usp.br/eindex.html
FAU - Faculdade de Arquitetura e Urbanismo	http://www.usp.br/fau/fau.html
Faculdade de Economia Administracao e Contabilidade - USP	http://www.usp.br/fea/fea.html
IF - Instituto de Fisica	http://www.usp.br/fisica/fisica.html
Instituto de Estudos Avancados	http://www.usp.br/geral/iea.html
IB - Instituto de Biociencias	http://www.usp.br/ib/ib.html
Instituto de Quimica	http://www.usp.br/iq/iq.html
Tampereen yliopisto / University of Tampere	http://www.uta.fi/
University of Toronto Home Page	http://www.utoronto.ca/uoft.html
Turun yliopisto - University of Turku Finland	http://www.utu.fi/
Uppsala University	http://www.uu.se/
Servidor WWW de la Universitat de Valencia	http://www.uv.es/
University of Vaasa	http://www.uwasa.fi/
University of Vaasa Info Page	http://www.uwasa.fi/samjay/index.html
UWinfo — University of Waterloo	http://www.uwaterloo.ca/
The University of Western Ontario	http://www.uwo.ca/
Welcome to the Liberec University of Technology	http://www.vslib.cz:80/
Victoria University of Wellington	http://www.vuw.ac.nz/
SISMOLOGiA - ZARAGOZA	http://zar.unizar.es/

Universities-US

MIT Media Arts and Sciences	http://alberti.mit.edu/mas/mas.html
Alcom Home Page	http://alcom.kent.edu/ALCOM/ALCOM.html
Archives of the University of Notre Dame	http://archives1.archives.nd.edu/guidecon.htm
Temple University Home Page	http://astro.ocis.temple.edu/
The Ohio State University at Marion	http://beetle.marion.ohio-state.edu/
The Digital REST Area at SUNY Plattsburgh	http://bio420.hawk.plattsburgh.edu/
UC Irvine Home Page	http://bookweb.cwis.uci.edu/
University of Washington Bothell - Welcome	http://booster.u.washington.edu/
World Wide Web for the STARRS	http://browndwarf.ucs.indiana.edu/
UCLA Home Page	http://cad.ucla.edu/repository/UCLA/UCLA.html
Rutgers University - Camden INFO	http://camden-www.rutgers.edu/
Valdosta State University Home Page	http://catfish.valdosta.peachnet.edu/home.html
International Studies Pages	http://ccat.sas.upenn.edu/isp/ispages.html
CMSU WWW Home Page	http://cmsuvmb.cmsu.edu/
University of Arkansas at Monticello WWW Home Page	http://cotton.uamont.edu/
Computing and Network Services at the University At Albany	http://cscmosaic.albany.edu/
Abilene Christian University Home Page	http://cteserver.acu.edu/
University of Colorado at Boulder Home Page	http://culine.colorado.edu/
CUTL WWW Server Home Page	http://cutl.city.unisa.edu.au/
USCWeb the University of Southern California	http://cwis.usc.edu/
World-Wide Web Home at BGSU	http://dad.bgsu.edu/BGSU.html
Disability Services at the University of Minnesota	http://disserv.stu.umn.edu/
Tullius Lab Home Page	http://dna.chm.jhu.edu/
The Dolphin Web Server	http://dolphin.csudh.edu/
Mechanics of Materials	http://ecsel.engr.washington.edu/main.html

Additional Sites

Phi Mu Alpha Sinfonia	http://eec.psu.edu/~panulla/pma/
ECSEL Coalition (Penn State)	http://eec.psu.edu/ecsel
Cornell Cooperative Extension	http://empire.cce.cornell.edu/
Wesleyan University Student Net	http://emu.con.wesleyan.edu/
Davis / Etcheverry Computing Facility	http://euler.berkeley.edu/
Phi Mu Home Page	http://gizmo.cac.psu.edu/sororities/phimu/home.html
Globin Gene Server home page	http://globin.cse.psu.edu/
UT Austin Center for Relativity Home Page	http://godel.ph.utexas.edu/
University of Idaho GN Server — A Httpish Gopher Server	http://gopher.uidaho.edu/
University of Idaho Information & Services	http://gopher.uidaho.edu/1/UI_gopher
Student Clubs and Organizations	http://gopher.uidaho.edu/1/UI_gopher/clubs
Electronic Green Journal	http://gopher.uidaho.edu/1/UI_gopher/library/egj
Prairie View HEP Home Page	http://hp73.pvamu.edu/
Unofficial University of Tulsa home page	http://hpserv.keh.utulsa.edu/home.html
IUPUI Home Page	http://indyunix.iupui.edu/
University of Arizona	http://info-center.ccit.arizona.edu:80/
The University of Alabama in Huntsville	http://info.uah.edu/
University of Tasmania WWW Service	http://info.utas.edu.au/
Cornell University Instructional Web Server	http://instruct1.cit.cornell.edu/
Stern School Information Systems Department	http://is-2.stern.nyu.edu/
Information Systems departmental WWW server	http://is.rice.edu/
UCI Registrar's Office/SAIS	http://ka.reg.uci.edu/
Ateneo Home Page	http://kilaw.admu.edu.ph/
Virtual Brain	http://lenti.med.umn.edu/BRAIN/brain.html
MSUE Home Page	http://lep.cl.msu.edu/msueimp/
CARD Laboratory Home Page	http://logos.ualr.edu/
The University of Tennessee	http://loki.ur.utk.edu/
Space Institute	http://loki.ur.utk.edu/campus/spac.html
THE UNIVERSITY OF TENNESSEE BOARD OF TRUSTEES	http://loki.ur.utk.edu/catalog/admin.html
Program in Animal Behavior at Indiana University	http://loris.cisab.indiana.edu/
Florida State University Physical Education Department	http://mailer.fsu.edu/~rrider/phy.html
MIT-LNS Home Page	http://mccool.cbi.msstate.edu/
Clinical Decision Making Group Homepage	http://medg.lcs.mit.edu/
UT-MENIC	http://menic.utexas.edu/menic.html
UVM Office of Audit Services Home Page	http://moose.uvm.edu/~auditwww/index.html
Project Muse Home Page	http://muse.mse.jhu.edu/
Administrative Computing Services Home Page	http://nimue.adcom.uci.edu/
Student Union	http://nimue.wustl.edu/~su/
Virtual Media Lab	http://philae.sas.upenn.edu/
UT-REENIC Home Page	http://reenic.utexas.edu/reenic.html
Rhetoric Index	http://rhetoric.agoff.umn.edu/
RiceInfo: Rice University WWW server	http://riceinfo.rice.edu/
Rocky's Home Page	http://rocky.humboldt.edu/
RSO Info	http://rso.union.wisc.edu/rsoinfo/homepage
PCF Home Page	http://sally.ucs.indiana.edu/index.html
UNH-Durham - campus-wide information	http://samizdat.unh.edu:70/1/unh
Florida Institute of Technology	http://sci-ed.fit.edu/
UCS Support Center	http://scwww.ucs.indiana.edu/
Welcome to SEP	http://sepwww.stanford.edu/
The Associated Students of the University of California	http://server.berkeley.edu/asuc/
Nicholls State University Home Page	http://server.nich.edu/
University of Canberra WWW Information Service	http://services.canberra.edu.au/home.html
SFSU WWW Home Page	http://sfsuvax1.sfsu.edu/
MU Main Menu	http://showme.missouri.edu/
Showroom and Solutions Home Page	http://showroom.doit.wisc.edu/
Office of Research Services Home Page	http://solar.rtd.utk.edu/default.html
Friends and Partners	http://solar.rtd.utk.edu/friends/home.html
The University of Tennessee - WWW Demonstration Server	http://solar.rtd.utk.edu/utwww/utwww.html
East Central University Home Page	http://student.ecok.edu/
Schoolyear 2000 Home Page	http://sy2000.cet.fsu.edu:70/0/WWW/SY2000/Home.html
Symbolic Systems Program	http://symbol.stanford.edu/
Not Stetson Web Home	http://thoth.stetson.edu/
Welcome to UBU	http://ubu.hahnemann.edu/
Louisiana State University Home Page	http://unix1.sncc.lsu.edu/
Boston University Home Page	http://web.bu.edu/
Florida A&M University -	http://web.fie.com/web/mol/fice/001480/index.htm
Clark Atlanta University -	http://web.fie.com/web/mol/fice/001559/index.htm
The MIT Home Page	http://web.mit.edu/
MIT SEA GRANT	http://web.mit.edu/afs/athena/org/s/seagrant/www/mitsg.htm
TechInfo main menu	http://web.mit.edu:1962/tiserve.mit.edu/9000/0
Michigan State University Home Page	http://web.msu.edu/
William James Hall Home Page	http://wjh-www.harvard.edu/
Loyola University Chicago Home Page	http://www.luc.edu/
Mississippi State University	http://www.msstate.edu/
Intro to the University of Illinois at Urbana-Champaign	http://www.ncsa.uiuc.edu/General/UIUC/UIUCIntro/UofI_intro.html
NTU Home Page	http://www.ntu.edu/
New York University Home Page	http://www.nyu.edu/
Beginning Screen for UCCS Computing Services.	http://www.uccs.edu/
The University of Chicago	http://www.uchicago.edu/
University of California servers	http://www.ucla.edu/ucservers.html
InfoPath	http://www.ucsd.edu/